Systems
and
Theories
of
Psychology

Systems
and
Theories
of
Psychology

second edition

J. P. Chaplin
University of Vermont

T. S. Krawiec
Skidmore College

Holt, Rinehart and Winston, Inc.

New York   Chicago   San Francisco   Atlanta   Dallas
Montreal   Toronto   London

Copyright Acknowledgments

The authors wish to make grateful acknowledgment for permission to adapt the copyrighted material below. Publishers are listed in alphabetical order, and authors not mentioned here are identified in the references for each chapter.

FIGURES AND TABLES

AMERICAN JOURNAL OF PSYCHOLOGY, for Fig. 9-8 on p. 337, copyright 1927, Fig. 9-9 on p. 338, copyright 1946, and Fig. 9-12 on p. 341, copyright 1924.

AMERICAN PSYCHOLOGICAL ASSOCIATION
    American Psychologist, for Fig. 5-8 on p. 166, copyright © 1963 and Fig. 12-4 on p. 467, copyright © 1958
    Journal of Abnormal and Social Psychology, for Fig. 5-11 on p. 181, copyright 1947.
    Psychological Bulletin, for Fig. 14-5 on p. 530 and Fig. 14-6 on p. 531, copyright 1942.
    Journal of Comparative and Physiological Psychology, for Fig. 11-9 on p. 440, copyright 1950.
    Journal of Experimental Psychology, for Fig. 5-1 on p. 154, copyright 1929, Fig. 5-2 on p. 156, copyright 1932, Fig. 8-1 on p. 298, copyright 1948, and Fig. 9-1 on p. 323, copyright 1938.
    Psychological Monographs, for Fig. 9-4 on p. 332, copyright 1937, Fig. 9-5 on p. 333, copyright 1922, Fig. 9-11 on p. 340, copyright 1945, Fig. 10-9 on p. 368, copyright 1945, and Fig. 10-10 on p. 381, copyright 1920.
    Psychological Review, for Fig. 3-5 on p. 106, copyright © 1957, Fig. 9-2 on p. 324, copyright 1935, Fig. 9-3 on p. 330, copyright 1949, Fig. 9-10 on p. 339, copyright © 1957, Fig 9-13 on p. 346, copyright © 1959, Fig. 13-15 on p. 506, copyright 1945, and Fig. 14-7 on p. 533, copyright 1930.

APPLETON-CENTURY-CROFTS, INC., for Fig. 7-6 on p. 260 and Fig. 7-11 on p. 267, copyright © 1957.

BLACKWELL SCIENTIFIC PUBLICATION, for Fig. 13-13 on p. 500, copyright 1954.

CAMBRIDGE UNIVERSITY PRESS, for Fig. 5-1 on p. 154, copyright 1932.

CLARK UNIVERSITY PRESS, for Fig. 3-1 on p. 99, Fig. 3-2 on p. 100, and Fig. 3-3 on p. 101, from Hecht, S. The Nature of the Photoreceptor Process. In C. Murchison (ed.) *Handbook of General Experimental Psychology.* Worcester, Mass.: Clark University Press, 1934.

COMPARATIVE PSYCHOLOGY MONOGRAPHS, for Fig. 13-5 on p. 482, copyright 1936.

HARPER & ROW PUBLISHERS, INC., for Fig. 10-2 on p. 362, Figs. 10-3 and 10-4 on p. 363, Fig. 10-5 on p. 364, Fig. 10-6 on p. 365, Fig. 10-7 on p. 366, and Fig. 10-8 on p. 367, from *Productive Thinking* by Max Wertheimer. Copyright 1945 by Valentin Wertheimer. Used by permission of Harper & Row, Publishers. Also for Fig. 13-18 on p. 509, copyright 1949.

HOLT, RINEHART & WINSTON, INC., for Fig. 3-13 on p. 119, copyright 1954, Fig. 7-1 on p. 231, copyright 1946, and Fig. 9-6 on p. 334, copyright 1954. Also for Table 10-1 on p. 385, Table 10-2 on p. 386, and Table 10-3 on p. 387, from "The Psychology of Creativity" by Frank Barron from *New Directions in Psychology II* by Frank Barron, *et al.* Copyright © 1965 by Holt, Rinehart & Winston, Inc. Reprinted by permission of Holt, Rinehart & Winston, Inc.

HUMANITIES PRESS, INC., for Fig. 6-4 on p. 221, copyright 1927.

BRUCE HUMHRIES (formerly J. W. Luce), for Table 11-1 on p. 409, copyright 1921.

JOURNAL OF COMPARATIVE NEUROLOGY, for Fig. 13-9 on p. 487, from Fig. 1, N. R. F. Maier, J. Comp. Neur., *56:*181

JOURNAL PRESS
    Journal of General Psychology, for Fig. 10-11 on p. 382, copyright 1946, and Fig. 13-7 on p. 485, copyright 1938.

J. B. Lippincott Co., for Table 9-1, reprinted by permission from *Psychology of Learning* by John F. Hall, published by J. B. Lippincott Company. Copyright © 1966 by J. B. Lippincott Company.

Liverpool University Press, for Figs. 13-10 and 13-11 on p. 489, copyright © 1958.

The Macmillan Company, for Fig. 6-2 on p. 203 and Fig. 6-3 on p. 204, copyright 1911, and for Fig. 13-12 on p. 490, copyright 1950.

McGraw-Hill Book Company, Inc. for Fig. 14-8 on p. 537, Fig. 14-9 on p. 538, Table 15-6 on p. 594, and Table 15-5 on p. 597, from *Psychology: A Study of a Science*, Vol. 2, by Koch. Copyright © 1959, McGraw-Hill Book Company. Used by permission of McGraw-Hill Book Company. For Fig. 14-14 on p. 546 and Fig. 14-15 on p. 547, from *Computers and Thought* by Feigenbaum and Feldman. Copyright © 1963. Used by permission of McGraw-Hill Book Company. Also for Fig. 15-3 on p. 573, copyright 1950.

David McKay Company, Inc. (formerly Longmans, Green & Co.), for Fig. 9-5 on p. 332, copyright 1952.

M. I. T. Press, for Fig. 3-12 on p. 117, copyright © 1961.

Oxford University Press, Inc., for Fig. 9-4, from *Explorations in Personality,* edited by Henry A. Murray. Copyright 1938 by Oxford University Press, Inc., renewed 1966 by Henry A. Murray. Reprinted by permission of the publisher.

Prentice-Hall, Inc., for Fig. 8-6 on p. 312, from Julian B. Rotter, *Social Learning and Clinical Psychology,* © 1954. Reprinted by permission of Prentice-Hall, Inc., Englewood Cliffs, New Jersey.

Random House, Inc., for Figs. 5-12 and 5-13 on p. 185, from *The Body Percept,* by Seymour Wapner and Heinz Werner. © Copyright 1965 by Random House, Inc. Reprinted by permission. Also for Fig. 13-14 on p. 502, copyright © 1958.

The Ronald Press Company, for Fig. 11-5 on p. 419, from Neal E. Miller—"Experimental Studies of Conflict" in *Psychology and the Behavior Disorders,* edited by J. McV. Hunt. Copyright 1944, The Ronald Press Company, New York.

Routledge & Kegan Paul, Ltd., for Fig. 6-4 on p. 221, copyright 1927.

Scientific American, Inc., for Fig. 3-9 on p. 111 and Fig. 3-10 on p. 112, copyright © 1964, and for Fig. 14-11 on p. 543 and Fig. 14-12 on p. 544, copyright © 1960.

Teachers College Press, for Table 6-1 on p. 198, Table 6-2 on p. 199, and Fig. 6-1 on p. 200, copyright 1913.

Time Inc., for Fig. 5-10 on p. 171 by Eric Schall—*Life* Magazine © Time Inc.

University of Notre Dame Press, for Fig. 14-13 on p. 545, copyright © 1963.

D. Van Nostrand Company, Inc., for Fig. 9-7 on p. 336, from McClelland's *The Achieving Society*. Copyright 1961, D. Van Nostrand Company, Inc., Princeton, N. J.

John Wiley & Sons, Inc., for Fig. 8-5 on p. 304, copyright © 1960, Table 8-2 on p. 306, copyright © 1960, Fig. 11-2 on p. 416, copyright 1946, Fig. 11-7 on p. 438, copyright © 1961, and Fig. 11-8 on p. 438, copyright © 1964.

Yale Univesity Press, for Fig. 3-8 on p. 110, copyright © 1955, and Table 8-1 on p. 295, copyright © 1956.

QUOTATIONS

Appleton-Century-Crofts, Inc., for McClelland's material from *The Achievement Motive* by David C. McClelland, *et al.* Copyright 1953 by Appleton-Century-Crofts, Inc. Reprinted by permission of Appleton-Century-Crofts. Also for Hull's postulates.

J. B. Lippincott Company, for Watson's material.

Liverpool University Press, for Penfield's material.

David McKay Company, Inc., for Carr's material.

Oxford University Press, Inc., for Murray's material on needs.

Prentice-Hall, Inc., for Rotter's material.

Psychological Monographs, for Duncker's material.

In addition, we gratefully make acknowledgment to Dr. Cattell for Table 15-4 on pp. 568–569 and Table 15-5 on p. 571; Dr. Hall for Table 9-1 on p. 321; Dr. MacLean for Fig. 13-18 on p. 509; Dr. Sheldon for Table 15-1 on p. 562, Table 15-2 on pp. 564–565, and Table 15-3 on p. 565; and John B. Titchener for material in his father's book.

Preface to the Second Edition

In preparing the second edition of this book, we have been guided by the same basic principles we followed in developing the first edition. Once again we have presented systematic psychology as an evolving field whose contemporary theoretical formulations grew out of philosophy, the natural sciences, and the classical schools of psychology. Since publication of the first edition, psychology has undergone rapid expansion in virtually all areas. Many new developments are reflected in emerging theories and models, and in the consolidation of older theories, many of which were formulated during the decade after World War II. We have attempted to represent these more recent trends in theorizing and systematizing fairly, and at the same time to retain the contributions of the older schools and to show wherever possible how the new evolved from the old.

Once again we have made no attempt to be all-inclusive; nor have we sought to discuss all the latest developments within a given theoretical area. Our cutoff point is generally 1960, and our guiding principle has been to treat representative points of view in some depth rather than to undertake a necessarily more superficial treatment of all systems and theories. Whenever possible, however, we have indicated bibliographic sources which will enable the reader to pursue fields of special interest.

The greatest change in the second edition has been the inclusion of three new chapters, two in the areas of learning and one in physiological psychology. The first of the new learning chapters (Chapter 8) deals with derivative theories, including those of Spence, Miller, Mowrer, and Rotter, and with current issues in contiguity, effect, and reinforcement theory. We believe these theories are the most influential to evolve from the now classical miniature systems of the thirties and forties. In the chapter on quantitative theories (Chapter 14), the mathematical model of Estes has replaced the Bush-Mosteller model because it has become the most prominent of mathematical models.

Chapter 9, the second of the two new chapters on learning, is concerned with selected theoretical issues in verbal learning. We believe that this area now looms so large in the field as a whole that it has earned a place in systematic and theoretical psychology alongside theories which emerged primarily from the animal laboratory.

The chapter on physiological theories of behavior (Chapter 13) reflects the great upsurge of research and theorizing in this field during the past fifteen years, particularly in the area of central processes.

Among other additions is the recent work by MacNichol and others on specialized cone types in the retina. We have summarized the growing body of work in environmental restriction and stimulation and its significance for perceptual development. Also included are the recent California studies of creativity, Harlow's work with infantile love in monkeys, and the theoretical significance of the work in exploratory and manipulatory behavior. In the chapter on personality (Chapter 15), we have brought Allport's and Cattell's positions up to date and have included a new section on Rogers' self theory, in recognition of its widespread influence in both American and European clinical psychology as well as personality theory.

It is hoped that these additions and changes will make the volume an even more useful introduction to systematic psychology and that it will provide the necessary background for advanced undergraduates and graduate students in this traditional and fascinating area of psychology.

Burlington, Vermont
     and
Saratoga Springs, New York
March, 1968

J. P. C.
T. S. K.

Preface to the First Edition

The present volume grew out of the authors' conviction that an introduction to the field of systematic psychology was needed which emphasizes the evolution of contemporary theoretical concepts from their historical origins in philosophy and the natural sciences. Most texts are oriented around the schools of the early part of the present century, leaving the student with the impression that systematic theorizing was strictly a by-product of psychology's early developmental period and no longer plays a significant role in the evolution of the science. Although the professional psychologist is aware that theorizing plays an active and significant part in contemporary psychology, there has been no convenient way to introduce the undergraduate major to this important aspect of the discipline.

In keeping with our evolutionary frame of reference, we have organized our book around the traditional topics of the mental processes. In each case we have begun with the emergence of the concept during the prescientific period and traced its evolution through the first half of the present century. For the most part, we have tried to emphasize contemporary trends without neglecting · the contributions of the schools. While our cut-off point is generally the beginning of the 1950's, we have not hesitated to ignore our self-imposed limitation whenever it seemed desirable to include a particularly good theoretical or experimental illustration that has emerged during the past ten years.

We should also like to point out that we have followed a "sampling technique," striving to present representative theoretical points of view in some depth rather than to undertake what would be a highly superficial survey of all major and minor systems. In keeping with this selective orientation, we have deliberately emphasized systems and theories in the areas of perception and learning, devoting two chapters to each. We believe that this is a fair reflection on contemporary interest in these two important areas of psychology.

Finally, by way of limitations, we have made no attempt to cover those developments in Continental European philosophy and psychology that are not directly related to the emergence of American experimental psychology. In no sense does this represent a value judgment on our part as to the relative worthwhileness of the various schools of thought. Certainly every psychologist would agree that the French clinical school, which we have excluded from the present volume, has played a significant role in the evolution of contemporary concepts in abnormal and clinical psychology. Rather, our aim has been to hew to the line of the empirical tradition which gave rise to the dominant experimental psychology of the contemporary American scene.

It is a pleasure as well as an obligation to acknowledge our indebtedness to our colleagues whose many suggestions and criticisms have been of immeasurable assistance. We are especially grateful to Bennet B. Murdock, Jr., for his critical reading of portions of the manuscript and for his many helpful suggestions through the course of the project. Professors Albert H. Hastorf and John W. McCrary of Dartmouth College reviewed the entire manuscript and made a number of valuable recommendations. Thanks are also due to Carolyn Long, Louraine Collins and Miriam J. Benkovitz for their assistance in the preparation of the manuscript. Finally, we wish to express our gratitude to the administrations of the University of Vermont and Skidmore College for making available grants-in-aid to assist in the final phases of our joint undertaking.

Burlington, Vermont
    and
Saratoga Springs, New York
May, 1960

J.P.C.
T.S.K.

Contents

xiv

Systems
and
Theories
of
Psychology

1

The Evolution of the Scientific Method in Psychology

The story of science is a record of one of man's greatest intellectual achievements. It is a dramatic history of a continuous struggle against ignorance, fear, and superstition—a struggle which has not always been successful in any given age but which over the span of recorded history is a proud and Promethean accomplishment. During his brief tenancy of this planet man has reached out far beyond the solar system to chart the fringes of outer space and to unravel the mysteries of the creation of the galaxies. And, here on earth, he has kindled those stellar fires which only yesterday seemed forever beyond his reach. Even the darkest mystery of all, the nature of life itself, seems well within his grasp, for, within the short span of a few generations, the geneticist has learned the secret of the transmission of living matter and is on the threshold of being able to modify it at will. So rapid has been the march of science in our time, it has been estimated that we have learned more about our universe and the inhabitants of our planet in one generation than was learned through the accumulated total of all scientific knowledge up to the twentieth century.

Meanwhile, what have we learned of man with his unrivaled mind and complex behavior patterns? Part of the recent mushrooming of scientific endeavor has been the coming of age of psychology, the science of human behavior. It was less than a century ago that man first turned the powerful weapons of the scientific method against his own ignorance of himself. Of course scholars have always been interested in human nature. Philosophers, artists, writers, and theologians have sought to interpret human conduct from their particular points of view, and many of our valued insights into human nature have come from these sources of

1

knowledge. But the challenging idea that those methods of investigation which won so much knowledge and understanding for the natural scientist could be applied to the study of human behavior is relatively recent. In a sense, the task of psychology has been to take over the problems and questions about human nature that were its heritage from the prescientific past and to seek the answers in the light of modern science. In view of recent political and military developments, thoughtful people would agree that there is no more pressing, urgent task to which science could address itself. Ours is a century of unlimited power with dangerously limited knowledge of how to control it and utilize it for man's benefit. We have too much knowledge, it seems, of the physical world and too little knowledge of the world within.

Psychologists have not always been in agreement as to just how they ought to proceed with their investigations and theoretical formulations. Some, as we shall see, believe psychology ought to ally itself with the natural sciences, while others believe it belongs with the social sciences. Among the early psychologists there were those who felt that the best way to develop a science of psychology was to construct elaborate theoretical or systematic skeletons on which to hang the facts that were rapidly emerging from the experimental laboratories. These systematic-minded psychologists were convinced that a thoroughly worked-out point of view would shed new light on old problems, direct research into fruitful channels, and provide a theoretical schema within which to interpret the results of such research. There was considerable precedent in the record of the natural sciences for this chain of reasoning. Darwin's theory of evolution had revolutionized biology. Newton's conceptualizations of physical laws had made possible several centuries of rapid advance in physics, as well as providing a working theory of the solar system. Even the more restricted or miniature systems among the other sciences, such as Mendelyeev's periodic table of the elements, provided ample evidence for the scientific value of an orderly and systematic orientation in the pursuit of knowledge.

It would be wrong to give the impression that theoretical viewpoints are merely remnants from the past of the natural sciences or little more than growing pains in the formative stages of a new science such as psychology. Nothing would be farther from the truth, for a mere accumulation of facts without some frame of reference for their interpretation would be chaos, or blind belief and not science. Every science grows through the development of theory as well as by accumulating factual information. Indeed, the gathering and systematizing of facts is really a complementary process since the absence of either leads to confusion and wasted effort. Theory without a factual foundation is a structure founded on sand, and fact without theory is a meaningless jumble of information useless for building an orderly scientific structure. Therefore, both contemporary psychology and contemporary science in general are an admixture of fact and theory, and since theory attempts to bridge gaps in factual knowledge, or to go beyond what is known, it is necessarily someone's point of view.

Because systematists and theoreticians must take into account not only facts when erecting their conceptual structures, but also any existing theories which may be relevant, it follows that theoretical viewpoints rarely spring into existence full-blown; rather they are the result of an evolutionary process. Each new theory or system is partly new and partly old, and the past, present, and future in science are a continuum. It will be the burden of this book to demonstrate the continuity of psychological systems by tracing the evolution of contemporary points of view or concepts in psychology from their ancestry in the past. Since the scientific past extends back into philosophy, the mother of all sciences, our search will span the centuries back to ancient Greece, the fatherland of modern philosophy.

SCIENCE AND METHODOLOGY

It has become a truism to say that science not only begins with a method but that its very essence *is* its methodology. More specifically, the heart of science is a set of rules which must be followed by anyone who aspires to be a scientist. Contrary to a widespread popular view, this statement implies that any science such as chemistry, biology, geology, or psychology is not so much a compilation of facts or a collection of impressive apparatus as it is an attitude or willingness on the part of the scientist to follow the rules of the scientific game. Facts have an annoying way of changing, and what is truth today may be error tomorrow. Therefore, facts alone are the transient characteristics and not the enduring stuff of science. Apparatus, too, however imposing it may appear, is not science but only the tool of the scientist—a tool whose application may or may not be scientific. Anyone can purchase a white robe and a laboratory full of "scientific" paraphernalia, but the possession of such equipment does not qualify him as a scientist. Rather, both his scientific status and the value of the information he is collecting are evaluated according to the manner in which he *plans* his investigations, the *procedures* he employs in collecting data, and the way in which he *interprets* his findings. It is his standing on these three fundamental steps in scientific methodology which reveals whether he is a scientist, an amateur riding a hobbyhorse, or possibly a pseudoscientist. So crucial is the methodology followed in any scientific investigation that no reputable scientist will accept a fellow scientist's results as valid until he knows precisely what procedures were employed in arriving at those results. This cautious, conservative attitude has been dignified by the special name, *operationism*, and has been elevated into a basic working principle of the natural sciences. In formal terms we may define operationism as follows: *The validity of any scientific finding or concept depends on the validity of the procedures employed in arriving at that finding or concept.* In effect, this means that both the results of an experiment and the conclusions the investigator derives from it can never transcend the methodology employed.

Bearing in mind this brief analysis of the importance of methodology, it becomes clear that in order to understand systems, schools, and theoretical points of view in psychology we must first have some appreciation of the methodology which lies at their foundation. In the last analysis, the exposition of a systematic point of view is a statement of its *aims, methods,* and *findings.* From what has already been said, the value of the findings is contingent upon the validity of the methods used in the investigation. Aims, too, however, tend to be inextricably interwoven with methods. For example, it is obvious that if the scientist's goal is to investigate the nature of the solar system, his methodology will be quite different from that which he would employ if he were embarking on a study of Australian mammals. As a consequence of this close, interdependent relationship between aims and methods, it becomes apparent that while it is correct to speak of *the* scientific method, each science has, in addition, its own specialized methodology. It is largely this specialization in aims and procedures which distinguishes each science from every other.

To summarize, it seems logical to begin our survey of systematic psychology with a study of the aims and methods which were instrumental in establishing the various systems, for this approach alone makes possible an operationistic frame of reference. Because, however, psychology and the methods employed in psychological investigations evolved slowly over the centuries, we shall begin by relating the evolution of the scientific method in psychology to the development of science in general. With this broader perspective as a background, we shall see that the problems and methods involved in the understanding of human behavior are not new, but represent the evolution of generations of thought, research, and debate.

PSYCHOLOGY WITHIN THE FRAMEWORK OF SCIENCE

In attempting to relate psychology to her sister sciences as these evolved from their common ancestor, philosophy, we are immediately faced with a dilemma. Is psychology a natural science or a social science? Would it be best to look for the roots of psychology in the history of chemistry, physics, and zoology, or should our search begin with those intellectual movements which led to the development of sociology, anthropology, economics, and political science? If we turn to the history of psychology for the solution to our problem we find that psychology evolved out of a coalescence of natural science and that branch of philosophy known as *epistemology,* or the theory of knowledge.

To put it another way, great thinkers have always been interested in the problems associated with the validity of human knowledge; and, as a result, an entire branch of philosophy, epistemology, came to be devoted almost exclusively to the study of such problems. But when the question is raised as to how we obtain knowledge of our environment, it quickly becomes involved with such corollary questions as: What are the avenues of knowledge? What organ is the repository of knowledge? How well does our mental picture of the physical world correspond to reality? While these are legitimate philosophical questions, their answers require an understanding of the sense organs, which are the avenues of knowledge, and the brain as the interpreter of sensations and the repository and integrator of experiences. Moreover, we need to know something of the physics of light, sound, and of the stimuli for the sense of smell as well as the other sense modalities. We also need to know how nerves and neurons work and how faithfully the brain can reproduce mental pictures of physical objects from nervous impulses generated in the sense organs by the stimuli from those objects. Obviously what we have here is the beginning of a hybrid science that must concern itself with relational problems—problems of how the physical, physiological, and psychological all relate to each other. And, in its beginnings, psychology was such a three-way synthesis of physics, physiology, and mental philosophy.

As the new science grew out of its infancy, many psychologists became impatient with restricting psychological research to the threefold problem of mind-body-physical relationships and insisted on broadening the young science to include the social, cultural, and interpersonal problems of human behavior which make up such a large segment of psychology today. As a consequence of this division of interests within the field, it is impossible to be black-and-white in categorizing psychology as a natural or a social science. It is allied to both of these broad areas of knowledge, and, according to their own interests and theoretical leanings, psychologists tend to divide themselves along similar lines. Some, notably the physiological psychologists with their strong interest in the workings of the nervous system, resemble physiologists more than they do psychologists. On the other hand, some psychologists, at least in the kind of work they do, are more appropriately described as social rather than natural scientists, and at a dinner party would find it easier to keep up a conversation with a social anthropologist than with a physiological psychologist. In the face of such a dilemma it seems wise to beat a strategic retreat and let the future decide whether psychology will ultimately become a pure natural science, or go over into the camp of the social sciences, or simply remain as it is. In any case, we can resolve the issue for our purposes by examining both sides of the question, first considering the working assumptions of the psychologist as a natural scientist and then examining those he must embrace as a social scientist.

PSYCHOLOGY AS A NATURAL SCIENCE

In general, although there are exceptions among individuals, natural scientists subscribe to the following credo of four fundamental assumptions about the processes of nature which constitutes their philosophy of science: (1) *natural monism*, (2) *mechanism*, (3) *operationism*, and (4) *determinism*. Each of these concepts will be discussed briefly in turn.

Natural monism.   Natural monism holds that the natural sciences form a family tree with physics, chemistry, and the other physical sciences at the roots and with biology, physiology, and psychology branching off from the top. Stated somewhat differently, physics and chemistry deal with matter in its simplest and most fundamental forms, while biology and psychology study nature's most complex organic compounds. If all sciences lie along a single continuum, then, according to this point of view, psychology can theoretically be reduced to physiology; and physiology in turn may be reduced to the physics and chemistry of organic compounds. Of course no one has demonstrated that mental processes are literally reducible into the physics and chemistry of brain matter, but such a hypothesis has led to many interesting discoveries in the area of psychoneural relationships. Moreover, this monistic view does not mean the psychologist must sit back with folded hands until the physiologist is ready with a complete explanation of glandular and nervous processes to which behavior can be related. Instead, the increasingly popular view among even the most natural-science-minded psychologists is to study behavior *at the level of behavior,* seeking to establish valid predictive principles without necessarily attempting to ground them in underlying glandular or nervous processes. By analogy, many people make good automobile drivers and could learn a great deal of predictive value about a new model's performance characteristics without knowing much about the engine. By contrast, the earlier psychologists who were interested in developing psychology as a natural science felt that a close kinship existed between psychology and the biological sciences, and many of them, as will be demonstrated later, made some attempt to relate psychological theory to underlying physiological mechanisms. This point of view, it might be noted, has often been called "reductionism."

Mechanism.   Mechanism has many shades of meaning, some of which have acquired a bad name. As applied in its most literal sense, mechanism means that the scientist looks upon the universe as a vast machine peopled by machines. Human behavior, in turn, would be no more than the functioning of the bodily machine. According to some of the more extreme proponents of this point of view, life itself will ultimately be created in the laboratory out of inorganic compounds. Mechanism enjoyed considerable popularity in the early 1900's, as a result of the teachings of Jacques Loeb (1859 to 1924), a prominent physiologist of the day, who vigorously championed the mechanistic viewpoint in biology. He was dedicated to the goal of demonstrating that all living things are elaborate chemical machines and are consequently understandable solely in physio-chemical terms. Loeb and his associates were fully confident that they were on the track of creating life in the laboratory out of inert chemicals. Such radical views generated considerable opposition during the first two decades of the present century. Today, such a position seems far less extreme in the wake of recent scientific advances. Psychologists, however, are not concerned with the validity of mechanism in its original sense. Rather, from the point of view of contemporary psychology, mechanism is the attitude that man's behavior, or the functioning of any other subject of scientific inquiry, can best be understood *without an appeal to external explanations;* in short it denies the validity of the *deus ex machina* as an explanatory concept. As a result of the general acceptance of this point of view, contemporary psychologists do not postulate evil spirits to account for bad dreams or demoniac possession to explain abnormal behavior. Rather, just as the astronomer seeks to understand the universe in terms of natural law, the psychologist attempts to account for man's behavior without going outside the laws of the natural sciences to achieve this end.

Operationism. Operationism has already been defined as the principle which holds that the validity of a scientific finding or theoretical construct is contingent upon the validity of the operations involved in arriving at that finding or construct. Operationism came into modern science in 1927 and was championed by Percy W. Bridgman (1882 to 1961), a well-known physicist and mathematician (*4*).[1] Psychologists are in general agreement that this principle is applicable in psychological as well as in physical research. Some psychologists have argued that certain concepts in psychology have proved useful even though it has not been possible to identify their corresponding operations. Nevertheless, at some point the investigator must be prepared to define his concepts in terms of the operations used to formulate them or he will fail to obtain general acceptance for his conclusions and generalizations. The student, too, as he examines the systematic viewpoints in subsequent chapters would do well to keep this principle in mind, asking

---

[1] Italicized numbers in parentheses refer to the references at the end of the chapter.

himself such questions as: What is the evidence for this theory? Are the experiments which led to this concept or generalization valid? Is this conclusion justified? By cultivating the operationistic point of view, the student, like the mature scientist, will acquire a critical spirit, which is the first mark of scientific sophistication.

It is also worth pointing out that the operationistic attitude is in part a reflection of the more general spirit of self-criticism and self-correction so characteristic of science. Each facet of human endeavor has its critics. There are art critics, literary critics, drama critics, and so on. But science is unique in being self-critical and therefore self-correcting. The scientist expects criticism of his hypotheses, methods, and findings, indeed invites it from his fellow scientists, since only his peers are capable of relevant and intelligent criticism. Naturally, this does not imply that scientists never make mistakes or that science alone holds the final answer to every question. Rather, it means that the scientist opens his work to criticism, that he is willing to change his mind, and that science is not likely to perpetrate error for very long. All of this may seem rather obvious, but a moment's reflection on how different the case has been in recent decades for political, economic, or philosophical systems (and "science") under totalitarian regimes will reiterate its importance.

Determinism.   Determinism is the assumption that everything that happens in the universe can be accounted for by definite laws of causation. As applied to human behavior the principle holds that all actions are subject to natural laws and must, therefore, be explained in terms of causative factors lying within the individual's heredity and environment. Consequently, from the deterministic point of view freedom of action is an illusion. All choices, great and small, are determined by the chain of causes and effects that reach back over the individual's entire life history, and even beyond into the genetic determiners inherited from his parents.

Largely because of its antithetical position to free will, determinism is sometimes confused with predestination. The latter, however, is a theological concept which holds that, irrespective of what the individual does, his ultimate fate after death is already determined.

Psychological determinism implies no such fatalistic view of the individual's post-mortem destiny, since scientific determinism deals only with earthly matters and does not concern itself with spiritual or theological issues. Neither should determinism be used to rationalize a philosophy of irresponsibility by those who argue that if one's behavior is determined by his past he is not a free agent and consequently is not responsible for anything he does. Such a notion is embodied in the story of the slave who was caught stealing by the philosopher Zeno. When Zeno got out the whip, the slave protested, "Master, according to thy teachings it was determined that I would steal from thee and thou should not beat me for that which I am not responsible." Zeno replied, "It is also determined that I will beat thee."

The answer to these difficulties lies in appreciating the position that determinism is a point of view or a working principle in science which has led to fruitful research, but is not to be construed as a guide for individual conduct. In fact, the ethical tradition of Western civilization is one of self-determinism in conduct. This, too, is a useful point of view within its own sphere, which, if carried over into the sciences, would become ridiculous. For example, any astronomer who "explained" the earth's rotation around the sun as due to the earth's desire to go around the sun would be expelled from the fellowship of scientists.

In summary, psychology as a natural science subscribes to four broad scientific principles: monism, mechanism, operationism, and determinism. Their function is to provide the psychologist with working hypotheses to guide him in the conduct of research and in the interpretation of research results. Each, as we have seen, is useful within its own frame of reference, but none is to be construed as an established fact or as an ethical principle for the guidance of individual behavior.

PSYCHOLOGY AS A SOCIAL SCIENCE

There is no commonly accepted set of scientific assumptions to which social scientists adhere; and, as a result, the individual scientist has considerable latitude in formulating aims, designing studies or experiments, and in interpreting results. The greater flexibility that is characteristic of the social sciences derives in part from the fact that, as established and recognized areas of knowledge, most of the social sciences are relatively young compared to the natural sciences. Consequently, they are comparatively free from the restraints of tradition. Secondly, the social sciences deal with highly complex economic, political, sociological, and psychological processes in which there is greater room for divergent views on just how investigations should be conducted. In a sense, this means that each investigation must stand on its own merits, often without the advantage of an evaluation based on prior experience or upon broad theoretical principles. For the most part, however, the social scientist, like the natural scientist, makes use of studies or experiments, is careful to observe all precautions of scientific observation and control, and interprets his results with the aid of quantitative or statistical techniques.

Perhaps the most striking differences, at least in psychology, between the psychologist as a natural scientist and the psychologist as a social scientist lie in the philosophical orientation and in the nature of the theoretical constructs which each employs. In general, the social psychologist fails to see the necessity for grounding psychology in physiology and is therefore not reductionistic in his explanations. Moreover, he is less interested in tracing the antecedents of present behavior back to earlier periods in the individual's development. Instead, he tends to emphasize the contemporary nature of causative factors in behavior. For this reason, he rarely stresses the deterministic point of view, even though he recognizes the necessity for it. His is a "soft" rather than a "hard" determinism. Finally, it may be pointed out that his research interests are likely to lie in such areas as social psychology, personality, or group dynamics rather than in the traditional fields of experimental or physiological psychology.

It has often been said that all generalizations are intrinsically invalid, and we would have to admit that exceptions could readily be found for any of the above characterizations of either the naturalistic or social science points of view in psychology. It is impossible to establish absolute categories into which scientists can be neatly fitted, just as it is impossible to type people into extroverts and introverts or some similar dichotomy. Still, such broad generalizations have their value as aids in thinking, provided it is recognized that they may not fit individual cases.

NOMOTHETIC AND IDIOGRAPHIC PSYCHOLOGY

Another useful way to describe the aims, procedures, and theoretical orientation of psychologists is in terms of nomothetic and idiographic points of view. Nomothetic psychology seeks to establish the general laws and principles governing mental and behavioral processes. This is the traditional manner in which psychologists have investigated the processes of development, sensation, perception, learning, motivation, and emotion. In striving to formulate laws of general applicability which pertain to the psychological processes, the psychologist must necessarily ignore the individual. Indeed, he will do his best to overcome the effects of individual differences among his research subjects which might obscure the validity and general applicability of his findings. He accomplishes this primarily by utilizing a large number of subjects who are carefully selected as being a representative sample of the population as a whole. When the data have been collected and are undergoing analysis, elaborate statistical safeguards are employed to insure that the inferences or generalizations drawn from the experiment are warranted by the data on hand.

The idiographic point of view stresses the understanding of a particular individual or event. Here the psychologist's emphasis is on the discovery of the laws of the individual case; consequently, he focuses his investigation on the person. Many clinical psychologists who favor the idiographic point of view emphasize that each individual is unique and therefore must be understood in terms of his own set of laws. They argue that to study generalized mental or behavioral processes is to force the individual into a mold or a type and to overlook the very differences which, in the final analysis, make him unique.

Of course, the study of large numbers of individuals from the idiographic point of view will reveal many similarities as well as differences among them. And so the clinician in striving to account for behavioral disorders is likely to formulate general laws of personality development and deviation, thus becoming something of a nomothetic psychologist. This is particularly true of clinicians who are strongly research-oriented Similarly, the differential psychologist who studies intellectual and personality differences in terms of standardized tests will also generalize his findings, sometimes stressing likenesses among individuals as well as their differences. For this reason the two approaches, nomothetic and idiographic, often complement each other.

Closely related to the division of the field in terms of nomothetic and idiographic psychology is the type of laws which the psychologist seeks to establish. The nomothetic or general psychologist strives to formulate laws of the type $R = f(S)$, or more simply, S-R laws. Thus, given certain observable responses (R), he seeks to establish the functional (f) relationships between those responses and the antecedent stimulating conditions (S). If he can accomplish this he has achieved a major objective of science; since, given the antecedent conditions, he will then be able to predict the response, and if this were considered desirable, to control it.

The idiographic or clinical psychologist searches for R-R laws or laws which govern the relationships among response variables. As an example, the clinician may wish to establish a functional relationship between conflict and anxiety, operating on the hypothesis that conflicts lead to anxiety states. Because he cannot directly control the environmental conditions which promote the development of conflicts in people, he must investigate the relationship between the variables he has chosen either by administering tests or measuring such variables and then correlating the results. For example, he might assess the presence of conflicts by means of a clinical test or projective technique, quantify the results, and then measure anxiety in the same group of subjects by means of an appropriate anxiety scale. Finally, he calculates the coefficient of correlation between the two variables. A significant correlation between two sets of responses does not guarantee that a causal relationship exists, but it does enable the psychologist to predict from one variable to another and to contribute to the prediction, understanding, and control of behavior.

There are some psychologists who have objected to a strict S-R formula as a model for psychology. They regard any system predicated on such

a formula as dealing with an "empty organism." Instead, they prefer the
S-O-R formula in which S represents stimuli, O the organism, and R the
responses. From this point of view psychology is the study of those intervening variables within the organism which mediate between stimuli and
responses. For example, the process of memory is an intervening variable
whose investigation must be undertaken by utilizing various stimuli (word
lists, nonsense syllables, etc.) and then measuring the subject's responses
under various conditions of memorizing. Therefore, the psychologist never
investigates memory directly, but only indirectly through the subject's
responses. He *infers* information about the memory process by studying
the subject's responses. The investigation of intervening variables is not
limited to psychology. Physicists and chemists often study intervening variables in much the same manner. Resistance, for example, is an inferred
variable which is measured by the flow of current through electrical circuits.

Each of these points of view is useful in psychology. We have already
pointed out how the important work of the clinical psychologist is furthered
by an idiographic, R-R orientation. Strongly behavioristic and operationistic psychologists tend to favor an S-R approach, arguing that little is
gained by adding hypothetical intervening variables to the formula. All
we can *measure,* they emphasize, are responses, and that which cannot be
measured cannot be dealt with scientifically. Others, particularly those
who take a more organismic point of view, believe that psychologists should
keep the individual or the organism in the picture even though general or
behavioral processes are under study.

We shall be considering many examples of these different points of
view in the pages to follow. Meanwhile we shall return to a consideration
of the origins of the scientific method, with a view to discovering just how
psychology came to be launched as an independent science and to seeking
a better understanding of the evolution of the scientific method in psychology.

THE ORIGINS OF SCIENCE

The dawn of science was far from a dramatic and sudden burst of
illumination which forever dispelled the darkness of ignorance and superstition. Instead, science as a whole, as **Ebbinghaus**[2] (1850 to 1909) once
said of psychology, has a long past but a short history. In fact, the point
of view to be presented here envisages modern science as a relatively recent

---

[2] For those persons whose names appear in boldface in Chapters 1 and 2, the reader will find
brief biographies at the ends of the respective chapters; these biographies are arranged alpha-
betically. Ebbinghaus was an important contributor to the early experimental psychology of
learning; a discussion of his contributions appears in Chapter 6 of this book.

system of thought which gradually evolved partly out of and partly parallel within two antecedent systems—animism and religion. This, of course, does not imply that science has supplanted religion and that religion in turn has displaced animism, for both religion and animism are still in abundant evidence throughout the world. Rather, it suggests that as social orders began to take shape among primitive prehistoric tribes, animism was the first organized and more or less universal system of thought. Religion evolved much later, whereas science is a relatively recent product of the human mind. Each earlier system remained in force, however, even though its explanatory power was diminished. Let us trace these developments by considering briefly how each system of thought was related to the other in terms of their historical antecedents.

Animism.   Animism is the primitive belief system characteristic of early totemic social orders and is still found in primitive societies today. As men began to form social groups, they organized into clans whose guiding spirit and supreme authority was a totem. The totem might be a bear, rain, a river, or whatever natural phenomenon appeared to have potential power over the weal and woe of the clan. The totem was consulted as an oracle, was offered sacrifices to propitiate its wrath, and in general was worshiped as a kind of primitive god. Animism also meant attributing spirits to clouds, plants, or to anything that moved or seemed potentially powerful. This naive conception of causality is sometimes found in children's explanations of why clouds move or why the wind blows (*12*). However erroneous, animism was nevertheless the first faltering step on the road to science, since it involved an attempt to understand, predict, and control nature. These are the very aims of contemporary science, but the methodology and interpretations of scientists are, to be sure, totally lacking in animism.

Religion.   As is true of animism, the origins of the ancient religions are obscured by the mists of antiquity. There is good reason, however, to believe that religion evolved as a natural outgrowth of animism (*8*). When specialization of function began to take place in the clan society, some members became warriors, others hunters, and still others assumed the position of medicine men. And those who specialized in priestcraft took over the office of dealing with the totem. Theirs was the job of interpreting the wishes of the clan to the totem and the totem to the clan. Gradually a body of ritual, symbolism, and dogma accrued to the priestly office, and in this manner a primitive religion took form. Still later, new religions came into existence largely through revelation to individuals who then became the prophets and promulgators of the new creeds. Primarily because of their origins, most of the major religious systems are characteristically authoritarian, dogmatic, and founded on revelation rather than on rationalistic speculation or experimentation. As a consequence, religion and science are grounded on antagonistic principles. On the positive side, however, many great theologians have attempted to rationalize religious beliefs and in the process have made searching inquiries into human nature and its relationship to the deity. This technique for seeking knowledge is the rational method so familiar to the philosopher. Rationalism in religious (and secular) philosophy has carried over into science, and every scientific deduction or hypothesis is an inquiry that must be put to nature for an answer. Thus, religion is not necessarily antagonistic to the spirit of inquiry, since this selfsame spirit in a different frame of reference becomes the quest for scientific knowledge.

Science.   Unlike animism and organized religion, science is essentially a Western concept. Science, especially science as a sacred cow, in no sense occupies such a prominent place in the Orient as it does in our culture. This geographical dissimilarity in attitudes extends into other areas such as politics, economics, and agricultural systems. In part, this is a reflection of the fact that our Western heritage in its various manifestations stems from a common intellectual ancestor, ancient Greece. Moreover, the Oriental thinker puts more emphasis on intuitive knowledge and on paradoxical and mystical approaches to ultimate reality. However valuable these modes of thinking may be in other spheres, they tend to stifle scientific progress.

Finally, in attempting to interrelate animism, religion, and science we may borrow from the philosopher Hans Vaihinger (13), who suggested that in the evolution of thought an ideational shift takes place in the direction of myth→ dogma→ hypothesis→ myth. Thus, what at first is animistic myth becomes religious dogma, but with increasing knowledge such dogmas are challenged successfully and retreat into hypotheses. Those unable to stand the test of time finally return once again to myths. Such, certainly, has been the fate of the old Greek and Roman religions. But in a sense science, too, is no more than a set of fictions or myths which work in practice. The physicist, chemist, or psychologist constructs elaborate theoretical or "fictional" systems which "explain" only in the sense that they hang together and account for scientific observations. This is why what was once considered truth in science has now been discarded and has reverted to the status of myth.

Insofar as we have any records of its early beginnings, science as we know it appears to have originated among the ancient civilizations of both the old and new worlds. We find evidence of scientific accomplishments, often striking in their intellectual sophistication, among the Sumerians, Egyptians, Aztecs, and Greeks (6). Each of these ancient peoples realized a relatively high degree of civilization which is a prerequisite for the emergence of science. Here, however, we shall be concerned only with the development of science among the Greeks, since it is to them that the origins of European thought, and incidentally psychology, can be traced.

Science among the Greeks.[3]   There were two branches of Greek thought significant for the development of modern science. These were cosmology and rationalism. Cosmology is the study of the cosmos—how it originated, its evolution, and structure. This school of thought was typified by the teachings of the philosopher **Democritus,** one of the later cosmologists, who postulated an atomic theory of the universe. In general, the cosmologists were reductionists, and were striving to resolve the physical universe into the irreducible elements of which they believed it to be fashioned. Some of Democritus' predecessors, however, were enlightened enough and broad enough in their interests to give a correct explanation of eclipses, to formulate a gas condensation theory of the origin of the universe, to argue that the stars are balls of fire, and finally to antedate Darwin's theory of the origin of the species by assuming a process of natural selection to account for the diversity of living forms. To maintain a proper perspective, however, it must be admitted that much of Greek science was also childish and unworthy of a modern high school student.

Generally speaking, the speculations of the cosmologists were materialistic in keeping with their attempts to formulate mechanistic models of the universe. This empirical trend in philosophy never disappeared from Grecian thought. For a time, however, it was obscured by the rationalists, typified by **Plato,** and by the Sophists, noted for their love of argument and their devotion to tricky reasoning. But the empirical spirit reemerged in **Aristotle,** who has often been called the world's greatest thinker. Whether or not he deserves such an exalted title, it is true that he tried to span the scope of knowledge as it existed in his time. He was a logician, aesthetician, biologist, ethical theorist, and the administrator of an educational institution. He wrote dozens of works not only in philosophy but also in physics, biology, meteorology, psychology, and politics. For our purposes it is noteworthy that he wrote a psychological treatise in which he systematically dealt with the various mental processes of sensation, perception, and memory. The modern writer and educator, Will Durant, in his *Story of Philosophy,* calls Aristotle "the *Encyclopaedia Britannica* of ancient Greece." So powerful was the domination of his intellect that he is generally acknowledged to be the father of modern science, and his word was law among scholars up to the time of the Renaissance.

---

[3] The account of Greek science and philosophy has been drawn from Boring (2), Murphy (11), Brett (3), and Durant (7).

Plato and the rationalistic movement. The rationalists sought enlightenment on philosophical problems by exercising the kind of thinking which we today call deductive as opposed to inductive. To put it another way, the rationalist is convinced he can get at the truth by the use of reason, and believes that knowledge derived from reason is just as valid as, and often superior to, knowledge originating from sense perceptions. Such, for example, was the basis for Plato's philosophy, which because of its subjective orientation is something of a mixture of poetry, science, and art.

Plato is most widely known for his *Republic* and for his interest in an ideal state—or Utopia, to use the name made famous by Sir Thomas More in 1516. It was his desire to found a brave new world which led him into psychological speculation, for in order to create the Utopian conditions necessary for bringing about the betterment of man, a prior knowledge of human nature is demanded. It is interesting to note that in the course of his speculation on human nature Plato concluded that man's behavior stems from three sources: *desire,* primarily sexual in nature; *emotion,* which arises from the heat of the blood; and *knowledge,* stemming from the head. In a Utopian society the man of desire would be assigned the job of running business enterprises; the man of emotion would be trained as a soldier; the man of reason would become a philosopher; and, understandably enough, philosophers would govern Utopia.

Plato also posed a psychological problem which we shall see has persisted down through the ages to contemporary psychology. This was the problem of the nature of mind and body and their relation to each other. Plato took a dualistic position separating the two and asserting that they were different entities. He, of course, failed to resolve the dilemma by separating them, but he was clearly more interested in the nature of mind than of body. The material body, he pointed out, perishes all too soon, but mind is permanent in the sense that ideas may live on for generations after the body has turned to dust. For this reason, in Utopia mind is to be cultivated by education so that ideals and worthwhile generalizations might bring order and reason into man's too often chaotic ideas.

By way of summarizing the contributions of this classic society to the development of the scientific method, we may credit the cosmologists with originating both naturalistic observation and the notion of understanding the unknown by reducing it to its constituent elements. Both of these methodological approaches are fundamental first stages in every science, whether ancient or modern. From Aristotle we have the idea of organizing the phenomena of nature into broad descriptive categories, which is the second stage in scientific endeavor, since before we can explain natural phenomena we must describe them and put them into some kind of order. Plato and the rationalists were less the scientists and more the philosophers, yet their rationalistic approach has its counterpart in the hypothetico-deductive method in modern science wherein the scientist attempts to postulate a rational set of assumptions to be tested by experiment.

Finally, we ought to mention the fact that one school among the ancient philosophers recognized the value of quantitative, or mathematical, methods. Mention of this group was omitted in the previous discussion since they belonged to neither the cosmologists nor the rationalists, but constituted a school unto themselves. Euclid and Pythagoras, two prominent Greeks who interested themselves in mathematical methods, are universally known at least by hard-pressed high school students who must learn their theorems. Today quantitative methods play a crucial part in both the natural and the social sciences. Thus, the Greeks in essence recognized the significance of what we believe to be *four* important stages in the scientific method: (1) naturalistic observation, (2) analysis and classification of natural phenomena into meaningful descriptive categories, (3) the formulation of hypotheses of cause and effect on the basis of such analyses, and (4) the value of quantitative methods. All that remains is to test the hypotheses by experiment or by critical observations. In this the Greeks were quite limited, although they did carry out a few crude experiments. The experimental attack on nature had to wait for many centuries before coming into its own. However, it is to the great credit of this ancient people that they were able to develop what in essence amounts to a sophisticated scientific methodology more than 2000 years ago.

SCIENCE IN THE MIDDLE AGES AND RENAISSANCE

With the death of Aristotle and the collapse of the Greek city-states, Greek science and philosophy suffered a decline. Barbarian invasions swarmed down over Europe, and at the same time Christianity began to catch fire and spread out from the Middle East. These political and religious upheavals led to an intellectual darkness in the West that is popularly characterized as the Dark Ages. The atmosphere was dominated by authoritarianism, both political and theological; and consequently scientific progress came to a virtual halt. The science of Aristotle was considered law in its sphere, and the Church actively discouraged independent scientific inquiries, which might embarrass or challenge the teachings of canon law.

But the Dark Ages were not entirely dark. There were a few thinkers and scholars who were willing to challenge dogmatism and risk the wrath of the Church. Those who stand out in the history of science during the 1400's and 1500's will be mentioned briefly. First there was Leonardo Da Vinci—artist, engineer, geologist—in fact, all-around genius. Copernicus, too, belongs to this period. He postulated a heliocentric theory of the solar system in opposition to the ancient Ptolemaic view which had erroneously placed the earth at the center of the solar family. Galileo is, of course, famous for his experiments with falling objects at the Leaning Tower of Pisa, but his astronomical observations in support of Copernicus were even more significant. Finally, Francis Bacon, the British scholar, ought to be mentioned since he successfully challenged the notion that classical science had already discovered everything of importance and thus led the break away from Aristotle. None of these intellectual giants is directly related to the evolution of psychology, but indirectly these and men of similar caliber created an atmosphere in which scientific inquiry could once again flourish. Consequently, they are important in the general evolution of modern science.

There was, however, one medieval scholar who is an exception because he stands in a direct relationship to the history of modern psychology. This was the French philosopher and mathematician, **René Descartes** (1596 to 1650). In many ways Descartes symbolizes a transition in human thought from the Renaissance to the modern period. Torn as he was between the safe, dogmatic beliefs of the medieval Church and the revolutionary ideas which were taking shape in his own mind, he took the crucial step and became a man of enlightenment. His philosophical method of doubting every proposition carried him even to the brink of disbelief in God, but he retreated from that extreme position. Because he could not doubt that he thought, he was able to assert the primacy of existence (*Cogito, ergo sum*). His reasoning led him to distinguish clearly between existence or consciousness and body or material substance, thus reaffirming Plato's dualism. But he was a special kind of dualist who believed that although mind and body are separate, they nevertheless interact with each other. For this reason Descartes is called an interactionist. He decided that the site of interchange between mind and body is the pineal gland, located at the base of the cerebrum. We still are not certain just what this gland's function is, but no modern psychologist believes it is a two-way gate between body and mind. In other respects Descartes anticipated modern psychology more accurately. He championed the mechanistic point of view and urged physiologists to use the empirical method of dissection in order to discover the machinery of the body. To some extent he must have engaged in this then-frowned-upon practice since he left amazingly accurate descriptions of the nervous system. While he stuck to the old Greek notion of the nerves as conductors of "animal spirits," he did nevertheless anticipate modern discoveries by arguing that the nervous impulses which travel out over nerves originate in the brain.

Descartes is also considered the father of modern philosophy, particularly by the existentialists. His distinction between existence and material essence led to the dichotomy between scientific abstractionism and humanistic existentialism which has become a focal conflict in modern philosophy, literature, and art. The study of abstractions and essences culminated in the development of modern mathematics and the physical sciences. Following Descartes the great systems of philosophy and science concerned themselves almost exclusively with building the abstract and symbolic edifices which have changed the face of Western civilization and given rise to our dominantly scientific and technocratic society. But doubt in the wisdom of the primacy of essence over existence remained a kind of dormant filament in philosophy which found responsive soil in Soren Kierkegaard (1813 to 1855) and Friedrich Nietzsche (1844 to 1900) and their followers. And, in the decades immediately following World War II, existentialism, which asserts the primacy of the individual, his consciousness, and his freedom of will became the dominant philosophy in Europe and profoundly influenced American philosophy and theology.[4]

As we have pointed out, from Descartes onward the development of modern science was rapid and prolific. It would not be feasible to trace its further progress in a general way; rather, we shall narrow our perspective to encompass only those intellectual developments which are directly related to the emergence of psychology. Indeed, for a while we shall turn away from science altogether in favor of pursuing certain developments in British philosophy which, as was pointed out earlier in this chapter, coalesced with physiology, ultimately to produce psychology. When we have completed our survey of British philosophy we shall return briefly to the further developments in natural science which are relevant for psychology.

BRITISH EMPIRICISM [5]

The ancient Greek modes of thought, empiricism, and rationalism, are reflected in British and Continental philosophy in the seventeenth and eighteenth centuries. Descartes, as we have shown, was mechanistic in his thinking and leaned toward empirical observation in studying nature. Yet he also had a rationalistic side, since he believed in the value of a priori axioms in philosophical speculation. In general, the British philosophers associated themselves with the empirical tradition, whereas on the continent of Europe both points of view had their adherents. Several of the British empirical philosophers' contributions will be considered in some detail, since they deal with psychological problems which have a bearing

[4] For a more detailed account of the development of existentialism and its place in philosophy, literature, and psychology see Barrett (*1*).
[5] For a more detailed account of the British Empiricists the reader should consult Boring (*2*) or Murphy (*11*).

on both the methodology and the systematic structure of modern psychology.

We may begin with **Thomas Hobbes** (1588 to 1679), who opposed Descartes' notion of innate ideas and instead held that sensations are the source of all knowledge. Memory and imagination he explained as decaying sense impressions which are held together by association. These teachings enabled British philosophy to break completely with the Middle Ages and initiated the philosophical school of empiricism which paved the way for the psychological school of associationism. Empiricism places the origin of mind in sensation and accounts for the higher mental processes, such as memory, thinking, and imagination, as complexes of persistent impressions held together by association. The associations in turn are said to arise because of certain conditions which existed at the time of impression, such as repetition and contiguity. For these reasons "grass" brings to mind "green," because we repeatedly experience visual and auditory sense impressions of the two ideas in close temporal contiguity. We shall return to the problem of the association of ideas in the chapters on learning, where associationism as such is treated more fully. Meanwhile, we may reiterate that Hobbes' importance lies in the fact that he provided a foundation for the empirical and associationistic movements in British philosophy, which ultimately carried over into psychology.

John Locke (1632 to 1704) extended Hobbes' principle of the empirical sources of human knowledge. In his *Essay Concerning Human Understanding,* Locke put the essence of his doctrine in the now famous comparison of the infant's mind to a *tabula rasa,* or blank paper, upon which experience writes. By holding that the infantile mind is a blank, Locke was denying the existence of innate ideas and asserting instead that all knowledge derives from experience and all knowledge is therefore empirical in origin. Simple, uncompounded ideas originate directly in sense experience, and the mind by combining simple ideas forms complex ideas. Part of his doctrine had to do with another problem of interest to psychology, and this was a distinction which he drew between "primary" and "secondary" qualities. The primary qualities are characteristics such as solidity, extension, mobility, and number. Primary qualities are inherent in external objects, while secondary qualities, such as color or odor, are dependent upon the mind. Thus, the size of a house is a primary quality inherent in the physical structure of that house. The color of the house or the recognition of the architectural period to which it belongs is dependent on the experiencing person.

The problem with which Locke was struggling is often heard in another setting in the old folk puzzle which is stated somewhat as follows: If a tree falls in the woods and there is nobody around to hear it, does it make any noise? The answer depends on the frame of reference one assumes.

Physically, sound waves are present in the sense that the tree certainly creates a molecular disturbance in the atmosphere, but psychologically there is no "sound" if there is no one to hear it. Locke's position has reappeared as a distinction in modern psychology between the physical situation and the psychological field (9). All people listening to the same radio or viewing a beautiful landscape are experiencing identical physical stimuli. This is the physical situation, but each perceives the situation differently according to his interests, past experience, and intelligence. Each individual's perception is a psychological field unique for each perceiver.

The importance of Locke's work lies in the fact that he presented the first completely worked out empirical theory of knowledge. Many of the issues first raised by him are still current in philosophy.

George Berkeley (1685 to 1753), Locke's successor in British empirical philosophy, carried the problem of inherent versus secondary qualities to its logical extreme by denying the validity of Locke's distinction. He asserted that there were no primary qualities, but that *all* knowledge is dependent upon the experiencing person. This would mean that even those seemingly well-entrenched physical qualities of shape, size, and position are in effect man-made constructs which we attribute to the environment. The only "reality" is mind. Berkeley's extremist position never gained popular support either in his own field of philosophy or in science. This is understandable in view of the fact that such a position essentially precludes the possibility of any kind of collective philosophy or science, since there would be no constancies upon which to base these disciplines. One could not be certain that anything exists except individual ideas.

In addition to this philosophical tour de force Berkeley also contributed the first book primarily devoted to the analysis of a psychological problem. This was his treatise entitled *A New Theory of Vision*. In it he dealt with the problem of how we perceive depth in space in spite of the two-dimensional nature of our retinas. His solution anticipated modern scientific knowledge quite accurately, since he included what we today call the physiological cues of convergence and accomodation and the psychological cues of interposition, shadows, and aerial perspective.

Finally, it is worth mentioning that Berkeley subscribed to the principle of association of ideas in accounting for the more complex process of the relation of experiences and ideas to each other. Thus, he continued the associationistic tradition originating with his predecessors Hobbes and Locke.

David Hume (1711 to 1776) not only agreed with Berkeley as to the nonreality of matter apart from the experiencing mind, but went a step further. He abolished "mind" entirely as a true entity or substance. Mind, Hume argued, is only a name for the flow of ideas, memories, imagination, and feelings. Moreover, mind, like matter, is a "secondary quality" observable only through perception. When we think we are perceiving mind we are merely perceiving separate ideas or internal sensations.

Not satisfied with applying the coup de grace to mind, Hume proceeded to abolish any notion of lawfulness in nature. Scientific laws, he argued, are in no sense the children of nature, but fictional constructs in the minds of men. Even general ideas, such as the idea of triangularity, are no more than concepts which designate collections of similar particular experiences that we have had in the past. Thus, we arrive at the position where nature, mind, and natural law are no more than ideational phenomena. In Hume's time such ideas were shocking and spelled radicalism with a vengeance, for they destroyed the very foundations of rational thought, science, and psychology. The dogmas of religion and the principles of science were no longer the eternal truths that men had traditionally believed them to be.

Even though Hume had done away with mind, there remained the problem of differentiating among the processes of ideation, memory, and imagination. It seems one cannot do away with "mind" completely! Hume distinguished between ideas of memory and ideas of imagination. Ideas of imagination were less distinct than ideas of memory, since the imaginative processes are less closely related to the original source of stimulation. Hume went on to discuss simple and complex ideas, the latter of course posing the problem of what causes ideas to cohere into complex cognitive structures. In keeping with his philosophical predecessors, Hume invoked the doctrine of associationism to account for the connectedness of complex ideas. Associational attraction could in turn be reduced to the "laws" of association, which for Hume were ultimately reducible to the principles of resemblance and contiguity. This aspect of Hume's psychology we shall deal with more fully in the chapters on learning. For the present it is sufficient to reiterate the strong affinity between the philosophical position of empiricism and the psychological doctrine of associationism. In a sense each demands the other, for both views are mechanistic in their attitude toward mind. Moreover, both are reductionistic and highly analytic in their approach to both epistemological and psychological problems, and these same trends were carried over into psychology when it came of age.

Hume's *Treatise on Human Nature* proved to be a rich source of inspiration for succeeding generations of philosophers. His strongly empirical side not only supported the established empirical tradition but can be found in contemporary systems of logical positivism and linguistic analysis. His extreme skepticism about the nature of reality has had an impact on both contemporary philosophers and theologians. His psychological analyses influenced both the pragmatists and the instrumentalists, such as James and Dewey. Many philosophers regard the *Treatise* as the most profound work written in the English language.

In this same tradition we may briefly mention **David Hartley** (1705 to 1757), who is considered by Boring (2) to be the founder of associationism as a distinct school within philosophy and psychology. Hartley, Boring adds, was an "important" but not a "great" man. This characterization our historian justifies on the grounds that Hartley systematized and organized the various threads of thought from Hobbes to Berkeley, formulating them into the formal doctrine of associationism, but was not the originator of new ideas or insights into the nature of mind. For this reason we need only mention that Hartley's formal laws of association were contiguity and repetition, and pass on to James Mill and his son John Stuart Mill, the last of the philosophers in our survey of the empirical-associationistic tradition.

James Mill (1773 to 1836) was the greatest associationist of them all, and carried the doctrine to its logical extreme in a kind of *reductio ad absurdum*. He began by subscribing to the by now familiar notion that sensations and ideas are the primary material of mind. Knowledge begins with sensation, whereas perceptions or ideas are derived processes or complexes. Thus, once again we have the familiar argument that mind is developed from elements and can therefore be reduced to elements by analysis. Perhaps no better illustration of this kind of thinking occurs than in the following often-quoted passage from James Mill's *Analysis of the Phenomena of the Human Mind,* Vol. I, p. 115.

> Brick is one complex idea, mortar is another complex idea; these ideas, with ideas of position and quantity, compose my idea of a wall. My idea of a plank is a complex idea, my idea of a rafter is a complex idea, my idea of a nail is a complex idea.
> These, united with the same ideas of position and quantity, compose my duplex idea of a floor. In the same manner my complex ideas of glass, wood, and others, compose my duplex idea of a window; and these duplex ideas, united together, compose my idea of a house, which is made up of various duplex ideas. How many complex, or duplex ideas, are all united in the idea of furniture? How many more in the idea of merchandise? How many more in the idea called Every Thing?

So extreme were James Mill's doctrines that his own son, **John Stuart Mill** (1806 to 1873), took issue with them on a very fundamental point. This was to argue that elements may *generate* complex ideas, but the ideas thus generated are *not* merely the sum of the individual parts. James Mill had previously argued that simple ideas *combine* into complex ideas. But in John Mill's way of viewing the matter a new quality emerges which may be unrecognizable as a mere conglomeration of elements. If, for example, we add blue, green, and red lights in proper proportions we get white. But the naïve observer would never have predicted such an outcome, and even the sophisticated observer cannot see the separate colors in the final product. John Mill's critique of his father's doctrine anticipated an important principle of Gestalt psychology, which is often quoted in the catch phrase "The whole is greater than the sum of its parts."

It would be well, before we leave the empiricists and associationists, to recapitulate the various lines of thought that came down to psychology from this philosophical tradition by the third quarter of the nineteenth century. To begin with, the problem of the nature of mind first formulated by the Greeks had already undergone considerable evolution from its inception to the time of the Mills. The Greeks provided general answers, but answers which were in themselves largely fresh problems. To recognize that mind and body differ in nature, to suggest that analysis into elements accounts for the problem of combinations of the many into one unitary whole, and to pursue two opposed methodological approaches—empirical and rational—in many ways raises more questions than it answers. In a phrase, we might say the Greeks posed the problems for the future to answer.

When philosophy freed itself from dogmatism and subservience to the rationalistic approach, the same old problems presented themselves anew: What is mind? How does it develop its complex cognitive structures? What are the laws of memory? The empirical-associationistic tradition found the answers in elementalism and associationism. Mind is built from sense experiences. These experiences provide simple ideas or memories which coalesce into complex ideas by virtue of associations which in turn arise through contiguity, repetition, similarity, and so on. In understanding mind, then, the most promising approach was held to be the empirical, atomistic, and mechanistic. In short, philosophy was becoming "scientific" and turning away from its traditional rationalism. What was needed was an *experimental* or *observational* approach to these problems and issues. Philosophy had done all it could. The stage was set for the introduction of the methods of the natural sciences to provide an experimental attack on the problems of mind.

THE PHYSIOLOGICAL INFLUENCE

We left the evolution of natural sciences at the Renaissance when we began our excursion into philosophy. We must now return briefly to developments in physiology during this same period which had a profound influence on the fate of the new psychology. In doing so we span three quarters of a century—from 1800 to the 1870's—the period when the physiological foundations of modern medicine were being laid. Great strides were being made in the understanding of the nervous system, that most complex of all physiological problems. At the same time, in their research interests physiologists were moving more and more into the bailiwick of psychology. This was the beginning of an interdisciplinary approach or the development of a physiological psychology devoted to the task of discovering the nervous mechanisms which underlie the mental processes. Such an approach seems promising for psychology on purely logical grounds. After all, the philosopher can speculate on and rationalize the nature of mind indefinitely, but this does not convince the natural scientist that the answers offered are correct. More valid from a scientific point of view would seem to be a direct attack on the sense organs to discover the nature of sensation and a direct study of the brain to uncover the neural equivalents of mental processes. This is the task of physiology.

Experimental physiology.   Physiology became an experimental discipline in the decade of the 1830's. Major responsibility for this development is assigned to two outstanding men of the period, **Johannes Müller** (1801 to 1858) and Claude Bernard (1815 to 1878). Both were strong advocates of the experimental method in physiology, and each made significant and lasting contributions to his chosen field. Müller is noted for two contributions. First, he wrote a *Handbook of Physiology* (which came out in several volumes between 1833 and 1840) in which he summarized the physiological research of the period, thus presenting an impressive body of knowledge in support of the new standing of physiology as an independent science. Second, he is also famous both in physiology and psychology for his doctrine of the specific energies of nerves. In his statement of the doctrine, Müller pointed out that we are only indirectly aware of our world through stimuli arising from the environment, which in turn generate nervous impulses in our sense organs and nerves. But even more important was the principle contained in the doctrine that each sensory nerve has its specific energy so that the arousal of a given nerve always gives rise to a characteristic sensation. The optic nerve when stimulated generates a sensation of light, and stimulation of the auditory nerve gives rise only to auditory sensations. Even if nerves are stimulated by inappropriate stimuli they still respond with their characteristic sensation, provided they respond at all. William James, the famous philosopher-psychologist, put Müller's doctrine in this fashion: If a master surgeon were to cross the optic and auditory nerves we would see the thunder and hear the lightning.[6]

The principle of specificity of function in Müller's doctrine that is most important, since it stimulated a good deal of research, is the establishment of a functional localization within the nervous system and the specificity of sensory organs on the periphery of the body. As it turns out, it is not that nerves are specific in their energies but that the brain centers where

[6] Paraphrased: *Briefer Course*, p. 12.

they terminate specialize in their functions. We shall return to this problem again in connection with our study of sensory processes in Chapter III.

Claude Bernard was an early French physiologist who experimented in an area which in recent years has turned out to have considerable significance for psychology. Broadly speaking, we refer to his work on the endocrine processes, which along with the nervous system are important integrating mechanisms in the body. Bernard correctly identified the sugar-storing function of the liver and related it and other physiological effects to what he called the "constant internal environment." He saw the blood stream with its relatively stable thermal, carbohydrate, and saline levels as an internal environment which maintains a steady state for the cells. A great deal of subsequent work on the physiological mechanisms of constancy was done by the Harvard physiologist, **Walter B. Cannon** (1871 to 1945) (5), who called the overall process homeostasis. The study of steady states is a lively area of research in contemporary psychology, especially in the study of food selection and thirst, both of which are believed to be influenced by homeostatic processes (10).

Brain functions and methods. Several men contributed to the experimental study of brain functions. They discovered functionally specialized areas and introduced what were to become widely used research methods in physiological psychology.

First, a Scots physician, Marshall Hall (1790 to 1857), pioneered in the investigation of reflex behavior. He observed decapitated animals, noting that they continue to move for some time if appropriately stimulated. From such observations Hall concluded there are several levels of behavior dependent upon certain broadly localized brain areas: (1) voluntary movement, a function of the cerebrum, or large brain; (2) reflex movement, dependent on the spinal cord; (3) involuntary movements, dependent on direct muscular stimulation; and (4) respiratory movements, dependent upon the medulla.

Pierre Flourens (1794 to 1867) extended Hall's experiments to include the systematic destruction of the cerebrum, midbrain, medulla, cerebellum, and spinal cord in animals. He concluded, on the basis of alterations in the animals' behavior following such destructions, that the higher mental processes are mediated by the cerebrum. The midbrain in turn contains centers for the visual and auditory reflexes, whereas the cerebellum governs coordination. The medulla is a center for the control of respiration, heartbeat, and other vital functions.

Hall's and Flourens' conclusions, though very broad, are still accepted. But more important than the conclusions themselves is the fact that these men attacked the functions of the brain experimentally, in opposition to the unscientific procedures of the phrenologists, whose doctrines were popular at the time. The importance of Hall and Flourens also lies in the fact that they introduced into psychology the method of extirpation of parts, whose essence consists of studying a part's function by removing it and then observing consequent changes in the animal's behavior.

The midpart of the nineteenth century saw the introduction of two new approaches to the understanding of the brain. One of these was the clinical method discovered by Paul Broca.(1824 to 1880) in 1861, and the other the method of electrical stimulation announced by Fritsch and Hitzig in 1870. Broca discovered the speech center, and for this reason it is often called "Broca's area." It happened quite by chance that he was given the care of a patient who for many years had been hospitalized because of an inability to speak intelligibly. Shortly before the patient died Broca examined him carefully, and after the man's death performed an autopsy. He discovered a lesion in the third frontal convolution of his former patient's cerebral cortex and announced this as the speech center. This marked the introduction of a new method, the clinical method, as well as the discovery of a new brain center. The clinical method has proved a valuable supplement to the method of extirpation. Because it is not possible to perform extirpations on human beings, psychologists are forced to accept the next best thing from nature in the way of lesions caused by tumors or injuries.

G. Fritsch (1838 to 1927) and E. Hitzig (1838 to 1907) worked jointly to explore the cerebral cortex with weak electrical currents. Contrary to the prevailing opinion of the day, which held the brain to be unresponsive to stimulation, they found that stimulation of certain frontal areas gives rise to motor responses. Because stimulation of the rear portion of the brain behind the central fissure failed to result in muscular responses, they concluded that motor processes are located in the frontal lobes just ahead of the central fissure. The usefulness of the electrical method has been greatly extended since its introduction by Fritsch and Hitzig; and with the invention of precise electronic equipment in recent years, this method has become the single most important technique for studying brain functions.

The work of Fritsch and Hitzig was confirmed and extended by David Ferrier (1843 to 1928), who utilized the methods of electrical stimulation and extirpation to discover localized sensory areas, particularly those for vision and audition, in the occipital and temporal lobes respectively.

This, in brief, is the story of the main developments that were occurring in physiology just prior to those events which established psychology as an independent science. Thus, while the philosophers were paving the way for an experimental attack on the elements of mind and their interrelationships in the form of higher mental processes, the physiologists were tackling the neural mechanisms underlying behavior. Both trends are clearly revealed in the methods and systematic orientation of the initiators of the new experimental psychology. To these men we turn our attention in the following chapter.

REFERENCES

1. Barrett, W. *Irrational man.* New York: Doubleday, 1958.
2. Boring, E. G. *A history of experimental psychology,* ed. 1. New York: Appleton, 1929.
3. Brett, G. S. *History of psychology,* abridged ed. R. S. Peters (ed.). London: G. Allen, 1953.
4. Bridgman, P. W. *The logic of modern physics.* New York: Crowell-Collier-Macmillan, 1927.
5. Cannon, W. B. *The wisdom of the body.* New York: Norton, 1939.
6. Ceram, C. W. *Gods, graves and scholars.* New York: Knopf, 1951.
7. Durant, W. *The story of philosophy,* rev. ed. New York: Simon and Schuster, 1933.
8. Freud, S. Totem and taboo. In *Basic writings of Sigmund Freud.* New York: Modern Library, 1938.
9. Krech, D., and R. Crutchfield. *Theory and problems of social psychology.* New York: McGraw-Hill, 1948.
10. Morgan, C. T., and E. Stellar. *Physiological psychology.* New York: McGraw-Hill, 1950.
11. Murphy, G. *Historical introduction to modern psychology,* rev. ed. New York: Harcourt, 1949.
12. Piaget, J. *The child's conception of physical causality.* New York: Harcourt, 1930.
13. Vaihinger, H. *The philosophy of 'as if': A system of theoretical, practical and religious fictions of mankind.* New York: Harcourt, 1924.

In addition to the above the following books will be found helpful:

Brown, C. W., and E. E. Ghiselli. *Scientific method in psychology.* New York: McGraw-Hill, 1955.
Conant, J. B. *Modern science and modern man.* New York: Columbia University Press, 1952.
Heidbreder, E. *Seven psychologies.* New York: Appleton, 1933.
Keller, F. S. *The definition of psychology.* New York: Appleton, 1937.
Marx, M. H., and W. A. Hillix. *Systems and theories in psychology.* New York: McGraw-Hill, 1963.
Pratt, C. C. *The logic of modern psychology.* New York: Crowell-Collier-Macmillan, 1939.

BIOGRAPHIES

Aristotle

Aristotle was born in 384 B.C., at Stagira, a Macedonian city about 200 miles north of Athens. His father was a court physician, and as a youth Aristotle had both opportunity and encouragement to develop a scientific turn of mind. At eighteen he went to Athens to become a pupil in Plato's school. Plato, the great teacher, spoke of his brilliant pupil as the *Nous* or very intellect of the Academy. Plato, in turn, exerted a profound influence on his pupil—an influence which is reflected in the happy balance of Aristotle's interests. His love of science, inspired by his physician-father, was tempered under Plato's tutelage by an equal appreciation of philosophy, politics, and metaphysics.

After leaving Plato's school Aristotle founded an academy of oratory, numbering among his pupils a wealthy young man, Hermais, who was to become the ruler of the city-state of Atarneus. After achieving this position, Hermais rewarded his former teacher by inviting Aristotle to the court and arranging a marriage between the philosopher and his sister.

About a year later Aristotle was called to Pella to the court of Philip, King of Macedonia, to undertake the education of young Alexander, destined to become Alexander the Great. When Alexander laid aside his books to take up the sword, Aristotle returned to Athens and started a school which he called the Lyceum. Here he walked about as he taught, hence the name Peripatetic by which his school and sect are known. For a dozen years he dominated the field of learning while Alexander conquered empires. When Alexander died and an anti-Macedonia party came into power in Athens, Aristotle fled to Chalcis, where he died in 322 B.C.—some say by drinking hemlock.

With Aristotle's death Greece lost her greatest philosopher, for his contributions were manifold. His works include treatises in the physical and biological sciences, psychology, politics, aesthetics, metaphysics, and logic. He is considered to be the father of modern science. Many historians rate him as the greatest intellect that ever lived.

George Berkeley

George Berkeley, Bishop of Cloyne, was born on March 12, 1685, in a cottage near Dysert Castle, Thomastown, Ireland. He began his schooling at age eleven, and four years later entered Trinity College, Dublin. There he came under the influence of Descartes and Locke, whose works were the subject of lively discussion. Upon graduation he remained at the college as a fellow and tutor. During this period, and while still in his twenties, he published his principal philosophical works. The two most important, the *New Theory of Vision* (1709) and *Principles of Human Knowledge* (1710), contain the essence of his system, a subjective idealism in which mind is made the center of the universe.

After writing his major philosophical treatises, Berkeley traveled extensively on the Continent and, upon returning to Ireland, held a variety of posts. He became financially independent upon being given a fortune by Miss Vanhomright, the lady Swift addressed as "Vanessa." Apparently Berkeley had met her only once at a dinner. With his newly-won independence he began to devote himself in earnest to the idealistic project of founding a college in Bermuda for colonists and Indians. Accompanied by his bride and friends, he sailed for Rhode Island, where he remained for three years hoping for promised governmental support. When the grant was denied, Berkeley gave up the plan, bequeathed his farm to a scholarship fund at Yale, and gave the institution a thousand volumes from his personal library. He returned to London for several years, and in 1734 was elevated to the Anglican bishopric of Cloyne in County Cork, Ireland. The remaining years of his life were devoted to philosophical speculation and writing. He died on January 14, 1753, and was buried in Christ Church, Oxford.

Walter Cannon

Walter Cannon of Harvard University was born on October 19, 1871 in Prairie du Chien, Wisconsin. His early education took place in the public schools of Milwaukee and St. Paul. When Cannon was fourteen, his father took him out of school because of the son's failure to apply himself to his studies, and found him a position in a railroad office. Two years later Cannon returned to school with a new appreciation of the value of time and determined to complete secondary school as quickly as possible. He finished the course in three years and won a scholarship to Harvard. He was graduated from that institution *summa cum laude* in 1896. Cannon remained at Harvard to enter medical school and eventually to join the faculty in 1899, where he remained until a few years before his death on October 1, 1945.

In a charming little autobiography Cannon relates how much of his considerable success in research was the result of "serendipity," a term coined by Walpole and adopted by Cannon to express the role of fortunate chance in scientific discoveries. However, Cannon's important contributions to the physiology of thirst and hunger, his research with Bard in support of the thalamic theory of the emotions, and his work on the mechanisms of homeostasis testify to his dedication to arduous work as well as to his belief in serendipity.

Though primarily a physiologist, Cannon's contributions to our understanding of the primary motives and his research in the area of the emotions have earned him a permanent niche in the psychological hall of fame.

Democritus

Democritus, regarded by some authorities as the greatest of the Greek physical philosophers, was born in Abdera in Thrace between 470 and 460 B.C., making him an older contemporary of Socrates. His biography is based largely on untrustworthy tradition. However, it seems certain that he inherited considerable wealth, which he spent traveling widely in the East in search of knowledge. He spent seven years in Egypt pursuing his interest in the mathematics and physics of the ancient schools. Of his subsequent life little is known. One tradition has it that he died impoverished at the age of about ninety. Others give his final age as over one hundred, and state that he became insane in his later years and was treated by the great Hippocrates.

Besides formulating the first atomic theory of matter, Democritus contributed to ethics, theology, and psychology. Of particular interest are his views of perception, in which he held that sensations are the result of atoms emanating from the surface of objects. These, he believed, passed through pores directly into the body eventually to reach the mind. He also attempted to explain color vision and postulated four primaries, black, white, red, and green, other colors being mixtures of these. The breadth of his knowledge and the impact of his thought on subsequent Greek science have led many to regard him as the Aristotle of the fifth pre-Christian century.

René Descartes

René Descartes, the son of a French parliamentary counselor, was born on March 31, 1596, at La Haye, in Touraine. As a boy of eight he was sent to a Jesuit school, where he showed considerable talent, especially in mathematics. Because of a weak constitution Descartes was allowed to remain in bed as long as he liked and, as a result, developed a life-long habit of meditating in bed. Upon completing his education, Descartes apparently spent several years in military service in Holland and Austria, though some of his biographers deny this.

In 1623, he returned to France and for the next five years lived in Paris, where he came into contact with a number of learned men of his age and pursued his favorite study, mathematics. But the distractions of Parisian life were too much for him and in 1628 he moved to Holland, seeking seclusion. So precious was his solitude that he changed his residence twenty-four times between 1628 and 1649 in order to avoid all but his most intimate friends.

His growing fame led Queen Christina of Sweden to invite him to her court to instruct her in the new philosophy. It was arranged that the lessons were to be held three times a week at five in the morning. This regimen, coupled with the rigors of the Swedish climate and his delicate constitution, was too much for Descartes. He contracted pneumonia and died on February 11, 1650.

Descartes has been described as a pioneer in modern mathematics and as the father of modern philosophy. In the field of mathematics, he was the first to lay the foundations of modern analytic geometry; he made important contributions to the theory of equations and is responsible for the algebraic convention of using the initial letters of the alphabet for known quantities and the last letters for unknowns. It is said that his insights in geometry came to him in a series of dreams.

In philosophy Descartes affirmed the value of the deductive method, no doubt influenced by his love of mathematics. He emphasized the primacy of consciousness and deductive reasoning over empiricism and the inductive method. In his famous doctrine *Cogito, ergo sum* he made the ultimate test of certainty the individual consciousness, or existence, thus anticipating one of the fundamental tenets of contemporary existentialism.

Hermann Ebbinghaus

Hermann Ebbinghaus was born in Barmen, in the Prussian Rhine, on January 24, 1850, the son of a merchant. Like many other young men of his day, Ebbinghaus attended several universities—Bonn, Halle, and Berlin. While at Berlin his studies were interrupted by the Franco-Prussian war, in which he served as a volunteer. After the war he returned to Bonn to take a doctor's degree in philosophy.

For the next seven years Ebbinghaus studied independently. During this period he chanced upon Fechner's *Elemente der Psychophysik*. Fechner's mathematical approach to psychological problems stimulated Ebbinghaus to undertake the quantitative measurement of the higher mental processes. Without the help of a university setting he invented the nonsense syllable and, using himself as a subject, conducted a series of experiments on the factors influencing learning and retention. After spending several years repeating and verifying his results, in 1885 he published *Über das Gedächtnis,* one of the most original works in experimental psychology.

Ebbinghaus was not a prolific writer; however, he published several highly successful textbooks and, with Arthur König, founded the *Zeitschrift für Psychologie.* He is also noted for devising the completion test now widely used in objective scales of intelligence and in the measurement of scholastic achievement. Ebbinghaus died suddenly of pneumonia in 1909, after a distinguished career at the Universities of Berlin, Munich, and Breslau.

David Hartley

David Hartley, the founder of associationism, was born in Armley, Yorkshire, August 30, 1705, the son of a minister. Hartley was educated by his father for the church; but his conscience forbade him to sign the Thirty-nine Articles, and he turned to the study of medicine, practicing for some years at Newark, Bury St. Edmunds, and Bath. According to his son, Hartley was a kindly, unassuming man who treated both rich and poor with equality, dispensing a little kindly philosophy with his medicines.

Hartley's *Observations on Man* (1749) was the first systematic treatise on associationism. In it he drew on Newtonian physical theory and the works of John Gray, a clergyman-philosopher of the time. This dual influence is reflected in his system, since his explanation of sensation and nervous activity leaned heavily on Newton's theory of vibratory action in the nerves. His conception of mind, however, based as it was on associationism, was free from the mechanism of his sensory theories. Hartley died at Bath in 1757.

Thomas Hobbes

Thomas Hobbes was born prematurely in Malmesbury, on April 5, 1588, the second son of a vicar. Hobbes' premature birth was occasioned by his mother's fright at hearing reports of the arrival of the Spanish Armada. The boy's early education was obtained in a church school. He then entered Oxford, where he became discontented with traditional learning and devoted his leisure hours to books of travel and the study of maps. It is probably due to this unsatisfactory college experience that he boasted of doing little reading, arguing that had he read as much as other men, he would have known as little as they did. However, his activities and interests were varied. He enjoyed travel, especially in France and Italy, and at one time acted as secretary to Sir Francis Bacon. For some years he was tutor to the Cavendish earls.

In the course of his reflections, Hobbes came to the conclusion that sensation was made possible only because of motion. On the basis of this concept he is the precursor of modern materialism and therefore a direct antagonist to the doctrine of innate ideas postulated by Descartes. Because he referred the content of mind to prior sense impressions, he anticipated Locke's doctrine of the *tabula rasa*. On the whole, however, his greatest contribution was in the field of politics with the publication of the *Leviathan*. His contemporaries found little significance in his works, yet his profundity, sparkling style of writing, clarity of expression, and trenchant observations made him a writer and observer of lasting influence. He died on December 4, 1679.

David Hume

David Hume, British philosopher, historian, and economist, was born in Edinburgh on April 26, 1711, the second son of a family of three children. His father died while he was very young, leaving Hume's upbringing in the hands of his devoted mother. Little is known about his early education. He entered the University of Edinburgh in 1723 to prepare for the law, but did not earn a degree, and left to enter the world of business.

After working for a few months in a business house in Bristol, he spent several years in France, devoting this period to intellectual pursuits. His reflections were collected into his famous *Treatise on Human Nature*, published in 1739 when he was just twenty-eight years of age. He was a restless, ambitious, sensitive man who was prone to perfectionism; consequently, the poor reception accorded to the *Treatise* was a bitter disappointment. Nevertheless, this early philosophical work is considered by many to be his major contribution to psychology and philosophy. In it he stated his radical doctrine that mind has no independent existence apart from experiences such as ideas, memories, and feelings. Upon reading a German translation of the book, Kant reported that he was shocked out of his "dogmatic slumber."

Hume's ambition was to be a literary man, and in his later years he did succeed in becoming a successful writer. His early attempts to obtain a university position failed; instead he held many occupational roles, including tutor, companion, judge-advocate, secretary, and librarian. In 1761 his *History of England* appeared. It was well received and proved to be a financial success. Ironically, Hume did not think very highly of it, although through it he is best known to the general reader. He died on August 25, 1776.

John Locke

John Locke was born on August 29, 1632, at Wrington, Somersetshire, the son of a country attorney. After attending Westminster he was sent to Christ Church, Oxford. Locke found little satisfaction in his studies at Oxford and became convinced that self-education was the best education. After serving as a tutor in Greek, rhetoric, and philosophy for several years, Locke began the practice of medicine, though he continued to be increasingly concerned with problems of ethics, morals, and philosophy. Through his medical practice he became adviser to Lord Shaftesbury and tutor to his son.

During 1670 to 1671, at meetings of friends for the discussion of social problems, Locke suggested that they should first determine how the mind acquires knowledge, what questions it is capable of dealing with, and what its limits are. Locke devoted seventeen years to a study of these problems and embodied his results in his famous *Essay Concerning Human Understanding* (1690), still regarded as one of the world's great classics.

When Shaftesbury left England after fomenting Monmouth's Rebellion, Locke came under suspicion and, like his patron, fled to Holland, at that time a sanctuary for those seeking political asylum. When it became possible to return to England, Locke lived mostly at Oates in Essex, publishing tracts on education, religion, economics, and adding chapters and emendations to his *Essay Concerning Human Understanding*. He died on October 28, 1704.

James Mill

James Mill was born on April 6, 1773, in Northwater Bridge, Scotland. His father was a shoemaker, his mother a farmer's daughter. Mill's early education was in a parish school. He then attended Montrose Academy and finally entered Edinburgh University, where he obtained his M.A. in 1794. While at Edinburgh he distinguished himself as a Greek scholar.

James Mill had high intellectual ability and an indomitable capacity for work. It is reported that his typical working day lasted from six in the morning until eleven at night, with an interval between ten and one devoted to tutoring and to the short walks that were his only relaxation.

Although he was licensed as a preacher of the Gospel, he did not pursue this vocation, but instead turned to tutoring and literary work. He was instrumental in organizing the *Literary Journal* in 1803. In it he endeavored to present a summary of the leading departments of human knowledge. He also contributed articles for the *Encyclopaedia Britannica* and over a period of eleven years wrote a *History of India*, his outstanding literary work. This latter project resulted in Mill's appointment to the India House, where he eventually became the head of the department of Examiner of India Correspondence.

His greatest contribution to psychology was his *Analysis of the Phenomena of the Human Mind*, which appeared in 1829. In it he attempted a precise, systematic exposition of the principles of association following in the tradition of Berkeley, Hume, and Hartley.

He was the father of nine children, one of whom, John Stuart, became one of the most brilliant men of the nineteenth century. He died on June 23, 1836.

John Stuart Mill

John Stuart Mill, the eldest son of James Mill, was born in London on May 20, 1806. As a boy Mill was educated by his father. He began the study of Greek at three, added English and arithmetic to his curriculum at five as secondary subjects, and at eight began the study of Latin. By his tenth year he had undertaken calculus and at fourteen was thoroughly familiar with the basic principles of logic, psychology, and political economy.

At fourteen, apparently as a vacation from his rigorous education, Mill went to France, where he learned the language, met a number of distinguished men, and became interested in French literature and politics. Upon returning to London he took a position as a clerk in the Examiner's office of the East India Company. During his thirty-three years with the Company, he rose to become head of the department dealing with the native states.

From his early years Mill wrote a number of articles on economics for the *Westminster Review*, and from 1835 to 1840 was editor and joint owner of the *London and Westminster Review*. His *System of Logic*, published in 1843, established him as a leading empiricist and one of the foremost thinkers of his time.

In his writings Mill revealed himself as a champion of individual liberty. He devoted himself to the amelioration of working class conditions, served in Parliament, and wrote several articles urging the extension of suffrage to women. His humanitarianism undoubtedly stemmed in part from revulsion against his stern, uncompromising upbringing.

Upon leaving Parliament in 1868, Mill retired to a cottage at Avignon and resumed a literary life. Here he devoted his time to writing and his favorite avocations of reading, walking about the countryside, and playing the piano. A stepdaughter was his constant companion. He died at Avignon on May 8, 1873.

Johannes Müller

Johannes Müller, the father of modern experimental physiology, was born in Koblenz, Germany, on July 14, 1801, the son of a shoemaker. Müller's brilliant early career in primary and secondary school gave promise of his future pioneer accomplishments in biology and physiology.

Upon receiving his medical degree, Müller began his professional career at

Bonn, where he taught from 1824 until 1833. In 1833 he was appointed to the chair of anatomy and physiology at Berlin, and in that same year began his monumental *Handbook of Physiology,* in which he summarized current knowledge in the field and strongly advocated the use of the experimental method in medical and physiological research. The final volume appeared in 1840. In the latter part of his life Müller devoted his attention to comparative anatomy, studying marine life on the Mediterranean and Scandinavian coastal waters.

Müller was not only a great systematizer and exact researcher, he was also an outstanding teacher. Among his pupils were many who became famous in biology and psychology, such as DuBois-Reymond, Helmholtz, and Wundt.

His personality was a curious mixture of nervous unrest, pride and deep melancholia—so much so that without any previous indication of illness, he was found dead on the morning of April 28, 1858, presumably a suicide.

Plato

Aristocles, better known as Plato, was born in Athens on May 26 or 27, 427 B.C. of distinguished lineage. He received the usual education of a high-born Athenian in athletics, music, and literature. It is recorded that he distinguished himself in both poetry and athletics. When Plato was twenty he became a disciple of Socrates, whose philosophy we know largely through Plato's writings. After the death of his teacher, Plato traveled extensively in Egypt, Italy, and Sicily. He is said to have been captured and sold as a slave in Aegina, from which bondage he was ransomed by friends.

Shortly afterwards he established his famous Academy in Athens, where he taught philosophy for forty years to a small band of disciples. Among his distinguished pupils were Aristotle, Demosthenes, and Lycurgus.

Plato's philosophy developed largely from that of his teacher, Socrates. Under their influence Greek philosophy shifted its focus from problems of the physical world to ethics, politics, knowledge, and ideas. In his great books, the *Laws* and the *Republic,* Plato elaborated his doctrines of education, the role of laws and the structure of the ideal state.

Plato died at a wedding feast in 347 B.C., in his eighty-first year. Tradition tells us that the old philosopher retired to a corner to rest and was found dead in the morning when the revels had ended. All Athens mourned her distinguished scholar.

2

Schools
of Psychology

Four men were intimately associated with the debut of psychology as an experimental science. They were: **Ernst Weber** (1795 to 1878), **Gustav Fechner** (1801 to 1887), **Herman von Helmholtz** (1821 to 1894), and **Wilhelm Wundt** (1832 to 1920). All were Germans and therefore fully aware of the impressive developments in European physiology that were taking place in the middle decades of the nineteenth century. Indeed, each had considerable training in this discipline in the course of his professional education, and it was through this avenue that he became interested in psychological problems. But in addition to this common core of interest in physiology, each contributed something unique to the development of psychology.

Weber's special contribution was to demonstrate the feasibility of applying experimentation to the investigation of psychological processes. Fechner was a curious mixture of physicist, mathematician, and philosopher, which, as we shall see, turned out to be highly significant for the development of the embryonic science. Helmholtz, though primarily a physicist, was an all-around genius who, like Weber, had a passion for exact knowledge derived from experimentation. When his great intellect was brought to bear on psychological problems, the result was a significant advance in the understanding of the structure and functions of the eye and ear. Wundt's special talent was that of an organizer and systematizer. He brought together the various lines of research and theoretical speculation of his day in the first systematic textbook of psychology, published in 1873 to 1874, which, significantly enough, he entitled *Physiological Psychology*. Wundt also founded the first

36

experimental laboratory of psychology in Leipzig in 1879.[1] Because of the critical and timely importance of these pioneers, we shall examine the special contributions of each in some detail.

Weber. We may point to two specific contributions made by Weber in the cause of the new science. First, as we have already pointed out, he carried over the experimental methods of physiology to the investigation of psychological problems. This took place in connection with his systematic investigation of the sense of touch and the kinesthetic sense. The details of his work need not concern us here, but it should be noted that these experiments marked a fundamental shift in the status of psychology. The new science had at last severed its ties with mental philosophy, and the court of last resort for the resolution of psychological issues was no longer philosophical dogma. Weber thus allied psychology with the natural sciences and blazed the way for the *experimental* investigation of human behavior.

His second and more significant contribution was a discovery which ultimately led to the first truly quantitative law in psychology and indirectly to the development of the psychophysical methods which we shall take up in the following section. Weber's discovery developed out of an investigation of the muscle sense by means of weight-lifting experiments. He found that the just noticeable difference between two weights is a certain constant ratio (1:40) of the standard stimulus. Thus, a weight of 41 grams would be just noticeably different from a standard weight of 40 grams, and an 82-gram weight just perceptibly different from a standard weight of 80 grams. Weber extended his investigation of difference thresholds into the area of visual brightness discrimination and the two point threshold on the surface of the skin, but he never formulated his results into a general law. However, his discoveries stimulated considerable interest in sensory processes among contemporary physiologists and psychologists. In fact, Weber's fame is primarily the result of Gustav Fechner's further development of his basic discoveries. In the following section we shall trace the evolution of Weber's concepts in his successor's work.

Fechner. Fechner repeated and extended Weber's careful work on sensory discriminations. In addition, he carried out a large number of experimental tests of what he called "Weber's Law," namely, that *the j.n.d., or just noticeable difference between two stimulus magnitudes, is a certain constant ratio of the total magnitude.* In the symbolic language of mathematics the

---

[1] Wundt's laboratory was the first of any significance. William James had a small laboratory at Harvard as early as 1871. Wundt is credited with the "founding" partly because of his intent to found a laboratory and partly because of the official administrative recognition accorded to the laboratory by the University of Leipzig.

law reads, $\Delta R/R = K$, where ΔR is a stimulus increment, K a constant, and R the standard stimulus magnitude.

At the same time, Fechner had been puzzling over the age-old enigma of the relationship between mind and body. His interest in this problem stemmed partly from his unusual background and partly from an obsessive and somewhat mystical preoccupation with the problem of the relationship between the material and the immaterial. He began his academic career as a physician, but turned to physics and mathematics, accepting an appointment as a professor of physics at Leipzig. But Fechner had a humanistic, philosophical bent along with his materialistic and scientific interests. He exercised his humanism by writing satires on the science of his day and by publishing serious philosophical works, many of which dealt with the place of mind in the material world. Indeed, for Fechner the *nature* of the relationship between the spiritual and the material was a consuming passion. One morning, following a long incubation of the problem, he had a Eureka experience in which he found the long-sought answer to his problem. This was the simple and forthright solution that mind and body are identical. This view has since been known as Fechner's *identity hypothesis*.

Fechner attempted to establish the validity of his hypothesis through the mathematical manipulation of Weber's Law. He reasoned that because we can measure stimuli directly, such as the physical intensity of sounds or the brightness of lights, then *physical* measurement is possible. What was lacking was *psychological* measurement. Fechner reasoned further that *if it can be assumed that j.n.d.'s are equal* along the range of sensations measured by Weber's Law, then j.n.d.'s can be used to measure sensation *indirectly* by a process of summation and scaling. After manipulating Weber's Law mathematically[2] he came out with the equation $S = K \log R$, where S = sensation, K = a constant, and R = stimulus (*Reiz* = German for stimulus). Sensation is thus measured, and the identity hypothesis is proved!

Fechner's tour de force of measuring the seemingly unmeasurable stirred up a controversy that lasted for years. Most of the arguments centered around his assumptions about j.n.d.'s being equal and therefore logically additive.[3] However, Fechner's place in psychology does not rise or fall with the validity of his formula, but with his psychophysical methods, which became milestones in mental measurement, and because he directed the new science into a large-scale study of sensory and perceptual processes. Since we are concerned in this chapter with the evolution of methodology, it is appropriate that these methods be discussed in detail.

---

[2] The mathematical processes involved are complex and involve a knowledge of calculus. Consequently, we shall not attempt to go into them here. Those interested in the derivation of Fechner's formula may find it in Boring (*4*, pp. 287–289).

[3] For an account of the controversy see Boring (*4*, pp. 289–295).

The Method of Average Error

The most basic of Fechner's methods is the method of average error, since it is a procedure employed in virtually every type of psychological experiment. It assumes that in a sense every measurement in psychology is an error for the simple reason that we can never measure the true value of anything. Our instruments and sense organs are subject to trial-to-trial variability which prevents us from obtaining a single "true" measure of any variable. Instead, we obtain a large number of approximate measures which are distributed on either side of a mean in the form of a normal probability curve. The mean of these measures represents the best single approximation that we can make to the true value. From this point of view, the mean is the average of the individual "errors" or measurements, and for this reason the method is aptly called the "method of average error." The standard deviation of the measurements gives us an estimate of how reliable the obtained mean is. Moreover, techniques are also available for calculating any constant errors or tendencies for the measurements to fall more on one side of the mean than the other. This technique is especially useful in measuring reaction time, visual or auditory discriminations, the extent of illusions, and the like. More generally, every time we calculate an average or mean we are employing the method of average error.

The Method of Constant Stimuli

Fechner's method of constant stimuli, with the many variations worked out by subsequent investigators, is also a broadly useful method. It is applicable whenever we have situations where a response can be treated according to a dichotomy, such as "right" or "wrong," "heavier" or "lighter," "more" or "less." For example, in determining the two-point threshold, we stimulate the skin by applying two points simultaneously, with the points sometimes a few millimeters apart and sometimes widely separated, perhaps ten or twelve millimeters apart. The problem is to find the minimal separation which the subject reliably recognizes as "two." In such an experiment, five to seven *constant* settings are employed. These are presented in random order a large number of times; hence the name "constant method." When sufficient data have been collected, the stimulus separation is calculated for that point at which the subject correctly discriminates "twoness" 75 percent of the time. Several methods are available for performing the necessary calculations.[4] The 75 percent level is chosen

---

[4] For an account of the various statistical procedures available, see Guilford (*13*), or Woodworth and Schlosberg (*37*).

because the subject could guess correctly 50 percent of the time. Therefore the 75 percent level is actually half way between chance and a perfect discrimination. There are many variations of the basic procedure outlined above, and these have been found useful in the wide range of measurement problems encountered in the determination of sensory thresholds and the measurement of aptitudes.

The Method of Limits

The third of Fechner's original methods, known as the method of limits, is a more specialized technique chiefly useful in the determination of sensory thresholds. When, for example, we are testing the range of pitches a child can hear on the audiometer, we are using the method of limits. As we approach the upper limit (around 20,000 c.p.s.), the stimuli presented are higher and higher in pitch until they can no longer be heard. Similarly, on the lower end of the scale we present tones in a descending series until they are no longer heard as tones. We have now established the upper and lower limits for pitch. However, in the method of limits one determination is not sufficient to establish a threshold. Many ascending and descending series are run, and the threshold is taken as that point at which the subject can discriminate correctly 50 percent of the time. With slight modifications the same method is also useful for the determination of difference thresholds.

The complete story of the psychophysical methods is long and involved. Many variations of the basic methods were developed by Fechner and others, and a definitive description of these may be found in Guilford (13). It is only necessary to point out here that the methods have stood the test of time to become fundamental procedures in psychophysical measurements, mental testing, and attitude scaling to assure Fechner a permanent niche in the psychological hall of fame.

Helmholtz.   Helmholtz was not a psychologist, and psychological problems were not his main interest. Nevertheless, he is important in the annals of psychology for measuring the rate of conduction of the nervous impulse, for his work on the eye and ear, and for his famous theories of color vision and hearing. His contributions to the psychology of vision and audition will be taken up in Chapter 3. Meanwhile, we may note that his research in sensory physiology and his measurement of the rate of the nervous impulse provided not only worthwhile knowledge of these processes for their own sake, but also lent impetus to the embryonic psychology of the day by demonstrating that the old problems of how we sense and how we know are amenable to experimental investigation. Moreover, it is important to note that in his writings on perception (a psychological process in which he became interested through his work in physical optics), he allied himself with the empirical tradition by subscribing to the association theory of meaning. In doing this he flew in the face of German tradition, which held the opposite view of nativism, which is the doctrine that the meaning of percepts may be inherent or a priori ideas, as, for example, ideas of space and time—two percepts which are often held to be inherent by the nativists. Finally, as Boring (4) points out, Helmholtz's views on the perceptual processes probably influenced Wundt, with whom he was associated at the University of Heidelberg some years before Wundt founded the laboratory at Leipzig.

In summary, then, this great physicist contributed an important body of knowledge to sensory psychology, helped strengthen the budding experimental approach to the investigation of psychological problems, and, finally, contributed indirectly to systematic psychology by espousing the empirical tradition and thus helping it to gain momentum on the European continent.

Wundt. It has already been said that Wundt was the founder of psychology as a formal academic discipline, and that this event took place in 1879 at Leipzig, Germany, where he established the first experimental laboratory. Aside from this important achievement, Wundt's place in the evolution of psychology may be considered from two points of view. First, he may be evaluated in terms of the nature of his system—what he believed psychology to be and what its aims and methods are. On the other hand, Wundt's contribution may be considered from the point of view of his influence as a leader in the new scientific discipline which he founded. For this aspect of the man, the reader is referred to the histories (4, 27). Here we shall confine our analysis to Wundt the systematist.

Wundt believed that the subject matter of psychology is experience—immediate experience—to be studied by self-observation, or, more technically, by *introspection,* an objective, analytic observation of one's own conscious processes. The primary aim or problem of psychology is the analysis of conscious experience into its elements. Thus, Wundt associated himself with mental chemistry and the empirical-associationistic tradition. Once this systematic analysis into elements had been accomplished, the manner in which the elements are interrelated or compounded could be determined. Consequently, Wundt set a twofold task for himself: first, the *analysis* of consciousness, and second, discovering the laws of *synthesis.*

It might be noted that a system such as Wundt's, which seeks to analyze the contents of consciousness, is known as *Content Psychology* as opposed to *Act Psychologies,* which take as their unit of study mental acts or processes. This distinction will be developed further in Chapter 4.

It is unnecessary to go into a fuller summary of Wundt's system at this point, since we shall shortly consider it in considerable detail as it was developed and expounded by Wundt's pupil, Titchener. It would be well, however, to point out that Wundt's general definition of psychology and his analytic approach show the culmination of the various trends we have been emphasizing in the preceding chapter. First, the concept that mind is reducible to elements and that these elements cohere in some lawful way is obviously a heritage from the empirical-associationistic tradition. Secondly, the use of experimental observation and analysis for understanding mental phenomena is the culmination of the trend begun by Weber and Fechner to utilize physiological and physical methods in psychological investigations. Finally, Wundt's choice of introspection as the method of psychology places him in the tough-minded category with those psychologists who favor highly objective, "scientific" techniques for the study of human nature.

One of the immediate reactions to the new laboratory was a migration to Leipzig of young men interested in this promising new approach to the study of the human mind. As a result, Wundt became the leader of a "school" of psychologists whose common purpose was mental analysis by means of introspection, with the ultimate aim of discovering the laws of mind.

The term "school," as it is used in psychology, refers to the groups of psychologists who associated themselves both geographically and systematically with the early leaders in the new science. For the most part, the psychologists who made up a school worked on common problems and shared a common systematic orientation. For these reasons it is proper to speak of a "Leipzig school" in the sense that Wundt and his associates at Leipzig shared the aims and methods of structuralism. Freud and his associates founded a school of psychoanalysis in Vienna in the first decade of the present century. The school became the focal point of the psychoanalytic movement. Similarly, the psychologists who were attracted to the "Chicago school" of functionalism were typically in agreement in their aims and research programs.

As psychology began to spread, either as an offshoot from the Leipzig laboratory or by indigenous growth outside of Germany, other schools were formed, composed of psychologists with common systematic interests. For several decades, from 1900 to 1930 approximately, this was the most conspicuous characteristic of the new psychology, and it was through these schools that contemporary psychology took shape. Because of their central importance in the evolution of modern psychology, we shall examine five of these schools in some detail: Structuralism, Functionalism, Behaviorism, Gestalt Psychology, and Psychoanalysis. We do not mean to imply that these are the only "schools" of psychology which developed early in the twentieth century. Rather, those we have selected for presentation have been, in our opinion, most influential in shaping the course of contemporary psychology. Moreover, most of the others are variations or offshoots of those we are about to consider, and the interested reader can readily find detailed accounts of any variants in which he may be interested by consulting sources given at the end of the chapter, especially *4, 15, 17,* and *36.*

THE SCHOOLS OF PSYCHOLOGY

Wundt's psychology was transplanted to the United States by his most outstanding pupil, **E. B. Titchener** (1867 to 1927). In Titchener's hands the master's conception of psychology underwent its fullest development. Thus, for most purposes, a study of Titchener's psychology provides a reasonably accurate view of Wundt's system. This does not mean the two systems are identical. There were differences of opinion between teacher and pupil, but in a general way it is fair to say that Titchener's system is Wundtian in spirit, in method, and in the types of problems investigated.

Titchener's structuralism. Our primary concern in this chapter is with Titchener's aims and methods. Other aspects of his psychology will be met with from time to time as we take up sensation, emotion, thinking, and other mental processes in chapters to follow. Therefore, what we hope to do here is make clear his definition of psychology and its place among the sciences.[5] Let us start, logically enough, with Titchener's definition.

Titchener begins by relating psychology to science in general. He takes a monistic view, arguing that in the last analysis all sciences have the same subject matter—"some aspect or phase of the world of human experience." The biologist deals with living forms; the physicist studies nonliving forms. In the study of nonliving forms the physicist specializes in those facets of experience concerned with energy changes, electricity, magnetism, and the like. The chemist, on the other hand, investigates the elements and their compounds. In the realm of living forms the botanist specializes in the study of plants, while the zoologist concentrates on animals. What, then, of psychology? The subject matter of psychology is human experience from the special point of view of *experience as dependent upon the experiencing person.* Thus, both the physicist and psychologist may be investigating light and sound; but the physicist is concerned with these phenomena from the viewpoint of the physical processes involved, whereas the psychologist is interested in how they are experienced by the observer.

Conscious experience, then, is the subject matter of psychology. But conscious experience is a private affair and can only be observed by the experiencing person; consequently, a special technique is needed for psycho-

[5] Our exposition of Titchener's psychology is based on his *Textbook* (*29*), first published in 1896.

logical observation. The method is *introspection,* which, of course, Titchener took over from Wundt.

Introspection, as Titchener employed the process, is a highly specialized form of self-observation in which the psychologist attempts to study his own consciousness scientifically. His aim is to observe the *contents* of consciousness—not in the dreamy, informal manner of everyday reflection, but in a detached, objective and systematic manner. Because of the difficulties inherent in a situation where the observed and the observer are, in a sense, one and the same, the introspectionists require considerable laboratory training in this special method of observation before their results can be considered valid. As we take up Titchener's system in detail, some of the special problems confronting the introspectionist will be brought out more fully.

Titchener next goes on to deal with the broad question of the aim of psychology which, he believes, is to answer the tripartite question of the "What," "How," and "Why" of experience. The question of *What* is to be answered by systematic introspective analyses of the mental processes. The question of *How* is the problem of synthesis: How are mental processes interrelated or combined? In other words, when the various elements of consciousness have been discovered through introspective analyses, the next problem is to find out how they are combined into compounds. And so Titchener's psychology, like Wundt's, was mental chemistry.

Titchener then considers the problem of *Why* by first arguing that the answer is *not* to be sought in the mental processes themselves. One mental process, he points out, cannot be regarded as the cause of another. If, for example, one runs afoul of some painful or noxious stimulus, the consciousness of pain is not due to past consciousnesses but to present stimuli. This line of reasoning would seem to suggest that *stimuli* must be the cause of consciousness, but this, too, is a false conclusion. Stimuli belong to the physical world; pain, to the mental; and a science that must go outside of its own boundaries for explanations is committing the error of accounting for its phenomena by invoking a *deus ex machina.*

Perhaps, Titchener suggests, we ought to look to the nervous system for the cause of consciousness. Is it not logical to assume that activities in the brain cause corresponding changes in consciousness? To this commonsense question Titchener answers with a resounding No! Brain is part of body; consequently both are aspects of the same physical world. Consciousness *parallels* nervous processes in the brain, but one is not the cause of the other. Thus, Titchener embraces a dualistic position on the mind-body problem in the form of *psychophysical parallelism.* This seems to leave psychology bereft of those cause-effect relationships so dear to the heart of the scientist. But Titchener gets around the difficulty this way:

Physical science, then, explains by assigning a cause; *mental science explains by reference to those nervous processes which correspond with the mental processes that are under observation.*[6] We may bring these two modes of explanation together, if we define explanation itself as the statement of the proximate circumstances or conditions under which the described phenomenon occurs. Dew is formed under the condition of a difference of temperature between the air and the ground; ideas are formed under the condition of certain processes in the nervous system. Fundamentally, the object and the manner of explanation, in the two cases, are one and the same (*29*, p. 41).

To recapitulate Titchener's position up to this point, psychology is the study of consciousness by the method of introspection for the purpose of answering three questions about mental phenomena: What? How? Why? The overall program for psychology is essentially similar to that of the other natural sciences. When the scientist has decided what aspect of nature he is going to study, he then proceeds to discover its elements, shows how these are compounded into more complex processes, and finally formulates the laws which govern the behavior of the phenomena under study.

Titchener then addresses himself to certain problems resulting from the special method of introspection. He admits that, at first glance, introspection as a method smacks of subjectivity. How can there be an objective, "scientific" psychology if the very process under observation is also doing the observing? The answer, Titchener believes, is to be found partly in training and partly in the observer's attitude. The introspectionist needs considerable laboratory experience under supervision before he can qualify as a psychologist. He must learn to take on an objective attitude while in the laboratory —to step outside himself, so to speak, and look back within. In addition, he must be on guard to avoid the "stimulus error"— an insidious trap for introspectionists—which is the description of a stimulus object in terms of everyday language instead of a report on the conscious content to which the stimulus gives rise. For example, to see and report an apple as an apple is to fall victim of the stimulus error. To describe the hue, brightness, and spatial characteristics in one's consciousness when an apple or other object is under observation is valid introspection.

Another vexing problem arises when one is attempting to observe an emotional consciousness. In this case the calm, scientific attitude which is necessary for laboratory work destroys the very process under observation. Titchener readily admits the difficulty and suggests that in such instances introspection must become *retrospection.* To put it another way, the psychologist allows the emotional experience to go on uninterrupted by introspection and then describes his conscious memory of the experience when it is

[6] Italics ours.

completed. Clearly this is a second best procedure which is subject to distortions of memory, but it is the only one possible in such instances.

The question also arises of how the psychologist can study the conscious processes of children, animals, and mentally disturbed individuals. Clearly, subjects such as these cannot be trained in introspection. Titchener's answer in these and similar cases is "introspection by analogy." The psychologist, after carefully observing the behavior of the subject, must put himself in the subject's place and try to interpret what the individual under consideration is experiencing. It might be noted parenthetically that in reading Titchener on this point, one gets the impression he was aware that this method was roundabout and unsatisfactory. Such an impression is suggested by the amount of space he devotes to arguments in support of the validity of introspection by analogy. This weak spot became a prime target for attack by Watson, the behaviorist (see "The behavioristic revolt" below).

It is beyond the scope of this chapter to attempt any extended discussion of what Titchener and his associates discovered in their pursuit of introspective psychology. Their contributions were many and varied; some we shall meet in subsequent chapters on sensation, perception, and thinking. Here we shall be content with a brief summary of the findings in order to convey some notion of how structuralism worked in practice.

True to his aim, Titchener and his associates proceeded to analyze consciousness into its elements. These were found to be three in number: *sensations, images,* and *affective states.* Each of these is an element with attributes such as quality, intensity, and duration. From these three building blocks all the complex and varied higher mental processes are derived. As this work was progressing, it became clear to Titchener that in spite of their differences the several elements were nevertheless all related to a "common mental ancestor." In view of Titchener's intellectual heritage it is not surprising that this ancestor appeared to be sensation—the basic "element" of mind in the associationistic-empirical tradition.

After devoting approximately half of his text to the sensory processes, Titchener takes up the affective states, attention, perception, memory, and thought. In each case the exposition is centered around the data derived from the introspective work of psychologists who associated themselves with Titchener's point of view. The discussions on memory and retention, for example, bear only faint resemblance to the treatment typical of a modern textbook in general psychology. There are no behavioristic reports of animal learning; there is nothing on conditioning; whereas memory and retention are treated as manifestations of the mental image.

Generally speaking, Titchener's structuralism was the most consistent and tightly knit of all the early systems. In fact, it has often been said that it remained *too* narrow because of Titchener's refusal to change with the times. American psychologists were not content to restrict psychology to the introspective analysis of consciousness. Consequently, structuralism weakened and finally collapsed. Structuralism as a movement, however, had brought science to psychology and established psychology as a science. This alone was a great contribution, and the fact that its method and scope proved too narrow to contain psychology cannot detract from its accomplishments.

Functionalism. Functionalism is the name given to a system of psychology promulgated by a number of prominent American psychologists whose primary interest was the study of mind as it functions in adapting the organism to its environment. The roots of this point of view extend back to the evolutionary biology of **Charles Robert Darwin** (1809 to 1882) and the pragmatic philosophy of **William James** (1842 to 1910). When the functionalistic point of view came into psychology, it developed into a movement which took on the attributes of a school whose nerve center was the psychology department at the University of Chicago. Here the school came under the leadership of **John Dewey** (1859 to 1952) and **James Rowland Angell** (1869 to 1949) in the early days of the 1900's and later, in the 1920's, under **Harvey Carr** (1873 to 1954), who was Angell's successor at Chicago.

Functionalism, then, ranges over a long period from the mid-1850's to contemporary times. Indeed it has been said that, broadly speaking, American psychology today *is* functionalistic (*5*, p. 10) because of its emphasis on learning, testing, perception, and other such "functional" processes. Moreover, functionalism, unlike structuralism, developed under the influence of a number of leaders with varied interests and backgrounds. Undoubtedly, it was partly this flexibility in leadership which kept the movement from ultimately becoming stultified and suffering the same fate as structuralism. At the same time, and for the same reason, it is a less sharply defined system than structuralism. Because of this it is difficult and perhaps unfair to select any one psychologist's work as a definitive statement of functionalism, yet the risk must be run for the sake of presenting the system in a coherent form. Harvey Carr's 1925 exposition (*7*) has been chosen, since it represents functionalism at its maturity and in its most definitive form. In order to provide a perspective for appreciating Carr's system, we shall first outline briefly the chief contributions of his predecessors, James, Dewey, and Angell.

William James's academic career in psychology at Harvard University spanned the years from 1872 to 1907. Something of the man's versatile intellect and personality is indicated by the fact that during this period he was in turn a physiologist, psychologist, and philosopher. In psychology, his outstanding contribution was his brilliant *Principles of Psychology,* published in 1890, in which he analyzed and criticized the structuralistic psychology originating in Germany. James made it clear that his was a *functional* psychology whose aim was not to reduce mind to elements, but to study consciousness as an ongoing process or stream. Mind, as it is revealed in habits, knowledge, and perception, is constantly engaged in active give-and-take relations with the environment. Mind, therefore, is useful or functional in adjustment; it is anything but a collection of static conscious states. Moreover, mind is highly personal and consequently cannot be subjected to the objective and scientific analyses favored by structuralists without destroying this personal flavor.

James's position put him in fundamental opposition to the highly objectified German psychology of the day. As a result, he performed the service of clarifying issues which arose between structuralism and its opponents. In addition, James's remarkable insights into human nature stirred up a great deal of interest in psychology and also left a heritage of hypotheses for the coming generation of experimental psychologists to test in their laboratories.

Dewey, who succeeded James as the Dean of American philosophers, was also his spiritual successor in psychology. In fact, Dewey is credited with sparking functionalism as a definite movement in psychology. Specifically, he wrote an article (9) in 1896 on the reflex-arc concept, in which he attacked psychological molecularism and reductionism. In his article Dewey argued the thesis that the behavioral act involved in a reflex response cannot be reduced to its sensory-motor elements and still remain a meaningful act. All that is left after such a dissection are abstractions of its sensory and motor phases existing solely in the minds of psychologists. He went on to argue that reflexes and other forms of behavior ought to be interpreted in terms of their significance for adaptation and not treated as artificial scientific constructs. In short, Dewey believed that the study of the *organism as a whole functioning in its environment* was the proper subject matter for psychology.

The Olympic torch of functionalism lighted by James and Dewey was passed on to James Rowland Angell at the University of Chicago. He molded the functionalistic movement into a working school, and, incidentally, made the psychology department at Chicago the most important and influential of his day. This scholarly heritage was taken over by Harvey Carr, Angell's successor as chairman of the psychology department, and the new leader of functionalism. From the time that Dewey gave the "keynote address" in his 1896 article to the time of Carr's administration during the 1920's and 1930's, functionalism had become a well-established and recognized school of psychology.

Carr and functionalism.   Carr defines psychology as the "study of mental activity." Mental activity, in turn, "is concerned with the acquisition, fixation, retention, organization, and evaluation of experiences, and their subsequent utilization in the guidance of conduct" (7, p. 1). Here is a functional point of view indeed! Not only is there heavy emphasis on learning (a highly functional process) in the wording of the definition, but Carr also specifically states that the functionalist is interested in how the mental processes are *utilized* in conduct. If this were not sufficiently functional, he points out in a subsequent paragraph that mind is concerned with "attaining a more effective adjustment to the world" (7, p. 2). Clearly, in functionalism we have an *"is for"* psychology as compared to Titchener's *"is"* psychology.

Carr then deals with the various traditional problems confronting systematists, beginning with his views on the mind-body problem. He admits that these two aspects of the individual must be taken into account in any analysis of behavior and that all mental activity is psychophysical in the sense that both mind and body are involved in any given task. He feels, however, that any ultimate resolution of the problem is a task for philosophy rather than for psychology.

In discussing the problem of methodology, Carr recognizes the necessity for introspection (to get at the conscious side of mind), but gives more emphasis to objective observation. And in the research programs at Chicago, fewer and fewer problems were attacked by introspective techniques as time went on. The inevitable result was that objective methods became the favored techniques of the functionalists.

With regard to scope, Carr's psychology is much broader than Titchener's—at least as far as Titchener's program worked out in practice. Functional psychology, Carr believes, is closely allied with physiology, since both disciplines study the animal organism; but, in addition, psychology should feel free to call on sociology, neurology, education, anthropology, and related sciences for facts and methodological contributions which might add in any significant way to psychology. He also makes it clear that, whenever possible, psychology in turn ought to contribute freely to other disciplines. In this way he opens the door to the possibility of an applied psychology.

Turning from aims and methods, Carr presents a survey of the nervous system and sense organs as a basis for understanding the higher mental processes. To this extent, at least, his exposition follows the traditional pattern of approaching the complex by way of the elementary. It is in the fourth chapter of his text, however, that Carr's functionalistic position is most clearly developed. In this chapter, entitled "Principles of Organic Behavior," Carr discusses the nature of an adaptive act. Such an act results from motivating conditions arising either in the individual as drives or in the environment as stimuli. The stimulation from such conditions persists until the individual responds in such a way as to achieve satisfaction. Consequently, behavior is adaptive in the sense that the individual's responses result in a better adjustment to the environment. It is interesting to note, parenthetically, that Carr's analysis of adaptive behavior is very similar to that found in most present-day textbooks of the psychology of adjustment. Such texts typically analyze an adjustive act as one arising from a drive accompanied by tension. When the drive is satisfied, the tension subsides and equilibrium is restored.

Carr goes on to deal with learning, which, as has been pointed out earlier, he considers a central problem in psychology and one which he treats as a "perceptual-motor" process. The organism when confronted with a problem for which it has no habitual or immediate solution engages in a persistent and varied attack on the situation. This problem-solving behavior is neither blind nor random, but instead utilizes previous experience and thus demonstrates that the learner perceives the relevant relationships in the elements making up the problem. When a solution is found it is fixated and becomes a part of the organism's repertoire of responses.

The strongly functionalistic nature of Carr's psychology is revealed in two additional ways. First, he argues that adaptive acts involve two stages: a *preparatory stage* of attentive adjustment, making for more efficient perception by excluding irrelevant and distracting stimuli, and a *response stage* which is the adaptive act itself. Therefore, attention in Carr's system is considered in terms of its functional utility in dealing with the environment. Second, his functionalistic bias is revealed by his interest in perception. Not only do the perceptual processes occupy a central position in the text from which we are drawing this summary of functionalism, but it is also significant that he wrote an advanced textbook on perception (8). For Carr, perception is a basic process in adjustment, since it is largely how we perceive our environment and its challenges that determines the manner in which we respond to it.

Surely a functionalistic psychology ought to emphasize those aspects of mind such as learning, attention, perception, and intelligence which are useful and which aid us in adaptive behavior. In this respect, Carr's psychology, along with the functional movement as a whole, lives up to expectation. In "classical" functionalism it is precisely these processes that received the major emphasis both in theory and research. Today, a large segment of contemporary functionalists are pursuing research in human learning (23). Moreover, the success of the mental testing movement in the United States is ample testimony to the functionalistic flavor of American psychology. As a systematic point of view functionalism was an overwhelming success, but largely because of this success it is no longer a distinct "school" of psychology. It was, so to speak, absorbed into contemporary psychology. No happier fate could await any point of view.

The behavioristic revolt. While structuralism was at its height, and during the two decades that functionalism was developing into a mature system, a revolution directed against both of these systems was brewing in the mind of a young American psychologist, **John B. Watson** (1878 to 1958). Watson began his career in psychology as a graduate student at the

University of Chicago during the formative years of the functionalistic movement. He became interested in animal research, founded an animal laboratory at Chicago, and carried his interests with him to Johns Hopkins where he accepted an appointment in 1908.

Watson's strong bias in favor of animal psychology weaned him away from the functionalism on which he had been nurtured and led him to embrace the position of a strict behaviorist. So completely was he converted to this new point of view that he strongly opposed the analysis of consciousness by introspection as a suitable aim for a scientific psychology, and in its place emphasized the study of behavior by objective, experimental procedures.

Watson's stand on these issues had all the earmarks of a revolt as opposed to mere disagreement on matters of principle. His youthful optimism and strong personality, coupled with a trenchant style of writing, admitted no compromise with existing systems of psychology, which, from his point of view, were totally unsatisfactory. His stand was formally published for the first time in 1913 as an article in the *Psychological Review* entitled, "Psychology as the Behaviorist Views It." In addition, he developed his systematic position in lectures at Columbia and Johns Hopkins, in various journals, and in several books. His two most important books are: *Behavior, an Introduction to Comparative Psychology* (1914) and *Psychology from the Standpoint of a Behaviorist* (1919). A third, semipopular exposition of the behavioristic position came out in 1925 and was entitled, simply, *Behaviorism*. The following summary of Watson's behaviorism is drawn primarily from the first two books just mentioned.

In the introductory chapter in his comparative text, Watson sounds the tocsin for the coming of a millennium in psychology. The state of psychology in 1914 he found "unsatisfactory" for several reasons. To begin with, a psychology whose method is introspection excludes, for all practical purposes, contributions from the animal laboratory. It is, Watson states, no answer to argue that data from comparative studies can be collected by analogous introspection. Such an alternative he dismisses as "absurd." Secondly, he believes that mentalistic concepts such as "mind," "consciousness," "image," and the like have no place in a *scientific, objective* science; they are a carry-over from the days of mental philosophy. Moreover, Watson points out that the introspective study of conscious processes such as sensations, affective states, and imagery had resulted in disagreement and confusion even in the stronghold of the inner camp of the structuralists. Indeed, Watson charges the structuralists with an inability to resolve such a fundamental problem as how many independent attributes are associated with the elements of consciousness—sensation, images, and affective states. Again, where introspectionists failed to obtain reliable results, the blame, Watson argues, was *mis*placed on the observer. He refuses to accept the validity of such excuses as "faulty training" or "poor introspection," offered by the structuralists to account for these difficulties. In reality, Watson asserts, the fault was with the *method*. If introspection were abolished in favor of objective, experimental observation, such difficulties could not occur.

Watson makes it clear that he is no more satisfied with functionalism than he is with structuralism. The functionalists, too, employ terms which are "elusive," such as "emotion," "volition," and "process" and, of course, are guilty of using introspection—an already discredited method from Watson's frame of reference.

Turning to the constructive side, Watson states what he believes to be a proper definition for psychology. It is "the science of behavior," and behavioral acts are to be described objectively in "terms of stimulus and response, in terms of habit formation, habit integration, and the like" (*31*, p. 9). Psychologists need never go back to such mentalistic concepts as consciousness, mind, imagery, and affective states.

The aim of behaviorism, as stated by Watson, is characteristically forthright and objective: *given the stimulus, to be able to predict the response, and given the response, to be able to predict the antecedent stimulus.* To take a simple example, every fundamental reflex in the body has a specific appropriate stimulus. The knee jerk, elicited by tapping just below the patella with a small rubber hammer, is familiar to everyone. Now there is very little psychology involved in predicting kick from tap or tap from kick in an experiment on the knee jerk. Nevertheless, it illustrates in minuscule form the essence of the behavioristic program. More complex forms of behavior might involve a complex of stimuli rather than a single stimulus. Similarly, most responses studied by psychologists are far more complex than simple reflexes. Nevertheless, the principle is the same, and putting Watson's argument in a formula, psychology is the science of *S-R*, where *S* represents the stimulus and *R* a response.

The methods proposed by Watson for the behaviorists' research programs are four in number (*32*, p. 24):

1. Observation, with and without instrumental control
2. The conditioned reflex method
3. The verbal report method
4. Testing methods

While Watson's methods are largely self-explanatory, Numbers 2 and 3 require further comment. The conditioned response was taken over from the Russian physiologist, Pavlov. In a limited way, conditioning was already in use in psychology before the advent of behaviorism; however, Watson was largely responsible for its subsequent widespread usage in American psychological research. As we shall find in Chapters 6 and 7, conditioning has also played a prominent role in a great deal of subsequent theory construction (*16*). However, of all psychologists who have sought the explanation of human learning in conditioning theory, Watson went to extremes in his enthusiasm:

> Give me a dozen healthy infants, well-formed, and my own specified world to bring them up in and I'll guarantee to take any one at random and train him to become any type of specialist I might select—doctor, lawyer, artist, merchant-chief and, yes, even beggarman and thief, regardless of his talents, penchants, tendencies, abilities, vocations, and race of his ancestors (*34*, p. 82).

Not only does this passage reveal his extreme behaviorism, but it also points up his environmentalism, leaving as it does very little room for heredity as an explanatory concept in human behavior by attributing so much to learning.

The verbal report method is also of special interest; for, in admitting the validity of such reports by the subject, Watson was letting a kind of introspection in the back door after having thrown it out the front. But let it be noted that he looked upon the verbal report as an "inexact" method (*32*, p. 42) at best, and a poor substitute for objective observation. The only reason for allowing verbal reports in the laboratory is expediency. After all, it would be cumbersome and inefficient to go through an elaborate conditioning process in order to determine whether a human subject could distinguish between two stimuli. How much simpler to ask him. Furthermore, Watson promises to treat verbal reports purely as objective data which are in no way fundamentally different from any other response or reaction given by the subject. He also makes it clear that the verbal report is entirely different from introspection. In introspection the psychologist and the subject are one and the same. In the use of verbal reports, the psychologist does not report on his own behavior or mental processes but utilizes subjects whose reports become data for the psychologist.

Here, then, is the new psychology—a real *science*, free from mentalistic concepts and subjective methods. It is a psychology capable of ultimate reduction to the stimulus-response level and as objective as chemistry or physics. And, in keeping with its new status as a natural science, it is forever free and independent of its philosophical ancestry.

Like all systematists before and since, Watson develops his psychology in line with his fundamental theses. Emotions and feelings—such knotty problems for the introspectionist—he treats as behavior patterns or reactions, predominantly visceral, and largely acquired through conditioning during childhood. Even thought, which might appear to be the last stronghold of the psychology of consciousness, is reduced to "laryngeal habits." In support of this conception he suggests observing a deaf-mute's fingers or attaching a suitable recording device to a normal person's larynx. In either subject, while "thinking" is taking place muscle movements can be seen and recorded. This, for Watson, *is* thinking. While admitting that such experiments are not always successful, he believes failures can be eliminated by more delicate instruments which will detect faint, "implicit" forms of behavior and make them explicit. Assuming the validity of these arguments, man's complex thought system is reducible to laryngeal habits which are no more mysterious than a rat's maze habits and acquired in essentially the same manner—through conditioning.

Finally, in this brief survey of the program of the behaviorists, it should be pointed out that Watson was favorably inclined toward applied psychology. One aspect of this broad field is concerned with the practical problem of handling children. Watson contributed a great deal of fundamental research in the area of child psychology, as well as publishing a guide for parents on the psychological care of infants and children (*33*). But in addition to borrowing from allied disciplines, Watson felt that a behavioristic psychology had much of value to offer such fields as advertising, law, industry, and education. Moreover, he believed that such professions would be ideal testing grounds for a psychology interested in discovering the principles involved in prediction and control of behavior. On this practical and hopeful note we shall leave behaviorism as a system. However, we shall meet with some of Watson's specific contributions throughout this volume. Meanwhile, it seems worth while to cast a backward glance by way of summary and interpretation.

Behaviorism, as Watson formulated it, represents the end point in the evolution of certain concepts and issues which we have been tracing in both this and the preceding chapter. We have seen how the dilemma of the relationship between mind and body returned again and again—always demanding but never reaching a satisfactory solution. Watson solved the problem by disposing of mind altogether. Moreover, with his deterministic, mechanistic, and superscientific attitude toward human nature Watson was reflecting what Boring (*4*) has called the *Zeitgeist*, or spirit of the times. It was a time for the ascendance of a mechanistic-determinism not only in psychology but in science in general. The preceding century had witnessed incredible scientific successes in every branch of knowledge, and science either seemed to have found—or given enough time, could find—the answer to everything. In keeping with this ascendance of science, literature, art and philosophy also turned to realistic, material themes. It was the beginning of an era where tender-mindedness and idealism began to give way to a tough-minded realism. There are those who feel that Watson went too far. But most observers believe that his crusade for an objective behaviorism did American psychology a service *at that time* by shifting the emphasis from an overconcern with consciousness to the broader horizons of the behavioral studies. Finally, while Watson's ambitious program remained primarily a *program* and never realized all that he claimed for it, the behavioristic point of view has remained a strong force in contemporary psychology. We shall meet it again.

Gestalt psychology.[7]   To trace the development of the next school of psychology, we must return to the continent of Europe after our long excursion into developments in American psychology; for, about the time that Watson was closing in on his battle with both structuralism and functionalism in the United States, a new movement was getting underway in Germany. It began as a revolt against Wundtian structuralism; but once it had gained momentum, it also took up arms against behaviorism. In essence, then, the new school was against *analysis* of the reductionistic variety, whether such analysis was structuralistic or behavioristic in origin.

This antianalytic school was Gestalt psychology, and its founder was **Max Wertheimer** (1880 to 1943). Closely associated with Wertheimer at that time were two other Germans, **Wolfgang Köhler** (1887 to 1967) and **Kurt Koffka** (1886 to 1941), who contributed a great deal to the new program—so much, in fact, that it has become conventional to think of all three as "founders." The new movement had its inception as a result of Wertheimer's interest in the "phi phenomenon," an illusion of movement. This occurs when two lines such as

$$\mathsf{L}$$

are exposed in rapid succession. The effect on the observer is not

$$\mid \text{ followed by } \underline{}$$

but

$$\mathsf{L}$$

or the apparent movement of the vertical line through an arc. A similar phenomenon occurs in moving pictures, for what is shown physically is a rapidly exposed series of still pictures with short blank intervals between them. The psychological effect, however, is smooth movement—illusory, it is true, but just as "good" as real movement.

Here, Wertheimer believed, was a phenomenon for which structuralism had no adequate explanation. Introspection of the test figure ought to give two successive lines and nothing more. But, instead, the illusion of a single line in motion persists no matter how hard one tries to introspect the

[7] There is no single textbook which serves as a standard reference for Gestalt psychology such as those we have drawn upon for definitive statements of the preceding schools. Our sources will be found at the end of the chapter. (See especially *4, 15, 17, 18, 19, 27,* and *36.*)

separate exposures. Here was a case where analysis failed—where, indeed, a fundamental Gestalt principle was strikingly illustrated, namely, *that the whole is greater than the sum of its parts.* In fact, in the eyes of its discoverers, this relatively simple finding seemed to challenge the traditional empirical-associationistic-structuralistic psychology which had held sway for so many years.

The Gestalt psychologists were quick to seize upon other perceptual phenomena in support of their thesis that analysis often fails to explain experiences, and they found ample grist for their mill in the perceptual constancies. In object constancy, for example, the table remains a table in appearance in spite of wide variations in viewing conditions. Look at it edge-on from one corner; it forms an oblique rectangular image on the retina, but perceptually remains a conventionally rectilinear table. Such object constancy is scarcely explicable in terms of structuralism, for if the elements of perception change, the perception ought to change with them. Similarly, in brightness and size constancy, the sensory elements may change radically under different viewing conditions, yet the percept keeps its quality of unique wholeness. Other examples abound in everyday experience. Transpose a tune into another key, and it is still the same tune even though the elements are all different. Dismantle a chair, and you no longer have a chair but a mere bundle of sticks.

Hence, the Gestalt psychologists could argue that experiences carry with them a quality of wholeness which cannot be found in the parts. For this reason, the name "Gestalt" is appropriate to characterize their system, since it denotes form, figure, or configuration and carries with it the connotation that reductional analysis destroys a figure or "Gestalt." The Gestalt psychologists quickly extended their observations and theoretical interpretations into other areas—learning, thinking, problem solving—in fact to the whole of psychology.

As the new movement grew in strength, Wertheimer and his group proposed nothing short of the complete overthrow of the traditional psychology represented by structuralism and also found themselves just as strongly opposed to behaviorism. Specifically, they deplored the "brick and mortar" psychology of Wundt, meaning elements ("bricks") bound by associations ("mortar"), and were equally dissatisfied with the reductionism of the behaviorists. In either case, they argued, the psychologist is dealing only with artifacts and abstractions as the end products of analysis; and it makes little difference whether the analysis is in terms of introspection on the one hand, or in terms of the reduction of behavior to conditioned or natural reflexes on the other hand. Perhaps the best summary of this fundamental aspect of Gestalt psychology is that it represents a *molar* as opposed to *molecular* point of view.

Equally objectionable to the Gestalt psychologists were attempts to seek the physiological foundations of behavior in a machine-like nervous system in which a point-for-point correspondence was assumed to exist between the environmental stimulus and sensory excitation in the cortex. This so-called machine view of the nervous system arose in connection with behavioristic explanations of learning in which the brain was likened to a telephone switchboard, where each new habit was represented by a neural connection between two cortical centers, just as a telephone operator establishes a connection by plugging in circuits. Experimental evidence opposed to this theory was to be found in Gestalt studies of transposability. For example, an animal can learn to discriminate in favor of the darker of two shades of gray, A and B, where A is light and B dark. If a new shade C is introduced, which is darker than B, and the animal then is tested for his ability to discriminate between B and C, he readily makes the discrimination in favor of the darker C—this despite the fact that he had been previously responding to B as "darker."

Finally, on the negative side of the ledger, the Gestaltists took issue with the behaviorists' denial of the validity of introspection as a psychological method. This is not to say that the Gestalt school approved the kind of introspection employed by Wundt and Titchener. Far from it; but they did favor the study of conscious experience in a phenomenological sense and frequently made use of critical demonstrations which appeal to direct experience for their validity.[8]

On the positive side, it has already been pointed out that the Gestalt psychologists utilized phenomenological analysis and favored the study of behavior as molar. In addition it should be noted that they took a "dynamic" or "field" view of the nervous system in place of the behavioristic machine view. While they did not deny a correspondence between cortical processes and outside stimulation, the relationship was "isomorphic" instead of the point-by-point correspondence implied by the S-R formula. The situation here would be similar to the manner in which a road map corresponds to the countryside. The map differs in many respects from the actual landscape; but, nevertheless, the essential correspondence is valid or the map would be useless as a guide. This problem will be dealt with more fully in Chapter 4, on perception. Meanwhile, we may turn our attention from these methodological considerations to outline some of the more important findings in support of the principles which we have been considering.

In the area of perception the Gestalt program provided many valuable and original contributions which at the same time lent support to the molar viewpoint. Specifically, we refer to the principles of organization of perceptual fields. Among these are the familiar principles of figure-ground so

---

[8] Numerous examples of such demonstrations can be found in any Gestalt source book.

fundamental in all perceptual experiences and the organizing factors of proximity, continuity, similarity, and closure. (See Figure 4-2.)

It should be noted that while these principles of organization are most obvious in visual perception, they are equally important in other sensory fields and in the "higher" mental processes of learning and thinking. Indeed, among the classical experiments of the Gestalt school is Köhler's work on insight learning in apes (*37*, p. 820). The ape's insightful solution of a box and banana problem[9] can be interpreted as "closure" of the gap in the animal's psychological field. Similarly, Wertheimer brought the Gestalt techniques to the field of education where he demonstrated with considerable success that when the teacher arranged problems so as to organize the elements of classroom exercises into meaningful wholes, insight would occur. This he contrasted sharply with the usual educational practices of blind drill and rote learning. Moreover, he was able to demonstrate that once the principle of a problem had been grasped it would carry over or transfer to other situations (*35*).

Since these earlier, more or less classic, experiments were carried out, Gestalt psychology has made its influence felt in ever widening circles. There have been extensions of the Gestalt point of view into child psychology, especially by Kurt Lewin (*22*), and into social psychology (*20*). Meanwhile, research in the area of perceptual phenomena has continued to occupy the attention of the group (*1*, pp. 131–134), and the primary influence of the Gestalt school on contemporary psychology has been in the fields of perception and learning—especially perception. Indeed, it is impossible today to find a chapter on perception in any general or experimental textbook of psychology that does not show the influence of this school.

Psychoanalysis.[10]   The last of the "schools" which we shall consider in this chapter is known as *psychoanalysis*. However, psychoanalysis was never a "school" or a systematic theory of psychology comparable to those we have been considering. This is true largely because the psychoanalytic movement developed outside of academic circles and, further, because this group has never attempted to take a systematic position on all of the mental processes. For example, the psychoanalysts have shown little interest in sensation, attention, depth perception, learning, and a variety of other processes which have been the traditional areas of concern for the other schools. They neglected these academic fields primarily because their aim was the very practical one of providing therapeutic aid for neurotic patients.

---

[9] The problem confronting the animal is to reach a banana suspended from the ceiling by stacking boxes until he is within reach of the fruit.

[10] For those interested in pursuing this system further, the *Introductory Lectures* and *New Introductory Lectures* make an excellent introduction to the system and have the advantage of being written by Freud himself. (See references *11* and *12*.) For additional references see Munroe (*26*). Our account has been drawn from a number of primary and secondary sources.

As a consequence, psychoanalysis *as a theory* is primarily centered around the etiology, development, and treatment of mental disorders. Psychoanalysis *as a practice* is a nonexperimental clinical technique for treating patients suffering from disorders which are psychogenic in origin.

However, despite the restricted theoretical position of psychoanalysis with its nonexperimental and nonacademic background, modern psychology has been profoundly influenced by this school. Moreover, the social sciences, philosophy, ethics, and the arts have also felt the impact of psychoanalytic theory. In fact, of all the schools of psychology, psychoanalysis has captured the imagination of the general public to the extent that many laymen erroneously equate psychology with psychoanalysis.

This highly influential movement got underway in Vienna near the end of the last century under the leadership of **Sigmund Freud** (1856 to 1939). At that time Freud was a practicing physician who specialized in diseases of the nervous system. He became aware that many of his patients with "nervous" diseases were in reality suffering from mental conflicts and neurotic states which manifested themselves as physical disorders or as complaints of extreme fatigue, "nervousness," insomnia, and the like.

At that time an honest recognition of this problem left the physician in a dilemma. Treating the patient's physical symptoms failed to get at the root of the problem, yet there was no real alternative. Clearly, what the patient needed was psychotherapy rather than physical therapy, but psychotherapy had not yet been developed as a recognized branch of clinical medicine. While Freud was puzzling over these difficulties, it came to his attention that a French practitioner, Jean Martin Charcot (1825 to 1893), and a German, Joseph Breuer (1842 to 1925), had been experiencing considerable success with the hypnotic treatment of hysterics who were suffering from paralyses, anesthesias, and mental confusion—all caused by psychogenic factors. The therapeutic technique consisted of hypnotizing the patient and then encouraging him to "talk out" his difficulties. This reliving of the troublesome experiences which appeared to be at the root of the symptoms frequently resulted in considerable improvement in the patient.

Freud studied the technique of hypnotherapy and collaborated for a time with Breuer in treating patients with this new clinical weapon. However, Freud discovered that some patients could not be hypnotized deeply enough to enable the physician to take them back to the source of their emotional difficulties. Even more discouraging was the discovery that in many cases where the therapy had been initially successful and the patient's symptoms relieved, the illness subsequently broke out in another form with a different set of symptoms. Evidently the "cure" had been superficial—nothing more than a temporary alleviation of symptoms.

To make a long story short, Freud eventually recognized that the real value in hypnotic treatments lay in the psychic analysis involved and had nothing to do with the hypnotic trance as such. The problem then became one of discovering a therapeutic technique rendering hypnosis unnecessary, but at the same time making possible a deeper and more complete analysis of the patient's psyche. This end was achieved by having the patient relax on a couch and freely tell whatever came into his mind. This is the method of *free association*. The psychoanalyst, meanwhile, listens to the patient and observes him as unobtrusively as possible for emotional reactions, signs of distress, and resistance to the treatment. Following such a session, the therapist will discuss with his patient interpretations of the material brought to light during the analytic hour.

In the course of his practice Freud also became convinced that dreams were of special significance for the new therapy, since, if properly analyzed, they revealed hidden wishes. Indeed, Freud considered the dream a main-line route into unconscious mental processes. For this reason, dream interpretation subsequently became an important part of both the therapeutic process and of psychoanalytic theory.

When Freud published accounts of his revolutionary technique and the discoveries he was making in his clinical chambers, a number of young medical men were attracted to Vienna to become students of the new therapy. As might be expected, an association for the development of psychoanalysis was soon formed (1902). Most of the original leaders in the school became famous either by virtue of their efforts in behalf of Freud's theories or because they dissented from their leader's doctrines and promulgated psychotherapeutic systems of their own. Of those who broke away from the master, the most important were **Alfred Adler** (1870 to 1937), founder of Individual Psychology, and **Carl Jung** (1875 to 1961), founder of Analytical Psychology. Of the two, Jung remained much closer to Freud's original position in both theory and practice, while in most respects Adler's views came to be diametrically opposed to Freud's. For recent and exhaustive comparative treatments of the various schools of psychoanalysis the reader is referred to Ford and Urban (*10*) or Munroe (*26*).

To return to Freud, our main concern in this chapter is with his contribution to the methodology and aims of psychology. Clearly, both psychoanalytic aims and methods are highly specialized for clinical work and, as a consequence, are not directly comparable to those of the academic schools. Perhaps the simplest and most valid generalization that can be offered is that neither Freud's methods nor his aims have appreciably influenced the evolution of *experimental* psychology. They created, it is true, a revolution in the treatment of mental disorders, but this occurred in psychiatry rather than in academic psychology. On the other hand, Freud's systematic theories did profoundly influence academic psychology in several ways.

To begin with, academicians had devoted relatively little attention to the psychology of motivation, particularly unconscious motivation, before the advent of psychoanalysis. The stimulation from Freud's writings did much to remedy this deficiency, since his system heavily emphasized this aspect of mental life. Freud did not, as some people suppose, "discover" the unconscious; nor was he the first to struggle with the problems of human motivation. However, it was Freud who emphasized these processes and who recognized that, traditionally, man's rational side had been over-emphasized in accounting for behavior. Perhaps, as some of his critics believe, Freud went too far in the opposite direction of explaining behavior almost entirely in terms of man's irrational nature. No final evaluation can be given at this time, since his hypotheses have proved difficult or impossible to test. They were formulated on the basis of clinical practice from a highly selected sample of the population (neurotics) and are frequently cast in such a form as to make experimental verification impossible (28).

Freud is also indirectly responsible for a great deal of the contemporary interest in child psychology and child development. His conclusions that neurotic disturbances originate in early childhood have made virtually everyone who has anything to do with the care or training of children extremely child-centered. Before Freud's influence was so widely felt, the child was thought of as a miniature adult who had to be indoctrinated and trained according to adult standards. Today, interest centers more in the child's own nature, needs, and potentialities, and in discovering how these may be developed at the least cost to his individualism and with the least risk of doing him psychological harm.

Freud and his followers are also largely held responsible for the radical change that has taken place in sexual mores since the end of the Victorian era. The change, needless to say, has been in the direction of increased freedom in sexual behavior. To some extent Freudian psychology is used as a rationalization instead of a true reason for the new sexual ethic. As has been true of other scientific theories as they percolate down to the grass roots, Freudian psychoanalysis has become greatly oversimplified in the public mind. Just as the whole of Darwinian evolution was reduced to the catch phrase, "Man descended from apes," in everyday parlance, so Freud's position on the sexual basis of the neuroses is oversimplified to, "It is psychologically harmful to repress sex." As we shall see (Chapter 11), Freud actually considered sexual repression necessary if civilization and culture were to survive. Whether rightly or wrongly, the notion of sexual freedom is attributed to Freud, and the end result has been a general loosening of sexual restraint in literature, art, the media of entertainment, and behavior in general.

Finally, there can be little doubt that psychoanalysis has played an important part in creating the strong interest exhibited by a large number of psychologists in the relatively new field of clinical psychology. This branch of psychology has grown rapidly in recent years primarily as a result of the impetus provided by World War II. Thousands of soldiers returning from battle zones were suffering from combat fatigue or more serious mental disturbances. Because of the shortage of psychiatrists it was necessary to train hundreds of psychologists to help provide skilled therapists for work in government hospitals. Moreover, the keener awareness on the part of the general public of the desirability of obtaining psychological assistance for adjustment problems has resulted in a great increase in counseling agencies, both public and private, whose personnel, in part, are clinical psychologists.

The clinical psychologist is rarely a psychoanalyst, and equally rarely is he committed exclusively to Freudian theory. His academic training is typically grounded in experimental psychology with specialization in psychometrics, abnormal psychology, and psychotherapy. We do not mean to imply that he is indoctrinated *against* Freudian theory, but rather that he is imbued with an eclectic point of view which recognizes the worth of various approaches and whose guiding principle is to test the value of any clinical principle or method by experimental techniques whenever this is feasible.

To summarize, we have taken the position that Freudian free association, dream analysis, and psychoanalytic theory and technique in general have largely developed outside of the scope of traditional academic and systematic psychology. Its methodology is specialized and thus far appears to be irrelevant for experimental psychology. On the other hand, Freud's theories of human motivation and psychogenic development have profoundly influenced academic psychology and, in addition, have resulted in a great deal of research, debate, and interest in the areas of personality and adjustment.

CONTEMPORARY DEVELOPMENTS

The collapse of the schools. The heyday of the schools passed with the end of the third decade of the twentieth century. The reason was simple: psychology had outgrown schools. With the great increase in research results pouring into the general fund of knowledge from all sides, it became increasingly difficult not to recognize that *all schools* and systematic positions were making valuable contributions. Moreover, it had become virtually impossible for any one psychologist to attempt to encompass the entire science in a single comprehensive system. The inevitable result was specialization, which, in turn, led to the development of miniature systems, theories, and models.

Because miniature systems, theories, and models occupy a central position in contemporary psychology, we shall discuss and compare each of these conceptual tools for the organization of factual and theoretical material before outlining contemporary trends in systematic psychology. In this way we shall be in a better position to illustrate how the older, more programmatic systems have been replaced by miniature systems, complex theories and models.

Miniature systems. A miniature system attempts to provide a framework for a particular area within the broad field of psychology, such as learning, motivation or perception. These miniature systems differ from the older global systems that were associated with the schools of psychology in being restricted to a single behavioral process or more often to some aspects of a behavioral process. For example, a miniature system which attempts to organize the factual and theoretical information in the field of learning concerns itself only with learning or with a particular type of learning, such as verbal learning, conditioning, or maze learning. Similarly, a miniature system in personality is likely to be organized around factual information and theory which represent a particular approach to personality, perhaps through factor analysis, the study of traits, or of constitutional types.

The miniature system begins with a definition of the process under consideration, states the postulates which it is undertaking to verify, specifies the nature of its data and the units of description and measurement to be employed, and finally organizes the data around the postulated theoretical framework. The essential steps in developing a miniature system are the same as those employed in developing a global system. The difference is one of range or scope. The global systems associated with the schools attempted to organize the field as a whole; whereas, as has been pointed out, the miniature system deals only with a single behavioral process. It might also be noted that the originators of miniature systems are specialists in their areas; consequently, the systems that they construct are typically formulated around large bodies of empirical data from their own laboratories.

Theories. The term *theory* is often used interchangeably with the concept of a miniature system, since the latter essentially is a compound theory made up of a number of interlocking limited theories. A theory, like a miniature system, attempts to relate a restricted range of phenomena by making use of postulates to fill in gaps in knowledge wherever empirical information is lacking. Very often the postulates in a theory may be no more than elaborate hypotheses to be tested, thus keeping the theory close to experimental testing or verification. In this book the two concepts will be used interchangeably.

Models.   The term *model* is employed in two ways in psychology. First, a model may be a mechanical copy of a physiological or anatomical entity designed in such a way as to show how the various parts function and relate to the whole. For example, models of the neuron, eye, ear, and brain have been developed in various degrees of complexity as aids to our understanding of these organs. Second, models are sometimes a particular subclass of theory. Used in this way a model, in contrast to a theory, is purely abstract and makes no pretense of being a copy of nature. For example, a statistical model of learning utilizes abstract mathematical symbols which represent the learning process. The model is chosen in such a manner as to stimulate research and to provide a better understanding of the learning process. It must be emphasized, however, that the model does not attempt to explain the processes underlying learning but only to represent them. Theories, on the other hand, do strive to explain psychological processes and so are "reality directed."

In general, psychologists are coming more and more to favor limited theories and models rather than complex theories and systems. Limited theories can be kept closer to the level of empirical data and experimental verification. Broad, programmatic theories and systems are useful in the early or developmental stages of a science. They define aims and specify methods. They provide useful guidelines for initiating research programs. But they do not reach down to the grass roots level of mental or behavioral processes which, in the final analysis, is the heart of psychology. It is primarily because of the greater sophistication of psychology as a science that theorizing has come to be closely related to experimental research programs.

Contemporary trends.   In subsequent chapters in this book many examples of miniature systems, theories and models will be presented. However, to lend perspective to both our past treatment of the traditional schools and our subsequent discussion of the evolution of contemporary concepts and limited systems and theories, we shall briefly summarize the main trends in systematic theory of the past several decades. These will be outlined under six headings: (1) learning theories, (2) perceptual theories, (3) intelligence and quantitative psychology, (4) model construction and information theory, (5) personality theory, and (6) the physiological basis of behavior.

Learning theories.[11] Learning theory and research constitute a large proportion of the output of contemporary psychologists. In keeping with the broad picture we are painting here, we may say that, following the dissolution of the schools, learning theorists divided themselves along two familiar systematic lines: first, those who followed the old *associationistic* tradition which goes back to the empirical philosophers, and second, those who stressed the *cognitive* approach typical of Gestalt-like theories. To put it another way, there are the *"S-R"* (stimulus-response) theories, and the more or less antithetical *"O"* (organism) theories. The latter tend to emphasize cognitive processes in accounting for learning as opposed to *S-R* processes. Naturally, such absolute distinctions are made for the sake of convenience rather than because they account with perfect exactitude for divisions in modern learning theory.

The associationistic position is broad enough to encompass, first of all, the functionalists, whose work in recent years has been primarily in the area of human verbal learning. In general, their explanations of learning have been developed in terms of associationism. Secondly, the behaviorists can also be classed under this heading, since they emphasize conditioning as a key to learning, which in turn leans heavily on the old associationistic principle of contiguity. The functionalists, it might be noted, are less concerned with the development of elaborate theoretical constructs than are the behaviorists. The former are willing to study such important areas of learning as retroactive inhibition, transfer of training, and forgetting without the necessity of immediately relating their findings to some overall theory of learning. The behavioristic group, especially those whose theoretical and research tool is conditioning, tend, on the other hand, to develop elaborate and comprehensive miniature systems.

Those who are most closely associated with cognitive theory are: Gestalt psychologists, psychologists who emphasize "expectancy," "understanding," "sign" learning, and wholism rather than atomism in theory building, and those who feel there is an intimate relationship between perception and learning. In chapters to come we shall meet representatives of each of the principal types of learning systems.

Contemporary emphasis in research and theorizing in the area of learning has taken three broad lines. First, the development of statistical or probability models of learning has grown in favor over theoretical explanations in terms of the traditional principles of contiguity and reinforcement. Secondly, considerable excitement has recently been generated by work in the area of the neural basis of learning. More specifically, the discovery of DNA (deoxyribonucleic acid) and RNA (ribonucleic acid)

---

[11] For a more detailed treatment of learning theory see Chapters 6 and 7, this volume, or Hilgard (*16*).

has raised the distinct possibility of explaining learning at the molecular level in terms of modifications of protein molecules as a direct result of practice. Third, a large number of psychologists have interested themselves in research on the effects of early experience on the development of human and infrahuman organisms. A considerable body of literature is already available on the effects of sensory deprivation, enriched environments, and experimental isolation on early development and adult behavior. These studies have evolved out of an older theoretical problem, namely, the relative importance of learning and maturation in development. The long recognized theoretical importance of the problem has been reinforced by the recent practical interest stimulated by space travel where astronauts must face long periods of relatively complete isolation. Recent work among psychologists has centered on controlled studies which attempt to identify the environmental and experimental factors responsible for learned behavioral modification in early development. We shall have more to say about each of the rapidly developing areas in Chapter 5.

Perceptual systems. In the traditional systems and schools of psychology, the emphasis in perceptual research and theory was on "S" factors. By S factors are meant those stimulus conditions important in visual depth perception, in attention, and in auditory and cutaneous localization. We might also include here the psychophysicists, since many of the problems brought under investigation in their laboratories were perceptual as well as sensory in nature. But here again, as was true in early learning theories, the emphasis was on an S-R orientation to the psychology of perception.

In recent years, one of the most significant developments in both perceptual theory and research has been to put an "O" in the traditional S-R approach. Shortly after World War II, when this movement became strong enough to make itself felt throughout the field, it was dubbed the "new look" in psychology. A few examples from the research laboratory will suffice to show the general direction of the new perceptual psychology.

Levine *et al.* (*21*) presented ambiguous stimuli on a ground glass screen to both hungry and nonhungry subjects. Some of these stimuli could be interpreted as food objects. The hungry subjects perceived a significantly greater number of the stimuli as food objects than did the nonhungry subjects.

Similarly, it has been shown by Bruner and Goodman (*6*) that under certain conditions the magnitude and brightness of perceptual stimuli can be influenced by values. Specifically, coins may be perceived as larger or smaller depending upon the subject's economic status.

Finally, a good deal of recent research within this same frame of reference has been directed toward testing the possibility of "perceptual defense" (*24*). Some experimental studies have suggested that it is possible for a subject to fail to perceive certain "threatening" stimuli even though he reveals "unconscious" perception of such stimuli through autonomic and other implicit reactions. If such subthreshold perception can be verified, psychologists will have evidence for an important ego-defense mechanism. These and related experiments show that the recent emphasis in perceptual research is on motivational, emotional, and personality factors. Perception from the point of view of those who study such inner determinants cannot be understood solely in terms of the traditional approach by sensory analysis, for O factors are at least equally important as determiners of human perception. In short, *what* we see or perceive is, in part, O-determined at the outset.

The Gestalt psychologists, in keeping with their traditional interests, have remained active in perceptual theory and research. In recent years they have attempted to link perceptual and cortical brain fields in order to substantiate experimentally the theory of isomorphism, which we considered earlier in this chapter.

Similarly Hebb (*14*), a behavioristically oriented psychologist, has sought to formulate a perceptual theory that takes as its point of departure neurological mechanisms in the visual cortex. In support of his program, Hebb reviews cases of cataract patients who have had their vision restored after being blind for years. Such individuals have great difficulty in making what seem to be simple discriminations such as those involved in distinguishing between triangular and rectangular stimuli. Along with similar results from the animal laboratory, this evidence suggests that our most fundamental perceptions are learned. Hebb also postulates a cortical mechanism to account for such perceptual learning. (See Chapter 5 of this volume.)

The neofunctionalists have been studying perception in terms of how it functions in a subject's basic adjustment in certain laboratory situations. They have been able to demonstrate that many of the successful adjustments involved in our interaction with objects in the environment are based on strongly developed perceptual frames of reference acquired during childhood. From our early experiences we come to *expect* that rooms are rectilinear, that plates are round, and that tennis balls are larger than golf balls; consequently, we deal with them according to our expectations. As a result of perceptual expectancies, when subjects are placed in *ambiguous* situations in which the cues allow them to interpret the situation in terms of past experience, this immediately and unconsciously happens even though the end result may be seriously distorted perceptions. (See Figure 5-10.)

These and other developments in recent perceptual theory show that, along with learning, this highly challenging field has continued to attract the systematists and theorists. It is not as easy to categorize perceptual theorists as it is learning theorists, and we shall make no attempt to do so here. However, it seems fair to say that the one clear-cut trend has been the shift from *S*-oriented perceptual theories to *O*-oriented theories.

The quantitative psychologists. The intelligence testing movement, which gained such impetus from the mass testing programs of World War I and the introduction of the Binet Test into the United States in 1916, inevitably gave rise to the question of what do the intelligence tests measure. Indeed, it seemed possible that much could be learned about the nature of intelligence from a searching analysis of the tests themselves. Some years later, when personality tests came into wide use, the same question was asked in connection with these tests, namely, could analyses of the tests reveal anything about personality?

As early as 1914, Charles Spearman (1863 to 1945), a British psychologist, began to attack the problem in regard to intelligence with correlational techniques. If a large number of different intellectual tasks are given to a group and the scores on the various tasks are intercorrelated, then high correlations between tasks can be interpreted to mean that the successful completion of such tasks depends upon the presence of a common intellectual factor. Spearman found moderately high correlations, around +0.70, among *all* cognitive tests; and on the basis of these findings he formulated his *G* and *s* theory of intelligence. *G* stands for the intellectual factor common to all tasks, and *s* represents the specific factor required for any given task. Since these *s* factors are independent or uncorrelated, each task requires its special *s*, or specific ability; consequently, there is one *G*, but there are many *s*'s.

From this beginning, interest in the quantitative approach to the understanding of aptitudes and personality increased rapidly. Newer and better mathematical tools were developed to analyze both intelligence and personality tests. In the United States, L. L. Thurstone in the area of intelligence, and R. B. Cattell in the area of personality, have been leaders in the development of factor analytic theories. From factor analyses of intelligence and personality test results they have developed comprehensive theories of intelligence and personality. Thurstone and his associates are also responsible for modifying the old psychophysical techniques to make them useful in the measurement of attitudes and opinions. Still other psychologists with an interest in quantitative methods have directed their efforts to the discovery of appropriate mathematical techniques for the analysis of all types of psychological data.[12]

Psychologists pursuing the mathematical approach to the solution of psychological problems stand apart in a kind of "school" in the broadest sense of the term. However, since they make no attempt to systematize the

[12] For a more detailed discussion of factor theories see Chapter 14.

whole field of psychology, we shall consider in subsequent chapters only those whose work has led to "miniature" systems in the areas of intelligence and personality.

Model making and information theory. In some respects those psychologists who design models of the brain or of a behavioral process, such as learning, and those whose research interests lie in information theory might well be grouped with the quantitative psychologists. Such a classification would be justified on the grounds that model makers and information theorists utilize mathematics extensively in their programs. However, their purpose is not so much to study a behavioral or mental process by means of mathematical techniques as it is to show how such processes *might* work in terms of models or to utilize mathematics in the *measurement* of communications processes.

Model making on a grand scale is relatively new in psychology, yet this type of research stems from a long past. As early as 1885 Ebbinghaus began a program of systematic research in memory which led to his mathematical formula $R = 100 \, K/[(\log t)^c + K]$, to account for his findings in the retention of nonsense syllables. This formula, in a broad sense, is a model, for it attempts to provide a generalized working construct for the prediction of the course of memory in time.

An early mechanical model of interest to physiological psychologists was constructed in 1920 by the physiologist R. S. Lillie, who succeeded in fashioning a working model of a neuron. He suspended an iron wire in nitric acid. When the initial chemical reaction stopped, the wire was coated with a "membrane" of ferric nitrate. If a stimulus such as a scratch were applied to the wire, an "impulse" in the form of a propagated breakdown of the "membrane" traveled over the entire wire. Lillie's demonstration suggested that a similar mechanism might be involved in the transmission of the nervous impulse. More recent electronic research has shown that a rapid, propagated breakdown of the neuronal membrane does indeed occur during nervous conduction.

From these early beginnings, there have been rapid developments in model making partly due to advances in electronics and partly as a result of the increase in data coming from psychological laboratories which serve as the foundation of such models. As a result, we have a number of recent mathematical models in learning theory along with some rather startling machines, called digital computers, which are capable of carrying out complex mathematical calculations at high speeds. Such devices have been popularly called "electronic brains."

Information theory is not a theory but an interdisciplinary area of research which draws upon mathematics, electronic engineering, psychophysics, and perceptual psychology for the solution of problems which involve the measurement, transmission, detection, and reception of messages or communications. Since World War II scientists have been increasingly concerned with the problems involved in telemetery, data processing, encoding, decoding, and transmitting signals and messages. In our modern world machines—automata—are doing humanlike tasks. The machine, like the human perceiver, must selectively receive signals from its environment, transmit those signals to a central processing station, and, depending upon the "decision" arrived at in that station, carry out some action affecting the environment.

There are many broad analogies which are possible between the human "machine" and electronic receivers and computers and the processes in which they engage. However, if information theory did not go beyond drawing analogies it would have remained no more significant for psychology than any other model. Information theory becomes of special interest to the psychologist when he is called upon to help the engineer design machines to replace human functions or to make them more efficient. To do this he must understand those functions. His knowledge of the sense organs and central nervous processes must be approached from new perspectives and in the process his understanding is broadened and deepened. In recent years psychologists in the fields of learning, perception, psychophysics, and social psychology have shown considerable interest in information theory and have made significant contributions to its empirical and theoretical literature (3). In Chapter 14 we shall review some of these developments in more detail.

Finally, the rapid advances in communication and information theory have resulted in remarkable devices which are largely used in military and space operations for guiding planes, missiles, antiaircraft shells, and space vehicles to their targets. The new science which has recently been developed to meet the need for bridging the gaps between the engineering, psychological, mathematical, and other fields that contribute to, or might benefit from, research along these lines is known as "cybernetics," from the Greek word meaning "steersman." It would be difficult to find better illustrations than these to show how psychology has specialized since Wundt set up his modest program for discovering the elements of consciousness!

Personality theory.   As we pointed out earlier in this chapter, the development of personality theory was given great impetus by Freud. The past half century has been characterized by a rapid proliferation of theories, some of which are offshoots of Freudian theory, while others have developed within academic circles. Generally speaking, deviations and modifications of psychoanalytic theory have taken a socially oriented point of view as opposed to the original biological orientation of Freud. In other words, the neo-Freudian theories have tended to minimize the importance of "instincts" or drives as important factors in psychogenic development while maximizing the importance of interpersonal relationships. It has recently been pointed out by Ansbacher and Ansbacher (2) that it would be more correct to label the major contemporary neo-Freudians "neo-Adlerians," since Alfred Adler's Individual Psychology either anticipates or was godfather to most of the recent personality theories.

According to the Ansbachers Adler's "striving for superiority" in compensation for feelings of inferiority has, in many recent theories, become a "striving for security." In addition, Adler's emphasis on the self as opposed to Freud's character structures of the id, ego, and superego, his emphasis on social relations and his stress on the present instead of the past, are characteristic of the so-called neo-Freudian theories of Karen Horney, Harry Stack Sullivan, Erich Fromm, and others. For these reasons they are often collectively referred to as "social psychoanalysts."

Among the academically nurtured personality theories, there are such widely divergent viewpoints as virtually to defy any simple classification. There are representatives of Gestalt or field theory, constitutional or body-type theories, factorial theories, conditioning theories, an eclectic theory, and several personalistic or individual-centered theories. Personality, in a sense, is a way of looking at the individual as a whole; and, because a molar point of view invites many possible approaches and interpretations, psychologists with different orientations have investigated personality along different lines. As a consequence of such diversity we have the complex picture just described.

Yet, in spite of these divergent points of view, personality theory reflects many of the same basic cleavages in systematic psychology with which we are already familiar. There are the biologically oriented as opposed to socially oriented theories; the molecular as opposed to molar, and the old S-R as opposed to self- or O-oriented points of view. Representatives of these points of view will be considered further in the chapter on personality theory.

The physiological basis of behavior. We pointed out (Chapter 2) that as an independent science psychology evolved out of a coalescence of philosophy, physiology, and the early work in sensory psychology carried out by Weber, Fechner, and others. We also noted that Wundt's first textbook in psychology bore the title, *Physiological Psychology.* Therefore, from its very inception the new science enjoyed a close affinity with physiology, particularly neural physiology or neurology. Moreover, a specialized area within the field, *physiological psychology,* rapidly developed into one of the most important research areas in psychology.

During the developmental years, physiological psychologists depended largely on the method of extirpation and the use of electrical stimulation to the surface of the cerebral cortex for their investigations of cortical functions. Most of our fundamental knowledge of brain localization has come through these avenues of research. During this same period the phylogenetically older and relatively inaccessible parts of the brain lying under the cortex took a secondary place in research interest largely because of the difficulty of utilizing extirpation on subcortical centers and because of the lack of appropriate stimulating techniques.

The recent discovery of permanently attached and implanted electrodes capable of stimulating centers deep within the brain has revolutionized our understanding of these centers. Many centers formerly assumed to be associated with olfactory processes are now known to play a role in the regulation of motivational and emotional processes. Psychologists have discovered "pleasure centers," centers for the regulation of hunger, thirst, sex, and emotional behavior. Moreover, with the introduction of high fidelity electronic equipment, the old method of electrical stimulation of the cerebral cortex is yielding much new information about brain localization.

These dramatic discoveries have been paralleled by equally promising developments in the area of neural pharmacology and brain biochemistry. Working in conjunction with biochemists, psychologists are carrying out qualitative and quantitative studies of brain chemistry to determine what changes occur as a result of psychological variables such as intensive practice or experience. Others are utilizing chemical techniques to investigate the possible role of DNA and RNA in learning and intelligence.

Because of the great potential significance of these research programs, we shall devote an entire chapter (Chapter 13) to summarizing and interpreting their significance for psychology.[13] At the same time we shall also discuss the relationships of some of the older theories of cortical function and localization to these recent discoveries.

REFERENCES

1. Allport, F. H. *Theories of perception and the concept of structure.* New York: Wiley, 1955.
2. Ansbacher, H. L., and R. Ansbacher. *The individual psychology of Alfred Adler.* New York: Basic Books, 1956.
3. Attneave, F. *Applications of information theory to psychology: A summary of basic concepts, methods, and results.* New York: Holt, Rinehart, and Winston, 1959.
4. Boring, E. G. *A history of experimental psychology,* ed 2. New York: Appleton, 1950.
5. Boring, E. G., H. S. Langfeld, and H. P. Weld. *Foundations of psychology.* New York: Wiley, 1948.

[13] For a discussion of the empirical findings in the areas of subcortical stimulation see Morgan (*25*, pp. 324–333, and Chapter 20).

6. Bruner, J. S., and C. D. Goodman. Value and need as organizing factors in perception. *Journal of Abnormal and Social Psychology,* **42,** 1947, pp. 33–44.
7. Carr, H. A. *Psychology: A study of mental activity.* New York: Longmans, Green, 1925.
8. Carr, H. A. *An introduction to space perception.* New York: Longmans, Green, 1935.
9. Dewey, J. The reflex arc concept in psychology. *Psychological Review,* **3,** 1896, pp. 357–370.
10. Ford, D. H., and H. B. Urban. *Systems of psychotherapy.* New York: Wiley, 1963.
11. Freud, S. *New introductory lectures on psychoanalysis.* New York: Norton, 1933.
12. Freud, S. *A general introduction to psychoanalysis.* New York: Boni & Liveright, 1920. (Also available in a reprint: Permabook #202 New York: Permabooks.)
13. Guilford, J. P. *Psychometric methods.* New York: McGraw-Hill, 1936.
14. Hebb, D. O. *The organization of behavior.* New York: Wiley, 1949.
15. Heidbreder, E. *Seven psychologies.* New York: Appleton, 1933.
16. Hilgard, E. *Contemporary theories of learning,* ed 2. New York: Appleton, 1956.
17. Keller, F. S. *The definition of psychology.* New York: Appleton, 1937.
18. Koffka, K. *Principles of Gestalt psychology.* New York: Harcourt, 1935.
19. Köhler, W. *Gestalt psychology.* New York: Liveright, 1929.
20. Krech, D., and R. Crutchfield. *Theory and problems of social psychology.* New York: McGraw-Hill, 1948.
21. Levine, R., I. Chein, and G. Murphy. The relation of the intensity of a need to the amount of perceptual distortion. *Journal of Psychology,* **13,** 1942, pp. 283–293.
22. Lewin, K. Behavior and development as a function of the total situation. In L. Carmichael (ed.), *Manual of child psychology.* New York: Wiley, 1946.
23. McGeoch, J. A., and A. L. Irion. *The psychology of human learning,* rev. ed. New York: Longmans, Green, 1952.
24. McGinnies, E. Emotionality and perceptual defense. *Psychological Review,* **56,** 1949, pp. 244–251.
25. Morgan, C. *Physiological psychology,* ed. 3. New York: McGraw-Hill, 1965.
26. Munroe, R. L. *Schools of psychoanalytic thought.* New York: Dryden, 1955.
27. Murphy, G. *Historical introduction to modern psychology,* rev. ed. New York: Harcourt, 1949.
28. Sears, R. R. *Survey of objective studies of psychoanalytic concepts.* New York: Social Science Research Council, 1943.
29. Titchener, E. B. *A textbook of psychology.* New York: Macmillan, 1910.
30. Watson, J. B. Psychology as the behaviorist views it. *Psychological Review,* **20,** 1913, pp. 158–177.
31. Watson, J. B. *Behavior: An introduction to comparative psychology.* New York: Holt, 1914.
32. Watson, J. B. *Psychology from the standpoint of a behaviorist.* Philadelphia: Lippincott, 1919.
33. Watson, J. B. *The psychological care of the infant and child.* New York: Norton, 1928.
34. Watson, J. B. *Behaviorism.* New York: Norton, 1930.
35. Wertheimer, M. *Productive thinking.* New York: Harper, 1945.
36. Woodworth, R. S. *Contemporary schools of psychology.* New York: Ronald, 1948.
37. Woodworth, R. S., and H. Schlosberg. *Experimental psychology,* rev. ed. New York: Holt, 1954.

BIOGRAPHIES

Alfred Adler

Alfred Adler, the son of a grain merchant, was born on February 17, 1870, in a suburb of Vienna. When he was five years of age, Adler became seriously ill with pneumonia. As a result of this experience he decided to pursue a medical career. He obtained his M.D. degree in 1895 at the University of Vienna and began his early medical practice as an eye specialist.

In 1902 Adler met Freud and became a member of Freud's inner circle. However, in 1911 he parted with the Freudians because of theoretical differences and established his own rival school of Individual Psychology. Adler's strong democratic outlook and love of people won him many devoted adherents, among whom was the British novelist Phyllis Bottome, who subsequently wrote a number of novels dealing with the problem of mental disorders. One of these, *Private Worlds,* achieved international prominence.

Adler and his associates founded a number of clinics for the guidance of children. Several of these are still active in Vienna. His daughter, Alexandra Adler, is associated with the Adlerian Consultation Center in New York City, while his son, Kurt, is also a practicing psychiatrist.

In 1927 Adler lectured at Columbia University. In 1932 he became associated with Long Island University, occupying the first chair of medical psychology in the United States. While on a lecture tour in Aberdeen, Scotland, Adler died suddenly on May 28, 1937.

James Rowland Angell

James Rowland Angell, the champion of functionalism, was born in Burlington, Vermont, on May 8, 1867. He was the descendant of nine generations of Rhode Islanders. His grandfather had been President of Brown University; his father was President of the University of Vermont at the time of James's birth and later President of the University of Michigan.

Angell's early education was in the public schools of Ann Arbor, and his undergraduate work was at the University of Michigan, where he studied under Dewey. He went on to do graduate work under James for a year at Harvard, where he obtained his M.A. in 1892. He then went to Germany for advanced study at Halle, and despite the fact that his thesis was accepted with the proviso that it be rendered into better German, he never obtained his Ph.D. degree. Because an offer to teach at the University of Minnesota proved too tempting, he left Germany in order to accept the position. Ironically, although he never returned to complete work on the thesis, in subsequent years he was instrumental in conferring many doctorates on others. After a year at Minnesota, Angell accepted an appointment at the University of Chicago, where he remained for twenty-five years, fourteen as a teacher and eleven as an administrator.

Following in the tradition of his grandfather and father, he became president of Yale University, the first non-Yale man to hold that position. There he was instrumental in the development of Yale's Institute of Human Relations. During his tenure as president of Yale, he was honored with doctorates by twenty universities and became the fifteenth president of the American Psychological Association. Upon his retirement from academic life he served as an executive of the National Broadcasting Company. He died on March 4, 1949.

Harvey A. Carr

Harvey A. Carr was born April 30, 1873, on a farm in Indiana. His early education was in country schools. At the age of eighteen he enrolled at De Pauw University, but at the end of his second year became seriously ill and was forced to remain at home for some time, regaining his health and earning money to finance his education. At the age of twenty-six he entered the University of Colorado, where he obtained a master's degree in 1902.

Upon leaving Colorado, Carr accepted a fellowship to study at the University of Chicago with Dewey, Angell, and Watson. There, in 1905, he was granted the Ph.D. degree in psychology. Failing to obtain two available university positions in psychology, he taught for a year in a Texas high school and then for two years at Pratt Institute in New York.

When Watson left Chicago in 1908, Carr was invited to become his successor. He remained at Chicago until 1938, succeeding Angell as department chairman. During his tenure some 130 doctorates in psychology were conferred by the University of Chicago. He was a teacher who was readily accessible to his students and vitally concerned with their welfare. He knew his students as individuals and frequently published jointly with them. His publications number about fifty, including a text in general psychology and a volume on space perception. He died at Culver, Indiana, on June 21, 1954.

Charles Darwin

Charles Darwin, English naturalist and author of *Origin of Species,* was born on February 12, 1809, at Shrewsbury, England. He was the son of Dr. Robert Darwin and the grandson of Erasmus Darwin, philosopher, physician, and poet. His mother was the daughter of Josiah Wedgewood, manufacturer of the fine china which bears his name.

Darwin attended school in his native town, and after two terms at Edinburgh entered Cambridge, where he took his B.A. degree in 1831. At that time the British government was preparing H.M.S. *Beagle* for a scientific cruise around the world. Professor John Stevens Henslow, a distinguished botanist and one of Darwin's instructors, urged his appointment as a naturalist. The now famous voyage lasted from 1831 to 1836. It began in South American waters, where Darwin made his monumental observations on the Galapagos Islands, then proceeded to Tahiti, to New Zealand, and, on the return trip, to Ascension Island and the Azores. Darwin returned with an immense amount of data, part of which was published in 1839 under the title *Journal of a Naturalist.*

In 1837 he had retired to the country because of poor health, which he struggled against for the remainder of his life. His biographers record that his working day was but four hours in length. Despite this severely curtailed program, in addition to *Origin of Species,* published in 1859, Darwin wrote numerous scientific papers and books including one of particular interest to psychologists, *Expression of the Emotions in Man and Animals.*

Darwin's *Origin of Species,* announcing his theory of evolution in comprehensive form, was eagerly awaited by his scientific colleagues, since in 1858 Darwin and Alfred Wallace had jointly announced the theory of evolution to the Linnean Society. All 1,250 copies of the first printing of the *Origin* were sold on the day of publication.

Darwin, whose epoch-making work has profoundly influenced every department of contemporary thought, is regarded as one of the outstanding figures of the nineteenth century. He died April 19, 1882, survived by two daughters and five sons, four of whom achieved scientific eminence in their own right.

John Dewey

John Dewey, American philosopher and educator, was born October 25, 1859, in Burlington, Vermont. His father was a storekeeper known for his Yankee wit and gentle humor and respected for his sound judgment. Young Dewey's early life was that of a average boy of his day. He had a paper route, worked part time in a lumber yard, and in no way distinguished himself in grammar school or high school. At the age of fifteen he entered the University of Vermont. Again he showed no great promise until the latter part of his junior year. In his autobiography Dewey relates that the reading of Huxley's *Elements of Physiology* brought about a transformation in his attitude. He began his search for the same marvelous integration in philosophy which Huxley had portrayed in the living organism.

After his graduation from the University of Vermont in 1879, Dewey taught high school in Pennsylvania and then at a private academy in his native state of Vermont. Meanwhile he continued his study of philosophy and succeeded in publishing several articles in the *Journal of Speculative Philosophy.* Dewey was so encouraged to become a professional philosopher that in 1882 he borrowed $500 from an aunt to pursue work in philosophy at Johns Hopkins. Two years later he obtained his Ph.D. degree and accepted an appointment to teach at the University of Michigan, where he remained until 1888. During this period he wrote his first textbook in psychology, which appeared in 1887. In 1888 he accepted an appointment at the University of Minnesota, but a year later returned to Michigan for six more years.

He was then invited to the University of Chicago, where in 1896 he established his experimental or laboratory school, a bold new venture in American education, which became the foundation for modern progressive education. However, he failed to enlist the support of the president of the university in his experimental program and resigned in 1904. With the aid of friends he obtained a position at Teachers College, and remained there teaching and writing his highly influential books on philosophy until his retirement in 1930. He died in New York City on June 1, 1952.

Gustav Fechner

Gustav Fechner was born on April 19, 1801, in Gross-Särchen, a small village in southeastern Germany. He attended the *Gymnasium,* then matriculated in medicine at Leipzig, where he took his degree in 1822. But even before graduating from medical school Fechner's humanistic side was rebelling against the prevailing materialism of his scientific training. Under the pseudonym of "Dr. Mises" he began a series of satirical essays lampooning science and medicine. He continued publishing the essays intermittently for the next twenty-five years, betraying a continual conflict between two sides of his dual personality.

After earning his degree in medicine, Fechner's interest in the biological sciences began to wane in favor of research in physics and mathematics, and within the next decade he had made his reputation as a physicist. Near the end of the decade, however, the versatile Fechner began to develop an interest in the psychology of sensation and seriously injured his eyes by exposing them to the sun in his studies of after-images. Unable to work, he went into a deep depression for a period of three years.

Upon recovery, Fechner's humanistic side sprang into ascendancy; he became more and more the philosopher and less the physicist. A by-product of his philosophical development was a growing interest in the relation between the material and the mental, which led to his founding of psychophysics and the writing of the monumental *Elemente der Psychophysik.*

Fechner lived to be eighty-six years of age. He spent the closing decades of his life in research in experimental psychology, esthetics, and philosophy. He died in Leipzig, November 18, 1887.

Sigmund Freud

Freud was born on May 16, 1856, in Freiberg, a small town in Moravia. At the age of four he was taken to Vienna, which became his home for most of his adult life. Following the completion of a traditional primary and secondary German education, he debated between entering the law or specializing in science. He chose the latter, earning his medical degree at the University of Vienna in 1881. His chief fields of interest during his early medical studies were botany and chemistry. Later he became interested in physiology and comparative anatomy. Upon graduation from medical school, Freud planned a professional life devoted to research in neurology, but lack of means compelled him to engage in clinical practice.

Freud's interest in mental disorders began in 1884 after Josef Breuer told him of a case in which the symptoms of hysteria were alleviated when the patient, under hypnosis, was encouraged to relate the long-buried memories which had given rise to the disorder. A year later Freud visited Charcot, the eminent French neurologist, who encouraged him to investigate hysteria from the psychological point of view. Freud returned to Vienna and collaborated with Breuer on *Studies in Hysteria,* but even before its publication parted with Breuer and replaced hypnotic therapy with free association.

The rest of Freud's life is customarily divided into two periods: the early decades, during which he developed psychoanalysis both as a theory and as a therapy, and the later phase (*Weltanschauung* period) in which he extended his theories to religion, social psychology, anthropology, and the problems of civilization. The change in his interest is revealed in the titles of his publications over the years. Among the early works are *The Interpretation of Dreams* (1900), *Three Contributions to the Theory of Sex* (1905), and *General Introduction to Psychoanalysis* (1916). Among his later works are *Beyond the Pleasure Principle* (1920), *The Future of an Illusion* (1928), and *Civilization and Its Discontents* (1930).

Freud's working day was arduous. He devoted the morning hours to his patients and lectures. After the midday meal he took a walk, during which he planned his writing. The afternoon and evening hours were devoted to patients, organizational work, and writing. He usually retired after midnight.

In the critical year of 1938, when the Nazis carried out their "bloodless invasion" of Austria, with the help of his associate and biographer, Ernest Jones, Freud escaped to England. However, his property was confiscated and his books burned. He died of cancer on September 23, 1939.

Hermann von Helmholtz

Hermann von Helmholtz, one of the greatest scientists of the nineteenth century, was born on August 31, 1821, at Potsdam, near Berlin. His mother was a direct descendant of the Quaker, William Penn. His father, a teacher of philology and philosophy, was instrumental in guiding the early education of his son, whose health was delicate during his early years. At the age of seventeen Helmholtz entered a medical institute in Berlin, where he took his degree.

He began his professional life as an army surgeon. However, since his first love was pure science, he left the army to accept an academic position in physiology at Königsberg. In the course of the next thirty years he held academic appointments in physiology at Bonn and Heidelberg, and in physics at Berlin. Among his outstanding accomplishments during this period were the measurement of the nervous impulse, providing the mathematical foundation for the law of the conservation of energy, the invention of the ophthalmoscope, and the formulation of his famous theories of color vision and hearing. His two most important books are *Physiological Optics* (1856–1866) and *Sensations of Tone* (1862). Both are considered outstanding contributions to modern science.

Helmholtz was a man of simple tastes, somewhat austere in manner and deeply devoted to the empirical point of view in science. Yet his empiricism was tempered by a broad philosophical outlook on the problems of science. Helmholtz died in Charlottenburg, September 8, 1894.

William James

William James, the great American philosopher and psychologist and brother of Henry James, the novelist, was born in New York City, January 11, 1842. His early education was sporadic and interrupted by extensive travel in the United States, France, England, Switzerland, Germany, and Italy. Throughout his early education he was profoundly influenced by his father, a Swedenborgian theologian of independent means, especially in terms of indifference to worldly success and concern with the fundamental problems of life.

After rejecting the idea of becoming a painter when he concluded that he lacked the necessary talent, James entered the Lawrence Scientific School of Harvard at the age of nineteen. Two years later he matriculated in medical school and at the age of twenty-three, left to accompany the zoologist Louis Agassiz on a research expedition. This proved to be a disappointing experience because the members of the expedition sought only factual information, whereas James preferred the search for underlying causes of phenomena. Following the close of the expedition he resided in Germany for a year and a half, where poor health prevented him from doing more than intermittent independent study.

During this period, James became deeply depressed and contemplated suicide. The experience proved to be a turning point in his life and led to his deep interest in philosophy. However, upon returning to the United States, he reentered Harvard to complete his medical training, and to hold positions as an instructor in anatomy and physiology. In later years he turned to psychology and philosophy and held professorships in both subjects.

In 1878 James began his *Principles of Psychology*, which did not appear until 1890. While working on the book he made numerous trips to Europe, so that what he originally planned to complete in two years actually took twelve. It is one of the truly great classics in the field.

As a philosopher James is associated with pragmatism, a system of philosophy which he developed after reading an essay of Charles Peirce in *Popular Science Monthly* on "How to Make Our Ideas Clear." James's pragmatism, with its central theme that the value of ideas must be tested by their consequences in action, profoundly influenced John Dewey. James died in New Hampshire on August 26, 1910.

Carl Jung

Carl Jung was born in Kesswil, Switzerland, on July 26, 1875, the son of a liberal Protestant clergyman. His early education was in Basel, and his advanced study at the University of Basel, which he entered in 1895. He obtained his M.D. degree in 1900 and two years later worked with Janet in Paris. Later he collaborated with Bleuler. From these experiences Jung developed his famous Word Association Test.

Jung met Freud in 1906 and became a member of Freud's inner circle. The association developed into a strong friendship and resulted in a fruitful exchange of ideas between the two men. However, in 1913 Jung resigned from the International Psychoanalytic Society, broke away from Freud, and founded his own school known as Analytical Psychology.

His research into the nature and phenomena of the racial unconscious led him to study the mental processes of primitive people. In pursuit of his objective he traveled in North Africa in 1921 carrying out field studies of the natives. Later he made similar studies of the Pueblo Indians in Arizona and New Mexico, and in 1926 revisited Africa to observe the behavior of the natives in Kenya.

His deep concern with man's unconscious, his religious nature, and his emphasis on archetypal modes of thought lend a flavor of mysticism to Jung's writings that has made him less appreciated in America than in Europe. His profound understanding of human nature and his vast knowledge of mythology, anthropology, and literature have led many to regard him as one of the world's great scholars. Jung died on June 6, 1961, at the age of eighty-five.

Kurt Koffka

Kurt Koffka was born on March 18, 1886, in Berlin. He came from a long line of lawyers but did not choose to pursue the family profession. Koffka's early education took place in Berlin from 1892 to 1903. It was during this period that a maternal uncle aroused his deep interest in the fields of science and philosophy. While he was at Edinburgh in 1903 to 1904, his interests were further developed under the influence of British scientists and scholars. After returning to Berlin he decided to pursue a career in psychology. He took his Ph.D. degree with Stumpf, writing a thesis on rhythm.

There followed a series of postgraduate positions as an assistant to Von Kries, Külpe, Marbe, and finally to Schumann at Frankfurt, where he met Köhler and Wertheimer and became a member of the triumvirate that founded Gestalt psychology. In 1911 he was appointed *Privatdozent* at the University of Giessen, where he remained until 1924. During World War I he worked with patients suffering from brain injuries and aphasias in the Psychiatric Clinic in Giessen. In 1924 he came to the United States to accept a visiting professorship at Cornell and later at Wisconsin.

In 1927 he was appointed William Allen Neilson Research Professor at Smith College, where no demand was put upon him to publish or teach. Instead his time was devoted solely to experimental work in the field of visual perception.

In 1932 Koffka joined an expedition originating in Russia to study the people of Central Asia. The results of the studies were never published. On the expedition he contracted a relapsing fever, and, while recuperating, he began his *Principles of Psychology*, an erudite and difficult book originally intended for the layman. After its publication he worked primarily in the field of experimental psychology but continued to maintain interest in art, music, literature, and general social and ethical questions.

Koffka never sought personal recognition and always felt indebted to his Gestalt colleagues for his successful career in psychology. He died on November 22, 1941, in Northampton, Massachusetts.

Wolfgang Köhler

Wolfgang Köhler was born on January 21, 1887, in Revel, Esthonia, then part of Russia. The family moved to north Germany when Köhler was five years of age, and his early education took place in a humanistic *Gymnasium*. His university studies were pursued at Tübingen, Bonn, and finally at Berlin, where he obtained his Ph.D. degree in 1909. In 1910 he went to Frankfurt as an assistant in psychology, and in 1911 he became a *Privatdozent*. It was in Frankfurt that Köhler and Wertheimer met and began their early experiments in Gestalt psychology.

In 1913 Köhler received an invitation from the Prussian Academy of Science to study chimpanzees on the Spanish island of Tenerife. After he had spent six months on the island, World War I broke out and Köhler attempted to leave, but fortunately for psychology he was denied permission to do so. Had he succeeded in reaching international waters, he probably would have been interned by the British. Köhler remained on Tenerife from Christmas, 1913, to June, 1920. He found his work on insight learning in chimpanzees not always sufficiently challenging and devoted a considerable amount of his time to the study of mathematics.

In 1920, Köhler returned to Germany. He was invited to succeed Müller at Göttingen, but instead accepted an appointment as director of the laboratory at Berlin to succeed Stumpf. He remained there from 1923 to 1935. During the years 1934 to 1935, he delivered the William James lectures at Harvard and decided to come to America permanently, since he was in continual conflict with the Nazis. He was made research professor of philosophy and psychology at Swarthmore College, an appointment he held until his retirement. Then he held a position as research professor at Dartmouth College until his death. He died on June 11, 1967, at his home in Enfield, New Hampshire.

Edward Bradford Titchener

Edward Bradford Titchener was born on January 11, 1867, at Chichester, England, of a family that had shown unusual ability for several centuries. His early schooling was in his native town. After obtaining his degree at Oxford in 1890 he went to Leipzig to study under Wundt. There in 1892 he was awarded the Ph.D. degree.

That same year Titchener began his long and productive career at Cornell as an assistant professor. Within three years he was made Sage Professor of Psychology. Meanwhile he translated important texts in psychology from German into English and wrote the original books on structuralism which bear his name. His most important work was his *Experimental Psychology*, which appeared in two volumes during the years 1901 to 1905. He presented the work to Oxford University for the degree of D.Sc., which was granted in 1906.

Although Titchener was British by birth and spent most of his professional life in America, he remained German in outlook throughout his career. He followed the European custom of lecturing in his academic robes and required members of his department to attend his lectures in general psychology, where they could become acquainted with his latest dogmatic pronouncements on structuralism. When it became apparent that introspectionism had lost the day, Titchener refused to change with the times and became increasingly less interested in psychology. During the last ten years of his life he developed a deep interest in coin collecting. He died of a brain tumor on August 3, 1927.

John B. Watson

John B. Watson was born in Greenville, South Carolina, on January 9, 1878. As a boy he attended a one-room schoolhouse where his teachers remembered him as "an indolent, argumentative boy, impatient of discipline and content if he barely passed his studies." He entered Furman University as a subfreshman, at the age of sixteen, to remain for five years, taking an M.A. instead of a B.A. The reason for his protracted stay was the infraction of a rule made by a teacher, Professor Moore, to the effect that any student who handed in a paper backwards would be failed. (Apparently Watson and his peers had discovered an unusual way to annoy their professors.) Watson turned in such a paper in civics, and Professor Moore kept his word by failing him in his senior year, even though he was an honor student.

Watson's graduate work was done at the University of Chicago, where he obtained a Ph.D. degree in 1903. He remained there as an instructor until 1908, during which time he helped found the animal laboratory. At Chicago he was associated with Angell, Donaldson, and Dewey. Watson, no lover of philosophy, remarked that he never understood Dewey, in spite of the fact that he was well grounded in philosophy as an undergraduate. He enjoyed his associations at Chicago and was reluctant to leave for Johns Hopkins, but the financial offer of $3500 a year, a large salary in those days, proved too attractive to reject.

It was during his stay at Johns Hopkins that he developed the central concepts of behaviorism. His success as a teacher and writer promised a long and brilliant career. However, because of the publicity associated with his divorce in 1920, Watson was forced to resign. With the help of friends he entered the advertising business, in which he was employed until 1946.

His final book, *Behaviorism*, a semipopular exposition, appeared in 1925 after he had left the field of academic psychology. It generated more criticism than any other book of that day. Strangely enough, Watson never replied to any of the criticism. Though he left academic circles after a professional career of less than two decades, his influence on contemporary psychology had been profound. He died after a long illness, in New York City, on September 25, 1958.

Ernst Weber

Ernst Weber was born in Wittenberg, Germany, on January 24, 1795, the son of Michael Weber, a professor of theology. After completing his early studies in Wittenberg, Weber was awarded the doctorate in 1815, at Leipzig, where he became a *Privat-*

dozent two years later. In 1818 he was appointed assistant professor of anatomy and physiology, and in 1821 was granted his full professorship. He served in this double capacity at Leipzig until 1866, when he gave up his duties as a physiologist. In 1871 he relinquished his chair of anatomy and retired from academic work.

Weber's outstanding contributions were in physiology. There was scarcely any specialty in the field to which he failed to contribute. His publications include research on the physiology of the circulatory system, the ear, the eye, the liver, and notably the skin. His collected papers on these topics were published in three monographs in 1851. Earlier, in 1834, Weber had published a Latin monograph, *De Tactu* (on touch), and in 1846, an article for Wagner's *Handbook of Physiology* in which he further elaborated his findings on the skin senses. Both are considered classics in the field of sensation. In *De Tactu*, Weber announced his discovery of what came to be known as "Weber's Law," namely that the just noticeable difference between two weights is a certain constant proportion of the total magnitude.

Aside from his primary interest in physiology, Weber contributed several articles on the improvement of medical education. In these he emphasized the view that future progress in medicine depends upon the adoption of exact, scientific methods. Weber's sympathies for more precise anatomical knowledge took the concrete form of addressing a petition to the Saxony parliament requesting a change in the laws to permit surrender of the bodies of suicides to anatomists. In his later years Weber urged the application of scientific findings to the arts and trades and became a cofounder of the German Polytechnic Society. He died January 26, 1878, in Leipzig.

Max Wertheimer

Max Wertheimer was born on April 15, 1880, in Prague, Czechoslovakia. His father was the director of a commercial school. The boy's early education was in Prague, where at the age of eighteen he completed the *Gymnasium*. For two and one-half years he studied law but finally gave it up in favor of philosophy. He did postgraduate work at Prague, Berlin, and eventually at Würzburg, where he obtained his Ph.D. degree under Külpe.

He held an appointment as *Privatdozent* at Frankfurt and Berlin, an assistant professorship in Berlin in 1922, and finally a professorship at Frankfurt, occupying Schumann's chair. Because of political unrest in Germany during the 1930's, he was among the first group of refugee scholars to arrive in New York, where in 1934 he became affiliated with the New School for Social Research.

In 1910, while on a vacation trip from Vienna to the Rhineland, it occurred to Wertheimer that apparent movement offered difficulties to the structuralistic point of view. He left the train at the next stop, which happened to be Frankfurt, went in search of a toy stroboscope, and in his hotel room tested the hypothesis that apparent movement could not be explained in terms of its elements. In Frankfurt also he met Köhler, his first experimental subject, and in the following year Koffka, who served as his second subject in perceptual investigations. These three, in their development and extension of Wertheimer's ideas, founded Gestalt psychology.

Wertheimer was a restless man whose real satisfaction came from striving toward, yet never quite reaching, a goal. He was also at heart a romantic, a poet, and a musician. His restless searching, coupled with his broad knowledge and interests, led him to direct psychology away from the current vogue of elementalism and toward the study of the phenomenal wholes. He died on October 12, 1943.

Wilhelm Wundt

Wilhelm Wundt was born on August 16, 1832, at Neckarau in Baden, the son of a Lutheran pastor. He spent two years in a local *Volkschule,* following which he was tutored by a vicar, his father's assistant. Although he had brothers and sisters, Wundt led the life of a solitary and imaginative boy, unquestioningly performing the tasks assigned to him by his tutor. As a young man he attended the University of Tübingen for one year and then entered Heidelberg. Although he took a degree in medicine, he turned to physiology in his early postgraduate research. During his seventeen years at Heidelberg he changed his professional affiliation from that of a physiologist to a psychologist.

In 1874, Wundt accepted an appointment at Zurich, and the following year he went to Leipzig, where he was to remain for the next forty-six years. At Leipzig he founded the first laboratory of psychology, wrote and experimented extensively, and developed his systematic psychology. Although he injured his eyesight in the course of his introspective research, he was able to continue his work with the help of his daughter.

Wundt's knowledge was encyclopedic. He wrote not only on psychology, but also in the fields of logic, ethics, and scientific metaphysics. In his publications he was a repeater, not in the sense of quoting himself but rather in restating the same ideas in different connections. He also put great emphasis on the definitions of concepts, collecting those of other authorities and then proceeding to point out how they differed from his own views. It is an astounding fact that during his professional career he published about 54,000 pages of psychological material. He died in his eighty-eighth year on August 31, 1920.

3

Sensation
in Systematic
Psychology

The evolution of method and theory in sensory psychology extends over the entire period of recorded history. In Chapters 1 and 2 we found that the empiricists from Aristotle to Mill sought the key that would explain the complexities of mind in the analysis of the sensory processes. The basic premise of this school of philosophy assumed that mind was compounded of simple ideas originally derived from sense experience. For this reason, sensory psychology found favor among the empiricists and their descendants, the objective psychologists of the early scientific period. But we also noted that the empirical tradition allied itself with associationism, for to argue that mind was no more than an unrelated conglomeration of simple ideas was logically indefensible as well as a violation of common sense. Therefore the principles of association were invoked by the empiricists in order to account for the complexities of mind. Consequently, in relating sensation to the empirical-associationistic tradition, we may consider all three to be inexorably interwoven, each lending meaning and support to the others. Considered from this point of view empiricism demands sensationism, and both logically lead to associationism. This tripartite alliance is the philosophical antecedent of modern sensory psychology, an area which for many years was the dominant theoretical and research area within the field.

However, in contemporary research and theorizing the study of sensation no longer dominates the field as it did throughout the prescientific period and during the heyday of structuralism. There are two principal reasons why the study of sensation has been relegated to a secondary position. First, contemporary psychologists draw a sharp distinction between sensation and perception. Historically, however, these two mental processes were not always treated separately, and much that went under the name of sensory psychology was, in fact, perceptual psychology. During the past several decades sensation has become a highly circumscribed field primarily concerned with the neurology and electrophysiology of the sense organs. It might be noted parenthetically that while the field of sensation has become more restricted in recent years, it has enjoyed at the same time a rebirth of interest on the part of physiological psychologists. This revival of interest is a result of the tremendous advances in the design of electronic equipment that have taken place over the past several decades. The availability of highly sensitive amplifiers and recording devices has made possible direct electrophysiological studies of the sense organs and their centers in the brain (*10*). On the whole, however, sensory psychology has gradually lost out to perceptual psychology as the lines of theory and research have diverged more and more sharply during the modern period. Perception, for the time being at least, has won the day in terms of research interest and the quantity of experimental literature published in the field.

The second reason for the decline of sensory psychology was the fall of structuralism as the dominant system of American psychology. The structuralists, following the old empirical tradition of mental analysis, conducted a vast research program on the sensory processes utilizing the introspective method. The newer schools, on the other hand, looked with disfavor on the analysis of consciousness, particularly atomistic analysis. As a consequence, sensory psychology, traditionally reductionistic and molecular in its aims and methods, suffered a decline along with the collapse of structuralism.

SENSATION AND THE SCHOOLS OF PSYCHOLOGY

We shall begin our study of systematic sensory psychology by examining its position in the literature of the schools which flourished during the first third of the present century. The student may review for himself the place of sensation in British empirical philosophy and the development of the quantitative methods for the measurement of sensory processes in Chapter 2. Meanwhile, we shall begin with Titchener's treatment of sensation in his system of structural psychology.

Structuralism and sensation.[1]   It will be recalled that Titchener's psychology took for its aim the analysis of consciousness into elements by the method of introspection. (See Chapter 2.) We also pointed out that sensations were one of Titchener's three elements of mind, the other two being images and affective states. With this as a starting point let us consider his position on sensation in detail.

[1] Our exposition is based on Titchener's *Textbook of Psychology* (*23*).

Titchener defines sensation as "an elementary mental process which is constituted of at least four attributes—*quality, intensity, clearness,* and *duration*" (*23*, p. 52). Let us analyze both parts of this definition in turn. First, what does Titchener mean by an elementary process? As he uses the concept, it means *irreducible* or incapable of analysis into anything simpler. His criterion for determining whether a conscious process is elemental is to subject the process to "rigorous and persistent" introspection. If, under these conditions, it remains unchanged—if it refuses, so to speak, to break down into something simpler—it is a true element. In essence, both Titchener's definition of elements and his test for their genuineness are analogous to chemists' criteria for establishing chemical elements. To cite a specific example, if the conscious experience aroused by a rose proves to be a compound of the elementary sensation of smell and a reaction of pleasantness, then the experience is not elementary but a complex of two more elementary processes. Similarly, if the chemist can reduce common salt to something simpler—in this case sodium and chlorine—then salt is not an element but a compound.

However, while elements are the primary, irreducible stuff of consciousness, they can nevertheless be classified or put into groups, just as the chemical elements can be organized into classes such as metals, heavy earths, rare gases, and halogens. In other words, in spite of their simplicity, elements possess *attributes* which enable us to make distinctions among them, and this brings us to a consideration of the second part of Titchener's definition of sensation.

Titchener puts *quality* at the head of his list of sensory attributes. Quality is the most important attribute which permits us to distinguish one elementary process from another. Thus, we discriminate salt from cold, yellow from blue, or middle C from green, on the basis of quality differences. In simpler terms, quality is the attribute from which every sensation takes its particular name; and for this reason it is the most fundamental attribute of all sensations.

The second attribute, *intensity,* is familiar from everyday experience. This is the attribute responsible for the distinctions and comparisons of strength or degree which we make among sensations of both the same and different qualities. To exemplify, when we have several shades of blue paper the attribute of quality is the same, namely, the quality of blueness. But the papers also differ in brightness or brilliance of color; hence we can distinguish between them on the basis of intensity differences. Similarly, we are able to make cross-comparisons between, say, a "bright red" and a "dark blue." In this instance we are either ignoring quality or holding it constant while concentrating on intensity. More generally, when we use terms like "brighter," "duller," "louder," "softer," "stronger," "weaker," and the like, we are referring to the experienced attribute of intensity.

Turning to *clearness,* Titchener held that this attribute characterizes a sensation in terms of its place in consciousness. The clear sensation is dominant and in the foreground of consciousness; the less clear sensation is subordinate and in the background. To cite a simple example, if in the course of a laboratory investigation we are studying tones introspectively, our consciousness of those tones will be clear. However, the same tones coming over the radio while we are at home and absorbed in a book might go entirely unheard, or, if noticed at all, form part of the obscure background noise found in the best of homes. We shall have to return to the attribute of clearness for it proved to be involved with the problem of attention to be considered later in this chapter. But meanwhile we shall go on to Titchener's fourth attribute, *duration*.

Duration describes the temporal course of a sensation. In Titchener's words, it marks the sensation's "rise, poise, and fall as a process in consciousness" (*23*, p. 53). Duration also makes the temporal course of one sensation characteristically different from the temporal course of another. Thus, a sustained tone or noise is characteristically different from a short click of the same pitch and intensity.

The attributes of quality, intensity, duration, and clearness are basic characteristics of *all* sensations. They are the essential four, always present to some degree in every sensory experience. However, Titchener points out that some sensations may also possess the attribute of *extensity*. The sensation aroused by a long strip of blue paper, for example, can be characterized by extensity in addition to the four fundamental attributes. Tones, on the other hand, do not possess extensity, but they, too, may have a special attribute, in this case, *volume*.[2] Volume is best exemplified by comparing the sound of an explosion to the tone of a piccolo. The explosion appears to fill all space, while the piccolo produces a highly circumscribed sound. Moreover, there is always the possibility that two or more attributes may join or concur in consciousness to produce what Titchener defines as a "second order" attribute. Here we shall once again quote Titchener in a highly characteristic paragraph which gives both the flavor of his trenchant style and at the same time conveys a picture of consciousness from the structural point of view in the words of the greatest introspectionist of them all. In the passage quoted, Titchener is describing "insistence," a second-order attribute resulting from a blend of either intensity or clearness and one of the other attributes.

> They are self-assertive and aggressive; they monopolise consciousness, as a forward and pushing guest will monopolise conversation at a social gathering. We speak of the penetratingness of odours like camphor and naphthaline; of the urgency or importunity of certain pains or of the taste of bitter; of the obtrusiveness or glaringness of certain lights and colours and tones (*23*, p. 55).

[2] Volume, as it turned out, proved to be a troublesome attribute to isolate. For a detailed history of the problem the reader is referred to Boring (*3*), who also presents an extensive treatment of the methodology involved in separating and isolating attributes.

Having defined sensations and their fundamental attributes, Titchener devotes nine chapters to the psychology of sensation. For each of the major senses he first enumerates and describes the attributes already established by introspective studies. Then he goes on to discuss various experimental problems and unresolved theoretical issues which remain to be investigated and decided upon by the structuralists' future program of research. Much of this material makes familiar reading for anyone with a background in general psychology. There are discussions of the laws of color mixture, rod-and-cone vision, sound waves, and tonal qualities. Also included are descriptions of the chemical senses of taste and smell and the important phenomena associated with them. A surprisingly complete treatment of cutaneous, kinesthetic, and vestibular sensitivities is included in the chapters concerned with these modalities. Finally, Titchener discusses the quantitative methods for the measurement of sensory processes, and in the same section goes into the derivation of the Weber-Fechner Law from Weber's equation. In fact, Titchener proves himself something of a prophet with honor, for he states that the textbooks of the future will bristle with mathematical formulas as psychology becomes increasingly quantitative in its methods.

However, no mere enumeration of topics is adequate to convey a picture of Titchener's dedication to his system and the vigor with which he tackled unresolved problems. Many of the gaps in the structuralists' system found a place in his *Textbook* in the chapters on sensation. These areas of ignorance are frequently discussed in special sections set apart in fine print. Here Titchener confesses his lack of knowledge or presents the various differences of opinions on some controversial point, and in a spirit of fairness cites whatever evidence is available whether or not it is in agreement with his point of view. However, the underlying implication is always that unresolved problems are not impasses for the structuralists' program but temporary difficulties which will ultimately yield to more carefully designed experimental studies. Irrespective of the status of a problem, the treatment is essentially the same. The problem or phenomenon is described, its known characteristics are enumerated, and the results of relevant studies are analyzed. Finally, wherever possible a physiological "explanation" is given in keeping with Titchener's promise to answer the question "why" by reference to the underlying neural processes involved.

Before concluding this summary of Titchener's treatment of sensation, a brief discussion of his position on the process of attention will be presented. While attention is typically not included under sensation in contemporary texts, Titchener, as implied earlier in the chapter, held that attention is closely related to the sensory attribute of *clearness*. For this reason we have chosen to include his treatment of attention in this chapter.

Titchener introduces the topic of attention by summarizing the confusion that has traditionally surrounded the concept. He points out that attention has been considered a "power," a "faculty," a "feeling," or even a "functional" activity by various authorities. To add to this chaotic state of affairs, common sense "explains" attention as an act of will or in terms of some inner force or agency which we employ when "we want to pay attention." In dealing with the multitude of definitions, Titchener argues that this difficulty will be resolved by experimental introspection, while the question of "will" or inner determination he dismisses as unworthy of a scientific psychology. By denying the possibility of inner controls, Titchener clearly takes a deterministic point of view. This is also revealed in his principle that the *description* of attention as a form of consciousness must be made in terms of the elementary mental processes themselves—sensations, images, and affective states—and the *explanation* of attention is to be discovered in parallel nervous processes, *not* in will power.

Taking up the challenge of the complex problems of attention, Titchener reports that introspective studies distinguish between passive or involuntary attention and active or voluntary attention. The former type is most readily experienced as a result of stimuli "that take consciousness by storm" (*23*, p. 268). All intense stimuli, such as pistol shots, bright lights, or sudden pain, give rise to passive or involuntary attentiveness. In addition, that which is novel or anything which fits into habits of attention gives rise to involuntary attentive states. In this way he accounts for both the compelling effect of the strange or unusual and for the common observation that our individual habits predispose us to attend to certain aspects of our environment. Titchener summarizes all such instances under the category of "primitive attention."

Active or voluntary attention is characteristically experienced whenever we have to "force" ourselves to attend, as frequently occurs when we are tired, distracted, or engaged in some uninteresting task. At first glance it may appear that Titchener is falling into the commonsense approach of describing secondary attention as a "power" or as dependent upon an act of will. But in employing terms such as "active" or "force" he is deliberately reverting to everyday language in order to state the problem clearly for his readers. He hastens to explain that in such secondary attentive states the experience of strain or the necessity of forcing concentration is due to a "conflict of primary attentions" (*23*, p. 272). Again we have a deterministic psychology, for, it will be recalled, primary or involuntary attention is aroused by strong, compelling stimuli or ideational impressions, and not by acts of will. Therefore, what seems to be an active striving within is, in reality, the feeling or affective state associated with the conflict in our consciousness and its underlying parallel processes in the cerebral cortex. When the conflict has been resolved and the "strain" disappears this does not imply that "we" have resolved the conflict, but that one of the excitatory processes has, to quote Titchener, "won the day" (*23*, p. 273).

Fundamentally the essence of Titchener's position as we have summarized it is this: Attention *is* clearness and therefore is nothing more or less than a state of consciousness wherein some sensory experience or mental image is in the foreground, while all other processes are for the moment in the background. No new elements are involved, but instead what appears at first glance to present a complex and difficult problem for introspection is analyzable into the familiar elementary processes of clear sensations or images!

Finally, Titchener undertakes an explanation of attention in terms of the nervous system. Here again we shall quote a particularly characteristic passage from the *Textbook*.

> Now take a case that lies nearer home. Suppose that you are in your room, preparing for to-morrow's examination, and that you hear an alarm of fire in a neighbouring street. Both ideas, the idea of examination and the idea of fire, are imperative; there is a conflict. The cortex is set in one part for work: and this setting is reinforced by a large number of associated excitations,—the nervous processes corresponding to ideas of the examination mark, the consequences of failure, and so on. The cortex is set in another part for going to the fire: and this setting is similarly reinforced, by the processes corresponding to the ideas of a run in the fresh air, an exciting scene, a possible rescue, and so on. The struggle may last some little time, and its effects may persist for a while after you have made your choice. So long as there is any trace of it, your attention is secondary or "active" attention (*23*, pp. 272–273).

We can only add that this is *descriptive* psychology at its best. Still, Titchener's parallelistic "explanation" in terms of cortical "sets" raises more questions for the modern reader than it resolves. Titchener, in a manner of speaking, is hiding behind the nervous system.

By way of summary, sensations for the structuralist are elements which possess the attributes of quality, intensity, clearness, and duration. The important classes of sensations are visual, auditory, olfactory, gustatory, cutaneous, and kinesthetic. In the structuralists' program each modality is analyzed introspectively to reveal its unique attributes, if any, and to describe and explain its important phenomena. Finally, the complex mental process of attention is reducible to the attribute of clearness. And by way of a parting comment, we might add that introspective psychology was most successful in the area of sensory psychology.

Functionalism and sensation.   In our discussion of the aims and methodology of functionalism in Chapter 2, it was pointed out that this system is characteristically an *is for* psychology in contrast to the *is* psychology of the structuralists. Moreover, functionalism represents a transition from the philosophical tradition of Wundt and Titchener to the biosocial orientation of an adjustmental psychology. Clearly, by embracing an adaptive or utilitarian frame of reference, the functionalist cannot afford to ignore the sensory processes completely. If mind functions to adapt the organism to its environment, then the senses are important adjuncts to mind, for they make possible awareness of the environment, and without awareness there can be no behavior, adaptive or otherwise. However, this is the extent of the functionalists' interest in sensation. It is to be investigated from the point of view of the first stage in an act of interaction with the environment. The second stage is perception or the actual knowing of the environment; and unlike structuralistic psychology, where the emphasis is on sensory processes, functional psychology stresses the perceptual processes, since it is through perception that the individual comes to adapt to his environment.

A second reason for the functionalists' lack of interest in sensation is their concern with *mental activities* as opposed to conscious content. For the functionalist sensation smacks of statics, while perception is dynamic. Moreover, the functionalists' interest in learning and their description of learning as a "perceptual-motor" process again emphasize their concern with the behaving organism, rather than with the organism's states of consciousness. With these general principles in mind, let us turn to Carr, who is our spokesman for the functionalistic point of view.[3]

In passing from Titchener to Carr one is immediately struck by the brevity with which the latter treats the sensory processes. Carr devotes but a single, brief chapter to "Sensory and Motor Equipment," whereas, it will be recalled, Titchener required ten chapters for his exposition of the same topic. Moreover, the flavor of Carr's approach is quite different. The emphasis is primarily on the basic anatomical details of the sense organs and only secondarily on the experiences to which they give rise, though the latter aspect of the sensory processes is not entirely neglected. Titchener, on the other hand, puts experience first, while physiology and structure are relegated to the background.

However, the most characteristically functional aspect of Carr's exposition is his concern with the utilitarian value of the sensory processes. In an introduction to the chapter on sensation, he points out the close relationship between the organism's flexibility in adapting to its environment and the degree of differentiation and specialization of its sense organs. The more highly adaptable the species, the more differentiated that species' sense organs. Primitive organisms possess only undifferentiated sensitive spots which respond equally well to all kinds of stimuli and affect the organism in much the same manner. In the higher organisms, behavior is varied according to the kind of stimulation. There is increased capacity to react to stimuli in a discriminating and differential manner. Following this general statement, he briefly outlines the structure of the various sense organs and

---

[3] The exposition follows Carr's *Psychology: A Study of Mental Activity* (6).

the characteristic experiences to which they give rise. Then, near the end of the chapter, he returns once more to the theme of the adaptive value of well-developed sensory capacities for animals and men with particular emphasis on the attentive processes as preparatory stages in the adjustment of the organism to its environment.

Specifically, Carr treats the adaptive value of the sensory processes for living forms under the broad heading of *spatial ability,* under which he includes discriminative ability. In developing his theme, Carr first notes that, as we move up the phylogenetic scale, animals show an increasingly well-developed ability to localize objects in space. At the same time, capacity for form and size discrimination increases with the organism's phylogenetic level. And, finally, under spatial discrimination, he points to the fact that as we move from primitive to advanced forms we find increasing emphasis on distance receptors, such as the eye and ear, and decreasing emphasis on contact receptors, such as are found in the cutaneous senses. The animal with distance receptors is able to deal with space far more effectively by anticipating threats or sensing food supplies at long range than an organism with poorly developed distance receptors.

The relevance of these evolutionary modifications of spatial capacities for better adaptive reactions is undeniable. Because successful adaptation involves dealing with objects in space, the better the organism's equipment the more successful it will be in adjustments involving both locomotor and manipulative acts. Indeed, in adapting to nature in the raw one misperception might well prove fatal. For similar reasons, the finer the animal's discriminative ability, the more successful it is likely to be in selecting a balanced diet, sensing potential enemies, and identifying objects in general.

After summarizing his position on sensation in terms of these principles of adaptation, Carr turns from sensation to those psychological processes of greater interest to the functionalistic program. Clearly, as has been pointed out previously, the brevity of the treatment of sensation reflects the school's greater concern with the other mental activities, notably perception and learning. Nevertheless, despite its brief treatment of sensation, the strong evolutionary point of view characteristic of this school is clearly developed. It is, in short, a Darwinian psychology whose orientation is the activity of the *whole organism* in its give-and-take relations with the environment. With this précis of Carr's position we shall leave this school for the time being and turn to the behavioristic view of sensation.

Behaviorism and sensation.[4]   It may seem strange at first reading to discover that Watson devoted considerable space to the sensory processes in

<hr>

[4] Our account is drawn from Watson's *Behavior: An Introduction to Comparative Psychology* (25) and *Psychology from the Standpoint of a Behaviorist* (26).

his first exposition of behaviorism. Six chapters of his comparative text deal with problems of definition and methodology in the area of sensation, and in addition he includes a summary of experimental results. In his later book, *Psychology from the Standpoint of a Behaviorist,* only one chapter is given to sensory psychology; it is, however, a substantial one several times longer than the equivalent chapter in Carr's text. On the surface, this much emphasis on the sensory processes seems more appropriate in a structuralist's text. If, as was brought out in discussing methods and aims of behaviorism, Watson was primarily interested in *behavior* as revealed by experimental observation, how, we may ask, can such aims and methods be reconciled with a heavy emphasis on sensory psychology?

The answer lies in two factors. First, it must be remembered that in his early work Watson was attempting to beard Titchener in the latter's own den. If he could demonstrate that sensory processes, which at first glance are open only to introspective methods, are in reality amenable to investigation by behavioristic techniques, he would have weakened the structuralists' position and in doing so strengthened his own. Second, the objective methods of the natural sciences which Watson favored were (and to a considerable degree still are) most useful in reductional analysis. Because sensation lends itself to this kind of treatment more readily than intelligence, personality, thinking, and such "higher" mental processes, it is natural that Watson found the study of sensation congenial to his overall aims and methods.

However, because of his affinity with animal research, Watson had to face certain methodological problems at the outset in his comparative text. How is it possible to investigate an animal's sensory capacities? There is no way for the psychologist to question animals about what they see, hear, taste, or smell, and even if such were possible, this would be going over to the structuralists' camp by admitting that introspection is a legitimate technique of investigation. The answer, Watson believes, is to be found in studying the animal's *motor* responses. For example, if the psychologist is interested in determining whether a certain species of animal can discriminate red from blue, he must arrange experimental conditions in such a way that the animal can *respond differentially* to the two colors. The animal must be motivated to learn the discrimination either by rewards for correct responses or punishment for incorrect responses, or possibly by a combination of both.

In his earlier book (the comparative text), Watson is able to marshal an impressive collection of plans and descriptions for apparatus that both he and other psychologists had already employed in testing animals' reactions in sensory discrimination problems. Moreover, he devotes the last four chapters of the book to a summary of experimental results from comparative laboratories. In the section on apparatus, Pavlov's conditioning technique is given prominence as a research method of great potential importance for psychology. His forecast that conditioning would have great potential for psychology proved correct, since the method assumed a central position in the behaviorists' research programs and theoretical systems. Watson also describes discrimination boxes already in use by pioneers in animal work, such as Yerkes and Yoakum. Such techniques, he points out, proved successful even before the advent of behaviorism in studying every one of the major senses in animals. Such problems as the animal's range of both quality and intensity discriminations proved amenable to testing by such methods for the visual, auditory, cutaneous, and kinesthetic modalities.

Watson, therefore, was able to demonstrate that insofar as the sensory processes were concerned, behaviorism was more than a mere theoretical program; it could already offer concrete results gathered by its methods, if not by its proponents. And these results were in the traditional bailiwick of the structuralists—the senses. Moreover, as we shall find in Chapter 6, Watson's methods also proved highly useful in the fields of learning and problem solving.

We may, therefore, credit Watson with broadening sensory psychology to include the study of animals and with contributing to the methodology of comparative psychology. However, Watson is not noted for any outstanding or specific discoveries in sensation. As a contributor to the experimental literature of psychology, his work on infantile emotions and the conditioning of fears (see Chapter 12) is much more widely known than his earlier work in comparative psychology. This, in part, reflects a shift in his research interests from the area of animal to child psychology, a change of interest that occurred in the mature phase of Watson's career. We may therefore leave Watson's treatment of the sensory processes with the conclusion that his chief contributions were in the direction of broadening the methodology and scope of sensory psychology to include work in the comparative area.

Gestalt psychology and psychoanalysis.   Gestalt psychologists and psychoanalysts have shown little concern with the sensory processes. Their lack of interest can best be understood in terms of their aims and methods. Because the study of holistic units of behavior through a molar approach is the chief concern of Gestalt psychology, molecular analyses at the level of sensation fall outside the scope of their program, while the study of perception offers a more rewarding field—indeed, becomes their major area of research. In the case of the psychoanalysts, essentially the same question of relevance applies. In short, sensory psychology proved irrelevant to their program. On the purely theoretical side, their main areas of interest lie in development, motivation, and personality—processes which have obvious significance for abnormal psychology and psychotherapy. Because neither of these schools contributed in a significant way to the psychology of the sensory processes, we shall pass them by for the time being, and turn instead to contemporary trends in sensation. However, because we are concerned with the evolution of concepts and methods in this volume, it seems wise to pause at this transition point and try to summarize in a general way the contribution of the traditional schools to the evolution of the sensory psychology.

Clearly, the outstanding contribution to sensory psychology was made by the structuralists, especially in terms of their *descriptive psychology* of the phenomena of sensation. Within this frame of reference Titchener and his associates mined the field of sensation thoroughly, and little or nothing was added by the subsequent schools to this aspect of the evolution of sensory psychology. In the realm of *methodology*, Watson's behavioristic approach offered the most significant contribution. This is not only true in terms of the healthy shift of emphasis he provided at a period when psychology had become overly mentalistic, but also because the heritage Watson and the comparative psychologists of his day left in the form of theoretical and methodological approaches has carried over into contemporary psychology. In contemporary work on sensation (as we shall see in the following section), the study of the lower forms through the use of empirical techniques dominates the field, for it is primarily on animals that the direct neurophysiological studies favored by contemporary psychologists are most feasible.

Carr and the functionalists, having fitted sensation into the strong adaptive orientation of their system, contributed nothing new or original to the field. And, as has just been pointed out, the virtual exclusion of sensory psychology from the Gestalt and psychoanalytic programs precluded significant contributions from either of these schools. To conclude, then, the descriptive psychology of consciousness had fully answered the What and How of the sensory processes. The behaviorists provided a methodology for investigating the mysteries of the neurological correlates of sensory experience.

CONTEMPORARY TRENDS IN SENSORY PSYCHOLOGY

We have already taken the position that contemporary interest in sensation is primarily along neurophysiological lines. This, in part, reflects the rapid advances in recent years in the development of high-fidelity electronic amplifiers, microstimulators, and recording devices. For decades the old method of extirpation, first developed over one hundred years ago, was the chief tool of the physiological psychologist. As applied to sensory problems, the method involves the establishment of a sensory discrimination habit in animal subjects following which destructions are made in cortical or subcortical centers—sometimes in one center, sometimes in another in different animals—until the center mediating the habit is found. This is evidenced by the animal's inability to perform the habit postoperatively once the critical center has been localized and destroyed. But the method suffers from difficulties, some of which are methodological, some theoretical. For example, if the animal fails to perform a discrimination following a brain lesion, the question arises as to whether he no longer has the sensory capacity or whether his memory for the habit has suffered. Again, in many cases the limits of a cortical area responsible for mediating a sensory or discriminative process cannot be established with accuracy.

While electronic techniques for investigating sensory processes are not a panacea for the ills or deficiencies of other methods, it is our contention that they have made available a more direct approach to the study of the neurological foundations of sensation. Not only are such methods more precise, but they also make possible the recording of electrical activities going on in the sense organs, nerves, and cortical centers while the animal is actually responding to stimulation. This in turn means that learned discriminations as an intermediate stage in sensory research can be dispensed with. Psychologists armed with these newer techniques have addressed themselves to the broad questions of how the sense organs work and how sensory impulses are communicated to the brain and there interpreted. More specifically, the old problems of quality and intensity as related to their underlying neurological mechanisms have been attacked with considerable success for audition and vision and to a lesser degree for the other senses.

Since this is not a handbook of experimental research, we shall confine ourselves to examples of recent research in vision and audition as illustrations of the methodological and theoretical problems involved. In so doing we shall be able to give a fair sample of the experimental findings obtained with such techniques in the two most important areas of sensory research. We shall, however, begin with a brief historical summary of the field of sensory neurology in order to set the stage for our dip into the contemporary literature.

The historical setting.   One of the oldest theoretical principles in physiological psychology is that which attributes *quality* to the sense organ stimulated and *intensity* to the number of sensory neurons aroused by the stimulus. For example, when the ear is stimulated appropriately, sounds of various qualities are experienced depending upon the stimulus-object from which the sound emanates. For the sake of simplicity let us assume that the stimulus-object is a tuning fork of 256 vibrations per second. The effect as experienced is a tonal quality of medium pitch. If another fork vibrating at 60 cycles is substituted, the resulting experience is a low-pitched tone. In either case the quality dimension is pitch, and our ability to sense pitch has traditionally been associated with the particular portion of the inner ear and auditory cortex aroused by the stimulus. In short, specific sense cells mediate specific qualities.

In the case of intensity, stronger stimuli (or in our example of the tuning forks the greater amplitude sound waves) arouse more sense cells or cortical cells to activity and thus give rise to more intense auditory experiences. These in turn are experienced as "louder" sounds.

The specific end-organ theory of sensory function was given great impetus by Johannes Müller's doctrine of the specific energies of nerves which, as we pointed out in Chapter 1, held to a strict specificity of qualitative experiences as dependent upon the sense organ stimulated. Later Max von Frey (1852 to 1932), a physiologist who had done considerable work on the skin senses, announced a specific end-organ theory of cutaneous sensitivity in a series of papers published between 1894 and 1896. Such was von Frey's prestige that the specific end-organ theory was not only greatly reinforced, but also a considerable amount of research was devoted to the investigation of the skin during the next generation in a search for the specialized sensory organs presumed to lie in the subcutaneous tissues.

With this summary of the traditional attitude toward the two most important dimensions of sensory experience—quality and intensity—to serve as a background, we may now turn to the development of systematic visual and auditory theories in contemporary psychology.

Contemporary trends in vision.   Visual theory and research divides itself along the lines of the *duplicity theory* formulated by Johannes von Kries (1853 to 1928). The theory assumes that there are two types of receptors in the retina, rods and cones, each with separate properties and functions. The rods are presumed to function in scotopic or twilight vision, or more generally at low levels of illumination. The cones function in photopic or daylight vision. Because the cones are more numerous in the fovea or central portion of the eye, this then is the center of clearest daylight vision. Outside of the fovea toward the periphery rods become increasingly numerous until they are the only receptors represented. Moreover, the cones are typically connected to the visual centers by single, point-to-point neuronal chains while many rods converge on a few ganglion cells. These neurological correlates suggest that the cones are more specialized for fine spatial discrimination and color vision while the rods are for intensity vision and vision under conditions of very weak stimulation.

The discovery that many nocturnal animals possess only rod retinas and that many diurnal animals possess only cones led to the widespread acceptance of the duplicity theory as essentially true. For the past century psychological research has divided itself according to this theory, with some psychologists concerning themselves with the nature of scotopic vision and others with the mechanisms of photopic vision. Those who are primarily interested in scotopic vision have shown little interest in attempting to formulate comprehensive systematic theories of vision. Rather, their research has been concerned with the establishment of laws governing the tripartite relationships among the stimulus, psychological, and neurological variables in brightness vision. Similarly, those who are primarily interested in photopic vision have been almost exclusively preoccupied with color vision.

While the duplicity theory represents a generally valid description of the dualistic nature of the visual processes, recent research has shown that there are exceptions to it, and we shall cite some of these in this chapter. However, accepting its broad outlines as essentially valid, we shall begin with a description of Selig Hecht's (1892 to 1947) photochemical theory (12, 13) as representative of systematic work in the area of scotopic vision, following which we shall consider recent theoretical and empirical work in color vision.

Hecht began his long and fruitful series of researches on vision in 1919. His overall aim was to formulate precise quantitative laws for the prediction of visual phenomena. More specifically, he attempted to account for all the important phenomena of brightness vision such as light adaptation, the threshold behavior of the retina in various organisms, and the influence of metabolic factors on adaptation and threshold phenomena.

Hecht takes as his starting point the principles of photochemistry exemplified by the behavior of photographic films or plates. With these for a foundation, he makes assumptions about the behavior of the retina and then attempts to verify his assumptions by collecting empirical data on human and animal subjects. Most of his hypotheses are cast into mathematical equations, and hypothetical curves are then drawn from the equations. In this way, Hecht can test the goodness of fit of his curves with empirical data from the laboratory.

Hecht first assumes that the photochemical process is reversible.[5] Some such assumption is, of course, demanded by the phenomena of light and dark adaptation. In these processes the eye, unlike a photographic film, can "recover" from exposure to light and so be ready to "take" another impression. On the other hand, once a photographic film has been exposed, its photosensitive substance is "used up" in a nonreversible reaction. Hecht identified the photosensitive substance in the eye as S, and postulated that it was decomposed into certain by-products by light. At least two such products, identified by Hecht as P and A, result from the response to light. Employing these symbols Hecht expressed the basic photochemical reaction of light-dark decomposition and resynthesis as follows:

$$S \underset{\text{dark}}{\overset{\text{light}}{\rightleftarrows}} P + A$$

---

[5] Technically a "pseudoreversible" chemical reaction. The entire presentation of Hecht's theory has been simplified.

In other words, the assumed photosensitive substance in the retina decomposes when the eye is exposed to light and resynthesizes when the eye passes from light into darkness. Carrying the argument a little further in order to take into account the *intensity* of the light and the *duration* of exposure—both important factors in threshold and summation phenomena —Hecht developed two additional equations.

First, he expressed the equation of the rate of the photochemical reaction in light adaptation as follows: $dx/dt = I(a-x)$, in which I is the intensity of light; a is the original concentration of the photochemical substance; x is the amount broken down; and t represents time. In mathematics the symbol d means "an increment of." Expressed in nontechnical language, the equation states that the rate of adaptation at any point in time is dependent upon two factors: (1) how much photochemical substance was present in the retina originally, and (2) the intensity of light to which the eye is exposed.

Second, the dark reaction is expressed as follows: $dx/dt = x^n$, where the rate of the regeneration process in the dark-adapting eye is a function of the amount of material x, raised to the power n, where n is the number of by-products resulting from light adaptation.

Another way of demonstrating the general nature of the relationships involved is to express them graphically. Figure 3-1 shows threshold values for the dark-adapting eye plotted against time. With increasing time in

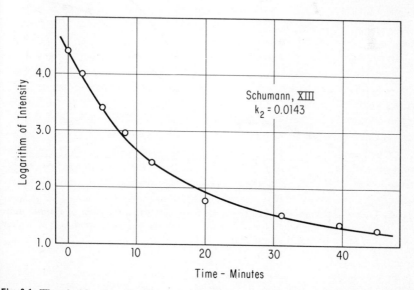

Fig. 3-1. Threshold values for the dark-adapting eye. Tests were confined to the rods. (From Hecht, *12*.)

darkness, the threshold for brightness vision falls rapidly at first. This is because of the availability of a large amount of the by-products of the light reaction. Then the threshold falls more slowly as increasingly less material is available for resynthesis. A careful study of Figure 3-1 reveals that within thirty minutes the eye can become 100,000 times more sensitive to light.

In light adaptation the reverse occurs, so that the eye becomes increasingly less sensitive to light with continued exposure. In other words, light adaptation is essentially a fatigue process, whereas dark adaptation is a recovery process. Hecht makes use of his basic equations in developing more complex equations with which he can predict the various thresholds, summative and discriminative retinal reactions. He then fits the hypothetical curves drawn from his equations to actual data collected from experimental studies on the eye of both human and animal subjects.

Flicker functions, Figure 3-2,[6] are of particular interest to psychologists because they permit a breakdown of visual functions into rod and cone responses. In pure rod eyes or pure cone eyes, flicker functions are continuous. But in mixed eyes, a rod component appears at the lower limb

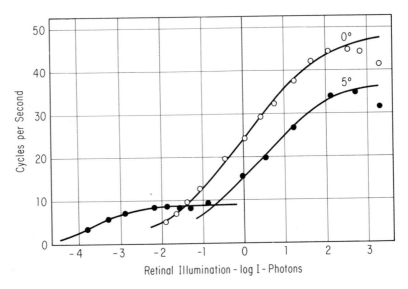

Fig. 3-2. Theoretical curves of flicker-fusion frequency as a function of illumination fitted to empirical data. The lower lefthand curve is for rods; the other curves are for cones in the fovea (0°) and 5° off center. (From Hecht, *12.*)

[6] Flicker functions refer to studies of the perception of stimuli which are alternating on and off or flickering. At low rates of alternation the stimulus is perceived as flickering. As rate of flicker is increased, a critical point is reached where the light appears to be continuous. This is called the critical flicker-fusion frequency.

of the sigmoid curve indicating that rods are functioning only at low levels of illumination as demanded by the duplicity theory. At higher levels of illumination their functioning is evidently inhibited by the cones or by chemical bleaching.

Measures of the relationship of visual acuity to the intensity of illumination, Figure 3-3, also show the duplex function clearly. As illumination

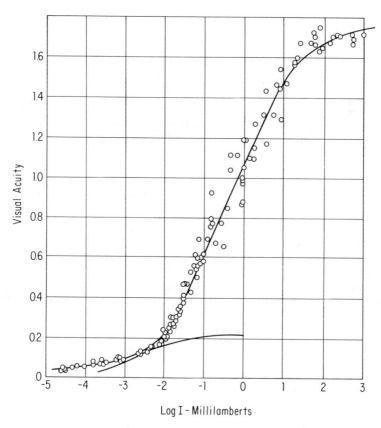

Log I - Millilamberts

Fig. 3-3. The relationship between visual acuity and illumination. The steep upper curve is for cones; the shallow curve at the bottom, for rods. (From Hecht, *12*

increases, the rod limb of the curve fails to increase, showing that there is little visual acuity contributed by the rods.

A study of Figures 3-1, 3-2, and 3-3 will demonstrate that Hecht's assumptions and rational equations are remarkably accurate predictions. However, it must be admitted that there are other instances in which his equations do not fit the data with the high degree of accuracy demanded by a "perfect" theory. Moreover, a note of warning must be interjected to the effect that when hypothetical equations are employed in this way some of the constants must be manipulated to fit the empirical data. Consequently, there is always a possibility that a different set of equations might fit equally well. What we are dealing with in the last analysis is a *model,* and all models have the defect of being representations rather than the real thing.

The merit of Hecht's theory for our purposes lies in the fact that it is our first example of a "miniature system," or elaborate theory, developed in a restricted area of psychology. Moreover, it is an excellent example of the combination of rational and empirical methods, or, in the more popular current phrase, the *hypothetico-deductive method,* in which a complex theory can be systematically evaluated by developing hypotheses from it which are then subjected to experimental verification. We shall meet with additional examples of this method in subsequent chapters.

To return to the more general problem of the contemporary treatment of brightness vision, Hecht's and other theories have served to stimulate investigations of light and dark adaptation, spatial and temporal summation, metabolic influences on visual phenomena, and electrical correlates of various scotopic processes. It is no longer demanded of a visual theory that it "explain" everything or fall by the wayside. Instead, any theory is considered useful so long as it leads to fruitful investigations of even limited aspects of visual phenomena. Psychologists who have devoted years of research effort to the task of uncovering the complex psychophysical and neurological relationships in brightness vision can point with pride to the impressive fund of information now available as the result of research designs based on limited or miniature theories. (See *10, 19, 21.*)

Contemporary trends in color vision.   Contemporary research in color vision stems from a number of classical theories, three of which are widely known and influential: the Young-Helmholtz, the Ladd-Franklin, and the Hering. Before reviewing these traditional theories it would be well to bear in mind the basic phenomena of color vision which any theory must explain if it pretends to be comprehensive. Briefly, the phenomena in question are:

1. Color mixture
2. Complementary colors
3. The psychological uniqueness of red, green, blue, and yellow
4. Color blindness
5. Color zones
6. Adaptation and contrast phenomena

To account for primary and intermediate experiences, the Young-

Helmholtz theory, as formulated by Thomas Young (1773 to 1829) and modified by Hermann von Helmholtz (1821 to 1894), postulates that there are three types of cones in the retina—red, green, and blue—which correspond to the physical primaries. Each type of cone is aroused by *all* wavelengths but is maximally excited by the wavelength to which it is most sensitive. (See Figure 3-4.) For this reason, primary experiences are the result of the excitation of the appropriate conal processes in the retina. Complementary experiences arise when all three processes are stimulated simultaneously. Mixtures of wavelengths give rise to intermediate color experiences, since two or more wavelengths arouse two or more cone types simultaneously. The theory makes no attempt to explain the psychological uniqueness of yellow.

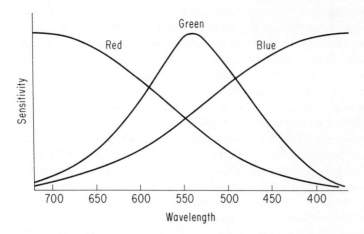

Fig. 3-4. Relative sensitivity of the primary retinal processes to the different wave lengths.

The chief limitation of the theory is its failure to explain red-green color blindness. In order to account for red-green blindness, the theory in its original form would have to assume the congenital absence of the red and green processes. This would explain the absence of both red and green experiences in the red-green color blind. However, since yellow is presumably a mixture of red and green, such individuals should not see yellow, but they do. This difficulty can be overcome by assuming not an absence of cones but a weakness in the red-green processes so that singly they may fail to give the appropriate response but when aroused simultaneously they are still capable of exciting the yellow experience. Color zones could be accounted for on the assumption of an appropriate zonal distribution of the cone processes. However, yellow is typically seen farther out on the retina than the outer limits of red and green; hence, the theory suffers from essentially the same limitation in explaining color zones as was true in the case of color blindness.

Adaptation and successive contrast (negative after-images) are explicable in terms of fatigue. Adaptation is the result of fatigue in a given cone process, which in turn raises the threshold for that hue. Negative afterimages are associated with complete fatigue of one or two cone types with the result that only the remaining processes can be aroused by white light. This, at the same time, accounts for the fact that the resultant experience is complementary to the original stimulus color. Finally, simultaneous contrast was only inadequately explained by the theory as an "unconscious inference," presumably dependent upon higher level neural centers.

The Young-Helmholtz theory has the advantage of parsimony in that it assumes only three cone types which correspond to the physical primaries. The chief limitation of the theory as originally formulated is its failure to explain color blindness, color zones, and contrast. But despite these limitations, the theory has served as a reference point for most subsequent theories and in addition has stimulated a great deal of research.

Christine Ladd-Franklin (1847 to 1930) avoided the difficulties of the Young-Helmholtz theory by postulating four primaries: red, green, *yellow*, and blue. Moreover the corresponding retinal processes were assumed to be zonally distributed to conform with the typical distribution outlined in the preceding section. Mrs. Ladd-Franklin rationalized these two basic assumptions by assuming that an evolution of cone cells had taken place over the course of human development. In the eye of primitive man there were only rods, a state of affairs that is reflected today in the cone-free peripheral portions of the human retina which are color blind. But as evolution proceeded, the primitive rod evolved into the more highly developed cones that are sensitive to yellow and to blue. Again, these are the hues which are seen farthest out on the periphery of the retina in modern man.

As evolutionary development continued, the yellow cone differentiated into red and green types. These most highly developed processes are nearest the fovea, which is the portion of the retina sensitive to all colors and which is the area of greatest visual acuity in photopic conditions.

Mixtures, after-images and adaptation effects are accounted for by the Ladd-Franklin theory in much the same way as they were explained by the Young-Helmholtz theory. The chief advantage of the Ladd-Franklin theory is its ability to account for the yellow zone and for yellow sensitivity in red-green blindness. Obviously, if the red-green processes are absent in red-green blindness, this in no way precludes the possibility of yellow sensitivity, which is assumed to be mediated by a different process. The chief difficulty is the necessity of assuming the additional primary, yellow. There is a further logical limitation to the theory in that it fails to account for red-green vision in the rare condition of yellow-blue blindness, since it is hard to understand how red and green vision could exist in the absence of its evolutionary antecedent, yellow.

The Hering theory formulated by Ewald Hering (1834 to 1918) postulates three processes in the form of paired opponent qualities: black-white; red-green; blue-yellow. Further, these are presumed to depend on the existence of three substances in the retina which are excitable in two opposite ways. Catabolic, or destructive, excitation gives rise to white, red, and yellow color sensations, whereas anabolic excitation gives rise to black, green, and blue. Mixtures resulting in the complementary phenomenon of gray are explained by the simultaneous arousal of any two antagonistic processes. Mixtures of noncomplements give rise to incomplete fusion colors (for example, orange) when nonantagonistic processes are aroused. Color zones are accounted for by assuming a zonal distribution of the three substances. Color blindness is explained by postulating anatomical defects involving the red-green or blue-yellow substances.

The chief weakness of the Hering theory is the assumptions involving anabolic-catabolic processes in the retina. The assumptions are complex and involve the postulation of events for which there is no physiological evidence. The theory also suffers from the limitation of having to account for certain aspects of brightness phenomena in color mixing in a highly complex manner. The problems involved are beyond the scope of this volume, but the interested reader will find a more detailed discussion of the theory in Boring (3, pp. 208–209), or in Stevens (21, p. 831 ff).

A revival of interest in the Hering theory has occurred in recent years. This interest has resulted from the theory's modification by Hurvich and Jameson (14) and because of the discovery that the neural coding of the receptor processes which carry the "color messages" from the retina to the brain may be represented by opponent processes involving antagonistic paired responses.

The Hurvich-Jameson theory presents two possible models of the opponent processes in the visual system (Figure 3-5). Model I assumes that there are three different receptor processes in keeping with the Young-Helmholtz theory. As Figure 3-5 indicates, these are linked with the neural units in such a manner as to account for all possible responses, including black and white. Green and red receptor excitation, for example, would yield yellow. Blue is not only linked to blue neural coding processes but also to red, since there is no true spectral red but instead a yellowish red, and therefore a certain amount of blue must be added to red in order to complement the yellow and so account for visual experience. White is the simultaneous excitation of all receptors. Black is a complex experience resulting

Neural Responses

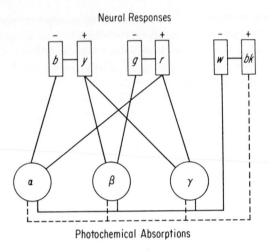

Photochemical Absorptions

Neural Responses

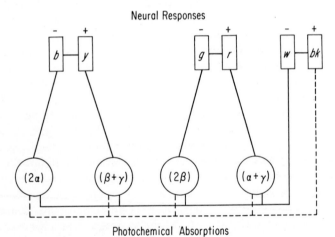

Photochemical Absorptions

$$y - b = k_1 (\beta + \gamma - 2a)$$
$$r - g = k_2 (a + \gamma - 2\beta)$$
$$w - bk = k_3 (a + \gamma + \beta) - k_4 (a + \beta + \gamma)$$

Fig. 3-5. Two alternative hypothetical explanations of the photochemical processes in color vision according to the Hurvich-Jameson theory. For explanation see text. (From Hurvich and Jameson, *14.*)

from simultaneous or successive contrast following or during light stimulation on some part of the retina. The absence of visual stimulation yields a homogeneous or neutral gray such as may be perceived upon being in a darkroom after adaptation.

Model II of the Hurvich-Jameson theory is essentially the same as Model I except that it has been simplified by adding a fourth receptor type (yellow) and assuming that the impulses from the four converge at some point in the visual system to form the appropriate opposing pairs.

There are numerous other theories of color vision which the interested reader will find summarized in Stevens (21). Rather than attempt at this point in our exposition to evaluate the three major theories that we have presented here, we may say that the test of time has left the Young-Helmholtz theory with the most supporters and that the Hering theory as modified is running a close second. However, in the following section we shall see that, paradoxically, both leading contenders may be correct depending upon which level of the visual system is under consideration.

The search for underlying neurological mechanisms. Understandably, those interested in either substantiating or verifying the various theories began the search for "cone types" to correspond to the three or more primary colors postulated by the theorists. To represent this type of systematic approach to the psychophysiology of color vision, we may begin with the pioneer researches of Ragnar Granit, a Scandinavian physiologist, who has for many years has been investigating the relationship between observed psychophysical functions and their underlying neurological correlates. (See 11, especially Chapter IV.)

Granit makes use of the excised eyes of animals in which the anterior structures (cornea and lens) are removed to allow direct access to the retina by microelectrodes. Figure 3-6 shows a highly diagrammatic view of the posterior portion of an eye with a microelectrode in position for recording neural impulses from the retina. Microelectrodes are made of finely drawn hollow glass tubes in which a silver wire or other conductor for recording electrical activity has been incorporated. So fine is the tip (a few microns in diameter), that it can pick up impulses from single neurons. Because the retina is "upside down," with the optic neurons leading to the brain forming the top retinal layer while the actual sensory cells—rods and cones—form the bottom layer, Granit's technique records third-order retinal responses rather than first-order rod or cone activity. (See Figure 3-6.) This must be borne in mind as a possible limiting factor in evaluating the results. However, "seeing" is ultimately dependent upon the occipital cortex, and because this center receives its "messages" from the optic neurons the underlying logic of the technique seems sound.

With eyes prepared in this fashion it is possible to study the comparative responses of pure rod retinas such as the guinea pig's, pure cone retinas such as the reptile's, and the mixed rod-and-cone retina of the cat, the latter being analogous to the mixed human retina. Whichever type is under investigation, the retina can be stimulated by various wavelengths and the

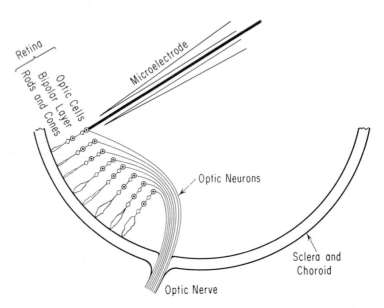

Fig. 3-6. A highly schematic cross section of the eye with the retina greatly enlarged with respect to the outer coats. Note that the microelectrode stimulates the optic neurons.

electrical response, if any, recorded. The results can be plotted on a graph with relative excitability as a function of wavelength. See for example, Figure 3-7, which reproduces Granit's findings for the guinea pig retina, a scotopic eye. This group of curves shows how the retina responds when stimulated by the various spectral wavelengths identified along the abscissa. It should be noted that the scotopic curve peaks at 500 millimicrons, falling off rapidly on either side of this value. By studying the cells which give this response under conditions of light and dark adaptation, it is possible to demonstrate that the behavior of the cells corresponds very well with the behavior of visual purple, or rhodopsin, believed to be the photochemical substance responsible for rod activity. So far, then, the cone-free eye of the guinea pig behaves as a pure rod eye ought to behave according to the duplicity theory.

A word of warning is in order, however. No one *knows* precisely what an animal experiences, and these results should not be interpreted to mean that the animal "sees" greens and blues in the human sense of the term. Rather, the results suggest that the intact guinea pig experiences a whitish sensation most readily if stimulated by wavelengths around 500 millimicrons. But the surprising discovery in Granit's work on the guinea pig is shown in the photopic curves in Figure 3-7. Here, indeed, is evidence for *color* receptors in the pure rod eye despite the fact that the duplicity theory implies the contrary. The secondary peaks around 525 and 460 milli-microns strongly suggest a "green" receptor and a "blue" receptor. This finding can be interpreted to mean that the animal is capable of sensing these wavelengths as "colors." The importance of this finding is obvious; psychologists may have to revise their thinking about the supposed scotopic functions of rods and admit the possibility that they may have a conelike function.

More generally, Granit has identified two types of response units in the retina, *dominators* and *modulators*. Dominators are response units with broad sensitivity, although they do show peaks of sensitivity in certain parts of the spectrum. Modulators are response units with narrow spectral sensitivity, responding only over a restricted part of the spectrum. In the typical vertebrate eye Granit has found two dominators, one with a peak at 500 mμ, the other around 560 mμ. The first corresponds with scotopic and the second with photopic sensitivity, as measured by curves of spectral sensitivity for rhodopsin or visual purple and iodopsin, the corresponding pigment for photopic vision.

Granit has also found a number of different types of modulators de-

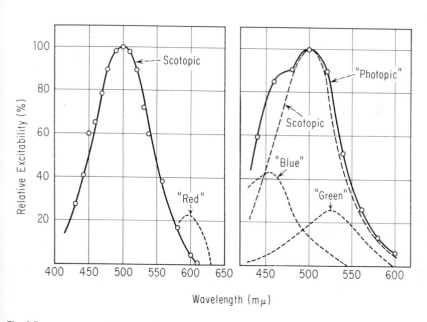

Fig. 3-7. Sensitivity curves for the guinea pig retina. Scotopic (rod) curves are shown on the left. On the right, peaks in the blue and green region of the spectrum are shown separately. The peaks combine to make the photopic curve shown as a solid line above. (After Granit, *11*. Reproduced by permission from *Physiological Psychology*, by C. T. Morgan and E. Stellar. Copyright 1950. McGraw-Hill Book Company, Inc.)

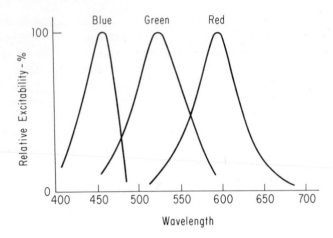

Fig. 3-8. Photopic components from the cat retina. (After Granit, *11.*)

pending upon the type of eye studied. Figure 3-8 presents the photopic components from the cat retina which, like the human retina, is mixed. It will be noted that the modulator or excitability peaks correspond remarkably well with what might be predicted from a trichromatic theory of color vision such as the Young-Helmholtz.

Even more direct evidence in favor of the Young-Helmholtz theory at the receptor level has been provided during the past several years by direct measurements of spectral sensitivity in single cones. E. F. MacNichol, Jr. (*15, 16, 17*) at Johns Hopkins University and P. K. Brown and George Wald (*4*) at Harvard have independently made direct spectral sensitivity tests involving single receptor cells in the retina.

MacNichol, whose work will be described here as representative of this type of investigation, utilized a microspectrophotometer. This device permits the casting of a tiny dot of light on a single receptor cell and records the response of the cell by means of an elaborate computer arrangement which actually prints the retinal responses on a spectral sensitivity graph. Figure 3-9 shows the sensitivity curves for both monkey and human retinas as originally recorded by the microspectrophotometer. Figure 3-10 shows the smoothed and combined curves with peaks at 445, 435, and 570 mμ respectively. Although the "red" curve peaks at yellow, it extends far enough into red to sense adequately all wave lengths that give rise to the experience of red.

These direct measurements of single receptor cells are convincing evidence of the essential validity of the Young-Helmholtz theory, at least at the receptor level. But there are many remaining questions concerned with how information arising in the retina is coded, sent over the optic system

Wavelength
(Millimicrons)

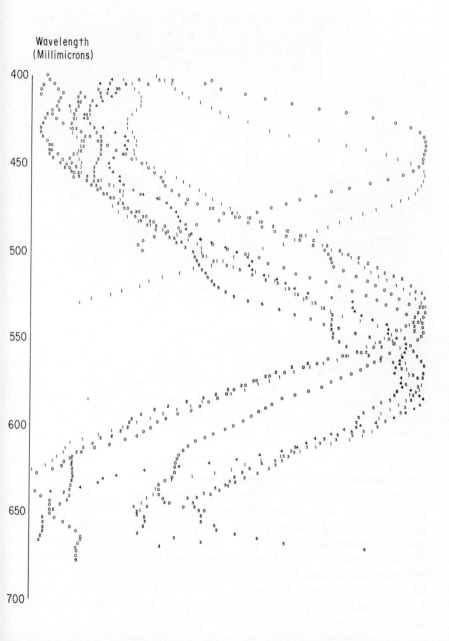

Fig. 3-9. Sensitivity curves for monkey and human retinas as recorded by the microspectrophotometer. Note the peaks at 445, 535, and 570 mμ. (After MacNichol, *16*.)

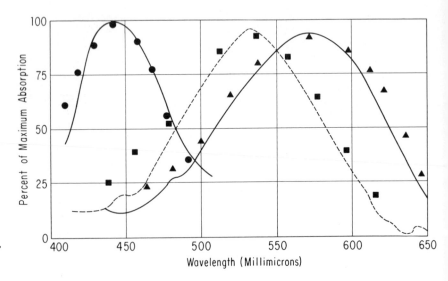

Fig. 3-10. Smoothed curves from the microspectrophotometer showing peaks in the blue, green, and "red" regions of the spectrum. (After MacNichol, *16.*)

and decoded in the brain. Indeed, it has been suggested that visual centers in the lateral geniculate body and beyond may function according to a coding system best represented by an opposing process theory. Developments in this area are taking place with explosive rapidity, and any attempt to review the mass of empirical data is far beyond the scope of this book. The interested reader will find summaries of the more recent work in references at the end of this chapter. See especially reference numbers *5*, *8*, and *18.*

Contemporary trends in auditory theory.   Auditory theorists, like visual theorists, have traditionally sought to account for the major sensory dimensions of quality and intensity. Moreover, as was true in visual theory, auditory theorists have generally taken as their point of departure one of the "classical" theories. The most famous and influential of these is the "resonance theory" formulated by Helmholtz in 1863. Let us first review the basic assumptions of this theory as a background for our study of contemporary developments in audition.

Helmholtz argued that the organ of Corti—the basilar membrane with its hair cells—functions as a resonator. That is, the fibers of the membrane vibrate in sympathy with external sounds coming into the ear by way of the tympanic membrane and auditory ossicles. Because the basilar membrane is trapezoidal in shape, or narrow at one end increasing gradually to maximum width at the other end, Helmholtz reasoned that the narrow end, which is near the base of the cochlea, is tuned to high pitches while the wider end, near the tip of the cochlea, vibrates in resonance with low pitches. By assuming that pitch is dependent on the *place* of stimulation, Helmholtz had accounted for the *quality* dimension of auditory experience. The mechanism for the appreciation of loudness or the intensity dimension of audition remained to be explained. This was eventually accounted for by assuming that: (a) auditory nerve fibers respond with more nervous impulses per second to more intense sounds, or (b) more fibers respond per unit of time to sounds of greater intensity. It was also necessary for Helmholtz to account for beats and combination tones. Beats he explained by postulating that sounds close together in pitch set up vibrations in overlapping portions of the basilar membrane. Finally, combination tones were accounted for as artifacts or subjective experiences arising in the auditory ossicles.

We have stated the Helmholtz theory in its definitive form as if all major facets of the theory had been worked out by 1863. In reality, the theory was originally announced in an incomplete form, and nearly a decade passed before Helmholtz had evolved his theory as it now stands. However, it was the more definitive form of the theory to which criticism was directed and which also served as a reference point for the formulation of alternative theories. For this reason we have avoided any attempt to trace the theory from its inception to its final form.

As Boring (*3*, p. 408) points out, very little criticism was leveled at Helmholtz's theory during its first twenty years. Then a variety of criticism and alternative theories were suggested (and are still being suggested), as more and more factual knowledge accumulated about the auditory mechanism. Boring (*3*, Chapter 11) summarizes twenty-one theories of hearing, many of which came into existence as a result of Helmholtz's theory. Of the post-Helmholtzian theories those which stand most directly in opposition to the original are the pure-frequency theories. In essence, a pure-frequency theory holds that the cochlea responds like a telephone transmitter to sounds entering the external ear; that is, it simply transmits nervous impulses along the auditory nerve at the same rate as incoming stimulus frequencies. For this reason the original frequency theory formulated by William Rutherford (1839 to 1899) in 1886 is known as the "telephone theory." Boring suggests that Rutherford was influenced by two factors in choosing a frequency hypothesis to account for auditory mechanisms. One was the invention of the telephone in 1886, and the other was his experiments on frog nerve-muscle preparations. In the course of his investigations he found that muscle preparations gave off tones when stimulated with sufficient rapidity to result in tetanic or sustained contractions.

A frequency theory such as Rutherford's places the burden of analysis on the auditory cortex, in contrast to a resonance or place theory which assumes that the analysis takes place in the cochlea. In reality, either alter-

native is theoretically possible. However, the chief difficulty with Rutherford's theory is its failure to account for loudness. Because the intensity
dimension of sensation is traditionally associated with the frequency of
nervous discharge, Rutherford's theory, by attributing pitch to frequency,
leaves no mechanism with which to explain loudness. It is the old dilemma
of trying to have one's cake and eat it, too.

However, the real limiting factor in the understanding of auditory
mechanisms during the several decades following Helmholtz's announce-
ment of his theory was too much theorizing in the absence of adequate
neurophysiological knowledge. Any valid body of information on the physiology of the auditory nerve and higher centers had to wait on the development of modern electronic equipment. The problem involved is very similar
to that met with in vision. Dozens of *logical* theories of either visual or auditory mechanisms can be postulated. But theorizing in the absence of adequate anatomical or physiological information only adds to the fund of
theories, not to factual knowledge.

With the invention of techniques capable of probing the mysteries of
nervous transmission from the cochlea to the brain, auditory research developed in a new direction in which the search for basic factual information
took precedence over theory. The high-fidelity amplifier and the oscillo-
scope make it possible to pick up, amplify, and photograph the nervous
impulses which arise in the cochlea, travel over the auditory nerve, and
eventually terminate in the auditory cortex after passing through several
subcortical centers.

Much of the recent neurological work in audition stems from an ingenious experiment conducted by Wever and Bray in 1930 (*27, 28*). These
investigators were studying the behavior of the auditory nerve in cats.
Their technique consisted of placing electrodes on the exposed auditory
nerve of the anesthetized cat so as to pick up electrical potentials which
were then amplified and eventually fed into a telephone receiver in a separate room. The dramatic moment in the experiment occurred when Wever
and Bray discovered that both human speech and various tonal frequencies
up to 5000 cycles per second could be heard in the receiver after being
directed into the cat's ear. There they were changed into nervous impulses
and were picked up and amplified by the electronic equipment. The implications of the experiment were far-reaching, for if the auditory nerve were
faithfully following the frequency of incoming sounds, Helmholtz's popular
resonance theory appeared inadequate to account for this phenomenon.

Further research by Wever and Bray and by Davis (see *22*, Chapters
13 and 14) revealed that, although the auditory nerve does follow the stimulus frequency within certain limits, Wever and Bray were also dealing with
an entirely different phenomenon which has since come to be known as
cochlear microphonics. Let us consider the latter phenomenon first and then
return to the question of transmission along the auditory nerve.

Cochlear microphonics are electrical potentials generated by the cochlea as it is converting sound waves into nervous impulses. Perhaps the most interesting aspect of the cochlear microphonic is its localization along the cochlea to correspond in a general way with what might be expected from Helmholtz's analysis of pitch localization on the organ of Corti. See Figure 3-11, which reproduces a map of cochlear microphonics as determined by E. A. Culler (7) for the guinea pig's ear.

It is now believed that cochlear microphonics are essentially generator potentials originating in the hair cells and functioning as excitors of the afferent neuronal endings of the auditory nerve, which terminate in the hair cells. The research of Von Békésy (24), for which he was awarded the Nobel prize, shows that during acoustic stimulation a traveling wave or bulge moves along the cochlea and exerts a shearing force at the point at which the hair cells are attached to the basilar membrane. Von Békésy has also shown that the wave travels along the cochlea according to its frequency with low frequency waves traveling farther toward the apex than high frequency waves, as would be predicted by a place theory. Although low frequency waves exert a broad stimulating influence on the cochlea, Von Békésy has utilized models to demonstrate that localization is sufficiently sharp to account for pitch discrimination.

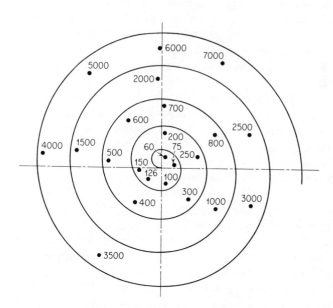

Fig. 3-11. Frequency localization in the cochlea as determined by the position where the cochlear microphonic is maximal. (After Culler, 7. Reproduced by permission from *Physiological Psychology*, by C. T. Morgan and E. Stellar. Copyright 1950. McGraw-Hill Book Company, Inc.)

In summary, then, acoustic stimulation generates a traveling wave in the cochlea. The pressures exerted by that wave stimulate the hair cells to generate potentials (cochlear microphonics) which, in turn, generate auditory impulses along the VIIIth nerve.

While Wever and Bray's original experiment failed to separate cochlear microphonics from auditory nerve impulses, this has since been done. An analysis of the two phenomena reveals that the VIIIth (acoustic) nerve does follow stimulus frequencies, but not so faithfully as Wever and Bray were led to believe by the results of their original experiment. The situation is this: synchronization of stimulus and VIIIth-nerve action potentials is very close up to 1000 cps; good up to 3000 cps; poor up to 4000 cps; and lacking above 4000 cps. The surprising, and at the same time puzzling, aspect of these findings is that there should be any following at all above 1000 cps, since neurons are not capable of firing at such high rates of speed. Whereas different types of neurons do respond faster than others, it is doubtful that even the largest, most high speed fibers, can exceed 500 cps (*19*, pp. 69, 213). Speeds such as these are far lower than the minimum "following" frequency of the VIIIth nerve.

To account for synchronization at speeds above the refractory period of the auditory neurons, Wever and Bray postulated a volley theory, in which it is assumed that the neurons of the VIIIth nerve fire in "volleys" analogous to the manner in which platoons in an infantry company might fire their weapons in successive volleys. In other words, instead of firing in a stepwise manner, the neurons of the VIIIth nerve fire in rotation, and in this way are able to transmit more impulses over a given period of time than if all fired at once.

In order to clarify the picture, the reader might imagine a large number of infantrymen, each with a single-shot rifle, requiring reloading after discharge in much the same way that a neuron must "reload" following an all-or-none response. Obviously if all our soldiers fire at once, reload, fire again, and so on, we shall have an "intense" discharge but a slow rate of fire. If, however, number one fires, instantly followed by two, then three, and so on, we shall have a much faster but weaker volley of shots. Now let us impose one further condition on our hypothetical soldiers. Let number one squad fire, followed by number two squad, and so on, and while the second squad is firing let the first squad reload and fire, and we shall have both high speed and a choice of intensity of fire according to the number of soldiers making up the squads.

The importance of postulating "squad firing" in the case of the auditory nerve is this: *It accounts for the mechanism of intensity,* and in this way avoids the stumbling block that Rutherford's frequency theory could not avoid. Indeed, Wever and Bray's volley principle has been woven into a duplex theory of hearing which accounts for pitches up to 3000 to 4000 cps in terms of the frequency principle and for pitches higher than 4000 cps in terms of the place or resonance principle.

There are, however, many traps and pitfalls awaiting the auditory theorist in the behavior of the cochlea, auditory nerve, and cortical centers. For this reason no contemporary theory of hearing can account for all the phenomena discovered in recent years by researchers in the field. We now seem to have a reversal of the original situation where there was too much theory and too few facts; now there are too many facts for any one theory to comprehend. Still, one set of facts that stands out above all the rest is that which has to do with localization throughout the entire auditory system. There is, as we have already shown, localization in the cochlear response. But there is also a complex kind of localization or specialization of fibers in the auditory nerve. Roughly speaking, fibers from the basal, middle, and apical portions of the cochlea preserve their identity by forming bundles as they travel toward the medulla and cortex. Moreover, it has been found that some *tonotopic* or spatial organization persists at the level of the subcortical and cortical centers for hearing, as would be demanded by a place theory.

Galambos and Davis (9), using microelectrode techniques, have found specialization of fibers for a restricted band of frequencies in the auditory system of the cat. In the thalamus, the great relay station for sensory fibers on the way to the cortex, Ades and his co-workers (1) discovered a tonotopic organization of responses to frequency. Finally, a number of investigators have offered evidence for such organization in the auditory cortices of various animals. See Figure 3-12 for a tonotopic map of the auditory cor-

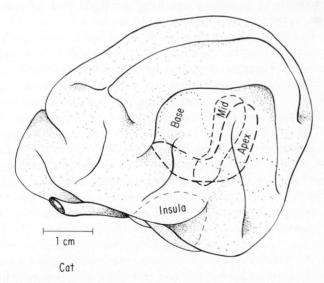

Fig. 3-12. Tonotopic organization of the temporal cortex of the cat. (From Woolsey, *30*.)

tex which represents a synthesis of recent findings. It will be noted that the cochlea appears to be "unrolled" on the surface of the cortex, although the relationship is a complex one with the cochlea being represented by two areas which are spatially the mirror images of each other with respect to localization. (See also *19*, pp. 217, 223; and *21*, pp. 1119–1133.) For a highly technical but comprehensive summary of research on auditory mechanism by leading experts in the field see Reference *24* especially Chapters 9, 10, and 12, which deal with problems of organization.

In summary, the weight of the evidence from recent electrophysiological studies of the ear has confirmed, *in principle,* Helmholtz's theory that quality or pitch depends upon the locus of stimulation of the hair cells along the organ of Corti. Moreover, this tonotopic organization of auditory mechanisms is preserved in some degree all along the conduction pathways and in the auditory cortex itself. What remains is to reconcile these findings with the fact that the auditory nerve shows synchronization of firing with outside frequencies at least along a restricted range of stimuli. There can be little doubt that this problem will eventually be resolved—perhaps in the form of a resonance-frequency theory. Meanwhile, we may conclude our survey of contemporary auditory theory with the comment that recent research has carried us far along the road to a comprehensive understanding of our second most important sensory modality.

Specialized receptors and the other senses. It will be recalled that both Müller's doctrine of the specific energies of nerves and von Frey's specific end organ theory of cutaneous sensitivity predicted that for each of the senses a specialized receptor organ would be discovered. It would be beyond the scope of a general account such as ours to attempt to review the extensive literature and vast body of empirical research for which these theories have been responsible. However, it may prove worthwhile to summarize briefly the present status of the special end organ theory for the more important remaining senses in order to round out our survey of sensory processes.

The two most important chemical senses are gustation and olfaction. Because of its greater accessibility, the sense of taste has been more widely and more definitively investigated than has the sense of smell. As Figure 3-13 shows, there is good reason to believe that the taste buds are specialized for the mediation of the primary tastes of sweet, salt, sour, and bitter. Largely due to the work of Pfaffmann (*20*) we also know that there are certain fiber types in the taste nerves which mediate those sensations, although the types are complex, some mediating more than one quality.

There are many theories of olfactory sensitivity, none of which are definitive. As has been pointed out, the inaccessibility of the olfactory epithelium makes it extremely difficult to investigate this sense. Henning's well-known classification of salient odors is given in Figure 3-14. Little is known of the central olfactory pathways.

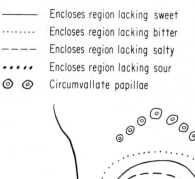
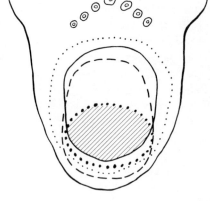

——————— Encloses region lacking sweet
·········· Encloses region lacking bitter
— — — — Encloses region lacking salty
• • • • • Encloses region lacking sour
◎ ◎ Circumvallate papillae

Fig. 3-13. Regions of the tongue sensitive to the primary gustatory stimuli. (From Woodworth and Schlosberg, *29.*)

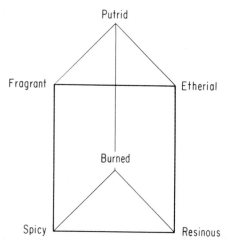

Fig. 3-14. Henning's classification of the salient odors.

Much more is known about the peripheral and central mechanisms of the somatic senses. The specific end organ theory has held up well except in the case of thermal sensitivity, which has proved puzzling to generations of researchers. As Figure 3-15 shows, encapsulated end organs serve touch and deep pressure while free nerve endings are the receptors for pain. Recent research (*19*) indicates that similar receptors may be responsible for temperature sensitivity instead of Krause bulbs and Ruffini cylinders.

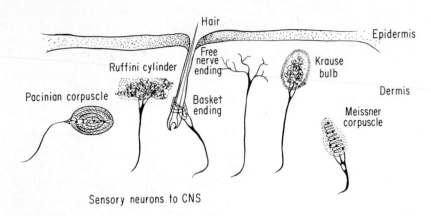

Fig. 3-15. A diagrammatic representation of the more important subcutaneous receptors. Basket endings and Meissner corpuscles mediate light touch. Pacinian corpuscles mediate deep pressure, free nerve endings pain. Traditionally, warmth has been ascribed to Ruffini cylinders and cold to Krause bulbs.

The proprioceptors are also specialized end organs which serve the muscles, tendons, and joints. The muscle spindles and Golgi tendon organs are responsive to stretch, the Pacinian corpuscles to movements of the joints.

SUMMARY AND EVALUATION

In casting a backward glance over the evolution of theory and research in sensation, one is immediately struck by a strong sense of the historical depth of sensory psychology. Along with associationism, sensory psychology formed the core of the prescientific psychologies; and, in terms of a descriptive system, reached its culmination in Titchener's structuralism. Then for a time sensation faded into the background of psychological research and systematizing. This, in part, was the result of its displacement by interest in other aspects of behavior and experience, and, in part, because evolution slows down or stops when there is no place for further improvement.

When modern electronic techniques became available, a burst of progress followed immediately and is still going on. But the direction of research has shifted from the description and measurement of sensation on a purely psychological level to a concerted attack on the underlying neuro-physiology of the sense organs themselves. We have attempted to show the general lines of advance of the new approach in the areas of vision and audition. Much the same pattern has been typical of recent research on the gustatory, olfactory, and cutaneous senses, where significant gains are being made in accounting for the physiological substrata of these modalities.

In a sense, then, the wheel has come full circle in sensory psychology, for sensation was the mainstay of the early "physiological" psychologies of Weber, Fechner, Wundt, and Titchener. Today it is back in the hands of the physiological psychologists where it once again has found a sympathetic home.

REFERENCES

1. Ades, H., F. Mettler, and E. Culler. Effects of lesions in the medial geniculate bodies in the cat. *American Journal of Physiology*, **125**, 1939, pp. 15–23.
2. Bartley, S. H. *Vision*. Princeton, N. J.: Van Nostrand, 1941.
3. Boring, E. G. *Sensation and perception in the history of experimental psychology*. New York: Appleton, 1942.
4. Brown, P. K., and F. Wald. Visual pigments in single rods and cones of the human retina. *Science,* **144,** 1964, pp. 45–52.
5. *Brown symposium on receptor mechanisms*. Providence, R. I.: Brown University, 1964.
6. Carr, H. A. *Psychology, a study of mental activity*. New York: Longmans, Green, 1925.
7. Culler, E. A. An experimental study of tonal localization in the cochlea of the guinea pig. *Annals of Otology, Rhinology, and Laryngology,* **44,** 1935, pp. 807–813.
8. Enoch, J. M. Physical properties of the retinal receptor and response of retinal receptors. *Psychological Bulletin,* **61,** 1964, pp. 242–251.
9. Galambos, R., and H. Davis. The response of single auditory-nerve fibers to acoustic stimulation. *Journal of Neurophysiology,* **6,** 1943, pp. 39–57.
10. Geldard, F. A. *The human senses*. New York: Wiley, 1953.
11. Granit, R. *Receptors and sensory perception*. New Haven: Yale University Press, 1955.
12. Hecht, S. The nature of the photoreceptor processes. In C. Murchison (ed.), *Foundations of experimental psychology*. Worcester, Mass.: Clark University Press, 1929.
13. Hecht, S. The photochemical basis of vision. *Journal of Applied Physiology,* **9,** 1938, pp. 156–164.
14. Hurvich, L. M., and D. Jameson. An opponent-process theory of color vision. *Psychological Review,* **64,** 1957, pp. 384–404.
15. MacNichol, E. F. Jr. Retinal mechanisms of color vision. *Vision Research,* **4,** 1964, pp. 119–133.
16. MacNichol, E. F. Jr. Three-pigment color vision. *Scientific American,* **211,** 1964, pp. 48–56.
17. Marks, W. B., W. H. Dobelle, and E. F. MacNichol, Jr. Visual pigments of single primate cones. *Science,* **143,** 1964, pp. 1181–1182.
18. McConnell, D. G. Chemical theories. *Psychological Bulletin,* **61,** 1964, pp. 252–261.
19. Morgan, C. T. *Physiological Psychology*, ed. 3. New York: McGraw-Hill, 1965.
20. Pfaffmann, C. The sense of taste. In Field, J., H. W. Magoun, and V. E. Hall. *Handbook of physiology,* Vol. 1. Washington, D. C.: American Physiological Society, 1959.

21. Stevens, S. S. (ed.). *Handbook of experimental psychology.* New York: Wiley, 1951.
22. Stevens, S. S., and H. Davis. *Hearing.* New York: Wiley, 1938.
23. Titchener, E. B. *A Textbook of Psychology.* New York: Macmillan, 1910.
24. Von Békésy, G. Experimental models of the cochlea with and without nerve supply. In Rasmussen, G. L., and W. F. Windle (eds.), *Neural mechanisms of the auditory and vestibular systems.* Springfield, Ill.: Charles C Thomas, 1960.
25. Watson, J. B. *Behavior, an introduction to comparative psychology.* New York: Holt, 1914.
26. Watson, J. B. *Psychology from the standpoint of a behaviorist.* Philadelphia: Lippincott, 1919.
27. Wever, E. G., and C. W. Bray. The nature of the acoustic response: The relation between sound frequency and frequency of impulses in the auditory nerve. *Journal of Experimental Psychology,* **13,** 1930, pp. 373–387.
28. Wever, E. G., and C. W. Bray. Action currents in the auditory nerve in response to acoustical stimulation. *Proceedings of the National Academy of Science,* **16,** 1930, pp. 344–350.
29. Woodworth, R. S., and H. Schlosberg, *Experimental psychology.* New York: Holt, 1954.
30. Woolsey, C. N. Organization of Cortical Auditory System. In Rosenblith, W. A. (ed.), *Sensory communication.* Boston: The M.I.T. Press, 1961.

4

Perception: The Classical Heritage

In his *New Theory of Vision* the philosopher Berkeley likened sensations to the sounds of language, which have no intrinsic meaning but which must be interpreted by the listener. From this point of view sensations have no inherent meaning and are but the raw materials of experience to which mind contributes understanding. But, it may be objected, we do not hear "sounds" in everyday life which have to be "translated" into meaningful concepts; nor do we experience masses of qualities, extents, and intensities from which we consciously construct a meaningful world of objects and events. Instead, under ordinary conditions, meaning seems to come instantaneously. It is as if we never *sense* stimuli out there but *perceive* objects, space, time, and events; our brains, it seems, are geared for perception, not sensation. Naturally, this does not deny the obvious fact that we must sense before we can perceive. Rather, it means the entire process of observation is so telescoped that we are rarely aware of sensory activity as such. Just as a good reader grasps ideas and meanings rather than words and letters, so the observer perceives meaningful objects instead of experiencing crude sense impressions. And this principle brings us to the fundamental problem for classical perceptual psychology: *to account for the orderly arrangement of objects in space and time in the world of the perceiver.*

The British empiricists, it will be recalled, taught that all knowledge comes to mind by way of the senses. But as an explanation of the meaningfulness of experience this doctrine begs the question, since the empiricists also held that sensations in and of themselves are not knowledge but only the elements from which knowledge is derived. Thus far, we seem to have a variation on the old puzzle of the primacy of the chicken or

123

the egg. To resolve the dilemma, the empiricists employed the principles of the association of ideas to account for meaning. Their argument ran somewhat as follows: Simple sense experiences eventually "go together" in mind through repetition and contiguity. For example, the experience of a certain wave length of light stimulating the eye of the child is frequently accompanied by a second experience, the spoken color name, and eventually one comes to mean the other. Sensation, then, is only the basis for perception; the role of experience in providing meaning is crucial.

On a more complex level general or abstract ideas can also be explained by means of associationism. The philosopher Hume asks us to consider the concept of a triangle. How do we come to have such a general idea which applies to such a diversity of geometric forms? His answer is that the concept of triangularity is built up slowly on the basis of individual sensory experiences with particular triangles. The general or abstract concept is the result of the association in memory of many experiences with various kinds of triangles.

For many years the empirical account of perceptual meaning was accepted as an adequate explanation of the process. However, its adequacy was eventually challenged on the ground that it failed to take into consideration motivational and other dynamic factors. For example, in abnormal perceptions, such as hallucinations or delusions, the effect of powerful motivational factors on perception is evident. In these cases, frustration, conflict, or strong desire determines the meaning of a percept just as surely as the stimulus factors or past experiences which may be involved. Similarly, in recent decades a great deal of emphasis has been put on attitudes, physiological states, personality traits, and even cultural factors as perceptual determinants. Because of the gradually increasing range of recognized determinants, perceptual theory has grown broader over the years to include more and more such factors. Today it is fair to say that virtually every other mental process is being investigated in terms of its possible role in influencing perception.

Because perceptual theory has come to occupy so prominent a position in contemporary psychology, we shall devote this and the following chapter to tracing its evolution from sensory psychology to its present status as one of the most important and central concepts in the entire field. In this chapter we shall deal with the origins of perceptual psychology in philosophy, its subsequent development in the early experimental period, and its place in the systematic structures of the schools. In the chapter to follow we shall be concerned exclusively with contemporary perceptual systems.

PERCEPTION IN PRESCIENTIFIC PSYCHOLOGY[1]

The Scottish philosopher, Thomas Reid (1710 to 1796), first formulated the distinction between sensation and perception. He referred sensations to the activities of the sense organs as these are experienced in consciousness. Perception he held to be dependent on sensation but different from the former in that the perceiver is aware of objects or events in his environment and not merely sense impressions. Moreover, Reid pointed out that awareness of what is out there carries with it a strong sense or conviction of the objective character of events, situations, time, and space. Reid called this objective aspect of perception an "invincible belief" in the existence of external objects. The objectifying of percepts is, therefore, a product of mind. Going beyond his descriptive definition of perception, Reid tried to account for the *why* of perceptual experience, and in doing so posed a fundamental question that subsequent generations of philosophers and psychologists sought to answer. Reid's own solution was simple and forthright but not very satisfying to the modern reader. He attributed the "existence quality" of perception to an "instinctive tendency" in the human constitution. The perception of both spatial extension and temporal duration, two fundamental dimensions of perception, he held to be "intuitive."

While Reid failed to formulate an acceptable explanation for perceptual meaning, he did set the stage for further inquiry into the problem along two major lines. These took the form of *nativism* and *empiricism*. The nativists, following Reid, postulated innate ideas or hereditary predispositions as the explanation of the perceptual processes, while the empiricists, in general, subscribed to associationism as the key to perceptual meaning. The empirical view was sponsored by Berkeley, Lotze, Helmholtz, and Wundt, while nativism was championed by Kant, Johannes Müller, Hering, and Stumpf.

We shall examine the specific contributions of each of these representatives of the empirical and nativistic traditions in more detail in paragraphs to follow. However, a word of explanation is in order for the contemporary student of psychology in regard to the emphasis on space and object perception in prescientific and early scientific writings on the subject. The modern reader, fresh from a general psychology course, is likely to think of perception in terms of motivational and emotional influences, the working principles of the Rorschach Test, or some similar topic of current interest. In the face of these highly challenging contemporary developments, it may be difficult to appreciate that the *fundamental* problem of perceptual psychol-

[1] Our account has been drawn from a variety of secondary sources. (See References *1, 2, 3, 6, 9, 12, 17, 21* and *24*.)

ogy is to account for the perception of objects in space. It was natural, therefore, that early perceptual theorists expended most of their efforts on this primary problem. With this in mind, let us begin by examining the contribution of the empiricists, who were particularly concerned with the specific cues employed in space perception.

PERCEPTION AND THE EMPIRICAL TRADITION

We have already seen (Chapter 1) how the empiricists, starting with Hobbes, brought the doctrine of innate ideas under attack. It was natural, therefore, for Berkeley in his *New Theory of Vision* to account for space perception on the basis of experience. He argued that distance, or the third dimension, is not directly perceived, since the stimuli that come to the eye terminate in a point on the retina, which in no way varies with the distance of the stimulus object. It makes no difference as far as the retinal image is concerned whether the point of light on the fovea originates in a star a million light-years away or comes from a source a few yards from the observer. Having only two dimensions itself, the retina has no mechanism for the direct appreciation of depth. Depth, then, must be the result of experience—experience of past contacts and movements employed in dealing with objects in space. Moreover, Berkeley argued that the kinesthetic strain set up in the extrinsic and intrinsic ocular muscles could serve as cues for distance. Again, the process is essentially one of association, for if we frequently experience the tensions associated with strong convergence of the eyes on near objects, these tensions presumably come to mean "near," while relaxed muscles and low tensions stand for "far." A similar mechanism holds for accommodation of the lens as a possible cue of depth.

In addition to reducing distance perception to nonspatial cues, Berkeley undertook an analysis of object size or magnitude which is, of course, closely correlated with distance. Object size, he pointed out, varies with the distance of an object from the retina; but in spite of variation in distance, the perceived size of objects remains relatively constant (size constancy). Berkeley related perceived size or magnitude to distance by arguing that his own distance from the object is taken into account by the observer, thus making for relative constancy in perceived size despite wide variations in viewing distance.

Finally, Berkeley came to grips with the problem of perceptual meaning, which he explained in terms of associationism. Specifically, he held that any given perception is meaningful only in the light of past perceptions, whose meaning in turn is carried into the present in the form of ideas. Similarly, present perceptions become the ideas of the future to be associated with tomorrow's perceptions.

The empirical tradition, as was brought out in Chapter 1, continued in British philosophy from Berkeley to Mill. But empiricism also took root on the continent of Europe and eventually found a place in Wundt's psychology. Because Wundt's system is in the mainstream of our evolutionary approach, we shall turn our attention to Continental empiricism beginning with a study of Lotze's theory of space perception.

Lotze and "local signs." Rudolf Lotze (1817 to 1881), an early German philosopher-psychologist, is in many ways reminiscent of Gustav Fechner. Like Fechner, Lotze was a blend of humanist and scientist, attracted on the one hand to the delights of philosophical and metaphysical speculation, and on the other to the exactitudes and the discipline of science. Although Lotze had been trained as a physician, he devoted a great deal of time to philosophical studies and, as was true of Fechner, became interested in the mind-body problem. His interest in psychology eventually resulted in a book entitled *Physiological Psychology*. It was in this volume in the section on space perception that Lotze presented his famous "local sign" theory which proved to be highly influential in nineteenth- and early twentieth-century psychology. In fact, Boring (2) argues that Lotze was responsible for the great interest in empiricism shown by Wundt and his immediate predecessors.

Lotze assumes that mind is inherently capable of perceiving space. However, space perception depends upon sensory cues which in and of themselves are nonspatial. For example, when the surface of the body is stimulated by anything larger than a point, the individual is able to perceive the spatiality of the stimulus. This, Lotze argues, depends upon cues generated by the pattern of excitation of the skin receptors. Objects larger than a point excite many receptors simultaneously thus giving rise to experiences of length and breadth. Moreover, because the skin is elastic, it is depressed by tactile stimuli; but the degree to which it is depressed is related to underlying conditions in the subcutaneous tissues. Over bony areas the pattern of depression (and its attendant sensory excitation) differs from the pattern over more yielding fatty or muscular tissues. Such differential intensity patterns are *local signs* which furnish the basis for space perception.

In applying his theory to vision, man's most highly developed spatial modality, Lotze places great weight on eye movements as cues for the appreciation of space. That is, our visual apparatus is in almost continuous motion as we attempt to bring external objects into clear focus on the fovea. Because of the effort involved, patterns of kinesthetic sensations are continually arising from the eye muscles. These sensations Lotze calls "changing feelings of position." The kinesthetic sensations generated as the eye sweeps around an arc of regard establish the local signs for the retinal points which are associated with such movements. If the quiescent eye is subsequently stimulated at two or more separate points, the associations of frequently experienced "feelings" of movement from the past come into consciousness, and the result is a sense of experienced space. In essence, then, the perception of space is learned through associations of movement in space with local sensory spots which are stimulated in the course of such movements.

Auditory spatiality is explained by assuming that stimuli which are not in the midplane of the head affect the two ears differentially.

Clearly, Lotze's theory is limited to explaining spatial perception for those senses in which movement of the sensory apparatus is possible (vision), or for those modalities where stimuli may be moved over the sense organs or are able to stimulate spatially separated organs (touch, audition). For this reason, the adherents of a strict local sign theory do not attribute spatiality to olfaction or taste.

The publication of Lotze's theory resulted in a controversy. The empiricists, as has been said, claimed the theory for their side; but the nativists, by pointing to Lotze's original premise that the brain is inherently capable of perceiving space, could argue that spatiality is an inherent or native process. We shall, of course, consider the opposite or nativistic view in more detail in a later section of this chapter. But the point to be emphasized here is that Lotze's theory was by no means unambiguously empirical. However, it was an attractive theory; and the early texts in psychology, whether on the side of empiricism or nativism, gave it extended consideration. Indeed, traces of the theory in a highly modified form can be found in contemporary associationistic accounts of perception.

Helmholtz and "unconscious inference." Helmholtz, with whom we are already familiar from our study of his famous theories of hearing and color vision, became involved in perceptual problems through his interest in sensation and optics. In his writings on these subjects, he clearly and forthrightly embraced empiricism, thereby placing himself in opposition to German tradition, which was strongly nativistic.

In essence, Helmholtz's theory of space perception centered around the concept of "unconscious inference." By the latter he meant that the experience of space is not a given or inherent characteristic of mind, but an *inferred* quality brought to present perception from the individual's past experiences with objects in space. Just as one infers that ice is cold when it is perceived visually because of memories of past tactual experiences with ice, so we may infer "seen" space on the basis of our past interaction with objects in space. Thus, if one is touched on the arm with his eyes closed, he can tell whether it was his right or left arm which was touched and the approximate location of the contact. This spatial localization is possible because of many prior experiences of the same kind in which touch on the arm has acquired a local sign.

Helmholtz, moreover, believed in local signs in the sense that he held that the various sense organs and nerves have their characteristic qualities, or as Müller had argued, "specific energies." But for Helmholtz such specific sense qualities are not in and of themselves spatial or intrinsically meaningful. They are bare sense impressions to which associations must be added (unconsciously inferred) to render them meaningful. Actually, in the child, or in the case of novel experiences in the adult, such associations would, at first, be conscious. It is frequent repetition which makes them rapid and automatic to the point where they eventually become "unconscious." For example, as children we were conscious of the greater strain associated with lifting large objects as compared to small objects. If as adults we are confronted with two objects identical in weight but greatly differing in size, the larger will seem much *lighter* than the smaller because we unconsciously associate greater effort with lifting heavy objects. Our "surprise" at the speed with which the larger rises makes it seem abnormally light. A pound of feathers can be made to appear lighter than a pound of lead through unconscious inference! Helmholtz referred to the compelling quality of such inferences as their "irresistibility."

In summary, Helmholtz's treatment of perception extended Lotze's local-sign theory, and at the same time attempted to make it congruent with Müller's doctrine of specific nerve energies. But of even greater importance was Helmholtz's clear-cut stand on the issue of nativism and empiricism itself. His strong support of empiricism carried great weight with the physiologists and embryonic psychologists of his day. Consequently, it is not surprising that Wundt, who was Helmholtz's assistant for four years at Heidelberg (1858 to 1862), was strongly influenced not only by the desirability of empiricism as a general point of view in psychology but also more specifically by the doctrine of unconscious inference.

Wundt on perception. Here we shall take up only a special aspect of Wundt's perceptual theory, since we shall consider the overall structuralistic treatment of perception in detail when we come to discuss Titchener's system. In general, Wundt adheres to the empirical-associationistic tradition which held that mind is a compound of elemental processes bound together by associations. Since he considered perception a complex process involving sensations and meaning, he had to face the problem of showing how meaning accrues to sensory experience, and it was his effort in this direction that led to his special "doctrine of apperception." By apperception Wundt means any conscious content which is clearly comprehended or grasped. Stated differently, Wundt argues for a distinction between a passive, "pure perception" without logical meaning, and the more active apperception which is pure perception plus preexisting ideas. It is the preexisting ideas which make perceptions meaningful. The total complex of preexisting ideas, or memories, make up what Wundt calls the "apperceptive mass."

But it would be a mistake to think of apperception as a passive process which automatically accrues to perception. Quite the contrary, it is accompanied by a conscious feeling of activity—an awareness of tension and excitement. It is, so to speak, a reflection of the excitement of "discovery" which is experienced as one clearly grasps the meaning of a perceptual situation and its relationship to the totality of present and past experience. Thus, *feeling* is an integral part of apperception from Wundt's point of view.

Finally, an important aspect of the doctrine of apperception is the role played by attention in the overall process. Wundt distinguishes between the whole range or field of consciousness on the one hand, and the focus or momentary "point" on the other. Because apperception involves a clear grasp or comprehension of conscious content, it is only those processes at the focus of attention which are apperceived. However, to avoid confusion, it is important to note that the heart of the doctrine is his belief that *the complex of ideas from past experience* form "apperceptive masses" which give meaning and interpretation to present consciousness.

Wundt took the doctrine of apperception from Johann Friedrich Herbart[2] (1776 to 1841), one of the Continental philosopher-psychologists of the nineteenth century. Herbart, in turn, got the idea from the mathematician Leibnitz. Therefore the doctrine of apperception was already well entrenched in psychology when Wundt made it a part of his system. Moreover, it crept into systems other than structuralism and became a lively and controversial issue in early German and American psychology. What we wish to emphasize here, however, is the fact that Wundt made experience and an active consciousness the central themes in his psychology of perception. Wundt's explanation of meaning in terms of past experience is clearly on the side of empiricism.

In summary, the empiricists, whether dealing with the relatively simple matter of space perception or the more general process of perceptual meaning, sought to demonstrate the validity of empirical explanations of the perceptual processes. Moreover, even in this brief summary of the empirical position it is possible to recognize the tendency for perceptual psychology to broaden gradually to allow for the inclusion of more and more complex processes. In fact, William James might well have been criticizing contemporary perceptual psychology when he complained that perception in becoming apperception allowed "innumerable" individual factors to enter into the meaning of perceptual experience. In short, James felt that the

---

[2] Herbart was deeply interested in education and urged that teachers strive to develop "apperceptive masses" in their pupils for the better comprehension and understanding of new experiences. Today, it is difficult to see just how the average teacher would proceed with such a project.

concept of perception had become so broad as to be meaningless. Whatever the merits of the case, the empiricists had claimed that the explanation of all perceptual processes was to be found in experience—not only for simple visual extents but for the complex cognitive processes as well. But there was another side to the argument, the nativistic, with an equally strong tradition—a tradition which has its counterpart in contemporary psychology. We must now consider this aspect of the controversy.

NATIVISM AND PERCEPTION

As we pointed out earlier in this chapter, nativism was sponsored by Kant, Müller, Hering, and Stumpf. Before we consider the individual contributions of these men, a brief general statement of the concept of nativism itself will be presented to serve as a frame of reference for the discussion of individual nativist contributions.

Nativism originated in philosophy as a parallel concept to rationalism and, like rationalism, is frequently employed as a bipolar opposite to empiricism in accounting for perceptual meaning. Nativism opposed the *tabula rasa* view of mind in which sensation gives rise to memory and, by association, memory in turn gives rise to ideas. The rationalists, on the contrary, believed that mind possesses inherent or a priori ideas—ideas of right and wrong, of space, time, and, some believed, of God. If this conception of mind is correct, then the materialistic philosophy of the empiricists is founded on error. The "pure reason" (to borrow Kant's famous phrase) of the empiricists failed to take into account the limitations of their own philosophy.

Because the doctrine of empiricism occupied a central place in prescientific psychology, it was natural that an opposition movement arose to question the idea that mind is derived from experience. Moreover, it is understandable that the controversy began in the field of perception—the key process in the understanding of mind. Finally, we might note that the controversy did not await the formal founding of psychology, but got underway as a result of Kant's great philosophical treatise, *The Critique of Pure Reason*.

Kant and nativism. In choosing the title, *The Critique of Pure Reason*, Kant (1724 to 1804) did not mean to imply that he was against reason. Rather, he took as his thesis the argument that the British empirical school of philosophy represented by Locke and his followers had fallen into the error of erecting their systems on false premises. Specifically, he charged that they had failed to realize that philosophy and science must recognize the validity of absolute truths arising out of the innate content of mind.

These truths, Kant believed, are not only independent of empirical proof, but also are true *before* experience, or in other words, are true a priori. Kant went on to argue that mathematics is replete with such absolute, a priori truths. The basic axioms of the mathematician are not dependent on experience for proof, but are the inevitable consequence of the nature of the human mind.

Space and time, to cite examples more relevant to psychology, are not born of sensations, but are a priori forms of perception which coordinate and make meaningful incoming sensations. Sensations arising from objects in the environment do not, as the empiricists believe, automatically take on a kind of unity or order and so become meaningful perceptions. Rather, according to Kant, *mind* imposes a selectivity on sensations, accepting some and rejecting others, depending on its purpose. "Mechanical" principles of association, such as frequency, recency, contrast, and the like, are inadequate to account for the order of mind. For Kant, mind is the master of sensations; sensations are not the masters of mind.

Kant's philosophy becomes psychology in the sense that two of his a priori attributes of mind are space and time. Because mind is inherently spatial, sensations are ordered on a continuum of space; and since mind can appreciate time, time, too, lends order to experience. Mind, therefore, contributes to experience as much as it takes. But in another sense, this is not psychology at all, for it is impossible to subject a priori ideas or innate "givens" to experimental tests. As a psychology, Kant's *Critique* provided no advantage over Descartes' doctrine of innate ideas. For this reason, Kant's importance to psychology consisted primarily in his having provided a focus for empirical attacks on the nativistic point of view. However, this is not to say that nativism itself stands or falls with Kant, for in some form or other it has persisted in psychology up to the present time, especially in the Gestalt tradition.

Johannes Müller.   Müller came into the empirical-nativistic controversy by way of his doctrine of the specific energies of nerves, which we considered in connection with the historical development of physiology (see Chapter 1). The argument that special experiential qualities are associated with specific nerves is, of course, far removed from Kant's doctrine of innate categories of mind or a priori truths. Instead, it simply states that nerves impose their innate or structurally determined qualities on mind. Since nerves are native equipment, Müller's doctrine is necessarily a primitive kind of nativism.

To relate the doctrine to perception, it can be argued that mind has no direct contact with the environment, but instead is aware only of nerves. Because of the spatial arrangement of the nerves which make up the optic tract, space is directly perceived from the tract. More specifically, the image from an external object is projected on the retina, and the retina, by way of the optic tract, "projects" the resulting nervous impulses on the brain in a pattern which mirrors the objective stimulus complex. Finally, it should be noted that Müller accepted the Kantian doctrine that mind is spatial. Such an assumption is a necessary part of Müller's argument, since patterns of nervous impulses cannot in and of themselves give a sense of space unless mind in some way *interprets* the pattern as spatial.

Although Müller accepted a Kantian-nativistic view of perception, it would be unfair to think of him as a pure nativist. His overall orientation was closer to empiricism than to nativism. This follows from the fact that he was struggling to put physiology on a sound experimental basis, and experimentation is in the empirical rather than the nativistic tradition. As Boring (*1, 2*) frequently points out, the complicating factor running through the entire empirical-nativistic controversy is that every nativist is something of an empiricist and every empiricist something of a nativist. In this connection, one is reminded of the heredity-environment controversy of more recent vintage where, it turns out, no one is willing to ascribe all individual differences to either factor but must admit that both play a part. In fact, it is typical of psychologists' controversies that they revolve around questions of emphasis rather than absolute differences.

Hering and Stumpf. Ewald Hering (1834 to 1918) is most famous in the annals of psychology for his theory of color vision, which we considered in the preceding chapter, while Carl Stumpf (1848 to 1936) is best known for his pioneer studies in the psychology of tone. We shall consider Hering's and Stumpf's theories of space perception only briefly for two reasons. First, both embraced the local-sign theory formulated by Lotze with which we are already familiar. Both, however, argued for a nativistic interpretation of Lotze's signs. Second, theories such as Hering's and Stumpf's which attribute inherent spatiality to the retina did not win general acceptance in the face of the far more popular empirical explanations. As a result, the strict nativistic point of view on retinal spatiality failed to evolve into an acceptable form in contemporary psychology. The nearest thing to nativism in modern perceptual theory is represented by the Gestalt point of view, which will be considered later in this chapter.

Hering holds that the retina, besides furnishing sensations of light and color, is capable of imparting three spatial qualities: height, breadth, and depth. These, in turn, he relates to retinal points or local signs. While adopting the local-sign foundation of space appreciation, Hering stipulates that spatiality is an inherent property of the retina. He then goes on to elaborate the theory, taking into account directional ability, binocular factors in depth perception, and the relationship between depth perception and kinesthetic cues arising from the eye muscles. We need not enter into the details of the theory here. It is exceedingly complex and has no counterpart in contemporary perceptual theory. The interested reader may consult Titchener (20) for a summary and critical interpretation of this theory.

In regard to Stumpf's theory we need only mention that, like Hering, he argued for a nativistic interpretation of Lotze's local signs. Moreover, he accepted Hering's argument that the retina possesses an inherent mechanism for the appreciation of visual space. Indeed, Stumpf held that space is just as directly perceived as sensory quality.

The difficulty with these theories is the a priori nature of their assumptions. The nativist, by making space inherent, more or less cuts the ground from under the opposition. Theoretically, in order to evaluate the nativistic position one would have to test the infant's perceptual ability to determine whether or not he has an inherent sense of space.[3] The empiricists, however, labor under no such limitations. And, because the empiricists' hypotheses could be subjected to experimental tests, the empirical view found favor in the experimentally oriented atmosphere of the late nineteenth century.

As we take leave of this old controversy, it is worth pointing out that it has some value for the contemporary student of psychology in emphasizing the desirability of appealing to experimentation instead of speculation and authoritarian doctrine for the resolution of theoretical issues. The controversy is an excellent, albeit unfortunate, example of too much theorizing and too little research. Moreover, the influence of the "weight of authority" is clearly evident as a factor which served to intensify and prolong the controversy. Kant's and Müller's great stature undoubtedly influenced Hering and Stumpf on the nativist side, just as Locke's and Helmholtz's fame must have attracted followers for the empirical camp. But in a sense, neither personal stature nor authority has any place in science which, theoretically at least, is impersonal. However, being a product of the human mind, science cannot completely free itself from the limitations of human nature.

PERCEPTUAL PSYCHOLOGY AND THE SCHOOLS

The leaders of the schools of the late nineteenth and early twentieth centuries varied widely in their general approach to perception and in the emphasis which they gave the perceptual process in their systems. For Wundt and his American exponent, Titchener, perception was a crucial problem. Watson, in keeping with his strict behaviorism, ignored perception. The Gestalt school, having originated as a result of a perceptual experiment, went on to make the study of the perceptual processes the very heart of

[3] In the following chapter we shall see that psychologists have recently made an attempt to do just this with, however, ambiguous results.

psychology. Moreover, each of those schools that developed systematic interpretations of perception took a stand on the nativistic-empiricistic controversy, which, in a sense, was their heritage from prescientific psychology.
The lines of division were no longer so clearly drawn, and the exponents
of the schools did not employ the traditional terminology. Nevertheless,
whether implicitly or explicitly, each had to resolve the issue for his own
system. Finally, it should be noted that perception proved to be a critical
test of the old method of mental analysis. In fact, the whole question of
the validity of perceptual analysis became one of the central issues in the
disputes among the schools. But we will let the schools speak for themselves,
beginning with Titchener's structuralism, which, in many ways, represents
a culmination of the tradition of interpreting perception in terms of associationism.

Titchener and structuralism.[4]   Titchener, it will be recalled, developed
his system around the three elements of consciousness—sensations, images,
and affective states. In view of his elementalism, perception, as well as the
other higher mental processes, posed a critical test for structural psychology.
If the perceptual process could be resolved into a single element or a combination of elements by introspection, then the original elements were adequate to explain perception. If, on the other hand, perception proved to
be irreducible, a new element, "perception," would have to be granted
coequal status with the original three. However, Titchener found that his
elements were equal to the task of accounting for perception and announced
his position in his famous "core-context" theory.

Titchener begins his exposition of the theory by asking his readers to
assume with him that perception might be analyzed into sensations "without remainder." It would then have to be admitted that such a "mere
enumeration" of sensations would be inadequate to account for perception.
To begin with, the particular sensations involved in any perception form
a cluster or a special group of impressions, which are selected out of the
total possible complex of stimuli impinging upon the individual at any
given moment. This selective aspect of perception Titchener explains on
the basis of attention. The grouping, the clarity, and the focusing involved
in perception are reducible, therefore, to the determinants of attention.
But while this may account for selectivity, it still fails to render a complete
picture of perception. Common experience tells us that perceptions are
meaningful, and in attempting to explain meaning Titchener comes to grips
with the heart of the problem. Let us go directly to Titchener: "Perceptions
are selected groups of sensations, in which images are incorporated as an
integral part of the whole process. But that is not all: The essential thing

---

[4] The exposition of Titchener's position is taken from his *Textbook* (20).

about them still has to be named; and it is this,—that perceptions have meaning" (*20*, p. 367). In the next paragraph he goes on to define meaning as "context." In other words, one mental process is the meaning of another.

In essence, Titchener's core-context theory is this: Sensations are the core of perceptions, but images accrue to the core to lend meaning to the complex of sensations. In contemporary terms this could be further simplified to read that memory or past experience makes present experience meaningful.

In elaborating his theory, Titchener argues that meaning is originally a kinesthetic process. At first, the individual takes a bodily attitude when confronted with a situation. For example, a child who comes too close to a fire and burns himself will take the bodily attitude of withdrawal and at the same time will experience pain. Fire, then *means* withdrawal accompanied by pain in this concrete situation. In future experiences the original sensations of pain and muscular movement (which in the meantime have become memory images) are added to the perception of a fire with the result that the meaning of "pain," "burn," and "get away" instantly come to the child's consciousness. These memory images *are* the context which makes the child's present perception meaningful.

Titchener admits that verbal as well as concrete images play an equally important role in conveying meaning. However, he argues that words at first are only meaningful as kinesthetic attitudes in the form of gestures or other overt responses. But with the passage of time overt attitudes become abstract images. Thus, irrespective of whether the imagery is kinesthetic or verbal, the process is the same, namely, one of telescoping or abstracting. In fact, Titchener points out that the whole process can become so telescoped that meaning itself becomes unconscious, as is true in the auditory perception of a well-learned foreign language. Upon first becoming acquainted with the language, we consciously and laboriously "translate" what we hear, but as our facility with the language improves, meaning comes swiftly and without conscious effort.

To summarize, Titchener's core-context theory is subsumed under four cardinal points. First, sensations form a cluster or group according to the principles of the selectivity of attention. Second, the sensations are supplemented by images. Third, the context provided by the imagery which accrues to the sensory complex *is* meaning. Fourth, in well-established perceptual situations meaning may "lapse from consciousness" and instead be mediated by habitual nervous sets.

Titchener also deals with the more specialized problem of space perception. In general, he explains depth perception in terms of the physiological cues furnished by retinal disparity, accommodation, and convergence, and by the secondary cues of linear and aerial perspective, interposition, apparent magnitude, and so on. In all essential respects, the discussion closely parallels that in contemporary texts; hence, we need not go into the details of his account here. In this same connection, it might be noted that Titchener is a mixture of nativist and empiricist in the sense that he holds extensity or spatiality to be an inherent capability of mind. But at the same time he emphasizes the importance of learning or experience in depth perception. Titchener, therefore, was attempting a synthesis of the traditional empiricist-nativist controversy. However, he is most famous for the core-context theory of meaning and not for his attempted resolution of nativistic and empirical factors in depth perception. His highly characteristic treatment of the complex processes involved in perception bears testimony to the versatility of his elements and to his own ability as a systematizer.

Functionalism and perceptual psychology.[5]   Harvey Carr, who is our representative of the functional point of view, was interested in the area of perceptual psychology above and beyond the call of duty. Besides treating it at considerable length in his general text, he wrote an advanced textbook on the subject. Since functionalism emphasizes mental activities from the point of view of their adaptive significance, and because attention and selectivity as attributes of perception are crucial in adaptation to the environment, it is no surprise that a functionalist would show considerable interest in perception.

In his general text, from which we are drawing the functionalist account of perception, Carr begins with a definition—a definition which sets the tone of the two chapters which he devotes to the perceptual processes. To quote Carr: "Perception may be defined as the cognition of a present object *in relation to some act of adjustment*"[6] (*4*, p. 110). The characteristically functional part of the definition is, of course, the second half. Carr is making the definition of perception commensurate with his original definition of psychology as the study of mental activities which are "concerned with the acquisition, fixation, retention, organization, and evaluation of experiences, and their subsequent utilization in the guidance of conduct" (*4*, p. 1).

Carr further points out that any act of perception involves two stages. First, there is a preliminary phase of attention which ensures selectivity and clarity of incoming sense data. Second, perception involves an interpretive phase in which there is an arousal of meaning. Meaning, in turn, is dependent upon both past experience and present or contemplated conduct. In essence, then, perception is *selective;* it is *organized;* and it is *meaningful.* Let us consider each of these aspects in more detail from the functionalistic point of view.

---

[5] Our account follows Carr's *Psychology* (*4*) and his *Introduction to Space Perception* (*5*).
[6] Italics ours.

As has already been pointed out, attention for Carr is the process which ensures selectivity of perception. This is accomplished partly by suppression or inhibition of some stimuli and in part by the synthesis of other stimuli. Suppression or inhibition functions in eliminating irrelevant or distractive stimuli such as noise. By synthesis Carr means the whole complex of cooperative adjustments in the sense organs (such as turning the eyes for foveal fixation), and in the body in general (such as bending over when searching for a lost object). All such activities must be synthesized into an integrated whole for maximal effectiveness and efficiency of perception.

The organization of incoming sensory data depends upon past experience. The force of this process is best revealed in negative examples. When first experienced, picture puzzles and the sounds of an unfamiliar language are disorganized jumbles of visual and auditory sense data. Irrespective of how attentive the observer may be, until he has had sufficient experience with the stimuli in question, they remain disorganized and meaningless. When he is shown the hidden figure in the puzzle (or discovers it himself), or when he learns the language, the organizing effect of experience is so strong that the individual can no longer *stop* seeing the hidden figure or, in the case of the language, hearing meaningful words.

Meaning is also dependent on the arousal of previous experiences. However, associations from past experience need not be in the form of complete redintegrations of experience in order for meaning to occur. In many cases a partial or indirect reactivation of associations is sufficient to arouse meaning. Precisely how complete a reactivation of previous experience takes place for any given perception depends upon how well-practiced the associations in question are. Small segments of well-established associations need not be reactivated completely to carry meaning; the first few notes of "Yankee Doodle" are sufficient to redintegrate the perception of the entire piece. Finally, the nature of the whole perceptual complex is dependent upon additional factors such as the environmental situation, the individual's purposes and activities at the moment of perception, and the sensory modality involved.

Although Carr did not elaborate upon the importance of "*O*" variables such as purposes or goal sets, he did include these factors as possible perceptual determinants. His recognition of such motivational influences is highly significant, for this marks the beginning of a trend which has become one of the central themes in contemporary psychology. This development will be brought out fully in the following chapter, but it should be noted here that the functionalists' broadening of perception to include purposes and goal sets proved to be a popular development. Psychologists were no longer willing to restrict the concept of perception to the narrow confines of space appreciation, but instead increasingly looked upon perception as a meeting ground for motivational, attitudinal, and personality variables.

Turning to Carr's analysis of space perception, we may begin by noting that his account follows the familiar empirical-associationistic tradition. He introduces the topic by arguing that space perception depends upon local signs. Consequently, the essential problem for the psychologist is to enumerate and describe these signs for each of the senses which mediate spatiality. In his general text, Carr confines his discussion to visual and auditory localization. Let us consider each of these modalities briefly.

In audition, the local signs for distance perception are *intensity* and *tonal complexity*. In other words, the nearer the sound, the more complex and intense it will be when it reaches the ear. Distant sounds, on the other hand, are weak and lacking in complexity by the time they reach the observer. Auditory localization is dependent upon differential binaural stimulation. In this case Carr emphasizes phase differences in sound waves as the chief binaural cues.[7]

In the section on visual space perception, the familiar local signs (or cues) of accommodation, convergence, interposition, and perspective are each discussed briefly. Carr's treatment of this topic is not different in any essential respect from Titchener's or from that to be found in other standard texts of 1900 to the 1930's. Apparently space perception had ceased to be a controversial issue. While this must not be interpreted to mean that psychologists of that period considered all the facts to be in, it does mean the main outlines were clear—the empiricists, for the time being at least, had won the day. The Gestalt movement had yet to be felt in its full force, and when it was, the old controversy had a rebirth.

Finally, Carr faces the question of how space perception is acquired and gives as his opinion that the weight of the evidence favors learning. He cites studies of individuals blind from birth who recover their sight in maturity as a result of surgical operations. In such cases the individual's visual space perception is poor, and cues for space must be interpreted in terms of the more familiar modalities of touch and hearing. In addition, he points to Stratton's classic experiment on the inversion of the retinal image.

Stratton wore a lens designed in such a way as to "turn things upside down" and reverse right and left. At first his movements were confused and uncoordinated. Objects seen on the right were heard on the left. Objects perceived to be below eye level were in reality above. In reaching for objects, Stratton had to employ a trial-and-error process of approximations. But after only three days his initial helplessness and confusion gave way to

---

[7] It is now believed that differences in time and intensity are of greater importance than phase differences (*18*).

unpremeditated, skilled movements in the new visual frame of reference. In fact, he became so familiar with his new visual world by the end of the experiment (eight days) that he felt the world was right side up. This must not be interpreted to mean that he *saw* things right side up. Rather, objects were felt, seen, and heard in a coordinated, logical relationship to each other. Carr, in his book on space perception, argues that Stratton's experiment, if it had been conducted on an infant from birth onward to adulthood, would have demonstrated that the subject as an adult would see the world as right side up. In other words, Carr concludes that objects have no spatial significance for the infant. Rather, the child *learns* up, down, right, left, and other spatial frames of reference as a result of his experience with objects in space. Despite the inversion of the retinal image, touch, kinesthesis, and vision are gradually coordinated so that what is *felt* in one position in space is also *seen* in that position.[8]

By way of summarizing Carr's position on perception, we need only reiterate the principle that perception is a form of mental activity in which the meaning of present situations, objects, and events is determined, in part, by past learning. But meaning is also related to a present or contemplated act of adjustment. The initial stage in perception is the attentive phase, characterized by receptor and bodily adjustments which make for selectivity of perception. Past experience provides organization and interpretation for the incoming stimuli. For Carr, then, perception is a highly functional or useful process in adaptation.

Behaviorism and perception. The student of systematic psychology will search in vain for the term "perception" throughout Watson's *Behavior: An Introduction to Comparative Psychology* or his *Psychology from the Standpoint of a Behaviorist.* However, the omission should not come as a complete surprise in the light of our previous discussion of his aims and methods. Despite his stand that concepts such as "meaning," "perception" and "images" are mentalistic and consequently unworthy of a scientific psychology, Watson had two possible avenues of approach to perception had he elected to use them. His verbal-report method and the Pavlovian technique of discriminative conditioning can both be adapted for behavioristic investigations of perception. For example, the contemporary psychologist who is interested in studying personality by means of projective techniques obtains a verbal report of the subject's reaction to ink blots, pictures, cartoons, or similar material. The subject's verbal productions are treated as raw data to be evaluated by the psychologist according to objective and preestablished criteria. Similarly, if an animal or human subject can learn to

---

[8] This experiment has been repeated several times both with human and animal subjects. The results are not in agreement. For a critical account of a number of such experiments see Munn (*15*, pp. 259–265).

discriminate between two stimuli, this may be taken as evidence that the subject is able to perceive the stimuli, or at least the difference between them.

While classical behaviorism did not exclude the possibility of the study of the perceptual processes, both Watson and those who followed in the behavioristic tradition were primarily interested in response, or "R" psychology. In effect, this has meant an emphasis on learning as opposed to perception among the proponents of the school. As is true of all generalizations, the foregoing is an oversimplification of the picture. Still, on the whole it represents the behavioristic attitude toward this area; and because of their preoccupation with other aspects of psychology, the behaviorists failed to make significant contributions in the field of perception. For this reason we shall pass on to the Gestalt school, which, by way of contrast, made its greatest contributions in the area of perceptual psychology.

Perception and Gestalt psychology.[9] There is general agreement among contemporary psychologists that the Gestalt school exerted a greater influence on the evolution of modern perceptual psychology than any other group. As we pointed out earlier in this chapter, the Gestalt movement developed out of Wertheimer's study of perceptual phenomena; and its leaders went on to devote a great deal of their research efforts to the field of perception. This must not be taken as an implication that Gestalt psychologists have failed to make significant contributions to other areas of psychology. Rather, it means the school's *most* significant and *characteristic* contributions were in the field of perception.

It will be recalled from our discussion of the aims and methods of Gestalt psychology in Chapter 2 that the starting point of the movement was Wertheimer's research with the phi phenomena, the results of which led him to challenge the existing tradition of elementalism which had dominated the thinking of the structuralists. In Chapter 2 we also brought out additional "protests" on the part of Wertheimer and his associates, Köhler and Koffka, which were directed against the established psychology of the day. We must now turn to the positive side of the Gestalt program. In this chapter we shall examine the basic, classical principles which the school offered in support of their systematic approach to perception, and in the following chapter we shall return to a discussion of contemporary developments in Gestalt psychology.

The fundamental law and *raison d'être* of Gestalt psychology is revealed by the school's name. *Gestalt* psychology is *form* psychology. According to its proponents, our perceptual experiences arise as *Gestalten* or *molar* con-

---

[9] For primary sources see Koffka (*13*) and Köhler (*14*). Good secondary accounts may be found in Heidbreder (*9*) and Woodworth (*24*).

figurations which are not mere aggregations of sensations but organized and meaningful wholes.

The "bundle hypothesis" is completely fallacious according to the Gestalt psychologists, since it treats complex perceptions as though they were nothing more than a bundle of simple sensations. Similarly, the meaning accruing to a complex percept cannot be treated as a "bundle" of simple meanings. The determinants of organization and meaning are related in turn to certain fundamental laws of Gestalten, the most important of which is *isomorphism*. The principle of isomorphism states that there is no one-to-one relationship between stimuli and percepts, but that the form of experience corresponds to the form or configuration of the stimulus pattern. Gestalten, then, are "true" representations of the physical world, but not photographic copies of it. They are not identical in size and shape. Just as a map is not a literal copy of the geographical terrain which it represents, so an experience is not a literal copy of the world out there. There are point for point correspondences, it is true, and each feature of the terrain is represented on the map. But there are also distortions. The map is only a fraction of the size of what it represents. Curves in the road map may be less sharp than in reality. Minor features may be omitted altogether. But, because the map is *iso* (identical in) *morphic* (form or shape), it can be used as a guide for travel. Similarly, mental or cognitive maps must "mirror" the form of the physical world or life would be chaos.

Isomorphism also frees psychology from treating the percept as nothing more than the collection of sensations from which it arises. Everyday experience is good Gestalt psychology in the sense that we see objects which are perceived as objects and not as aggregates of sensations. The perception of a table is the perception of a molar object, not a collection of color patches, intensities, spatial extents and the like. Moreover, it is important to recognize that this holds true even for the child who has not yet acquired the concept "table." Provided he is attending to the table at all, it is an object—an object which is perceived against a background.

Gestalt psychology looks upon the world as psychophysical. As we have seen, the world of experience is not the same as the physical world, and to emphasize the distinction, Gestalt psychologists are in the habit of referring to the *psychological field* to represent the perceiver's view of reality. In contrast the world of the physicist is referred to as the *physical situation*. By way of illustration see Figure 4-1, which shows an old perceptual illusion. No matter how long one looks at it, the lines appear to spiral in toward the center. The spiral effect is the observer's psychological field. However, if the observer starts at point *A* and follows the twisted line 360° he will arrive back at *A*. The spirals, it turns out, are all circles. This is the physical situation. While illusions provide dramatic and extreme illustrations of the absence of any one-to-one relationship between the situation and field, we

Fig. 4-1. The spiral illusion. For explanation see text. (From E. G. Boring, H. S. Lang-feld, and H. P. Weld, *Foundations of Psychology.* New York: John Wiley & Sons, Inc., 1948.)

need only go to everyday experience for hundreds of equally valid, if less obvious instances. Mother's valuable antique chair may be perceived as a piece of junk by her modern-minded daughter-in-law. Or consider the strikingly different reactions shown by people of different political persuasions as they listen to a politician during the heat of the campaign.

We are now in a position to consider certain subprinciples under the general law of isomorphism. These are the well-known Gestalt principles of perceptual organization. The laws have sometimes been called *laws of primitive organization* because they are presumed to describe inherent features of human perception. Put somewhat differently, the Gestalt psychologists argue that the child or the savage can experience meaningful, patterned perceptual fields on the basis of these principles.

The most fundamental of these principles of primitive organization is that of figure-ground. Figure-ground is the familiar principle which states that every perception is organized into a figure which stands out from a background. The figure not only stands out but also has well-defined contours, depth, and solidity. It must be emphasized, however, that these figural characteristics are not properties of the *physical* stimulus-object, but are characteristics of the psychological field. An object such as a block of ice has solidity, contours, depth, and other qualities in the physical sense, but if the object is not in the focus of attention it is part of ground and consequently lacks solidity, well-defined contours, and depth. If the observer turns his attention toward the block of ice it will then become the figure, taking on solidity, depth, and the like, and objects previously in the foreground of consciousness will become ground.

We do not mean to give the impression that the Gestalt principle of figure-ground is merely the equivalent of attention in other systems. It must be borne in mind that the traditional account of attention and perceptual meaning emphasized the role of experience as an explanatory concept. The Gestalt psychologists, on the other hand, emphasize figure-ground as a spontaneous and native organization which does not depend upon learning, but is an inevitable consequence of man's perceptual apparatus.

The Gestalt position on the fundamental nature of figure-ground perception was strengthened by experiments with animals which respond to test situations in such a way as to suggest that they are able to perceive a figure on a ground. In a test of the European jay's ability to respond to a figure-ground pattern, Hertz (*10*) arranged a number of inverted flower pots in a large ellipse, placing an additional "odd" pot outside the ellipse. On test trials the bird watched the experimenter put food under one of the pots and was then allowed to fly to the pattern and search for the reward. If the food was placed under the "figure" or odd pot, then the jay had no difficulty; if it had been placed under any of the "ground" pots in the circle, the bird became confused and experienced great difficulty in finding the correct pot.

The Gestalt position on isomorphism and figure-ground perception puts the school in the nativistic camp. However, contrary to a widespread misconception, the Gestalt psychologists did not take an extreme position in which the role of learning in perception is ignored. Rather, it is de-emphasized in favor of contemporaneous principles which emphasize immediate, spontaneous percepts and meanings. This position is further brought out by certain less fundamental but equally compelling organizing factors which can be readily illustrated by simple visual diagrams (see Figure 4-2).

More characteristically Gestalt is the principle of *Prägnanz,* which holds that percepts take the best form possible under the circumstances. They make, so to speak, good Gestalten. In Figure 4-2 (*d*), for example, the figure on the right is perceived as a square despite the fact that physically

Fig. 4-2(a). Proximity. The three birds on the left form a group while the two on the right form another group.

Fig. 4-2(b). Continuity. Both the straight line and the wavy line are seen as continuous despite the fact that each is broken by the other.

Fig. 4-2(c). Prägnanz. A vague, disjointed figure is perceived as "good" as circumstances will permit.

Fig. 4-2(d). Closure. In spite of gaps, the figure on the left is seen as an arrow and the figure on the right as a square.

it is four disjointed lines. The same figure also illustrates a corollary principle, that of *closure,* which is a special case of the law of *Prägnanz.* The gaps, so to speak, are "closed" by the perceiver. More generally, *Prägnanz* and closure operate in all sensory modalities to give the best definition, symmetry and form to perceptual figures.

Prägnanz and closure also occur in everyday life as organizing factors in complex experiences which may depend upon the simultaneous contribution of both present and past experiences. Sets, past experiences, present motivations, and other O factors are all determinants which influence the perceptual field. We shall consider these at length in the next chapter, but it is worth noting here that the Gestalt psychologists did not confine their perceptual principles to simple drawings. There is a tendency to form this impression because of the widespread use of simple visual illustrations in texts which deal with Gestalt principles.

Finally, among the fundamental laws[10] of the classical Gestalt school is the law of *transposition*. This principle states that because Gestalten are isomorphic to stimulus patterns they may undergo extensive changes without losing their identity. Thus, a tune transposed to another key remains the same tune even though the elements (notes) making up the melody are all different. In a classic and often verified experiment, Köhler trained apes and chicks to respond to the darker of two shades of gray for a food reward. Let us call the brighter stimulus "*A*" and the darker "*B*." After a number of repetitions, a new gray, "*C*," was introduced where "*C*" was darker than "*B*." The animal immediately responded to "*C*" even though this meant shifting from the shade which was so well practiced in previous trials.

Perception, then, is flexible; and, just as a map can be expanded, shrunk, or presented in different types of geographic projections and remain recognizable as the same map, so the elements of our perceptions may be changed—often markedly—and still yield the same perception. Naturally, there is a limit beyond which change in elements may not go without producing a complete transformation in the percept. The structuring of the elements may be changed markedly without destroying the Gestalt only so long as the *relative* spatial and temporal relationships are preserved.

The principles summarized in the preceding paragraphs are closely related to a broad and fundamental concept which runs through the whole of Gestalt psychology—that of *equilibrium*. The perceptual field and its underlying isomorphic field are dynamic wholes which, like a magnetic field of force, tend toward equilibrium. And, as is true of a magnetic field, when the psychological field is "disturbed" by the introduction of new forces, the whole undergoes a realignment of forces until equilibrium is once more established. In short, it is a fundamental property of percepts to tend toward stability and to remain as stable as conditions permit.

Though the Gestalt psychologists never emphasized adaptation to the environment as a systematic theme, their psychology is nonetheless func-

---

[10] There are literally hundreds of laws, principles, and corollaries in Gestalt source books if the various offshoots of the Gestalt school are included. We have included only the basic laws in our summary.

tionalistic in spirit, for, to the extent that the laws of Gestalten are valid, they make for stability and constancy in an ever-changing world. This is especially true of the principle of equilibrium, since, as the functionalists themselves frequently pointed out, the problem-solving organism by virtue of its motivation is in a state of disequilibrium. When it has surmounted the problem, the organism returns once more to a state of equilibrium.

We shall return to Gestalt psychology in the following chapter and again in the chapters on learning, where recent work on perception and learning will be summarized. Meanwhile, we shall conclude our discussion of Gestalt perceptual psychology with a brief evaluation of the school's contribution to psychology.

It is not an exaggeration to say that perceptual psychology was never the same once it had experienced the impact of the Gestalt movement. Such a generalization can, of course, be applied to the effect of *any* school or system in any area of psychology. But Gestalt psychology, like behaviorism, was a revolution which, as is true of all successful scientific revolutions, shook the very foundations of the traditions to which it was opposed. The school's challenge in the area of perception was so successful that the Gestalt principles of perceptual organization are now widely recognized as fundamental. But it is also true that classical Gestalt psychology left an equally strong impression on the overall orientation of psychologists to their subject matter. The theoretical correctness of the whole *vs.* part principle has been accepted as valid. In short, elementalism and molecularism had been successfully challenged as broad methodological points of view. This is not to say that there were no anticipations of the Gestalt holistic or molar approach. But no individual or group had protested with such force and so comprehensively. Moreover, it must be emphasized that the Gestalt psychologists made positive contributions as well as offering criticisms and protests. While it is not incumbent upon the critic to offer alternatives for what he considers unsound, it is to the Gestalt school's credit that it has gone far beyond mere criticism to become a positive influence on modern psychology.

Psychoanalysis and perception. It should come as no surprise to anyone with some knowledge of psychoanalysis that Freud showed no concern with perceptual psychology in the sense in which we have been using the concept throughout this chapter. Traditional psychology is a cognitive psychology, whereas Freudian psychology is a conative psychology. Freud emphasized drives, instincts, personality development, and unconscious processes; hence his system was a "low perception" theory. In general, we traditionally associate perceptual processes with conscious processes, but Freud considered the perceptual conscious relatively unimportant in comparison with preconscious and unconscious aspects of mental life. Man the rational became man the irrational, in Freudian psychology. As Frenkel-Brunswick (7, p. 357 f) puts it, there was a shift from "surface to depth" in Freud's account of the dynamics of human behavior. (See also Chapter 11 on motivation.)

However, it would be a serious mistake to dismiss the whole of the psychoanalytic movement as lacking in perceptual psychology. Starting with Alfred Adler, a one-time associate of Freud's in the early days of the psychoanalytic movement, a radically different view of human nature has been elaborated by those who dissented from Freud's teachings but who are nevertheless considered to belong within the psychoanalytic movement. This neo-Freudian school has (either directly or indirectly) put a great deal of emphasis on perceptual factors in both normal and abnormal patterns of psychological development. Such practitioners as Karen Horney (11), Harry Stack Sullivan (19) and Erich Fromm (8), who constituted the vanguard of the so-called neo-Freudians (or, as they are sometimes called, the "social psychoanalysts"), emphasize *goal perception* and *self-perception* in relation to the individual's life goals as basic factors in psychological development and adjustment to the environment.

It is beyond the scope of this book to present even a superficial summary of each of the many variants of psychoanalysis, since, with the exception of Sullivan, the leaders of the neo-Freudian movement have written prolifically in expounding and defending their particular views.[11] However, it is posible to summarize the general position of the neo-Freudians on the role of perception in development. Stemming from Adler's original conceptions of human personality, the group has put heavy emphasis on the individual's self-image. Adler called this individual conception of self the "guiding fiction." Others prominent in the movement have used different terms;[12] but the important point is that all are in agreement as to the basic importance of self-perception in shaping the developing personality. Individual physical limitations or a harsh environment during childhood may result in an unrealistic and distorted picture of the self. Goals, too, under these circumstances may become unrealistic or more and more fictional, with the result that the individual grows increasingly more alienated from the real self.

The task for the therapist is to make the patient aware of his distorted conception of the self and to point out how, as Adler put it, his whole "style of life" involves the creation and maintenance of neurotic symptoms as defenses. By means of his defenses the neurotic seeks to harmonize the real self with the fictionalized self. In essense, then, neo-Freudian therapy involves a Gestalt-like reorganization of self-perception in order to make

[11] See Munroe (16, Chapters 8–11).

[12] Horney, "idealized image"; Fromm, "striving for individuation"; Sullivan, "self-dynamism."

self-appraisal more realistic and to establish sound and harmonious inter-personal relations.

This must not be taken as an implication that successful psycho-therapy involves nothing more than a dramatic, insightful reorganization of personality which effects a total and permanent cure. Rather, as Horney (*11*) puts it, the neurotic, with the help of the therapist, must explore every ramification of his neurosis in order to understand his real feelings and desires and to resolve his inner conflicts which are the core of any neurosis.

The foregoing summary of the neo-Freudian point of view, while in no way pretending to do justice to the movement, does serve to bring out the fact that these theories are "high perception" systems in contrast to Freud's, which leaned so heavily on unconscious drives and dynamisms. It is both interesting and significant that therapeutic "schools" which em-phasize perception also give great weight to cultural and interpersonal factors in both normal and abnormal development.[13] We shall, however, have more to say about the motivational aspects of both Freudian and neo-Freudian systems in the chapter on motivation.

SUMMARY AND EVALUATION

An overview of the evolution of perceptual theory during the period covered in this chapter reveals that the field has undergone both intensive and extensive development from its first formulation in the writings of Reid. Nevertheless, the central theme of perceptual psychology has re-mained unchanged—to account for the meaning of human experiences. In the early stages of its development as a separate field the problem of perception was narrowly conceived, in the sense that most writers under-took the task of explaining the mechanisms of space perception. We have seen how the philosophers and psychologists of the prescientific period sought the answer to this question along two major lines, empiricism and nativism.

With the development of the academic schools, the field of perception broadened to include the study of cognitive factors such as sets, habits, and attitudes. However, this was only a hint or foretaste of the great expansion of perceptual psychology that was to occur in the contemporary period. In their stand on the nativistic-empiricistic controversy, most of the schools recognized the importance of *both* native and empirical factors, though each tended to place more emphasis on one set of variables than on the other. In our account of the academic schools, we have emphasized the contributions of the structuralists, because of their historically important

[13] See especially Sullivan (*19*).

core-context theory, and of the Gestalt psychologists for their unique re-formulation of the entire field of perceptual psychology. Finally, we touched on the place of perception in the psychoanalytic school in order to point out basic differences in emphasis between the Freudian and neo-Freudians. While Freud minimized perception, the neo-Freudians have made self-perception and interpersonal perceptions of central importance in the development of their theories.

REFERENCES

1. Boring, E. G. *A history of experimental psychology,* ed. 1. New York: Appleton, 1929.
2. Boring, E. G. *Sensation and perception in the history of experimental psychology.* New York: Appleton, 1942.
3. Brett, G. S. *History of psychology,* abridged ed. Peters, R. S. (ed.). London: George Allen & Unwin, 1953.
4. Carr, H. A. *Psychology, a study of mental activity.* New York: Longmans, Green, 1925.
5. Carr, H. A. *Introduction to space perception.* New York: Longmans, Green, 1935.
6. Durant, W. *The story of philosophy.* New York: Simon and Schuster, 1933.
7. Frenkel-Brunswick, E. Personality theory and perception. In Blake, Robert R., and G. V. Ramsey, *Perception. An approach to personality.* New York: Ronald, 1951.
8. Fromm, E. *Escape from freedom.* New York: Holt, Rinehart and Winston, 1941.
9. Heidbreder, E. *Seven psychologies.* New York: Appleton, 1933.
10. Hertz, M. *Zeitschrift für vergleichende physiologie.* Vol. 7, 1928. Summarized in considerable detail by Köhler (*14*).
11. Horney, K. *The neurotic personality of our time.* New York: Norton, 1937.
12. Keller, F. S. *The definition of psychology.* New York: Appleton, 1937.
13. Koffka, K. *Principles of Gestalt psychology.* New York: Harcourt, Brace, 1935.
14. Köhler, W. *Gestalt psychology.* New York: Liveright, 1929.
15. Munn, N. L. *The evolution and growth of human behavior.* Boston: Houghton Mifflin, 1955.
16. Munroe, R. L. *Schools of psychoanalytic thought.* New York: Dryden, 1955.
17. Murphy, G. *Historical introduction to modern psychology,* rev. ed. New York: Harcourt, Brace, 1949.
18. Stevens, S. S., and H. Davis. *Hearing.* New York: Wiley, 1938.
19. Sullivan, H. S. *The interpersonal theory of psychiatry.* New York: Norton, 1953.
20. Titchener, E. B. *A textbook of psychology.* New York: Macmillan, 1910.
21. Warren, H. C. *A history of the association psychology.* New York: Scribner, 1921.
22. Watson, J. B. *Psychology from the standpoint of a behaviorist.* Philadelphia: Lippincott, 1919.
23. Watson, J. B. *Behavior, an introduction to comparative psychology.* New York: Holt, 1914.
24. Woodworth, R. S. *Contemporary schools of psychology.* New York: Ronald, 1948.

5

Perception: Contemporary Trends

Kurt Koffka, the Gestalt psychologist, once observed that the basic problem of perceptual psychology was to answer the question: Why do things look as they do? Koffka did not, of course, intend to restrict perception to visual processes. Rather, he meant that, fundamentally, to perceive is to experience stimulation—to see, taste, feel, smell—to discriminate among stimuli, and to obtain meaning from our sensory experiences.

We have seen how classical perceptual psychology emphasized the problem of spatiality and the organization of stimuli into meaningful groupings. Following this tradition the schools maintained the traditionally close relationship between sensory and perceptual psychology. The answer to Koffka's question was sought entirely within the framework of the associationistic and empirical tradition except, of course, for the Gestalt group who favored a nativistic interpretation of perceptual processes.

But there were hints of dissatisfaction with the state of perceptual psychology from time to time by those who favored broadening its scope to include the study of how central determinants—motives, emotions, attitudes, and the like—influence our interpretations of raw sensory data. Perceptual experience, they pointed out, is only partly a function of stimulus conditions and the associations which they call up from memory to make them meaningful. But it was not until after World War II that the field of perception underwent a kind of revolution in which the traditional types of perceptual experimentation and theorizing were overshadowed by the search for central determinants. For some years afterwards the field was dominated by the investigation of the role of both relatively simple central determinants, such as mood and motives, and highly complex determinants, such as attitudes and personality traits.

151

Moreover, the old problems of analysis and synthesis underwent reformulation. Analysis was carried farther and farther away from the sense organs and sensation to higher brain centers and to more complex mental processes. Half a century after William James had pointed out that part of what we perceive comes out of our own head, the postwar psychologists were arguing that meaning, which is the end product of perception, does not derive from experience but is largely brought to it by the observer. Things, therefore, are not what they seem. Our perceptions of the world and the people in it are determined by attitudinal, emotional, motivational, and evaluational factors as surely as they are determined by stimuli from the world out there.

Yet, despite these revolutionary developments, perceptual psychology retains its linkage with history, and it is still possible to discern the evolutionary sources and foundations of contemporary theory in the past. Following our customary procedure we wish first to examine recent developments within the familiar framework of the Gestalt, behavioristic, and functionalistic points of view. Then, we shall proceed to the more revolutionary directive state theories and other current developments of interest within the field.

CONTEMPORARY GESTALT THEORY

Our summary of Gestalt theory in the preceding chapter covered the fundamental laws of Gestalten. By employing these principles the Gestalt psychologists attempted to account for the organized and meaningful nature of the perceptual processes. But taken only to this point the theory is incomplete. First, there remains the problem of relating perceptual phenomena to underlying cortical processes in accordance with the principle of isomorphism. Isomorphism, it will be recalled, is the Gestalt psychologist's answer to the traditional mind-body issue in which he seeks to link the neurological and psychological fields. Secondly, there is the problem of relating perceptual processes to memory. The Gestalt psychologist, true to his molar orientation, refuses to erect fences between psychological processes and, in the best traditions of the school, has sought the laws of interrelation among the various mental processes. We shall address ourselves to the latter problem first, then return to the question of isomorphism and brain fields.

The memory trace.   When we perceive an event and subsequently recall our experience after an interval of time, we may infer that the original perception left a "trace" in the cerebral cortex. For the time being it is not necessary to undertake a neurological explanation of such traces. This we shall consider more fully later. For the present we may think of memory traces as *some kind of physiological modification* of the brain, probably at the neuronal level. Thus far, our analysis is not peculiar to the Gestalt school but represents a general point of view held by most psychologists. Indeed, some such hypothesis is demanded by common sense, since it is difficult to understand how memory could function in the absence of some kind of structural modification in the brain. However, at this point we part company with tradition, since the naïve or commonsense view of memory goes on to explain forgetting as a gradual fading of traces with the passage of time. Such a "disuse" theory in a somewhat more sophisticated form also gained support in scientific circles (see Chapter 9).

The Gestalt psychologists, on the other hand, reject any such passive, decay-like theory of retention. Indeed, just the opposite view is taken, namely, that memory is an active or dynamic process where *traces undergo progressive changes according to the same principles of organization which govern original perceptions.* Imperfect or vague traces tend to become better Gestalten just as incomplete perceptual stimuli tend to be perceived as "good" figures. On more complex levels, poorly organized clusters of traces become better organized to form stronger "cognitive structures."[1] Moreover, memory constellations may become enmeshed with subsequent experiences—a process which associationistically oriented learning theorists call retroactive inhibition[2]—or even with attitudinal or emotional processes, with the result that considerable reorganization of the original percept may take place over a period of time.

The basic experiment which illustrates the nature of changes in mnemonic traces was carried out by Wulf (*77*). In his investigation, Wulf used simple geometric figures of irregular shapes which were shown to his subjects for five seconds. The subjects were subsequently requested to draw the figures from memory at intervals of thirty seconds, twenty-four hours, and one week. Wulf's findings are summarized under the principles of "sharpening," "leveling," and "normalization." In cases where the original figure was "weak" the subject tended to "sharpen" it into a better figure. Conversely, an overly sharp figure would undergo "leveling" in memory. In summary, the general tendency was to "normalize" figures.

Wulf's original experiment has been repeated with varying results. On the positive side Gibson (*27*) found that when subjects were presented simple visual forms and asked to recall them some time later there were, indeed, distortions. Similar results were found by Bartlett (*6*) who obtained successive reproductions of figures by different subjects in the same manner in which rumors are transmitted. Figure 5-1 shows samples of Gibson's and Bartlett's results. Similar results were obtained by Bartlett (*6*) and by All-

---

[1] We are borrowing the term "structure" as an "intervening variable" from Krech and Crutchfield (*48*).
[2] See Chapter 9.

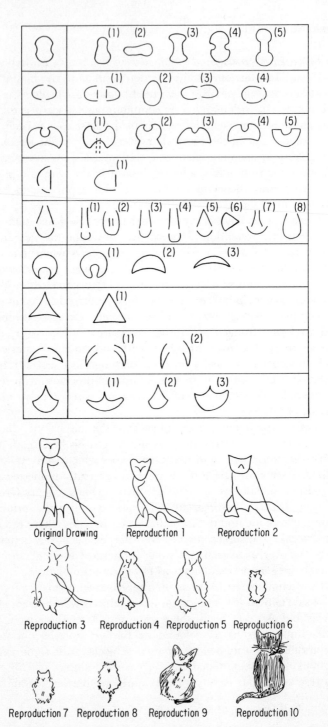

Fig. 5-1. Showing changes in the reproduction of visual forms. (After Gibson, *27*, and Bartlett, *6*.)

port and Postman (2) with verbal materials. Stories or "rumors" were related to subjects and then recalled after varying periods of time. Considerable distortion was evident, and the results tend to support the Gestalt position.

However, as Carmichael, Hogan, and Walter (16) have shown, some of the obtained distortion may come from assumptions made about the figures at the time of perception. As Figure 5-2 demonstrates, if perceptual forms are given a label, the subsequent reproductions are assimilated into the suggested form. It is quite possible that at least some subjects label inspection figures even though not explicitly instructed to do so.

Another difficulty lies in the fact that in testing subjects' memories the method employed—whether recognition or reproduction—makes a great deal of difference in the results obtained. For example, Rock and Engelstein (59) required some subjects to recognize visual inspection figures and others to reproduce them, each subject being tested after only one interval following the original exposure. In the recognition tests the subjects showed little or no decline in accuracy up to a month, while those who attempted to reproduce the figures showed a marked decline.

Critics have also pointed out that in experiments which involve repeated tests of memory, each test represents not only an assessment of memory but in effect a kind of practice period which reinforces errors and distortions. Clearly, in the face of these and other criticisms, considerable additional research will be needed before the issues of methodology and theory can be resolved.

Isomorphism and the brain.   We may now return to the second part of the Gestalt program—the problem of cortical mechanisms in perception. After having established phenomenologically that percepts are organized wholes and that the dynamics of remembered percepts are the same as the dynamics of perceived Gestalten, the Gestalt psychologists turned to the task of formulating a theory of the neurological correlates of perceived Gestalten. Here they were attempting to substantiate the general hypothesis that cortical fields behave according to Gestalt-like principles. It will be recalled from our previous discussion (Chapter 4), that in order to clarify their position the Gestalt psychologists contrasted isomorphism with the "machine" (43) view of the nervous system. The latter is a more or less "static" conception of cortical processes which likens nervous activity to the workings of a machine incapable of organizing or modifying what is fed into it. Thus, a "memory machine" or computer would faithfully reproduce a percept without sharpening, leveling, or normalization according to the laws of perceived Gestalten. Moreover, a machine view, according to the Gestalt psychologists, implies a one-to-one correspondence in size, form, and configuration between the percept and its cortical counterpart. Carried to its

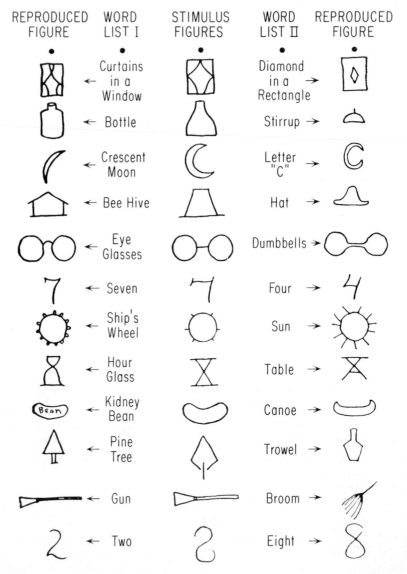

REPRODUCED FIGURE	WORD LIST I	STIMULUS FIGURES	WORD LIST II	REPRODUCED FIGURE
	Curtains in a Window ←		→ Diamond in a Rectangle	
	← Bottle		Stirrup →	
	← Crescent Moon		Letter "C" →	
	← Bee Hive		Hat →	
	← Eye Glasses		Dumbbells →	
	← Seven		Four →	
	← Ship's Wheel		Sun →	
	← Hour Glass		Table →	
	← Kidney Bean		Canoe →	
	← Pine Tree		Trowel →	
	← Gun		Broom →	
	← Two		Eight →	

Fig. 5-2. A figure showing the influence of verbal labels on memory for visual forms. The stimulus figures are shown in the center; the reproductions as a function of attached labels are shown to the right and left of the stimulus figures. (From Carmichael, Hogan, and Walter, *16*.)

logical extreme, such a view would postulate an exact cortical "picture" which would correspond to the physical stimulus configuration in every perception. Specifically, if one were looking at a cross, the cortical neurons in the visual area would be activated in the form of a cross with a one-to-one correspondence between the retinal image and the cortex, and with a similar correspondence of retinal image and stimulus figure. It was in opposition to any such literal mirroring of percept and cortical field that isomorphic brain fields were postulated to relate percepts to their neurological foundations.

For many years Wolfgang Köhler, one of the original founders of Gestalt psychology, has conducted a research program designed to investigate various facets of the Gestalt conception of isomorphism and cortical brain fields. In formulating his hypotheses Köhler has taken as a point of departure the concept that cortical processes behave in a manner which is analogous to fields of electrical force. Perhaps the simplest illustration is the behavior of an electromagnetic field of force around a magnet (see Figure 5-3).

In undisturbed magnetic fields the lines of force are in equilibrium; if a disturbance is introduced, the field will be temporarily thrown into a state of disequilibrium. However, a rapid realignment of the lines of force will occur and equilibrium will be reestablished. It is also important to recognize that such a field is a continuum, and whatever affects one part of the field affects all parts to some degree.

As applied to the cerebral cortex, Köhler (44) suggests that electromechanical processes in the brain may establish fields of neuronal activity in response to sensory impulses coming in over afferent neurons. For example, if one fixates a simple figure-ground stimulus, such as a white cross on a background of uniform gray, electrochemical events in the visual area of the occipital cortex will be activated which are isomorphic to the stimulus pattern. The cross would be represented by rather strong electromotive forces

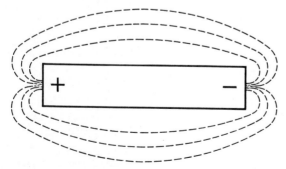

Fig. 5-3. A magnetic field of force.

in the cortex shading off from the boundary outward. In effect, then, a neurological figure-ground would be set up in the cortex because of the potential differences existing between adjacent areas of tissue. The cortical figure-ground would in turn correspond isomorphically to the phenomenally observed figure and ground.

Now, the only *direct* proof of such a theory would have to be nothing short of an examination of the living brain with oscilloscopes sensitive enough to demonstrate such effects if they do indeed occur. To date there is no feasible way of carrying out this experiment; consequently, the appeal must be to indirect methods.

The nearest thing to a direct demonstration of cortical fields is Köhler and Held's (*46*) electroencephalographic studies in which potential differences in the visual cortex were shown to occur as a test object was moved across the subject's visual field. To some extent the expected configuration was found, but unfortunately the electroencephalogram can measure only relatively gross and complex electrical signs of cortical activity as they appear on the surface of the head, and is therefore unable to trace the outline of a "cortical" figure-ground if such, in fact, exists.

However, Köhler and Wallach (*47*) have also approached the problem from the phenomenological side. Their logic in brief is this: if it can be shown that the brain behaves *as if* it were developing cortical fields isomorphic to test patterns, then it has been demonstrated that such a theory is at least plausible and consistent with perceptual phenomena. Such demonstrations have been made in terms of *satiation* phenomena, especially interesting aspects of which are *figural after-effects* first studied by J. J. Gibson in 1933 (*28*).

Köhler further proposes that if the visual cortex does develop electrical fields isomorphic with stimulus configurations, then such fields in the cortex should undergo changes if kept active for long periods of time. This effect can, in fact, be shown in isolated neurons in which various electrotonic changes can be demonstrated to occur with prolonged stimulation (*24*, p. 69f.). Going back to the perceptual side, let us suppose a figure is fixated for a much longer period of time than is normally true in the course of our rapid everyday glances at objects around us. Will changes in the appearance of such figures occur which are explicable in terms of cortical processes? That this is the case Köhler and Wallach believe to be true of figural after-effects. The reader may demonstrate for himself the phenomenon of figural after-effects by following the directions given under Figure 5-4.

In relating such after-effects to cortical events, Köhler and Wallach propose that the cortical area stimulated by the black squares becomes "satiated," and, as a consequence, the white squares are distorted away from the area of original stimulation. Or, in physiological terms, the part of the cerebral cortex which is polarized becomes satiated with direct currents as

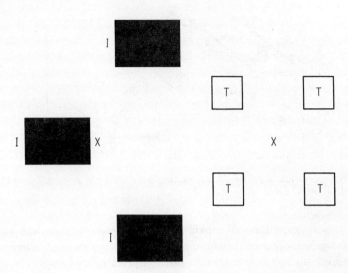

Fig. 5-4. A demonstration of the figural after-effect (after Köhler and Wallach 29). Fixate the X in the inspection figure for 35 to 40 seconds. Shift the fixation directly across to the X in the test figure. The left-hand squares of the test figure will be seen to be spread apart while the right-hand squares will appear closer together. Since the black rectangle in the extreme left of the inspection figure falls between the left-hand test squares when the gaze is shifted, the test squares "move away" from the satiated area. Similarly, when the gaze is shifted, the two black rectangles on the right-hand side of the inspection figure fall outside the test squares on the extreme right and "squeeze" them together. It may be necessary to repeat the experiment if it does not work the first time.

a result of prolonged stimulation from the visual receptors as the inspection figure is fixated. Increasing resistance develops in such areas; and when new stimulation arrives at the cortex as a result of examining the test figure, the resulting cortical currents will flow away into less satiated areas of lower resistance. A similar explanation is utilized in accounting for the reversible figures (see Figure 5-5). When the visual cortex becomes satiated the figure "escapes" by changing both phenomenally and cortically.

Other equally striking demonstrations have shown that fixation of curved lines will make a subsequently observed straight line appear curved. Angles can be made to change and even illusions may disappear (45) because of such satiation effects. These findings have been extended to other sensory modes. Spitz (67) has recently reviewed the research in this area.

Not all psychologists have been willing to accept figural after-effects as convincing demonstrations of the reality of isomorphic processes in the cortex. This critical literature is too extensive to review here. The interested reader is referred to Allport (1) and Spitz (67). As is usual in cases of conflicting opinion in regard to the validity of research findings, only time and

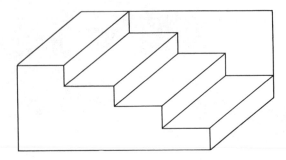

Fig. 5-5. The reversible staircase. Fixate on the figure for a few moments, and the staircase will be seen "upside down."

further experimentation will provide the final answer. Meanwhile, we shall leave these developments in neo-Gestalt research on the neurology of perception and turn our attention to other aspects of contemporary Gestalt psychology which are related to perceptual theory.

Gestalt theory and social psychology.   About the time that Wertheimer, Köhler, and Koffka were launching the Gestalt program in Berlin, a young German psychologist, Kurt Lewin (1890 to 1947), began a line of work that has since come to be known as "field theory." Because it is closely related to the mainstream of Gestalt psychology, Lewin's system is often treated as part of the Gestalt movement. On the other hand, it is sufficiently autonomous to be considered an independent system. We have chosen the former course. However, because field theory took motivation as its point of departure, our examination of Lewin's system will be deferred to Chapter 11, which deals with motivational concepts. We are introducing the system here because of Lewin's strong interest in social psychology and because he was the first Gestalt-oriented psychologist to attempt to extend this viewpoint into social psychology.

A contemporary movement directly related to Lewin's field theory and to social psychology in general is *group dynamics*. The name "group dynamics" covers an ever-widening field in psychology which is concerned with such seemingly unrelated areas as psychotherapy, industrial relations, small-group research, and communication problems. As early as 1923, J. L. Moreno became interested in the dynamics of small groups and developed a special technique known as *sociometry* for analyzing group processes. (Moreno is also well known for his therapeutic technique of the psychodrama.) Sociometry is essentially a type of group analysis based on the study of functional contacts and interactions between various members of a group. It enables the investigator to discover powerful, popular, isolated, and other types of individual members.

Meanwhile, other group dynamicists have devoted considerable effort to the study of role playing in committee work, industrial relations, and education. For example, a foreman by playing a role (in this case a worker's) can better perceive his own relationship to the group under his jurisdiction. According to its proponents, the technique is especially valuable for obtaining insight into another's needs and point of view.

Finally, we shall mention briefly E. C. Tolman's interesting attempt to wed Gestalt theory with the behavioristic point of view. The best exposition of Tolman's position is his book *Purposive Behavior in Men and Animals*. A good summary of the theory is available in Hilgard (*36*). Since Tolman's system leans heavily on the learning process we shall consider it in detail in Chapter 7, which deals with recent trends in this area of psychology. However, it is worth noting here that despite its emphasis on behavioristic studies of learning, it is a *cognitive* theory of *how* learning occurs. This cognitive approach again emphasizes the perceptual orientation of Gestalt psychology even when dealing with behavioral processes.

With these brief hints of the divergent areas in which contemporary psychologists are seeking to extend classical Gestalt theory, we must leave this productive school. We shall meet with the Gestalt viewpoint again when we discuss learning, thinking, and motivation, since Gestalt psychologists have traditionally interested themselves in these processes. Meanwhile, we must turn our attention to developments which fall within the behavioristic frame of reference. We shall find the transition not at all difficult, since we have chosen the neurologically-oriented theory of D. O. Hebb to represent the behavioristic approach to contemporary perceptual theory. We shall find Hebb's treatment of perception paralleling Gestalt theory in many ways.

A CONTEMPORARY BEHAVIORISTIC MODEL OF PERCEPTION

Hebb, while agreeing with Gestalt psychologists that wholes in perception possess characteristics which transcend the parts, believes that the Gestalt school has overemphasized the completeness of perceptual organization. Even more significantly, Hebb denies that the Gestalt assumption of organized brain fields can account for perceptual organization on the neurological level. Instead, it is a fundamental postulate of Hebb's that perception is largely learned. Thus, he associates himself with the empirical tradition—especially the associationist arm of that tradition. Moreover, in the construction of his neurological model of perceptual processes, Hebb relies on essentially associationistic principles, and in doing so further alienates himself from the Gestalt point of view.

Hebb makes it clear, however, that he is also in opposition to any explanation in terms of point-for-point cortical connections or pathways to which perceptual experiences are assumed to be related. In this he is in agreement with Gestalt theory, which also found the "telephone exchange" view of cortical processes totally unacceptable. In fact, Hebb's perceptual theory is somewhat difficult to classify. He accepts the validity of the Gestalt notion of figure-ground perception as inherent and is equally in agreement with Gestalt opposition to a cortex that is merely a telephone exchange. On the other hand, he denies the validity of the Gestalt field theory of cortical activity and insists instead on specific localization of function at *some* place in the cortex at *some* stage of perceptual learning. While Hebb in no sense calls himself a behaviorist, his theory draws heavily on behavioristic principles and is certainly in the associationistic-empirical tradition of favoring learning as the basis of perception. This is our justification for classifying the theory as behavioristic despite a certain degree of eclecticism in his overall orientation.[3] Our discussion of Hebb's perceptual system is drawn from his *Organization of Behavior* (*32*).

The most fundamental postulate in Hebb's entire theory is the concept of a "cell assembly." A cell assembly is a group of cortical neurons which bear a functional relationship to each other or, more simply, are circuits in the cerebral cortex made up of interconnected neurons. Now the most interesting and challenging of Hebb's postulates is the further assumption *that such assemblies can be developed through practice.* Indeed the very foundation of Hebb's theory is the assumption that neurons can become functionally associated with each other through learning.[4] More specifically, he suggests that learned neuronal associations may come about through the development of synaptic knobs on neuronal endings which are in close proximity to active cell bodies or to the dendrites of other neurons (*32*, pp. 62–66).

Let us suppose, for example, that a sensory neuron leading into a primary area in the cortex gives rise to excitation in that area. The activity will also spread into adjacent "association" areas (see Figure 5-6). Now in the highly schematized situation represented in Figure 5-6, Neurons A, B, C, D, E, and F will be excited in turn. Let us further suppose that Neuron X, while lying in close proximity to the termination of Neuron C and the cell body of B, has insufficient synaptic knobs to be fired by C. With repeated activity in C, however, knobs may be developed analogous to the manner in which plants will develop new rootlets if "stimulated" by electrified rods which have been sunk in the ground. When such knobs have proliferated in sufficient numbers, X becomes active and in turn can fire B. When this becomes possible we have a functional cell assembly. Moreover, in this case we also have a *reverberatory circuit,* B-C-X-B, and so on, capable

[3] Hebb's own account of how his theory came into being is given in Koch (*42*, pp. 622–627).
[4] This notion is not new. See Morgan (*53*, pp. 518–525) for a discussion of neural basis of learning.

of maintaining activity for a period of time even though external excitation has died down.

This highly simplified scheme does not do justice to either Hebb or the cerebral cortex. To begin with, Hebb makes it clear that there are other possible ways of accounting for the development of functional connections. But whatever the precise mechanism, the main point is that the development of such assemblies is an essential hypothesis in Hebb's account of perceptual learning. We shall return to this problem shortly. It is also necessary to emphasize that no simple circuits consisting of a few neurons are really typical of cell assemblies. The reader must remember that the cortex has approximately 9,000,000,000 neurons and even the most limited cell assemblies involve thousands of neurons.

To continue Hebb's account of perception, we are asked to consider an extremely simple figure—a triangle. How do we come to perceive it as "a triangle"? Do we have some inherent sense of "triangularity" or do we learn it in one simple act of visual fixation? Hebb argues that either explanation is adequate. Indeed, he presents evidence to suggest that far from being a simple affair, the perceptual learning involved is extremely complex and depends on the development of a number of cell assemblies.

In order to simplify matters let us first deal with the evidence which suggests that the perception of a triangle and recognition of it as such is a complex process. In support of this contention Hebb cites the work of Senden, who collected records on individuals who had been blind from birth and whose vision was restored at maturity by surgical operations. Such

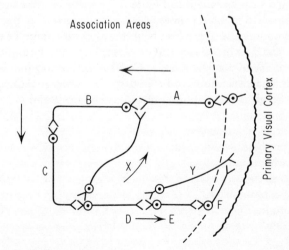

Fig. 5-6. Diagram of a cell assembly and reverberatory circuit in the visual area of the cerebral cortex. For explanation see text.

people were found to have extreme difficulty in distinguishing simple geometric figures from each other, such as triangles and squares. Even more
incredible, such patients have difficulty learning to associate the concept
"triangle" with visually presented triangles—this in spite of the fact that
they do recognize solid triangular figures by touch. When at last they do
learn the name for a visual figure which has been presented many times,
they still fail to recognize it if it is presented in a slightly altered form.

Similar results are reported by Hebb for animals reared in darkness
until they are sufficiently mature to be tested on visual discrimination problems. He cites Riesen's research with chimpanzees and his own work with
rats. In each case Hebb finds the experimental evidence from animals in
line with clinical evidence on human subjects; that is, such animals have
great difficulty with problems which are readily solved by normal animals.

Hebb goes on to suggest that the normal human baby must go through
a similar stage of gradual learning in the development of his perceptual
processes. In other words, as children it was necessary for all of us to have
many experiences with triangles before we grasped the concept "triangularity." It is not a simple concept acquired in one experience and easily transferred to similar situations. Rather, it involves first the growth of cell
assemblies to act as mnemonic traces for *parts* of the original triangle and
then the establishment of what Hebb calls "phase sequences" to mediate
the *total* experience of a triangle. The former, it will be recalled, are functional cortical circuits developed through learning. The latter are essentially
assemblies of cell assemblies. By way of illustrating and relating cell assemblies
and phase sequences, let us return to the perception of a triangle.

A triangle such as shown in Figure 5-7 consists of three angles, a hori-
zontal line, and two oblique lines. As a subject examines the triangle he
might fixate on angle A. This results in a sensory discharge in the subject's
occipital cortex which, in turn, at least initiates the formation of a cell
assembly designated by Hebb as a. Our subject, as people normally do,
tends to shift his fixation to C and B in turn. The order makes no difference,
but the end result is the initiation of cell assemblies c and b.

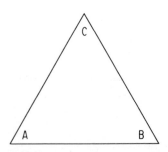

Fig. 5-7. A triangle to illustrate Hebb's theory. For explanation see text.

Moreover, as the eyes move around the lines from angle to angle, assemblies will be initiated as a result of stimuli activating the retina from the lines of the three sides of the triangles. Because of their contiguity in space and time, and further because they are linked by eye movements, the motor processes involved in scanning a triangle aid in facilitating the formation of a *phase sequence* made up of the six separate cell assemblies involved in cortical responses to the three angles and the three sides. With repeated fixations of the triangle, the cell assemblies initiated in early trials become well established. Hebb believes this process is aided by reverberatory circuits which maintain neuronal activity even though external stimulation has stopped.

To make a long story short, the end result is a complex of the separate cell assemblies in the form of a "phase sequence." The acquisition of a functional phase sequence means that the subject has added a new unitary perception "t" (triangle) to his repertoire of perceptual concepts. Through further facilitation, activiation of any part of the sequence will activate the entire sequence. For example, a figure such as

△

immediately gives a sense of "triangularity" by activating the appropriate phase sequence even though the figure is not a complete triangle.

Similarly, transfer will occur whenever test figures closely resemble the original figure and consequently can excite the appropriate phase sequence. Hebb believes this explanation holds for a rat's ability to respond to a variety of "equivalent" stimuli in a discrimination experiment, provided the new stimuli are not too dissimilar to the original. Returning to human learning, Hebb can also account for the well-known phenomenon of *generalization* in both learning and concept formation. For example, if little George acquires the concept "kitty" as a result of the formation of an elaborate phase sequence because of repeated visual stimulation by the family cat, it is easy to understand how he can mistake a skunk for "kitty." Needless to say, hard experience will establish a phase sequence in Georgie's cortex for "skunk" which differs in certain essential aspects from the "kitty" sequence. Finally, it is worth noting that Hebb's theory is able to explain the remarkable ability of an animal to continue to discriminate, say, a triangle from a circle, even though a large part of the animal's occipital cortex has been destroyed. Interpreted in Hebbian terms, this means that the phase sequence of cell assemblies in the cortex which mediate the discrimination are still sufficiently intact to allow the animal to remember the discrimination.

It is important to recognize that Hebb does not conceive of cell assemblies as dependent upon the activity of certain specific neurons each of which is vital to the assembly. Rather, as assemblies are formed, their organization becomes highly complex as a result of the addition of new links in the neuronal change. For example, if neurons A, B, C, D, E, F, and X in Figure 5-6 represent an assembly, E could be destroyed and the assembly would still function through Y, which would serve as an alternate path. In this way Hebb avoids the "telephone exchange" conception of cortical activity where, if a "wire" (neuron) is cut, the whole circuit is out of order. At the same time he can utilize the concept of specific associations of patterns of neurons to explain the same cortical processes that the Gestalt psychologists interpret in terms of less specific concepts such as "cortical fields" or "gradients."

More recently, Hebb (*33*) has found evidence to support his theory that cell assemblies are to some degree autonomous processes capable of firing for at least brief periods independently of sensory excitation in observations made on stabilized retinal images. Stabilized retinal images can be produced by having a test object mounted on a contact lens which is applied directly to the eye. Such an arrangement stabilizes the image by rendering ineffective the normal fluctuations due to tremors of the extrinsic eye muscles.

The surprising result of such observations is that images do not disappear as a whole as a result of prolonged fixation, as might be predicted by Gestalt satiation theory, but instead show complex changes. Figure 5-8 shows some of the changes observed in test figures of varying degrees of

Fig. 5-8. Target figures (left) and observed forms of fragmentation of the target figures (right) showing the influence on the target figures of straight lines on the perception of a circle. (From Hebb, *33*.)

complexity. Hebb interprets these and similar results utilizing other test figures as evidence in favor of what he calls "semiautonomous" processes in perception. That is, perceptions of even simple figures must be regarded as more than simple S inputs followed by invariable R outputs. Instead, the cortical cells, through complexly interconnected assemblies, are capable of mediating at least partially autonomous changes in perception.

Following a five-chapter exposition of his perceptual model, Hebb devotes the rest of his *Organization of Behavior* to extensions of his theory into other psychological areas, such as motivation, emotion, and intelligence. This phase of Hebb's theory is beyond the scope of a chapter devoted to perception. The interested reader is referred to Hebb's book (*32*) for further details.

Learning and experience in perception: an extension of Hebb's theory. We pointed out in the first chapter that theory provides a framework upon which the results of experimental studies are organized. We have also seen how theories can stimulate research—indeed, this is perhaps their most important function. Hebb's theory is no exception. Because of its essentially empiricist position on perceptual development, it has generated a great deal of research on the effects of early experience on subsequent learning and perceptual development. If, as Hebb suggests, perceptions are mediated by cell assemblies and phase sequences which, in turn, are developed through experience, subjects who are placed in enriched environments in infancy ought to show an increased ability to learn subsequent perceptual discriminations, particularly if these involve certain elements that were present in early experience. Contrariwise, if subjects are kept in severely restricted environments, they should show decreased ability to learn perceptual discriminations, possibly suffering permanent retardation.

A large number of studies have been carried out employing both of these broad experimental designs. Indeed, the area has become so lively a research field that hundreds of papers have been published in the past decade. Extensive bibliographies are available in recent reviews (*25, 75*) and in a volume devoted to experimental and clinical analyses of isolation (*11*). R. H. Forgus in his recent book on perception (*23*) has included a chapter (Chapter 9) on the relationship of learning and experience on the development of perceptual processes. We cannot review so extensive a literature, but will attempt to summarize the general results from research on enriched and deprived environments citing typical experiments.

Forgays and Forgays (*21*) carried out an extensive early investigation of the effects of varied infant environments on adult behavior utilizing hooded rats as subjects. The animals were selected immediately after weaning and divided into several groups. All animals were maintained in the same *general* environment in a four-story structure which permitted some animals to be reared in a free environment—that is, an environment allowing a free run of one of the stories of the four-layered structure. Some of the free environment animals had "playthings" and some did not. Other groups of animals were reared in small mesh cages within the larger cages, and some of these had playthings and others did not. Further, some of the animals in the restricted cages were maintained in layers of the apparatus in which free environmental animals were present with and without playthings to test whether the opportunity to see a free environment and objects in it could significantly improve subsequent learning ability. Finally, some rats were maintained in restricted environments consisting of solid metal cages with small wire mesh doors.

When the animals were mature they were tested in the Hebb-Williams closed field test of rat intelligence. Figure 5-9 shows the type of equipment used in the study. The results were as follows. The free environment rats that had the playthings as part of their early experiences were significantly

Fig. 5-9. The equipment used in the study of the effects of early experience on subsequent learning in rats. (Photograph courtesy of Dr. Donald G. Forgays.)

better at solving problems than members of any other group. Moreover, the free environmental animals without playthings were better than all remaining groups who were restricted to some degree. The severely restricted group was the poorest of all on subsequent tests in the Hebb-Williams maze.

These results have been confirmed by a series of subsequent studies by Forgays and by other investigators (25, 26, 75). There is general agreement among these investigators that the effects of early enriched environments are not specific but general. That is to say, no evidence was found to support the hypothesis that giving animal subjects experience with specific perceptual forms such as triangles, circles and squares will enable them to perform better than controls on subsequent discrimination problems. For example, Gibson et al. (26) provided rats with exposure to a circle and an equilateral triangle. Subsequent discrimination tests involved an isosceles triangle and an ellipse. The experimental subjects were superior to control animals who had not enjoyed enriched experiences. However, because the experimental and test stimuli were different, the investigators concluded that the subjects' general learning ability rather than their specific ability was improved.

However, Forgus (22) reports evidence to show that under certain conditions it may be possible for animals to benefit from specific training. Rats reared with triangles and circles on the walls of their cages were subsequently found to be superior to control rats in tests of discrimination involving these same figures. These interesting results have not been confirmed by independent investigators at this writing.

Turning to the negative side of the question, what happens when subjects are reared in restricted environments? We have already shown that Forgays and Forgays found significant decrements in performance among restricted animal subjects. Moreover, the reader will recall the work of Senden and Reisen which was cited earlier in this chapter. In addition, there have been a number of experiments and clinical studies on sensory deprivation and isolation on human subjects (11). In general, experimental subjects are kept in isolation with their limbs encased in cylinders stuffed with cotton bats, or are kept in aquatic environments in diving equipment. All such subjects report their experiences as unpleasant. After sleeping excessively during the early part of the experiment, they become bored. They sing or talk to themselves. Some count, tap on the walls of their chambers or otherwise try to distract themselves. Some experience hallucinations, or dream-like scenes. Few subjects are willing to spend more than a few days in such environments even though they are being well paid for their participation (11, pp. 99-134). These results suggest that: (1) the brain needs stimulation from the environment in order to function normally; and (2) in the absence of normal environmental stimulation, the cortex generates its own stimulation, possibly as the result of the spontaneous operation of phase sequences.

These experiments involving enriched environments and sensory deprivation or isolation do not, of course, prove the existence of cell assemblies and phase sequences, but they do lend indirect support to the hypothesis that the neurological bases of our perceptions are learned, as Hebb proposes, and that the cortex is able to function autonomously at the level of self-generated perceptions in the absence of sensory stimulation. This again suggests the presence in the cortex of some kind of semiautonomous cellular process.

We need only add a final thought: this is, that in addition to providing a highly sophisticated associationistic model of perception, Hebb and his associates have revitalized the role of learning in perception. Possibly because of the dominance and novelty of Gestalt psychology, the systematic development of perceptual theories formulated on learning principles suffered a decline in recent times. These contributions restore learning to its ancient heritage in the psychology of perception.

CONTEMPORARY FUNCTIONALISM IN PERCEPTION

The shoulders of functionalism are broad enough to support a variety of viewpoints in any area of psychology including the field of perception. It will be recalled from our discussion of classical functionalism in Chapter 2 that this system favors the study of mental processes or behavior patterns as they are instrumental in functioning in man's adaptation to his environment. Because perception is inevitably involved in all adaptive behavior, *any* perceptual theory might logically be included under the category of functionalism. However, there is the danger of broadening a point of view to such an extent that it loses all meaning. We shall avoid the latter danger by selecting for detailed presentation the contemporary perceptual theory which, in our opinion, has been formulated in the original spirit of the functionalistic point of view. Specifically, we refer to "transactional functionalism," a system formulated by Ames and his associates at the Hanover Institute for Associated Research.[5] Following our discussion of transactional functionalism, we shall briefly summarize several other contemporary perceptual theories which are also functionalistic in their general orientation.

Ames and his associates have not only drawn heavily upon classical functionalism in erecting their theoretical structure, but also have devised some of the most remarkable perceptual experiments in the entire history of experimental psychology. The experiments themselves are highly functionalistic in design in the sense that the subject is put in the position of

[5] See primary sources (*3, 14, 15, 38, 39, 40* and *41*). See also Allport (*1*).

interacting with experimental setups so elaborate that they virtually constitute "environments." In short, the Ames group has wed theory to practice as closely as possible under the necessarily artificial conditions of the laboratory.

Let us begin with their best-known experimental demonstration, shown in Figure 5-10. It should be noted that the camera in taking the photograph was placed in the same position as a subject's eye in viewing the room. Clearly something is wrong. The boy appears to be taller than the adult, while the room *looks* normal. However, the room is far from the rectilinear room of everyday experience; instead, it was constructed with trapezoidal floors and walls (the right wall being smaller than the left), so as to *reproduce the retinal image of a room as seen by an observer standing in the left-hand corner of a normal room.* With this background information we can explain the distortions experienced by an observer or demonstrated in photographs. Our past

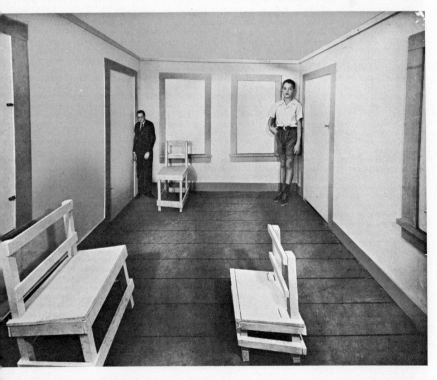

Fig. 5-10. Distorted perception induced by the Ames room. When the camera is placed in eye position so that the light rays from the right and left walls reflect equally on the film, the walls are perceived as equal in size. The people in the room are then distorted to conform to our past experience with "normal" rooms. (Photo by Eric Schaal. Courtesy LIFE, copyright 1950, Time, Inc.)

experiences with rooms tell us that when we are viewing a room from a corner angle, the room has equally high walls with a rectangular floor and ceiling *in spite of the fact that our retinal image is distorted*. Relating this to the Ames experiment, our experiences with past rooms at the moment of looking into the experimental room are all in favor of the room's being perceived as normal—so much so that the people in it are distorted.

By means of similar experimental setups, the Ames group has devised demonstrations where marbles appear to roll uphill, familiar objects are distorted in size and shape, jumbled patterns look like meaningful objects and a window which seems to be oscillating back and forth is, in reality, rotating 360°.

At first glance such experimental demonstrations seem to be in opposition to the functional point of view which holds that perception aids in the organism's adjustment to its environment. However, such illusory perceptions actually demonstrate the strength to which normal human beings develop perceptual constancies and interact with their environments on the basis of these constancies. This is entirely consistent with functionalism, for in dealing with rooms, it makes sense that we perceive them as rectangular in spite of distortions in our retinal image. After all, with the exception of "crazy houses" at carnivals and psychologists' experimental rooms, rooms *are* rectilinear. The exceptions in this case only serve to demonstrate the worth of the rule. If our perceptions changed with every change in viewing conditions, the world, as James once said, would truly be "one great blooming buzzing confusion." Or, as Stagner and Karwoski put it, "Illusions are the price we have to pay for this (constancy) mechanism" (*68*, p. 229).

The theoretical explanation employed by Ames and his associates to account for the results of the experiments just described is relatively straightforward. It is formulated in a system of concepts which are directly related to the philosophical antecedents of the classical school of functionalism championed by Dewey, Angell, and Carr discussed in Chapter 2. Going back one step, it will be recalled that the intellectual antecedent of Dewey, Angell, and Carr was William James, author of the philosophy of pragmatism. In essence, pragmatism holds that ideas which work in practice are true. To put it another way, the real test of the value of principles, concepts, or ideas is how well they actually work out in daily living. As James once said in his inimitable style, "Truth is the cash value of an idea."

Returning to functionalism in perception, it may be argued that our perceptions, especially the constancies which we develop through experience, are "pragmatic truths" in the sense that they work for us in practice. And in a very general way this principle is the bulwark of functionalistic perceptual theory. As Brunswik[6] has pointed out, our perceptions are never

---

[6] Brunswik is not a member of the Ames group. His "probabilistic functionalism" is very close to transactional functionalism, and we are making use of some of Brunswik's concepts in the present discussion.

completely valid representations of the physical world of objects, sizes, shapes, colors, and the like (*14*). On the other hand, neither do we "distort" objects to the extent of achieving perfect constancy. Our give-and-take relations with the environment are a compromise wherein things are perceived neither as demanded by the retinal image nor as perfectly constant. As Brunswik puts it, we come to establish "hypotheses" or "probabilities" which we unconsciously bring to perceptual situations.

Applying this argument to the distorted-room situation, we find that our assumptions about the rectangular character of a room are so strong that the probabilities are virtually certain that it will be seen in terms of perfect constancy. In more lifelike situations, however, constancies are not so perfect. Colors have a way of appearing different on our living room walls after we make a "perfect" match at the paint store. Similarly, near objects do look somewhat larger than distant objects, and if we go out of our way to choose odd or unusual viewing conditions, constancy is very poor indeed. Anyone who has looked from a tall building at people and cars in the street below will recall how small and ant-like they appear. Presumably a child reared in such a way that he experienced objects only from the vertical perspective of tall buildings would have trouble on street level. In either case the old hypotheses and probabilities about the perceptual world would not apply.

The theoretical assumptions underlying the preceding argument ought to be testable from a·frame of reference other than that of devising illusory demonstrations. Since the theory places a heavy burden on learning and experience, constancy ought to follow a developmental trend in children. That this is the case has been demonstrated (*69*, Chapter 6; *76*). Secondly, it ought to be possible to demonstrate that, through learning, a subject could overcome illusions or otherwise alter percepts. Again there is ample testimony to this effect, going back as far as Stratton's classic work on the inversion of the retinal image, and more recently in demonstrations that the perfect constancy of the Ames room can be overcome by subjects who are given an opportunity to interact with the room and thus *learn* its spatial characteristics.

To summarize, the transactional functionalists, true to their tradition, emphasize *learning* as basic to perception. In effect, they are empiricists rather than nativists in their thinking. In this sense they are in opposition to Gestalt theory, at least to the extent that Gestalt psychologists claim so much for inherent organizing factors, while tending to ignore the role of experience and the importance of interactions between stimuli and observer which occur in perception. In fact, the interactive nature of perceiving is so heavily emphasized in the Ames variety of functionalism that the theory is aptly called "transactional" functionalism. In other words, perception is developed out of the transactions of man with his environment.

To avoid misunderstanding it should be emphasized that transactional functionalists do not propose that in our interactions with environmental objects, distances and the like, we *consciously* say to ourselves, "My past experience tells me rooms are square; therefore this room must be square." On the contrary, the whole process is an unconscious and instantaneous *inference* rather than a conscious rationalization of the situation. Moreover, it would be wrong to give the impression that Ames and his associates are solely interested in looking backward to account for present perceptions. While this is a necessary part of their interpretation of the experimental work, they also emphasize that the "transactions" of the individual with his environment determine his future course of action. Thus, the theory attempts to be predictive in addition to accounting for present behavior. And in this respect the theory once again demonstrates a close relationship to its ancestral philosophy of pragmatism, for James once wrote, "Habit is the great flywheel of society." In terms of contemporary perception, James's statement can be taken to mean that constancies found expedient in the past become habitual and are carried into the future.

In concluding this brief survey of neofunctional perceptual theory, we should like to mention several related theories which are functionalistic in a broad sense. Already referred to earlier in this section is Brunswik's "probabilistic functionalism" (*14*), which, as was previously pointed out, is closely related to "transactional functionalism." A rather specialized perceptual theory which deals primarily with the quantitative estimates we continually make in our daily lives is Helson's "adaptation-level" theory (*34, 35*). Helson, in essence, argues that our experiences with magnitudes, distances, brightnesses, and the like, leave a residual "average" or "adaptation level" upon which future estimates are made. Here again we sense the functionalistic nature of the perception of everyday living.

Less obviously functionalistic is Gibson's (*29*) "gradient theory," which deals with the problem of depth perception. The theory relies heavily on the concept of "texture gradients" in accounting for depth in perception. Gibson points out that the closer portion of a surface directly in front of the observer (such as a wall) has homogeneous or uniform gradients. Gibson also attempts to show how lines, angles, and shadows produce patterns which enable the individual to perceive a three-dimensional world. The most significant aspect of Gibson's theory is his charge that spatial depth is *not* lost when projected on the retina, but that the order of stimulation of retinal processes by environmental stimulus gradients can convey a sense of depth without the necessity of assuming that learning is the key to the whole process. In other words, retinal gradients may correspond in an orderly way with physical gradients—more closely, indeed, than psychologists have traditionally assumed. Again, such an interactive approach which utilizes lifelike problems is functional.

Finally, Witkin's (*73, 74*) work with "tilted rooms" and "tilted chairs" and their influence on the individual's perception of test figures, while primarily directed toward the investigation of individual differences in perception, is nevertheless broadly functional in the sense that it utilizes subject-environmental interactions in research. We shall have more to say about this theory toward the end of the chapter when we deal with personality and perception. Meanwhile, we must leave functionalism with the hope that we have conveyed some impression of the vigor and variety of contemporary developments in this traditional approach to human nature.

CENTRAL DETERMINANTS IN PERCEPTUAL THEORY

As we pointed out in the introduction to the present chapter, one of the strongest trends in recent perceptual research has been to put the "O" back in the old S-R formula. Indeed, it might be said that the same perceptual determinants which the classical psychophysicists sought to eliminate from their experiments have become the experimental variables in a large segment of contemporary research. In the days of Weber and Fechner any psychologist would be considered a poor experimentalist who allowed the subject's attitudes, needs, values, or similar O factors to affect the experimental results. Today, experiments on the effect of such variables are in the forefront of research in the field of perception. This movement appeared so radical when it first got underway, after World War II, that it was dubbed "the new look" in psychology. By now it already has all the earmarks of tradition, so rapid has been the flow of events in the past quarter-century in contemporary psychology.

Speaking somewhat more technically, this movement is known as "directive state" theory (1) on the ground that the *direction* of perceptual experience is influenced by such O factors as sets, attitudes, values, needs, and similar intervening variables. In reality this conception of central determinants in perception is not new, for both literature and philosophy are full of allusions to inner "determinants" in perception.

Motives, needs, and sets as perceptual determinants. The general design of experiments falling under this category is as follows: The experimenter chooses some measurable verbal or motor reaction which is dependent on perception and establishes the subject's average level of response under "normal" conditions. Then, he induces a need, set, or motive in the subject and repeats the measurements. The difference in response is attributed to the influence of the induced determinant on the subject's perception. In this type of experimental design the subject serves as his own control. It is also possible to use equated groups, and measure the difference between the performance of the experimental group under the influence of the determinant and the control group which is not subjected to the experimental variable.

As examples of such experiments on *needs,* there have been several in which subjects are deprived of food until hungry and then tested for their tendency to perceive food-relevant objects in perceptual test fields. Even before the era of the "new look" in perception, Sanford[7] (*61, 62*) showed that hungry subjects completed word stems in such a way as to make more food-relevant words than did nonhungry subjects. For example, the word stem ME—was more likely to be completed as MEAT or MEAL by hungry subjects than by nonhungry. There have been a number of similar studies by subsequent investigators, the results of which have been in general agreement with Sanford's (see references *1, 50, 58,* and *63*).

Since sets are essentially temporary states of motivation which alert the subject to perceive or respond in accordance with the set, it might be predicted that such states would exert perceptual influences of the same type as just discussed in connection with needs. A study of Siipola (*64*) demonstrates that sets influence perception as expected. In the experiment the subjects were required to respond to words presented tachistoscopically at 0.10 second. The stimulus words were as follows:

1. horse	6. monkey
2. baggage	7. pasrort
3. chack	8. berth
4. sael	9. dack
5. wharl	10. pengion

One group of subjects were told they would be dealing with words having to do with *animals or birds,* while the other group were informed they would be responding to words in the category of *travel or transportation.* Since all "words" except Numbers 1, 2, 6, and 8 are ambiguous, the hypothesis was that the responses would be in keeping with the set. For example, the first group might perceive *sael* as "seal," *wharl* as "whale," and so on, while the second group might perceive the same words as "sail" and "wheel" respectively.

The results confirmed the hypothesis. Subjects in the first group perceived six times as many *animal-bird* words as did the subjects in the second group, who, incidentally, perceived five times as many *travel-transportation* words as the first.

Among more recent experiments in this general area, Schafer and Murphy's (*63*) on the perception of reversible figures will serve to illustrate how *motive* satisfaction influences perception. The experimenters devised drawings in such a way that either half of the drawing could be seen as

[7] Sanford's experiments were published in 1936 and 1937.

a face. The faces were then cut out so that either could be presented separately. A training series was then initiated in which members of one group of children were "rewarded" with small sums of money every time they were shown one face and "punished" by losing a few pennies every time they were shown the alternate face. The faces were then combined and presented tachistoscopically at exposure times short enough to prevent the perceptual alternation which usually occurs if ambiguous figures are fixated for relatively long intervals. A significant difference was found in the direction in which directive-state theory would predict, namely, the rewarded face was seen—the punished unnoticed.

To summarize, we have outlined three representative experiments in support of the position that *needs, sets,* and *motives* influence perception. This must not be taken to mean that there is a simple one-to-one relationship between perception and the intervening variables just mentioned. Indeed, we know from both animal and human experiments in the area of food selection that organisms do not always make beneficial choices when given an opportunity to do so (*78*). We may logically assume that such subjects do not "perceive" in accordance with their needs. In such cases habit or other factors may dominate needs and the subject's perception of the problem as well. Moreover, structural or stimulus factors are always present in perceptual situations and must not be ignored.[8] It is merely a matter of experimental convenience that psychologists "divide" people into separate mental processes. But it must be remembered that the individual as a whole is the unit of response in real-life situations.

Emotional states and moods as perceptual determinants. It does not require a parade of scientific findings to demonstrate that emotional states and moods tend to influence perception. Folk wisdom has recognized this relationship from time immemorial. The lover, we say, looks at the world through "rose-colored glasses." The child's happy optimism makes the world appear to be his oyster. While such generalizations may seem to have face validity, we must appeal to the experimental literature for the precise relationships involved.

Experiments designed to investigate the influence of moods and emotional states are relatively straightforward. The experimenter induces a mood or emotional state in the subject and then compares his responses in a perceptual test situation either to the subject's normal responses or to those of a matched control group not under the influence of an emotional state. Let us begin with an experiment on the effect of moods.

Leuba and Lucas (*49*) hypnotized three subjects and by means of

---

[8] See Postman and Crutchfield (*58*) for an experiment on the interaction of needs, sets and stimulus factors in perception.

suggestion induced three different moods in each subject: "happy," "critical," and "anxious." While in each mood, the subjects were presented with six pictures which they were asked to describe following a brief observation period. In general, the descriptions corresponded to the induced moods. The following example is from the experimental protocols presented by Leuba and Lucas.

The picture shown was that of a wounded man being carried on a litter by soldiers to an airplane. Subject A in a "happy attitude" gave the following description: "Wounded soldier. Good thing men were there to help him and get him to a hospital. The men in this war are well taken care of." When Subject A was put in a "critical attitude" this was his description of the same picture: "Wounded or killed soldier; one more in a million who are just killing each other off. That's war, I guess. We must think it's fun or we wouldn't do something so useless as murder and destruction." Finally, while in an "anxious attitude" the same subject described the picture in this fashion: "He is wounded and they're taking him to a plane but he's in bad shape and may not live even though the plane will rush him to a hospital."

When we turn to the closely related problem of emotional determinants in perception, we are entering one of the most challenging and controversial areas in the entire literature of perceptual research. More specifically, recent research suggests the possibility of subthreshold perception—perception below the conscious level but nonetheless sufficiently complete to result in emotional reactions, in delayed recognition of stimuli, and frequently in misperception of stimuli.

The literature on this problem goes back to a study by McGinnies (52) reported in 1949, in which subjects were presented with a list of words—eleven of which were neutral and seven of which had emotional connotations. Among the emotional words were the following: "raped," "whore," "penis," and "bitch"; and among the neutral, "apple," "child," "river," "music," and "sleep." Eight male and eight female college students were presented with the eighteen words in a scrambled order. The words were viewed by the subject in a tachistoscope which allowed McGinnies to expose the words for duration periods of 0.01 second upward. At the same time, a psychogalvanometer was connected to the subject to record emotional reactions, if any. The subjects were instructed that they would be shown words and were to judge what the word was, but not report until signaled to do so by the experimenter. In this way the subjects' psychogalvanic response could be noted *before* they reported. Thus, two measures were possible: the subjects' threshold, in seconds, for recognition; and the galvanic response for the trials preceding correct recognition. Presumably, if the emotional words resulted in high galvanic responses *before* they were correctly recognized on a conscious level, this would indicate prerecognition on an unconscious level. Finally, McGinnies was also able to make a qualitative study of the kinds of verbal responses made to the neutral as opposed to critical words. If there were more cases of misperceiving emotional words, especially in the direction of making them "harmless," this, too, would indicate the operation of an unconscious perceptual determinant. An example of such misrepresentation would be reporting "whose" for "whore" or distorting it into an entirely dissimilar word or even into a nonsense syllable.

In short, McGinnies found significant differences between the neutral and critical words along all three dimensions measured. Specifically, the thresholds for emotional words were higher, the PGR responses greater, and there were more distortions among the emotional words than the neutral words. He interpreted his findings as an anxiety-avoidance reaction in the form of a "perceptual defense" mechanism which protected the subjects from the unpleasant meanings of the critical words.

The critics were quick to charge that McGinnies had failed to control for several possible factors. Solomon and Howes (65) pointed out that the critical words appear less frequently in writing, speaking, and reading and on this basis alone might be harder to recognize, consequently generating mild emotional reactions which could be mistakenly interpreted as "perceptual defense." Aronfreed et al. (4) found that in cases where the subjects were females and the experimenter a male, the recognition threshold was longer and the emotional reaction greater for emotional words, thus demonstrating that embarrassment might be a factor. Moreover, it is possible that student subjects might simply be surprised that such words were utilized in an experiment and delay responding until they were certain of their recognition, with a consequent increase in recognition thresholds.

To obviate some of these difficulties McCleary and Lazarus (51) utilized nonsense syllables half of which were accompanied by shock in a pretest conditioning series. When the shocked syllables were subsequently presented with nonshocked syllables the emotional reactions were found to be higher for the crucial syllables. But again the critics have pointed to additional difficulties of interpretation and control. Bricker and Chapanis (9) argued that subliminal presentation of nonsense syllables does convey some information to the subject and that syllables which are more familiar to the shocked syllables result in an increased galvanic skin response. Murdock (54) utilizing nonsense syllables also demonstrated the possibility of partial recognition—a factor which other investigators had not taken into account in experiments involving all-or-none recognition thresholds. Finally, in any discussion of subception or perceptual defense, the work of C. W. Eriksen (17, 18, 19, and 20) ought to be mentioned. Eriksen has criticized the use of the Thorndike-Lorge word list as a source of materials for constructing balanced lists of equally familiar neutral and taboo words for perceptual defense experiments. He believes that the Thorndike-Lorge list is inadequate in respect to underestimating the frequency of the so-called taboo words in the language. Thus, experimenters using this list might not find evidence for perceptual defense simply because their taboo words were not, after all, taboo to the subjects. Eriksen has also pointed out that there may be statistical artifacts in subception experiments which have not been controlled adequately.

Obviously the issue of perceptual defense and subception remains unsettled. However, it may be that in the near future an entirely new interpretation will have to be put on studies involving perceptual defense. Recent work on encoding and storage of information in the eye shows that psychologists who utilize tachistoscopic presentation in experiments such as have been reported here will have to take into account information storage and erasure in the visual process. The reading in of bits of information into the visual processes is relatively fast, but short term storage in the visual mechanisms is only on the order of a quarter second. New information coming in "erases" the old. As yet the precise mechanisms of scanning, storage, erasure, and central decoding are not known. It is possible that with additional knowledge on these processes new interpretations of experimental findings on vigilance, subception, and perceptual defense will have to be offered.

By way of final comment, we would add that if "subception" and "perceptual defense" mechanisms become experimentally established beyond reasonable doubt, a most valuable and far-reaching technique will be available for exploring the dynamics of perception. Moreover, such techniques will also have challenging implications for psychotherapy and personality theory.[9] For further elaboration and a critical interpretation of this facet of directive-state theory the reader may consult Allport (1, pp. 319–337).

Attitudes and values as perceptual determinants. In dealing with such complex cognitive processes as attitudes or values, the experimenter must first screen his subjects by means of a test or socioeconomic survey in order to set up two groups which are widely divergent along some attitudinal or value dimension. Then he brings his experimental variable to bear in order to determine whether or not the preexisting intervening variables of value, attitude, and the like have a demonstrable effect on the subject's reaction. We shall present two experiments to illustrate the basic designs in this area, both of which gave positive results in support of directive-state theory. In fact, the first experiment by Bruner and Goodman (12) is something of a "classic" in directive-state perceptual theory.

[9] See Rogers (60) for a more extended discussion of the latter aspect of this possibility.

Bruner and Goodman selected two groups of ten-year-old children, one group from "rich homes" and one from "poor homes." The subjects' task was that of estimating the physical size of coins ranging from one to fifty cents. Estimations were made by the manipulation of a knob which in turn controlled a diaphragm regulating the size of a circular patch of light on a ground-glass screen. The actual sizes of the coins were the standards, and the averages of the subjects' light settings were compared to the standards in order to obtain a measure of the magnitude of under- or over-estimation. Essentially the technique was the old psychophysical method of average error. A control group made similar estimations using cardboard disks as the standard stimuli.

The "poor" children overestimated the size of every coin to a greater degree than the "rich" children, though all subjects tended to overestimate coins, especially the five-, ten-, and twenty-five-cent denominations. There is less overestimation, incidentally, when the coins are absent and estimations made from memory. Figure 5-11 shows the subjects' estimations in terms of deviations from physical size.

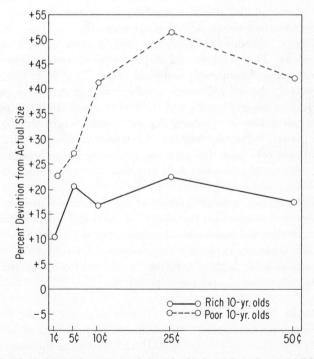

Fig. 5-11. The deviation in the perceived size of coins by rich and poor children. (From Bruner and Goodman, *12*.)

This experiment has been repeated with other value objects and with adults as well as with children. The results have not always been in agreement with Bruner and Goodman, but in general valued objects or objects which have acquired temporary value through experimental manipulation have been overestimated in respect to size. Objects with no value or with negative values induced by experimental manipulation have been underestimated. Thus, the directive state theorists have shown that the relation between size and value can be manipulated experimentally and may be mediated by motivational and culturally determined values.

Instead of using concrete objects or symbols which have values associated with them, it is possible to investigate the subject's more complex, general values by means of verbal tests. The Allport-Vernon Study of Values gives a comparative index of the following broad categories of values: "theoretical," "economic," "esthetic," "social," "political" and "religious." By plotting an individual's results on the test in the form of a psychogram, the psychologist can compare the relative strength of the testee's values to each other and to standard norms.

Postman, Bruner, and McGinnies (57) administered the test to twenty-five college students who were subsequently asked to identify words tachistoscopically. Some of the words related to the Allport-Vernon categories. The stimulus words were presented at durations from 0.01 second upward, and the subjects' thresholds were determined for both "valued" and "nonvalued" words. The prethreshold responses were also recorded by the experimenters and subsequently analyzed.

In general, the valued words required shorter exposure periods for recognition than neutral words, and there were fewer contrary (opposite in value area) or nonsense responses for the valued words during the prethreshold period.[10] Putting together the results of the two phases of the experiment, we find that the data are consistent with the directive-state theory of perceptual selectivity as a function of needs, values, personality traits, and the like—in this case values.

Psychologists are not yet certain of the mediating mechanisms that result in lowered recognition thresholds for need and value related words. But it is clear that the experimental results support the directive-state position that the organism is not a sponge which soaks up stimuli indiscriminately. Instead it is highly selective in its reactions depending upon underlying motivational and value processes.

Personality traits and perception.   The final aspect of the problem of central determinants in perception which we shall examine in this chapter is the research in the area of personality variables as influences on perception. The notion that the individual's perceptions are influenced by his

---

[10] Compare to the McGinnies experiment described earlier in this chapter.

personality characteristics is, of course, not new. Anyone familiar with the projective techniques knows that these are based on the hypothesis that responses to vague or unstructured stimuli are revealing of the individual's personality. Rorschach's Ink Blot Test and Murray's Thematic Apperception Test are the most familiar contemporary examples of this avenue of approach to the evaluation of personality. Binet, the originator of the intelligence test, made use of cloud pictures for similar purposes. However, in recent years the traditional clinical-psychometric approach has been complemented by experimental investigations which attempt to apply laboratory methods to the study of individual differences in perception.

Within this rapidly growing area of psychology, a body of theoretical and experimental literature has developed in recent years, so large that it defies any attempt to reduce it to a brief summary of the sort possible here. Within the past decade alone, several symposia have appeared on perception and personality (8, 13); and, in addition, an entire volume devoted to an experimental report of the relationships among certain space orientation tests and personality variables has been published (73). In addition to these reports, a new Rorschach method has been developed (56), and a number of investigations have been carried on in which the factor-analytic approach to personality traits was employed.

Because our aim in this volume is to relate theory and empirical research as closely as possible, we shall once more invoke the "sampling technique" and present in some detail the results of a series of investigations spanning nearly two decades in which basic experimental investigations of the interaction of sensory and motor processes in perception has led to broad techniques for the investigation of personality.

The fundamental research on sensory-motor interaction in perception is the work of Werner and Wapner and their associates. Its extension into the area of personality is the work of H. A. Witkin and his associates.

The theory of perception developed by Werner and Wapner (70, 71, 72) assumes that all perception involves the interaction between sensory and motor processes.[11] The motor processes in which Werner and Wapner have been most interested are the tonic muscle contractions and their proprioceptive feedback processes. Sensory processes, of course, refer to all other types of afferent stimulation. Because it emphasizes these two basic sets of factors, the theory is known as the *sensory-tonic theory of perception*. Moreover, Werner and Wapner emphasize the relationship between the perceptual processes and the bodily image of the observer. In their words

we assume that there can be no perception of objects "out there" without a bodily framework and, conversely, we assume that there can be no perception of the

---

[11] For a recent account of the work of Witkin and his associates and Werner and Wapner see (72) Chapters 2 and 3 which contain extensive bibliographic references to both early and recent studies.

body-as-object without an environmental frame of reference. Thus, one basic feature of this "body:object" relationship pertains to the interaction constantly going on between them. The central notion here is that the appropriate unit to be dealt with is not the organism *per se,* but rather, the organism in its environmental context, i.e., the organism in relation to objects. The consequence of this conceptualization, then, is that the variability of stability of the biological unit, "body:environment," reflects itself in body perception as well as in object perception (*72*, p. 10).

The evidence in support of sensory-tonic theory comes from situations in which tonic and sensory factors are made to interact under controlled conditions. In their basic experiment Werner and Wapner showed that subjects' perceptions of verticality were influenced by the condition of their musculature. In the experiment in question the subjects were asked to state when a luminescent rod in a dark room appeared vertical, the experimenter starting the rod 30° off vertical and changing it in steps of 3° until the subject reported that it appeared vertical. Tonic stimulation in the form of an electric current applied to the neck musculature or an auditory stimulus applied to the ear was provided on some trials, while on others (control series) no special stimulation was applied. When stimulation was applied to the left side the rod was set further to the right and with stimulation to the right side the rod was set further to the left, thus demonstrating the interaction of tonic and sensory factors in perception.

In another experiment the effect of body tilt on the perception of rod verticality was studied, the judgments being made under two conditions of body tilt, 15° and 30° off vertical respectively. As might be predicted, the 30° off vertical position of the body had the greater influence on the perception of rod verticality.

Werner and Wapner have recently extended their techniques to the investigation of differences between children and adults with respect to their ability to differentiate external and internal influences on perceptions. Figure 5-12 shows in diagrammatic form the experimental arrangements and the essential results. It will be noted that the adults showed a greater angular discrepancy between true bodily position and its apparent position. This increased discrepancy is attributed by the investigators to "increasing polarization of body and object space with increase in age." In other words, the child makes less of a distinction between the inner and outer frames of reference which influence all perceptions.

Finally, as typical of Werner and Wapner's extensive research we shall cite an interesting experiment on the effect of surrounding environmental space on arm length. Figure 5-13 shows the experimental situation in which the subject is placed with one outstretched arm toward open space and the other toward a wall (Subjects A, B). In two control conditions, the subjects stretch out both arms either toward open space (Subject B) or toward a wall (Subject D). The subject is then asked to examine the situation and

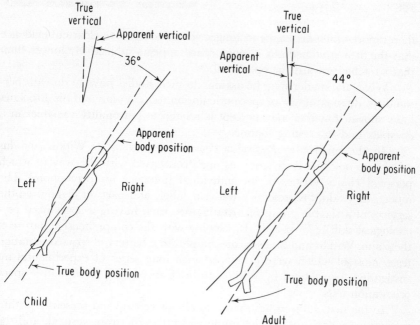

Fig. 5-12. A diagrammatic representation of the child's and the adult's perception of verticality as influenced by body position. Note that the child's perception of verticality is less influenced by body position than the adult's. (From Werner and Wapner, *72.*)

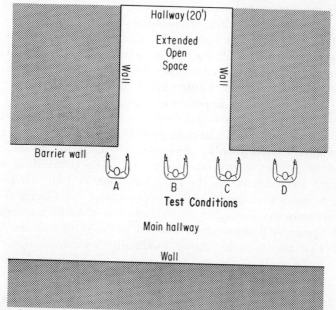

Fig. 5-13. The experimental arrangements used to test the effect of surrounding environmental space on perceived arm length. (From Werner and Wapner, *72.*)

then report which arm appears longer. The findings give clear-cut evidence that the arm stretched out in open space appears subjectively longer than that stretched toward the open wall.

What, the reader may be asking, do such studies have to do with personality? By making use of space orientation tests, Witkin and his associates have shown that the body percept is related to personality variables in a complex and interesting manner.

In the preface to *Personality through Perception* (*73*), Witkin and his colleagues describe their study as one "concerned with the way in which personal characteristics of the individual influence his perception." The report, they add, "represents a ten-year labor, and parts of it required the services of a sizable group of investigators, each having a specialized psychological skill" (*73*, p. xxi). In keeping with the comprehensive nature of their aim, Witkin and his associates employed a battery of space orientation tests, most of which were developed in a long series of experimental investigations carried out by Witkin. In brief, there were three main[12] space orientation tests.

In the first, subjects adjusted a luminous vertical rod presented within a frame in a dark room. The frame was tilted 28° from vertical, and the subject's task was to set the rod to true verticality by instructions to the experimenter, who slowly moved the rod until the subject was satisfied that it was vertical. In essence, the subject's problem is to overcome the effect of the distorted frame of reference created by the tilted frame.

In the second, the tilting-room-tilting-chair test, the subject himself might be tilted while the framework remained vertical. Or the subject could be kept vertical while the "room" and frame were tilted. On some trials the subject was instructed to make the room upright; on others he was required to adjust the chair to true vertical. In this way the subject's use of his own bodily orientation in perception could be evaluated.

The third test was a rotating-room test, in which essentially the same tasks of adjusting the room and chair to verticality were presented but with the additional complication for the subject of having to take into account the pull of gravity—partly downward and partly outward—due to the centrifugal force created by the room's rotation at 18.8 revolutions per minute. In every case the measures employed were the subjects' deviations in degrees from true vertical of the rod, room, or chair for a series of trials.

The perceptual adjustments involved in the three tests are far more complex than appear at first glance. Essentially they involve, first, "part-of-a-field" tasks, such as the rod-and-frame test, and, second, "field-as-a-whole" tasks as represented by the room-adjustment problems. Thus, when

[12] A two-hand coordination test, a body steadiness test, and a figure-embeddedness test were also employed. However, our summary is confined to the more important perceptual tests. The interested reader may consult Witkin and his associates (*73*) for results on the other tests.

the subject is confronted with a part-field problem, he has the advantage of a normal frame of reference which he may employ to correct the item that appears to be distorted. On the other hand, when the whole field is distorted, the task is similar to that faced by the viewer in the Ames demonstrations discussed earlier in this chapter. In other words, if the subject "accepts" the whole field as his frame of reference, then objects in it will suffer distortion. However, it must be emphasized that the subject in the space orientation tests is not *compelled* to accept the whole field "passively" as he is in the Ames demonstrations. In the experiments under discussion, the subject at least has the possibility of adjusting the field as a whole, as for example, by moving the room instead of the rod or his own body. The room is the field-as-a-whole, while the rod or the subject's body is the bit or part of the field-as-a-whole.

We shall return to the space orientation tests later. Meanwhile, we shall summarize the chief techniques used to evaluate the personality dimensions involved in the study. These were an autobiography, a clinical interview, a personality questionnaire made up of items selected from the Minnesota Multiphasic Inventory, a sentence completion test, a figure-drawing test, a word association test, and the Rorschach and Thematic Apperception Tests. Thus, a multidirectional design was employed in order to ensure a relatively complete analysis of each subject's personality.

The subjects selected for the experiment were of both sexes. The adult groups consisted, in part, of normals as represented by college students and, in part, of psychiatric patients who were hospitalized at the time of the study. By including extreme or deviant personalities, the investigators sought to obtain a kind of independent check on the validity of the personality measures employed and, at the same time, were able to investigate the possibility that the perceptual processes of maladjusted individuals are deviant on space orientation tests just as their behavior in general is "deviant." Finally, the experimenters also tested small groups of children in an attempt to cast light on the problem of perceptual development.

We shall consider first the results obtained on the space orientation test and then turn to the findings from the personality tests, attempting to formulate the general relationships between the two sets of measures.

In regard to the space orientation test, Witkin and his associates found that, on the average, the visual field in each test exerted a significant effect on the subject's perception of the task involved as revealed by his adjustments of the apparatus. For example, in the rod-and-frame test, subjects generally did not adjust the rod to true vertical, but moved it instead in the direction in which the frame was tilted. It is interesting to note that on this and the other perceptual tests, male subjects showed smaller deviations in their adjustments than did females. We shall return to this sex difference presently; meanwhile, several other findings will be considered first.

On the various perceptual tests, the influence of the visual field was greater when the "position of the field as a whole was to be determined than when the position of an item within the field was to be established . . ." (*73*, p. 60). To illustrate, if the room in the tilted-room-tilted-chair test were being adjusted by the subject, the deviations were greater than if the subject were adjusting the position of his own body in the adjustable chair. This seems reasonable, since the larger portion of our perceptual environment is apt to dominate what we see.[13]

Another general result from the experiments involving body adjustment (the tilting-chair test) was the finding that the body was less influenced by the visual field than was an external item such as the rod. The authors suggest that the strong kinesthetic sensations from the body may cause the subject to resist displacement in this case, whereas in the rod test the subject gets only visual cues arising from external sources which are consequently overcome more readily.

It will be recalled that Witkin and his associates also studied children and hospital patients. We shall briefly summarize the results for these groups on the space orientation tests. The hospital patients, as might be expected, were more deviant in their adjustments than normals. Indeed, the statistical analyses showed that these individuals tended toward opposite extremes on the space orientation tests in the sense that there was a greater proportion of individuals in this group who were either highly *dependent* on the visual field, on the one hand, or extremely *independent* and *analytic,* on the other hand, with proportionately few cases falling in the intermediate range. Put another way, normals in general tend toward dependence on the visual field, but show a normal range of reactions from heavy dependence to relative independence. However, only a few cases are represented at the extremes among normals; most are in the intermediate range of deviations. The hospital cases, on the other hand, tend to group themselves on the more extreme ends of the range of individual differences.

Perhaps the most significant general finding with the children was a tendency for field dependence to decrease with age. Evidently the adult is less likely to accept things as they are but takes instead a more analytic attitude toward his environment. As was true with adult women, the female subjects among the children were more "passive" in accepting the visual field and as a result made more deviant adjustments at all ages. The authors suggest this may be due to the more passive cultural and biological roles imposed upon the female in our society. At any rate, there is no evidence to suggest that such differences are inherent.

Turning to the personality tests, we shall outline a sample of the find-

[13] An everyday example occurs when large, fluffy clouds are racing across a moonlit sky. Frequently it is the moon which appears to be racing. The large clouds are "forcing" the small moon to move, since they provide a more stable frame of reference.

ings based on the interview, the Rorschach Test, and the figure-drawing tests.

In the clinical interview, the field-dependent subjects showed a lack of insight into their own mental processes, tended to repress their feelings and impulses, and were inclined to suffer from inferiority feelings. This finding was generally confirmed by the subjects' figure drawings. The field-dependent subjects drew immature, inadequate figures of people, whereas the analytic, independent subjects drew more capable-looking and mature-appearing figures.

On the Rorschach, the field-dependent subjects tended to be dominated by the blot as a whole, or to put it another way, yielded to their "environment" as represented by the blots, without analyzing or looking beyond the "popular," more obvious interpretations. In fact, a "coping" score which can be derived from the Rorschach responses showed that those who demonstrated relatively low deviations on the space-orientation tests were high in the ability to cope with their environments, whereas the field-dependent or high-deviation group on the space tests had low coping scores.

In general, the other personality-test results were consistent with the picture presented in the preceding paragraphs, although not all tests and subtests were significantly related to scores on the space orientation battery.

More recently, Witkin and his associates (74) have utilized figure drawings obtained from ten-year-old boys which were analyzed along the dimension of the child's ability to show good figure articulation, the latter being evaluated along a five-point scale taking into account the level of the form drawn, the role portrayed, sex differentiation (the children were asked to draw a picture of both sexes), and the level of detail.

> In a number of studies, scores for the figure-drawing test have been shown to relate significantly to scores for the orientation tests. In the drawings of children whose performance in the orientation tests is field dependent, we find very little detail and unrealistic representation of proportioning and of parts. Sexual characteristics are shown minimally or not at all, so that in some pairs of drawings it it difficult to tell which is male and which is female. In most cases there is no attempt at role representation. On the other hand, in the drawings of a child whose perceptual performance is at the opposite extreme—that is, field-independent—we find such characteristics as these: The body is typically drawn in realistic proportion. The parts of the body are presented in some detail and fairly realistically. There is clear representation of sex and sex differences. Aside from indication of sex through body characteristics, the sex of the figure is indicated by such externals as clothing, and, for example, a male or female name written on the clothing. We also find attempts at role representation, suggesting a sense of the uses to which the body may be put. These differences among children in the way in which they represent the body on paper are significantly related to how they perform in the orientation tests in the laboratory. (74, pp. 34–35).

By way of summary and interpretation, Witkin and his associates believe that the interrelationships discovered in their study of perceptual and personality variables reveal that there are three important personality dimensions significant for the individual's interactions with his environment. First, there is the degree to which the individual possesses the ability to cope *actively* with his environment as opposed to accepting it *passively*. The active individual shows mastery in social and physical situations and has less need of environmental support for his decisions. The passive individual, on the other hand, accepts authority, seeks support for decisions, and fails to show an analytic attitude toward his perceptual world.

Second, the individual's perception of his body and his handling of his own impulses and strivings appeared to show a clear-cut relationship with performance on the spatial tests. The field-dependent, passive individual revealed a lack of awareness of his inner life, a fear of his own impulses, and poor control over his feelings and impulses, with the result that his anxiety level was higher than normal. Field-dependent children also show poor awareness of bodily articulation. Aggressive and sexual impulses presented special problems for the field-dependent individual. On the other side of the picture, the active, independent subjects who showed smaller deviation on the space tests also demonstrated good insight and reasonable mastery over their own motivational and emotional processes as revealed by the personality measures.

Finally, the individual's self-esteem and role-awareness were found to be significantly related to scores on both spatial and personality tests. The field-dependent individual revealed low self-esteem, difficulty in accepting the self and his own body; whereas the independent, analytically-minded subject was relatively high in self-esteem.

SUMMARY AND EVALUATION

With these general conclusions summarized from the report by Witkin and his associates, we shall take leave of the field of perception. In this and the preceding chapter, we have witnessed a continuous (and recently rather remarkable) broadening that has taken place in this area of psychological theory and research. Specifically, the shift has been in the direction of emphasizing the interrelations among O factors or intervening variables. This does not mean that contemporary psychologists show no interest in the investigation of S factors in perception. On the contrary, a glance at experimental textbooks or journals will quickly demonstrate that such is not the case. Two recent volumes in this area by Gibson (25) and Bartley (7) demonstrate that research and theory on the role of S factors is far from a dead issue. Indeed, Gibson deplores the lack of rapport between psychologists interested in structural factors, on the one hand, and those interested in O variables, on the other hand. Nevertheless, we have chosen to emphasize the latter since this reflects the contemporary picture more accurately. It may be that there are fads or cycles in science, and in the future it is quite possible there will be a shift back to emphasis on *S*-factor perceptual psychology.

Finally, it seems to us that, irrespective of which systematic position contemporary psychologists take, the broad trend over the past several decades has been more and more toward a *functionalistic* approach to perception. For the most part, experimental design and theoretical structures have tended more and more in the direction of treating perception as a key process in man's interaction with his environment. This, we believe, is not only true in the more obvious cases, as seen in the work of the Ames group, but is also a strong element in the Witkin program, the directive-state work and, in a more limited way, in the Gestalt and neo-behavioristic approaches. If our analysis is correct, it may well be that the effects of this will spill over into areas of psychology such as learning, thinking, and intelligence. If such an eventuality comes to pass, we may expect broader, more complex research programs which seek to interrelate and synthesize a number of psychological processes with decreasing emphasis on analytic and reductionistic research.

REFERENCES

1. Allport, F. H. *Theories of perception and the concept of structure.* New York: Wiley, 1955.
2. Allport, G. W., and L. Postman. *The psychology of rumor.* New York: Holt, 1947.
3. Ames, A., Jr. Reconsideration of the origin and nature of perception. In S. Ratner (ed.), *Vision and action.* New Brunswick, N. J.: Rutgers University Press, 1953.
4. Aronfreed, J. M., S. A. Messick, and J. C. Diggory. Reexamining emotionality and perceptual defense. *Journal of Personality,* **21,** 1953, pp. 517–528.
5. Auerbach, E., and A. S. Coriell. Short term memory in vision. *The Bell System technical journal,* Monograph number 3756, January, 1961, pp. 309–328.
6. Bartlett, F. C. *Remembering: An experimental and social study.* London: Cambridge University Press, 1932.
7. Bartley, S. H. *Principles of perception.* New York: Harper, 1958.
8. Blake, R. R., and G. V. Ramsey (eds.). *Perception, an approach to personality.* New York: Ronald, 1951.
9. Bricker, P. D., and H. Chapanis. Do incorrectly perceived stimuli convey some information? *Psychological Review,* **60,** 1953, pp. 181–188.
10. Brown, W. Growth of memory images. *American Journal of Psychology,* **47,** 1935, pp. 90–102.
11. Brownfield, C. A. *Isolation.* New York: Random House, 1965.
12. Bruner, J. S., and C. C. Goodman. Value and need as organizing factors in perception. *Journal of Abnormal and Social Psychology,* **42,** 1947, pp. 33–44.
13. Bruner, J. S., and D. Krech (eds.). *Perception and personality—a symposium.* Durham, N. C.: Duke University Press, 1950.
14. Brunswik, E. Organismic achievement and environmental probability. *Psychological Review,* **50,** 1943, pp. 255–272.
15. Cantril, H. *The "why" of man's experience.* New York: Macmillan, 1950.

16. Carmichael, L., H. P. Hogan, and A. A. Walter. An experimental study of the effect of language on the reproduction of visually perceived form. *Journal of Experimental Psychology,* **15,** 1932, pp. 73–86.
17. Eriksen, C. W. Subception: Fact or artifact? *Psychological Review,* **63,** 1956, pp. 74–80.
18. Eriksen, C. W. An experimental analysis of subception. *American Journal of Psychology,* **69,** 1956, pp. 625–634.
19. Eriksen, C. W. Discrimination and learning without awareness: A methodological survey and evaluation. *Psychological Review,* **67,** 1960, pp. 279–300.
20. Eriksen, C. W., and C. T. Brown. An experimental and theoretical analysis of perceptual defense. *Journal of Abnormal and Social Psychology,* **52,** 1956, pp. 224–230.
21. Forgays, D. G., and J. Forgays. The nature of the effect of free-environmental experience in the rat. *Journal of Comparative and Physiological Psychology,* **45,** 1952, pp. 322–328.
22. Forgus, R. H. The effect of different kinds of form pre-exposure on form discrimination learning. *Journal of Comparative and Physiological Psychology,* **51,** 1958, pp. 75–78.
23. Forgus, R. H. *Perception.* New York: McGraw-Hill, 1966.
24. Fulton, J. F. (ed.). *Howell's textbook of physiology,* ed. 15. Philadelphia: Saunders, 1946.
25. Gibson, E. J. Perceptual learning. *Annual Review of Psychology,* **14,** 1963, pp. 29–56.
26. Gibson, E. J., R. D. Walk, H. L. Pick, Jr., and T. J. Tighe. The effect of prolonged exposure to visual patterns on learning to discriminate similar and different patterns. *Journal of Comparative and Physiological Psychology,* **49,** 1956, pp. 239–242.
27. Gibson, J. J. Reproduction of visually perceived forms. *Journal of Experimental Psychology,* **12,** 1929, pp. 1–39.
28. Gibson, J. J. Adaptation, after-effect, and contrast in the perception of curve lines. *Journal of Experimental Psychology,* **16,** 1933, pp. 1–31.
29. Gibson, J. J. *The perception of the visual world.* Boston: Houghton Mifflin, 1950.
30. Gibson, J. J. Theories of perception. In W. Dennis (ed.), *Current trends in psychological theory.* Pittsburgh: University of Pittsburgh Press, 1951.
31. Hastorf, A. H., and A. L. Knutson. Motivation, perception and attitude change. *Psychological Review,* **56,** 1949, pp. 88–97.
32. Hebb, D. O. *The organization of behavior.* New York: Wiley, 1949.
33. Hebb, D. O. The semi-autonomous process: Its nature and nurture. *American Psychologist,* **18,** 1963, pp. 16–27.
34. Helson, H. Adaptation-level as a basis for a quantitative theory of frames of reference. *Psychological Review,* **55,** 1948, pp. 297–313.
35. Helson, H. *Adaptation level theory.* New York: Harper & Row, 1964.
36. Hilgard, E. R. *Theories of learning,* ed. 2. New York: Appleton, 1956.
37. Howie, D. Perceptual defense. *Psychological Review,* **59,** 1952, pp. 308–315.
38. Ittelson, W. H. *The Ames demonstrations in perception.* Princeton, N. J.: Princeton University Press, 1952.
39. Ittelson, W. H., and H. Cantril. *Perception: A transactional approach.* New York: Doubleday, 1954.
40. Kilpatrick, F. P. *Human behavior from the transactional point of view.* Hanover, N. H.: Institute for Associated Research, 1952.
41. Kilpatrick, F. P. (ed.). *Explorations in transactional psychology.* New York: New York University Press, 1961.
42. Koch, S. (ed.). *Psychology: A study of a science,* Vol. I. New York: McGraw-Hill, 1959, pp. 622–643.

43. Köhler, W. *Gestalt psychology*. New York: Liveright, 1929.
44. Köhler, W. *Dynamics in psychology*. New York: Liveright, 1940.
45. Köhler, W., and J. Fishback. The destruction of the Müller-Lyer illusion in repeated trials: I. An examination of two theories. *Journal of Experimental Psychology*, 40, 1950, pp. 267–281.
46. Köhler, W., and R. Held. The cortical correlate of pattern vision. *Science*, 110, 1949, pp. 414–419.
47. Köhler, W., and H. Wallach. Figural after-effects: an investigation of visual processes. *Proceedings of the American Philosophical Society*, 88, 1944, pp. 269–357.
48. Krech, D., and R. S. Crutchfield. *Theory and problems of social psychology*. New York: McGraw-Hill, 1948.
49. Leuba, C., and C. Lucas. The effects of attitudes on descriptions of pictures. *Journal of Experimental Psychology*, 35, 1945, pp. 517–524.
50. Levine, R., I. Chein, and G. Murphy. The relation of intensity of a need to the amount of perceptual distortion. *Journal of Psychology*, 13, 1942, pp. 283–293.
51. McCleary, R. A., and R. S. Lazarus. Autonomic discrimination without awareness. *Journal of Personality*, 18, 1949, pp. 171–179.
52. McGinnies, E. Emotionality and perceptual defense. *Psychological Review*, 56, 1949, pp. 244–251.
53. Morgan, C. T. *Physiological psychology*, ed. 1. New York: McGraw-Hill, 1943.
54. Murdock, B. B., Jr. Perceptual defense and threshold measurement. *Journal of Personality*, 22, 1954, pp. 565–571.
55. Osgood, C. E. *Method and theory in experimental psychology*. New York: Oxford, 1953.
56. Piotrowski, Z. A. *Perceptanalysis*. New York: Macmillan, 1957.
57. Postman, L., J. S. Bruner, and E. McGinnies. Personal values as selective factors in perception. *Journal of Abnormal and Social Psychology*, 43, 1948, pp. 142–154.
58. Postman, L., and R. S. Crutchfield. The interaction of need, set, and stimulus structure in a cognitive task. *American Journal of Psychology*, 65, 1952, pp. 196–217.
59. Rock, I., and P. Engelstein. A study of memory for visual form. *American Journal of Psychology*, 72, 1958, pp. 221–229.
60. Rogers, C. R. *Client-centered therapy*. Boston: Houghton Mifflin, 1951.
61. Sanford, R. N. The effects of abstinence from food upon imaginal processes. *Journal of Psychology*, 2, 1936, pp. 129–136.
62. Sanford, R. N. The effects of abstinence from food upon imaginal processes: a further experiment. *Journal of Psychology*, 3, 1937, pp. 145–159.
63. Schafer, R., and G. Murphy. The role of autism in visual figure-ground relationship. *Journal of Experimental Psychology*, 32, 1943, pp. 335–343.
64. Siipola, E. M. A study of some effects of preparatory set. *Psychological Monographs*, 46, 1935, pp. 28–37.
65. Solomon, R. L., and D. Howes. Word frequency, personal values, and visual duration thresholds. *Psychological Review*, 58, 1951, pp. 256–270.
66. Sperling, G. The information available in brief visual presentations. *Psychological Monographs*, 74, 1960, pp. 1–29.
67. Spitz, H. H. The present status of the Köhler-Wallach theory of satiation. *Psychological Bulletin*, 55, No. 1, January, 1958, pp. 1–29.
68. Stagner, R., and R. T. Karwoski. *Psychology*. New York: McGraw-Hill, 1952.
69. Thompson, G. G. *Child psychology*. Boston: Houghton Mifflin, 1952.
70. Werner, H., and S. Wapner. Sensory-tonic field theory of perception. *Journal of Personality*, 18, 1949, pp. 88–107.
71. Werner, H., and S. Wapner. Toward a general theory of perception. *Psychological Review*, 50, 1956, pp. 315–337.
72. Werner, H., and S. Wapner (eds.). *The body percept*. New York: Random House, 1965.

73. Witkin, H. A., H. B. Lewis, M. Hertzman, K. Mackover, P. B. Meissner, and S. Wapner. *Personality through perception.* New York: Harper, 1954.

74. Witkin, H. A. Development of the body concept and psychological differentiation. In Werner, H., and S. Wapner (eds.). *The body percept.* New York: Random House, 1965.

75. Wohlwill, J. F. Perceptual learning. *Annual Review of Psychology,* **17,** 1966, pp. 201–232.

76. Woodworth, R. S., and H. Schlosberg. *Experimental psychology.* New York: Holt, 1954.

77. Wulf, F. Über die Veränderung von Vorstellungen. *Psychologische Forschung,* **1,** 1922, pp. 333–373.

78. Young, P. T., and J. P. Chaplin. Studies of food preference, appetite and dietary habit. *Comparative Psychology Monographs,* **18,** 1945, pp. 1–45.

6

Learning I: The Classical Heritage

In introducing the topic of sensation (Chapter 3), we pointed out that the study of the sensory processes dominated psychology during its formative years. At the same time we emphasized the close relationship that existed between sensationism and associationism. Philosophical empiricism made sensations the elementary processes out of which ideas are formed, and ideas, in turn, coalesce into more and more complex ideas because of the attractive power of associations. But we also indicated that sensory psychology suffered a decline with the collapse of structuralism. Associationism, on the other hand, continued its progressive evolution into modern learning theory. Through the work of Ebbinghaus in the 1880's on human verbal learning, philosophical associationism became experimental associationism; and experimental associationism, in turn, evolved into the field of contemporary learning around the turn of the century, largely as a result of the pioneer efforts of the early comparative psychologists. In the decades that followed, the field of learning enjoyed a steady growth until today it is the single largest field of psychology in terms of the quantity of productive research and theory construction.

Because learning has come to occupy such a central position in modern psychology, several chapters will be devoted to tracing its evolution from its origin in classical philosophy to its present status in psychology. In this chapter we shall first touch on the older, associationistic views of learning. Second, we shall consider in some detail the pioneer experimental programs of Ebbinghaus and Thorndike. Finally, we shall trace the development of learning theory as it underwent further evolution within the schools of psychology. In the chapter to follow we shall deal with those learning theories which were stimulated by the earlier

195

schools and which developed into "miniature" systems. In the third chapter devoted to learning we shall consider those contemporary systems which have evolved from the miniature systems, and in the fourth chapter devoted to learning we shall examine theories in human verbal learning, a field which absorbs the experimental and theoretical interests of an enormous number of American psychologists.

THE ASSOCIATIONISTIC TRADITION

We have already examined the associationistic point of view in some detail in connection with the evolution of the scientific method (Chapter 2) and the development of sensory and perceptual psychology (Chapters 4 and 5). Therefore a brief review will suffice here.

The first of the associationists, in spirit if not in name, was Aristotle. His laws of memory—contiguity, similarity, and contrast—were, in effect, laws of association. Moreover, true to his empirical orientation, Aristotle linked these laws to sense experience, arguing that the content of mind arises out of sensations which, in turn, become ideas that are bound together by the principles of association.

Aristotle's principles served as the foundation of the British school of associationism of the eighteenth and early nineteenth centuries. Thomas Hobbes (1588 to 1679) restated Aristotle's laws and attempted to reduce them to a single law, contiguity, largely on the logical ground that, in the absence of contiguity, similarity and contrast are not sufficient conditions for associations to be formed. Hobbes also distinguished between free and controlled association—a distinction which was to become important many years later when free association was employed by the psychoanalysts as a method for investigating unconscious mental processes.

John Locke, whose philosophy we examined in Chapter 1, greatly strengthened associationism by announcing his highly influential doctrine that at birth the human mind is a *tabula rasa* upon which experience writes and also by espousing mental analysis as a method for reducing complex ideas to simple associations.

Locke was followed by Berkeley, Hume, and Hartley, each of whom evolved within his philosophy an empiricist-associationistic psychology. Berkeley, however, is best known for his contributions to visual space perception (Chapter 1), and Hume for his analysis of ideas (Chapter 1). Both subscribed to associationism, but neither made it a central concept in his system of psychology. The elevation of associationism to a true system was Hartley's contribution, and for this reason the historians (2, 3, 4, 16, and 18) attribute the "founding" of the "school" of associationism to him. As we pointed out in Chapter 1, Hartley systematized and organized the ideas of his predecessors, formulating them into a system of associationism. We also indicated that associationism as a system persisted in British psychology until it reached its fruition in the Mills, father and son (Chapter 1).

There were others,[1] in both the British and Scottish schools of philosophy, who made contributions to associationistic theory, but we need not go into the many variations and ramifications of associationism here. What we wish to emphasize is this: Associationism was a well-established system in British empirical philosophy by the middle of the eighteenth century. The philosophers had undertaken the Herculean task of reducing the complexities of mind to the sensory-association continuum. In doing so, they set the stage for the evolution of modern learning theory and for an experimental attack on the higher mental processes. While no one would deny the importance of these contributions, the great weaknesses of associationism as a psychology were threefold. First, the highly general nature of its claims broadened the doctrine to the point of superficiality. To reduce ideas, memories, space perception, and thinking to associations greatly oversimplifies the complexity of the human mind. Second, little or nothing was offered by way of explaining the processes of acquisition and forgetting, both topics of great importance in modern learning theory. Third, such variables as the influence of motivation, individual differences, and methods of learning on the formation of associations were not systematically explored by the philosophers largely because the investigation of such problems demands the use of experimental techniques.

In summary, then, the associationists had set the stage for the experimental attack on the higher mental processes. What remained was for someone to turn speculative philosophical empiricism into scientific experimentalism. A German psychologist, Hermann Ebbinghaus, undertook the pioneer labor of forging the necessary techniques.

EBBINGHAUS AND THE EXPERIMENTAL STUDY OF MEMORY

Ebbinghaus became interested in the quantitative investigation of the mental processes as a result of chancing upon a copy of Fechner's *Elemente* while engaged in a program of independent study. The experience marked a turning point in his career. He was deeply impressed by Fechner's careful experimental analysis of the sensory processes and became convinced that the same techniques could be adapted to the study of the higher mental processes. During a five-year period (1879 to 1885), Ebbinghaus devoted himself to his self-appointed task and in 1885 published the results of his

---

[1] See References 2, 3, 4, 16, 27, and 31 for more complete accounts of associationism.

experiments in a little volume entitled *Über das Gedachnis*.[2] This book was destined to become a landmark in the literature of psychology.

Ebbinghaus launched his research program by devising a revolutionary kind of material for use in learning sessions. The material in question was nonsense syllables which he fashioned by combining consonants and vowels in such a way as to avoid meaningful words. For example, *vol, rux, noz* and *lut* are readily pronounceable nonsense syllables which have little resemblance to real words. By employing such material Ebbinghaus could "start from scratch" and thereby avoid the ever-present danger involved in meaningful material, namely, the possibility of inadvertently selecting passages once studied but now "forgotten." As his own results subsequently demonstrated, material once learned may be relearned with less effort and fewer errors even though it has been forgotten in the conventional sense.

Ebbinghaus went on to design a number of experiments to test the influence of various conditions on both learning and retention. In these experiments he served as both experimenter and subject, and it is to his great credit that he worked so carefully that the results of his experiments have never been seriously challenged. We shall consider his findings under two main headings: first, his studies of factors influencing learning and, second, his investigations of conditions influencing retention.

Ebbinghaus found that the length of his lists greatly influenced the number of repetitions necessary for an errorless reproduction and, of course, increased the time required to learn a given list. Analyzing his data further, he also found that the *average time per syllable* was markedly increased by lengthening the list. His results are summarized in Table 6-1.

While any high school student could have predicted the outcome of Ebbinghaus' experiment *in a general way*, its significance lies in his careful

Table 6-1.
Learning Time and Length of List[a]

No. of syllables in list	No. of readings required	Time for total list (seconds)	Average time per syllable (seconds)
7	1	3	0.4
12	17	82	6.8
16	30	196	12.0
24	44	422	17.6
36	55	792	22.0

[a]After Ebbinghaus, *8*.

[2] An English translation is available under the title *Memory* (see reference *8*).

control of conditions, his *quantitative* analysis of his data, and the not so readily predictable finding that *both* the total time for learning *and* the time per syllable increase with longer lists. Indeed, the magnitude of the difference in time for memorizing longer lists is surprisingly large. An examination of Table 6-1 will show that adding only five syllables to a list increases the total time for learning twenty-seven fold and the average time per syllable seventeenfold. This finding—that proportionately more time is required per unit of material in longer lists—has been confirmed by subsequent investigators, although the relationship between the variables depends upon the nature of the material and the degree of learning (*30*). The greater number of repetitions and increased total time required for learning longer lists is explicable on the basis of intrasyllable inhibitory effects. That is, the longer the list, the greater the likelihood of both forward and backward interference effects between associations.

Ebbinghaus also investigated the relationship between the degree of learning and subsequent retention. Since his criterion for mastery was one errorless repetition,[3] he repeated the lists "by heart" a number of times beyond bare mastery in order to test the effect of overlearning. His measure of overlearning was the saving in time to achieve once again a perfect repetition of the original list following a twenty-four-hour retention period. This technique is now known as the *savings method,* or *method of relearning.* Table 6-2 reproduces Ebbinghaus' results with various lengths of lists.

Many repetitions and variations on Ebbinghaus' experiment have since been carried out by psychologists and the results are in general agreement. Overlearning, up to a point, results in a saving of both time and errors upon relearning. In fact, the savings method is so sensitive an index

Table 6-2.
Savings in Repetitions and Percent of Requirement for Original Learning after a Twenty-four-hour Interval for Three Lengths of Lists[a]

NO. OF SYLLABLES IN SERIES	NO. OF REPETITIONS FOR ORIGINAL LEARNING	SAVING IN REPETITIONS IN RELEARNING AFTER 24 HOURS	SAVINGS IN PERCENT OF REQUIREMENT FOR ORIGINAL LEARNING
12	16.5	5.5	33.3
24	44	21.5	48.9
36	55	32	58.2

[a]After Ebbinghaus, *8.*

[3] Contemporary psychologists who work in the field of learning generally require two perfect consecutive repetitions.

of retention that some saving in subsequent learning may appear years after the material has been "forgotten" in the ordinary sense (5).

Ebbinghaus went on to investigate a number of additional variables which influence the curves of learning and retention, such as the effects of near and remote associations within lists, review or repeated learning, and the influence of the passage of time. We shall make no attempt to summarize all of Ebbinghaus' results. The interested reader may consult the original work (8) or Woodworth's (30) excellent summary, which also includes the results of subsequent studies bearing on these same questions. However, it would be a grave omission not to mention Ebbinghaus' famous curve of retention, which has been used to illustrate the general process of forgetting in every major textbook of experimental and general psychology published within the last half-century. The curve is presented in Figure 6-1 as drawn from Ebbinghaus' original data (8, p. 76).

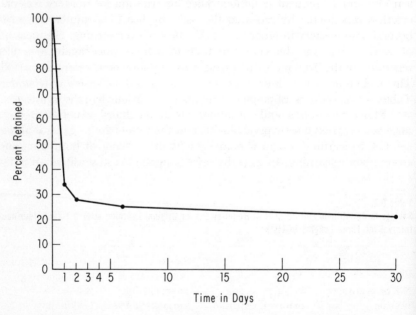

Fig. 6-1. Ebbinghaus' curve of retention for nonsense syllables obtained by the savings method. (Plotted from Ebbinghaus, 8.)

Ebbinghaus' curve of retention is interesting not only because it shows the general nature of forgetting—the initial rapid drop-off followed by negatively accelerated loss with increasing time—but also because it is one of the major pioneer attempts in psychology to reduce experimental data to mathematical form.[4] Ebbinghaus' logarithmic relationship is known as an *empirical* equation because it was based on an actual set of experimental data to which an equation was fitted by the method of least squares. In effect, this means the parameters employed by Ebbinghaus have no rational significance. They are, as the modern phrase has it, "purely empirical."

By way of contrast, there have been a number of attempts to formulate *rational* equations for learning curves which are not merely descriptive of the data obtained, but are based on a study of the fundamental nature of learning and retention, and which attempt to provide a rational basis for the type of equation that has been selected. We shall have more to say about such equations in the next chapter, but we are introducing the concept here partly to clarify the nature of Ebbinghaus' equation and, in part, to reveal its limitations. Clearly, it is a dubious procedure to make predictions beyond the limits of an empirical curve since there is no assurance that additional samples would yield similar results. With rational curves, on the other hand, deductions and hypotheses can be made by extrapolations beyond the observed limits of the data. Hypotheses formulated on the basis of such extrapolations can and should be subjected to subsequent verification by experimental tests.

In a sense, Ebbinghaus' failure to formulate a rational basis for his results brings out his limitations as a theorist, for the essence of theory *is* to go beyond the observed data by hypothesis and deduction. But Ebbinghaus was not a systematist, nor was he a theoretician on the order of Fechner. His great strength lay in his careful sense of controlled experimentation and (within the limits of the times) experimental design. In the last analysis, we can only reiterate what has often been said before, that those who provide the instruments and weapons of research contribute just as significantly as those who provide theories and systems.

THORNDIKE AND THE EXPERIMENTAL STUDY OF LEARNING

In moving from Ebbinghaus to Thorndike we are jumping from Germany to the United States and, at the same time, are turning from experiments on human verbal learning to studies of animal learning. Moreover, the contrast between the two men is heightened by the fact that, whereas Ebbinghaus is known for his model experiments, Thorndike's fame in the

[4] The Ebbinghaus curve may represent a spuriously rapid loss because of his extensive work with nonsense syllables leading to the build-up of considerable proactive inhibition. See Chapter 9 for a further analysis of the problem of retention in highly practiced subjects.

field of learning is primarily the result of his theoretical explanations of his research findings. Indeed it may be said that Thorndike offered the psychological world the first miniature system of learning—a system which proved to have a profound influence on the course of learning theory for the next half-century. In fact, Thorndike's theory may be considered a *contemporary* theory of learning, and is so treated by Hilgard in the several editions of his *Theories of Learning* (9). From the point of view of the present account it is a *transitional* theory characterized on the one hand by its associationistic foundations and on the other hand by its behavioristic approach to experimentation. For this reason, we have chosen to include it in this rather than in the following chapter.

Thorndike's theory of learning takes as its point of departure the results of his own experiments with chicks, cats, fishes, dogs, and monkeys. Of these, the most famous and influential are those in which the subjects were cats and chicks. It was on the basis of the experiments with cats that Thorndike described *trial-and-error learning* as a fundamental type of learning, while the chick experiments, as we shall see, had profound significance in assessing the validity of his laws of learning.

Let us first consider the experiments with cats. Thorndike employed a variety of puzzle boxes which required different kinds of manipulations on the part of the animal for a successful solution. The simple boxes required only that the cat pull a loop in order to open the door, whereupon he could escape from the box and obtain a reward of fish. One of the more complex boxes is illustrated in Figure 6-2. In this case three separate acts were required to open the door. Both bolts had to be raised, one by depressing the hinged platform, the other by clawing the exposed string; and either of the bars outside the door had to be turned to the vertical position. The door then opened automatically as a result of the pull exerted by a weight attached to a string fastened to the outside of the door.

The following description of the animals' behavior in the puzzle box is quoted from Thorndike's *Animal Intelligence*. It is a general summary of his results with twelve cats ranging from three to nineteen months of age.

The behavior of all but 11 and 13 was practically the same. When put into the box the cat would show evident signs of discomfort and of an impulse to escape from confinement. It tries to squeeze through any opening; it claws and bites at the bars or wire; it thrusts its paws out through any opening and claws at everything it reaches; it continues its efforts when it strikes anything loose and shaky; it may claw at things within the box. It does not pay very much attention to the food outside, but seems simply to strive instinctively to escape from confinement. The vigor with which it struggles is extraordinary. For eight or ten minutes it will claw and bite and squeeze incessantly. With 13, an old cat, and 11, an uncommonly sluggish cat, the behavior was different. They did not struggle vigorously or continually. On some occasions they did not even struggle

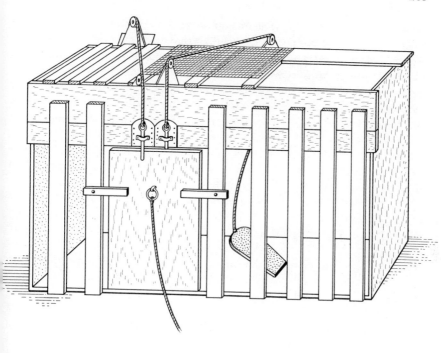

Fig. 6-2. One of Thorndike's puzzle boxes. (Redrawn after Thorndike, *19*.)

at all. It was therefore necessary to let them out of the box a few times, feeding them each time. After they thus associate climbing out of the box with getting food, they will try to get out whenever put in. They do not, even then, struggle so vigorously or get so excited as the rest. In either case, whether the impulse to struggle be due to instinctive reaction to confinement or to an association, it is likely to succeed in letting the cat out of the box. The cat that is clawing all over the box in her impulsive struggle will probably claw the string or loop or button so as to open the door. And gradually all the other non-successful impulses will be stamped out and the particular impulse leading to the successful act will be stamped in by the resulting pleasure, until, after many trials, the cat will, when put in the box, immediately claw the button or loop in a definite way. (*19*, pp. 35–40.)

Thorndike's description of the cats' behavior epitomizes what has since been known as "trial-and-error" learning. Reduced to the fundamental stimulus-response patterns involved, trial-and-error learning means that the animal must learn to associate one or more responses with a certain stimulus pattern. It is important to note that the animal does not learn a new response. Rather, he must *select* an appropriate response out of his repertoire of responses, and must learn to associate this response with a certain stimulus pattern. The gradualness with which the appropriate response is selected convinced Thorndike that the animal does not reason out the solution but proceeds in a blind or random manner. Finally, his assumption that "unsuccessful responses will be stamped out" and "the successful act will be stamped in by the resulting pleasure" is an informal statement of his highly influential Law of Effect, which we shall consider as a formal law after a brief description of the experiments with chicks.

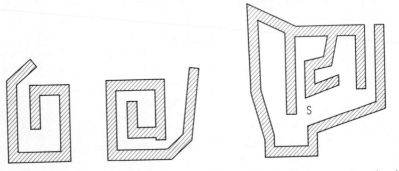

Fig. 6-3. Three mazes used by Thorndike in his studies of trial-and-error learning in chicks. (Redrawn after Thorndike, *19*.)

Figure 6-3 is a reproduction of the floor plan of several of Thorndike's "pens" which he employed in studying the course of learning in chicks. In contemporary terms, these were essentially simple mazes which in a more elaborate form are now widely used in learning experiments with rats. In studying the chick's behavior, Thorndike placed the bird somewhere in the center of the maze (say at S), and the problem for the chick was to find the exit which led to food and other chicks. In general, Thorndike found that the chicks' behavior was essentially of the same trial-and-error variety as that exhibited by the cats in the puzzle boxes. The main differences, according to Thorndike, were: (a) the chicks were "very much slower in forming associations," and (b) they were less able to solve difficult problems.

Finally, Thorndike's interest in comparative psychology led him to test dogs and monkeys on a variety of problems. In general, the results were closely correlated with the animals' phylogenetic level. That is, the monkeys solved problem boxes with relative ease and rapidity and at the same time showed more planning in their attack on the escape mechanism. Dogs were more comparable to cats in their behavior, yet their learning curves were somewhat smoother than those for the cats, indicating that the dogs were less variable in their problem-solving ability. However, it is important to note that the higher animals' greater speed and superior performance in no way led Thorndike to modify his view that animals in general do not solve problems by a process of reasoning. In Thorndike's own words, "There is also in the case of the monkeys, as in that of the other animals, positive evidence of the absence of any general function of reasoning" (*19*, p. 186).

Thorndike's findings with the various species that he tested were sufficiently consistent to lead him to generalize his results into two fundamental laws of learning—perhaps the most widely known and influential laws ever formulated in this area of psychology. These were his "Law of Effect" and "Law of Exercise."

The statement of the laws follows that given in *Animal Intelligence*.

The Law of Effect is that: Of several responses made to the same situation, those which are accompanied or closely followed by satisfaction to the animal will, other things being equal, be more firmly connected with the situation, so that, when it recurs, they will be more likely to recur; those which are accompanied or closely followed by discomfort to the animal will, other things being equal, have their connections with that situation weakened, so that, when it recurs, they will be less likely to occur. The greater the satisfaction or discomfort, the greater the strengthening or weakening of the bond.

The Law of Exercise is that: Any response to a situation will, other things being equal, be more strongly connected with the situation in proportion to the number of times it has been connected with that situation and to the average vigor and duration of the connections. (*19*, pp. 244–245.)

Thorndike explains what he means by "satisfaction" and "discomfort" in the following terms (*19*, p. 245):

By a satisfying state of affairs is meant one which the animal does nothing to avoid, often doing such things as attain and preserve it. By a discomforting or annoying state of affairs is meant one which the animal commonly avoids and abandons.

In his *Animal Intelligence*, Thorndike added a statement which in a subsequent publication[5] was to become the "Law of Readiness." In the account we are following, he gave it only the status of a "provisional hypothesis." As originally formulated, the hypothesis held that neuronal synapses are capable of modification through exercise. This, he felt, might be brought about by chemical, electrical, or even protoplasmic changes which could be the consequences of such activity. The law of readiness was subsequently formulated in terminology closely paralleling that of the Law of Effect. As given in Thorndike's *Educational Psychology*, the law states: "For a conduction unit ready to conduct to do so is satisfying and for it not to do so is annoying." Thorndike also added: "For a conduction unit unready to conduct to be forced to do so would be annoying" (*20*, p. 127).

[5] *Educational Psychology*, 1913. (See reference *21*.)

While Thorndike spoke about neurons in his first formulations of the Law of Readiness, the law makes little sense if taken literally. Indeed, it is actually contradictory to speak on the one hand of "forced" conduction as detrimental to the establishment of bonds and on the other hand of neuronal connections being established through exercise, since conduction, whether forced or "voluntary," would be a form of exercise and should therefore strengthen connections. Moreover, there is no physiological basis for the neurological hedonism implied by the law. Broadly speaking, Thorndike's Law of Readiness makes sense only if interpreted to mean that a preparatory set on the part of the organism as a whole is an important condition influencing learning. If the animal is set for a given kind of behavior, then engaging in that behavior pattern is rewarding or reinforcing. Conversely, when an animal (or a person) is forced to do what he does not want to do, the experience is annoying. The forgoing modification of the principle of readiness is the one generally utilized by those psychologists who consider readiness an important condition of learning.

In addition to his three primary laws of exercise, effect, and readiness, Thorndike advocated various subsidiary laws and principles over the years (20, 21, 22, and 25), several of which are sufficiently important to warrant our attention. These are the principles of: (1) *multiple response,* (2) *set or disposition,* (3) *selective responses,* (4) *response by analogy,* and (5) *associative shifting.* Each of these will be discussed briefly, in turn.

The principle of *multiple response* states that when one response fails to produce a satisfying state of affairs it will trigger a new response. In this way the animal continues to respond until some response finally results in satisfaction. Thus, the cat in the puzzle box described earlier in this chapter unleashes its repertoire of responses until one releases the latch. The adaptive significance of the animal's ability to vary responses is obvious. The animal that gave up after the first failure would die of starvation if not released by the experimenter. In some cases, as Thorndike points out, fatigue or extraneous factors may intervene to distract the animal from his attempts to escape. As a rule, however, the animal's own varying behavior pattern brings about his release.

The principle of *set* or *disposition* is Thorndike's equivalent of the concept of motivation or drive in contemporary learning systems. The hungry cat will struggle to get out of the box; the satiated animal is likely to go to sleep. Thus, set or disposition to engage in activity is fundamental for the initiation of responses and, indirecly, for learning.

The law of *selective responses* holds that as learning proceeds the animal responds selectively to certain elements in the problem situation while ignoring others. The cats in the problem boxes, for example, concentrated on the general area of the door, the latch, or the pulley, as the case might be, even in the first few trials. The relevance of such selectivity of response and discrimination is obvious. An animal that is incapable of discrimination will never learn an escape route.

The principle of *response by analogy* is a transfer principle. The cat that has experienced one problem box will, when placed in a different box, utilize whatever responses are appropriate, provided the new situation contains some elements which are identical with elements in the previous situation. In formulating the principle of analogy, and in his more general treatment of transfer of training, Thorndike subscribed to an "identical elements" theory. This is to say that transfer will occur if, and only if, there are elements in common between the two learning situations involved. More generally, his theory of learning was permeated with "connectionism," a concept that spread into his writings on intelligence, educational applications of learning theory and social psychology.

Associative shifting is the Thorndikian equivalent of conditioning. In essence, the principle states that responses learned to one set of stimulus conditions may be learned to a new set of stimuli provided the overall situation is kept relatively intact during the substitutive learning. By way of illustration, the reader may call to mind any of the many tricks which animals can be taught to perform. If, for example, the child wishes to teach his dog how to sit up at command, he proceeds by holding a biscuit out of the dog's reach (or he forces the animal into a sitting position) and at the same time verbally orders the dog to sit up. After a number of trials the animal sits up on command, even when the child does not offer food. Essentially this is a form of conditioning which is no different in principle from Pavlov's bell-saliva experiment.

The five subsidiary principles just discussed plus the three fundamental laws of exercise, effect, and readiness constitute Thorndike's fundamental systematic views on learning. Most of the laws and principles were elaborated on the basis of his early animal experiments, but with slight modifications they are theoretically applicable to human learning situations. In fact, Thorndike himself generalized his laws to the human level, and his growing interest in educational psychology eventually led him into research in the field of human learning. However, as Thorndike continued with his experimental program, his own findings made it clear that the laws of exercise and effect required modification. In fact, the Law of Exercise had to be abandoned altogether as originally stated, and the Law of Effect turned out to have a much narrower range of generality than he originally believed.

The Law of Exercise was disproved by Thorndike in experiments where exercise was made the independent variable while other factors were held constant. For example, he had college students draw a three-inch line while blindfolded. Some subjects were allowed over a thousand trials, and the measure of learning was the increase in accuracy from the beginning to the end of the session. On the average there was no improvement from the first to the final trial. Practice without knowledge of results failed to produce improvement. The line-drawing test employed by Thorndike would be exactly parallel to requiring soldiers to shoot at targets without informing them of their scores. No improvement could be expected. For the human subject, knowledge of results acts as a reinforcing agent, or in terms of Thorndike's system, provides an opportunity for the operation of the Law of Effect. Despite these negative findings on the value of practice per se, Thorndike did not take the absurd position that learning could occur in its absence. Rather, he held that exercise or practice provides an opportunity for other factors to operate. In short, it is *rewarded* practice that strengthens bonds— not practice alone.

The Law of Effect came under fire as a result of experiments designed to test the relative efficacy of reward and punishment in strengthening and weakening responses. It will be recalled that the law was a two-part law wherein a connection is strengthened if it leads to satisfaction or weakened if it leads to annoyance. In an often-cited experiment with chicks, Thorndike employed a simple maze where the correct pathway led to "freedom, food, and company," while incorrect choices led to confinement for a period of thirty seconds. In terms of the Law of Effect, the responses which led to a large enclosure where there was food and "company" (in the form of other chicks) should have been stamped in, while incorrect responses should have been stamped out since they led to a state of solitary confinement as well as the annoyance of prolonged hunger.

By keeping track of the tendency of the chicks to repeat preceding correct choices if rewarded and avoid preceding choices if punished, Thorndike was able to test both aspects of his Law of Effect. The outcome of this experiment and a number of other experiments along similar lines with both animal and human subjects was clear. Reward strengthens connections, but punishment fails to weaken connections. As a result of these negative findings with respect to punishment, Thorndike had to abandon the second half of the law insofar as any direct effects of punishment are concerned. He did continue to hold that punishment retained some *indirect* value in the sense that it may cause a "shift to right behavior" for which there is a reward. Or, in the case of undesirable behavior, punishment can act as a barrier to the attainment of a reward, thus indirectly weakening a connection. But even in the case of such indirect effects, the influence of punishment is in no way comparable to that of reward.

Meanwhile, he formulated a new principle, that of *belongingness,* and discovered a phenomenon (the spread of effect) which he believed to be a crucial and independent test of his modified Law of Effect. We shall consider each of these more recent aspects of Thorndike's position in turn.

Belongingness is a principle which was formulated on the basis of verbal learning experiments with human subjects. In a typical experiment bearing on belongingness he read the following list of sentences to his student subjects ten times.[6]

> Alfred Dukes and his sister worked sadly. Edward Davis and his brother argued rarely. Francis Bragg and his cousin played hard. Barney Croft and his father watched earnestly. Lincoln Blake and his uncle listened gladly. Jackson Craig and his son struggle often. Charlotte Dean and her friend studied easily. Mary Borah and her companion complained dully. Norman Foster and his mother bought much. Alice Hanson and her teacher came yesterday.

Immediately following the last reading the subjects were asked the following questions:

1. What word came next after rarely?
2. What word came next after Lincoln?
3. What word came next after gladly?
4. What word came next after dully?
5. What word came next after Mary?
6. What word came next after earnestly?
7. What word came next after Norman Foster and his mother?
8. What word came next after and his son struggle often?

If mere contiguous repetition governed the formation of bonds, then all sequences of words should have been remembered equally well. However, this was not the case. Even though "Edward" follows "sadly" just as frequently as "Davis" follows "Edward," the "belongingness" of "Davis" to "Edward" outweighs the mere contiguity of the "Edward-sadly" connection. In summary, the average percentage of correct associations from the end of one sentence to the beginning of the next was 2.75, while 21.5 percent correct responses were obtained, on the average, for the first and second word combinations in the same sentences. Obviously, we are more accustomed to associating words within sentences than between sentences, and, in addition, there is the functional belongingness of subjects and their verbs. In effect, Thorndike is arguing that rewards and punishments, to be maximally effective, must be relevant to the situation to which they apply.

The spread of effect principle states that reward strengthens not only the connection to which it belongs but also connections which precede and follow the rewarded response. So strong is the spread of effect that *punished* responses three to four steps removed from the rewarded connection are made with greater than the expected frequency (22). There is, however, a gradient involved so that the effect on any given response becomes weaker the farther that response is from the rewarded connection. The gradient effect was demonstrated in experiments where a number of responses could

---

[6] Quoted from *The Fundamentals of Learning* (*23*, p. 66).

be given to certain stimuli. For example, stimulus words were presented by Thorndike to which the subject responded by saying any number between one and ten. The experimenter arbitrarily "rewarded" responses to certain stimuli regardless of the response given, and in the same series "punished" other responses. The "reward" was simply hearing the experimenter say "*Right*," and the "punishment," "*Wrong*." A typical series might be diagramed as follows: W W W W R W W W. In general, the effect of the reward is strongest on the rewarded connection but may spread or scatter to connections several steps removed from the rewarded connection.

In discovering the spread of effect, Thorndike believed he had come upon independent evidence for the Law of Effect (*24*), and at the same time had strengthened his position that rewards operate mechanically—a position which is consistent with his essentially behavioristic trial-and-error conception of learning. However, Thorndike's interpretation of his results has been questioned by other investigators. Furthermore, a long-standing controversy has developed over the reality of the phenomenon itself (some investigators have failed to find it in attempts to duplicate Thorndike's original experiment) and over its interpretation in those cases where such effects have been duplicated. We cannot undertake to review this extensive literature here. The interested reader is referred to Postman (*17*), McGeoch and Irion (*14*), and Hilgard (*9*) for a variety of experimental tests and interpretations of the spread of effect phenomenon.

Whatever the ultimate status of Thorndike's basic laws and principles, there is general agreement among psychologists that his theory of learning heralded the rise of modern learning theory to its position of preeminence in contemporary psychology. Its greatest strength lies in the fact that the various tenets of the theory were stated with sufficient specificity and in such a form as to render them subject to experimental investigation. But in a sense, this same specificity proved to be Thorndike's greatest weakness. His emphasis on bonds or connections, his elementalism in accounting for transfer, the mechanical operation of the Law of Effect and his rote-drill conception of human learning have, in the opinion of many psychologists, greatly oversimplified the nature of the learning process. This, of course, does not mean that psychologists disapprove of exactitude in the exposition of theoretical and systematic positions. Rather, it means that subsequent experimentation failed to confirm Thorndike's expectations. While this may be disappointing to the theorist, it is of enormous value to the science as a whole in the sense that research has been stimulated and alternative hypotheses and interpretations have been offered to account for experimental findings. In this respect Thorndike's pioneer efforts rank among the greatest in the history of psychology. As will be demonstrated more fully later, his theoretical interpretation of learning has profoundly influenced two generations of psychologists.

LEARNING AND THE SCHOOLS

Following our usual plan, we shall consider how the topic of learning was handled by the representatives of structuralism, functionalism, behaviorism and Gestalt psychology. However, in beginning our survey with Titchener, it will seem as if we are moving backward; for while Thorndike's was an associationistic psychology in principle, it looked beyond traditional associationism. Titchener's psychology of learning, on the other hand, is old-fashioned by comparison. It would be difficult to conceive of two systems founded on the same basic principles of associationism that are more different in all essentials. Titchener's associationism has an aura of eighteenth- and nineteenth-century British philosophy about it, whereas Thorndike's connectionism has all the earmarks of a contemporary experimentally oriented system.

Undoubtedly the primary explanation of the great difference between the two systems lies in the general aims and methods of their proponents. Titchener's analytic introspectionism favored associationism—associationism as a conscious higher mental process involved in perception, ideation, attention, and other mental processes. Thorndike's objectives, especially in the early years, were akin to Watson's. Therefore Thorndike, like Watson, hoped to demonstrate that by the study of behavior within the S-R framework the science of psychology could be objectified and applied to practical affairs, which in Thorndike's case meant educational applications. Since Titchener's account of learning was developed in terms of the older associationism, we shall give it only summary treatment and pass on to the other schools where the topic of learning found a more congenial atmosphere for its development.

Titchener and associationism.[7] Titchener introduces his chapter on association by briefly recapitulating the history of the concept in British philosophy. He reviews the traditional laws of association and the empiricists' attempts to reduce them to the single law of contiguity. He then summarizes Ebbinghaus' work, stating that "the recourse to nonsense syllables, as a means to the study of association, marks the most considerable advance, in this chapter of psychology, since the time of Aristotle." Ebbinghaus' results are presented with considerable emphasis on the conditions under which associations are formed. In the course of the discussion it becomes clear that Titchener favors contiguity as the primary condition for the formation of associations. Mention is also made of forward and backward linkage in serial associative learning, and even such matters of con-

---

[7] The exposition follows Titchener's *Textbook* (26).

temporary interest as retroactive inhibition, associative interference and mediated associations are touched upon briefly.

An entirely separate chapter is devoted to retention, but the treatment bears little resemblance to that found in modern texts. The entire section emphasizes introspective descriptions of memory images, after-images, types of imagery, and similar processes. In spite of his high regard for Ebbinghaus, very little of Ebbinghaus' experimental results found a place in Titchener's account, and what is presented is put into fine print as if he felt that experimental findings were of minor importance compared to his own long-winded descriptions of the associative and retentive consciousness.

We shall make no attempt to present Titchener's lengthy accounts of the memory consciousness. The material has little relevance for the understanding of contemporary learning theories. The interested reader will find an excellent summary of the memorizing process from the introspective or impressionistic point of view in Woodworth (30, pp. 23–35). Meanwhile, we shall go on to consider the functionalistic treatment of learning.

Functionalism and learning.[8]   Carr, it will be recalled, defined mental activities as those processes concerned with "the acquisition, fixation, retention, organization, and evaluation of experiences, and their subsequent utilization in the guidance of conduct." Clearly, this strongly functional definition of psychology places great emphasis on learning as a key process in adaptation. We have already pointed out (Chapter 2) Carr's interest in perception as another mental process of great significance in the organism's interaction with its environment. Indeed, he treats the two processes together in the fifth chapter of his *Textbook*, entitled "Perceptual-Motor Learning." In this book Carr deals with learning in a highly general way, more or less laying down the broad principles that govern learning from the point of view of adjustment. However, Carr and those who followed in the functionalistic tradition were also interested in the study of verbal learning and retention on the human level. Thus, the functionalists represent a continuation of the associationistic tradition in British philosophy as it came into experimental psychology through the pioneer work of Ebbinghaus. Carr's systematic approach to verbal learning is best represented in an article entitled "The Laws of Association," which was published by Carr in 1931 in the *Psychological Review* (7). Because of this twofold interest in learning on Carr's part—learning as adaptive behavior and learning from the viewpoint of associationistic psychology—we shall consider his systematic treatment of the topic under two headings: first, learning as an adaptive activity and second, learning from the associationistic point of view.

---

[8] Based on Carr's *Psychology* (6) except as otherwise indicated.

Learning as an Adaptive Activity

Carr begins by defining learning as the "acquisition of a mode of response" in a problem situation. Problems, in turn, are the result of a lack of adjustment brought about in one of several ways. First, the environment may be lacking in some needed substance or the individual may be confronted by obstructions which must be circumvented if a goal is to be reached. Second, an organism may lack the required skill to respond to a situation. The human infant, Carr points out, lacks the motor skills to satisfy its own needs. Finally, problems often arise out of conflicting response tendencies such as curiosity and fear. By way of illustration, Carr offers the example of the nesting bird torn between the impulse to stay on her eggs and her fear of an approaching intruder.

In solving such problems the organism employs a "variable, persistent, and analytical motor attack." All previously useful modes of behavior are tried, since, as Carr puts it, "the world is so constituted that acts that are adapted to one situation are usually somewhat appropriate to similar situations" (6, p. 89). Carr goes on to state that the animal's attack on the problem is neither aimless nor random but relevant to the situation and is, moreover, "selective and analytical." He believes, and he must have had Thorndike in mind, that other psychologists overemphasize the trial-and-error nature of animal learning.

Carr next considers a variety of factors which govern the success or failure of adaptive learning, such as the animal's capacity for learning, the strength of his motivation, the nature of the problem situation and the repertoire of previously learned modes of adapting which the animal has available and is bringing to a given problem situation. Clearly, the well-motivated organism with high capacity for learning that has had experience in solving similar problems is more likely to succeed in a given situation than the organism lacking such qualifications.

Carr then considers the knotty problem of how the correct responses in adjustmental learning are fixated while the incorrect responses are eliminated. He begins by stating the Law of Effect as a *descriptive* statement of what takes place, but does not agree with Thorndike that the sensory consequences of an act can either "stamp in" the act, if pleasant, or "stamp out" acts which are unpleasant. Carr offers the alternative hypothesis that the organism's behavior is controlled by the character of the sensory stimuli encountered by the animal *during* the problem-solving attack. In Carr's own words this relationship is stated as follows:

All acts alter the sensory situation, and the sensory stimuli necessarily exert some effect upon the subsequent behavior of the organism. Successful and unsuccessful acts can be differentiated on the basis of these effects. In the first case, the resultant sensory stimuli tend to reinforce, direct, and continue the act until the objective is attained, while the sensory stimuli resulting from an unsuccessful act operate to inhibit, disrupt, and discontinue that mode of attack. For example, a rat soon desists from further digging when the hard floor is reached, and the sensory results of gnawing at the wire mesh are not conducive to a continuance of this mode of attack. On the other hand, the sensory consequences of a success-ful act function to direct that act to the attainment of its objective. The rat lifts the latch, the open door entices the animal to enter, the rat approaches the food and begins to eat, and this act of eating is then continued until the animal's hunger is appeased. In fact, the continuance or discontinuance of any line of attack is almost wholly a function of the character of the sensory stimuli that are encountered during this time. (6, pp. 93–94.)

Carr concludes his discussion of learning as adaptive behavior by con-sidering the problems of *transfer, association,* and *habit,* and by relating these processes to his overall scheme of adjustmental learning. In dealing with transfer, he points out that all learning involves the utilization of previous experience. A dog that learns how to carry a cane through a gate by grasp-ing it at one end instead of in the middle, can transfer the solution to similar objects and situations. Or, the child who is frightened by a specific dog will exhibit fear of dogs in general. Carr also points out the practical utility of transfer and argues that as the organism is confronted with new situations it both utilizes and modifies habitual modes of behavior. In this sense, trans-fer is basic to all learning; for, even from the beginning, the organism is endowed with a "congenital repertoire of movements" which provide the basis of all future learning.

Carr relates his theory of adaptive learning to associationism by argu-ing that whenever two aspects of experience are associated they are organized in the form of an S-R relationship. In other words, once associ-ated, the presence of one will arouse the other. Generalizing to adaptive activity, Carr argues that such acts may be considered highly complex organizations of stimulus-response sequences. Thus, from Carr's point of view, learning may be regarded as a process involving the establishment of S-R connections. Carr then goes on to summarize the various laws of associ-ation, but because we shall take these up in the following section, we need not consider them further here.

Finally, Carr relates the concept of habit to his psychology of learning by emphasizing the "automatic" nature of habitual behavior. The well-established complex of associations is easily aroused, functions smoothly, and is relatively difficult to disrupt by the introduction of outside stimuli. Habit strength, in turn, is dependent upon: (1) the number of repetitions of an act, (2) the constancy of the environmental conditions under which it is performed, and (3) the degree to which competing activities have been eliminated.

It is fitting that Carr should conclude his discussion of adaptive be-havior with a discussion of habit, for one of the most brilliant passages in the entire literature of psychology is a description of the power of habit by Carr's intellectual ancestor, William James (*12*, p. 121).

Learning as Association

The functionalists' point of view on associative learning is developed in two classic expositions by Carr and Edward S. Robinson, a former stu-dent and associate of Carr's. We have already mentioned Carr's article, from which our summary of the functionalistic position will be taken. Robinson's views are to be found in a book published in 1932 (*18*). In most respects the two statements represent a common viewpoint; hence we have chosen to base the following summary on Carr's statement.

Carr begins by briefly reviewing the history of associationism in British philosophy, its entrance into experimental psychology, and its relationship to conditioning theory. In the course of the review, he denies the validity of any fundamental distinction between the laws of association and the laws of conditioning. The terms are different, but the meaning and application are the same. Therefore, at the outset he makes it clear that the laws of association are applicable to *all* types of learning which can be formulated in terms of stimulus-response connections.

Carr launches into his thesis proper by proposing a distinction between *descriptive* and *explanatory* laws. Descriptive laws are those which state the conditions under which sequences of associations tend to occur. For ex-ample, the traditional law of similarity states that the thought of one object tends to arouse the idea of a similar object. Explanatory laws are those which state relations of dependence between the observed variable and the antecedent condition(s) which are capable of being observed independently. Carr cites the law of contiguity as an example of an explanatory law. Theoretically, the conditions or factors which make for contiguity (temporal and/or spatial sequences) are prior to and are independently measurable of the associations to which they give rise. This independence justifies the designation "explanatory." Similarity, on the other hand, cannot be regarded as an explanatory law because similarity is merely a characteristic or attribute of a thought sequence and therefore cannot be observed independently of or apart from that sequence.

Carr adds that he is not interested in descriptive laws. Descriptive laws, he believes, are great in number and are reflections of all sorts of logical and grammatical relationships among words and consequently are of little interest to the psychologist. Explanatory laws, on the other hand, are of considerable importance for psychology and can be divided into three classes.

The first class deals with the *origin or formation* of associations. The law of contiguity belongs to this class and, in Carr's opinion, is the most important law of association. In conditioning theory, he points out, the law of simultaneity is the equivalent of the law of contiguity.

The second class of laws deals with the *functional strength* of associations. Simply stated, laws subsumed under this class purport to explain why some associations are stronger than others. The *law of frequency* is a specific example of this class of laws. The law states that associative strength increases as a function of the relative frequency of repetition. However, there is a point of diminishing returns beyond which frequency of repetition does *not* increase associative strength. Fatigue, boredom, and a host of other factors may make the operation of the law of frequency ineffective. Moreover, the various conditions of learning, such as distribution of practice, whole *versus* part, ordinal position in a list and the like, are also factors which influence the functional strength of associations. In fact, Carr states that the conventional associationistic laws of frequency, recency, and primacy "must be expanded to include many of the factors that are discussed under the heading of 'laws of learning.'"

A third class of laws is needed to explain the frequently observed phenomenon of variability in learning. The *law of assimilation*[9] exemplifies a very broad principle subsumed under this class. The law states that "any novel sense impression will tend to elicit those responses that are already connected with a similar sensory stimulus." The operation of the law may be exemplified in conditioning experiments where "incidental stimuli" are often associated with the conditioned response.

Pavlov, for example, found that the buzzing of a bee which had accidentally flown into his laboratory during a conditioning experiment elicited the salivary response in a dog which had been conditioned to the sound of a tuning fork. Pavlov and his followers referred to this phenomenon as stimulus generalization.

The law of assimilation, however, goes far beyond such cases of incidental learning, since, as Hilgard (*9*) points out, it is the framework in which the functionalist can investigate transfer, the equivalents of Gestalt insight and transposition, as well as generalization phenomena. In short, it is a kind of all-inclusive law which is broad enough to include virtually everything that may be subsumed under the topic of "learning." It is also important to recognize that Carr, by including the law of assimilation, denies that associative learning is explicable on a purely *S-R* basis. In order to include the factors subsumed under the law of assimilation, the *S-R* formula would have to be modified to become an *S-O-R* formula. In Carr's own words, "the character of the associations that are established is not wholly deter-

---

[9] Compare Thorndike's law of response by analogy.

mined by the sequence of objective events, but . . . is also materially influenced by the reaction of the organism to its environment" (7, p. 223).

Finally, it must be emphasized once again that Carr was not seeking to formulate a definitive set of laws of learning, but *classes* of laws organized on the basis of their function, of which the laws of contiguity, frequency, and assimilation are but specific examples. In other words, Carr sought to make the functionalist framework broad enough to include additional laws as needed.

By way of summary, Carr's systematic treatment of learning begins with the organization of the field into two broad subdivisions: primitive adaptive learning and verbal learning. Adaptive learning is best exemplified by adjustmental reactions in animals wherein the animal carries out a variable and analytic attack on a barrier to a goal. In such cases of adaptive behavior, the animal's reactions are governed by the immediate sensory consequences of his own activities. Under ordinary conditions the solution is found and the goal is reached. The consummatory activity associated with the goal reduces the animal's motivation, and the behavioral sequence is complete.

Verbal learning is handled from the point of view of association theory. Carr formulates laws of association in terms of two broad types—descriptive and explanatory. In elaborating a framework for the further development of explanatory laws, Carr believes that there are three basic functional types: first, laws dealing with the formation of associations, as exemplified by the law of contiguity; second, laws concerned with the strength of association, as exemplified by the law of frequency; and third, laws dealing with variability, as exemplified by the law of assimilation.

We shall return to the functionalistic point of view in the chapters to follow on contemporary trends in learning theory. Meanwhile, we may go on to examine the classical behavioristic position on learning as formulated by Watson. Before considering Watson's point of view, however, we shall summarize the background of behaviorism in animal psychology, a tradition which exerted a profound influence on Watson's entire system and research program, as well as on subsequent behavioristic systems.

Animal psychology as a forerunner of behaviorism. Animal psychology had its beginnings in the work of Charles Darwin. Upon the publication of his *Origin of Species* in 1859, man could no longer claim unique status in the animal kingdom. The wide divergence in both anatomical forms and behavior patterns which had lent support to the dogma of the individual creation of the specific species could now be accounted for on the basis of chance variation and selection by survival of the best adapted variants. Once the problem of the evolution of the body had been brought under attack, it was only a question of time until the possibility of the evolution of the mind came to the foreground of scientific investigation. In fact, Darwin, himself, brought the question of mental evolution under scientific scrutiny in his *Expression of Emotions in Man and Animals* (1872). In this volume he accounted for the behavioral aspects of human emotions by postulating that they are vestigial carry-overs from ancestral animal behavior. The human rage pattern, for example, bears a striking relationship to that found in lower forms.

A more direct approach to the question of mental evolution was championed by one of Darwin's countrymen, George Romanes, whose *Animal Intelligence* (1883) was the first book devoted to comparative psychology. Romanes collected and organized what amounted to anecdotal accounts of the behavior of fishes, birds, domestic animals, and monkeys. Because his work was based on anthropomorphic speculations, Romanes' conclusions fell far short of modern scientific standards. Nevertheless, he is respected for his pioneer efforts and the stimulation he provided to those who followed.

One of the outstanding British scholars who took up the challenge of animal psychology was C. Lloyd Morgan. Lloyd Morgan is famous for his "Canon," which was formulated as a criticism of Romanes' anthropomorphic interpretations of animal behavior. The Canon states that an animal's behavior must not be interpreted as the outcome of higher mental processes if it can be interpreted in terms of lower mental processes. In effect, the Canon is a law of parsimony in scientific explanation.

Lloyd Morgan published several books dealing with animal behavior and the relation of the animal to the human mind. In these publications he cites the results of studies and observations of animal behavior carried out by himself and others. His work was not truly experimental in the modern sense of controlled laboratory investigations, but, for the times, was a great step forward.

Interest in animal psychology grew rapidly toward the end of the nineteenth century. By this time Thorndike had started on his program of animal experiments in the United States. Loeb had announced his theory of tropisms in 1890 and launched his mechanistically oriented studies of the life processes. In France, Henri Fabre's world-famous studies of insects appeared, beginning in 1874; and in England, L. T. Hobhouse published his *Mind in Evolution* (1901), a volume which summarized his experiments on animals ranging in size from cats to elephants. Some of Hobhouse's experiments are quite modern in design, one of his investigations being strikingly similar to Köhler's studies of insight in chimpanzees. A monkey, "the Professor," was confronted with the problem of getting a banana out of a large pipe. By using a stick supplied by Hobhouse, "the Professor" succeeded in solving the problem after a few trials by pushing the reward completely through the pipe. Though Hobhouse does not use the term insight, he credits the monkey with "articulate ideas" (*10*, p. 247).

Of all the influences that lent impetus to the behavioristic movement in psychology, the work of Ivan P. Pavlov, the Russian physiologist, stands out most prominently. His careful, systematic series of experiments, his objectivism in interpreting his results and his use of conditioning as a technique for investigating sensory and higher mental processes were highly influential in determining the direction of Watson's behaviorism. Since Pavlov's experiments and his theoretical interpretations are treated at length in most general texts, we shall make no attempt to review them here.

With this brief historical sketch of the forerunners of behaviorism in animal psychology, we shall turn to Watson's treatment of learning, which, like much of the rest of his system, remained more of a program than a concrete set of accomplishments.

Watson on learning.[10] Watson's initial interest in animal research stemmed from his early association with the functionalists at the University of Chicago where he obtained his Ph.D. degree. His thesis research for the doctorate was concerned with the investigation of sensory mechanisms in maze learning in rats. His first book, *Comparative Psychology,* reflects his early interest in animal psychology, but, interestingly enough, gives but slight emphasis to Pavlov's conditioning experiments. He merely reports the method as chiefly useful in investigating animals' receptor processes. He even expresses doubt that "the method could be worked upon the primates" (*28,* p. 68), thereby proving himself a bad prophet.

With the publication of *Psychology from the Standpoint of a Behaviorist* in 1919, there could be little doubt that Watson's reservations about conditioning had disappeared. It was now one of the chief methods of the behaviorist and was employed by Watson himself in the famous Albert experiment where the child was conditioned to fear a rabbit. Moreover, Watson had come to lay unlimited stress on learning in the development and modification of human behavior.[11]

Despite this enthusiastic beginning and the favorable *Zeitgeist* which Watson himself helped to create, it comes as something of an anticlimax to learn that Watson never developed a satisfactory theory of learning. In his early work on maze learning in rats, he subscribed to a kinesthetic reflex theory to account for the animal's ability to run the maze successfully. In essence, he argued that the execution of one movement became the kinesthetic stimulus for the next movement (*28,* p. 212). However, he had to admit that the evidence for this view was largely negative in the sense that it was based on his own experiments in which the other senses were

[10] Our account is based on Watson's *Behavior* (*28*) and *Psychology from the Standpoint of a Behaviorist* (*29*).

[11] See the quotation, Chapter 2.

systematically destroyed with no significant effect on the animals' maze learning ability. Since the kinesthetic sense had not been destroyed, he concluded that this was the crucial sense in maze learning.[12] The question of how correct responses are fixated is discussed in Chapter VII of his comparative text. He holds that the animal learns the correct responses primarily through the operation of the law of frequency (exercise) and secondarily through the law of recency. He justifies his argument on the grounds that the animal runs along the true path more frequently than he enters the various blinds. The animal *must* run the true path at least once per trial, but he often skips blind alleys, thus gradually eliminating them. The principle of recency, Watson felt, applied more to problem boxes than to mazes. Since the last act of a series in the problem box *is* the correct one, it tends to decrease the probability of the occurrence of all other activities.

Therefore, in his early accounts of animal learning, Watson favored the age-old associationist principles, even as he denied the broader implications of associationism as it had been traditionally applied to ideation, memory, and imagination. He specifically denied the validity of the Law of Effect, calling it no law at all but "Thorndike's conviction." Watson, of course, objected to Thorndike's terminology, since phrases such as "satisfying state" and "followed by discomfort to the animal" were cast in the language of consciousness.

In his later work with the method of conditioning, Watson again emphasized the repetition of *S-R* sequences and failed to recognize what subsequently became a key issue in conditioning theory—reinforcement. In summary, then, Watson, despite his interest in the objective methods for the study of animal learning, belongs with the pre-Thorndikian associationists. Consequently, his views on learning failed to evolve into a form acceptable to contemporary behaviorists. With this rather paradoxical conclusion, we shall leave Watson and turn our attention to Gestalt contributions to learning theory.

Gestalt psychology and learning theory.   The Gestalt psychologists evidenced little interest in empirical research on learning and made few significant contributions to learning theory. Despite this harsh evaluation, it is something of a paradox that any enumeration of the most significant experiments in the literature of psychology would certainly include Köhler's studies of problem solving in apes. Nevertheless, our initial statement stands. As we pointed out earlier, the school's chief interest was in the field of perception, whereas learning remained a subordinate issue. Moreover,

---

[12] Watson was wrong. He failed to make *combination* destructions which reveal that the animal deprived of one sense falls back on those that remain. Thus, a blind, deaf, or anosmic animal can still learn a maze. But a blind-deaf-anosmic animal shows no significant learning. See Honzik (*11*).

Gestalt psychology from its very inception was antagonistic to the Thorn-dikian and Watsonian types of analyses. Indeed, the members of the Gestalt school considered that one of its major contributions to psychology was the attack on associationistic and S-R theories of learning. It might also be noted that Köhler's experiments on apes, significant as they are, are in many ways more properly classified as experiments in the area of thinking or reasoning rather than learning. However, it has become conventional to treat the experiments under the topic of learning, and we shall follow tradition and summarize them in this chapter. The Gestalt memory-trace theory, how-ever, is considered in Chapter 5.

Köhler's experiments with chimpanzees were carried out at the Uni-versity of Berlin Anthropoid Station on the island of Tenerife (one of the Canaries) during the years 1913 to 1917. The results were published in book form in 1925, and a second edition in English was issued in 1927 entitled *The Mentality of Apes* (*13*). The following account has been drawn from the latter edition. In this volume Köhler describes five types of problems which he employed in testing the apes' ability to solve complex problems. These were: (1) detour problems,[13] (2) problems involving the use of ready made implements, (3) problems in which the animal had to make implements, (4) building problems, and (5) problems involving imitation.

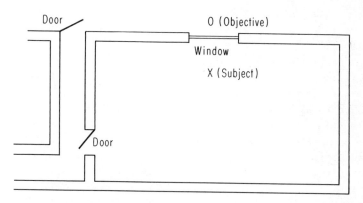

Fig. 6-4. A detour problem. (Redrawn after Köhler, *13*.)

A detour problem requires the subject to turn away from the goal in order to reach it (see Figure 6-4). In order to be credited with insight the animal must, according to Köhler, show evidence of perceiving the relation-ships involved by adopting the detour route quickly and smoothly. Köhler describes his human subject's solution for a similar problem as follows:

---

[13] In addition to apes, Köhler used a dog, hens, and a little girl as subjects for this problem.

A little girl of one year and three months, who had learned to walk alone a few weeks before, was brought into a blind alley, set up *ad hoc* (two meters long, and one and a half wide), and, on the other side of the partition, some attractive object was put before her eyes; first she pushed toward the object, i.e., against the partition, then looked around slowly, let her eyes run along the blind alley, suddenly laughed joyfully, and in one movement was off on a trot round the corner to the objective (*13*, p. 14).

But when tested on the same type of problem hens showed no evidence of reasoning or insight. The birds spent most of their time "rushing up against the obstruction." Some eventually achieved the solution in simplified problems if they extended their running sufficiently to hit upon the opening accidentally, where they could then see a direct route leading to the goal.

The dog and the chimpanzee did exhibit the ability to solve the detour problem in an insightful manner. Köhler reports that his subjects' behavior clearly reveals the dramatic moment at which insight occurs.

Köhler's second and third types of problems involved both the use of ready-made implements and the making of implements. In either case, the successful solution to the problems involves the animal's understanding of the implement as a tool. For example, if a banana is placed out of reach outside the animal's cage and several hollow bamboo sticks are provided inside the cage, then the animal must perceive the sticks in an entirely new manner—not as playthings—but as tools which he can use as extensions of himself.

When Sultan, Köhler's brightest ape, was confronted with this problem he failed at first. He tried to get the banana with one stick, then brought a box toward the bars and immediately pushed it away again. He next pushed one stick out as far as it would go, took the other stick and pushed the first with it until the first touched the banana. Sultan, Köhler adds, exhibited considerable satisfaction at this actual contact with the fruit. However, despite the fact that Köhler gave Sultan a "hint" by putting his finger in the bamboo stick while the animal watched, the ape did not succeed in the course of an hour-long trial. But immediately after that same trial, in the course of playing with the sticks, Sultan solved the problem. The following report is by Sultan's keeper who happened to be observing the animal at the critical moment.

> Sultan first of all squats indifferently on the box, which has been left standing a little back from the railings; then he gets up, picks up the two sticks, sits down again on the box and plays carelessly with them. While doing this, it happens that he finds himself holding one rod in either hand in such a way that they lie in a straight line; he pushes the thinner one a little way into the opening of the thicker, jumps up and is already on the run towards the railings, to which he has up to now half turned his back, and begins to draw a banana towards him with the double stick. I call the master: meanwhile, one of the animal's rods has fallen

out of the other, as he has pushed one of them only a little way into the other; whereupon he connects them again" (*13*, p. 127).

In subsequent experiments Sultan solved the problem quickly and was not confused even when given three sticks, two of which could not be fitted together. Köhler reports that the animal did not even try to put the inappropriate sticks together.

We may interpret the significance of this and similar tests with implements as follows. The chimpanzee does not exhibit "pure insight" in solving the problem in the sense that he needs no experience with the implements before demonstrating their use in an insightful manner. *Some* trial-and-error behavior is a necessary prelude before insight can take place.[14] Once the animal grasps the problem, he exhibits a high degree of understanding and good transfer.[15]

We shall conclude our summary of Köhler's studies by reporting briefly on the box-stacking problem—perhaps the best known of all of Köhler's experiments. The situation confronting the animal is the proper utilization of one or more boxes for obtaining a banana, which is suspended too high for the animal to reach directly or to grasp by jumping.

It turned out that the apes had considerable difficulty with this problem. Sultan needed repeated trials and several demonstrations of box-stacking by the experimenter before succeeding. But Köhler goes on to argue that the animal was actually confronted with two problems in one. First, he had to solve the problem of the gap between the floor and the banana. Essentially, this was a perceptual problem necessitating the perception of the box as a gap filler. The second aspect of the problem was the mechanical one of actually building the box structure, and it was on this phase of the problem that the animals experienced the greatest difficulty. They were, so to speak, poor builders. Even on the first trial Sultan quickly demonstrated that he knew how to bridge the gap by dragging boxes under the suspended fruit, but he stacked the boxes in so wobbly a manner that his structures kept collapsing. It is, after all, unnecessary for a chimpanzee to be a skilled builder in his natural surroundings when he is so agile in climbing trees. However, several of Köhler's animals eventually managed a three- to four-box tower which remained in place long enough for them to scramble up and seize the banana before the structure collapsed. Köhler concluded that the building problem was solved only by trial-and-error, but that the perceptual problem was solved by insight.

By way of a general summary, let us try to abstract from these experiments what the Gestalt psychologists mean by insight. Certainly, as Köhler himself points out (*13*, pp. 22–24), an important condition of insight is the

---

[14] See Birch (*1*) for a similar interpretation and an experimental confirmation.
[15] See Chapter 9 for a discussion of Harlow's work on learning to learn which is relevant to the problem of interpreting experiments on insight.

nature of the experimental situation. *The animal must be able to see the relation-ships among all parts of the problem before insight can occur.* Köhler criticizes Thorndike's work on the grounds that the cats in the puzzle boxes were frequently confronted with problems in which a survey of the entire release mechanism was impossible. Köhler believes that the various elements or parts of the problem must be perceived by the animal or it will be impossible for him to reorganize them into a large whole.

Secondly, these experiments clearly point out that insight follows a period of "trial-and-error" behavior. This does not mean the "blind, ran-dom attack" of Thorndike's cats, but a procedure more akin to what we might call "behavioral hypotheses" which the animal is trying out and dis-carding. In this connection, the animal's previous experience with either the specific elements involved in the problem under attack, or with similar problems in the past, is crucial. Past experience with similar problems leads to fruitful hypotheses in future problem solving.

Third, once the animal solves the problem by insight, there is a high degree of transfer to similar problems. Moreover, the animal shows a high level of retention and understanding which, of course, makes for good transfer.

Finally, insight is closely related to the animal's capacity to learn. Not *all* chimpanzees can solve the same problem. Moreover, there are differ-ences among species of animals. It will be recalled that dogs could readily solve the detour problem whereas hens could not. No one has made an exhaustive study of the matter, but it is doubtful if anything akin to "reasoning" or "insight" can be demonstrated lower on the phylogenetic scale than the rodents, and even here the problems must be so simple that it is a controversial matter whether they are properly characterized as "reasoning" problems in the first place (15).

To conclude, Köhler's studies of insight lent support to the Gestalt psychologists' molar interpretation of behavior as opposed to association-istic and behavioristic elementalism. Köhler's results were subsequently used to support the contention that learning of the insightful variety is essentially a perceptual reorganization or restructuring of the psychological field. The animal confronted with a problem is in a state of disequilibrium. There is a gap, so to speak, in his psychological field which closes at the moment that insight occurs. Thus, an insightful solution is analogous to closure in the area of perception.

SUMMARY AND EVALUATION

In this chapter we have attempted to show how philosophical associa-tionism evolved into experimental associationism and eventually into modern learning theory. In our opinion, the two most significant events which took place during the period covered in this chapter were the experimental investigations of memory by Ebbinghaus and the theoretical interpretations of acquisition and forgetting offered by Thorndike. Ebbinghaus' work evolved into the highly active field of verbal learning—a field which is essentially functionalistic in spirit. Thorndike's animal research was a part of the developing behavioristic movement which favored studies of animal subjects. The tradition of animal research has continued up to the present time among behavioristically oriented psychologists. However, while contemporary behaviorists in general have no fault to find with Thorndike's "trial-and-error" *description* of animal learning, they have been far less sympathetic to his theoretical *interpretation* of how learning takes place. Nevertheless, it is something of a paradox that Thorndike's Law of Effect has probably stimulated more controversy and research in the area of learning than any other single theoretical principle.

The Gestalt psychologists, as we pointed out, were more attracted by the field of perception than learning. The molar approach favored by this school is not congruent with the essentially molecular analyses required for studies of the course or progress of human and animal learning. For this same reason, the Gestalt psychologists found themselves in opposition to the traditional associationistic views favored by the other schools. However, ignoring evolutionary trends, Köhler's experiments on insight, along with his studies on transposition in learning discussed in Chapter 4, are numbered among the classics in the entire field of psychology. Moreover, the influence on the Gestalt movement as a whole has made itself felt in contemporary learning theories, as will be brought out in the next chapter.

REFERENCES

1. Birch, H. G. The relation of previous experience to insightful problem-solving. *Journal of Comparative Psychology*, **38**, 1945, pp. 367–383.
2. Boring, E. G. *A history of experimental psychology*, ed. 1. New York: Appleton, 1929.
3. Boring, E. G. *Sensation and perception in the history of experimental psychology*. New York: Appleton, 1942.
4. Brett, G. S. *History of psychology*, abridged ed. R. S. Peters (ed.). London: G. Allen, 1953.
5. Burtt, H. E. An experimental study of early childhood memory. *Journal of Genetic Psychology*, **58**, 1941, pp. 435–439.
6. Carr, H. A. *Psychology: A study of mental activity*. New York: Longmans, Green, 1925.
7. Carr, H. A. The laws of association. *Psychological Review*, **38**, 1931, pp. 212–228.
8. Ebbinghaus, H. *Memory: A contribution to experimental psychology*. 1885. Translated by Ruger and Bussenius. New York: Teachers College, Columbia University, 1913.
9. Hilgard, E. R. *Theories of learning*, ed. 2. New York: Appleton, 1956.

10. Hobhouse, L. T. *Mind in evolution.* New York: Macmillan, 1901.
11. Honzik, C. H. The sensory basis of maze learning in rats. *Comparative Psychology Monographs,* **13,** 1936, No. 64.
12. James, W. *The principles of psychology,* Vol. I. New York: Holt, 1890.
13. Köhler, W. *The mentality of apes.* Translated by E. Winter. New York: Humanities Press, 1927, and London: Routledge.
14. McGeoch, J. A. and A. L. Irion. *The psychology of human learning,* rev. ed. New York: Longmans, Green, 1952.
15. Morgan, C. T., and E. Stellar. *Physiological psychology,* ed. 2. New York: McGraw-Hill, 1950.
16. Murphy, G *Historical introduction to modern psychology,* rev. ed. New York: Harcourt, Brace, 1949.
17. Postman, L. The history and present status of the Law of Effect. *Psychological Bulletin,* **44,** 1947, pp. 489–563.
18. Robinson, E. S. *Association theory today: An essay in systematic psychology.* New York: Appleton, 1932.
19. Thorndike, E. L. *Animal intelligence.* New York: Macmillan, 1911.
20. Thorndike, E. L. *Educational psychology,* Vol. I. *The original nature of man.* New York: Teachers College, Columbia University, 1913.
21. Thorndike, E. L. *Educational psychology,* Vol. II. *The psychology of learning.* New York: Teachers College, Columbia University, 1913.
22. Thorndike, E. L. *Human learning.* New York: Appleton, 1931.
23. Thorndike, E. L. *The fundamentals of learning.* New York: Teachers College, Columbia University, 1932.
24. Thorndike, E. L. A proof of the law of effect. *Science,* **77,** 1933, pp. 173–175.
25. Thorndike, E. L., and I. Lorge. The influence of relevance and belonging. *Journal of Experimental Psychology,* **18,** 1935, pp. 574–584.
26. Titchener, E. B. *A textbook of psychology.* New York: Macmillan, 1910.
27. Warren, H. C. *A history of the association psychology.* New York: Scribner, 1921.
28. Watson, J. B. *Behavior: An introduction to comparative psychology.* New York: Holt, 1914.
29. Watson, J. B. *Psychology from the standpoint of a behaviorist.* Philadelphia: Lippincott, 1919.
30. Woodworth, R. S. *Experimental psychology.* New York: Holt, 1938.
31. Woodworth, R. S. *Contemporary schools of psychology,* rev. ed. New York: Ronald, 1948.

7

Learning II: Miniature Systems

In any survey of the major fields of psychology from the systematic point of view, the area of contemporary learning theory stands out in several important respects. First, with perception, learning shares the distinction of being one of the most active areas in the entire field of psychology in terms of theory development. So extensive is the literature in the area of learning that a detailed summary of the outstanding theories alone would require an entire volume.

Second, the field of contemporary learning theory offers one of the finest examples of the evolution of concepts in modern psychology. The chief reason for this clear evolutionary trend lies in the fact that contemporary theories of learning evolved directly from three main sources: (1) nineteenth-century associationism, (2) Thorndike's connectionism, and (3) the strong systematic viewpoints championed by the leaders of the traditional schools of psychology. Consequently, the ties that bind modern learning theories to their ancestral counterparts are stronger than those which link other contemporary areas to their evolutionary origins. This, of course, must not be interpreted to mean that learning theory is unique in this respect. On the contrary, the theme of this book is predicated upon the evolutionary point of view for psychology as a whole. Nevertheless, in such areas as intelligence, perception, motivation, and emotion, contemporary developments are more revolutionary than is true in the field of learning.

Third, theories of learning provide excellent examples of what have been called "miniature" systems in contemporary psychology. The contemporary learning theorist, in contrast to the leaders of the traditional school, strives to formulate comprehensive theories in a specific area of interest rather than for psychology as a whole. For this reason, contemporary learning theorists characteristically formulate elaborate sets of assumptions to aid in bridging gaps in our knowledge of the learning process, or to facilitate the formulation of empirical laws, which when verified, can ultimately be fitted into broader systems that seek to embrace the entire field of psychology.

Moreover, the contemporary learning theory has tended more and more in the direction of reliance on the hypothetico-deductive method. While the latter has always been the traditional approach to experimentation in all areas of psychology, in practice the early years of experimental psychology were characterized by a great deal of "exploratory" experimentation; and in some areas of psychology exploratory experiments are still the rule. In the field of learning, however, theorists are striving to design "crucial experiments" which are based on deductions from their own or rival theories. The outstanding example of the hypothetico-deductive approach in learning theory is Hull's *Systematic Behavior Theory,* which we shall consider later in this chapter. In this same connection, it might be noted that during the past decade learning theorists have begun a trend toward the extensive use of mathematical models. Mathematics has, of course, always been a part of the hypothetico-deductive method in the sense that descriptive and inferential statistics are the language of experimentation. But the widespread use of mathematical models is a recent development—a development, it might be added, that is particularly characteristic of learning theory.

Finally, the student will note that contemporary learning theorists have favored animal models both for their experimental programs and for the development of their theories of the nature of learning. This, in part, is a consequence of the fact that learning theory has attracted primarily behavioristically oriented psychologists who, as has been pointed out, believe that the use of animals promotes a more objective and scientific point of view.

Before taking up specific theories, we should like to outline our scheme for the exposition of the several theories with which we shall be concerned in the pages to follow. First, we shall indicate the theorist's overall systematic position—behavioristic, Gestalt, and others. Second, for each theory we shall summarize the chief laws or principles that bear upon the acquisition of learned responses. More specifically, we shall delineate the author's position on the relative role of practice and reinforcement (or reward) as determinants in learning. Third, the laws of generalization or transfer will be considered wherever applicable. Fourth, the laws of extinction or forgetting will be examined in light of the author's overall position. Finally, other important variables or laws not included in the preceding categories will be discussed briefly. In this way we hope to facilitate cross-comparisons between the several points of view which are represented. We shall begin our survey with Guthrie's system of *Contiguous Conditioning.*

GUTHRIE'S CONTIGUOUS CONDITIONING[1]

We have Guthrie's own admission that he has long favored the behavioristic approach in psychology. However, the designation "behaviorist" immediately brings to mind Watson and the revolution he directed against structuralism and functionalism. In contrast to Watson's iconoclastic program, Guthrie's is a mild-mannered and sober account of an associationistic-contiguity theory of learning. Indeed, at first reading Guthrie's theory appears simple and uncomplicated to the point of superficiality. This effect is heightened by Guthrie's engaging style and frequent use of anecdotes and homespun examples. But while the system appears simple in the sense that Guthrie (in contrast to most learning theorists) makes little use of formal laws, it is anything but simple in the range of phenomena it attempts to encompass and in the careful attention that Guthrie has given to measuring his position against those held by other prominent theorists. But let us turn to the theory itself, considering, first, Guthrie's laws of acquisition.

The laws of acquisition. The framework of Guthrie's system is based on conditioning; consequently, the development of the theory centers around the principle of contiguity of stimulus and response. Early in his book on learning (7, p. 23), Guthrie makes his position clear by announcing his primary and only formal law of learning: *"A combination of stimuli which has accompanied a movement will on its recurrence tend to be followed by that movement."*[2] The implications of the two terms, "movement" and "tend," in the law require further comment. As a behaviorist Guthrie is interested in the observable responses of the animal or human subjects. However, Guthrie makes a distinction between responses as acts and responses as movements. Psychologists ordinarily measure acts which consist of a series of movements that accomplish a result. Thus, the act of hitting a baseball involves a pattern of movements which, theoretically, can be recorded and measured, but which, in practice, are not. Only the act is considered important. However, it is particular movements, not acts, which are the true conditioned responses from Guthrie's point of view and are therefore the raw material of the system. Moreover, it must be emphasized that movements produce proprioceptive stimuli and that these stimuli serve as the conditioned stimuli to further movements. If we bear in mind that any learning situation involves both environmental stimuli and these internal stimuli which are carried by the organism from situation to situation, the

---

[1] The exposition is based on two primary sources: Guthrie's *Psychology of Learning* (7) and *Cats in a Puzzle Box*, by Guthrie and Horton (9). For shorter accounts of Guthrie's theory see references *0, 32*. For a bibliography of critical summaries see 7, p. 81.
[2] Italics in original.

stimulus pattern for any given learning situation is highly complex and difficult to identify. The use of the qualifying term *tend* recognizes the common finding that expected responses do not always appear because of a variety of "conflicting" or "incompatible" tendencies, as will be further elucidated later in this discussion.

It should be emphasized that Guthrie makes it clear that he does not subscribe to a law of effect or to reinforcement as an important condition of learning. He finds it unnecessary to postulate any kind of "confirmatory" explanation of conditioned associations, whether these take the form of Thorndikian satisfiers or reinforcers in the sense of drive reduction agencies. In short, *learning depends upon contiguity of stimulus and response patterns alone.*

Let us pause to illustrate Guthrie's primary law of acquisition by introducing Guthrie and Horton's experiment on cats in puzzle boxes (9). The experiment under consideration involved the use of a puzzle box of special design in which the front of the box was made of glass to provide for complete freedom of observation and photographic recording. A second feature was the inclusion of a special release mechanism consisting of a post suspended from the top (or in some models standing on the floor of the box). The post was designed in such a way that slight pressure by the animal *from any direction* caused the door to open. Movement of the post simultaneously activated a camera which took the cat's picture at the moment of responding. In order to control the animals' approach to the post's release mechanism, they were introduced into the box from a starting compartment in the rear. Finally, a dish of fish was placed outside the puzzle box. The glass door enabled the cat to see the fish at all times.[3] Let us follow a typical animal's progress in escaping from the box.

Guthrie tells us that upon entering the puzzle box the cat exhibited the traditional "trial-and-error" behavior to be expected of cats that have found themselves in psychologists' puzzle boxes since Thorndike's pioneer studies of this variety of behavior. To quote Guthrie:

> In general the cats, on being admitted to the box, paused at the threshold, entered cautiously, proceeded to the front door and clawed, sniffed, looked about. Any outstanding features such as the crack around the door got attention and were pushed at or bitten at. Approximately an average of fifteen minutes was spent in such exploratory behavior. This meant many excursions about the box.
>
> Eventually most cats did something that moved the pole and opened the escape door. The noise of the door was followed by the cat's looking at the door and then (usually) by its leaving the box through the open door (7, p. 265).

Guthrie and Horton were struck by several features of the cats' be-

---

[3] The student should compare the design of the Guthrie-Horton box to Thorndike's. See Chapter 6.

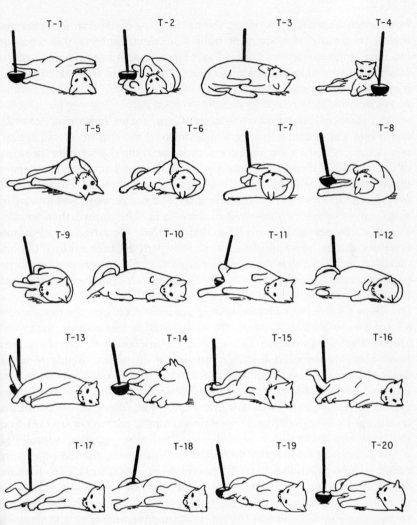

Fig. 7-1. The stereotyping of a single cat's responses over 20 trials in the puzzle box. From Trial 5 on, the animal uses its rear leg or tail to activate the release mechanism. Reproduced from tracings of original photographs made at the time of release. (From Guthrie and Horton, 9.)

behavior. First, there was a strong tendency for the animals to repeat the precise movements leading up to and including the escape movement. Some cats exhibited several "routines" or sequences of movements during the early trials, but typically settled on one routine during the latter phases of the experiment. Guthrie and Horton call the tendency for the animal to repeat successful movement patterns "stereotypy." Figure 7-1, taken from original photographs, shows the stereotyping of one animal's response during the course of a series of trials. The significance of this repetitive behavior is interpreted by Guthrie and Horton as strong evidence in favor of contiguity learning. The pattern of escape movements is repeated because it removes the animal from the box, *thereby preventing new and contradictory associations from being formed.*

In some of their animal subjects, Guthrie and Horton occasionally found new patterns of behavior which involved the appearance of entirely new solutions. Such idiosyncrasies are also accounted for by the principle of contiguity. Evidently, because the animal entered the puzzle compartment from a slightly different direction or angle, thereby setting up new proprioceptive and external stimuli patterns, *a new learning situation requiring a new escape response* was involved in these cases. The animal then went on to repeat the new sequence rather than the old; the latter, in effect, had been *unlearned* by the acquisition of the new pattern of responding. Guthrie and Horton believe that the priority of new over old responses supports the principle that associations *reach their full associative strength upon the first pairing.* In other words, learning is complete in one trial!

If, as Guthrie and Horton believe, learning occurs on the first successful trial, why, it may be asked, are so many trials necessary in the typical animal learning situation? The answer, Guthrie believes, lies along these lines: First, the simplest learning situation is, in reality, highly complex. Second, there are many stimuli confronting the animal. Some arise from external sources, others from proprioceptive organs in the animal's own muscles, tendons, and joints. Guthrie argues that "every action performed by the cat in the puzzle box is conditioned on the contemporary cues from the cat's own movements from the box and other external stimuli" (7, p. 271). Therefore, following the initial successful trial, the cat repeats the entire routine, including "errors" or irrelevant movements as well as the "correct" response. That irrelevant movements are gradually eliminated in favor of the increasingly stereotyped correct response is the result of relearning. The observer sees the cat shortening the time of escape, reducing irrelevant movements, and attaching the appropriate movement to the appropriate cue. Any given correct movement is learned on the first occasion it occurs, but with each new trial some movements drop out if they are not recurrent or essential to the action pattern.

Guthrie presents the following example of how this might take place for the simple act of entering one's home:

> If, for example, we are engaged in any one of those repeated action series that lead to stereotyped habit, such as entering our home, the first occasion involves many movements dependent on adventitious stimuli. The postman is leaving and we stop to exchange a word with him; the dog greets us at the street

and we respond to him. These are variable elements in the situation, and responses to them are generally eliminated from our final habit series. These
adventitious acts tend to be repeated, and are sometimes a part of the stereotyped
habit, but they are eliminated if successive homecomings offer other stimuli that
break them up, or if some of the external stimuli on which they depended are
lacking. On the second homecoming the serial tendency to stop where we chatted
with the postman gives way to our response to the sight of the entrance. We are
not on this occasion looking at the postman. All that is left is the trace of the
previous action which is a reminder of our meeting. We may think of the postman (7, p. 109).

Similarly, the cat in the puzzle box is judged by the external observer
to have "learned" only when the animal's performance is a smooth sequence
of the essential acts involved in the problem. In effect, the animal has eliminated all those associations which, from the observer's point of view, are
useless. Thus, practice results in improvement *only in the outcome* of learning
but does not affect the strength of any given association. With highly complex skills, such as learning to typewrite, drive an automobile, or play
basketball, there are so many movements which must be attached to their
appropriate cues that the learning of the tasks takes many trials.

To summarize Guthrie's theory up to this point, we may reiterate
his position that learned responses become associated with stimuli both
external and internal. Such associations reach full strength on the first
occasion that they occur. When the original stimulus pattern is repeated
there is a tendency for the response to be repeated, provided fatigue or
distractions do not interfere. Finally, as the cats in the puzzle box demonstrated, stereotyping of responses (especially those most intimately associated with the act of escape) occurs as a result of the elimination of
irrelevant or adventitious responses.

The role of reward and punishment.   We must now turn to the place of
reward and punishment in Guthrie's theory. It will be recalled from the
preceding description of the puzzle-box experiment that a dish of fish was
placed outside the box. At the same time we also indicated that Guthrie
does not subscribe to the Law of Effect or to reinforcement as a necessary
condition of learning. The cat learns the correct movements by *S-R* contiguity. What, then, is the role of reward? Rewards, according to Guthrie,
serve to prevent the animal (or human subject) from engaging in behavior
patterns which could break up previously learned patterns. Therefore, if
it were feasible to do so, putting the cat in a "cataleptic trance" the instant
the animal escaped from the box would be just as effective in preventing
forgetting as allowing it to eat the salmon. The act of eating the fish keeps
the cat from moving about and establishing new (and possibly disruptive)
S-R connections. In summary, then, the effect of reward is the purely mechanical one of preventing unlearning. It might be noted in this connection

that Guthrie and Horton observed that their cats often failed to eat the fish.

This raises the related problem of the role of drives or motives in learning. Why, it might be asked, make the animal hungry in the first place? The answer lies in the fact that the hungry animal is the more rest-less animal whose higher rate and greater variety of responses are more likely to lead to movements which, in turn, will result in escape. Thus, drive for Guthrie does nothing more than energize behavior in a general way and provide for vigorous movements. It has no place in his learning system other than as an overall regulator of behavior.

Transfer. Guthrie's position on transfer is virtually identical with Thorndike's. It will be recalled that Thorndike envisioned transfer in terms of identical elements. If, according to Thorndike, two learning situations, A and B, have elements in common, then transfer from A to B can occur. Guthrie deals with the problem of transfer in much the same way. If certain stimulus-response relationships are identical from one situation to another, then and only then is there a possibility of transfer.

In this same connection, it should be emphasized that Guthrie lays great stress on proprioceptive cues in skill learning. He argues that the learner carries over proprioceptive cue patterns from one learning situation to another. Because of this, there is always the possibility of positive transfer when previously learned proprioceptive response patterns are appropriate in the new learning situation. Clearly, in those cases where such S-R be-havior patterns are inappropriate, interference effects or negative transfer will occur and learning will be hindered. In extreme cases learning would be disrupted altogether.

In elaborating on the problem of transfer, Guthrie devotes an entire chapter in his *Psychology of Learning* (Chapter IV) to time factors in condi-tioning. The latter, he believes, are important in transfer. The burden of Guthrie's argument is that conditioning theory has greatly overemphasized the importance of the traditional conditioned stimulus (CS) and its asso-ciated external stimuli as the cues responsible for eliciting the response. As we emphasized under the laws of association, Guthrie believes that *movement-produced stimuli* (proprioceptive stimuli) are far more important in accounting for associations (especially remote and generalized associations) than are external cues. For this reason, when associations appear to be separated in time, as is true in trace and delayed conditioning situations, it is because intervening movements fill the gaps, and the true association is between events which occur simultaneously. In many ways Guthrie's position is reminiscent of Watson's earlier account of maze learning (see Chapter 6), and in another sense is in line with the recent emphasis by the cyberneticists on the importance of "feedback" in learning (see Chapter 14).

Forgetting. Psychologists who base their accounts of learning on conditioning theory distinguish between extinction and forgetting. Extinction, according to Pavlovian theory, is brought about by repeated nonreinforced trials. In such cases CS gradually loses its power to evoke CR. Forgetting, on the other hand, is typically considered to be the result of disuse.[4] However, many psychologists find disuse per se inadequate to account for forgetting, since this explanation of forgetting implies fading with the mere passage of time. The critics of the disuse theory argue that time is not a process or force that accomplishes anything. Rather, it is what goes on in time that weakens or obliterates memory traces.

Despite his general orientation in favor of conditioning, Guthrie does not agree that extinction results from nonreinforced practice or forgetting from disuse. In regard to extinction, it will be recalled that he does not subscribe to reinforcement theory; consequently, "extinction" simply has no meaning in his system. However, forgetting and the related problem of breaking undesirable habits are treated at considerable length. Forgetting occurs because new learning takes the place of what has been previously learned. If an established S-R connection is not displaced by a new association it will persist indefinitely. To support his position, Guthrie cites the stability of conditioned responses in dogs—responses which may last for months. Provided the dog is not subjected to bells, buzzers, tuning forks, or other stimuli similar to those used in conditioning experiments, there is nothing in the dog's normal routine to expose him to new learning which could interfere with what he has previously learned in the relatively artificial laboratory situation. Similarly, Guthrie points out that certain human skills such as are involved in skating or swimming may persist over years of disuse simply because nothing occurs to interfere with them.

Breaking habits. A problem that is closely related to the process of forgetting is that of unlearning undesirable habits. Life is full of instances where the individual's goal is to get rid of habits rather than to acquire them. New Year's is the traditional time for a tongue-in-cheek self-renunciation of pleasurable but harmful activities. However, on a more serious level, the parent, clinician, animal trainer, and teacher frequently desire to "break bad habits" in those under their control. Guthrie has long been interested in such practical applications of learning theory to problems in the guidance and control of behavior. Indeed, he conceives of much of

---

[4] See the discussion of Hull's system, this chapter.

the "undesirable behavior of the nervous breakdown, the anesthesias, paralyses, compulsion, tics, seizures, that make life a burden to the psychoneurotic" as habits (6, p. 71).

Although Guthrie's analysis of the problem is too extensive to do it justice here, we shall briefly outline the substance of his argument. For a complete discussion of this interesting application of learning theory, the reader should consult Guthrie's books (6, Chapters V and VII; 7, Chapter XI).

Essentially, the fundamental rule for breaking a habit is *to discover the cues that initiate the undesirable action and then to practice a different response to the same cues.* Guthrie offers several specific techniques for achieving this end. First, the conditioned stimulus may be introduced so gradually that the associated response is not evoked.[5] Thus, following this method in helping an individual overcome a fear of cats, the proper technique is to have him acquire a tiny kitten whose helplessness and small size fail to evoke the usual antagonistic reactions. Since the kitten's growth is so gradual, the individual acquires tolerance. The second technique involves repeating the stimulus cues until the response is fatigued. For example, by allowing the child to have his temper tantrum or the bucking horse to buck himself out, the subject is rendered temporarily tractable to reconditioning. The final technique involves pairing the undesirable response with a mutually contradictory response. Guthrie exemplifies this with the rather macabre example of tying a dead chicken around the neck of a dog guilty of habitually chasing chickens. The animal's violent reactions under these conditions will result in the development of an avoidance response.

Conclusion. Because of the limitations of space, many aspects of Guthrie's system of contiguous conditioning have been neglected in our highly condensed summary. However, within the limitations intrinsic to an account such as this, we have attempted to present the broad outlines of the theory.

By way of recapitulation, we may reemphasize Guthrie's behavioristic orientation and the grounding of his theory in the principles of conditioning. We found, however, that Guthrie either sharply limits the applicability of conditioning theory or modifies most of the traditional laws. The principle of contiguity is accepted outright and forms the basis of his system. Reinforcement is rejected entirely in the sense that it was employed by Pavlov to account for the strengthening of learned responses. Proprioceptive patterns are emphasized in favor of the traditional CS or external stimuli though the latter are by no means neglected. Transfer, too, is treated outside the bounds of traditional conditioning theory by considering it not

---

[5] Compare to Watson's conditioning of Albert, Chapter 12.

in terms of stimulus generalization, but as the carrying of previously learned appropriate cue-response associations into new learning situations. Finally, forgetting is considered as unlearning, which results from the acquisition of new responses that are incompatible with the old responses.

Independent attempts to test Guthrie's system in experimental situations have, as is so often true of psychological experiments, turned out to be divided in their support, some providing positive, some negative evidence. For example, V. W. Voeks, a student of Guthrie's who formalized the theory in a series of postulates (*40*), carried out experiments designed to assess the validity of the postulates. The best known of her postulates is the *principle of postremity*, a formalization of Guthrie's assumption that what the animal does last is learned. This assumption was tested by studying the learning of human subjects in finger mazes. The experimental hypothesis was cast into the form of a test of the relative predictability of frequency of prior choices at a choice point versus postremity or the last choice made. For all but one of fifty-seven subjects postremity was a better basis for prediction than frequency (*39*).

However, Seward (*22*) tested two groups of rats in a bar-pressing situation in which members of one group were permitted to eat the food while members of the other group were quickly removed from the situation after making the correct response. In this case the experimental design is obviously intended as a test of Guthrie's hypothesis that reward is irrelevant and that only contiguity produces learning. Indirectly, the experiment also is a test of postremity, since the animals that did not engage in eating behavior should be superior according to the principle. But Seward found that although both groups learned to press the bar, the rewarded group progressed significantly faster than the nonreward group.

These two examples are only representative of many contradictory sets of results which might be cited pro and con Guthrie's position. Hilgard (*10*, p. 75) summarizes a number of experiments bearing on the theory and Osgood (*21*, pp. 370–372) presents a critical analysis of the results of several experiments, including Voeks' mentioned above. In general it is fair to say that the apparent simplicity of the theory has proved illusory. Its very generality makes it difficult to subject it to a critical experimental test; and in those cases where its postulates have been cast into more precise form, results have been divided, some supporting, others failing to support the theory. Until future research assigns it a permanent place in learning theory, it remains as a challenging example of the wide range of phenomena which a pure contiguity theory can account for without invoking the principle of reward.[6]

For a final statement of Guthrie's theory by its originator, including a biographical summary, ce (*8*, pp. 158–195).

HULL'S HYPOTHETICO-DEDUCTIVE THEORY

Clark L. Hull's learning theory represents the work of a lifetime. Hull began to elaborate his theory in preliminary form as early as 1915, and at the time of his death in 1952 the system was still incomplete. By 1943 the theory was in a sufficiently advanced stage for it to be published in book form in a volume entitled *Principles of Behavior*. (A mathematical exposition of the theory by Hull and his associates had been published several years earlier, in 1940.) In 1951 a revision of his system entitled *Essentials of Behavior* was published, and in 1952 the final publication, *A Behavior System*, appeared posthumously. Hull had planned an additional volume in which he intended to report continued extension of his theory into the area of the analysis of social phenomena. As a result of his death before the completion of his plans, the system remains unfinished in the sense that its author hoped to apply the basic theory to a wide range of behavioral phenomena not covered in the latest statement of the theory. Because the system remained in a continuous state of evolution, it is, of course, impossible to present it in definitive form. In practice, however, this is not an insuperable obstacle for the simple reason that no system is ever "finished" in a literal sense except those systems that no longer have any proponent who are engaged in research. Such systems are extinct.

By far the most serious barrier to an understanding of Hull's system is its intrinsic difficulty. Because he was deeply impressed by the Newtonian approach to understanding natural phenomena, he employed the mathematico-deductive method in formulating his basic theory of learning. The theory is presented as a set of highly integrated postulates, theorems, and corollaries. These are stated in both verbal and mathematical form. As Hull continued to revise the system, he extended it into more and more complex areas of learning. As a consequence, the final volume, *A Behavior System*, is a work of forbidding difficulty and is virtually impossible to present in a highly condensed form without considerable "translation" and simplification. However, despite a great deal of simplification it is doubtful that the reader without a wide background in both learning theory and mathematics is in a position to understand the *Behavior System*.[7]

---

[7] As pointed out in the text, the beginner will find the *Principles of Behavior* (*11*) the least difficult of Hull's books. The *Mathematico-deductive Theory of Rote Learning* (*14*) by Hull and his associates is a highly technical mathematical statement of the theory. The *Essentials of Behavior* is a short book embodying Hull's revisions of the postulates in the *Principles*. It is considerably more difficult than the former. *A Behavior System* is the most difficult of the verbal expositions. For secondary sources the student may consult Hilgard (*10*), whose summary is based on the *Behavior System*; Osgood (*21*), based on the earlier works; and Thorpe (*32*), also based on the earlier works. Marx and Hillix (*18*) and Wolman (*42*) have interpretive summaries drawing on both the earlier and revised systems.

Because it seemed highly desirable to include Hull's system in *some* form in this introduction to systematic psychology, we have chosen to base our exposition on the *Principles of Behavior,* which, while more restricted in range than *A Behavior System,* can be rendered intelligible to the student with a background in general psychology. Moreover, the additional advantage will be gained of minimizing the simplification of Hull's original statements. In dealing with systems based on a highly integrated and logically deduced set of postulates, there is considerable risk in any attempt at simplification, since both the precision of the original language and the originator's symbolization are necessarily sacrificed for the sake of simplicity. However, after we have summarized the tenets of the original core theory, we shall attempt to indicate the major areas in which Hull sought to extend his theory and at the same time point out any important changes in the fundamental postulates. In this way it will be possible to present the theory without unduly sacrificing the precision which Hull himself believed to be one of his most important contributions. At the same time it should be possible for the serious student, with this introduction as a background, to consult the primary sources or more advanced secondary sources.

The background of Hull's system.   In attempting to understand a closely integrated deductive system of learning such as Hull's, it is important to know something of the author's general orientation to system building as well as those background influences that helped to shape the system. With regard to the former, Hull himself has provided a statement of the principles upon which his theory is predicated. In the first two chapters of *Principles of Behavior,* he discusses the nature of theories in general and the nature of his own system in particular.

Hull makes it clear that *theory,* as he employs the concept, means "a systematic deductive derivation of the secondary principles of observable phenomena from a relatively small number of primary principles or postulates. . . ." (*11,* p. 2). He goes on to exemplify his definition of a deductive theory by pointing out that the various principles and corollaries of Euclidean geometry are derived from a few definitions and axioms. On a more advanced level, he cites Newton's brilliant deductive system of celestial mechanics, which was formulated on the basis of seven definitions and three laws of motion. In support of the validity of such systems, Hull points out that many of Newton's deductions explained a number of astronomical phenomena that had been observed for centuries but which were never fully understood, such as the procession of the equinoxes.

It must be emphasized that the deductive method employed by Newton and favored by Hull for psychology does *not* begin with certain basic, well-established laws that have been previously derived from experimental observation. Hull strongly emphasizes that generalizations made on the basis of empirical observation are always uncertain. Every empirical obser vation of a given phenomenon only increases the probability that future observations will duplicate the original results. One might, he points out conclude that all heavenly bodies are spherical after looking at the moon While observation of the sun and a few planets might strengthen the con viction that all celestial objects are spherical, there may be many heavenly bodies as yet unobserved which are not round.

Hull does not, of course, deny the utility of observed data. Rather deduction and empirical observation go hand in hand in theory building The role of empirical observation is that of a check or test on the validity of the initial postulates formulated by deduction. Thus, the postulates in a hypothetico-deductive system are verified, discarded, or modified de pending upon the outcome of experiments designed to test the validity of the original assumptions. Clearly, Hull strongly favors the traditiona method of the physical sciences and their ally, mathematics.

As applied to psychology, the hypothetico-deductive method consist of postulating intervening variables. As we pointed out earlier, intervening variables are O factors or *unobservable* entities which the psychologist employ to account for *observable* behavior. Since intervening variables are function ally related to certain antecedent conditions, on the one hand, and observ able responses, on the other, then the hypothetico-deductive method in psychology demands *a hierarchy of intervening variables that are logically inter related, noncontradictory, and experimentally verifiable.* The antecedent condition (*A* factors) can be manipulated as independent variables to observe their effects on behavior (*R* factors). In diagrammatic terms: $A—f—(O)—f—R$

In addition to his admiration for Newton and the hypothetico-deduc tive method, Hull also expresses his indebtedness to Pavlov and Darwin He was profoundly influenced by Pavlov's writings when they first appeared in the United States. The Russian physiologist's behavioristic approach his statement of conditioning principles in terms readily adaptable for the formulation of additional hypotheses, and his careful program of empirica research were all factors which favorably disposed Hull toward utilizing conditioning principles in the elaboration of his own theory. In fact, the conditioned response became the focal point of Hull's theory and was regarded by him as the most fundamental form of learning by means of which more complex forms of learning could be investigated and explained

Hull was also influenced by Darwin, as revealed by his concern with providing a foundation for his learning-theory system in the framework of organisms' environmental interactions. Indeed, Hull hoped to show that his system could account for the basic laws involved in the "social" behavior of various species; that is, he sought to discover the *primary* principles of behavior valid alike for man and beast in their interactions with the phys ical world and the world of living organisms.

With this introduction to Hull's overall orientation in mind, let us turn to the system itself, following our plan of considering first the laws of acquisition followed by a consideration of laws of reinforcement, extinction, transfer, and other processes.

Laws of acquisition. Hull lays the groundwork for his laws of acquisition by anchoring his system in the neurological substrata of behavior. Adaptive behavior can occur only if the organism is aware of its environment through receptor activities which are conducted inward to the central nervous system over peripheral sensory nerves. Upon arriving in the central nervous system, impulses are routed to the proper muscular and glandular organs, thereby effecting adaptive behavior. However, the brain is not a simple bundle of in and out pathways which invariably produce a given response to a given stimulus. If this were the case, there would be little variation in behavior. Instead, neural impulses interact, and neurons sometimes discharge spontaneously; both processes result in variability of behavior.

In order to take the stimulus or antecedent conditions into account, as well as the possibilities of central nervous interaction, Hull's first two postulates are concerned with (1) afferent impulses essential for the appreciation of stimuli and (2) central nervous interaction. Postulate 1 is stated as follows:

Postulate 1

When a stimulus energy (S) impinges on a suitable receptor organ, an afferent neural impulse (s) is generated and is propagated along connected fibrous branches of nerve cells in the general direction of the effector organs, via the brain. During the continued action of the stimulus energy (S), this afferent impulse (s), after a short latency, rises quickly to a maximum of intensity, following which it gradually falls to a relatively low value as a simple decay function of the maximum. After the termination of the action of the stimulus energy (S) on the receptor, the afferent impulse (s) continues its activity in the central nervous tissue for some seconds, gradually diminishing to zero as a simple decay function of its value at the time the stimulus energy (S) ceases to act (*11*, p. 47).

In simpler terms, Hull is postulating that sensory impulses generated in receptor organs excite nervous tissue rapidly, but the effects gradually decrease and eventually die out altogether after stimulation has ceased. The most significant concept in the postulate is that of the gradual decay of nervous excitation. *This slow decay allows for the possibility of association by contiguity.* Thus, even though thunder follows lightning, association of thunder *with* lightning is possible, since the nervous excitations generated by the lightning persist for some time and thereby allow it to be experienced contiguously with the subsequent thunder. In conditioning, much the same process occurs. The excitations from CS persist long enough for them to overlap with those generated by US.

The second postulate, which deals with afferent neural interaction, is given as follows:

Postulate 2

All afferent neural impulses (s) active in the nervous system at any given instant, interact with each other in such a way as to change each into something partially different ($\bar{s}$) in a manner which varies with every concurrent associated afferent impulse or combination of such impulses. Other things equal, the magnitude of the interaction effect of one afferent impulse upon a second is an increasing monotonic function of the magnitude of the first (*11*, p. 47).

More simply, sensory impulses occurring together in the nervous system interact, and in the process of interacting, modify each other. The manner in which impulses are modified varies with any given set of impulses whether these occur in simple pairs or in combinations. The degree to which one impulse influences another depends upon the strength of the first.

The importance of Postulate 2 lies in the fact that it allows for the synthesizing effects of cortical processes, thus permitting Hull to deal not only with *patterns* of stimuli, but also to account for those configurational problems to which the Gestalt psychologists devoted so much attention. For example, if one fixates a small yellow square against a gray background, the resulting color experience is quite different from the sensation resulting when a yellow square is fixated against a blue background. More generally, combinations of stimuli are continually bombarding our receptors, but the effects are not isolated in our nervous system. Rather, each stimulus influences every other because of the resulting neural interaction.

Hull goes on to relate his system to needs by arguing that the general function of effector systems is that of bringing about need satiation. However, because environmental conditions vary a great deal, no one response can always be guaranteed to bring about needed relief. Consequently, Hull postulates that organisms are capable of demonstrating "hierarchies of response" in problem situations, thus ensuring a range of varied activities which have a high probability of successfully reducing needs. In postulate form the principle is stated as follows:

Postulate 3

Organisms at birth possess receptor effector connections ($_sU_R$) which, under combined stimulation (S) and drive (D), have the potentiality of evoking a hierarchy of responses that either individually or in combination are more likely to terminate the need than would be a random selection from the reaction potentials resulting from other stimulus and drive combinations (*11*, p. 66).

This postulate might be exemplified by the remarkable behavior of the excised fetal guinea pig described by Carmichael (2). If the animal (which is kept alive in a warm saline solution) is stimulated by touching its cheek with a horse hair, it will make avoidance movements with the entire head region. If the stimulus persists, the animal will make brushing movements with its paws, and finally under continuing stimulation will swim away with its attached placenta. Here, indeed, is a strikingly adaptive hierarchy of responses.

Thus far we have been examining the groundwork for what may be regarded as the most basic postulate in Hull's system, Postulate 4. Following our usual plan we shall quote the postulate as originally given, followed by a simplified statement.

Postulate 4

Whenever an effector activity ($r \rightarrow R$) and a receptor activity ($S \rightarrow s$) occur in close temporal contiguity ($_sC_r$), and this $_sC_r$ is closely associated with the diminution of a need ($\dot{G}$) or with a stimulus which has been closely and consistently associated with the diminution of a need ($\dot{G}$), there will result an increment to a tendency ($\triangle_sH_R$) for that afferent impulse on later occasions to evoke that reaction. The increments from successive reinforcements summate in a manner which yields a combined habit strength ($_sH_R$) which is a simple positive growth function of the number of reinforcements (N). The upper limit (m) of this curve of learning is the product of (1) a positive growth function of the magnitude of need reduction which is involved in primary, or which is associated with secondary reinforcement; (2) a negative function of the delay (t) in reinforcement; and (3) (a) a negative growth function of the degree of asynchronism (t') of $\dot{S}$ and R when both are of brief duration, or (b), in case the action of $\dot{S}$ is prolonged so as to overlap the beginning of R, a negative growth function of the duration (t'') of the continuous action of $\dot{S}$ on the receptor when R begins (*11*, p. 178).

Let us break this postulate into its two component parts, first considering that aspect which deals with temporal contiguity as an important condition of learning, and secondly the part that is concerned with the role of reinforcement. In simplified form the first part of Postulate 4 states that habit, or more precisely habit strength, which is the Hullian intervening variable for learning, depends upon close temporal contiguity of the receptor and effector activities involved. In essence, Hull is simply patterning this aspect of his postulate on the familiar conditioning experiment where CS (bell) must be closely associated with UR (salivation to food) before conditioning can occur. However, it must be emphasized that, while contiguity is a necessary condition for learning, it is not a sufficient condition. Consequently, we must next consider the critical role of reinforcement contained in the statement of the postulate.

Hull distinguishes between primary and secondary reinforcement. Primary reinforcement, as Hull originally formulated the concept, is a

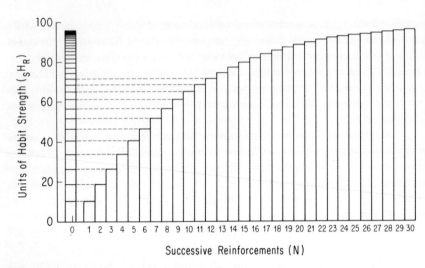

Fig. 7-2. A diagrammatic representation of habit strength as a function of successive reinforcements. (From Clark L. Hull, *Principles of Behavior*. Copyright, 1943, D. Appleton-Century Co., Inc. By permission of Appleton-Century-Crofts, Inc.)

process of need reduction.[8] The animal that jumps from a charged grid into a "safe" area, as one of a number of possible reactions to the shock, quickly establishes the habit of jumping and no longer exhibits the variety of other responses typical in such situations, such as urination, biting the bars, trying to climb the walls, and the like. The jumping reaction is reinforced because it is closely followed by need reduction, the need in this case being to avoid the injurious effect of the shock. Similarly, food in Pavlov's conditioning experiment is a primary reinforcer because it reduces the animal's need for food.

Secondary reinforcement results when stimuli closely associated with primary reinforcement become effective in reducing needs through learning. The infant, for example, ceases crying when it is fed. But because the mother typically picks up the infant and "cuddles" it during the process of feeding, the cuddling stimuli become associated with the primary reinforcement (food), and after a number of such experiences the infant will cease crying upon being picked up. The cuddling, then, may be said to have become a secondary reinforcer.

Turning to the aspect of the postulate which deals with habit strength, Hull specifies the manner in which summation of increments of habit strength depend upon repetitions of reinforcement. In addition, three variables which limit habit strength are stated. Figure 7-2, taken from Hull

[8] Hull subsequently changed his mind and defined primary reinforcement as drive-*stimulus* reduction. See "Major revisions and extensions of Hull's theory," this chapter.

(*11*, p. 116), shows a theoretical representation of habit strength as a function of successive reinforcements. The curve is a typically negatively accelerated learning curve in which gains are initially high and gradually diminish with successive reinforcements. A word of explanation is in order with regard to the stepwise growth of the curve; this is attributed to the fact that each reinforcement is a unit and is therefore theoretically indivisible in its effect on learning.

The limit of habit strength depends upon: (a) the magnitude of need reduction, (b) the delay between response and reinforcement, and (c) the time interval between the conditioned stimulus and the response. The variable of magnitude of need reduction theoretically operates as follows: The greater the quantity and the higher the quality of reinforcement, the higher the upper limit of the curve of habit strength.[9] Delay in reinforcement is negatively correlated with habit strength, which means that the longer reinforcement is delayed, the weaker its effect.

The problem of temporal patterning in conditioning is complex. Let us approach it by reviewing briefly the various possibilities involved. There are four temporal patterns normally employed in experimental work: (1) simultaneous, (2) delayed, (3) trace, and (4) backward. In simultaneous conditioning, *CS* and *US* are presented at the same time and continue together until *CR* occurs. In the delayed conditioned response, *CS* is presented anywhere from a few seconds up to a minute before *US* and may continue with it for a few seconds. In trace conditioning, *CS* is presented first, then after a brief delay *US* follows; and in backward conditioning, *US* is given before *CS*. These relationships are shown diagrammatically in Figure 7-3.

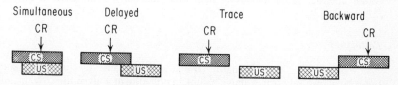

Fig. 7-3. Temporal relationships in conditioning. (Reprinted from *Elements of Psychology* by David Krech and Richard S. Crutchfield, by permission of the publisher, Alfred A. Knopf, Inc. Copyright 1958 by David Krech and Richard S. Crutchfield.) For explanation see text.

Without attempting to go into the detailed findings on the relative efficiency of the various time patterns—a problem to which Hull devotes an entire chapter—we shall simply indicate that conditioning is most rapid when *US* follows the onset of *CS*, as is true in delayed and trace condition-

[9] See also discussion in Chapter 8.

ing. If, however, the separation of *CS* and *US* in trace conditioning is too great, then habit strength is adversely influenced.

With this discussion of the role of contiguity, primary and secondary reinforcement and temporal patterns in conditioning, we have come to the core of Hull's theory: *The basic condition under which learning takes place is contiguity of stimuli and responses under conditions of reinforcement.* Because of its emphasis on reinforcement, Hull's has been called a "need reduction" theory, in contrast to Guthrie's contiguity theory and the purposive behaviorism of Tolman, which is known as a cognitive theory (this chapter). The student should also compare Hull's reinforcement principle to Thorndike's Law of Effect (Chapter 6) and to Carr's theory of adaptive learning (Chapter 6). Hull, in fact, has attempted to integrate the Law of Effect into Pavlovian conditioning. Finally, we would like to point out that, while Hull's is a behavioristic theory, his use of the intervening variable of reinforcement represents a departure from a strict behavioristically oriented *S-R* psychology which employs only the principles of frequency and recency to account for learning. Watson, in turn, surely would have objected to the O factor of reinforcement on the same grounds that he objected to consciousness, sets, motives, and other "unobservables."

In Postulates 6 and 7[10] Hull relates drives to learning by stating that drives activate effective habit strength into "reaction potentiality" ($_sE_R$). In essence, this means that learned habits are evoked only in the presence of drives, or, in short, that drive regulates performance. In Hull's terms, the two postulates are stated as follows:

Postulate 6

Associated with every drive (D) is a characteristic drive stimulus (S_D) whose intensity is an increasing monotonic function of the drive in question (*11*, p. 253).

Postulate 7

Any effective habit strength ($_s\bar{H}_R$) is sensitized into reaction potentiality ($_sE_R$) by all primary drives active within an organism at a given time, the magnitude of this potentiality being a product obtained by multiplying an increasing function of $_s H_R$ by an increasing function of D (*11*, p. 253).

Since the original wording of Postulates 6 and 7 is relatively simple, we need only emphasize that the magnitude of reaction potential is a multiplicative function of drive and habit strength. If, therefore, drive is zero, reaction potential will be zero. If drive is maximum, reaction potential will

---

[10] Postulate 5 deals with transfer and will be considered in the next section in order to preserve our announced outline of topics.

be high—how high depending, of course, on habit strength. Finally, we might note that because drives carry characteristic stimulus patterns (Postulate 6) the animal can learn to discriminate on the basis of drives.

Let us illustrate the factors given in Postulates 6 and 7 by means of simple examples. A rat that has been conditioned to press a bar in order to obtain a pellet of food will be stimulated to respond by a high level of drive, while the satiated animal will give few responses irrespective of how well he may have learned the bar-pressing habit. If the learning situation demands discrimination, as is true in the case of a T-maze in which the animal when hungry must turn right for food and when thirsty must turn left for water, then the stimuli associated with these visceral drives will evoke the proper response in proportion to the strength of the drives and the degree of effective habit strength.

Transfer. Conditioning theorists prefer to speak of generalization rather than transfer. The concept of generalization stems from the classical Pavlovian conditioning experiment in which the animal, after having been conditioned to respond to a certain stimulus, will respond to similar stimuli. In general, the greater the similarity between the stimuli, the greater the magnitude of the generalized response, and the more dissimilar the stimuli, the weaker the response. Consequently, there is a *gradient* of generalization which is directly related to the degree of similarity of *CS* and the generalization stimulus. Hull's fifth postulate expresses the relationship as follows:

Postulate 5

The effective habit strength $_S\bar{H}_R$ is jointly (1) a negative growth function of the strength of the habit at the point of reinforcement ($\dot{S}$), and (2) of the magnitude of the difference (d) on the continuum of that stimulus between the afferent impulses of $\dot{s}$ and s in units of discrimination thresholds (j.n.d.'s); where d represents a qualitative difference, the slope of the gradient of the negative growth function is steeper than where it represents a quantitative difference (*11*, p. 199).

In simplified terms, Postulate 5 states the relationship already discussed in the preceding paragraph. In addition, we might note that Hull attempted to quantify the relationships in terms of just noticeable difference thresholds and to present empirical data (*11*, p. 201) in support of his contention. We need not be concerned with this purely quantitative aspect of Hull's fifth postulate here.

The problems of inhibition, extinction, and forgetting. Thus far we have discussed the critical role of contiguity and reinforcement in habit strength. However, common experience tells us that the presence of adequate habit strength and drive is sometimes insufficient to assure an effective reaction. There are occasions when inhibition may prevent the appearance of an otherwise readily evoked response. If, for example, an animal has been responding for a long period of time in a conditioning experiment, fatigue will set in. In and of itself fatigue will generate a form of inhibition which Hull calls *reactive inhibition*, and the animal will cease to respond. If an arbitrary stimulus is presented at the same time that the response is gradually diminishing because of fatigue, conditioned inhibition will develop, and the associated stimulus will become capable of inhibiting the response. Because of the ever-present factor of variability in behavior, Hull also postulates that inhibitory potentials oscillate from instant to instant. The relevant postulates follow:

Postulate 8

Whenever a reaction (R) is evoked in an organism there is created as a result a primary negative drive (D); (a) this has an innate capacity (I_R) to inhibit the reaction potentiality $({}_sE_R)$ to that response; (b) the amount of net inhibition $(\dot{I}_R)$ generated by a sequence of reaction evocations is a simple linear increasing function of the number of evocations (n); and (c) it is a positively accelerated increasing function of the work (W) involved in the execution of the response; (d) reactive inhibition (I_R) spontaneously dissipates as a simple negative growth function of time (t''') $(11,$ p. 300).

Postulate 9

Stimuli (S) closely associated with the cessation of a response (R) (a) become conditioned to the inhibition (I_R) associated with the evocation of that response, thereby generating conditioned inhibition; (b) conditioned inhibitions $({}_sI_R)$ summate physiologically with reactive inhibition (I_R) against the reaction potentiality to a given response as positive habit tendencies summate with each other $(11,$ p. 300).

Postulate 10

Associated with every reaction potential $({}_sE_R)$ there exists an inhibitory potentiality $({}_sO_R)$ which oscillates in amount from instant to instant according to the normal "law" of chance, and whose range, maximum, and minimum, are constant. The amount of this inhibitory potentiality associated with the several habits of a given organism at a particular instant is uncorrelated, and the amount of diminution in ${}_s\bar{E}_R$ from the action of ${}_sO_R$ is limited only by the amount of ${}_s\bar{E}_R$ at the time available $(11,$ p. 319).

In addition to what has already been said by way of introduction to Postulates 8 and 9, it should be noted that in Postulate 8 (d), reactive inhibition spontaneously dissipates with time after the cessation of practice. A simple example may be found in the case of spontaneous recovery in conditioning experiments. In such cases the animal is extinguished by repeated nonreinforcement but recovers following a rest period. It should also be emphasized that conditioned inhibition does *not* spontaneously dissipate with time. Conditioned inhibition is *learned* inhibition, and, according to Hull, time per se has no effect on learned reactions. Only unreinforced repetition of conditioned reactions (including conditioned inhibition) could cause a diminution in response. Finally, it should be noted that according to Postulate 9, reactive and conditioned inhibition are additive in their effects in diminishing reaction potential.

Postulate 10, as was previously pointed out, deals with the oscillation of reaction potential. Hull believes there is evidence to show that these variations in inhibition take place according to the laws of chance and, when plotted, follow the normal probability curve. Finally, the second sentence in the postulate contains the hypothesis that two or more inhibitory potentials existing within the individual at the same time are not correlated, and the extent of the effect of inhibitory potentials is limited only by the amount of effective reaction potential available at the time.

Hull points to two important implications of the oscillation principle. First, he believes that it explains the frequently observed phenomenon that stimuli may elicit reactions which have never been conditioned to them. More specifically, such variable reactions occur because the oscillation process results in variations in the intensity of muscular contractions, thus making every coordinated act slightly different from every other. Second, oscillation implies that behavior can never be predicted with certainty at any given point in time. However, prediction is nevertheless possible, since oscillation follows the law of chance. As a result, predictions can be made in terms of the central tendency of behavior and, of course, this procedure involves collecting data from a large number of observations.

Hull has no postulate dealing directly with either extinction or forgetting. However, Postulate 4 deals with the problem of extinction in the sense that it *implies* that unreinforced repetitions of CS will lead to the disappearance of the conditioned response.[11] In such cases, extinction will follow a negative growth function. Data and curves are presented by Hull both from animal and human experiments demonstrating the occurrence of extinction under conditions of repetition. However, it is important to recognize that in such cases the cause of extinction *is the building up of conditioned and reactive inhibition.* In other words, extinction does not result from nonreinforced repetition per se, but from inhibitory effects.

Forgetting is presumed to be the result of a decay function. This is implied by one of Hull's corollaries (*11*, p. 296) which states: *"In the case of rote series learned by massed practice, reminiscence will rise at first with a negative*

[11] See also Postulate 14.

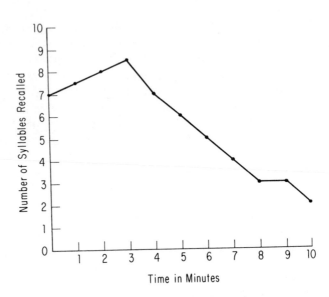

Fig. 7-4. Reminiscence. The subject practices until he can repeat seven syllables correctly. Reminiscence is shown by the initial rise in the curve without further practice.

acceleration, which will presently be replaced by a fall." Figure 7-4 shows a hypothetical retention curve for the rote learning of nonsense syllables. The brief rise in the curve following the cessation of practice is the result of reminiscence. The reminiscence effect is most marked, as Hull implies in the corollary quoted above, when practice is massed, presumably because of the more rapid buildup of inhibition under such conditions. A further study of the curve shows that the material undergoes a gradual decay with time, following the appearance of reminiscence.

Reaction thresholds and response evocation. The final concept we wish to introduce from Hull's 1943 system is that of the reaction threshold, $(s\bar{E}_R)$. It will be remembered that Hull's system of intervening variables is anchored to antecedent conditions, such as receptor stimulation and other general conditions that are essential for learning. However, in Hull's own words, "The pivotal theoretical construct of the present system [around which the various factors described in the postulates are oriented] is that of the effective reaction potential $(s\bar{E}_R)$" (*11*, p. 342). In his final six postulates, Hull attempts to anchor effective reaction potential to certain variables not yet considered which influence responses. At the same time, several basic problems of measurement are considered.

The two most important variables which govern the evocation of responses are thresholds and incompatible responses. Other things being equal, if the effective reaction potential is above threshold, then a response will appear. If effective reaction potential is below threshold, no response will appear. In the case of incompatible responses, the response whose reaction potential is greatest will be the response that is evoked.

Postulates 11 and 16 state these conditions in formal terms:

Postulate 11

The momentary effective reaction potential ($_s\bar{E}_R$) must exceed the reaction threshold ($_sL_R$) before a stimulus (S) will evoke a given reaction (R) (*11*, p. 344).

Postulate 16

When the reaction potentials ($_sE_R$) to two or more incompatible reactions (R) occur in an organism at the same time, only the reaction whose momentary effective reaction potential ($_s\dot{\bar{E}}_R$) is greatest will be evoked (*11*, p. 344).

Postulates 12, 13, and 14 deal with quantitative problems involved in the measurement of responses. Briefly, Hull advocates *probability of response, latency, and resistance to experimental extinction* as measures of effective reaction potential. Clearly, the stronger the habit the greater the probability of response, while short latency and high resistance to extinction indicate a high degree of effective reaction potential, and indirectly, a high degree of effective habit strength ($_s\bar{H}_R$). Long latency and low resistance to extinction indicate weak effective reaction potential and at the same time a low degree of effective habit strength. The relevant postulates are given as follows:

Postulate 12

Other things equal, the probability (p) of striated-muscle reaction evocation is a normal probability (ogival) function of the extent to which the effective reaction potential ($_s\bar{E}_R$) exceeds the reaction threshold ($_sL_R$) (*11*, p. 344).

Postulate 13

Other things equal, the latency ($_st_R$) of a stimulus evoking a striated-muscle reaction is a negatively accelerated decreasing monotonic function of the momentary effective reaction potential ($_s\bar{E}_R$), provided the latter exceeds the reaction threshold ($_sL_R$) (*11*, p. 344).

Postulate 14

Other things equal, the mean number of unreinforced striated-muscle reaction evocations (n) required to produce experimental extinction is a simple linear increasing function of the effective reaction potential ($_s\bar{E}_R$) provided the latter at the outset exceeds the reaction threshold ($_sL_R$) (*11*, p. 344).

Postulate 15 states:

Postulate 15

Other things equal, the amplitude (A) of responses mediated by the autonomic nervous system is a simple linear increasing function of the momentary effective potential $(_S\dot{E}_R)$ (*11*, p. 344).

In this postulate Hull deals with the special case of autonomic responses, such as the galvanic skin response or salivation, which, he believes, may involve somewhat different problems of measurement than striated muscular responses. Hull and his associates found certain experimental differences in the factors governing the amplitude of autonomic and striated muscular responses; hence a distinction is made between the two. We need not enter into the problems involved here, since the distinction is not a crucial one for our purposes. A discussion of the relevant issues can be found in Hull (*11*, pp. 339–340).

We have now traced in highly summarized form the major postulates that constitute the framework of Hull's 1943 system. We have made no attempt to present much of the detailed reasoning that lies behind the formulation of the postulates, nor have we attempted to summarize the many corollaries that Hull derived from the postulates. Finally, by way of further omissions, we have not attempted to discuss the quantitative units of measurement and the mathematical constants developed by Hull. We hope that despite these gaps a sufficiently detailed account of the primary postulates has been presented to convey the flavor of Hull's system and to give some appreciation of his hypothetico-deductive approach to the formulation of learning theory. By way of a final glance at the postulate system as a whole, the major theoretical constructs in Hull's theory may be related in terms of the following equation:[12]

$$_S\dot{E}_R = [_S\bar{H}_R \times D - (I_R + _SI_R)] - _SO_R$$

where $_S\dot{E}_R$ represents the momentary effective reaction potential or Hull's observable measure of learning, $_S\bar{H}_R$ is habit strength, D is drive, I_R is the amount of reactive inhibition, $_SI_R$ is the amount of conditioned inhibition, and $_SO_R$ is oscillation potential associated with $_S\bar{H}_R$.

The formula may be interpreted as follows: The effective reaction potential (in short, performance) depends, first of all, upon effective habit strength (learning) multiplied by drive. Thus, if *either* effective habit strength *or* drive is zero, no response can be evoked. Second, the product of effective habit strength and drive is diminished by the addition of two antagonistic

[12] We are indebted to B. B. Murdock, Jr., for this formulation.

factors, reactive and conditioned inhibition. The relationship is such that if either is zero, or very weak in magnitude, then reaction potential is high. If, since $I_R + {}_sI_R$ is *subtracted* from ${}_s\bar{H}_R \times D$, either reactive or conditioned inhibition is present, effective reaction potential will be adversely affected. Finally, the influence of the oscillatory potential ${}_sO_R$ is subtractive in its effect. Consequently, as oscillation decreases, effective reaction potential increases and vice versa.

This completes our summary of Hull's 1943 system of learning. As we previously indicated, our next task is to outline briefly the major revisions in the system and note its extensions into areas of behavior other than simple learning. We shall make no attempt to trace Hull's revisions as they were developed and published in the technical journals and books between 1945 and the final revision in *A Behavior System* (1952), but instead base our exposition on the 1952 system.

Major revisions and extensions of Hull's theory. Hull's revisions took several forms. In some cases postulates were dropped and in other cases underwent revision. Several new postulates were substituted for those which had been dropped. Without attempting to go into detail, we shall indicate the direction which the major changes took.

First, it will be recalled that habit strength (${}_s\bar{H}_R$) increases as a function of reinforcement. The magnitude of the increase depends, in turn, upon the degree of need reduction and the temporal factors involved. (See Postulate 4.) In the 1952 system these factors are no longer held to influence habit strength. Rather, only the number of reinforced contiguous repetitions of S-R relationships influences habit strength.

The second major revision involves increased emphasis upon secondary reinforcement, along with a closely related change in attitude toward the essential factor in reinforcement. It will be recalled that Hull emphasized primary reinforcement as the critical condition in habit formation in the 1943 system and, further, defined primary reinforcement as need reduction. In the 1952 edition, *drive stimulus reduction* is the essential factor in reinforcement. To clarify the point, let us consider the case of a hungry animal. He needs food, and his restless behavior indicates the operation of a drive for food. Accompanying the drive process are stimuli arising from the viscera, such as hunger pangs, which Hull refers to as drive stimuli. Now the critical factor in reinforcement may be considered to be either the reduction of the hunger drive in the sense of diminution of the need for food, or the reduction of the drive stimuli themselves. It is the latter process which the 1952 system held to be crucial. Obviously, under most conditions, secondary reinforcement is more effective in reducing drive stimuli than primary needs; consequently, secondary reinforcement becomes of much greater importance in the revised system.

Hull also emphasized two factors associated with $_s\dot{\bar{E}}_R$, or the response tendency. These were: V, or the stimulus-intensity dynamism, and K, or incentive reinforcement. In the case of the stimulus-intensity dynamism, it is assumed that for any given level of habit strength or $_s\bar{H}_R$, the greater the stimulus intensity, the greater the reaction potential or $_s\dot{\bar{E}}_R$. In the form of an equation,

$$_s\dot{\bar{E}}_R = V \times {}_s\bar{H}_R$$

Similarly, for any given level or habit strength, the greater the magnitude of the reinforcement, or K, the greater the reaction potential. In the form of an equation,

$$_s\dot{\bar{E}}_R = K \times {}_s\bar{H}_R$$

If we introduce these new variables into the basic equation for performance in a learning situation then:

$$_s\dot{\bar{E}}_R = [_s\bar{H}_R \times D \times V \times K - (I_R + {}_sI_R)] - {}_sO_R$$

By introducing incentive motivation into his system Hull allowed for the empirical finding that incentives regulate performance and, incidentally, brought his system closer to Lewin's Field Theory and other systems which emphasize incentives as arousers of drive and regulators of behavior.

Finally, we should like to mention Postulate 17, the last stated by Hull in the 1952 system. The wording is as follows:

Postulate 17

> The "constant" numerical values appearing in equations representing primary molar behavioral laws vary from species to species, from individual to individual, and from some physiological states to others in the same individual at different times, all quite apart from the factor of behavioral oscillation ($_sO_R$) (*13*, p. 13).

Clearly, by including a special postulate devoted to individual differences, Hull is giving formal recognition to an age-old problem in psychology. Individuals differ in respect to intelligence, learning ability, motivation, and so forth, and all theories of learning must take such individual differences into account. In practice, Hull and his associates had already done this for those portions of the 1943 system for which quantitative constants had been developed. This was accomplished by repeated measurements on large groups of animal or human subjects in order to eliminate individual variations statistically.

With regard to extensions or applications of the system into areas other than simple learning situations, the major portion of *A Behavior System* is devoted to this task. It is impossible in a chapter such as this to do more than broadly indicate the fields involved.

First, Hull extended his theory into the area of discrimination learning. He discusses both generalization of stimulus qualities and stimulus intensities, and concludes that the primary factor underlying discrimination learning of either type is differential reinforcement. In accounting for discrimination learning in this manner, Hull follows classical conditioning theory, for Pavlov found that by selective reinforcement differential conditioned responses could be established after generalization had occurred. Second, Hull extends the system into the area of maze learning. In dealing with this favorite topic of the animal psychologist, Hull reintroduces one of his early concepts, that of the *goal gradient* (1932). The goal-gradient hypothesis holds that learning will be most effective the closer the animal gets to the goal. Therefore, the hypothesis predicts that, other things being equal, the animal will eliminate blind alleys in reverse order. Similarly, long blind alleys are eliminated faster than short blinds, and short mazes are learned more readily than long mazes. Hull believes that the empirical evidence collected by himself and others supports the validity of the goal-gradient hypothesis (*13*, p. 304). Moreover, he argues that the principle of experimental extinction may be applied to maze learning, though, because of the complexity of factors operating concurrently in the maze situation, it is difficult to isolate experimentally.

Third, Hull seeks to extend his theory into the area of problem solving, a traditional stronghold of the Gestalt psychologists. Laying great stress on the stick-and-banana problem as a model, Hull believes that behavioral oscillation coupled with stimulus and response generalization can account for what the Gestalt school calls insight learning. Insightful behavior, according to Hull, is not as sudden as it appears to be on the surface, but, instead, occurs only after various stages of subgoals have been mastered through repetitive reinforcement. Birch's experiment with apes is cited in support of his position. It will be recalled that, in Birch's study, apes who had no previous experience with sticks were unable to solve the stick-banana problem.[13]

Hull's final extension of his system is in the area of values. After reviewing a number of philosophical approaches to the problem, Hull outlines his suggestions for a natural-science approach to the theory of values in terms of learning theory, but we shall make no attempt to summarize his tentative conclusions in this highly complex area.

---

[13] See Chapter 6, "Gestalt psychology and learning theory."

Summary and evaluation. The central concept in Hull's system has remained that of reinforcement. Around this basic concept Hull has erected
a tightly knit logical structure on the basis of deductive reasoning supplemented by empirical studies. The system is elaborated in the form of postulates, theorems, and corollaries. Though originally based on conditioning
principles, Hull was confident that his system could be broadened sufficiently to include such complex processes as problem solving, social
behavior, and forms of learning other than conditioning. He lived
only long enough to see part of his ambition realized, and it is, of
course, a highly controversial matter whether the extensions contained in
A Behavior System will prove to be significant contributions to psychological
theory.

More generally, the validity of Hull's entire system has been a controversial issue in the professional literature for several decades.[14] It is, of
course, premature to attempt any final evaluation of Hull's theory, but it is
generally agreed that his attempt to formulate precise quantitative laws of
learning represents a significant step forward over the older schools. The
latter were largely programmatic, in the sense that they attempted to define
the field of psychology and specify the general approach to the study of all
psychological processes. Hull, on the other hand, sought to formulate a
precise, self-correcting system within a limited field—a system capable of
evolution into broader and broader areas. As Hilgard (*10*) has pointed out,
a theory formulated in a highly precise postulate form is more vulnerable
to attack than theories whose aims are broad and whose purpose is largely
programmatic.

Perhaps the two most controversial aspects of Hullian theory are, first,
the generality of his parameters, many of which are founded on the basis of
limited sets of data derived from animal experiments and, second, the
assumption that drive reduction is the basic process in learning. In regard
to the problem of generality, a theory which seeks to discover principles
applicable to the entire range of mammalian behavior ought to utilize a
wide range of representative species in establishing its constants. Much of
Hull's system is based on experimental findings involving white rats. In
regard to drive reduction, we pointed out earlier, the current trend in learning theory is away from drive reduction and toward contiguity. However,
even his severest critics admit that Hull's Herculean effort to formulate a
deductive theory of learning represents a brilliant achievement irrespective
of what the final outcome may be with respect to the particulars within the
system. Hilgard (*10*) reminds us that even Newton was superseded, yet this
does not detract from the greatness of his accomplishments.

14 For a detailed criticism see Koch (*16*) and Hilgard (*10*).

SKINNER'S OPERANT CONDITIONING

In our study of the evolution of the behavioristic psychologies, we found that Watson favored a strict stimulus-response orientation to the analysis of behavior. For Watson the S-R formula was a kind of irreducible or minimal statement of the essential relationships between the organism and its environment. Guthrie, in adopting the behavioristic approach to learning, leaned heavily on pure contiguity, as reflected by his emphasis on movements as the unit of analysis. Hull, however, found a strict S-R formulation of organismic-environmental relationships inadequate to account for learning and favored instead an S-O-R psychology. Indeed, as we have seen, Hull's hypothetico-deductive approach to learning was organized around O variables, with S and R variables serving primarily as anchoring points to which the O variables might be related.

B. F. Skinner's system of operant conditioning is a *descriptive* behaviorism devoted entirely to the study of responses. It is an R psychology in contrast to Hull's S-O-R psychology, since Skinner leans toward an empirical system that does not demand a theoretical framework around which behavioral data are organized. At first glance, therefore, Skinner's orientation to learning seems to be essentially the same as Guthrie's. However, Guthrie formulated an elaborate theoretical statement of contiguous conditioning some years before his main supporting experiments were carried out, while Skinner's objective descriptions of his experimental results are atheoretical —representing a system which is descriptive rather than explanatory in its aims. Moreover, a central concept in Guthrie's system is the role of stimuli, especially kinesthetic stimuli, as mediators of learned behavior sequences. Skinner, on the contrary, believes the inclusion of stimulus analysis both unnecessary and undesirable. Here, then, is behaviorism with a vengeance —a behaviorism strictly descriptive in its approach, based on the study of responses, and opposed to the analysis of intervening variables.

Despite Skinner's conviction that the learning psychologist need not commit himself to a theoretical system in which explanation plays the major role, he nevertheless finds *some* framework necessary around which to organize empirical data from his learning experiments. The framework is conditioning. However, he favors a special variety of conditioning known as *operant conditioning,* which he believes to be clearly distinguishable from classical Pavlovian conditioning and which he holds to be more representative of learning in everyday life.

In his first attempt to write a system of behavior (*23*), Skinner distinguished between "Type S" and "Type R" conditioning. Type S conditioning is the classical Pavlovian variety wherein a known stimulus is paired with a response under conditions of reinforcement. In Type S conditioning, the behavioral response is *elicited* by the stimulus and may be called a *respondent*. In contrast, Type R conditioning utilizes *emitted* responses called *operants*. In Type R conditioning, the stimuli, if identifiable in the first place, are irrelevant to the description and understanding of operant behavior.

Skinner believes that most behavior is emitted behavior for which we either do not know the stimuli which are correlated with the response, or we must postulate them in order to account for the observations. For example, suppose we write a letter. The responses are certainly observable, but what are the stimuli which gave rise to the writing responses? Perhaps the letter was initiated by glancing at a picture of an absent loved one. Perhaps it was the receipt of a letter from the person to whom we are writing. Or we may have been impelled by "an impulse." Whatever the case, the example points up the difficulty of attempting to pinpoint the stimuli that give rise to every-day behavior.

Skinner grants that, in classical conditioning experiments conducted under highly circumscribed laboratory conditions, the stimulus which elicits the response may be identifiable—indeed must be identifiable before the experiment can proceed. The bell in Pavlov's experiment is clearly cor-related with the conditioned response of salivation. But, Skinner points out, the learned modification of visceral reflexes is not the type of behavior of greatest theoretical and practical interest to psychologists. In Skinner's opinion, the traditional conditioning theorists have greatly over-emphasized Type S conditioning. Skinner hopes to correct this imbalance. In his own words:

> The early contention that the concepts applicable to spinal respondents and to conditioned reflexes of Type S could be extended to behavior in general has delayed the investigation of operant behavior. There is, therefore, good reason to direct research toward obtaining a better balance between the two fields, especially *since the greater part* of the behavior of the intact organism is operant (*23*, p. 45).[15]

Because Skinner made operant responses the basic behavioral data in his system, he adopted a kind of instrumental conditioning experiment as the model for the study of variables which influence operants. The experi-ments are based upon the well-known "Skinner box," an early form of which is shown in Figure 7-5. In this case the operant behavior studied is bar pressing in rats. The lever is a small brass rod which, in response to slight pressure, moves downward, activating a food magazine (not shown) in such a way that a small pellet of food is released into the tray. The lever can be connected to a pen or stylus for recording each movement of the

---

[15] Italics ours.

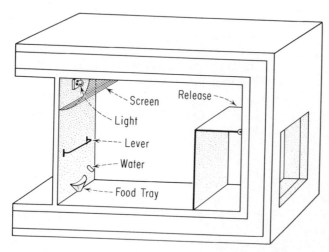

Fig. 7-5. An early form of the Skinner box. (From B. F. Skinner, *The Behavior of Organisms*. Copyright 1938, D. Appleton-Century Co., Inc. By permission of Appleton-Century-Crofts, Inc.)

lever. Finally, it might be noted that the construction of the box is such that all extraneous stimuli are eliminated as far as it is possible to do so.

In choosing bar pressing as his operant, Skinner believes that this particular response has certain advantages over other possible choices. First, it is a relatively easy response for the animal to make. Second, an untrained animal will, on the average, press the lever up to a dozen times an hour, thereby demonstrating sufficient "spontaneous" behavior upon which to base operant conditioning. Third, it is not included in other behavior patterns crucial for the organism; and therefore it can be isolated and recorded. If, for example, scratching were chosen as an operant, its high frequency of spontaneous occurrence and significant role in grooming would obscure the results. Fourth, the bar pressing response is unambiguous; hence there is little difficulty in deciding whether or not it has occurred.

The bar-pressing experiment, then, is Skinner's "model" experiment, just as puzzle boxes were models for Thorndike and Guthrie. In recent years, Skinner has worked with human subjects and animals other than the rat. However, the design of his recent experiments involving species other than rats is not essentially different from that employed in the "Skinner box." For example, pigeons have been used as subjects where the operant under investigation is pecking at a spot which acts as a key to trigger the reinforcement (see Figure 7-6), and human subjects where the operant is problem solving. For the pigeons, food is the reinforcement just as it is for the rat in the box, but with human subjects the reinforcement

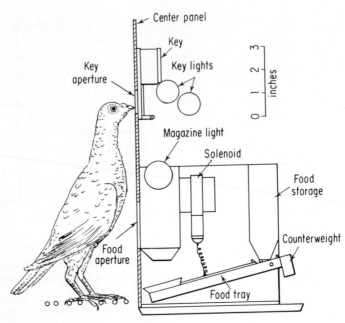

Fig. 7-6. The Skinner box as adapted for the pigeon. (From Skinner and Ferster, *28.*)

may be getting the right answer or a verbal expression of approval (*21*). However, because the designs are essentially the same, the following discussion of the laws of acquisition, extinction, and so on, will be based on Skinner's rat experiments from which his system originally evolved.

Laws of acquisition. The bar-pressing operant is conditioned by first allowing the unconditioned but hungry animal to explore the box. As previously indicated, the operant of bar-pressing will be emitted a number of times "spontaneously." Following a spontaneous response, the experimenter, by manually operating the food magazine, drops a pellet into the tray and allows the animal to eat. After a number of repetitions of food-in-the-tray, the animal has learned the habit of going to the tray immediately upon hearing the sound of the magazine. In the final stage the lever is connected to the food magazine in such a way that whenever the bar is pressed the animal obtains a pellet of food. From this point on, conditioning proceeds rapidly. Figure 7-7 shows the results from one of Skinner's experiments. As the slope of the curve indicates, the first few reinforcements were relatively ineffective, but after the fourth reinforcement, the rate of response is extremely rapid.

The experiment just described illustrates the law of acquisition which is stated by Skinner as follows: *"If the occurrence of an operant is followed by presentation of a reinforcing stimulus the strength is increased"* (23, p. 21).[16]

Clearly, both practice and reinforcement are basic in the establishment of high rates of bar pressing. However, practice per se does not increase rate of response, but merely provides an opportunity for repeated reinforcement to occur. At first glance, Skinner's law of acquisition might appear to be essentially the same as Thorndike's Law of Effect or Hull's Postulate 4. However, it must be borne in mind that Skinner makes no assumptions about the pleasure-pain consequences of reinforcement as Thorndike did, nor does he believe it desirable to interpret reinforcement as drive reduction—a position favored by Hull. Thorndike's and Hull's are *explanatory* systems, while Skinner's is a *descriptive* system. If the question is pressed as to why reinforcers are reinforcing, Skinner points to the obvious biological significance of reinforcers such as food and water. From a broad evolutionary point of view, any response which reduces deprivation is likely to be reinforced and thus lead to the repetition of that response. However, Skinner does not find that attempts to analyze the nature of reinforcement are of practical benefit in his system.

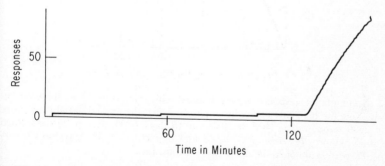

Fig. 7-7. A learning curve for original conditioning where all responses were reinforced. Note the rapidity of conditioning after the first few reinforcements which were relatively ineffective. (From B. F. Skinner, *The Behavior of Organisms*. Copyright 1938, D. Appleton-Century Co., Inc. By permission of Appleton-Century-Crofts, Inc.)

In a descriptive system such as Skinner's the problems of units of measurement and of recording the data are of crucial importance. The data *are* the system, so to speak, provided that they can be demonstrated to be lawful and predictable. Skinner's objective recording system has already been described. His measure of the progress of conditioning is *rate of response*. For any given animal the rate of response is obtained by finding the number of responses per unit of time by direct measurements taken

[16] Italics in original.

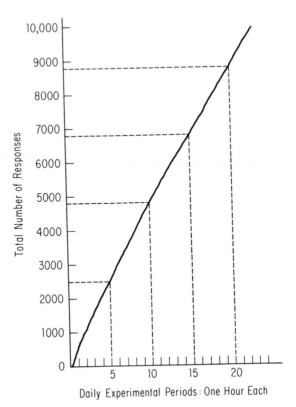

Fig. 7-8. A cumulative response curve obtained with reinforcement at three-minute intervals. Note the high rate of conditioning. At 5 days the animal has given approximately 2500 responses; at 10 days, 4800; at 15 days, 6800; and at 20 days, 8800. (From B. F. Skinner, *The Behavior of Organisms.* Copyright 1938, D. Appleton-Century Co., Inc. By permission of Appleton-Century-Crofts, Inc.)

from the animal's data curve, as illustrated in Figure 7-8. Obviously, steep curves represent high rates of conditioning, while slowly climbing curves are indicative of slow rates. When curves flatten out, this indicates that extinction has set in. Therefore, cumulative curves of operant conditioning are *not* to be interpreted as ordinary learning curves which, upon flattening out, indicate that the subject has reached mastery or is approaching his physiological limit. The laws of Skinner's descriptive behaviorism, then, are the laws that govern the rate of response; and as we have seen, the basic law is the law of reinforcement. However, before continuing with the variables centering around reinforcement, we should like to indicate briefly the role of drives as related to reinforcement.

According to Skinner, drive in animals is governed by depriving the animal of food or water—usually food. In his purely descriptive system, Skinner defines drive in terms of the *number of hours of deprivation* and does *not* consider drive as a "stimulus" or "physiological state." Hours of deprivation can be measured; drive cannot. Following Skinner's reasoning, drive is simply a set of operations which affect behavior in a certain way. The appropriate question concerning the role of drive becomes: How do *x* hours of deprivation influence rate of response? This is the only legitimate question that can be asked about drive in a purely descriptive system and has been answered by a number of experiments (*23*, pp. 341–405) in which hours of deprivation are correlated with rate of conditioning. In general, *rate* of conditioning is increased with increasing length of deprivation. It has also been demonstrated that the rate of extinction (another favorite measure of operant strength) is highly correlated with the *number* of reinforcements during learning, but not with the degree of deprivation during conditioning. Thus drive as a specified state of operations has been shown to affect rate of response but not the strength of the operant as measured by the number of trials to extinction under conditions of reinforcement.

A closely related problem in learning systems is the role of punishment in the acquisition of responses. It will be recalled that Thorndike first considered punishment as a kind of a negative reinforcer which stamped out undesirable responses, but subsequently modified his position in favor of regarding punishment as having no effect other than an inhibitory action in preventing a response. Skinner regards punishment in essentially the same way as did Thorndike in his later formulation. In other words, for Skinner punishment affects the rate of response, but does not weaken operant strength. Thus, if a rat has been well conditioned to press a bar for food and is then shocked for a number of trials every time he touches the bar, rate of response will rapidly fall off to approach zero. If the bar is then rendered harmless, rate of bar-pressing will once again go up sharply. Moreover, it has been demonstrated in extinction experiments that the total number of responses to extinction is not affected by punishment.

These effects on the operant define *positive reinforcement* and *negative reinforcement*. A positive reinforcer is any stimulus, such as food, which increases the probability of a response. A negative reinforcer is any stimulus, such as a shock, which decreases the probability of a response.

Variables associated with reinforcement. Aside from his basic bar-pressing experiment, Skinner is best known for his investigations of various schedules of reinforcement. Indeed, the studies of schedules of reinforcement by Skinner and his associates have produced such an extensive body of data that a large volume has recently appeared devoted to the results of research on this variable alone (*28*).

Let us approach the problem of schedules of reinforcement by considering the typical reinforcing situation in a classical conditioning experiment. *CS* is presented followed by *US*. During the period of acquisition, the *US* is always presented, and for this reason the reinforcement is continuous. But Skinner points out that, in the operant behavior more characteristic of everyday life, reinforcement is anything but continuous. Consider the gambler, for example, who for years responds to the lure of the horse races despite the fact that reinforcement in the form of picking a winner is all too infrequent. In more ordinary cases, life is replete with examples of intermittent rewards. The factory worker gets raises only periodically; the housewife does not expect paeans of praise for *every* culinary effort; and the mature scientist or artist may be willing to work for years with only occasional recognition.

The question immediately arises, which is more effective—continuous or intermittent reinforcement? Similarly, the related problem of what types of intermittent reinforcement are most effective in learning must also be considered.

To begin with, the least complicated situation is that in which the animal is reinforced according to a certain predetermined time schedule, say, every two minutes or every five minutes. Skinner classifies such schedules under the category of *interval reinforcement*, since the fundamental variable is the time interval involved. Figure 7-9 shows a graphic record of lever responses made by rats under four conditions of interval reinforcement. The records show lawful and relatively uniform rates of responding which are proportional to the intervals between reinforcements. Clearly, the shorter the interval, the more rapid the rate of response, with speed of acquisition falling off rapidly with the very long intervals. If, by a simple calculation, the rate of responding is related to the number of reinforcements, it can be shown that over a considerable range of intervals the animal makes about eighteen to twenty responses per reinforcement.

In regard to extinction, Skinner found that the curves for extinction fall off much more slowly where interval reinforcement is employed during acquisition than for those cases where reinforcement has been continuous. In one experiment, a pigeon gave 10,000 extinction responses after a special schedule of intermittent reinforcement. Skinner believes the explanation for this finding lies in the fact that with intermittent reinforcement the extinction trials resemble the conditioning trials much more closely than is true in continuous reinforcement. In the latter case, the animal moves from continuous reinforcement to zero reinforcement, but in the former many of the conditioning trials were not reinforced. Therefore the animal's responding is not rapidly disrupted by a series of nonreinforced trials at the beginning of extinction. The situation is analogous to the case of the child who, following a long period of finding cookies in a certain jar, never

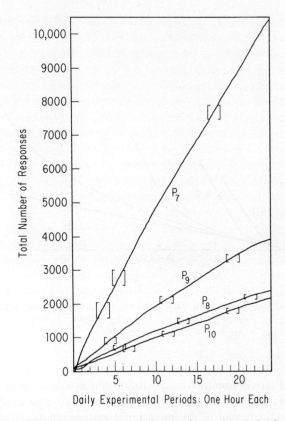

Fig. 7-9. A record of lever responses for 24 daily experimental periods of one hour duration. For P$_7$ responses were reinforced every three minutes; for P$_9$ every six minutes; for P$_8$ every nine minutes; and for P$_{10}$ every twelve minutes. (From B. F. Skinner, *The Behavior of Organisms.* Copyright 1938, D. Appleton-Century Co., Inc. By permission of Appleton-Century-Crofts, Inc.)

finds them after his mother decides to hide them elsewhere. Extinction of "looking for the cookies" would be quite rapid. On the other hand, if a child occasionally finds cookies in a jar, and then does not find them, it is reasonable to suspect he will go on responding much longer than the first child, since "not finding" has occurred before in the child's experience.

A second type of intermittent reinforcement makes use of *fixed ratio* schedules. Here the animal determines his own schedule of reinforcement in the sense that after so many trials—say twenty—the animal is reinforced. He must then press the bar another twenty times to obtain another reinforcement. The surprising result is the fact that with low rates of reinforcement relatively high rates of response are obtained. Figure 7-10

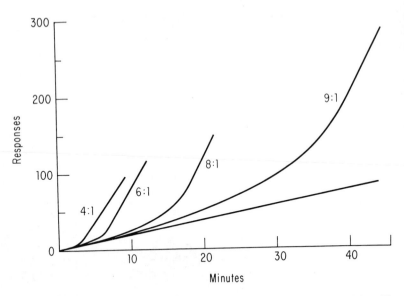

Fig. 7-10. Calculated curves from various fixed ratio reinforcement schedules. (From B. F. Skinner, *The Behavior of Organisms.* Copyright 1938, D. Appleton-Century Co., Inc. By permission of Appleton-Century-Crofts, Inc.)

shows several curves obtained under ratio reinforcement where cumulative responses are plotted against time. It may be noted that in this case the four-to-one ratio results in the most rapid rate of conditioning. It should also be noted that ratio schedules typically result in higher rates of responding than interval schedules. Because rapid rates of response on a ratio schedule bring larger amounts of reinforcement, whereas rapid response rates on an interval schedule do not, it is not surprising that animals on ratio schedules respond rapidly. Both fixed interval and fixed ratio reinforcement schedules result in a scalloping effect on the cumulative record curves. This is caused by the fact that rate of responding is slow after a reinforcement has occurred and then speeds up, reaching a maximum as the next reinforcement is due. Figure 7-11 shows a typical scalloping effect obtained with a fixed ratio reinforcement schedule.

It is also possible to set up schedules of reinforcement making use of variable intervals, variable ratios, and a variety of mixed schedules. Discussion of these more complex varieties of reinforcement schedules is beyond the scope of this book. For detailed presentations of acquisition and extinction rates under a variety of schedules of reinforcement, the reader is referred to Skinner and Ferster's Schedules of Reinforcement (28).

Secondary reinforcement. The Skinner box is well adapted to the study of secondary reinforcement. In secondary reinforcement a stimulus which is originally neutral may become reinforcing by being associated with a reinforcing stimulus. Let us suppose that when the animal presses the bar a light comes on followed by a pellet of food. The bar-pressing is, of course, reinforced by the food. Let us further assume that a number of trials with the light-bar-food sequence are given, following which the bar-pressing is virtually extinguished in the dark by nonreinforcement. The bar is then connected to the light in such a way that pressing the bar activates the light, but no food appears in the tray. The rate of bar-pressing immediately increases, showing that the light alone has become a reinforcer.

In discussing secondary reinforcement, Skinner prefers to emphasize the concept of *generalized reinforcers* (*27*, see especially p. 77f.), by which he means a variety of conditions that may become associated with primary reinforcers. Skinner suggests money as an example of "the generalized reinforcer par excellence" (*27*, p. 79), since money becomes associated with a variety of primary reinforcers of great significance to the individual, such as food, clothing, shelter, and the like.

In dealing with secondary or generalized reinforcers, Skinner points out that such reinforcers may be either positive or negative depending on the original emotional situation in which conditioning occurs. If the primary reinforcement is negative (punishment), then any secondary reinforcers associated with it will be negative. If the original primary reinforcer

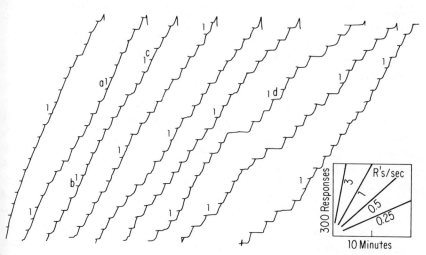

Fig. 7-11. The scalloping effect obtained with fixed ratio reinforcement. Every eleventh reinforcement was followed by a two-minute time-out period. (From Skinner and Ferster, *28*.)

is positive, then the generalized reinforcers are also positive. Moreover, Skinner notes that generalized reinforcers are effective even though the original reinforcers from which they were developed are no longer present. By making use of these principles Skinner can account for behavior which, on the surface, appears to be unrelated to reinforcement, such as the irrational emotional reactions that commonly occur in phobias. In the case of phobias, the original or primary conditions of reinforcement may no longer be present or remembered, but the presence of stimuli associated with the original reinforcement will reactivate the original emotional response. In such instances, the original traumatic experience need not recur in order to generate the anxiety. Rather, anxiety will occur if stimuli associated with the original fear-producing situation are present to act as secondary reinforcers.

Generalization. Skinner's equivalent for generalization or transfer is *induction*. By induction he means the tendency for stimuli with common properties to be effective in arousing behavior. If, for example, a pigeon has been conditioned to peck at a red circle in the Skinner Box, a yellow spot will evoke pecking behavior but at a much slower rate. An orange spot will evoke a more rapid rate of response than a yellow spot, but not as rapid a rate as the original red spot. Skinner refers to this decrement in rate as the induction gradient.[17]

Induction is explained by Skinner on the basis of the presence of "identical" elements in both the original and new stimulating situations. Similarly, induction can occur on the response side provided identical responses are possible in the two situations. In reinforcing a given response, similar responses are strengthened—responses with "identical elements." A common example of response induction may be found in mirror drawing, where the individual who acquires skill with one hand "transfers" a great deal of the acquired skill to the other hand without intervening practice.

In discussing stimulus and response induction, Skinner makes it clear that he believes that other theorists have placed too much emphasis on the discreteness of stimuli and responses. He suggests that neither stimuli nor reponses are separate, discrete units but instead are *classes* of events. Skinner finds it "difficult to conceive of two responses which do not have something in common" (*27*, p. 94).[18] Similarly, " a discrete stimulus is as arbitrary a notion as a discrete operant" (*27*, p. 132). Clearly, Skinner allows for a much greater degree of transfer than has been traditional in previous conditioning theories. Finally, we might note that Skinner's own usage of the concept of "identical elements" is very similar to Thorndike's conception of transfer as dependent upon identical elements (see Chap-

[17] In classical conditioning the parallel process is called gradient of generalization.
[18] See *27*, p. 94ff.; also *23*, Chapter V.

ter 6). However, Skinner provides for both discrimination among stimuli and differentiation among responses. Discrimination in operant conditioning is brought about in much the same manner as in Pavlovian conditioning, namely, by selective reinforcement. For example, if a pigeon is trained to attack another pigeon when a green light appears and to stop attacking when a red light appears by selectively reinforcing attack behavior only if it occurs in the presence of the green light, then discrimination among stimuli has been established. At the same time the *response* can be said to be differentiated on the basis of selective reinforcement.

Extinction. We have already included a number of Skinner's graphs showing cumulative responses during conditioning. (See Figures 7-7, 7-8, and 7-9.) It has been noted that in the cumulative response records employed by Skinner, extinction is demonstrated when the curve bends toward the base line or abscissa and eventually flattens out. This indicates that rate of response is zero, and extinction has taken place. Skinner has demonstrated that rate of extinction varies with various schedules of reinforcement. Generally speaking, extinction is more rapid with continuous, as opposed to intermittent, reinforcement.

Forgetting is distinguished from extinction in much the same manner in which Hull[19] differentiated between the two processes. That is, extinction results only from nonreinforcement, whereas forgetting is due to slow decay with the passage of time. Skinner reports (*27*, p. 71) that forgetting under controlled laboratory conditions is, indeed, a slow process. Pigeons may show operant responses six years after conditioning, even though no reinforcement was given during the interim.

Complex skills and the method of successive approximations. Skinner and his associates have taken cognizance of the fact that learning theories must account for more complex behavior than bar-pressing and pecking at spots. However, the Skinnerians believe that the principles of operant conditioning are sufficient to account for highly complex motor skills, and have demonstrated the validity of their claim in ingenious experiments with seriatim problems (*26*). For example, a rat may be trained to obtain a marble from a magazine by pulling a string. He must then pick up the marble in his paws and carry it to a tube which projects above the floor of his cage and there deposit it before obtaining reinforcement.

To accomplish so complex a program of training the *method of shaping or successive approximations* must be employed. That is, the animal is first reinforced for approaching the string. He is then reinforced for pulling on the string. Reinforcement is then given as he approaches the released

[19] See pp. 249–250.

marble and later upon his picking up the marble, and so on until only the complete act brings reinforcement. In an informal way the method has been used by animal trainers for centuries.

Skinner has shown how shaping can account for the hitherto uniquely human behavior of superstitions (24). If a pigeon is reinforced according to a fixed interval schedule regardless of what it is doing, some operant will be reinforced. Suppose, for example, that the bird happened to be bobbing its head upon being reinforced the first time. The response will tend to be repeated. If this occurs several times with reinforcement, head bobbing will come to dominate the pigeon's behavior during the course of conditioning.

The situation just described for the pigeon is exactly parallel to that found in human superstitions. For example, if a mother happens to be in her son's room looking at his picture and experiences a strong premonition that some misfortune has happened to him at the moment his picture happens to fall from the wall, she will adopt pictures falling from the wall as a sign of bad luck if she subsequently hears that her son, indeed, came to some misfortune at the time of her observation.

Verbal behavior.   Skinner's interest in verbal behavior spans over three decades and embraces such divergent problems as the design of the now famous teaching machine, the verbal summator (a device for producing vague, speech-like sounds which are interpreted by subjects as meaningful words and phrases, just as ink blots or other unstructured stimuli may be seen as meaningful objects), and an analysis of language in terms of operant conditioning.[20] Although any attempt to summarize Skinner's extensive work in this area would carry us far afield from the scope of this chapter, it may be pointed out that speech sounds are behavioral responses which can be reinforced by verbal reinforcers in the same manner that bar-pressing or spot pecking can be reinforced by food. Which sounds will be reinforced will depend, of course, upon the culture. Any normal human infant has the potentiality to learn any language in the world. We shall have more to say about the possibility of interpreting verbal behavior in terms of conditioning in Chapter 9. Meanwhile we shall conclude our summary of Skinner's theory with a few general observations.

Concluding statement.   In our brief survey of Skinner's descriptive behaviorism, we have attempted to summarize his position on the more important variables in simple learning. As we have indicated, Skinner takes as his point of departure what might be called "raw behavior," and to the

---

[20] For a detailed analysis of language and literary behavior according to the principles of operant conditioning see *Verbal Behavior* (29).

extent that the raw data are lawful and consistent, they form a system. It seems unlikely that anyone will seriously argue that Skinner's raw materials fail to demonstrate the kind of lawfulness upon which a descriptive system can be built. Moreover, Skinner has done a remarkable job of demonstrating the wide range of applicability of principles derived from operant conditioning research. In his book, *Science and Human Behavior* (*27*), which was designed as an introductory text, Skinner has extended his learning system into such areas as social behavior, religion, psychotherapy, education, and the personal and social control of conduct. Irrespective of one's attitude toward conditioning as a key process in the development of complex behavior, everyone would have to agree that Skinner has at least demonstrated the *possibility* of utilizing the laws of conditioning in elaborating a comprehensive behavior system.

Moreover, it is to Skinner's credit that he has not shunned the task of grappling with the ethical problem of the *control* of behavior so important in the world today. Throughout his *Science and Human Behavior,* the problem of controlling human nature comes up again and again in connection with religious, political, and educational systems, and other social agencies. As his own experiments have so clearly demonstrated, it is possible to bring an individual's behavior under control without that individual's awareness or volition.[21] The most fundamental issue which underlies the problem of control is the question of who shall control, or even more fundamentally, who shall control the controllers. The democratic tradition has cherished the conception of ultimate control residing in the individual, who, in fiction if not in fact, is considered a free agent. But science raises the possibility of realizing George Orwell's fictional *1984*—a terrifying new world wherein the methods of the behavioral sciences become the weapons of control. Skinner offers neither a counsel of retreat nor despair in the face of such frightening questions, but instead dispassionately examines the alternative —free man in the traditional sense, or man controlled by science.

Skinner's willingness to grapple with the age-old problems of human behavior demonstrates the lure of theory. Despite his "antitheory" (*25*) bias, Skinner, in company with every psychologist who has tried to organize and systematize the data of behavior, finds it necessary to bridge the all-too-frequent gaps in our knowledge of human behavior by appealing to theory. We do not mean to imply that Skinner has fallen into what he himself considers the traditional "errors" of seeking explanations in the nervous system, on the one hand, or appealing to intervening variables, on the other. Rather, Skinner's theorizing takes two forms: First, he accepts the ready-made skeleton of conditioning theory as the structural framework of his system, and, second, by a process of logical reasoning, he is

[1] See especially *29*.

willing to extend or extrapolate the principles of operant conditioning to everyday problems of human behavior. This, we submit, is theory.

Precisely what the final evaluation of Skinner's system will be only history will reveal. It is impossible to attempt an evaluation of a vigorously developing system while that system is in the process of evolving. Nevertheless, it seems safe to predict that Skinner's emphasis on operants is a significant and salutary departure from the traditional emphasis on Pavlovian conditioning. It is possible that Skinner's greatest contribution will ultimately be that which he himself hoped for his system nearly a generation ago—to turn the attention of psychologists to a new conception of learning as operant behavior.

TOLMAN'S PURPOSIVE BEHAVIOR

In the heyday of the schools of psychology, anyone who suggested that behaviorism and Gestalt psychology could make congenial bedfellows would have been considered a jokester or a madman. Yet this is precisely what Edward C. Tolman attempted to do and, it is generally agreed, with considerable success.

Tolman's system evolved slowly over the course of a quarter-century. The first important exposition of the system was his *Purposive Behavior in Animals and Man*, published in 1932. The system continued to evolve in a series of articles and two books, *Drives Toward War* (1942) and *Collected Papers in Psychology* (1951), the latter being made up largely of material previously published as journal articles. Tolman's final statement, entitled "Principles of Purposive Behavior," was published in 1959 in Volume II of *Psychology: A Study of a Science*. However, Tolman's system as a system has held fast to certain basic principles to be found in the *Purposive Behavior* It was in this first important exposition of the system that he announced his general orientation, programmatic aims and methods, and the systematic framework around which he believed experimental studies of animal learning could be organized. Indeed, so comprehensive was Tolman's initial statement that it can be considered as either a complete system of psychology analogous to Carr's, Watson's, or the Gestalt psychologists', or it may be treated as a theory of learning. The latter treatment is justified in the sense that the learning process is heavily emphasized within the system as a whole. Having chosen the latter course, we shall restrict our discussion of the system to the learning theory within the overall system Our exposition will be based largely on *Purposive Behavior* and certain significant articles[22] which have appeared since the initial publication of his first book.

---

[22] See *33*, *34*, *35*, *36*, and *37*.

As has been implied, Tolman's general orientation is at one and the same time behavioristic and Gestalt. Because this is something of a paradox, let us attempt to delineate the relative role of these traditional systems as they appear in Tolman's synthesis.

Tolman is a behaviorist in the sense that he is strongly opposed to a psychology of consciousness or pure phenomenology. In the prologue to his *Purposive Behavior,* he states: "The motives which lead to the assertion of a behaviorism are simple. All that can ever actually be observed in fellow human beings and in the lower animals is behavior" (*33*, p. 2). Moreover, in keeping with this behavioristic orientation, he favors the study of animals. Indeed, his *Purposive Behavior* is dedicated to *Mus norvegicus albinus,* the albino rat, whose kith and kin have given so generously to psychological research.

But despite his *predilection* for animal research and objective observation, Tolman is *not* a Watsonian behaviorist. He makes it clear that behavior in his system will be treated as a *molar* rather than a *molecular* phenomenon. A molar definition of behavior implies that the *behavioral act* is the unit for psychological study *without regard to underlying molecular components in the nerves, muscles, and glands.* Moreover, the molar orientation envisages behavior as goal seeking or purposive. The particular movements the animal makes in getting out of puzzle boxes or in running through mazes are of far less consequence than the fact that the movements lead to goals.

Molar behavior is also characterized "by the fact that it always involves a specific pattern of commerce-, engagement-, communion- with such and such intervening means-objects, as the way to get thus to or from."[23] In less technical terms, molar behavior makes use of environmental objects —tools, pathways, signs and the like—in arriving at goals. Finally, molar behavior is characterized by selectivity toward "means objects," which is to say the animal will make use of shorter as against longer routes in reaching goals.

Tolman's system is a Gestalt system in the sense that he characterizes molar behavior as *cognitive.* Evidence for the cognitive nature of purposive behavior is found in the animal's reactions to environmental means— objects in arriving at goals. He asks us to consider the well-practiced rat "dashing through the maze." As long as the maze is not altered, the rat's rapid, sure performance is operational evidence of the animal's cognitive expectancy that the maze is as it always has been. If the maze is altered, the rat's behavior breaks down. To anticipate a little in order to make the matter of cognition clear, Tolman's explanation of learning is centered around "sign learning." The animal in the maze or puzzle box learns the significance of signs along the route. For this reason, Tolman's theory is often called a "sign Gestalt" theory.

---

[23] Tolman's *Purposive Behavior* is sprinkled with neologisms and peculiar phrases which are at once colorful and annoying. The quotation appears on p. 11 of Tolman's book.

Finally, by way of orientation, Tolman emphasizes that molar behavior is "docile" or, in other words, teachable. The molecular reflex cannot be taught about goals; moreover, reflexes are not characterized by purposes. But, says Tolman, behavior "reeks of purpose." That is, behavior in the sense of behavioral *acts* is characteristically purposive. The importance of docility lies in the fact that it provides objective support for his contention that behavior is purposive. The animal that varies its behavior and shows the ability to select shorter and easier paths to goals *is* demonstrating cognitive and purposive behavior, in the Tolman sense.

In summary, Tolman's orientation is, at one and the same time, behavioristic and Gestalt. To use one of his own phrases, he is unwilling to have "commerce with" subjective or molecular approaches. Thus, he attempts to break through two traditions: the tradition of objective psychology as molecular (Watson, Titchener) and the tradition of subjective psychology as molar (Gestalt). In short, he believes that he can build a valid system by taking the best of the older traditions and discarding the worst.

With this brief orientation as a guide, we shall now consider Tolman's position on the major variables in learning—acquisition, transfer, extinction, and others.

Laws of acquisition. After a sixteen-page review of the experimental literature on the role of practice in learning, Tolman concludes that ". . . the law of exercise, in the sense of differentially more frequent or recent repetitions of one of the alternative responses as against any of the others as the cause of learning, plays little, if any role" (*33*, p. 362). Later in the same chapter, he goes so far as to suggest that *some* practice on *incorrect* choices in learning situations is probably necessary (*33*, p. 346). However, lest we have given the impression that Tolman discounts the value of practice altogether, we must emphasize that he believes practice is necessary for the building up of *sign Gestalts.* With this statement we have come to the heart of Tolman's theory of learning, for sign learning is the core around which the system revolves.

Sign Gestalts are cognitive processes which are learned relationships between environmental cues and the animal's expectations. In the maze the untrained animal has many cues available—auditory, visual, olfactory, tactile. If the animal is hungry he will move around the maze, sometimes on the true path, sometimes in blinds, and eventually will discover the food. In subsequent trials the goal gives purpose and direction to the animal's behavior; and, as he comes to each choice point, expectations are built up that such and such a cue will lead on to food. If the animal's expectancy is confirmed, the sign Gestalt of cue expectancy is strengthened. The entire pattern of sign Gestalts thus built up Tolman calls a "cognitive map." In the long run, then, the animal learns a cognitive map of the maze

—*not* a set of motor habits. The role of practice is to provide an opportunity for the building of the map, and the role of reward is to lend purpose to the animal's behavior.

The evidence upon which Tolman has erected his sign Gestalt theory of learning comes from experiments designed to test the relative role of motor habits versus sign learning in the maze. These experiments may be considered under three headings: (1) "place learning" experiments, (2) "reward-expectancy" experiments, (3) experiments on latent learning. We shall exemplify each type and attempt to show how the results support Tolman's sign Gestalt theory.

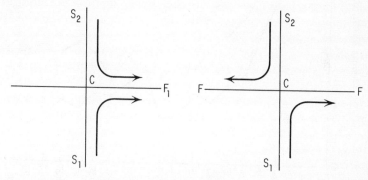

Fig. 7-12. A schematic representation of the place learning experiment. One group of animals always found food at the same place irrespective of the starting point. The other group was trained to make the same response at choice point C. Place learning was found to be superior to response learning.

Place learning. If, Tolman argues, we consider the question of what the animal learns in the maze, the alternatives appear to be (a) some kind of motor habit, possibly a chain of conditioned responses to either kinesthetic or external cues, or (b) a cognitive map made up of sign Gestalts. Now a test of these alternatives was designed by Tolman and Honzik (37) as follows: A maze was constructed in the form of a cross with two possible starting points and two alternative goals. (See Figure 7-12.) One group of rats was trained so that they always found food *at the same place,* say F_1, irrespective of whether they started at S_1 or S_2. Another group was required to make the *same response,* turning right, at the choice point C, irrespective of their starting point. The first group, or the "place learners," were significantly better in their performance than the "response learners." This result supports the cognitive theory in the sense that learning a place presumably requires a cognitive map of that place rather than a specific set of motor responses. By analogy, the individual who is thoroughly familiar with his town or city can take a variety of routes to a given goal and is not lost if his usual path is blocked.[24]

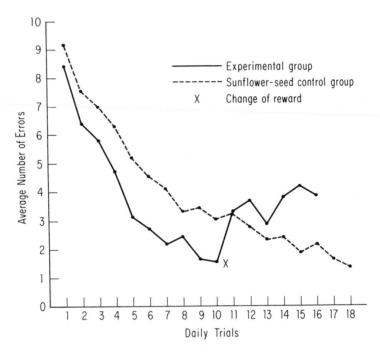

Fig. 7-13. The effect of change of reward on learning in the T-maze. For explanation see text. (From Edward Chace Tolman, *Purposive Behavior in Animals and Men.* Copyright 1932, The Century Co. By permission of Appleton-Century-Crofts, Inc., and the University of California Press.)

Reward expectancy. Reward expectancy in its simplest sense means that the learner comes to anticipate the presence of a reward (or in some cases a certain type of reward), and if that reward is absent or changed, behavior is disrupted. One of Tolman's associates, M. H. Elliott (5), employed a T-maze in which two equally hungry groups of rats were trained to find a reward of bran mash and sunflower seed respectively. Elliott called the bran-mash group the experimental group and the sunflower-seed group the control group. As Figure 7-13 shows, when sunflower seed was substituted for bran mash on Day 10 for the experimental group, learning was disrupted in the experimental group, as demonstrated by a marked increase

[24] This early experiment on place learning has been repeated a number of times under various conditions and with modifications in the apparatus. The results have not always supported Tolman's position. For a more detailed analysis of place learning with additional examples and bibliographic references to critical interpretations see Hilgard (*10*, pp. 192–195).

n errors. The hypothesis is that the animals had come to *expect* the bran mash—a more desirable reward, as demonstrated by the more rapid learning of this group—and when their expectation was not confirmed, behavior was disrupted. This experiment, among others, is Tolman's operational definition of reward expectancy and, at the same time, serves as objective support for the importance of reward expectancy as a factor in learning.

Latent learning.   Latent learning is a fundamental concept in Tolman's system and at the same time continues to be a controversial topic in contemporary learning theory. As the term implies, latent learning is hidden learning which goes on unobserved but which, under certain conditions, can be revealed in performance. One of the modern classics in the experimental literature is Tolman and Honzik's study of latent learning in rats (*38*). Three groups of rats were used: a no-reward group that was allowed to wander about in the maze but found no food in the goal compartment, a regularly rewarded group, and a third group that received no reward for the first ten days but on the eleventh and subsequent days found food in the goal compartment. As Figure 7-14 shows, no reward results in little apparent learning. But, as the curve for the delayed reward group demonstrates, learning was taking place though not manifested in performance until the introduction of the reward.

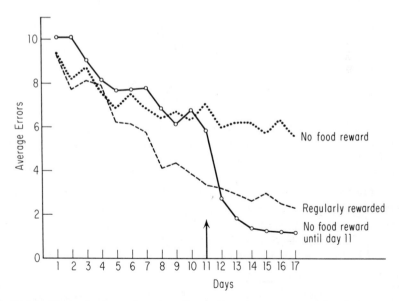

Fig. 7-14. Evidence for latent learning. For explanation see text. (After Tolman and Honzik, *38*. From Ernest R. Hilgard, *Theories of Learning*. Second edition copyright © 1956, Appleton-Century-Crofts, Inc., and the University of California Press.)

The importance of Tolman and Honzik's finding lies in the fact that it is in opposition to the older concepts of drive-reduction through reinforcement, or the Law of Effect. If reward acts as a reinforcer of those responses leading to the goal, then traditional reinforcement theories simply cannot account for the learning of the delayed reward group. Tolman, on the other hand, argues that the exploratory behavior of the animals in the delayed-reward group provided an ideal opportunity for the formation of sign Gestalts, since the animals thoroughly explored blind alleys as well as the true path. More recent reinforcement theories, such as Hull's 1952 version, argue that *amount* of reinforcement is irrelevant and attempt to account for latent learning by pointing to the operation of subtle, but nonetheless significant incentives, such as "curiosity," desire to return to the living cage, and the like, which are operative even though the animal is not hungry and no food is present. In such cases, learning is reinforced, but *performance* is poor because of the lack of direction provided by a single goal with a relatively high incentive value such as food.

Since the Tolman-Honzik study, there have been literally dozens of "latent learning" experiments with wide variations in design. A review of this large body of material has been provided by Thistlewaite (*31*) in 1951 who cites seventy-six relevant studies. A more recent review of the relevant literature is available in Kimble (*15*). The controversy is far too extensive to be reviewed here, but there is no longer much doubt about the reality of the phenomenon. The main problems with which most investigators are now concerned are: (a) under what conditions latent learning is demonstrable; and (b) in the light of those conditions, the bearing of latent learning on drive-reduction versus cognitive theories.

In summary, Tolman's position on the acquisition of learned behavior is oriented around sign learning. The animal learns a cognitive map of the maze which is "reinforced" by expectancy and confirmation. Practice is important only in providing opportunities for the acquisition of sign Gestalts; practice alone does not result in learning. Reward regulates performance but does not act as a reinforcer of correct responses.

Transfer. The problem of transfer and the conditions under which it occurs has not been one of the central issues in Tolman's system. However, the topic is not completely neglected, since transfer is considered as the carrying over of a sign Gestalt readiness from one situation to another. "Sign Gestalt" readiness is defined by Tolman as follows:

> . . . the organism is possessed of a generalized "universal" propensity whereby, in order to get to or from a given demanded type of goal-object, he is ready to have such and such positive or negative commerce with such and such means-objects (sign-objects) whenever particular instances of (i.e., the appropriate stimuli for) the latter are present (*33*, p. 454).

In simplified language, Tolman is arguing that, provided two situations are similar, the animal will carry appropriate sign Gestalts from one situation to another. He cites an experiment by Gengerelli wherein animals trained in one T-maze were able to transfer learned habits to a similar but not identical maze (*33*, pp. 33–34). Because Tolman favors a cognitive theory of learning, a high degree of transfer would be expected by him as a matter of course, provided the problem situations concerned were such that a general understanding of the essential elements was possible.[25] In practice, however, Tolman devotes very little space to the topic of transfer, and, as a consequence, the problem does not loom large in his system.

Forgetting. The topic of forgetting does not appear in the index of Tolman's *Purposive Behavior*. This omission is indicative of the fact that both he and his associates were more interested in the process of *acquisition* than in forgetting. Moreover, psychologists whose work has been primarily with animals have traditionally shown little interest in forgetting, as compared to those whose work is with human subjects. It seems likely that this difference in interests can be explained by the fact that verbal material lends itself to experiments on retention more readily than do mazes, problem boxes, and the like. Moreover, verbal materials are learned under conditions which favor forgetting. After learning a list of nonsense syllables, for example, the typical human subject goes from the laboratory to situations in everyday life where new learning is required. And, as has been so abundantly demonstrated in retroactive inhibition experiments, new learning interferes with the recall of old. The animal subject, on the other hand, is in a more isolated or "protected" environment where he is not confronted by the necessity of learning additional material once his responsibilities to the experimenter have been discharged. Forgetting, therefore, is less rapid in the animal subject and, for this reason, less often studied. *Purposive Behavior* does contain a brief reference to retentivity, however. Retention is treated under capacity laws as an ability which promotes more rapid learning (*33*, p. 375).[26]

Other laws of purposive behaviorism. In addition to the principles enumerated in the preceding sections, Tolman has postulated a large number of "laws" of learning to account for various types of learning within the sign Gestalt orientation. In keeping with psychological opinion in general, Tolman's laws vary with the nature of the learning situation. There are laws for conditioned-reflex learning, trial-and-error learning, and "inventive learning." Although the list of laws is far too extensive for detailed

---

[25] See also the Gestalt view of transfer, Chapter 6, "Gestalt psychology and learning theory."
[26] In his *Drives Toward War* (*34*) Tolman accepts repression as a special case of forgetting.

discussion, it will be possible to outline the general nature of Tolman's laws under three broad headings: (1) capacity laws, (2) stimulus laws, (3) laws relative to the manner in which material is presented.

Under capacity laws, Tolman includes six subcategories:

1. Formal means-end capacities
2. Dimensional means-end capacities and discriminanda and manipulanda capacities
3. Retentivity
4. Additional formal means-end capacities: alternativeness, roundaboutness, and the like
5. Consciousness—ability and ideational ability
6. Creativity (creative instability)

Laws 1 to 3 play a major role in conditioning; laws 1 to 4 in trial-and-error learning; law 5 refers to the animal's capacity or talent for learning; and law 6 applies particularly to inventive learning.

The means-end-capacity laws (1, 2, and 4) refer to the learner's ability to utilize signs, directions, distances and other variables and dimensions in his environment. The animal must be able to manipulate latches, make use of cues in mazes, adopt alternative routes, and the like, if he is to be successful in learning situations. More generally, the same capacities are necessary in dealing with things to be discriminated and manipulated in the learner's natural environment.

The law of retentivity simply implies that good retention is a necessary capacity in learning, for, if the organism were unable to retain, learning would be impossible. Ideational capacities and creative instability are primarily important in problem solving situations in which the ability to perceive new relationships is essential for the successful solution.

The second category, stimulus laws, concerns Gestalt-like laws having to do with conditions inherent in the material itself. Tolman postulates five such laws:

1. Togetherness
2. Fusibility
3. Other Gestalt-like laws
4. Interrelations among the spatial, temporal, and other characters of the alternatives
5. The law of presentations and characters favoring new closures and expansions of the field

Togetherness is a Gestalt-like law which holds that for efficient learning the sign Gestalts and the means-end relations must occur together as a kind of figure against a ground. For example, the dog in conditioning experiments must be presented with the *CS* and *US* together, or nearly so;

otherwise, conditioning will not take place. However, by togetherness Tolman does not mean mere contiguity. Rather, the concept is roughly equivalent to Thorndike's "belongingness" in that it implies a molar connectedness of stimulus and means to the goal (or reinforcement).

Fusibility is a closely related law which states that certain signs and their means-end correlates will more readily or naturally form a whole. For example, an olfactory stimulus is more likely to prove effective as a CS for a dog than is a noise which tends to evoke an avoidance reaction.

The third category, "other Gestalt-like laws," is a provision for the inclusion of new discoveries. Tolman suggests (33, p. 382) that possibly the law of Prägnanz, if verified, might fit into this category.

The fourth and fifth laws are more applicable to problem situations in which the perception of relationships is an important condition of learning. These laws apply in trial-and-error situations, such as studied by Thorndike (Law 4), and in insight problems, such as those employed by Köhler (Law 5).

Under the heading of laws relative to the manner in which material is presented, Tolman includes the following factors:

1. Frequency, recency
2. Revival after extinction, primacy, distributed repetitions
3. Motivation
4. Not "effect" but "emphasis"
5. Law of temporal orders and sequences in the presentation of the alternatives
6. Temporal relations between the presentation of certain of the already given alternatives and the true solution

Of the above, laws 1 to 4 apply to conditioning, 1 to 5 to trial-and-error learning situations, and all apply to inventive learning.

In regard to Numbers 1 to 3, we need only point out that, other things being equal, frequency, recency, good motivation (and other conditions which favor economy in learning) promote rapid acquisition of learned responses in conditioning or quick solutions in trial-and-error learning.

Law 4 reiterates Tolman's strong emphasis on learning by expectancy and confirmation as opposed to reinforcement, while Laws 5 and 6 recognize the fact that the manner of timing and the spatial conditions under which problems are presented are important variables in determining success in trial-and-error and inventive learning.

While we realize that it is impossible to convey an adequate picture of Tolman's many laws in such a highly summarized manner, we hope that our bare outline will at least convey some impression of the broad range of variables which he considers important in understanding learning. Indeed, the significance of the laws lies primarily in their broad delineation of the many variables which enter into the situational and behavior complex in learning. The generality of the laws and the absence of more precise quantitative definitions leave much to be desired.

A note on revisions in Tolman's system.   During the several decades before his death, Tolman made revisions in his theoretical position. Of these, the most important were published in an article in the *Psychological Review* (35). In this article Tolman asserts his belief that there are at least six basic types of learning, each of which has appropriate laws that are different from those of other types. While the postulation of these revised categories or types of learning does not indicate any fundamental change in the system, the types do provide an excellent capsule view of Tolman's theory. We shall, therefore, briefly discuss the following six types of learning as formulated by Tolman in 1949.

1. Cathexes
2. Equivalence beliefs
3. Field expectancies
4. Field cognition modes
5. Drive discrimination
6. Motor patterns

Cathexes are positive or negative relationships which develop between drives and goal objects. Positive cathexes are acquired "by trying out" food, sex objects, drinks, and so on, and "finding that they work." In other words, to satisfy his primitive drives the organism eventually learns to utilize a variety of goal objects by discovering through experience that those objects are need satisfying. Negative cathexes are acquired whenever pain or "some other noxious state" results from an experience with an object. Thereafter the object will have negative cathexis for the organism, and the need satisfied will be pain avoidance.

In accounting for positive and negative cathexes in terms of drive satisfaction, Tolman is closely approaching, if not accepting, the idea of positive and negative reinforcement. However, he feels that there is, as yet, insufficient evidence one way or the other to come to any final conclusion on the role of reinforcement in the formation of cathexes. But he also notes that cathexes are extremely resistant to forgetting, as is held to be true of conditioned responses by the conditioning theorists. On both points, therefore, he is approaching the position of the conditioning theorists.

Equivalence beliefs are learned connections between goals and subgoals which operate to make the individual behave toward the subgoal just as he would toward the original goal. Thus the animal will approach subgoals for which he has established positive equivalence beliefs and avoid those for which he has acquired negative equivalence beliefs. By way of illustration of a positive equivalence belief, Tolman cites the case of the student who works for A's in order to win parental love, but finds some degree of comfort in obtaining the A grade per se. The grades have become equivalent for love. Similarly, negative equivalence beliefs can be formed through a process of association. For example, a rat given a shock will cringe, urinate, and scramble about the apparatus. If a light is presented a few times along with the shock, the animal will acquire a negative equivalence belief for the light and engage in the same emotional reaction to the light alone as it formerly gave to the shock. As these examples show, Tolman's concept of equivalence beliefs is approximately the same as the principle of secondary reinforcement in conditioning theory. Finally, it should be noted that Tolman emphasizes that equivalence beliefs are more important in social learning than in learning situations involving visceral drives.

Field expectancies are the same as sign Gestalts discussed above; consequently we need not discuss them further here.

Field cognition modes are complex mental "structures" employed in learning situations. These modes depend upon the more basic mental processes of perception, memory, and inference. In simple language, the individual during the course of learning can acquire capacities (or make use of potential abilities) that will help him to learn. He may learn to employ perceptual cues to solve a perceptual problem, or he may remember something from a previous learning situation that can be applied to the present task. Again, the learner may make "inferences" on the basis of available cues to help him in a problem solving situation. In a sense, then, field cognition modes represent the ability to acquire field expectancies based on perceptual, mnemonic and inferential processes.

Drive discrimination is a type of learning in which the subject must learn to distinguish between drives. For example, the animal in a T-maze may have to learn to go right when hungry for a food reward and left when thirsty for water. However, aside from admitting the reality of experimental demonstrations of this type of learning, Tolman has no formal laws to apply by way of explanation of how the learner learns to discriminate between his drives.

Motor patterns refer to the type of learning required of the cats in the Guthrie-Horton experiment. Moreover, Tolman is willing to "take a chance" and accept Guthrie's simple conditioning explanation as the basic law of acquisition in this kind of learning *provided* it is recognized that such sensory-motor skills are "always imbedded in a larger goal-directed activity. . . ."

By way of comment we should like to stress once again that Tolman's 1949 analysis of the fundamental types of learning does not constitute a basic departure from his original emphasis on cognitive factors in learning. Rather, just as conditioning theorists such as Hull have come to recognize that they must modify their systems to include important phenomena of

learning if they wish to maintain comprehensiveness, so Tolman has soft-
ened his original position to admit the relevance of types of learning emphasized by rival theorists. Indeed, as we have seen, Tolman has gone far
toward admitting the validity of reinforcement theory for certain kinds of
learning.

A final formulation of Tolman's theory appeared in 1959, the year
of his death (36, pp. 92–157). In this article he again revealed that his
fundamental position had not changed in the nearly quarter-century since
his views had originally been published. The theory remains a cognitive
theory in spirit with increased emphasis on more logical and definitive
formulations. He continues to stress behavioristic methodology. We may
briefly summarize the major principles embodied in this final account by
discussing the independent and intervening variables which were emphasized by him.

He identifies the independent variables of purposive behaviorism as
the summation of conditions associated with any previous training that
the animal might have been given, including conditions of drive. Independent variables also include present stimuli, both those originating from
the environment and those arising from conditions within the organism.
Tolman accepts drive stimuli as important in learning, as did Hull, but
argues that other drives, such as the curiosity drive, may also be important
in cognitive learning, even though we cannot as yet recognize the stimuli
from which they originate.

There are two major classes of intervening variables: (a) means-end
readinesses, and (b) expectations, perceptions, representations, and valences. Means-end readinesses, the most important intervening variables
in cognitive learning, are essentially the animal's beliefs as established by
previous trials in the learning situation (or in similar situations). For example, the animal develops a means-end readiness or belief that a certain
stimulus complex in the maze signifies another stimulus, which in turn
becomes a stimulus-to-be-expected and so on to the end of the maze. It is
on the basis of such means-end readinesses that cognitive maps are learned.
Although the concept of means-end readinesses was formulated early
in Tolman's systematizing, it was not emphasized until the final statement.

Perceptions, expectancies, representations, and valences are all cognitive events within the organism which interact with means-end readinesses and upon which learning also depends. Tolman does not offer
detailed explanations of these concepts; nor does he propose a concrete program for measuring them in quantitative terms.

The dependent variable in a learning situation is, of course, the animal's response or, to use a more molar expression, the animal's performance.
The independent and dependent variables are the only variables which the

psychologist can measure directly. The intervening variables are inferred, and their effects are measured indirectly in terms of performance.

Tolman then presents hypothetical formulas for several paradigms of model learning situations—escape, avoidance, choice, latent, and incidental learning. Formal postulates cast in the language of abstract symbols show the relative importance to be given to independent and intervening variables in the five situations. A summary review of experimental research bearing on the system is also included. Tolman admits that his system has been most productive of research in the area of animal learning—as he intended that it should be. In discussing the scope of his system he concludes:

> I cannot do much . . . with the acquisition of sensorimotor skills in adults or with the way in which performance vectors govern and select from among such skills. Neither have I actually been able to do much with the higher mental processes of thinking, verbal communication, and the like in human beings, though I do feel that these latter processes will someday lend themselves more readily to a formulation of the (SR → S) type than to a simple S-R formulation (*36*, p. 151).

Concluding statement.   While it is impossible to render a final evaluation of Tolman's system at the present time, we shall attempt to summarize in a broad way contemporary professional reactions to this system. First, there can be little doubt that Tolman and his associates have, over the years, contributed a significant body of research to the field of learning. In general, of all his experiments, those directed toward the support of the place-learning hypothesis and those intended to demonstrate latent learning have excited the widest interest among psychologists and, even more important, have stimulated a great deal of independent research on the part of psychologists in no way affiliated with Tolman. Whatever the ultimate fate of the system, his many fruitful experiments in animal learning stand apart as significant contributions to the field, irrespective of whether his interpretation of the results is acceptable or not.

It was Tolman who first distinguished clearly between learning and performance on the basis of the latent learning experiments. By so doing he brought to the attention of learning theorists the importance of motivational variables as energizers and regulators of learned behavior. Tolman's early insight was to reach a definitive formulation in Hull's postulate relating performance to drive and habit strength:

$$s\dot{\bar{E}}_R = s\bar{H}_R \times D$$

Tolman is also known for his concept of the intervening variable which was discussed on page 240. Generally speaking, experimental psychologists have found explanations of behavior in terms of intervening variables a major step forward in the precise formulation of experimental designs developed to test such variables.[27] Indeed, the heart of experimental psychology has become the search for the relationships among intervening variables. It is to Tolman's great credit that he was the first to define clearly and point out the importance of this orientation to the study of behavior.

It is something of a paradox that the most frequently criticized aspect of Tolman's system is his own set of intervening variables. Psychologists in the area of learning have found such variables as "sign Gestalts," "means-end-capacities," "cognitions," and "expectations" difficult to accept. By their very nature, intervening variables such as these are difficult to anchor to measurable stimulus-response variables with any degree of precision. The molarity of Tolman's concepts makes them widely applicable but at the same time insufficiently definitive to test experimentally.[28] Perhaps time will deal kindly with this aspect of Tolman's system in the sense that, once the more elemental or molecular variables involved in learning have been clearly identified, it will prove possible to reformulate Tolman's more global variables as complexes of simpler variables. It may be that once the processes entering into cognitions, capacities, expectancies, and so on are better known, their manifestations in molar form can be subjected to more precise experimental manipulation. We shall touch on this problem again at the end of Chapter 8. Meanwhile, we must leave Tolman for a brief look at several other contemporary developments in the field of learning.

A NOTE ABOUT CURRENT FUNCTIONALISM

No contemporary psychologists prominent in the field of learning call themselves "functionalists" in the sense the term was used to refer to the school founded by Dewey, Angell, and Carr. Today, functionalism is a loosely used category which includes the large group of American psychologists who are more interested in promoting research than in developing elaborate theoretical systems. They are, in a manner of speaking, more favorably disposed to an orderly systematization of the experimental *facts* of learning than toward orderly systems based largely on theory. Moreover, the debates and quarrels of the strongly theoretical psychologists in the area of learning are likely to leave the functionalist unimpressed. If the contemporary functionalist can be said to favor any one traditional theory over another, that tradition is associationism.

The functionalist's ties with associationism are revealed, first of all, in his interest in human as opposed to animal learning. Unlike the behav-

[27] As exemplified by Hull, who adopted the concept of intervening variables from Tolman.
[28] For an attempt to render Tolman's programmatic principles into definitive laws see MacCorquadale and Meehle (*17*, pp. 177–266).

iorists and Gestalt psychologists, who have done so much in the animal field, the functionalist's main interest has been human verbal learning.[29] He is interested in studying such problems as retroactive inhibition, factors associated with the rate of learning (distribution of practice, recitation, amount of material, and the like), and transfer of training.

Moreover, the current functionalist is empirical-minded in his approach to the psychology of learning just as his intellectual ancestors, the associationists, were empirical in their philosophy. Following in the tradition of Ebbinghaus, the functionalist maps out a program of research in some chosen area of learning, such as transfer, and strives to identify the important conditions and variables that influence the process. While he may theorize and utilize the hypothetico-deductive design in his experimental program, the functionalist, unlike the "orthodox" theorist, makes theory subservient to experimentation, rather than experimentation subservient to theory.

It must not be concluded, however, that the functionalist is "anti-theory" or fails to make use of theoretical constructs in his research. Even a glance at a recent advanced text in the area of learning reveals a wealth of functionalistic theoretical explanations. Because we shall devote a special chapter to verbal learning, the reader will be able to judge for himself that functionalist theories are closely related to research results and are topical rather than global in scope. Meanwhile, we shall examine the more important contemporary theories which developed out of the miniature systems or which were heavily influenced by them. We shall defer any attempt to summarize and evaluate the area of learning until we have considered both these contemporary developments and verbal learning.

In summary, current functionalism represents a strongly empirical orientation to learning, with emphasis on human verbal learning. The functionalistic point of view is represented neither by a highly structured theory nor by the systematic writings of any one person. The functionalist is an investigator first and a theorist second, though, as we have indicated, theory plays a role in his program in the sense that he offers theoretical explanations of research findings.

REFERENCES

1. Bugelski, B. R. *The psychology of learning.* New York: Holt, 1956.
2. Carmichael, L. (ed.). *Manual of child psychology.* New York: Wiley, 1946.
3. Cotton, J. W. On making predictions from Hull's theory. *Psychological Review,* **62,** No. 4, 1955.

[29] For representative books on learning by those who favor the functionalistic approach, see reference numbers *4* and *19*. For an excellent article summarizing the entire area of learning and relating it to the functionalist point of view, see Melton (*20*).

4. Deese, J. *The psychology of learning.* New York: McGraw-Hill, 1958.
5. Elliott, M. H. The effect of change of reward on the maze performance of rats. *University of California Publications in Psychology,* **4,** 1928, pp. 19–30.
6. Guthrie, E. R. *The psychology of human conflict.* New York: Harper, 1938.
7. Guthrie, E. R. *The psychology of learning,* rev. ed. New York: Harper, 1952.
8. Guthrie, E. R. Association by contiguity. In S. Koch (ed.). *Psychology: A study of a science.* New York: McGraw-Hill, 1959.
9. Guthrie, E. R., and G. P. Horton. *Cats in a puzzle box.* New York: Rinehart, 1946.
10. Hilgard, E. R. *Theories of learning,* ed. 2. New York: Appleton, 1956.
11. Hull, C. L. *Principles of behavior.* New York: Appleton, 1943.
12. Hull, C. L. *Essentials of behavior.* New Haven: Yale University Press, 1951.
13. Hull, C. L. *A behavior system.* New Haven: Yale University Press, 1952.
14. Hull, C. L., C. I. Hovland, R. T. Ross, M. Hall, D. T. Perkins, and F. B. Fitch. *Mathematico-deductive theory of rote learning.* New Haven: Yale University Press, 1940.
15. Kimble, G. A. *Hilgard and Marquis' conditioning and learning,* ed. 2. New York: Appleton, 1961.
16. Koch, S., and Clark L. Hull. In Estes, W. K. *et al.* (eds.). *Modern learning theory.* New York: Appleton, 1954.
17. MacCorquodale, K., and P. E. Meehl. Edward C. Tolman. In Estes, W. K. *et al.* (eds.). *Modern learning theory.* New York: Appleton, 1954.
18. Marx, M. H., and W. Hillix. *Systems and theories in psychology.* New York: McGraw-Hill, 1963.
19. McGeoch, J. A., and A. L. Irion. *The psychology of human learning,* rev. ed. New York: Longmans, Green, 1952.
20. Melton, A. W. Learning. In W. S. Monroe (ed.), *Encyclopedia of educational research,* rev. ed. New York: Macmillan, 1950.
21. Osgood, C. E. *Method and theory in experimental psychology.* New York: Oxford, 1953.
22. Seward, J. P. An experimental study of Guthrie's theory of reinforcement. *Journal of Experimental Psychology,* **39,** 1949, pp. 177–186.
23. Skinner, B. F. *The behavior of organisms.* New York: Appleton, 1938.
24. Skinner, B. F. "Superstition" in the pigeon. *Journal of Experimental Psychology,* **38,** 1948, pp. 168–172.
25. Skinner, B. F. Are theories of learning necessary? *Psychological Review,* **57,** 1950, pp. 193–216.
26. Skinner, B. F. How to teach animals. *Scientific American,* **185,** 1951, pp. 26–29.
27. Skinner, B. F. *Science and human behavior.* New York: Macmillan, 1953.
28. Skinner, B. F., and C. B. Ferster. *Schedules of reinforcement.* New York: Appleton, 1957.
29. Skinner, B. F. *Verbal behavior.* New York: Appleton, 1957.
30. Spence, K. W. *Behavior theory and conditioning.* New Haven, Conn.: Yale University Press, 1956.
31. Thistlewaite, D. L. A critical review of latent learning and related experiments. *Psychological Bulletin,* **48,** 1951, pp. 97–129.
32. Thorpe, L. P., and A. M. Schmuller. *Contemporary theories of learning.* New York: Ronald, 1954.
33. Tolman, E. C. *Purposive behavior in animals and men.* New York: Appleton, 1932.
34. Tolman, E. C. *Drives toward war.* New York: Appleton, 1942.
35. Tolman, E. C. There is more than one kind of learning. *Psychological Review,* **56,** 1949, pp. 144–155.
36. Tolman, E. C. Principles of purposive behaviorism. In S. Koch (ed.). *Psychology: A study of a science.* New York: McGraw-Hill, 1959.

37. Tolman, E. C., and C. H. Honzik. Degrees of hunger, reward and non-reward, and maze learning in rats. *University of California Publications in Psychology,* **4,** 1930, pp. 241–256.
38. Tolman, E. C., and C. H. Honzik. Introduction and removal of reward, and maze performance in rats. *University of California Publications in Psychology,* **4,** 1930, pp. 257–275.
39. Voeks, V. W. Postremity, recency, and frequency as bases for prediction in the maze situation. *Journal of Experimental Psychology,* **38,** 1948, pp. 495–510.
40. Voeks, V. W. Formalization and clarification of a theory of learning. *Journal of Psychology,* **30,** 1950, pp. 341–362.
41. Voeks, V. W. Acquisition of S-R connections: a test of Hull's and Guthrie's theories. *Journal of Experimental Psychology,* **47,** 1954, pp. 137–147.
42. Wolman, B. B. *Contemporary theories and systems in psychology.* New York: Harper, 1960.

8

Learning III: Derivative Theories and Current Issues

Each major figure in the history of science has had his followers. The ideas of great men of the past evolve into the mainstream of present thinking through the works of their associates and students. We have seen how the schools of psychology centering around men such as Wundt, Titchener, Watson, Köhler, and Freud received their impetus from the founder whose immediate associates formed a nucleus of the "school" which, in turn, attracted ever-widening interest. But leaders in science rarely retain the loyalty of their followers for long. Followers tend to become leaders, founding systems and theories in their own right. If they should fail to do so, all progress in science would cease.

Some derivative systems remain close in aims, methods, and philosophy to their original prototypes. Others reveal that a process of reaction has occurred, and the new theory becomes in effect a rejection of the old. Most of Freud's immediate associates pursued the former course, adopting the aims and techniques of psychoanalysis for their own purposes but modifying both theory and practice in the light of their clinical experience. Adler, in contrast, rejected psychoanalysis to found an entirely new system whose spirit and methods were diametrically opposed to Freud's. Similarly, among academic psychologists, Titchener remained faithful to Wundt's structuralism while Watson, who was nurtured under functionalism, rejected it to found a new school.

We have seen how the more recent miniature systems of learning developed out of the systematic theorizing of leaders within that field of psychology. Clearly, the behaviorists—Guthrie, Hull, and Skinner—were all strongly influenced by Pavlovian conditioning, and in the very broadest sense their systems are derivatives of classical conditioning. Tolman, on the other hand, did not adopt conditioning as his model, and for many years stood alone as the outstanding champion of a cognitive approach.

Looked at from a different frame of reference, the miniature systematists may be divided into contiguity versus reinforcement theorists, with Guthrie and Tolman in the contiguity camp and Hull and Skinner (some would include Thorndike) in the reinforcement camp. In terms of research interests the latter categorization is the more meaningful. Most of the research in contemporary animal learning has centered, in one way or another, around the problem of reinforcement, its nature, and its necessity. Indeed, it was disagreement with respect to the role of reinforcement in learning that led to cleavages among close associates and the development of derivative and rival theories.

Because theories which have developed around current issues are of necessity vital and evolving conceptual schemas, it is important that the student of systematic psychology recognize them as incomplete. Indeed, in time some will become major, well-established theories. Others will enjoy only transient prominence and cease to be influential. Undoubtedly there are evolving theories which we have failed to include here which time will treat more kindly than some of those which constitute our sample. Time, unlike authors, has the advantage of hindsight. Moreover, any choice is of necessity arbitrary. We have tried to include for discussion in this chapter those theories which have already stood the test of time for a decade or more and which have stimulated a developing body of research. Quite arbitrarily we have chosen to defer treatment of one influential mathematical model (Estes') until the chapter on quantitative psychology where it can be examined within the frame of reference of other statistical models of learning.

SPENCE'S *S-R* REINFORCEMENT THEORY

In beginning our survey of current theories with Kenneth Spence's *S-R* reinforcement theory, we shall be on familiar ground, for it evolved out of Hull's systematic behavior theory. Spence was a former student and later an associate of Hull's and influenced the latter's thinking, particularly on the issue of incentive motivation, or *K*. However, while he accepts the validity of the Hullian stimulus-response analysis of learning within the larger framework of a conditioning model, Spence also differs with his former teacher and associate both on general theoretical issues and on the interpretation of empirical findings. In his *Behavior Theory and Conditioning* (26, pp. 54–59), he brings his points of disagreement with Hull to the foreground.

First, Spence believes that Hull's attempt to utilize the hypothetico-deductive method was, in fact, an erroneous conception of the method which gives a misleading impression of the state of development of psychology as a science. The system was, in reality, an intervening variable system and not a hypothetico-deductive system. The hypothetico-deductive method of the natural sciences begins with axiomatic statements and postulates which are logically consistent and which subsequently can be correlated with empirical findings. A *postulate* is a broad underlying principle which must be assumed in the absence of evidence because it is vital to the development of a system. But, argues Spence, psychology is not yet able to make such formal statements of principle. Rather, the psychologist utilizes *hypotheses*, which are conclusions made in advance to be verified or rejected by experimental tests and which are therefore closely bound to the results of empirical research. Intervening variables are then introduced by the experimentalist to interpret, organize, and explain the laboratory findings. For example, Hull's concept of habit strength although stated in postulate form is actually an intervening variable used to account for S-R relations in learning.

Second, Spence does not believe in defining intervening variables in neurophysiological terms. Hull justified his utilization of explanations in terms of hypothetical neurological structures and processes by arguing that further research could develop and evaluate the status of such constructs. Spence thinks not. While he favors physiological concepts which develop within the framework of physiological research, merely to add physiological names to such psychological concepts as habit strength does not aid in our understanding of them.

Third, Spence differs from Hull on the issue of reinforcement. Hull, it will be recalled, first adopted drive reduction and subsequently drive stimulus reduction as the physiological basis for the effectiveness of reinforcement. Spence does not attempt to specify the nature of reinforcement. Rather, he takes the position that it is unnecessary to the mathematical validity of a learning theory to make assumptions about the physiological basis for reinforcement. Clearly, Spence's second and third points of difference with Hullian theory are closely related and reveal his antipathy to physiologizing about the nature of the learning process.

Fourth, Spence criticizes Hull for his willingness to build an elaborate system on the basis of a minimal set of empirical data. Spence prefers to move more cautiously in developing a limited theory based on a step by step elaboration of hypotheses which are followed by experimental verification, rejection, or modification. Certainly most psychologists would agree that Spence has followed his self-imposed rule in his model experiments in conditioning (*26, 27*).

Turning to the positive contributions made by Spence to basic Hullian theory, we may begin by introducing the concept of the *fractional anticipatory*

oal response, or r_G, first developed by Hull but elaborated into a major contruct in conditioning theory by Spence and his associates. The fractional
nticipatory goal response is a form of antedating response, or a response
which occurs earlier in a sequence of events than it originally occurred, paricularly a response which occurs prior to the appearance of the stimulus
which originally evoked it. To begin with a very simple example of an
ntedating response we may consider the case of an animal, in learning a
naze, who may, upon arriving at a certain point in the entering arm of a **Y**
egment (let us assume the first point where the two arms diverge), begins
o bend toward the right. But as the learning goes on, the animal begins to
eer right—hugging the wall immediately upon entering the **Y**. The animal
s now showing an antedating or anticipatory response. In terms of a cogniive theory he is showing expectancy. Indeed, the concept of the antedating
esponse is the equivalent of expectancy in cognitive theories of learning.
imilarly, the fractional anticipatory goal response is a reaction that occurs
progressively early in a response chain during the acquisition of a condiioned response.

In his last book, *A Behavior System,* Hull referred to the complete unconlitioned response or UK as the goal response or R_G and any portion of it as
he fractional response or r_G. The rat that begins chewing movements upon
pproaching a goal compartment is showing a fractional anticipatory reponse. Now, because the r_G occurs in contiguous association with proprioeptive stimuli arising from the musculature and produced by r_G, Hull
rgued that $r_G \rightarrow s_G$ and that $r_G \rightarrow s_G$ sequences become important meditors and integrators of behavior.

Spence and his associates at the University of Iowa elaborated the
oncept of the fractional anticipatory goal response as an explanation of
atent learning as revealed in experiments with a simple **Y**-type maze (*28*).
These experiments had been undertaken in an attempt to find a crucial experiment in which the hypothesis that learning occurs in the absence of
einforcement could be tested. As it turned out, "motivationless" animals
efused to run the maze and "social" motivation in the form of a cage of
ats at the goal end of the maze had to be provided to insure activity on the
part of the experimental subjects. During the course of the training runs the
nimals were given an opportunity to experience finding water in one goal
ompartment and food in the other even though satiated. Forced trials
vere employed to insure that the animals entered both compartments the
ame number of times. On the first test trial on which the animals were
ither hungry or thirsty there was a significant tendency to choose the
orrect or appropriate side. A second test trial in which the motivation was
eversed again demonstrated latent learning, although the results were not
ignificantly different from chance expectations.

In experiments such as that just described, Spence and his associates stressed the importance of $r_G \rightarrow s_G$ sequences as integrators and organizers of behavior. Essentially, the act of reinforcement at the end of the maze produces the conditioning of fractional anticipatory goal responses to stimulus cues through the response chain. It is assumed that the sight or smell of food is mildly reinforcing even to a satiated animal. It can be further assumed that the evocation of an $r_G \rightarrow s_G$ sequence to food $(r_f \rightarrow s_f)$ is different from that evoked by water $(r_w \rightarrow s_w)$. It is further necessary to assume that when the animal arrives at a choice point in a Y or T maze it looks to the right and left, thus making motor responses. These motor responses need not be obvious but may be so weak or tentative as to be only implicit. Because these proprioceptive responses have been associated with eating or drinking—or in the case of latent learning experiments with the sight and smell of food, hence with r_G's—the induction of a thirst or hunger drive leads to the appropriate fractional anticipatory goal response and, at the choice point, to movement toward food or water. Therefore, in essence, *the r_G is a special kind of response in as much as it produces reinforcing effects and is capable of influencing the motivational level of the organism.* More simply, in the typical maze experiment the animals' sight and smell of food and water antedate the behavior patterns involved in manipulating or eating the same objects. The sight and smell of the goal objects come to elicit antedating fractional portions of the total goal reaction, and it is these reactions which come to signify the "eatability" or "drinkability" of the objects. The association of these antedating reactions with proprioceptive stimuli at choice points are assumed to be strengthened by the presence of reinforcement. On subsequent trials the presence of drive stimuli arouses the appropriate sequence of responses, and so the correct choice is made.

Closely related to the concept of the r_G is the concept of K or incentive motivation, which was adopted by Hull largely as a result of Spence's insistence on its central importance in learning. While Hull simply identified K with incentive motivation, and therefore with the level of habit strength depending upon its reinforcing value, Spence identified it with the fractional anticipatory goal response or r_G. In effect, K is the anticipated response based on $r_G \rightarrow s_G$ that the "food is near." In this sense K becomes very similar to Tolman's concept of the sign Gestalt.

Spence holds that the relationship between habit strength, drive, and K are additive, not multiplicative as Hull believed. Thus even though the level of drive was at zero or near zero (such as in a latent learning experiment), learning could still occur even though it might not be revealed in performance. The evidence to support this contention is complex and incomplete. It is reviewed by Spence in Chapter VI of his *Behavior Theory and Conditioning.* Essentially the evidence revolves around the related questions of whether or not the degree of learning and the level of performance vary as a function of the level of drive and the nature and the amount of the reward. The problem is therefore part of the larger issue of whether or not contiguity or reinforcement is essential for learning. Spence, in disagreement with Hull, believes that these are unsettled questions and cannot be resolved by the postulation of simple multiplicative relationships between habit strength and drive for all forms of learning.

To show the hidden complexity in even the simplest instance of the drive-performance relationship, Spence presents data from an eyelid conditioning experiment in which two groups of forty subjects were employed in a factorial design permitting the isolation and analysis of both drive strength and habit strength. One group of subjects was given thirty trials with a weak stimulus (*US*) and the other thirty trials with a strong stimulus. In a second session the two original groups were divided into subgroups with one-half given *US* at the same intensity as in the original series and the other half switched to the other intensity, either higher or lower. The frequency of conditioning of the original and the subgroups is shown in Table 8-1.

Note that both row means and column means differ, representing significant differences for both conditions of the experiment. The difference in row means indicates that differences in the intensity of the *US* given during the first series resulted in a difference in response strength during the second period. Because the level of intensity of the *US* in the second period was controlled by splitting the groups and giving both levels to all subgroups, this difference cannot reflect differences in drive strength resulting from a different intensity of *US* during this period. Spence suggests that possibly differences in habit strength were developed during the first series because of different intensities of the *US* and that performance under higher conditions of drive in the second series reflects this difference in associative strength rather than differences in drive. Thus, in this test *D* and *H* are not related multiplicatively, as Hull suggested, but only additively.

Data is also available from discrimination learning experiments and

Table 8-1.
Mean Number of Conditioned Responses in the Initial Twenty Trials of the Test Phase (Day 2) of a Factorial Design Used to Investigate the Action of the Unconditioned Stimulus on Eyelid Conditioning[a]

Day 1 *UCS* (lbs./sq. in.)	Day 2 *UCS* (lbs./sq. in.)		Row MEANS
	0.25	5.00	
0.25	5.65	8.80	7.23
5.00	7.45	13.00	10.23
Column means	6.55	10.90	

[a] From Spence, 1956. The differences between both the row and column means are significant, implying the involvement of both associative and motivational factors.

experiments involving delay of reinforcement (26, pp. 124–164) to suggest that in *instrumental* learning, as opposed to *conditioning*, contiguity and incentive motivation or K may be a more important factor than reinforcement or drive stimulus reduction. However, Spence is not willing to commit himself irrevocably to what would amount to a two-factor theory of learning[1] but with the adoption of K and $r_G \to s_G$ has gone far toward Tolman's position of contiguity learning.

In summary, then, Spence's theory is a stimulus-response reinforcement theory based on the Hullian model, but a modified reinforcement theory in which considerable emphasis is placed on r_G—s_G and K. With the introduction of r_G as essentially a cognitive anticipation of the reward, Spence has included in his system an important element of cognitive theory and has thus brought the two camps closer together.

MILLER'S REINFORCEMENT THEORY

Neal Miller, like Spence, has been strongly influenced by Hull but unlike Spence has not chosen to work within the confines of classical conditioning. His wide range of experimental and theoretical work spans the areas of drive acquisition, conflict, reinforcement, and the application of S-R theory to personality development.

Because the concept of drive is central to Miller's position in all areas of habit formation, from those involving simple bar-pressing responses to those intimately concerned with complex habits of personality, we may begin with an analysis of the nature of drive. A drive is any strong stimulus which arouses the organism into action. Drives may be either external or internal; and they may be primary, physiological drives related to the survival of the organism, or they may be secondary or acquired drives which have been learned in the course of development. Hunger, thirst, and pain exemplify physiological or primary drives with whose stimuli everyone is familiar. These drive states are capable of producing powerful internal stimuli which impel the organism to act in such a manner as to reduce the drive. Thus the hungry animal seeks food; the lion goaded by pain strives to remove the thorn from his foot.

But everyone also knows that the infant, while subject to strong drives, has not acquired the necessary behavioral patterns which will reduce those drives; and until he does, he must have help from his parents. Similarly, an adult in a novel situation may be strongly motivated or driven toward a goal but be unable to reduce his drive simply because he has not acquired the necessary habits of behavior to accomplish this. For example, many

---

[1] See "Mowrer's Two-Factor Theory," below.

adults are strongly impelled to express themselves in artistic media—by painting or writing. But the first tentative attempts standing at the easel or sitting before a stack of blank paper are more likely to produce frustration than to be drive reducing. Only after a long period of learning and self-discipline is the neophyte likely to find the satisfaction that he is seeking. Summarizing what we have said thus far in the form of a principle, *drives energize behavior while learning provides the behavior patterns that result in efficient drive reduction.*

Our last example of drive in the preceding paragraph not only serves to emphasize the importance of learning, it also emphasizes a distinction with which we are already familiar from our consideration of previous theories, namely, that of primary and secondary drives. Primary drives, it will be recalled, are those which arise out of the functioning of the organism's basic biological equipment. They do not have to be learned and are universal within a given species. It is, of course, true that the means of satisfying primary drives must be acquired, and it is in the particular manner in which the individual learns to satisfy his drives that individual differences in personality are developed.

Secondary drives are learned drives. Consequently they are culturally or individually determined and are usually not linked in any obvious way to physiological functions or to biological survival. The strong motives that many individuals exhibit to collect works of art, coins, stamps, or other material goods exemplify secondary drive mechanisms. A drive toward stamp collecting, to pick one example from the list, is not vital to anyone's survival; nor is it linked in any known way with biological mechanisms. Yet it can be a powerful drive for which the individual may make great sacrifices of time and treasure.

In their well-known books, *Social Learning and Imitation (14)* and *Personality and Psychotherapy (1)*, Miller and John Dollard, his collaborator and professional associate, have summarized the nature of the learning process as involving not only drives, but also cues, responses, and rewards (or reinforcement). We shall comment briefly on each of these facets of the learning process out of which habits of drive satisfaction are developed.

Cues are stimuli that serve to guide the responses of the organism. In a simple salivary conditioning experiment, the *CS* becomes a cue which elicits the response of salivation as a consequence of learning. Similarly, in the infant, the sight of the bottle becomes a cue for the cessation of struggling and crying and the initiation of sucking behavior.

The response is, of course, central to learning since it must occur before it can be associated with the cue pattern through reinforcement or reward. Miller and Dollard utilize Hull's concept of a hierarchy of responses (see Chapter 7), pointing out that some responses are innate, others derived or resultant as consequences of learning. Thus, to return to the familiar example of Thorndike's cats, the animals showed a hierarchy of innate responses involving struggling, clawing, biting, and the like, and a final resultant response consisting of loop pulling or pedal pushing which allowed them to escape from the box.

Again, we are already familiar with the principle that in a cue→response or *S-R* situation, the reinforcement or reward is the critical factor in determining which response will be linked to the cue or stimulus pattern. Here Miller follows Hull in assuming that reinforcement acts through drive reduction, strengthening those responses which reduce drive stimuli.

We shall return to the problem of reinforcement later in this chapter, but meanwhile we may illustrate the learning process according to Miller's *S-R* analysis by describing a basic and widely-cited experiment on fear as an acquired drive (*11*). Figure 8-1 shows the acquired-drive apparatus in which white rats were used as subjects. The animals were first put in both the white and black compartments where they could explore freely. They showed no fear of either compartment or of the grid on the floor of the white compartment. Next Miller administered shocks to the animals who were placed singly in the white compartment. The rats were allowed to escape the pain

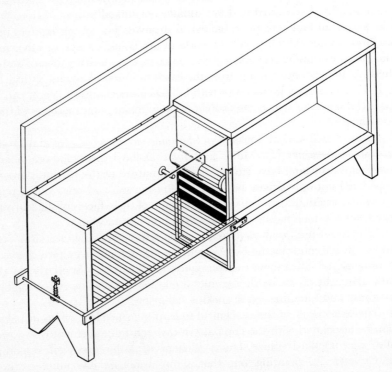

Fig. 8-1. Miller's apparatus for utilizing anxiety as a drive. (From Miller, *11*.)

by running into the black compartment, the experimenter meanwhile raising the door (painted with white and black stripes) by remote control. So far the experiment demonstrates only the well-known fact that animals can learn to escape a noxious stimulus. But Miller went on to demonstrate that later, without the grid being electrified, the animals upon being put into the white compartment showed signs of fear (urinating, defecating, crouching, and the like) and ran to the black compartment. The *stimuli* (cues) in the white compartment, consisting of the compartment itself plus the strong responses made by the animal itself, which also serve as cues, had become associated with the *response* of running to the black compartment as a result of the fear *drive*. The *reinforcement* in this case was the reduction of the pain stimuli.

To demonstrate that the acquired fear of the white box could serve as a drive in itself to motivate new learning, Miller arranged the experimental situation in such a way that the animals could only escape from the white compartment by turning a small wheel above the door. This the animals learned to do—not, it will be recalled, in response to shock, but to fear of shock. Indeed, Miller was able to demonstrate that a lever could be substituted for the wheel as a "key" to the door leading to the black compartment. The animals quickly learned to extinguish the wheel-turning response in favor of the lever-pushing response, again without the necessity of additional shocks.

This experiment with white rats suggests that similar mechanisms are operative in human beings in the course of development. Fear, a primary reaction to a noxious or painful situation, produces responses which we call emotional reactions which, in turn, can, through learning, serve as cues that guide or control behavior in subsequent situations. Phobias, anxieties, and other "irrational" fear responses in conflict situations in adults may thus develop through learning during childhood. We call such fears and anxieties irrational only because we have not been in a position to observe their development during the individual's childhood. Similarly, if we had not known that the rats were shocked in the white compartment, their behavior would seem equally irrational. Moreover, it should be obvious that the elimination of such fears could only take place through repetition of the original situation in which the organism is induced to make his fear response in the absence of reinforcement. Thus, the rat, if placed in the white compartment often enough without shock, will gradually extinguish his fear responses and running reaction. Verbal psychotherapy, by analogy, is the verbalizing of anxieties in the presence of a permissive therapist who helps to bring about extinction by nonreinforcement—reinforcement in this case being verbal statements or criticisms from friends and members of his family which strengthen the fear reactions.

Miller has also adopted *S-R* theory in an analysis of conflict situations

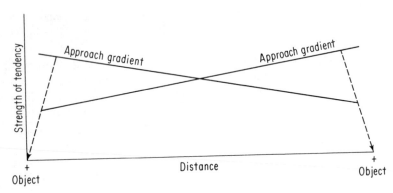

Fig. 8-2. A diagrammatic representation of the approach-approach gradient. As either positive object is approached, the gradient of approach becomes steeper.

(*13*). The theoretical foundation involves five basic assumptions. First, it is assumed that the tendency to approach a goal increases as the distance to the goal decreases. Second, the tendency to avoid a negative stimulus becomes stronger with decreasing distance between the organism and the stimulus. Third, it is assumed that the gradient for avoidance or negative stimuli is steeper than for approach or positive stimuli. Fourth, increase in drive increases the level of gradients of either approach or withdrawal. Fifth, if two response tendencies are in competition, the stronger will occur in behavior. Figures 8-2, 8-3, and 8-4 show theoretical representations of several types of conflict analyzed according to gradients of approach and avoidance and the strength of the tendency operating in the organism at any given period of time.[2] A number of empirical studies by Miller and others summarized by Miller (*13*) show that this type of analysis is a valid extension of the drive aspects of *S-R* learning theory into the area of conflict and personality.

Indeed, Dollard and Miller have elaborated their extension of Hullian theory into an entire system of personality development and psychotherapy (*1*). In doing so they follow the tradition set by Pavlov, Guthrie, and Skinner, who also attempt to utilize the basic principles of conditioning theory in order to account for the infinite complexities of behavior as found in life beyond the laboratory. The validity of such efforts to extend and generalize basic learning theory has been and remains a controversial issue among both learning theorists and psychologists in general. Essentially the conflict lies in the fact that physiology and biological science do explain the complex in terms of the simple or elementary. This has been the tradition of science

[2] The reader should compare this analysis with that given in Chapter 11. See section on Lewin's Field Theory.

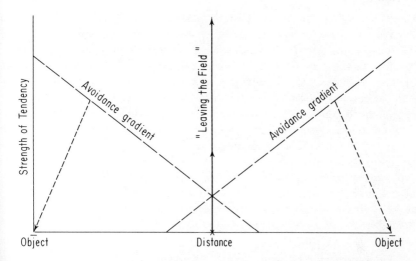

Fig. 8-3. A diagrammatic representation of an avoidance-avoidance gradient. As either object is approached, the gradient of avoidance becomes steeper. The gradient is least steep at maximum distance from the two negative goals. The arrow labeled "leaving the field" indicates a tendency for the subject to resolve such conflicts by escaping the situation.

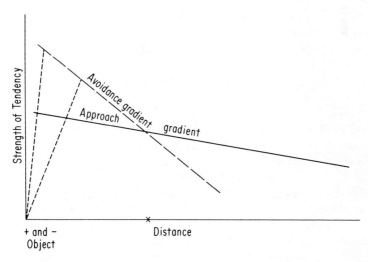

Fig. 8-4. Approach-avoidance gradients. As the individual approaches an object with both positive and negative qualities, the avoidance gradient becomes steeper and steeper eventually to overcome the approach tendency.

301

ever since it first emerged in Greek empirical philosophy. It has also been traditional for psychology to explain complex phenomena in terms of more elementary processes from the days of the British empiricists and the structuralists to the present time, with the exception of the Gestalt and other phenomenological schools. But the opponents of such systems of explanation either reject the *method* outright, as is the case of those who are persuaded of the phenomenological point of view, or they argue that it is too soon to attempt to generalize from the laboratory to life. Spence is representative of the latter group. Whatever the merits of the issue, we doubt that the critics will have their way. The desire to make psychology relevant to real human problems is too strong to be overcome by scientific caution. Few psychologists would disagree that at *some* stage of the development of psychology such an attempt ought to be made. Certainly most of the S-R theorists have done so with admirable caution and restraint.

MOWRER'S TWO-FACTOR THEORY OF LEARNING

For nearly a quarter of a century O. Hobart Mowrer has been emphasizing the dual nature of learning. Early in his theoretical attempts to account for learning he suggested that basically there are two forms of learning: *sign learning* and *solution learning*. Sign learning is the kind of stimulus substitution learning which goes on in classical conditioning, while solution learning is learning in situations where the correct response is selected under conditions of reward or reinforcement.

We are already familiar with the possibility that different factors operate in different kinds of learning. It will be recalled (Chapter 7) that Skinner dichotomizes conditioning into two types, Type-S and Type-R, with Type-S exemplified in experiments in which conditioned responses involving autonomic processes are elicited, and Type-R in situations involving operant behavior. It will also be remembered that Spence suggested that learning may involve two factors. From his point of view, in classical conditioning drive reduction and reinforcement may be more important than contiguity and incentives, whose importance, in turn, is emphasized in instrumental learning.

In his *Learning Theory and Behavior* (*16*), Mowrer develops his views historically from their origins in Hullian drive reduction (he was at one time associated with the Yale group under Hull's leadership) to their final formulation in a kind of sign-expectancy theory which bears many resemblances to Tolman's sign Gestalt theory of learning. In the third chapter of his book, he takes Hull's conditioning model of drive reduction as his point of departure. There he points out that Hull strove to reduce all learning to an S-R reinforcement model in what might appropriately be called a "one factor" theory. With this single factor of drive reduction (or drive stimulus reduction), Hull not only attempted to explain simple classical conditioned responses but also the acquisition of drives and the learning of complex discriminations. Admittedly, incentives (K) play a role in the Hullian system of learning, particularly in Spence's derivative theory, but the emphasis is on drive and reinforcement.

Mowrer detects a serious weakness in the Hullian position, because of what he believes to be its inability to explain certain forms of animal learning. Using Miller's experiment on the acquisition of fear as his example, he points out that there is an illogicality in attempting to account for the results in terms of drive reduction. Miller, it will be recalled, trained rats to escape from a white compartment into a black compartment, thereby avoiding shock. He argued that the animal's fear is strengthened by the sudden cessation of the shock upon escape. Therefore, as the experiment proceeds, the animal's fear becomes stronger and the drive better established and so can be utilized to energize wheel-turning or lever-pushing in an avoidance situation with no further primary reinforcement.

The illogicality in Miller's position, Mowrer believes, lies in assuming that the cessation of pain strengthens the fear. Common sense tells us that we are apprehensive about the coming of pain, not its cessation. Therefore, he asks, how is it possible for fear or anxiety—which is an anticipation of shock—to be strengthened by its elimination? In attempting to explain this phenomenon drive reduction theory appears paradoxical and self-contradictory.[3] Mowrer further asks us to consider the following design of an experiment which bears upon the issues between the Hullians and himself. Hungry rats are first trained to press a bar in a Skinner-type situation in order to obtain food. The act of bar-pressing activates a tone stimulus which has previously been paired with shock. If the bar-pressing is inhibited, upon presentation of the tone, then the tone has acquired the capacity to arouse fear. Five groups of rats were then used in the experiment proper (17), involving five different temporal sequences of CS and US, with the sequences and the results shown in Figure 8-5. Mowrer argues that if fear conditioning depends upon what happens when the shock comes on, then the least conditioning would occur under those conditions where the tone immediately precedes shock. However, if the conditioning of fear is dependent upon what happens when shock goes off, then the best conditioning should occur in the group in which the tone is presented just ahead of the termination of the shock. As Figure 8-5 shows, when the tone was paired with shock onset, the conditioning was most effective. Thus, the tone becomes a *sign* that the shock is approaching and the appropriate inhibitory behavior is initiated. Mowrer points out that according to Hullian theory the best conditioning should occur under the condition where tone precedes shock termination.

Mowrer presents considerable additional evidence in support of his

For Miller's rejection of Mowrer's interpretation see *12*.

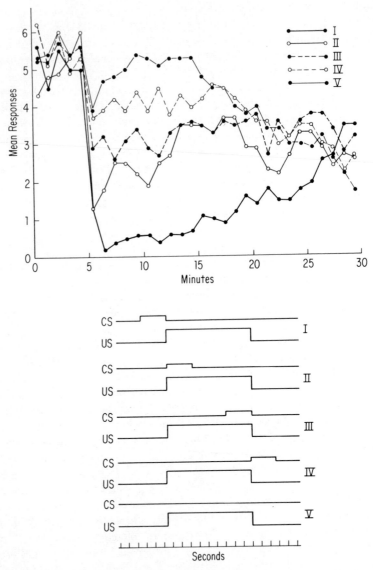

Fig. 8-5. Five different temporal sequences of conditioning a fear reaction in a bar-pressing experiment with the results obtained. (From Mowrer, *16*.)

original two-factor theory (*16*, pp. 83–89) and concludes that fear, other emotions and attitudes are conditioned as sign learning—the onset of a stimulus becomes, through practice, a sign which is effective in eliciting a certain response. The drive, so to speak, is *induced* rather than reduced. Similarly, in a Pavlovian bell-saliva experiment, the bell becomes a sign of food and the salivatory response is an anticipatory reaction to *US* or food-in-the-mouth. What is learned is stimulus substitution. Salivation occurs to the bell instead of waiting until the food is on the tongue.

In trial and error learning, such as in the Thorndikian model, reinforcement remains the important factor because the response is a voluntary one which must be given *before* the reinforcement occurs. The drive is thus reduced by the reinforcement following the response. What is learned in this case is the utilization of an appropriate response in a particular stimulus situation.

Mowrer admits that it would be a mistake to regard the avoidance learning of a fear response as pure sign learning involving no solution learning whatsoever. Both types of learning are typically involved. The animal must *do* something to escape the punishment. Simply *expecting* punishment is not enough to avoid it. Such an admission, however, does not prove a fatal weakness in the original statement of the theory. But it does suggest that perhaps the dichotomy needs a more searching analysis and further suggests that there may be only one kind of learning after all. Additional weakness, particularly in accounting for the problem of secondary reinforcement, led Mowrer to revise completely his theory between 1947, the date of its first publication, and 1960, the year of publication of *Learning Theory and Behavior*.

Secondary reinforcement, it will be recalled, involves the association of a stimulus pattern with a primary reinforcer in the presence of a drive. Thus, if an intermittent light is flashed while the bar-pressing rat is being reinforced, the presence of the light will take on reinforcing properties and the response will be more difficult to extinguish in the presence of the light than in its absence. However, consider an experiment involving the presence of a tone upon the cessation of shock. As we have already discovered from the Mowrer-Aiken experiment (*17*), the tone does not take on secondary reinforcing properties. Mowrer points out the difference in the two situations as follows: The reinforcing property of the light is tested in the presence of the primary drive—hunger. The reinforcing property of the tone is not tested in the presence of a primary drive—the shock has already ceased. If the tone is presented ahead of shock it will be considered a cue to do something and will take on reinforcing properties to become effective in producing inhibitory behavior. This kind of secondary reinforcement, the expectation that an event will occur, Mowrer calls Type-2 reinforcement.

It is important to recognize the responses themselves can become conditioned to primary and secondary reinforcement. Mowrer asks us to consider the case of a dog that a boy is teaching to "shake hands." The boy lifts the dog's leg, shakes it, and then rewards the animal with a pat on the

Table 8-2.
Present Version of Two-Factor Theory

Incremental reinforcement (punishment)		Decremental reinforcement (reward)	
Primary reinforcement		Primary reinforcement	
Secondary reinforcement		Secondary reinforcement	
Danger Signal on (fear)	Safety signal off (disappointment)	Danger signal off (relief)	Danger signal on (hope)

head or a bit of dog biscuit. The passive flexion of the leg arouses proprio-ceptive stimuli which become associated with the pat or the food and serve as secondary reinforcement in the form of an expectation of a reward. Soon the animal raises his paw with the associated expectation of food.

In summary, the problem of secondary reinforcement in avoidance conditioning is associational. Stimuli associated with the cessation of shock are secondary reinforcers. Sensations from the animal's own responses be-come "danger" signs just as the dog's paw lifting becomes a sign of "hope" or expectancy. Mowrer is thus led to postulate a revised two-factor theory in which all learning involves sign learning but reinforcement is considered dualistically as: (1) incremental reinforcement or punishment, and (2) decremental reinforcement or reward. In incremental reinforcement learn-ing, stimuli become signs of fear; in decremental learning, of hope. Table 8-2, as modified from Mowrer, summarizes the two-factor theory and shows the relationship of incremental and decremental reinforcement to the variables of learning.

In looking back on the derivative theories examined thus far, we have seen how increasing emphasis has been placed on cognitive factors with the exception of Miller's drive reduction theory, which hews to the Hullian line. In the theory to follow we shall find that expectancy plays a central role. Clearly, the struggle of the learning theorist with the relative contribution of contiguity, expectation, and reinforcement or reward is at the heart of their disagreements. By making the relative roles of reinforcement and ex-pectancy central to the evolution of his theory, Mowrer has undertaken a searching and comprehensive review of modern learning theory. Of these relative roles we shall have more to say after our examination of Rotter's Social Learning Theory.

ROTTER'S SOCIAL LEARNING THEORY

Julian Rotter's social learning theory constitutes a radical departure from the theories of learning which we have considered thus far. Without exception, beginning with Thorndike and carrying through the major derivative theories including Mowrer's two-factor theory, all systems that we have studied have evolved in the tradition of "pure" as opposed to "applied" science. In contrast Rotter's theory was developed in a clinical setting, and its avowed purpose is to provide a learning theory which will have relevance for the clinical as well as the academic psychologist. This is not to say that Rotter is antiexperimental in his attitude or that the theory is based on pure speculation. On the contrary, it is a rigorously worked out attempt to ". . . translate and relate the basic knowledge of experimental and theoretical psychology into the practical situation of the clinic, the hospital, and the school" (*21*, p. viii). Moreover, in the account of his basic position in *Social Learning and Clinical Psychology* (*21*), Rotter presents a great deal of experimental evidence to provide a foundation for his fundamental postulates, and in the past decade he and his associates and students have generated a vigorous research program in support of the theory.

Rotter's basic concepts are those of *behavior potential, expectancy,* and *reinforcement value.* Behavior potential is defined by Rotter ". . . *as the potentiality of any behavior's occurring in any given situation or situations as calculated in relation to any single reinforcement or set of reinforcements.*" (*21*, p. 105).

The term behavior as it is employed in the foregoing definition is a broad one, including any observable action of the organism in response to a meaningful stimulus. Both explicit and implicit forms of behavior are included. Moreover, complex patterns of behavior emphasized by the dynamic psychologists are covered by the definition. These include the Freudian defense mechanisms of repression, projection, fantasy, and the like, and the central Adlerian concept of compensation.

Expectancy is defined by Rotter ". . . *as the probability held by the individual that a particular reinforcement will occur as a function of a specific behavior on his part in a specific situation or situations. Expectancy is independent of the value or importance of the reinforcement*" (*21*, p. 107).

Expectancy is a central concept in the system, and it is used by Rotter to describe the degree to which the individual believes that he is the agent controlling his own behavior. The normal individual with a strong perception of himself as the agent of control, believes that he is the master of his fate and develops his expectancies accordingly. The depressed, the psychotic, the individual in an authoritarian situation may show a high perception of himself as the victim of external controls and the pawn of fates. Obviously, the individual's perception of the degree to which he is master of his own behavior has important implications for clinical diagnosis and psychotherapy.

Reinforcement values ". . . *may be ideally defined as the degree of preference for any reinforcement to occur if the possibilities of their occurring were all equal*" (*21*, p. 107).

By way of illustration of reinforcement value Rotter gives the example of a dollar-an-hour worker who would ideally choose to be paid at the rate of ten dollars an hour if the choice were his. Clearly, by including the con cept of *preference* in his definition of reinforcement, Rotter departs from the usual treatment of reinforcers as material agents, such as food or shock which psychologists apply to animals whose preferences are considered inaccessible or irrelevant. In a clinical situation preferences, wishes, the subjective expectancy of rewards, disappointments and level of aspiration are all important variables which theoretically ought to be modifiable by learning and experience.

In elaborating his definition of reinforcement Rotter adopts an em pirical law of effect. That is, reinforcement is any observable event which changes the potential of occurrence of a given behavioral pattern. Since the reinforcement results in a change in behavior, the effect of reinforce ment can be measured; and, what is more important, predictions about the effect of reinforcement on behavior can be made.

Rotter further distinguishes between internal and external reinforce ment. Internal reinforcement is a subject's perception that an event has taken place which has present or potential value for him. External re inforcement is the occurrence of an event which is known to an observer to have value for a given group or the entire culture to which a subject belongs. For example, praise, when experienced as a pleasant subjective feeling by a child, is internal reinforcement, but praise as an experimental variable to be given by an experimenter conducting research on the in fluence of rewards on learning is external reinforcement.

Immediately after defining his basic constructs Rotter presents five fundamental formulas (*21*, pp. 108–110):

$$\text{B.P. } _{x's_1'R_a} = f(E\ _{x'R_a's_1} \ \& \ \text{R.V.}_{\cdot a}) \tag{1}$$

The formula may be read as follows: The potential for behavior x to occur in situation 1 in relation to reinforcement a is a function of the expectancy of the occurrence of reinforcement a following behavior x in situation 1 and the value of reinforcement a.

Note the sign & is used as the only indication of the nature of the mathe matical relationship between expectancy and reinforcement value. The purpose of this is to avoid, for the time being, a more precise mathematical formulation because of an insufficient amount of experimental data. However, it seems fairly clear from data available that this relationship is a multiplicative one.

Prediction with such a formula does not lead to a statement of the potential occurrence of the behavior x in situation 1, since it considers only a single rein forcement a and not other possible consequences of behavior x. Should we be interested in calculating the potential of behavior x's occurring in situation we would have to combine a set of such behavior potentials, each determined for a specific reinforcement. This behavior potential is expressed in the formula below:

$$\text{B.P.}_{x's_1'R_{(a-n)}} = f(E_{x's_1'R_{(a-n)}} \ \& \ \text{R.V.}_{(a-n)}) \qquad (2)$$

This may be read as follows: The potential of behavior x's occurring in situation 1 in regard to all potential reinforcements for which the individual has expectancies is a function of the expectancies of the occurrences of these reinforcements (a to n) in situation 1 and the values of these reinforcements.

Should we wish to broaden our prediction to include a variety or group of situations, the formula would then include additional situations. This may be expressed as in the formula below.

$$\text{B.P.}_{x's_{(1-n)}'R_{(a-n)}} = f(E_{x's_{(1-n)}'R_{(a-n)}} \ \& \ \text{R.V.}_{(a-n)}) \qquad (3)$$

This may be read as follows: The potentiality of behavior x's occurring in relationship to the reinforcements a to n in situations 1 to n is a function of the expectancies of these reinforcements occurring in these situations and the values of these reinforcements.

We might wish now to broaden our prediction one more step and to include instead of a single behavior a group of functionally related behaviors $(x - n)$ and not all their possible consequences but the degree to which these behaviors are used to obtain one of a set of functionally related reinforcements $(a - n)$. This formula would be represented as follows:

$$\text{B.P.}_{(x-n), s_{(1-n)}'R_{(a-n)}} = f(E_{(x-n), s_{(1-n)}'R_{(a-n)}} \ \& \ \text{R.V.}_{(a-n)}) \qquad (4)$$

This may be read: The potentiality of the functionally related behaviors x to n to occur in the specific situations 1 to n in relation to potential reinforcements a to n is a function of the expectancies of these behaviors leading to these reinforcements in these situations and the values of these reinforcements.

These formulations are concerned with specific behavior-reinforcement sequences. From them we derive the broader constructs of *need potential, freedom of movement* and *need value* which are the important variables in what we refer to as psychological needs . . .

The rather complicated formula 4 above may be reduced to a formula for more general prediction that may be expressed as follows: The potentiality of occurrence of a set of behaviors that lead to the satisfaction of some need (need potential) is a function of the expectancies that these behaviors will lead to these reinforcements (freedom of movement) and the strength or value of these reinforcements (need value). This may be given in the formula below:

$$\text{N.P.} = f(\text{F.M.} \ \& \ \text{N.V.}) \qquad (5)$$

Need potential is a function of freedom of movement and need value. In clinical work it is usually this formula in which we are essentially interested; that is, it is these constructs we are trying to measure in clinical predictions. The more specific formulas are used primarily in the experimental testing of hypotheses.

We might point out that Rotter intends that the specific relationships indicated in the formulas to be only for specific situations, and that the *situation* is a basic variable in all formulas, thus itself requiring definition and description. By emphasizing the importance of the situation Rotter is acknowledging his indebtedness to Kurt Lewin's field theory with its stress on the life space and behavioral field in which a given behavior sample occurs.[4]

While Rotter is not dependent upon the concept of drive reduction as the explanation of why reinforcers reinforce, he does present a tenatative list of needs or need categories which give directionality to behavior and which lend themselves to measurement by means of empirical studies. These are given below (*21*, p. 132).[5]

> *Recognition-status:* Need to be considered competent or good in a professional, social, occupational, or play activity. Need to gain social or vocational position—that is, to be more skilled or better than others.
>
> *Protection-dependency:* The need to have another person or group of people prevent frustration or punishment and to provide for the satisfaction of other needs.
>
> *Dominance:* Need to direct or control the actions of other people, including members of family and friends, to have any action taken be that which he suggests.
>
> *Independence:* Need to make own decisions, to rely on oneself, together with the need to develop skills for obtaining satisfactions directly without the mediation of other people.
>
> *Love and affection:* Need for acceptance and indication of liking by other individuals. In contrast to recognition-status, not concerned with social or professional position of friends, but seeks their warm regard.
>
> *Physical comfort:* Learned need for physical satisfaction that has become associated with the gaining of security.

A list of needs such as the above immediately strikes the reader familiar with animal learning theories as being uniquely human and as having immediate relevance for personality theory and clinical applications.

A large part of Rotter's *Social Learning and Clinical Psychology* is concerned with evidence from empirical studies in supporting the general theory and in relating it to personality measurement, diagnosis, and psychotherapy. These considerations are beyond the scope of our summary of the theory as a learning theory. However, in order to give some idea of the design and scope of the research in support of the theory, we shall summarize a study by Rotter *et al.* (*24*) on expectancy, which is a central concept in the theory. Then we shall comment on *freedom of movement,* another basic concept in his theory which stands in opposition to the philosophic position of the traditional experimental psychologist.

In the investigation on expectancy four groups of undergraduate students ($N =$ thirty for each group) were used. The groups included proportionate numbers of both sexes. The subjects were first trained on a level of aspiration test developed by Rotter and M. B. Jensen. The task requires the subject to make symbol substitutions and it is possible for the experi-

---

[4] For a discussion of Lewin's field theory see pp. 413–423.
[5] Compare to Maslow's hierarchy of needs pp. 428–432.

menter to control the level of success on the test since it is timed and can be arbitrarily stopped at any given level of completion. Following a controlled preliminary level of training each of the four groups was provided with different instructions:

Group I members were asked to indicate the score they expected to make on the trial to follow with emphasis being placed on accuracy. The subjects were given a ten point scale and asked to indicate their level of expectation in terms of that scale.

Group II subjects were asked to rate in absolute terms on a ten point scale their actual probability of making a set of specific scores of 20, 25, 28, 30, 32, and 35. (A score of 28 was the mean score of the preliminary training series.)

Group III subjects were asked to rate their chances of making a score of at least 20 on the following trial and also give rating for making the remaining scores of 25, 28, and so on.

Group IV members were given 60 cents in six piles of 10 pennies each and were requested to bet up to a limit of 10 cents on making a score of at least 20 or more on the next trial and so on for the other scores of 25, 28, and the like.

The results are shown in Figure 8-6. The six possible scores on which the probability ratings were made are shown along the abscissa. The ordinate is the rating scale of probability of 1–10. It will be noted that the dot labeled I shows the mean level of expectancy of 28.2—a level which is only a little above the theoretical level of 28. Note that Group II members who rated their absolute probability of making a given score show a curve whose highest probability is also at the mean. While the curves for Groups III and IV appear similar they differ significantly at the 5 percent level of confidence using an analysis of variance technique. It may be noted that the curve for the betting group yields the highest expectancy levels in all cases. Evidently making the conditions of the experiment more gamelike added zest and a higher level of aspiration to the subjects' estimates. The general similarity of the curve for groups II to IV shows that the experiment was measuring the same function; however, the students making absolute judgments overestimated the probability for a given score.

Level of aspiration is a complex phenomenon dependent upon many factors, and it would be dangerous to generalize to the effect that any one measure can represent the individual's overall expectancy in all life situations. However, Rotter and his associates are currently engaged in further studies of expectancy and have given convincing demonstrations that a subjective phenomenon can be translated into objective measures.

Rotter's treatment of the concept of freedom of movement clearly places him in the category of those psychologists who do not emphasize determinism as a central concept in their systems. It will be recalled (Chap-

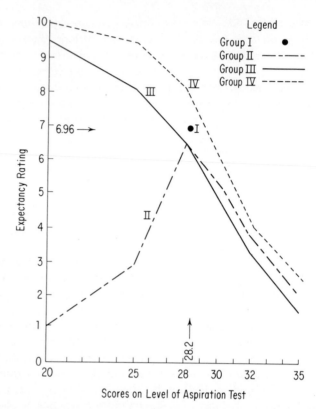

Fig. 8-6. Scores on a level of aspiration test plotted against expectancy ratings for four different groups of subjects who were provided with different instructions. For explanation see text. (From Rotter, *21.*)

ter 1) that socially oriented psychologists in general do not stress determinism. Rotter is no exception. H. M. Lefcourt, one of Rotter's former students, has developed the importance of the concepts of internal control freedom and expectancy for clinical theory within the framework of social learning theory (*8, 9*). In general it may be reemphasized that normal individuals feel as if they are internally determined. Psychotics and neurotics feel as if they are under the control of external forces which regulate their freedom of movement. Clearly, since freedom of movement is closely related to psychological needs, a high sense of freedom of movement involves a high expectancy of success in achieving goals, whereas a low sense of freedom, of course, implies failures.

It is too soon to say to what degree Rotter's theory will influence the mainstream of learning theory. As has already been pointed out it has generated a considerable body of research among its adherents. Many psychologists on both sides of the academic-applied fence have deplored the separateness of these two major groups, particularly the division that exists between the clinicians and the experimentalists. Rotter and his associates have offered a challenging model of how these two groups might be drawn closer together in applying experimental techniques to essentially clinical problems.

CURRENT ISSUES IN LEARNING THEORY: CONTIGUITY, EFFECT, AND EXPECTANCY[6]

In glancing back over the many theories of learning which we have reviewed, the persistent question which overshadows all others is the nature of learning itself. How is a stimulus-response bond learned? Or, speaking more generally, how is any acquired association learned? In the last analysis most of the controversies in learning theory revolve around this basic question. Beginning with Aristotle and stretching forward into the present and, no doubt, the future, we have seen that the principle of *contiguity* has either implicitly or explicitly played an important role in learning theory. Another influential view popularized by Thorndike has been the supposition that some form of a *law of effect* strengthens associations or *S-R* connections, and a third major principle has been that of *expectancy*. Because differences among theories as to the relative role of these factors or conditions play a major part in contemporary research and theorizing in learning, we shall conclude this chapter with an examination of each of these principles and attempt to indicate the trends that research has taken over the past decade.

Contiguity theory. Contiguity theorists hold that the essential condition for the occurrence of learning is the simultaneous (or nearly simultaneous) presentation of a neutral stimulus and the response with which it is to be associated. Such a position is most explicitly held by classical conditioning theorists. The *CS* and the *US* must occur simultaneously or nearly so, or the desired association will fail to develop. Theoretically, in classical conditioning learning is a process of stimulus substitution so that the *CS* comes to be the equivalent of the *US*. Either is then capable of evoking the desired response. In Pavlov's experiment, the bell (or tuning fork) came to elicit the salivation reaction which normally is elicited by food in the mouth. Pavlov saw no necessity for invoking a principle of motivation or effect

[6] Within the last decade a great body of literature has developed around current issues in learning. The *Annual Review of Psychology* and the *Psychological Review* are excellent sources for following the year-by-year developments. Hilgard (4) devotes three chapters of his *Theories of Learning* to current developments, and Osgood (20) has a chapter on controversial issues in the field.

in order to account for learning. His conception of learning was both behavioristic and mechanistic. Contiguity alone was held to be both necessary and a sufficient condition for learning in the conditioning situation.

However attractive conditioning may be to the classical conditioning theorist, critics have pointed out that even though Pavlov, Watson, and their successors believed that classical conditioning was the key that would unlock the door to the fundamental laws of learning, such a promise has never eventuated in reality. No one has denied that the conditioned response is a *form* of learning, but many psychologists would argue that it is not the only form—indeed, some (Skinner, for example) would go so far as to argue that it is a very special type of learning primarily applicable only to autonomic processes. Moreover, many theorists have pointed out that a contiguity theory of stimulus substitution as an explanation of conditioning is, in itself, insufficient to account for the facts. The conditioned response is not a mere substitute for the unconditioned response. The response is typically not as strong; it is more variable and is likely to show a longer latency period. Indeed, a strict stimulus substitution theory would demand that the animal behave toward the *CS* in the same way that it behaves toward the *US*—namely, the dog would attempt to eat the *CS* No such literal substitution of stimuli has been observed in conditioning research.

Turning away from conditioning, a pure contiguity theory should also be able to account for latent learning. However, the reality of latent learning is itself controversial, as we have indicated (Chapter 7). Certainly it does not occur in a clear-cut and unmistakable manner, as would be demanded by strict contiguity theory. As Spence has pointed out, completely "motivationless" animals are not impelled to transverse mazes in order to provide psychologists with tests of the contiguity (or expectancy) principle. Similarly, studies of "incidental" learning (20) and learning during sleep— kind of acid test of incidental learning (2)—have been disappointing in providing satisfactory evidence in favor of pure contiguity as a sufficient condition of learning.

Paradoxically, despite the lack of agreement about the sufficiency of contiguity for learning, few psychologists would seriously question its necessity. Long delays between *CS* and *US* are not conducive to learning, and common sense tells us that if thunder followed lightning by several days instead of a second, human beings might well still be wondering what causes celestial booms after summer storms. And everyone who has engaged in the rote learning of verbal materials, such as the learning of a foreign language vocabulary assignment, knows that contiguous repetition of the stimuli is the essence of learning. Thus, it seems that contiguity is a *necessary* condition for learning, even though it fails as a sufficient condition

tion. The remaining question concerns the relative role it plays in various forms of learning.

Effect. Some form of the law of effect has played a major role in learning theory since it was first clearly formulated by Thorndike nearly three-quarters of a century ago. Thorndike, it will be recalled, stated his law in both physiological and hedonic terms. Connections are strengthened by satisfiers; connections are weakened by annoyers. We have already seen (Chapter 6) how quickly the negative half of the law had to be abandoned and also how varied has been the fate of the positive half.

Initially much of the controversy centering around the law of effect was concerned with the use of the concepts of satisfaction and annoyance. The behaviorists were particularly scornful of mentalistic terminology, and even the most favorably disposed saw a circularity in the reasoning that satisfying states are what the animal seeks to prolong and annoying states are what the animal seeks to curtail. The explanation, they argued, is similar to that of explanation in terms of instincts. What is an instinct? An instinct is an unlearned form of behavior, such as nest building in the wasp. Because of dissatisfaction with the original wording, numerous expressions were offered in substitution by those favorably disposed toward the law in the hopes of finding a more operationally defensible statement. Reward, reinforcement, tension-reduction, maintaining stimuli, drive reduction, and homeostatic equilibrium are some of the terms which have been used and which have played a role in theoretical explanations of learning.

Some theorists have attempted to meet the problem by distinguishing between an *empirical law of effect* and a *theoretical law of effect*. The empirical law of effect states only that the occurrence of a response is necessary for learning to take place. About this fundamental fact of behavior there is no disagreement, even among such antidrive reductionists as Guthrie and Skinner. The controversy centers around whether some kind of drive reduction or drive stimulus reduction is a necessary part of reinforcement or reward. Those who maintain that it is subscribe to a theoretical law of effect. Their research is designed to demonstrate that in the absence of drive reduction or drive stimulus reduction, learning does not occur. There is, more simply, no such thing as latent learning or learning by pure contiguity.

An enormous body of research has been devoted to attempts to formulate a "critical" experiment which will reveal the precise nature of reinforcement. Such experiments may take the form of Tolman's place learning experiments, whose purpose is to show that drive-conditioned habits are not necessary to account for learning, or they may take the form of research designed to show that animals can learn in the absence of drive reduction. In an early experiment Sheffield and Roby (25) showed that animals can learn with saccharine as a reward. Similar results were found by Kraeling (7) who, using sucrose, showed that variations in the strength of drive as measured by speed of learning are a function of the concentration of sucrose employed. Since saccharine is inert metabolically, it theoretically cannot reduce drive. In the Sheffield-Roby experiment it would seem that we have a clear instance of reward without drive reduction. In Kraeling's experiment, taste rather than drive appears to be the critical factor. Unfortunately the matter is not as simple as it first appears. Murray (18, p. 31) has pointed out that rats prefed on saccharine do not eat as much and do not press a bar as often for food as rats not so prefed. Similarly, white rats will show learning with copulation in the absence of ejaculation[7] as a drive-reducing reward (5). However, such behavior becomes aversive if ejaculation is never permitted.

Some experimenters have approached the problem by designing a situation in which animals can be given reinforcement which is drive reducing but in which any possibility of "reward" or stimulation from the head receptors is ruled out. This can be accomplished by preparing the animals in such a manner that a food (such as milk) can be introduced directly into the stomach by way of a fistula or opening to the outside. Meanwhile the members of a comparison group receive their reinforcement in the usual manner, that is, by eating or drinking. Miller and Kessen (15) showed that rats prepared in this way can learn a discrimination problem where the reinforcement is milk injected directly if the animal makes the appropriate choice in a T maze, the incorrect choice leading to an injection of saline solution. And Kohn (6), one of Miller's associates, has shown that food eaten normally is less effective in a bar-pressing experiment than food which is injected directly via fistula. Food introduced into the stomach quickly reduces drive and depresses rate of bar-pressing.

To complicate the picture still further, we have the discovery of the "pleasure centers" in the subcortex of the brain by Olds and Milner (19). Animals will press bars for hours in order to stimulate these centers with mild shocks. Stimulation of the centers can also be utilized as a reward in maze learning. In this case we have a situation where no need existed or where sensory pleasure via the receptors can be ruled out. And it must also be borne in mind that studies[8] by Harlow (3) and others have shown that monkeys will learn to operate complex puzzles with the only reward being the successful solution of the problem itself. Clearly, if the satisfaction o

---

[7] It is characteristic of the male rat that mounting and insertion of the penis (intromission) ma occur several times before ejaculation or discharge of seminal fluid takes place and sexual be havior ceases. To study the role of intromission as a reward, the animals are allowed intromissior but not ejaculation and consequent drive reduction.

[8] See Chapter 13 for a further discussion of the brain implantation studies and Chapter 11 for the experiments bearing on curiosity and manipulatory motives.

a curiosity or manipulatory drive can serve as a motive for learning, it would be difficult indeed to test for "pure" contiguity or expectancy without the possibility of curiosity or manipulation operating as "hidden" motives.

It would be futile to attempt to resolve an issue here that can only be decided in the laboratory by future research. We can only confess that we do not know the reason why rewards are rewarding but only that both drive reduction and drive stimulus reduction are effective in producing learning. We must also admit that nonnutritive substances associated with stimulation of the receptors are also reinforcing. Thus, as is so often true when dealing with the complexities of behavior, there appear to be several reasons why reinforcement increases the probability of the recurrence of a response.

Expectancy. As we have already pointed out, expectancy theory was first formally espoused by Tolman and has moved into the camp of the drive reduction theorists and won converts there (Spence, Mowrer, Rotter). Expectancy is, as we have seen, related to incentive motivation and as such has roots in Gestalt psychology and field theory. Because our survey of expectancy theory has been largely within the confines of the present chapter, we need not review the evidence again. What we wish to emphasize is this: expectancy, a cognitive variable, has gained status in recent years to take its place along with effect and contiguity as a major explanatory construct in learning.

In summary then, we have a kind of "three-factor" learning theory—contiguity, effect, and expectancy—with most psychologists willing to grant *some* validity to each point of view. Which plays the greater role may, in the long run, turn out to be a function of the situation utilized as an experimental design. All we can safely conclude at the present time is that all three are significant variables in learning.

REFERENCES

1. Dollard, J., and N. E. Miller. *Personality and psychotherapy.* New York: McGraw-Hill, 1950.
2. Emmons, W. H., and C. W. Simon. The nonrecall of material presented during sleep. *American Journal of Psychology,* **69,** 1956, pp. 76–81.
3. Harlow, H. F., M. K. Harlow, and D. R. Meyer. Learning motivated by a manipulative drive. *Journal of Experimental Psychology,* **40,** 1950, pp. 228–234.
4. Hilgard, E. R. *Theories of learning,* ed. 2. New York: Appleton, 1956.
5. Kagan, J. Differential reward value of incomplete and complete sexual behavior. *Journal of Comparative and Physiological Psychology,* **48,** 1955, pp. 59–64.
6. Kohn, M. Satiation of hunger from food injected directly into the stomach versus

food ingested by mouth. *Journal of Comparative and Physiological Psychology,* **44,** 1951, pp. 412–422.

7. Kraeling, D. Analysis of amount of reward as a variable in learning. *Journal of Comparative and Physiological Psychology,* **54,** 1961, pp. 560–565.

8. Lefcourt, H. M. Internal versus external control of reinforcement: a review. *Psychological Bulletin,* **65,** 1966, pp. 206–220.

9. Lefcourt, H. M. Belief in personal control: research and implications. *Journal of Individual Psychology,* **22,** 1966, pp. 185–195.

10. Miller, N. E. Experimental studies of conflict. In Hunt, J. McV. (ed.). *Personality and the behavior disorders,* Vol. I. New York: Ronald, 1944.

11. Miller, N. E. Studies of fear as an acquirable drive: I. Fear as motivation and fear-reduction as reinforcement in the learning of new responses. *Journal of Experimental Psychology,* **38,** 1948, pp. 89–101.

12. Miller, N. E. Comments on multiple-process conceptions of learning. *Psychological Review,* **58,** 1951, pp. 375–381.

13. Miller, N. E. Liberalization of basic *S-R* concepts: extensions to conflict behavior, motivation, and social learning. In Koch, S. (ed.). *Psychology, a study of a science,* Vol. II. New York: McGraw-Hill, 1959.

14. Miller, N. E., and J. Dollard. *Social learning and imitation.* New Haven: Yale University Press, 1941.

15. Miller, N. E., and M. L. Kessen. Reward effects of food via stomach fistula compared with those of food via mouth. *Journal of Comparative and Physiological Psychology,* **45,** 1952, pp. 555–564.

16. Mowrer, O. H. *Learning theory and behavior.* New York: Wiley, 1960.

17. Mowrer, O. H., and E. G. Aiken. Contiguity *vs.* drive-reduction in conditioned fear: temporal variations in conditioned and unconditioned stimulus. *American Journal of Psychology,* **67,** 1954, pp. 26–38.

18. Murray, E. J. *Motivation and emotion.* New Jersey: Prentice-Hall, 1964.

19. Olds, J., and P. Milner. Positive reinforcement produced by electrical stimulation of septal area and other regions of rat brain. *Journal of Comparative and Physiological Psychology,* **47,** 1954, pp. 419–427.

20. Osgood, C. E. *Method and theory in experimental psychology.* New York: Oxford, 1953.

21. Rotter, J. B. *Social learning and clinical psychology.* New York: Prentice-Hall, 1954.

22. Rotter, J. B. The role of the psychological situation in determining the direction of human behavior. In Jones, M. R. (ed.). *Nebraska Symposium on Motivation.* Lincoln, Nebraska: University of Nebraska Press, 1955, pp. 245–269.

23. Rotter, J. B. Generalized expectancies for internal versus external control of reinforcement. *Psychological Monographs,* **8,** No. 1, 1966, No. 609, pp. 1–28.

24. Rotter, J. B., B. J. Fitzgerald, and J. Joyce. A comparison of some objective measures of expectancy. *Journal of Abnormal and Social Psychology,* **49,** 1954, pp. 111–114.

25. Sheffield, F. D., and T. B. Roby. Reward value of a nonnutritive sweet taste. *Journal of Comparative and Physiological Psychology,* **43,** 1950, pp. 471–481.

26. Spence, K. W. *Behavior theory and conditioning.* New Haven: Yale University Press, 1956.

27. Spence, K. W. *Behavior theory and learning.* New Jersey: Prentice-Hall, 1960.

28. Spence, K. W., G. Bergmann and R. Lippitt. A study of simple learning under irrelevant motivation-reward conditions. *Journal of Experimental Psychology,* **40,** 1950, pp. 539–551.

9

Learning IV: Selected Theoretical Issues in Verbal Learning

A casual glance over the preceding three chapters would give the impression that psychologists are more interested in the process of learning in animals than in man. And, although Ebbinghaus and Thorndike were interested in human learning, it would have to be admitted that the preponderance of *theories of learning* have developed around animal models. This, in part, is a reflection of the strong interest among American psychologists in conditioning—a learning paradigm which has dominated research and theory for nearly half a century. But it also reflects the psychologist's hope that in the study of relatively simple forms of animal learning lies the key to the more complex forms of human learning. This, it will be remembered, was the firm conviction of Pavlov, Watson, and Hull and remains the goal of the Skinnerians and others interested in the analysis of operant behavior. But a moment's reflection will also suggest that the associationism which lies at the heart of conditioning theory did not begin with the analysis of animal learning but with attempts to explain memory and the cognitive processes. Originating in the speculations of Aristotle and continuing through British empirical philosophy, associationism found its experimental justification in the research programs of Ebbinghaus and Thorndike.

Although neither of these men belonged to the functional school of psychology, their work was nonetheless functional in spirit. Both studied ongoing processes—a goal which is entirely appropriate to the functional definition of psychology as the study of mental and behavioral processes as they make possible the adaptation of the organism to its environment. We found, moreover, that under the leadership of Harvey Carr functionalism as a school expressed considerable interest in both animal and verbal learning (Chapter 6).

319

Elsewhere (Chapter 2) we have also pointed out that, with the passing of the schools, American psychology remained functionalistic in spirit, although it adopted the methodology of behaviorism. This characterization of the field is nowhere more valid than in the area of contemporary verbal learning. Psychologists working in this area approach their research objectively, with rigorous experimental methods and statistical analyses which are the hallmarks of contemporary psychology and a reflection of the behavioristic influence. But like the functionalists who went before them, the verbal learning psychologists are not interested in elaborating complex theoretical structures or systems comparable to those we have just reviewed in the immediately preceding chapters. Instead of seeking to establish basic laws of learning, they concentrate on the experimental investigation of variables associated with the acquisition of responses and the course of retention and forgetting. They are convinced that their colleagues in animal learning are jumping the gun, so to speak, by elaborating complex theories in the absence of sufficient empirical data.

Nevertheless, despite the atheoretical position of verbal learning psychologists, theory nonetheless creeps into their accounts of verbal learning. Even a classification of problems to be investigated involves *some* degree of theory. And dimensional analysis of variables to be investigated inevitably leads to hypothetical explanations to account for research findings. As a consequence, there are lively divisions of opinion about such issues as the cause of forgetting and the nature of transfer.

In keeping with the purpose of this volume we shall avoid any attempt to review the complex and massive literature in this field of psychology; instead we shall confine ourselves to selected issues which involve theoretical differences in interpretation. Wherever possible we shall attempt to relate these to familiar systematic positions.

THE FUNCTIONAL ANALYSIS OF ACQUISITION

In order to provide a perspective or overview for our first major topic, the functional analysis of acquisition, it will be helpful to outline the type of problems which have been investigated in this area. First, beginning with the work of Ebbinghaus, the variable of meaningfulness of the material learned has been an important area of research. Second, the distribution of practice—the size of the block of the material and the length of the practice period and interpolated rest periods—has come in for a large share of the investigators' attention. Third, the whole *versus* part variable (whether the material is gone over as a whole or in parts) has been extensively investigated for all kinds of material. Fourth, the question of various motivational variables, such as active recitation, knowledge of results, and the like has been analyzed both in theoretical and practical learning situations. We shall begin our discussion with the first of these, the variable of meaning-fulness.

Meaningfulness of material. Classical associationism would predict that meaningful material is more readily mastered and retained than meaning-less material. If memory consists of ideas held together by bonds developed through such principles of association as similarity, contrast, and belonging-ness, then meaningless, disjointed material with no relationship among its elements should not only be more difficult to learn but also should be more quickly forgotten. Common sense and common experience seem to verify the associationistic position. The average person if given a choice between learning a Shakespearian sonnet and a list of nonsense syllables would choose the former, knowing in advance that it would be easier to master.

However, the question immediately arises as to whether or not it is proper to compare poetry and nonsense syllables or any other such dissimi-lar material. It is theoretically possible that variables other than the relative meaningfulness of the material might account for any observed differences in relative ease of learning. This possibility can be avoided, at least in part, if nonsense syllables are compared to words of equal length or to digits. Moreover, nonsense syllables themselves vary in association value and have been calibrated for the use of psychologists interested in the variable of meaningfulness. For example, a list of syllables of high association value, such as LUV, LOS, RUF, can be compared to syllables which are relatively meaningless, such as XUY, ZER, YUT.

In an early study by McGeoch (*19*) the learning of three-letter words was compared to the learning of nonsense syllables of varying degrees of association values. Three-letter words are significantly easier to learn than 100 percent association value nonsense syllables, and with decreasing asso-ciation value nonsense syllables become increasingly harder to learn.

More recently Hall (*5*) has used the Thorndike-Lorge Word Fre-quency List to investigate the influence of association value or familiarity on learning. Table 9-1 shows that the mean recall value varies as a function

Table 9-1.
Learning as a Function of Thorndike-Lorge Word Frequency[a]

T-L FREQUENCY COUNT	MEAN RECALL
1 per million	12.04
10 per million	13.31
30 per million	15.02
50–100 per million	15.04

[a] From Hall, *5*.

of the frequency of the word count, with those words being more easily remembered which have a high frequency in the English language. Numerous other studies (*20*, pp. 468–480; *5*, pp. 292–329) both of long-term and short-term memory reveal that there is, on the whole, a positive correlation between meaningfulness and ease of learning and retention.

In attempting to account for the relationship between meaningfulness and ease of learning, some psychologists have invoked the concept of positive transfer. Positive transfer, it will be recalled, refers to those situations where the learning of *A* facilitates the learning of *B*. Thus, learning to drive a Ford insures that with little additional training the subject can drive any other car. The transfer is both positive and virtually 100 percent complete. McGeoch and Irion (*20*) assume that the same process accounts for the relative ease of learning meaningful as opposed to meaningless material. To encounter a word, such as *love* or a nonsense syllable such as LUV (which the subject actually remembers as "LOVE") is to recognize something already learned and is therefore a case of positive transfer of identical elements. The subject's only task is simply to remember the serial order of the list under study. On the other hand, to encounter such syllables as XEV, YIW, UEX (or lists of unrelated digits) is to begin the learning practically from scratch.

An alternative theoretical explanation for the advantage of meaningful material has been offered by the Gestalt-oriented psychologists in the form of the principle of differentiation. Differentiation refers to the fact that familiar terms have been discriminated from other terms in past experience whereas meaningless terms, because they have not been discriminated in past experience, do not stand out from other such terms until considerable practice has made them familiar. Evidence for this hypothesis comes from studies of serial learning in which the middle portion of the series proves the most difficult to master whether the material be nonsense syllables, lists of common words, or a maze. Figure 9-1 shows this effect as it is revealed in verbal rote learning (*9*). Taking cognizance of this effect, von Restorff (*31*) showed that a two-digit number was more readily learned if placed in a list of nonsense syllables than if mixed in with other digits. Similarly, if a nonsense syllable in the middle of a list is printed in red, it will be easier to learn than if printed in ordinary black and white (*39*). The Gestalt psychologists attribute these findings to *isolation*, or perceptual differentiation, a special case of the figure-ground effect.

An alternative hypothesis to account for the serial order phenomenon has been offered by those learning theorists who favor interference effects as the cause of forgetting. They argue that it is the result of inhibitory effects which build up as the subject progresses further and further into the list. Figure 9-2 shows Hull's hypothetical analysis of such effects for a list of nonsense syllables. Presumably the more meaningless the material the greater the interference effects. The von Restorff effect is accounted for simply on the basis that printing the middle syllable in a distinctive color is the equivalent of breaking the list into two parts and therefore minimizing interlist interference.

Distribution of practice. The importance of inhibitory and interference effects on learning is further emphasized by studies of massed versus distributed practice. In massed practice the learner is required to master the material in a single session. In distributed practice, blocks of practice are interspersed with blocks of rest. If the absolute learning time is computed, distributed practice is generally found to be superior to massed practice. This, at least, has been the preponderance of experimental findings in the older literature. Again, we refer to Figure 9-1, which shows a family of curves obtained by Hovland (9) for massed and distributed practice under two different rates of presentation. In both conditions, massed practice was found to be inferior to distributed practice. Similar effects, it might be noted, have been found with motor tasks such as in rotary pursuit learning, which consists of attempting to keep a stylus on a dot which is revolving near the edge of a turntable similar to a phonograph turntable. In fact, the phenomenon is more readily and reliably observed in motor or skill learning situations than it is in verbal learning.

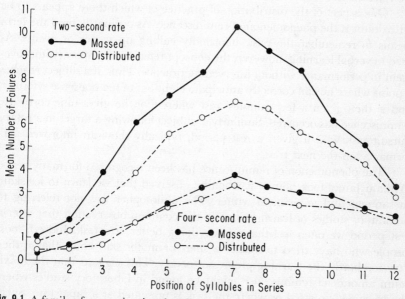

Fig. 9-1. A family of curves showing the effect of massed and distributed practice on the serial order position of nonsense syllables under two different presentation rates. Note the significantly increased difficulty of learning with massed practice under a high speed of presentation, especially for syllables in the middle of the list. (From Hovland, 9.)

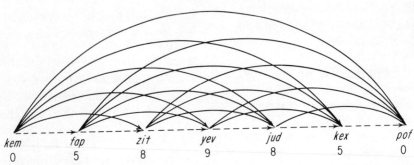

Fig. 9-2. A diagrammatic representation of both immediate and remote forward excitatory tendencies. The straight broken arrows represent immediate excitatory tendencies; the curved solid arrows, remote excitatory tendencies. The number of remote excitatory tendencies spanning the syllables is given below each. (From Hull, *10*.)

Distribution effects vary considerably with the nature of the task to be learned and with the relative length of practice periods and rest intervals. Unfortunately, it is not possible to generalize at the present time as to what the most economical distribution of practice and rest is for various types of learning. Those interested in reviewing the conflicting evidence in this area are referred to McGeoch and Irion (*20*, Chapter 5).

One aspect of the distribution of practice of which there appears to be little doubt is the phenomenon of reminiscence. As ordinarily used the term means to remember the past, informally calling up scenes or events. As used in verbal learning, however, the concept refers to a temporary improvement in performance without intervening practice. Thus, if a subject reaches a point where he can correctly anticipate eight out of ten nonsense syllables, and is then given a few minutes' rest whereupon he gives nine correctly, reminiscence has occurred. Similarly, a subject following a target in a rotary pursuit task will, if given a rest period, typically show an improved performance on the next trial.

The phenomenon of reminiscence has been recognized for many years. William James took note of it when he observed that we learn to ice skate in summer and to swim in winter. The philosopher was not referring to laboratory studies of learning, but to the common observation that after a rest period we often feel that we are doing better at a task. Indeed, most people who have tried to master a sport or motor skill know that if they "try too hard" the learning progresses poorly. This suggests that the maximum amount of reminiscence might be found in laboratory studies where the learning is massed or where the task is presented at a rapid rate. Such, in fact, is typically the case (*9*), which further suggests that reminiscence may be due to some kind of interference or inhibitory effect. Hovland, who did a considerable amount of the early work on reminiscence adopted this hypothesis. It will be recalled that in his study of the serial learning effect more errors were found under conditions of massed practice than under conditions of distributed practice. (See Figure 9-1.)

Massed practice favors reactive inhibition (Figure 9-1), and interlist interference effects are maximal near the middle portion of the list. Because reactive inhibiton and interference effects dissipate with rest, distribution of practice favors reminiscence and, therefore, makes for efficient learning.

More generally, the benefits of distribution of practice have been accounted for in terms of a number of theoretical alternatives. One widely favored theory is the retroaction or interference theory discussed in connection with reminiscence. Other investigators have assumed that motivation and fatigue are important variables in acquisition and that massing practice tends to tire the subject with a consequent drop in motivation. The discovery that reminiscence is most striking in motor tasks supports the importance of these variables as possible causative factors, since fatigue is more likely to occur in motor skills, particularly during the early stages of learning.

Another theory which found favor among the older investigators was the perseveration hypothesis (20, pp. 178–180). Perseveration theory argues that some form of persistent activity is necessary in the nervous system for consolidation of the memory traces to take place. We shall go into this hypothesis more fully when we examine theories of retention later in this chapter. Here we need only note that the concept has been invoked to account for distribution of practice effects. Clearly, if practice trials are massed or if high rates of presentation are used, the neural circuits will have little time for perseveration; consequently, the traces cannot become established. Rest, on the other hand, would obviously favor consolidation, since it would permit continued activity immediately following the cessation of practice.

Finally, brief mention may be made of rehearsal as a possible factor in accounting for distribution effects. If not otherwise instructed, there is the possibility that the subject may rehearse during rest periods in verbal learning situations and thus show superiority on the next trial without formal intervening practice. It is more difficult to understand how this could occur in motor tasks, unless some sort of "implicit" or "symbolic" rehearsal is assumed to have occurred.

In summary, the preponderance of opinion favors explanation in terms of interference or inhibitive effects in accounting for the inferiority of massed practice and the dissipation of such effects to account for both reminiscence and the general superiority of distributed practice.

It must be emphasized, however, that neither reminiscence nor superior performance under conditions of massed practice are consistently found in studies of learning. In several investigations Underwood (38) has been unable to find an advantage for distributed practice in verbal learning under certain conditions, particularly in paired associate learning. It now appears that the subject's level of sophistication in learning experiments and the kind of response habits which he brings to the laboratory from everyday life may have an important bearing on the results obtained. We shall have more to say about this problem when we come to examine retroactive and proactive inhibition as variables in retention and forgetting. Here we need only add that no one theory of distribution effects has proved adequate to account for the laboratory findings; and, as is so often true in psychology (and science in general), the effects obtained are a function of the operations or experimental arrangements which are used to obtain those effects.

Whole versus part learning. Whole learning means attacking the entire task and going over it in its entirety until it has been mastered. Part learning refers to learning in which the material is subdivided and each subdivision is learned to mastery. For example, a poem may be memorized as a whole by reading the entire poem from beginning to end until mastery is reached, or it may be attacked stanza by stanza.

It has proved to be difficult to obtain clear-cut results on the whole *versus* part issue in laboratory studies utilizing a variety of materials. Moreover, the issue generated very little theoretical controversy and does not appear to be related in any meaningful way to proactive and retroactive inhibition theories, which play such prominent roles in the analysis of laboratory findings. In addition, the dichotomy of whole *versus* part learning is somewhat artificial to begin with, since, as Woodworth and Schlosberg (42, p. 786) have pointed out, the task must eventually be performed as a whole even in those cases where the parts are learned separately. This would apply not only to poetry and similar verbal materials but also to mazes and other tasks involving serial learning.

Disregarding these difficulties it seems fair to summarize the experimental findings as follows: for tasks of short and moderate length the whole method has generally been found to be superior. For tasks of increasing length the part method has been found to be more economical of learning time. The issue is, however, a complex one and many other variables need to be studied before the problem can be resolved definitely.

Motivational variables. There is an enormous literature on the role of motivational variables in learning. However, by far the preponderance of motivational studies which are of theoretical interest has been in the area of animal models. For this reason a considerable portion of our discussions of the classical, miniature, and derived theories of learning in the preceding chapters was devoted to the role of motivation, drive, drive-stimulus reduction, and incentives.

In human verbal learning, relatively little attention has been paid to the role of motivational variables. We know that an active attitude where the subject participates by reciting and being aware of his progress favors learning (*42*, pp. 779–782). In verbal learning experiments, the experimenter attempts to motivate the subject by the instructions and in some cases by adding tangible rewards, such as monetary payments. However, assuming he has the subject's willingness to participate, little further effort is made to motivate him beyond giving him some indication of his progress. Typically no mention is made of motivational variables in the analysis and discussion of the data.

The dearth of motivational studies reflects, in part, the difficulties encountered in attempting to control human subjects. The psychologist is usually not in a position to deprive his subjects of food, water, or other physiological reinforcers; and if he were, the situation would be an artificial one, since such states are not typical of how subjects learn in everyday life. He is also limited in the use that he can make of incentives, and those that have been employed tend to have an artificial quality. However, in industry and education rewards and incentives have been utilized for generations. It is assumed that to some degree there is a direct relationship between motivational variables and the speed of learning or performance. Few of the studies qualify as direct investigations of the role of motivation on learning; most are concerned with regulating performance; and there seems to be little doubt of the efficacy of such factors. Unfortunately, the lack of rigid experimental controls makes the results of such studies of limited use to the theoretician or experimental psychologist.

Some psychologists have approached the problem indirectly by studying the effect of levels of anxiety on learning by using questionnaires, such as the Manifest Anxiety Scale. These instruments are given to large samples and high and low anxiety subjects are selected as experimental and control groups in learning situations (*2*, p. 117). A number of such studies have been carried out with eyelid conditioning as the learning variable. The results generally favor the conclusion that conditioning does occur more readily in individuals with high anxiety drives. However, we must be cautious in generalizing these results. Very high levels of anxiety disrupt learning in more complex situations (*33*, *34*). Most of us would expect such a result from our everyday experiences, since we know it is difficult to learn when we are emotionally upset.

Level of aspiration studies (*35*) also show that subjects who constantly experience failure become discouraged and show lower levels of aspiration on subsequent trials. However, the exact relationship between motivational variables on the one hand, and learning, performance, and retention on the other hand, are exceedingly complex and will require much more research.

TRANSFER OF TRAINING

When learning in one situation influences learning in another situation, we have evidence of the phenomenon of transfer of training. In general there are two types of transfer. First, learning in Situation A may favorably influence learning in Situation B, in which case we have *positive transfer*. Second, learning in Situation A may have a detrimental effect on learning in Situation B, in which case we have *negative transfer*. Both types of transfer are readily observable in everyday life. We learn to drive one automobile, confident that the skills acquired will transfer positively to other automobiles. We learn to roller skate and discover that it helps us in learning to ice skate, although in this case we find that the degree of transfer is not so great as in learning to drive.

We may also observe negative transfer when we carry out a skilled act such as attempting to do something for the first time while looking in a mirror. Our movements are jerky and uncoordinated. We may "block" completely, finding ourselves unable to move at all. We are bringing to the mirror situation all our previous practice in eye-hand coordination under normal conditions, with the result that severe interference occurs.

In the laboratory, transfer has been studied in a wide variety of situations using perceptual-motor skills and verbal materials. While we are primarily concerned with the latter in this chapter, we shall refer to other types of transfer in order to illustrate principles or to provide support for hypotheses of transfer.

The general design for a transfer experiment may be diagrammed as follows:

> Experimental group: Learn Task A→Learn Task B
> Control group: Rest→Learn Task B

The experimental and control groups must be equated.

The degree of transfer, whether positive or negative, can be determined by finding the difference in the learning for Task B for the experimental group. If the transfer has been positive, then the experimental group will take fewer trials to learn B. If the transfer is negative, the experimental group will require more trials than the control group to reach the criterion.[1]

In verbal learning, typical studies of transfer have employed paired associates which can be either S-R pairs of nonsense syllables, meaningful words or mixtures of the two. In general there are two extreme possibilities. The stimuli can be completely different in Task B with the responses re-

---

[1] There are many other possible designs for studying transfer. The interested reader may consult Woodworth and Schlosberg (*42*, pp. 735–738) for a discussion of additional types.

maining the same; or the responses in Task B can be changed completely with the stimuli remaining identical.

In schematic form the first possibility might be illustrated with the following pairs:

Task A Task B

S	R		S	R
glass	- - - - - - - - - - - -bell		nail	- - - - - - - - - - - -bell
sand	- - - - - - - - - - - -chair		boy	- - - - - - - - - - - -chair
cloud	- - - - - - - - - - - -book		pin	- - - - - - - - - - - -book
	etc.			etc.

The second design would look like the following illustration:

Task A Task B

S	R		S	R
girl	- - - - - - - - - - - -desk		girl	- - - - - - - - - - - -run
paper	- - - - - - - - - - - -floor		paper	- - - - - - - - - - - -dog
man	- - - - - - - - - - - -brick		man	- - - - - - - - - - - -toy
	etc.			etc.

In general terms the first situation is an $S_1 \rightarrow R_1 : S_2 \rightarrow R_1$ design, while in the second situation we have $S_1 \rightarrow R_1 : S_1 \rightarrow R_2$. The first situation gives slight positive transfer, the transfer arising from the subject's already having learned the responses. He must still learn the new stimuli, but the task is easier than if he had to learn both stimuli and responses.

When subjects are tested in $S_1 \rightarrow R_1 : S_1 \rightarrow R_2$ situations the transfer is strongly negative. The learning of competing or conflicting responses causes severe interference effects. If both the stimuli and the responses are identical $(S_1 \rightarrow R_1 : S_1 \rightarrow R_1)$ from Task A to Task B, the transfer will, of course, be strongly positive. All the subject has to overcome is whatever degree of forgetting may have occurred between the cessation of Task A and the initiation of learning of Task B.

There are, of course, other possibilities. The stimuli may be made similar and the responses identical, whereupon strongly positive transfer will be obtained. If the stimuli remain identical and the responses similar, there will be slightly positive transfer.

Some of the more recent studies (*14, 15*) have suggested that the general principles given above based on work extending over the first half of the century may have to be modified somewhat. In some instances, attaching an old response to a new stimulus may result in slightly negative transfer. Since the effect has been confirmed by several investigators, we must accept a modification of the general rule that $S_1 \rightarrow R_1 : S_2 \rightarrow R_1$ designs always lead to positive transfer. The reasons for this effect are not fully understood but it has been suggested (*15*) that the relative meaningfulness of the material is a factor in determining whether negative transfer will occur. If highly meaningful *S-R* pairs are used, the transfer is more likely to be negative; no doubt because the *S-R* connections are more unified if meaningful materials are used than if nonsense syllables are employed.

Osgood (*25*) has attempted to integrate the principles of stimulus-response transfer and the related phenomenon of stimulus generalization in conditioning experiments by developing a model with a three-dimensional surface. The surface, known as the transfer and retroaction surface, is shown in Figure 9-3. Decreasing response similarity is represented by the axis running from upper left to lower right, R_I standing for identical responses, R_S for similar responses; R_N for neutral, R_O for opposite, and R_A for antagonistic responses. Decreasing stimulus similarity is shown along the axis which runs from lower left to upper right with similar labeling. The amount of transfer to be predicted is shown along the vertical axis (positive upward; negative downward). The medial plane of the model represents zero degree of transfer.

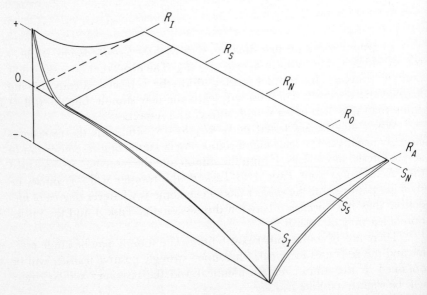

Fig. 9-3. Osgood's transfer surface. Decreasing response similarity is represented by the axis which runs obliquely from the upper left to the lower right-hand side of the figure. R_I represents identical responses; R_S similar responses; R_N neutral or dissimilar responses; R_O opposite responses; and R_A antagonistic responses. Decreasing stimulus similarity is shown on the axis running from lower left to upper right and is labeled accordingly. The amount of transfer to be expected in any given case is shown along the vertical axis on the left—+ representing high transfer; 0, low or no transfer; and —, negative transfer. (From Osgood, *25*.)

The reader will note that points on the surface which are close to the plus sign are indicative of the amount of transfer to be expected if both stimuli and responses are identical. Points near the minus sign are indicative of the amount of transfer to be expected in those cases where stimuli are identical but responses are different.

Osgood's surface is a model which attempts to describe and predict the relations between facilitation and inhibition and degrees of stimulus response similarity. It does not attempt to explain why transfer occurs and has yet to receive wide support from theoretical studies.

Theoretical explanations of transfer have emphasized two broad classes of responsible factors, general and specific. Under general factors we may include understanding, insight, and learning sets as explanations of positive transfer, and under specific factors we are dealing with stimulus-response elements which, as we have just seen, can be correlated with positive and negative transfer effects depending upon their arrangement and degree of similarity from one task to another.

Very early experiments (12) in transfer of principles showed that subjects could transfer a general understanding of a task from one situation to another. We found (Chapter 6) that the Gestalt psychologists strongly emphasized this factor in their experiments on insight learning in both animal and human subjects. While few psychologists would disagree that a kind of general understanding of a situation can be transferred from one situation to another, they are by no means in agreement that such concepts as "insight," "transfer of principles," or "understanding" add anything by way of explanation.

Harlow (7), working with monkeys, showed that the general transfer effect from one situation to another may be accounted for by the concept of "learning how to learn" or learning sets. In a number of experiments the animals were given a series of discrimination problems consisting of positive and negative cue objects presented in a random order over food cups. The animal obtained food only if the "positive" cue object was chosen. The monkey had to learn to pick up the positive object in spite of its varying position on a large number of trials. Hundreds of pairs of such objects were used. On the second trial following the presentation of the first few problems the monkeys were only 50 percent correct—no better than chance— in selecting the proper object. By the time 100 tasks had been mastered, the monkeys were 80 percent correct on Trial 2. By the end of 300 tasks they were 95 percent correct. A man from Mars entering the laboratory at this point might well have attributed insight to the animals, whereas a more parsimonious explanation in terms of learning to learn or learning sets is adequate to account for the data.

Similar results have been obtained by Postman (30) in verbal learning. Subjects who engage in the learning of paired associates and serial lists of

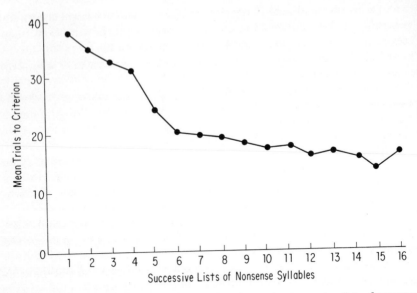

Fig. 9-4. The cumulative positive transfer effect in learning successive lists of nonsense syllables. (From Osgood, *26,* after Ward, *41.*)

nonsense syllables will do better on subsequent tests involving not only these specific tasks but others as well. However, while there is general transfer in these situations, the effect is limited. No evidence was found to indicate that rote learning improves the memory process in general. Rather, learning in the laboratory is a process which requires the development of certain skills and attitudes. Subjects who engage in nonsense syllable learning for the first time often lack confidence. They have not yet learned how to learn. When they acquire confidence and the necessary skills, these carry over into subsequent learning situations (*41*). See Figure 9-4. However, another word of caution is in order. Too much prior learning may result in proactive inhibition effects. Proactive inhibition refers to the learning of A having a detrimental effect on the learning of B. It is a form of negative transfer effect. Of this we shall have more to say in the following section which deals with forgetting.

Specific theories of transfer assume that any special skills or responses which can be carried from one situation to another will result in positive transfer, if similar or identical, and in negative transfer, if dissimilar or antagonistic. This hypothesis was first formulated by Thorndike. Since we have already extensively analyzed this type of transfer, we need not discuss it further here.

In summary, then, we have considered two main theoretical explanations of transfer: (a) transfer of general principles, including learning sets, and (b) transfer by means of identical elements. We also mentioned incidentally in connection with Osgood's surface that the process of generalization in conditioning (induction in operant conditioning) is invoked to account for transfer. The conditioning theory may account for positive transfer in cases of stimulus similarity by assuming stimulus generalization, and in cases of response similarity, by assuming response generalization. Negative transfer would presumably be the result of conflicting or incompatible responses.

RETENTION AND FORGETTING

Research on the nature and conditions of retention and forgetting began with the work of Ebbinghaus and has continued to be a challenging and well-developed empirical and theoretical area over the past three-quarters of a century. We are already familiar with Ebbinghaus' famous curves of retention which he obtained with nonsense syllables utilizing the savings method. Ebbinghaus' work was quickly followed by studies of retention as a function of (1) different methods of measurement, (2) the conditions under which the original learning took place, (3) type of material learned, (4) the extent and nature of related activity prior to original learning or interpolated between original learning and recall, and (5) the influence of various pathological and psychological conditions.

Different methods of measurement. A representative of this type of study is Luh's (*17*) classic investigation of retention curves obtained under different conditions of measurement. These curves are presented in Figure 9-5.

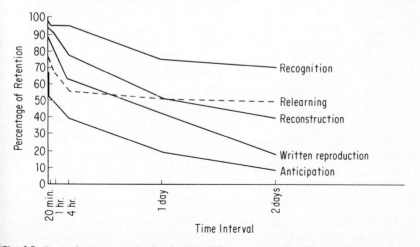

Fig. 9-5. Retention curves obtained with different methods of measurement. (From McGeoch and Irion, *20*, after Luh, *17*.)

Luh's results clearly demonstrate that retention is a function of the method by means of which it is measured. Recognition is the most sensitive index of the various measures employed, with anticipation the least sensitive and also the most difficult for the subject. The curve for the relearning method, it will be noted, first falls more rapidly than these for recognition and reconstruction and then levels out. This is undoubtedly due to the fact that the method is actually a combination of two methods, recall and relearning, which are negatively correlated, since the greater the recall at the first presentation, the less relearning is required.

Conditions of original learning.   Typical of studies which concern themselves with the conditions of original learning are those which investigate the effects of overlearning. Overlearning is defined as practice beyond one (or two) perfect recitations. Numerous studies have shown that overlearning up to a point of diminishing returns aids in retention (*16*).

Even more striking results are obtained when additional learning is spread over a long period of time in the form of reviews (See Figure 9-6). The results of such studies have been formulated into a law by Jost (*12*) which states that given two associations of equal strength but different ages, practice is more beneficial to the old. Jost's law is a reflection of the shape of the curve for retention. Clearly, an association which is recent is on a steeper part of the curve than an older association; consequently it will undergo a more rapid decline.

We have indicated that under most conditions of learning distributed

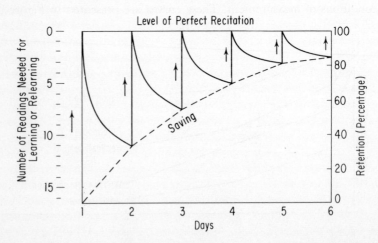

Fig. 9-6. A diagrammatic representation of Jost's Law. Each successive review (represented by the arrows) causes the curve of retention to fall less steeply and the savings in time needed to relearn increases sharply. (From Woodworth and Schlosberg, *42*.)

practice is superior to massed practice (see above). A similar general statement can be made for learning under conditions demanding active participation (42, pp. 779–782). Thus, the basic principle underlying these results is that whatever favors efficiency in original learning also favors retention.

Type of material learned.

Attempts to measure differential forgetting as a function of the types of material learned are fraught with difficulties of methodology and interpretation. Can the learning of a poem be directly compared to the learning of a list of nonsense syllables? Do motor skills undergo slower decay in retention than verbal skills, as seems to be the case from everyday observation. Can we compare insightfully learned problems to rote learning? In attempting to answer these questions, psychologists are not certain that investigators who have attempted to cross compare poetry, prose, nonsense material, and the like, have achieved sufficient control over the original degree of learning. We are not sure that a poem learned to the criterion of one errorless repetition has been learned to the same degree of mastery as a list of twenty nonsense syllables learned to the criterion of one errorless repetition. The same problem in accentuated form occurs when investigators attempt to compare retention for motor skills to retention for verbal skills.

Nevertheless, despite the formidable difficulties in the way of any final answer to the question, it has not gone begging. Figure 9-7 shows a composite curve reflecting a relative comparison of several types of material (4). It will be observed that materials which lend themselves to insight learning are retained better than poetry, connected discourse, and nonsense syllables. Poetry with its rhythm and rhyme schemes has an advantage over prose, and prose, in turn, over nonsense syllables. In addition to studies such as these, researchers working with animals have found that very simple motor skills, such as those acquired in conditioning experiments, are retained over very long periods (six years) if the animals are not subjected to additional training (8). This suggests that not only does the type of material influence retention but also what happens to the subject during the retention interval exerts an influence. We shall develop this point further in the section to follow.

We may add here that two reasons have been suggested why verbal materials are not retained as well as perceptual-motor habits. First, the latter are typically overpracticed. The boy or girl does not learn to ride a bicycle to the point of bare mastery and then stop practicing. Considerable overlearning occurs. Secondly, there is more opportunity for interference effects in the area of verbal learning than in motor learning, particularly among young adults who are in school and therefore amassing large blocks of verbal materials daily. The isolated laboratory animal, on the other

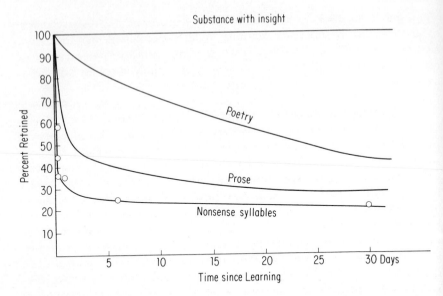

Fig. 9-7. Theoretical retention curves for material with varying degrees of meaningfulness from insightful to nonsense. (From Guilford, *4*.)

hand, is subjected only to the highly restricted environment of his living cage. If he is not the subject of research, there is little in his behavioral routine to interfere with a learned habit.

Interpolated material.   In studying the influence of extraneous or interpolated material on retention, the psychologist is investigating what is technically known as proactive and retroactive inhibition. Retroactive inhibition, as the name implies, refers to inhibitory effects generated by the interpolation of material between the original learning and recall. In terms of an experimental design, retroactive inhibition is studied by means of two equated groups as follows:

> Experimental Group: Learn A→Learn B→Recall A
> Control Group: Learn A→Rest→Recall A

The difference in recall is the measure of retroactive inhibition.

Proactive inhibition refers to the influence of previously learned material on the retention of the experimental material. In terms of a design:

> Experimental Group: Learn B→Learn A→ Recall A
> Control Group: Rest→Learn A→Recall A

Prior to World War II retroactive inhibition received the major share of research and theoretical attention as the factor primarily responsible for forgetting and interference effects. A wide variety of subjects ranging from cockroaches to man were studied by varying a number of parameters such as the degree of original and interpolated learning, the nature of the interpolated material, and the temporal placement of the interpolated material —that is, close to the original learning or just prior to recall.

Studies of the relationship between similarity of original and interpolated material have generally shown that the learning of moderately similar materials results in maximum interference, whereas if the interpolated materials are identical to the original or entirely dissimilar, interference is minimized (20). Taking account of a series of experiments of his own and those of E. B. Skaggs, E. S. Robinson formulated what has come to be known as the Skaggs-Robinson hypothesis which states: "As similarity between interpolation and original memorization is reduced from near identity, retention falls away to a minimum and then rises again, but with decreasing similarity it never reaches the level obtaining with maximum similarity" (32). The principle is shown in schematic form in Figure 9-8. Some of the early research carried out by Robinson and by Harden (6) verified the first half of the law but not the second. Dissimilar materials cause more interference than would be predicted by the hypothesis. However, a vast experimental literature has grown up around the problem of similarity and interference since 1941, and the problem itself has proved to be far more complex than Robinson's assumptions led him to believe. As we noted in connection with negative transfer experiments, not only must

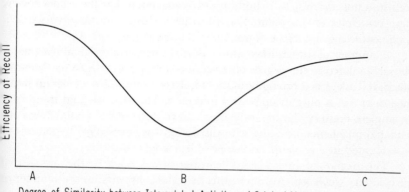

Degree of Similarity between Interpolated Activity and Original Memorization — Descending Scale

ig. 9-8. The Skaggs-Robinson hypothesis relating efficiency of recall to degree of similarity between interpolated activity and original memory. At A similarity is maximal; t B similarity is intermediate, and at C is minimal. (From McGeoch and Irion, 20.)

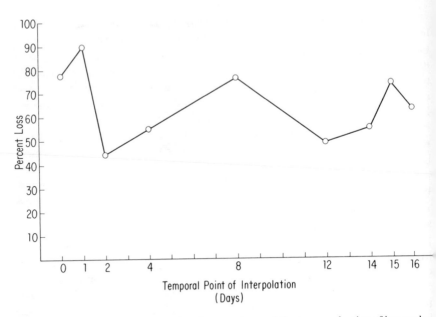

Fig. 9-9. The relationship between loss in retention and the temporal point of interpolation of interpolated material. (From Postman and Alper, *30*.)

general similarity be taken into account, it is also important to specify whether we are referring to stimulus similarity or response similarity.

It will be recalled in this connection that Osgood's surface also makes predictions about the degree of retroactive inhibition, taking into account both stimulus and response similarity. It is suggested that the reader review these principles at this point. For a further discussion of these varied and often conflicting results see *5*, pp. 592–633, and *20*, pp. 394–417.

A number of studies have shown that the degree of original learning is inversely related to the degree of mastery of interpolated learning. In other words, if Task *A* is thoroughly mastered, Task *B* has less detrimental influence than if *A* is only incompletely mastered. This suggests that in cases of incomplete mastery the memory traces have not become completely consolidated and hence are subject to disruption—an important hypothesis to be evaluated in any complete theory of learning.

The degree of interpolated learning also influences the amount of retroaction. McGeoch (*18*) tested this hypothesis by varying the number of trials of the interpolated learning while holding the number of trials of the original learning constant. The original material was presented for 11 trials, the interpolated for 6, 11, 16, 21, or 26. Retroactive interference increased from between 6 and 11 trials but not beyond that, suggesting again that recency effects in retroaction may be the most important variable.

Theoretically, it might be assumed that placement of interpolated ma-
rial directly after the original learning would maximize interference,
hereas placement later in the interval up to near recall time would show
ss interference, with a possible increase near recall time. Unfortunately,
e results are conflicting, with some investigators finding peaks of maximal
terference at various points along the curve of retention (Figure 9-9).
owever, the tentative conclusion appears to be justified that interference
maximized when the interpolated material is placed near the end of the
iginal learning session, thus lending support to an anticonsolidation
ypothesis (30).

Since World War II a number of studies of proactive inhibition have
en carried out by B. J. Underwood and his associates. Figure 9-10, which
as formulated by Underwood (38) from the results of a number of studies,
ows the effect of prior learning on recall. Figure 9-11 provides a com-
arison of the effects of proactive and retroactive inhibition on retention
7). While retroaction causes the greatest amount of interference, the two
rves are similar in all respects with regard to slope and general effect.

The importance of Underwood's findings for a theory of forgetting lies
the fact that he has shown that the retention of any given set of materials
a joint function of what has gone on before as well as interpolated learn-

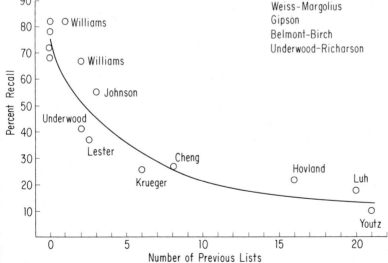

ig. 9-10. The effects of prior learning on recall. Note that with increasing numbers of
ior lists recall becomes less efficient. (From Underwood, 38.)

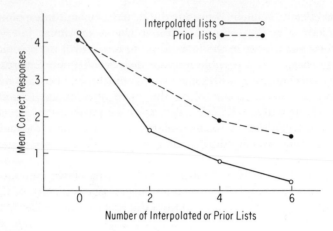

Fig. 9-11. Retention as a function of the number of interpolated lists (retroactive inhib tion) and prior lists (proactive inhibition). (From Underwood, *37*.)

ing which might come afterwards. It further suggests that some of the earl literature utilizing well-practiced subjects (Ebbinghaus, for example) ma show abnormally steep losses in retention following learning due to hidde proactive inhibition. In any case we must now recognize that any theory (forgetting must take both types of interference into consideration. Unde wood, moreover, has emphasized the subject's extra-laboratory experienc as possible influences on the course of forgetting, particularly in the case (college student subjects who are likely to be engaging in verbal learnin tasks similar to those demanded of them in the laboratory.

Pathological and other conditions. Any theory which ascribes a majc share of forgetting to activities interpolated between learning and recal needs to take into account the influence of various psychological states o retention. If, as interference theories presuppose, the failure of trace con solidation because of interpolated activities is the primary cause of fo getting, then studies which investigate the role of level of activity followin learning should provide direct evidence on the validity of the theory.

The classic studies on the problem were carried out by Jenkins an Dallenbach (*11*) and by van Ormer (*40*), who investigated the influence (sleep on retention. In the Jenkins-Dallenbach experiment, subjects learne lists of ten nonsense syllables and then engaged in one to eight hours (normal waking activity (control subject) or sleep (experimental subject Figure 9-12 shows the comparative level of forgetting during sleep an waking for two subjects. It will be noted that the curve for sleep drops rap idly—though not as sharply as that for waking—and then levels off at higher level than the curve for waking. The experiment furnishes no direct evidence as to why the sleep curve should show a rapid initial loss. Indirect evidence to account for this result comes from studies of the electroencephalographic recording of brain waves during sleep. These studies show that deep sleep is not achieved instantly. Presumably, the cortex remains more active for the first hour or so of sleep than during deep sleep. The Jenkins-Dallenbach results do clearly demonstrate that the differential forgetting during the waking state is due to the activity going on and not to mere "disuse" with the passage of time. These findings were confirmed in all essentials by van Ormer, who utilized the savings method rather than direct recall.

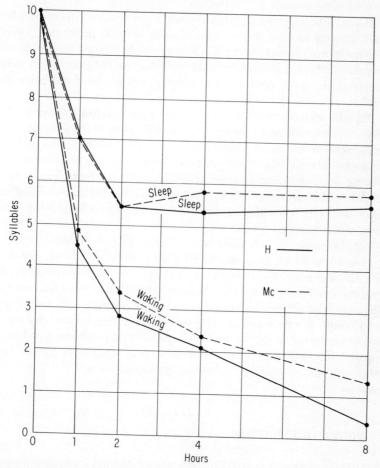

Fig. 9-12. Retention as a function of sleep and waking for two subjects. (From Jenkins and Dallenbach, *11*.)

Attempts to control the activity level of animal subjects to the point of "freezing" them physiologically immediately after learning have given mixed results. Drugs and anesthetics have been used for this purpose, but retention level is not improved by anesthesia, possibly because of the deleterious physiological effects of the drug itself. In an attempt to circumvent this difficulty Minami and Dallenbach (22) utilized the propensity of the cockroach to become inactive when subjected to extensive bodily contact, such as when crawling into a box containing tissue paper. Comparison of an experimental and control group (which was permitted activity in a small cage) on a simple maze problem showed that the active insects were significantly inferior to the inactive insects in retention, the inactives showing only a very moderate loss in retention.

It would be unwise to generalize from maze learning in cockroaches to verbal learning in man in the sense of attempting to prove that complete inactivity in man would result in better retention, but the results are interesting as a confirmation of the work with human subjects and a striking example of the great phylogenetic range of this fundamental principle of retention.

Equally instructive in accounting for the mechanism of retention are studies of retrograde and anterograde amnesia. Both of these conditions are due to blows to the head which produce varying periods of forgetting. In retrograde amnesia, the blow produces forgetting for events immediately following the injury and in anterograde amnesia, for events preceding the injury. In either case, the theoretical explanation is given in terms of interference from the physiological disturbance adversely affecting the consolidation of the memory traces.

Similar results are obtained when human subjects or animals are subjected to electroshock immediately after learning. If human patients under electroshock therapy are given lists of verbal materials to learn they cannot retain these following shock (47). Similar results have been obtained by investigators who subject animals to cerebral shock following learning (23, pp. 547–548). We do not know why shock causes amnesia (or why it brings about remission of symptoms in certain psychiatric conditions). It has been suggested that the attendant convulsions cause temporary anoxia in the brain, thereby disrupting neuronal pathways which mediate recent memories.

MOTIVATED FORGETTING

We are indebted to Sigmund Freud for the first systematic theory c motivated forgetting. In his famous *Psychopathology of Everyday Life* (3) h called attention to many instances of slips of the tongue (*Lapsus linguae* forgetting of appointments, functional amnesias, and similar states, which seem to have a psychological function in protecting the individual ego. Thus, to forget a name associated with an unpleasant experience is a kind of adjustive mechanism designed to protect the self from a painful memory. Or, for a husband to forget the opera tickets, when he really does not want to attend, expresses a subconscious wish which is carried out in behavior.

More generally, Freud and his followers postulated that in cases of memory involving painful or shameful experiences a process of *repression* inhibits memories from reaching consciousness. Repression, it must be emphasized, is not forgetting; repressed memories are only inhibited and constantly strive to find expression in dreams, neurotic symptoms, slips of the tongue, and the like.

While it is not possible for psychologists to experiment on repression directly by having children undergo threatening or humiliating experiences, it has been possible to design analogues of repression using verbal materials. Zeller (*44, 45, 46*), who has done considerable work in this area, utilized the broad outlines of a retroaction experiment to investigate repression. His experimental group learned Task *A*, then was given practice on Task *B* with ego-deflation and embarrassment (the experimenter informed the subjects that they had failed). There followed a recall test for Task *A* to determine whether repression had occurred. The subjects were then given more practice on Task *B* with praise from the experimenter (broadly analogous to a therapeutic session), and finally a test of Task *A* to discover if repression had been successfully removed. Zeller has reported that he obtained evidence of repression by comparing experimental groups with control groups who do not undergo ego-deflation. Similar experiments carried out by Aborn (*1*) gave similar results.

However, the experimental conditions in these experiments fall short of those demanded by Freudian theory, which presumed repression to be the result of an extremely traumatic experience, such as a sexual assault or a child's witnessing of intercourse on the part of the parents. Clearly, ego-deflation, while embarrassing and humiliating for some subjects, does not measure up to such highly charged experiences. More generally, in repression we may have an instance of a psychoanalytic concept which is almost universally accepted by psychologists but for which there is little concrete experimental evidence, largely because of the ethical barriers to carrying out research on the problem.

Problems of experimental design and interpretation are also sources of controversy in attempting to evaluate the famous *Zeigarnik effect*, or the tendency for subjects to remember interrupted tasks better than completed tasks. Zeigarnik (*43*), a pupil of Lewin's, gave subjects a series of twenty simple tasks. Half of the tasks were interrupted, the rest allowed to go on to completion. At the end of the session the subjects were asked to recall all tasks. On the average, about 50 percent could be recalled; but of the re-membered tasks 68 percent of the unfinished tasks were recalled with only 43 percent of the finished being remembered. This differential recall of unfinished tasks is known as the *Zeigarnik effect* and was attributed by her to the tensions associated with a subjective state of disequilibrium because of failure.

The experiment has been repeated a number of times with positive results. However, in some cases reversals of the effect may occur with com-pleted tasks being recalled better if the subject believes his intelligence is being measured. Failure becomes humiliating with an apparent tendency to wish to forget the "failed" tasks. Ego-defense, then, may be the critical factor rather than "tension" or "disequilibrium." A number of experiments bearing on the problem are interpretatively reviewed by Osgood (26, pp. 582–587). Here we need only note that regardless of the theoretical inter-pretation of the *Zeigarnik effect,* it appears to lend support to motivated fac-tors in forgetting.

AN INTEGRATED THEORY OF FORGETTING

Any theory of forgetting which pretends to completeness would have to take into account not only the various factors reviewed in this chapter but others as well. Let us briefly list these by way of a summary of this section.

1. Disuse.   Disuse has never proved to be a popular theory of forgetting. Nevertheless, we mention it as a possibility. It seems logical to believe that *some* degree of forgetting could be the result of disuse, especially because of fading traces due to metabolic changes in the cerebral cortex.

2. Interference effects.   Of these we have discussed (a) retroactive inhi-bition which has played a prominent if not the major role in theories of forgetting since the work of Ebbinghaus, and (b) proactive inhibition which also has come into increasing prominence with the studies of Underwood and his associates since World War II.

3. Pathological and other states.   Under this variable we may include retrograde and anterograde amnesia, shock effects, and the like as special kinds of forgetting which more generally support a perseveration or con-solidation theory of trace formation.

4. Motivational variables.   Important here are clinical cases of forgetting due to functional amnesia and repression which reveal the role of person-ality and ego-defense mechanisms in retention.

5. Gestalt factors. The reader will recall that the Gestalt psychologists emphasized that memories undergo systematic changes with the passage of time in accordance with the principles of perceptual organization (Chapter 5). These, too, would have to be included in a complete theory of forgetting.

Of these five possible causes of forgetting, we may add that interference effects are believed to be the single most important factor in ordinary forgetting. Moreover, retroactive and proactive theory has received the widest general experimental support.

A NOTE ON SHORT-TERM MEMORY

Within the past decade considerable interest has developed around the concept of short-term memory in regard to its possible differences from long-term memory. A short-term memory is illustrated by the memory span or the number of digits which can be recalled after a single presentation. Such a unit of material has been called a "chunk" (*21*) and may represent a kind of maximal amount which can be encoded on the brain in a single brief exposure. Individuals with long memory spans may be able to encode larger masses of information into a limited number of chunks by grouping techniques.

Peterson and Peterson (*27*) studied short-term memory by presenting the subject with a three-letter nonsense syllable followed by a number. When the subject heard the number he was instructed to count backward by threes from it until given a stop signal. This was done to prevent his rehearsal of the syllable. At the signal the subject tried to recall the syllable. Intervals between the presentation of the syllable and the signal for its recall were 3, 6, 9, 12, or 18 seconds. The frequencies of correct recalls are shown in Figure 9-13. It will be noted that forgetting is rapid with nearly complete forgetting having occurred by 18 seconds. These results show the very limited time in which storage can take place; and if it fails to do so, it is forgotten. Confirmation of these results was obtained by Murdock (*24*) utilizing paired associates made up from the Thorndike-Lorge word list. No difference was found in the subject's ability to remember three words as opposed to three digits, both being made up of an equal number of chunks.

It is tempting to speculate that short-term memory represents basic neural encoding by way of a process of perseveration for a brief period of time followed by a more or less permanent consolidation. Once consolidation has occurred the memory is much more resistant to change due to interference effects. More experimental evidence is needed before we know the exact relationship between short-term memory and neural processes,

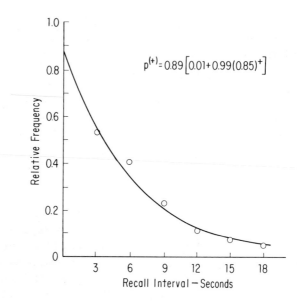

Fig. 9-13. A curve for short-term memory. Note that the relative frequency (of correct recalls) has dropped to nearly zero after only 18 seconds. (From Peterson and Peterson, *27.*)

but interest in the field has opened up a challenging possibility for the correlation of behavioral and neurological science.

REFERENCES

1. Aborn, M. The influence of experimentally induced failure on the retention of material acquired through set and incidental learning. *Journal of Experimental Psychology,* **45,** 1953, pp. 225–231.
2. Deese, J. *The psychology of learning,* ed. 2. New York: McGraw-Hill, 1958.
3. Freud, S. The psychopathology of everyday life. In Brill, A. A. (ed.) *The basic writings of Freud.* New York: Random House, 1938.
4. Guilford, J. P. *General psychology.* New York: Van Nostrand, 1939.
5. Hall, J. F. *The psychology of learning.* Philadelphia: J. B. Lippincott, 1966.
6. Harden, L. M. A quantitative study of the similarity factor in retroactive inhibition. *Journal of General Psychology,* **2,** 1929, pp. 421–430.
7. Harlow, H. F. The formation of learning sets. *Psychological Review,* **56,** 1949, pp. 51–65.
8. Hilgard, E. R. *Theories of learning,* ed. 2. New York: Appleton, 1956.
9. Hovland, C. I. Experimental studies in rote-learning theory. III. Distribution of practice with varying speeds of syllable presentation. *Journal of Experimental Psychology,* **23,** 1938, pp. 172–190.
10. Hull, C. L. The conflicting psychologies of learning—a way out. *Psychological Review,* **42,** 1935, pp. 491–516.

11. Jenkins, J. G., and K. M. Dallenbach. Obliviscence during sleep and waking. *American Journal of Psychology,* **35,** 1924, pp. 605–612.

12. Jost, A. Die Assoziationsfestigkeit in Ihrer Abhängigheit von de Verteilung der Widerholungen. *Zeitschrift für Psychologie,* **14,** 1897, pp. 436–472.

13. Judd, C. H. The relation of special training to general intelligence. *Educational Review,* **36,** 1908, pp. 28–42.

14. Jung, J. Transfer of training as a function of degree of first-list learning. *Journal of Verbal Learning and Verbal Behavior,* **1,** 1962, pp. 197–199.

15. Jung, J. Effects of response meaningfulness (m) on transfer of training under two different paradigms. *Journal of Experimental Psychology,* **65,** 1963, pp. 377–384.

16. Krueger, W. C. The effect of overlearning on retention. *Journal of Experimental Psychology,* **41,** 1929, pp. 432–441.

17. Luh, C. W. The conditions of retention. *Psychological Monographs,* **31,** 1922, No. 142.

18. McGeoch, J. A. The influence of degree of learning upon retroactive inhibition. *American Journal of Psychology,* **41,** 1929, pp. 252–262.

19. McGeoch, J. A. The influence of associative value upon the difficulty of nonsense-syllable lists. *Journal of Genetic Psychology,* **37,** 1930, pp. 421–426.

20. McGeoch, J. A., and A. Irion. *The psychology of human learning,* ed. 2. New York: Longmans, Green, 1952.

21. Miller, G. A. The magical number seven, plus or minus two: Some limits on our capacity for processing information. *Psychological Review,* **63,** 1956, pp. 81–97.

22. Minami, H., and K. M. Dallenbach. The effect of activity upon learning and retention in the cockroach. *American Journal of Psychology,* **59,** 1946, pp. 1–58.

23. Morgan, C. T. *Physiological psychology,* ed. 3. New York: McGraw-Hill, 1965.

24. Murdock, B. B. Jr. The retention of individual items. *Journal of Experimental Psychology,* **62,** 1961, pp. 618–625.

25. Osgood, C. E. The similarity paradox in human learning: a resolution. *Psychological Review,* **56,** 1949, pp. 132–143.

26. Osgood, C. E. *Method and theory in experimental psychology.* New York: Oxford University Press, 1953.

27. Peterson, L. R., and M. J. Peterson. Short-term retention of individual verbal items. *Journal of Experimental Psychology,* **58,** 1959, pp. 193–198.

28. Postman, L. Transfer of training as a function of experimental paradigm and degree of first-list learning. *Journal of Verbal Learning and Verbal Behavior,* **1,** 1962, pp. 109–118.

29. Postman, L. Studies of learning to learn. II. Changes in transfer as function of practice. *Journal of Verbal Learning and Verbal Behavior,* **3,** 1964, pp. 437–447.

30. Postman, L., and T. G. Alper. Retroactive inhibition as a function of the time of interpolation of the inhibitor between learning and recall. *American Journal of Psychology,* **59,** 1946, pp. 439–449.

31. Restorff, H. von. Über die Wirkung von Bereinschbildungen im Spurenfeld. In: Köhler, W., and H. von Restorff. Analyse von Vorgängen im Spurenfeld. *Psychologische Forschung,* **18,** 1933, pp. 299–342.

32. Robinson, E. S. The "similarity" factor in retroaction. *American Journal of Psychology,* **39,** 1927, pp. 297–312.

33. Sarason, I. Effect of anxiety, motivational instructions, and failure on serial learning. *Journal of Experimental Psychology,* **51,** 1956, pp. 253–260.

34. Sarason, S. B., G. Mandler, and P. G. Craighill. The effect of differential instructions on anxiety and learning. *Journal of Abnormal and Social Psychology,* **47,** 1952, pp. 561–565.

35. Sears, P. S. Levels of aspiration in academically successful and unsuccessful children. *Journal of Abnormal and Social Psychology,* **35,** 1940, pp. 498–536.

36. Twedt, H. M., and B. J. Underwood. Mixed versus unmixed lists in transfe studies. *Journal of Experimental Psychology,* **58,** 1959, pp. 111–116.
37. Underwood, B. J. The effect of successive interpolations on retroactive and pro active inhibition. *Psychological Monographs,* **59,** 1945, No. 3.
38. Underwood, B. J. Interference and forgetting. *Psychological Review,* **64,** 1957, pp 49–60.
39. Van Buskirk, W. L. An experimental study of vividness in learning and retention *Journal of Experimental Psychology,* **15,** 1932, pp. 563–573.
40. van Ormer, E. B. Sleep and retention. *Psychological Bulletin,* **30,** 1932, pp. 415–439
41. Ward, L. B. Reminiscence and rote learning. *Psychological Monographs,* **49,** 1937 No. 220.
42. Woodworth, R. S., and H. Schlosberg. *Experimental psychology,* ed. 2. New York Holt, Rinehart, and Winston, 1954.
43. Zeigarnik, B. Über das Behalten von erledigten und unerledigten Handlungen *Psychologische Forschung,* **9,** 1927, pp. 1–85.
44. Zeller, A. F. An experimental analogue of repression. I. Historical summary *Psychological Bulletin,* **47,** 1950, pp. 39–51.
45. Zeller, A. F. An experimental analogue of repression. II. The effect of individua failure and success on memory measured by relearning. *Journal of Experimenta Psychology,* **40,** 1950, pp. 411–422.
46. Zeller, A. F. An experimental analogue of repression. III. The effect of induce failure and success on memory measured by recall. *Journal of Experimental Psy chology,* **42,** 1951, pp. 32–38.
47. Zubin, J. Memory functioning in patients treated with electric shock therapy *Journal of Personality,* **17,** 1948, pp. 33–41.

10

Thinking

Thinking is closely allied to the process of learning inasmuch as our chief tools of thought—concepts—are learned. Moreover, a great deal of our thinking is based on memories, recollections, and memory images. Indeed, much of what is called thinking is actually remembering. For example, when the individual exclaims, "I wish I could think of his name," he is trying to remember something he has learned in the past. However, there are other cases in which thinking is clearly different from simple memory. The farm boy resting on a haystack and building air castles in Spain is engaging in *reverie,* a form of thinking which depends upon memory, but which goes far beyond memory to the imagining of events that have never happened and probably never will. Or, consider a scientist who is engaged in seeking the solution to a problem. He utilizes many learned concepts, but the characteristic thing about this variety of thinking is the resulting discovery of new relationships. Thinking, then, takes many forms. Let us attempt to classify the more important types here at the outset in order to have working definitions for the discussion of the systematic views on thinking that constitute the remainder of this chapter.

VARIETIES OF THINKING

Perhaps the simplest and most fundamental type of thinking is simple association, of which there are two subvarieties: *free* and *controlled.* Free association occurs whenever the thinker allows the stream of consciousness to wander where it will, as so often happens at night when we are dropping off to sleep. Frequently under these conditions the mind seems to drift, so to speak, from one thing to another, to the point where the individual may be surprised at the long chain of loosely related events which has passed through his consciousness from start to finish. It is also interesting to note that free association is employed in psychoanalysis. Theoretically the freely associating patient's "guard" is down; and, as a consequence memories and impulses which are ordinarily not admitted to consciousness can come to the foreground.

By contrast, in controlled association the individual's thinking is re stricted, since he is instructed to respond within a certain type or class o possible responses. For example, he may be told to respond to a set of stim ulus words by giving opposites. Thus, if the stimulus word "light" is spoken by the experimenter, the subject responds with "dark." In the case where opposites must be given, the degree of restriction is great. However, where the subject is required to give synonyms, he enjoys a somewhat greater degree of latitude.

In reverie, fantasy, and dreams (both of the day and night variety) the associations flowing through consciousness are not directed by the con scious efforts of the thinker. However, in any of these varieties of thinking the thought patterns are more highly organized and interrelated than i true of thinking in free association. There is, so to speak, a theme running through the thinker's mind. In fact, as common experience tells us, noc turnal dreams may be so highly structured and realistic that, upon awaken ing, the dreamer is not certain whether he has been dreaming or has experi enced a real chain of events. Most psychologists believe that the theme o story in reverie, in fantasy, and in dreams is related to the thinker's motiva tional processes. Often these varieties of ideational activity are wish fulfill ing in the sense that the individual is obtaining satisfactions in imagina tion that he cannot achieve in reality; or, as is frequently true in reverie the function may be purely recreational. One cannot "keep his mind" on reality all the time!

Autistic thinking is dominated by the thinker's needs rather than by the demands of reality. In this sense, autistic thinking is closely related to reverie, fantasy, and dreaming; and, for this reason, some psychologists use the terms more or less interchangeably. However, there are occasions when autistic thinking can be distinguished from reverie, fantasy, and dreaming For example, let us suppose that a scientist has a strong prejudice (and scientists do have prejudices) in favor of a particular theory. Quite uncon sciously his interpretations of his empirical findings may be distorted in favor of his theoretical position, even though he believes that he is being objective.[1] Therefore, in contrast to fantasy, reverie, and dreaming, which are usually conscious, autistic thinking is frequently an insidious, uncon scious process that is difficult to detect.

---

[1] Darwin once observed that he was always careful to record any information unfavorable to his theory of evolution, since, if he failed to do so, he often forgot it.

Animism is a form of thinking in which the individual projects life, or the attributes of life, into inanimate objects. As we shall see, this form of thinking is common in young children, who are prone to attribute life or conscious awareness to clouds, astronomical bodies, the wind, and other natural phenomena.

Creative thinking is a highly directed, goal-oriented type of ideational activity. In effect, the thinker is solving a problem. In some cases he may be engaged in reasoning in which new relationships are sought, or he may simply be trying to remember a formula which will enable him to solve a mathematical problem. Or, perhaps, he is a philosopher hard at work in his armchair trying to improve on a traditional ethical system. In still another instance he might be an artist attempting to develop a new form. As these few examples show, creative thinking takes many forms—so many, indeed, that an extensive breakdown of this broad category of thinking would alone constitute an entire volume in itself.

Our brief outline of the chief types of thinking should serve to demonstrate that ideation is a process with many facets; and, as a consequence, it is often necessary to specify what *type* of ideational activity is under consideration rather than to employ the loose term "thinking." As will be apparent in our examination of the systematic psychology of thinking, different investigators, aware of the many subvarieties of the thought processes, have developed theories or systems which seek to explain certain types or aspects of thinking, rather than systems which attempt to encompass the thought processes as a whole in a single, comprehensive theory.

HISTORICAL BACKGROUND

Much of what we had to say about the early psychology of perception and learning is, of course, equally relevant to thinking. The philosophers and early experimental psychologists who sought the answer to the nature of the higher mental processes in the form of elements were confident that thinking could be reduced to simpler processes. As we pointed out in previous chapters, mental chemistry was popular among the empiricists and associationists, and besides being responsible for the development of associationism as a school of philosophy, also led to the structuralistic psychology of Wundt and Titchener. Because the basic aim of the structuralists was the analysis of mental contents, we may include Wundt, Titchener, and their followers under the broad rubric of "content" psychologists.

However, during the same period that Wundt and Titchener were developing structuralism, an opposition movement was growing in psychology which found support both on the continent of Europe and in the United States. In Europe, the chief opponents of content psychology were a group of psychologists in southern Germany and Austria, collectively known as the Würzburg school. The Würzburg group stressed the study of *acts* and *functions* as the proper subject matter of psychology as opposed to content. The school was aided in its attack on content psychology by the American functionalists, James, Dewey, Angell, and Carr, who were opposed to structuralism for many of the same reasons that led to the development of the Würzburg movement. We shall begin our discussion of the systematic psychology of the thought processes by examining representative views of the proponents of these opposing schools of thought. Despite a certain chronological irregularity, we shall first consider the structuralistic view of thinking, following which we shall examine the position of the Würzburg school, and, finally, we shall review the closely related viewpoint of the functionalists.

THE STRUCTURALISTIC VIEW OF THE THOUGHT PROCESSES

Titchener's[2] account of "thought," which is the title of the ninth chapter in his *Textbook,* begins on a strongly controversial note. Titchener, it will be recalled, taught that consciousness was reducible to three basic elements: sensations, images, and affections. But it had come to his attention that other experimentalists were by no means in agreement with his position. There were reports emanating from various laboratories to the effect that introspection of the thought processes revealed the existence of "conscious attitudes," "imageless thoughts," and "elementary processes of relation." None of these ideational activities appeared to be explicable in terms of the structuralists' "elements," and, even more disturbing, they might have to be regarded as new "elements." The greater part of Titchener's account of thinking is devoted to an attempt to refute this challenge to structuralism, rather than to the development of an original point of view on the thought processes. We do not mean to impute prejudice to Titchener. He is fair in concluding that opinion alone is not sufficient to resolve issues which must wait upon further experimentation. What we do wish to emphasize is the weakness of the structuralistic contribution to the psychology of thinking. Titchener's simple elementalism was no match for the variety and richness of the cognitive processes. But let us summarize his arguments on the old controversies of the day, for it will help to introduce us to the issues which were central in the early systematic viewpoints on thinking.

Conscious attitudes may be exemplified by such everyday concepts as "hesitation," "vacillation," or "dissent." Can a strong conscious state of the

[2] Our exposition is based on Titchener's *Textbook of Psychology* (*37*).

attitude "this is novel" be analyzed into the familiar elements of consciousness? The initial introspective reports generally favored the stand that such an attitude was unanalyzable. Titchener holds the contrary view that such conscious attitudes are analyzable, and that the difficulties experienced by other investigators were the result of several experimental errors. First, he believes that psychologists working in the area of thinking had become victims of suggestion, in the sense that when observers found conscious attitudes unanalyzable, others more or less took their findings for granted and so failed to pursue their own investigations with sufficient rigor. Second, Titchener goes on to argue that attitudes "thin out" with repetition, so that the visual and verbal images which originally mediated the attitude are no longer present when the attitude is brought under laboratory investigation. As a result, the thought processes involved seem to be imageless and sensationless. In this same connection, it was this finding that led to the argument for new elements: since thought is not dependent upon the elements of consciousness, it must stand alone as a new element coequal with the original three. Third, Titchener believes that some observers had fallen into the error of reporting their ideas or attitudes *as ideas* instead of looking beyond to the elements out of which the idea or attitude is formulated. The situation here is similar to that found in describing an object in terms of its ordinary meaning (the stimulus error),[3] instead of the raw conscious processes which are generated by stimuli from the object.

Other difficulties connected with the analysis of ideational processes are discussed by Titchener, but the three which we have summarized are a sufficient indication of the problems and pitfalls of the introspective approach to the thought processes. Titchener, however, is certain that the difficulties are experimental artifacts and that more carefully controlled observations will eventually resolve them in favor of the structuralistic point of view. Indeed, he reports positive results from his own laboratory where a large number of attitudes were "pounced upon" at the moment they came to the observer's consciousness, "made focal, and examined as carefully as the circumstances allowed" (*37*, p. 516). In Titchener's opinion, there was little doubt of the result: "All the reports show the same features: visual images, pictorial or symbolic; internal speech; kinesthetic images; organic sensations. Nowhere a sign of the imageless component!" Thus, the problems of "conscious attitudes" and "imageless thoughts" are resolved by Titchener at one and the same time.

The "alleged elementary process of relation" is described as the conscious state which arises when such concepts as "if," "and," "but," and "is to" occur in the observer's consciousness. Some introspectionists were convinced that the conscious relations mediated by such terms are elementary

[3] See Chapter 2.

thought processes not reducible to sensations, images, and affections. In Titchener's own words, the problem and its possible solutions are described as follows (*37*, p. 512):

> The observer was asked, for instance, "London is to England as Paris is to _____?" or: "Eyes are to face as a lake is to _____?" He was required to answer these questions, in the sense of the relation obtaining between the first pair of terms, and then, afterwards, to give an introspective account of the whole experience. The results were of three kinds. The blank may be filled up, under pressure of the instruction, without any consciousness of relation; the transferred relation may be carried in visual images, or in internal speech; and, lastly, the relation may be present in consciousness, without any imaginal component simply as an "imageless thought." From these results the conclusion is drawn that "the feelings of relation are of the same order as feelings of sensory quali ties; each feeling of relation is a simple quality."

Titchener and his associates tackled the problem of ideational rela tions in their characteristically forthright manner, and the results from the laboratory in no way favored the supporters of "imageless relations" or "elementary processes of relation." Rather, the consciousness of relation was, in the great majority of introspective reports, accompanied by sensory or verbal images.

At the end of his discussion, he concludes that the structuralists' posi tion that there are three elementary processes—sensations, images, and affections—stands. He then goes on to deal with other cognitive processes such as language, abstract ideas, and judgment. We need not trace the development of Titchener's position on these topics, since in doing so we would only be multiplying examples. As he saw it, the problem throughout is the same: how to analyze the complex and often elusive thought processes into their more elementary components. It is truly a psychology of content whose fundamental method is mental chemistry. Nothing original was added to the psychology of thinking by the structuralists. Instead, ideational activities are reduced to the familiar, well-established elements from which all complex conscious processes are derived.

Act psychology and the Würzburg school.   As we pointed out at the be ginning of the chapter, about the same time that Wundt and Titchener were developing their content psychology, an opposition movement was getting underway in Europe. This movement eventually came to be known as the Würzburg school. Our next task will be tracing the development of the latter school of thought in relation to the structuralistic point of view.

A number of individuals[4]—philosophers, embryonic psychologists, and physiologists—were associated with the development of the Würzburg

---

[4] The interested reader may consult Boring (*3*) for a more detailed history of the school.

school, but we shall limit our discussion to the teachings of Oswald Külpe, under whose leadership the "school" developed. Külpe began his academic career in the field of history. However, he came under the influence of Wundt in Leipzig, in 1881, and, as a result, developed a strong interest in psychology. Eventually he became a professor of psychology at Leipzig, but in 1894 he was called to Würzburg, in Bavaria. There he and his associates addressed themselves to the problem of the analysis of thought—a problem which Wundt was finding increasingly difficult to deal with experimentally. Because of these procedural difficulties, Wundt, in fact, was turning to the study of social psychology in the hope that the record of man's thoughts and actions as revealed in folk psychology would cast light on the higher mental processes.

Külpe, on the contrary, felt that the thought processes must and could be studied experimentally. In keeping with their experimental orientation, he and his associates began a program of direct introspection of the thought processes, which, as it turned out, yielded surprising results. The structuralists, it seemed, were wrong in suggesting that thoughts could be reduced to sensory or imaginal elements. The Würzburg psychologists found evidence to support just the opposite point of view, namely, that thinking can go on without any sensory or imaginal content.[5] Moreover, some observers suggested that a new element—a "thought element"—ought to be introduced to account for their findings. Others suggested that the concept of "unanalyzable conscious attitudes" best described the results.

We have already seen that Titchener took issue with the "imageless thought" and "conscious attitude" school. Wundt, in support of his own position that man's language and social products were the proper avenue to the study of the higher mental processes, denounced direct introspective studies of thought as "mock experiments." Külpe, however, continued his observations, and was leaning more and more in the direction of abandoning content psychology altogether in favor of a functionalistic point of view. Whether or not this would have ultimately happened is difficult to say, for Külpe died before completing a revision of his systematic writings.

Summary. This, then, was the state of the structuralistic psychology of thought: Titchener, trained in the Wundtian tradition, championed the point of view that the thought processes could be successfully analyzed into the traditional elements of the introspectionists without the necessity of postulating a new "thought element." Külpe, from the same academic background, gained wide support for the "imageless thought" interpretation of the ideational processes, and, as a result, was gradually moving

---

[5] Külpe's findings were supported by Binet, the great French originator of the Binet Test, and by R. S. Woodworth, a prominent American psychologist. Woodworth subsequently denied the possibility of a pure state of imageless consciousness (*44*, p. 788).

toward a functionalistic position.[6] Consequently, the structuralists were under attack by their German colleagues as well as by the American functionalists, whose position we shall consider next.

FUNCTIONALISM AND THE THOUGHT PROCESSES

William James, the brilliant precursor of the American school of functionalism, sets the tone for the functionalistic view of the thought processes in one of the most famous passages in the literature of psychology. We refer to Chapter IX of the first volume of his *Principles of Psychology*. Significantly, the chapter is entitled, "The Stream of Thought." A few quotations from it are worth including, both for their excellent descriptive value and functionalistic flavor. Here, for example, is the famous paragraph in which James defines thought as a stream of consciousness:

> Consciousness, then, does not appear to itself chopped up in bits. Such words as "chain" or "train" do not describe it fitly as it presents itself in the first instance. It is nothing jointed; it flows. A "river" or a "stream" are the metaphors by which it is most naturally described. In talking of it hereafter, let us call it the stream of thought, of consciousness, or of subjective life.

A few pages further on James writes of the "flights" and "perchings" of thought:

> As we take, in fact, a general view of the wonderful stream of our consciousness, what strikes us first is this different pace of its parts. Like a bird's life, it seems to be made of an alternation of flights and perchings. The rhythm of language expresses this, where every thought is expressed in a sentence, and every sentence closed by a period. The resting-places are usually occupied by sensorial imaginations of some sort, whose peculiarity is that they can be held before the mind for an indefinite time, and contemplated without changing; the places of flight are filled with thoughts of relations, static or dynamic, that for the most part obtain between the matters contemplated in the periods of comparative rest.

Finally, in one of the best known of all passages from the *Principles,* James describes the consciousness of a set or tendency:

> Suppose we try to recall a forgotten name. The state of our consciousness is peculiar. There is a gap therein; but no mere gap. It is a gap that is intensely

---

[6] Franz Brentano, of the same period, developed an "act psychology" in opposition to structuralism. Brentano held that acts rather than contents were the proper subject matter for psychology. Clearly, an "act" psychology is functionalistic in spirit as opposed to structuralistic. For further details see *3,* pp. 431ff.

active. A sort of wraith of the name is in it, beckoning us in a given direction, making us at moments tingle with the sense of our closeness, and then letting us sink back without the longed-for term. If wrong names are proposed to us, this singularly definite gap acts immediately so as to negate them. They do not fit into its mould. And the gap of one word does not feel like the gap of another, all empty of content as both might seem necessarily to be when described as gaps. . . . But namelessness is compatible with existence. There are innumerable consciousnesses of emptiness, no one of which taken in itself has a name, but all different from each other. The ordinary way is to assume that they are all emptinesses of consciousness, and so the same state. But the feeling of an absence is *toto coelo* other than the absence of a feeling. It is an intense feeling. The rhythm of a lost word may be there without a sound to clothe it; or the evanescent sense of something which is the initial vowel or consonant may mock us fitfully, without growing more distinct. Everyone must know the tantalizing effect of the blank rhythm of some forgotten verse, restlessly dancing in one's mind, striving to be filled out with words.

As descriptive psychology James' prose is without parallel. However, we must take the long jump from James to Carr in order to examine the functionalists' position on ideation after functionalism had developed from a philosophy into a mature school of psychology. The leap, however, does not represent an extensive historical period, for only thirty-five years elapsed between the publication of the *Principles* and Carr's *Textbook;* but, in the meantime, functionalism had become experimental and developed the strong systematic point of view that *mental activities* were to be studied as they functioned in enabling the organism to adapt to its environment.

Carr's treatment of the nature and function of ideas[7] strongly reflects the school's adaptive frame of reference: "An idea or thought," Carr begins, "is a cognitive process in that it involves the apprehension of an object in the interest of some subsequent reaction in reference to it." The final phrase in the quotation conveys the potential utility value of ideas assigned to them by the functionalists in keeping with their overall orientation. After discoursing at length on various types of ideas, Carr returns to the characteristically functional position in a section entitled "The Function of Ideas." In his discussion, ideas are treated as substitutes for perceptual stimuli. Now if we bear in mind that he defines perception as "The cognition of a present object in relation to some act of adjustment" (see Chapter 4), then it is clear that ideas are capable of arousing response patterns which have an adaptive value for the individual. Carr exemplifies his argument by suggesting that the thought of a coming lecture may induce more adequate preparation, or that the individual in walking home at night may utilize his cognitive knowledge of the streets by taking advantage of a shortcut.

Ideas, therefore, have the same consequences in adaptive activity as

[7] Our exposition follows Carr (*4*, Chapter VIII).

perceptions. More particularly, Carr suggests three ways in which ideas may function in adaptive conduct. First, the object of thought may be the end or goal of adaptive behavior. The dress designer or architect has an ideational conception of the end product of his activities in mind from the beginning. In this same connection Carr adds that it is by means of ideas that we are able to strive for remote goals. Because of his ability to look ahead, the human organism is capable of creative ideational adaptive behavior. Inventions, bridges, dams, and similar complex and remote-goal adaptive projects can be undertaken for human betterment. Second, thoughts may serve as means to ends. To illustrate: We may think of a tool which will facilitate the completion of an ongoing do-it-yourself project and thus utilize an idea in bringing about a more nearly adequate adjustment. Finally, ideas may serve a vicarious function in taking the place of actual behavior. The chess player, for example, often makes many moves ideationally in order to foresee, if possible, their consequences when carried out in actuality.[8]

In addition to his chapter on ideas in general, Carr devotes a separate chapter to the specific topic of reasoning. The treatment, however, is so similar to his earlier account of perceptual motor learning (see Chapter 6) that one wonders why he bothered to separate the two. In essence, he considers reasoning as identical in all important respects with perceptual-motor learning. The reasoner is confronted with a problem which can be either perceptual or ideational. The solution is achieved by a "variable, persistent, and analytical ideational attack which is continued until the solution is more or less accidentally discovered" (4, p. 202). This definition of reasoning is virtually identical with that given previously for perceptual-motor problems, save in the latter the term "motor" is used instead of "ideational." Carr, indeed, goes a step further in arguing for the similarity of the two types of problem solving by emphasizing that reasoning problems require considerable repetition before the solution is fixated.[9] Finally, he briefly discusses the process of *generalization* of ideational solutions. Generalization corresponds to transfer, as he employs the latter concept in his previous discussion of perceptual-motor learning.

While the parallel is complete, Carr does not, of course, consider the two processes to be literally identical. Both the advantages and disadvantages of reasoning are pointed out by Carr and compared to those for motor behavior. In general, the great advantages of ideational problem solving over perceptual-motor solutions are its efficiency and the fact that abstract problems can be dealt with only in ideational thinking. However, he also points out that the consequences of our acts cannot always be foreseen.

[8] Tolman coined the colorful phrase "behavior feints" to describe such processes.

[9] In reading Carr, one is strongly impressed by his implicit lack of belief in insight and rather strong tendency to favor a trial-and-error conception of learning.

ind in such cases we must fall back on a motor trial-and-error attack. And
o, as we are leaving Carr's treatment of the reasoning process, we must
igain emphasize the strong affinity which exists for Carr between motor
ind ideational activity. Undoubtedly, much of the identity in the two
processes is the result of his emphasis on the adaptive nature of the activ-
ties in question. The goal of adaptation, therefore, is the important con-
ideration from the functionalists' point of view; the nature of the ideational
processes involved is of less consequence.

Finally, by way of a closing comment on Carr's treatment of ideas
ind reasoning, one cannot help but be struck by his largely programmatic
approach to thinking. Virtually no empirical laboratory experiments are
discussed, and the analyses throughout are almost entirely theoretical. It
s a *pure systematic* psychology entirely divorced from empirical problems
ind interpretations.

BEHAVIORISM AND THE GREAT REVOLT

When we come to examine Watson's views on thinking, we are face
to face with one of the most characteristic, challenging and controversial
of all his doctrines. We refer to his celebrated "peripheral theory of thinking." Since Watson's viewpoint is often contrasted to the "centralist" theory
of thinking, it will be convenient to consider the two together. As Figure
10-1 shows, the centralists contend that thinking is exclusively a cerebral

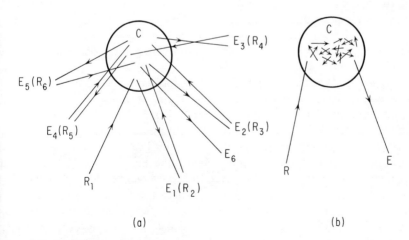

Fig. 10-1. The peripheralist (a) and centralist (b) views of the role of the brain in thinking. (From J. F. Dashiell, *Fundamentals of General Psychology.* Boston: Houghton Mifflin
Co., 1949.)

affair, while the peripheralists consider ideation to be a function of the body as a whole. The centralist position is, of course, the older, traditional point of view which is supported by common experience; that is, we seem to think with our heads. Moreover, we found that the structuralists argued that the image, a central, conscious process, is the mediator of ideas. All such central processes were held to be dependent upon the central nervous system.

As early as 1914, Watson had attacked "central images," or "centrally aroused sensations," in the introductory chapter of his *Behavior: An Introduction to Comparative Psychology*. In the latter, he defined the image as a form of *implicit behavior*, although he had to admit that no method was available at that time to demonstrate the existence of any such implicit behavior patterns and doubted that one would ever be devised. However, he strongly suggests that the muscles of the larynx and tongue are the probable foci of much of our implicit behavior because, of course, of the close association between language and thought. In his *Psychology from the Standpoint of a Behaviorist*, published in 1919, only five years after *Behavior*, Watson proves himself a poor prophet; the behaviorists *had* found a way to measure responses of the laryngeal musculature.

The procedure which he describes for recording implicit behavior is simple. A tambour is attached to the subject's neck in the region of the larynx. Whenever muscular movements occur, pressure changes are set up within the tambour and are transmitted to a recording device. Moreover Watson reports carrying out investigations on deaf-mutes. He found that their hands and fingers frequently move, just as the normal individual's lips are frequently active while he is reading or deeply engaged in thought. Even though his investigations of normal and deaf-mute implicit muscle movements sometimes failed to yield positive results, Watson was confident (*41*, pp. 324–326) that such movements nevertheless existed in all cases of thinking and awaited only the discovery of better instrumentation in order to be revealed.

Clearly, Watson recognized and emphasized the close correspondence between language and thinking. Indeed, the phrase, "laryngeal habits," *is* his equivalent for "thinking." Laryngeal habits are developed in early childhood out of the vocalizations which all infants display during the first year of life. Through conditioning, such vocalizations become words. For example, the child's "da-da" is attached to his father by conditioning and, through selective reinforcement, eventually becomes "daddy." As the child's verbal habits grow stronger, he no longer needs to speak the word "daddy," but may simply "think" it when he sees his parent. However, the child's "thinking" is nevertheless motor as revealed by his *subvocal* pronounciation of words.

In addition to laryngeal habits, the language function may also be mediated by gestures, frowns, shrugs, and the like, all of which "stand for" more overt reactions to situations. Similarly, writing, drawing, dancing, painting, and sculpturing may be considered motor forms of communication which represent ideas. Indeed, Watson goes so far as to argue that there is really little value in attempting to record thinking, because "it finally eventuates in action and in the second place most of it in mankind is worthless from the standpoint of society—any consistent series of thought processes which is of any social interest will, if sufficiently well-integrated with other bodily action systems, take issue finally in overt action" (41, p. 327).

Watson left the field of academic psychology before modern techniques for recording muscle potentials, brain waves, and nerve impulses were developed. It has since been demonstrated without doubt that we do think with our entire body and not with our brains alone (16, 22, and 23). The muscles of the arms, legs, and trunk are in constant tension or tonus; but during mental activity the tensions are increased—especially in those muscles which are closely associated with the content of the thought pattern. For example, if an individual imagines lifting a weight, strong bursts of action potentials can be recorded from his arms even though the limbs are apparently quiescent. The extrinsic muscles of the eyes are especially rich sources of such potentials during periods of waking thought (22) and, even more dramatically, can be used as an objective index of dreaming (5).

Despite abundant confirmation that peripheral mechanisms are involved in thinking, contemporary psychologists are inclined to take a middle ground on the centralist-peripheralist continuum, recognizing that both cortical and peripheral processes are involved in ideational activity. There is increasing evidence to show that consciousness, thinking, and muscular processes are complementary. Ideational activity often initiates muscular activity, but the relationship is reciprocal; and muscular contractions, by stimulating lower brain centers, indirectly affect the cortex. We are getting ahead of our story, however, and we must return to the teachings of the systematists, turning our attention to the contributions of the Gestalt school.

GESTALT PSYCHOLOGY AND THE THOUGHT PROCESSES

Generally speaking, the work of three Gestalt psychologists stands out in the area of thinking. We refer to Köhler's research on insight in chimpanzees, which we have already considered in Chapter 6; Wertheimer's experiments with children (42); and Duncker's modern classic on problem solving (6) carried out on University of Berlin college students. We shall examine both Wertheimer's and Duncker's research programs and their theoretical interpretations. The student may review for himself the account of Köhler's experiments on insight.

In introducing his experiments with young school children Wertheimer asserts that "productive thinking" is the exception rather than the rule. In large measure, he lays the blame for this unsatisfactory situation on the educational system, which, he believes, has been dominated by traditional logic and association theory. Traditional logic analyzes thinking in terms of formal definitions, propositions, inferences, and syllogistic reasoning. Since the days of Aristotle, the logicians have sought to ensure correct thinking by insisting on precise definitions, exact judgment, carefully formulated concepts, and the like. According to the logicians, the individual who is able to carry out the operations laid down by the science of logic *is* able to think correctly. But Wertheimer finds that in comparison with "real, sensible, and productive" thinking, the examples of traditional logic seem "barren, boring, empty, unproductive" (*42*, p. 10). Even more important, logical thinking does not guarantee either correct or productive thinking. One may be exact in his thinking if he follows logical procedures, but his thinking may nevertheless be senseless and sterile.

Similarly, from Wertheimer's point of view, traditional association theory leads to blind drill, chance discovery of the correct answers, and fixation of whatever is "reinforced" regardless of whether or not that something is meaningful and productive. The educational system operating under the philosophy of association theory, Wertheimer argues, is dedicated to the inculcation of rules and principles by rote memory, with the result that the pupil's thinking is rarely productive and more often a blind repetition of procedures dictated on a priori grounds by his teachers. When the child is subsequently confronted with a variation of a problem learned under this system of education, he is unable to solve it even though the same basic procedure applies.

To exemplify his argument, Wertheimer investigated the technique usually employed for teaching pupils how to find the area of a parallelogram. The procedure was as follows: (1) The teacher first reviewed the process for finding the area of a rectangle where area = altitude × base; (2) a parallelogram was then drawn on the blackboard such as that shown in Figure 10-2; (3) the pupils were next shown how to drop perpendicular lines, a–b and c–d, at the ends of the parallelogram, and extend the bottom

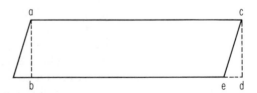

Fig. 10-2. From Wertheimer, *42*.

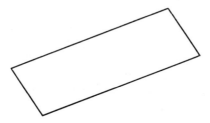

Fig. 10-3. From Wertheimer, *42*.

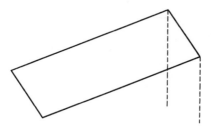

Fig. 10-4. From Wertheimer, *42*.

side d–e. They were then shown that the area is equal to the base times the altitude, since the parallelogram had been transformed into a rectangle.

Following a demonstration such as that outlined above, the pupils had no difficulty solving a variety of similar problems. But when confronted with the situation illustrated in Figure 10-3, many of the pupils either refused to attempt a solution or proceeded with logical but incorrect solutions such as those illustrated in Figure 10-4. A few rotated the figure to "normal" position and obtained the correct solution.

Going a step further, Wertheimer found that some children, after being instructed how to find the area of a parallelogram by the method outlined above, were able to find acceptable solutions for problems involving trape-zoids and similar figures such as those shown in Figure 10-5. In general, among children who attempted solutions, two types of responses were found which Wertheimer calls "A-responses" and "B-responses," respectively. In A-responses the children essentially shifted the triangles by proper use of auxiliary lines to arrive at a correct solution. In B-responses previously learned operations (dropping lines) are indiscriminately applied to arrive

A - responses:

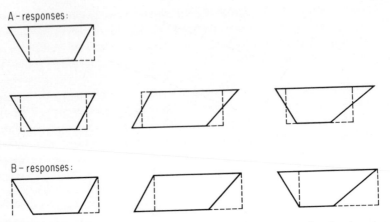

B - responses:

Fig. 10-5. Problems and solutions involving trapezoidal figures. In the A-responses the subjects change the figures into rectangles by shifting the triangles. In B-responses previously learned operations are applied indiscriminately. (From Wertheimer, *42*.)

at incorrect solutions. These are illustrated in Figure 10-5. On the other hand, some children refused to attempt solutions, asserting that they had never been instructed in the proper procedure for solving such problems.

Finally, Wertheimer presented other types of geometric figures in which "A-solutions" were possible by drawing auxiliary lines, and others in which A-solutions were not possible. See Figure 10-6. In the A-figures the child must realize that when lines are dropped to make rectilinear forms, the "remainders" do not matter since they are equal in area to the indentations. No such solution is, of course, possible with the B figures. Nevertheless, Wertheimer found that some children attempted to apply (indiscriminately) A-solutions to B-type problems.

Wertheimer is convinced that children do not necessarily approach geometric problems such as those we have illustrated in a blind, inappropriate manner, but have become victims of a pedagogic tradition which relies on a teacher-taught "correct" procedure which does not offer any real insight into the problem. Wertheimer adds that the validity of his interpretation is supported by the results of studies where pupils who had been instructed in the traditional manner were asked for proof of their solutions. The children, he found, were either dumfounded or attempted to "prove" the solution in terms of specific measurements for a particular case. What is lacking in such instances, Wertheimer continues, is a knowledge of the *inner relationships between the size of the area and the form of the figure.* He exemplifies his argument with a simple rectangle which is subdivided into little squares. See Figure 10-7. The squares are immediately organizable into an integrated whole. The solution then becomes meaningful in terms of the relations between area and form. The thinker perceives that the total area is equal to the total number of smaller squares, which can readily be obtained by multiplication.

For the application of the "squares-solution" to trapezoids, the figures must be restructured in such a way as to produce a "better figure," that is, a rectangle. Wertheimer found that children who had never been given formal training in geometry (and adults who had forgotten theirs), when shown how to obtain the area of a rectangle by the squares method, arrived at solutions to parallelograms and trapezoids with little or no assistance. "Some children reached the solution with little or no help in a genuine, sensible, direct way. Sometimes, after strained concentration, a face brightened at the critical moment. It is wonderful to observe the beautiful transformation from blindness to seeing the point!" (*42*, p. 48).

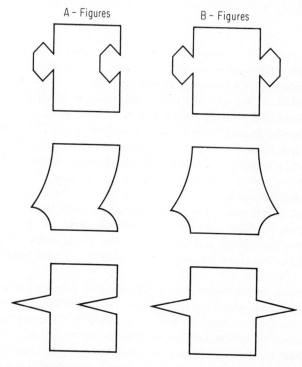

Fig. 10-6. Examples of figures in which A-solutions cannot be applied to B-figures. Some children saw no difference between A- and B-figures, attempting to apply the same solution to both.

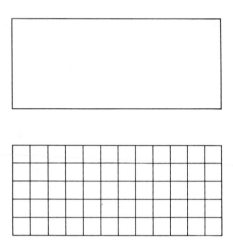

Fig. 10-7. From Wertheimer, *42*.

Wertheimer cites dozens of interesting examples of solutions of geometric problems by children—some as young as five years—all of which showed structural changes involving transformations of the figure. Moreover, he studied the thought processes involved in other types of problems such as proving the equality of the angles formed by the intersection of straight lines (see Figure 10-8); how to solve the series $1 + 2 + 3 + 4 + 5 \ldots n$ quickly and without adding the entire series; and finding the sum of angles of a polygon. In each case, he analyzed the types of solutions employed by his subjects in terms of the productiveness and insightfulness of the thinking involved.

Professor Wertheimer also devotes a chapter in his book to an account of the thought processes utilized by Albert Einstein, the great physicist, in developing his limited and general theories of relativity. The account is of special interest, since it is based on a series of personal interviews with Einstein.

As a result of his investigations, Wertheimer formulated a theory of productive thinking which constitutes the concluding chapter in his book. He begins by summarizing his general findings on the various types of problems which he utilized in his investigations (*42*, pp. 189–190). First he found that the individuals studied showed many instances of "genuine fine, clean, direct productive processes—better than some might have expected." Wertheimer is convinced that productive thinking is the natural way to think but is often absent because of blind habits, bias, and school drill.

Second, his subjects employed processes such as "grouping," "centering," and "reorganization" that had not been recognized by logicians and associationists in their analyses of the thought processes. Third, productive solutions were not perceived piecemeal but were related to "whole characteristics." This was true even though some operations favoring the traditional analyses were found; they, too, were utilized in a functional relationship to the whole characteristics of the problem.

Finally, and perhaps most importantly, productive solutions showed a "structural truth." They did not partake of "cheap plausibility," but were honest and sincere attempts to verify or prove the solutions utilized in solving problems. Moreover, Wertheimer strongly emphasizes that thinking cannot be conceived of as a purely intellectual operation, but rather as a process in which attitudes, feelings, and emotions also play a significant role. There must be a willingness to adopt an honest and sincere attitude that takes cognizance of the demands of the situation rather than a blind, egocentric view (43, p. 179).

On the basis of his findings, Wertheimer is convinced that productive thinking involves a grasp of the inner structural relationships of the problem followed by grouping the parts of the problem into a dynamic whole; any "gaps" or "disturbances" must be understood and dealt with in terms of the structural unity of the problems as a whole. The thinker must realize the difference between peripheral and fundamental aspects of the problem, and group each in a structural hierarchy.

Wertheimer is fully aware of the inherent difficulty and lack of definity in his terminology, but points out that his research was undertaken more in the expectation of exposing problems for further research than for providing answers to already formulated hypotheses. In fact, he had hoped to publish two additional volumes on thinking, but his goal was never realized.[10] We shall conclude our discussion of Wertheimer's work by sum-

Fig. 10-8. From Wertheimer, 42.

[10] *Productive Thinking* was published posthumously. An expanded edition (43) including other types of problems illustrative of Wertheimer's research and theoretical interpretations was published by his son, Michael Wertheimer, in 1959.

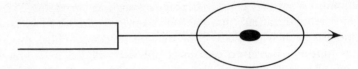

Fig. 10-9. A schematic representation of Duncker's tumor problem. The ellipse represents a cross section of the diseased area with the tumor in the middle. If the body is rotated, the radiation will be maximal in the center and minimal on the periphery. (From Duncker, *6*.)

marizing his suggestions for further research. In general, he believed that further study should follow three leads provided by his preliminary work:

1. The study of the laws governing segregation, grouping, centering, and transposibility in problem solving
2. The relations of parts to wholes
3. The nature of what constitutes good Gestalten

Now let us concern ourselves with Karl Duncker's studies of problem solving, which were highly similar to Wertheimer's, both in terms of experimental design and theoretical interpretation of the results. He worked with college students rather than with elementary school children and employed more "practical" problems as compared to Wertheimer's abstract geometric problems. Duncker's overall aim, however, was quite similar to Wertheimer's in that he sought to reveal the essential nature of the thought processes.

Duncker's most thoroughly investigated problem was the following: Given an inoperable stomach tumor and rays which at high intensity will destroy tissue (both healthy and diseased), how can the tumor be destroyed without damaging surrounding tissue? Typically, the subjects were also shown a schematic sketch of the problem while it was being presented verbally. Duncker's drawing is reproduced in Figure 10-9.

The following experimental protocol is quoted from Duncker's monograph to illustrate a subject's thought process in arriving at a solution.

Protocol

1. Send rays through the esophagus.
2. Desensitize the healthy tissues by means of a chemical injection.
3. Expose the tumor by operating.
4. One ought to decrease the intensity of the rays on their way; for example would this work?—turn the rays on at full strength only after the tumor has been reached. (Experimenter: False analogy; no injection is in question.)

5. One should swallow something inorganic (which would not allow passage of the rays) to protect the healthy stomach-walls. (E: It is not merely the stomach-walls which are to be protected.)
6. Either the rays must enter the body or the tumor must come out. Perhaps one could alter the location of the tumor—but how? Through pressure? No.
7. Introduce a cannula.—(E: What, in general, does one do when, with any agent, one wishes to produce in a specific place an effect which he wishes to avoid on the way to that place?)
8. (Reply:) One neutralises the effect on the way. But that is what I have been attempting all the time.
9. Move the tumor toward the exterior. (Compare 6.) (The E repeats the problem and emphasizes, ". . . which destroy *at sufficient intensity*.")
10. The intensity ought to be variable. (Compare 4.)
11. Adaptation of the healthy tissues by previous weak application of the rays. (E: How can it be brought about that the rays destroy only the region of the tumor?)
12. (Reply:) I see no more than two possibilities: either to protect the body or to make the rays harmless. (E: How could one decrease the intensity of the rays en route?) (Compare 4.)
13. (Reply:) Somehow divert . . . diffuse rays . . . disperse . . . stop! Send a broad and weak bundle of rays through a lens in such a way that the tumor lies at the focal point and thus receives intensive radiation. (Total duration about half an hour.)

Duncker analyzed the protocols obtained from his subjects according to certain stages revealed by the subject's reactions. First, there is the discovery of the "general or essential properties of a solution." Using the protocol quoted above as an example, when the subject begins thinking about the problem, he suggests sending the rays through the esophagus, desensitizing healthy tissue or lowering the intensity of the rays on their way to the tumor. (See Figure 10-9.) None of these solutions is practical, but they nevertheless reveal a general grasp of the problem and a reformulation of it in a goal-oriented direction. To borrow Wertheimer's terminology, the problem is being "restructured" by the subject.

Upon being advised of the impracticality of his first general proposals, the subject continues to formulate solutions which are still broad but which are more truly *solutions* as opposed to mere reformulations of the problems. These solutions Duncker groups under the heading of solutions with "functional value." (See Figure 10-10.) Out of functional solutions the subject develops specific solutions, one of which is acceptable—focusing the rays by means of a lens.[11]

---

[11] The idea is only correct in principle. X-rays are not deflected by a lens. In medical practice, several weak rays coming from different directions are made to focus on the tumor, or the subject rotated to minimize the exposure of healthy tissue and maximize the exposure of malignant tissue.

Of course, not every student-subject clearly showed all three stages during the course of problem solving, nor did each come up with the same functional and specific solutions. But Duncker argues that however primitive the solutions offered, they were not describable "in terms of meaningless, blind, trial-and-error reactions" (6, p. 2). A little further on (6, p. 9) he emphasizes that *"what is really done in any solution of problems consists in formulating the problem more productively. . . . The final form of a solution is typically attained by way of mediating phases of the process, of which each one, in retrospect possesses the character of a solution, and, in prospect, that of a problem."*[12] Put somewhat more simply, problem solving consists of hierarchically related stages of organization of the problem, starting with general solution-oriented reformulations of the problem to increasingly more specific solutions. Because each stage is related to those that have gone before, as well as to those that lie ahead, the process is a dynamic whole rather than a blind, trial-and-error affair.

Duncker went on to investigate mathematical problem solving, insight learning, and the process of transfer of solutions to new problems. Even a summary of Duncker's complete experimental program is far beyond the scope of a single chapter. However, because of its intrinsic interest and importance in thinking, we shall include a brief description of his concept of "functional fixedness" in problem solving. Functional fixedness is illustrated on a simple level by the ape who, after mastering a banana-stick problem cannot solve the problem in the absence of a stick because he fails to perceive that he can break off a small branch from a nearby tree. The animal has become "fixated," so to speak, on unattached sticks and is blind to the possibilities of utilizing other sticks which may be available.

On the human level, the same phenomenon has been investigated in *"Einstellung"* (set) experiments, wherein the subject is shown how to do a series of problems, all of which involve a certain fixed series of stages. If similar problems are introduced where the correct solution *cannot* be attained by the now familiar approach, subjects tend to continue to use the inappropriate method because of the strong set built up by the initial series of successful solutions. For example, Duncker requested his subjects to suspend several cords from a wooden shelf for "perceptual experiments." On a table were screw hooks, the cords, and a gimlet. The subjects readily used the gimlet to bore holes for starting the screw hooks but found there were one too few hooks to hang the required number of cords. They failed to perceive that the gimlet could be employed as a support after it had been used to start the holes for the screw hooks. The subjects' set toward the gimlet was as a tool and not as a support, even though nothing in the instructions prevented the latter use. In Duncker's terms, the subjects

[12] Italics in original.

search for an additional screw hook was "unprägnant," because restructuring of the problem failed to occur as a result of fixation.

Summary and evaluation. The experimental programs and theoretical interpretations offered by Köhler, Wertheimer, Duncker[13] and other Gestalt-oriented psychologists, have strongly emphasized the *perceptual* nature of problem solving. The problems employed have typically called for creative or reasoned solutions as opposed to "trial-and-error" solutions. Therefore, to some extent, their interpretations in terms of Gestalt prin-ciples have been favored by the Gestalt-like nature of the problems chosen, just as a "reinforcement" interpretation of animal learning experiments is favored if the initial design and conditions of the experiment preclude the possibility of insightful solutions. Because we have tried to follow closely Wertheimer's and Duncker's rather difficult original wording and inter-pretation, we shall conclude this section by attempting to bring together the essence of the Gestalt viewpoint in a highly summarized and simplified set of principles which we hope will clarify the Gestalt position without doing violence to the spirit of the original.

I. *Productive or creative thinking occurs when the organism is confronted with a problem that cannot be resolved by habitual means.* Köhler's and Duncker's problems are excellent illustrations of this principle. Apes do not habitually obtain their food by the aid of tools, nor do college students treat tumorous patients. Both are "original" problems, and both lend themselves to "thoughtful" solutions, in the sense that all elements of the problem are in the subject's perceptual field.

II. *Thinking takes the form of a perceptual reorganization of the problem in a series of hierarchically related solutions which tend to become increasingly more specific.* Both Wertheimer's and Duncker's protocols revealed such stepwise trans-formations in the subject's thought processes. It is impossible to know whether Köhler's apes were engaged in hierarchical thinking because, of course, it was not possible to obtain verbal reports from the animals.

III. *Perceptual reorganization during thinking tends in the direction of "centering" and "focusing," of "filling gaps," and seeking better Gestalten.* Köhler's apes, Wert-eimer's children, and Duncker's college students all demonstrated behavior which suggested increased focusing on the "missing parts" of the problem. The apes had to perceive the boxes as filling the gap between the floor and the banana before they were able to "solve" the problem. This the animals perceived early in the experiment, as revealed by their dragging the boxes under the fruit. However, the more difficult problem of statics (box stacking) remained to be solved. In his studies of human thinking,

N. R. F. Maier, an American psychologist, has conducted a number of similar experiments on reasoning in both animals and human subjects. His results and interpretations are entirely con-gruent with Wertheimer's and Duncker's.

Wertheimer found that his pupils often referred to something "missing" or something "messy" on the ends of parallelograms and trapezoids. A similar process occurred in Duncker's students, who often realized "something was needed" to protect healthy tissue even though they could not yet suggest just what.

IV. *The readiness with which the solution is found is related to the fixity of the perceptual field, motivational factors, and the subject's previous training.* Here we must rely mainly on Wertheimer's work with the children who had been given rigid, formal training in geometric problems. They experienced more difficulty in the solution of parallelograms than did naïve subjects. However, Duncker's studies of fixedness are also pertinent, since subjects with the incorrect "set" had difficulty with experimental problems.

V. *The final solution tends to occur as a sudden reorganization or transformation of the perceptual field.* "Suddenness" is, of course, a byword in Gestalt interpretations of problem solving. Once again we must emphasize that suddenness is not to be confused with rapidity. Some of Duncker's subjects required over thirty minutes for the solution of the tumor problem. What is meant is that the subject's reorganization of the perceptual field is stepwise; he "jumps" from one possible solution to another.

VI. *A high degree of transfer to similar problems may be expected if the subject is allowed to work out his own solutions to cognitive problems.* Both Köhler's apes and Wertheimer's subjects demonstrated high transfer provided they achieved insightful solutions. Such solutions depended, in turn, upon grasping the principle of the problem. Though not discussed in this chapter, Duncker's results on transfer are consistent with the work of other Gestalt psychologists.

PIAGET AND THE DEVELOPMENT OF UNDERSTANDING IN THE CHILD

Jean Piaget is a "school" unto himself. For many years he has been associated with the University of Geneva where he has carried out elaborate investigations on the development of the child's understanding of the physical and social environments. The results of this research and his challenging theoretical interpretations have appeared in nearly a dozen books since 1926. In addition, he has contributed a large number of articles to French technical journals. These publications range over such varied subjects as the development of language, judgment, intelligence, play, number concepts, and the appreciation of reality in the child. In recent years Piaget has extended his work into the experimental areas of perception and thinking in order to search out the more fundamental processes which underlie his descriptive categories and modes of thinking.

While Piaget stands aside from the traditional British-German-American schools of psychology, his work has made itself felt throughout the psychological world and has stimulated a considerable amount of research. Consequently, we have decided to include it here. We should also point out that both his results and theoretical interpretations are considered highly controversial. We shall make no attempt to review the extensive literature bearing on the controversy.[14] We might also note that the best original introductions to Piaget are his *Child's Conception of the World* (*30*) and *The Child's Conception of Physical Causality* (*32*). The present account has been drawn largely from these sources.

In his investigations of children's conceptions of the world, Piaget employed three general but not entirely independent methods. First, he followed the purely verbal procedure of asking the child questions about his relations to other people, to environmental objects and to natural phenomena; in the same category were questions designed to test the child's understanding of physical causality. For example, the child might be asked, "Where does the wind come from?" "What makes you dream?" "Is the air outside alive?" The second method was half verbal and half concrete. Concrete descriptions of natural phenomena were presented to the child orally, who was then asked questions designed to test his understanding of the phenomena in question. The third method was primarily concrete. Piaget and his associates arranged miniature experiments designed in such a way as to demonstrate fundamental physical relationships. For example, children were shown a toy engine run by steam generated by means of a small alcohol lamp. Water was placed in the boiler and the fire was lighted in the child's presence. When sufficient steam had been generated, a small piston caused a flywheel to rotate rapidly. The fire was then extinguished, and the flywheel gradually stopped. The child was then asked to explain the energy transformations involved.

The children tested by the several techniques just enumerated were of various ages from three to fourteen but mainly were in the age range from three to eleven. All subjects were either French-speaking Swiss children or French boys and girls. Since we are considering both the child's conception of reality and his conception of physical causality, we shall summarize Piaget's findings on these closely related processes separately.

The child's conception of reality.[15] Piaget found that the content of the child's thought processes varies according to certain stages. Briefly, up to the third year of age, the child's thinking is characterized by *autism*. Indeed,

[14] In Jersild (*25*) references appear throughout Chapters 13 and 14. Those who wish to pursue the literature in the area should consult the bibliographies in Thompson (*36*, pp. 234–238), in Jersild (*25*) and Berlyne (*2*).

[15] The exposition follows Piaget (*32, 33*).

the very young fail to distinguish between the internal and external world
Thus, clouds move because "We make them move by walking." Up t
seven or eight years of age the child's thinking is *egocentric* and characterize
by *animism*. Everything is alive for the child, and he believes that clou
and heavenly bodies move of their own volition, following people as the
walk. Beyond seven and eight, the child's thinking evolves into a stag
characterized by *mechanical causation* and *logical deduction*. External and ii
ternal processes are well differentiated. In short, the child has overcom
his egocentricity.

More specifically, Piaget believes that three complementary process
are at work in the evolution of the child's thought between the ages of thre
and eleven. First, thought moves from *realism* to *objectivity;* second, fror
realism to *reciprocity;* and third, from *realism* to *relativity*. The processes ar
simultaneous, and the stages overlap. By the evolution from realism to ot
jectivity, Piaget means that the child at first fails to differentiate betwee
the self and the external world. During the early years he "thinks with h
mouth," believes that his words are part of external things, and identifi
his breath with the wind. Moreover, the names of objects are confused wit
objects themselves. Dreams are believed to be actual events going on befor
the child which could be seen by anyone else who might be in the roon
It is only ". . . through a progressive differentiation that the internal worl
comes into being and is contrasted with the external" (*32*, p. 243).

In part, Piaget's evidence for the child's failure to differentiate the se
from external reality comes from his investigations of children's languag
(*29*). He found over one-third of the children's speech was egocentric i
content at three years of age, with decreasing percentages at older age
Thus, as measured by the frequency of occurrence of personal pronour
and references to self, the younger child is the more egocentric. Howeve
Piaget's generalization has been widely criticized by American psycho
ogists who have failed to duplicate his results on the language studies. O
the other hand, Piaget's questionnaire and experimental studies have nc
been seriously challenged, and, on the whole, the evidence supports h
contention of self-referent realism as the first stage in the evolution of th
child's thought processes.

The transition from realism to reciprocity is marked by a transforma
tion in the child's thinking, away from a point of view in which the se
is absolute, to one in which other points of view are possible. The nine-yea
old child has discovered that the sun follows everybody and not him alon
At this stage the child regards his dreams as true inner manifestations c
the self and no longer believes the same dream is experienced by everyon
as if it were out there in objective reality. Balloons do not ascend "becaus
they want to fly" but "because they are light."

The transition from realism to reciprocity blends into the transitio from realism to relativity in which absolutes in thinking are dropped in favor of relative standards. Boats are no longer heavy and pebbles light; instead, their weight depends on the surrounding medium. A boat on land is heavy and in the water is light, whereas a pebble on land is light and in the water is heavy. Thus, in the third stage, beyond seven or eight years, the child's perception of the world is rapidly taking on the characteristics of the adult mode of thought.

The child's conception of causality.   According to Piaget, the development of the child's conceptions of causality follows much the same pattern as his conceptions of reality. However, Piaget's analysis of the various types of causal relationships in children's thinking is much more complex in that he distinguishes seventeen types of causal relations in children's thinking. We need not examine each of these types in detail since many are so closely related that the seventeen can be grouped into three main functional categories according to the ages at which they occur:

1. Psychological, realistic, and magical: ages one to six
2. Artificial, animistic, dynamic: ages six to nine
3. The more rational types: ages ten to seventeen

Psychological, realistic, and magical thinking refers to strongly egocentric modes of thought. The child may explain the motion of clouds by saying that they move because we are bad (motivational). Or he may explain cloud movement on the basis of his own motion (realism), or again that perhaps the clouds move because he wants them to (magical).

In artificial, animistic, and dynamic types of thinking, the child may attribute life to inanimate objects (animism), or he may give dynamic force to objects without attributing life to them (the rock flies through the sky by iself). And, in artificial thinking, he may explain natural events in terms of attributing desire to physical objects (the clouds move because they want to).

In rational types of thinking the child gives logical, adultlike explanations based on empirical observation or knowledge gained from books.

More recently (34) Piaget has cast his theoretical explanations of children's thinking into a developmental form involving several age periods ranging from preconceptual stages to sophisticated, operational stages of thinking characteristic of adolescents and adults. In the first stage, which lasts from birth to two, there are no concepts or true representative processes. This stage Piaget calls the sensory-motor stage. The child is learning the bare rudiments of space and time in reference to his own bodily reactions in the environment. The sensory-motor stage is succeeded by the period of pre-conceptual thought, which lasts until approximately four.

During the period of pre-conceptual thought the child cannot gene
alize meanings; nor can he think either inductively or deductively. Hi
thinking is transducive or simply specific from one experience to anothe
He may, for example, have a kind of proto-concept of *cat* from his experi
ence with the family cat but not a true generalized idea of "catness" suc
as that possessed by a high school student. For this reason many youn
children mistake similar animals (skunks, porcupines, and the like) fo
cats—sometimes to their considerable embarrassment and dismay.

From four to seven the child enters a period of intuitive thought i
which he can reason, but only on a limited basis. At this stage of develop
ment he is still dominated by perceptions and so comes to erroneous con
clusions if given abstract problems. For example, if he watches th
experimenter pour beads from one glass into a taller and thinner glas
he is likely upon being questioned to say that there are now more bead
in the second glass than there were in the first because the level is highe
or that there are fewer because the second glass is narrower.

From seven to eleven years of age he enters the stage where he i
acquiring a set of operational concepts which are organized into system
of thought. This process, if developed more formally, starts about age twelv
and becomes the kind of thinking which is characteristic of the adult.

It must be emphasized that not all psychologists are in agreement wit
Piaget's analysis of the child's conception of physical causality. Attempt
to repeat his studies with American children have been inconclusive. Som
investigators have found similar stages in the children studied; others hav
failed to confirm Piaget's findings. Some have even found evidence of ani
mistic thinking in adults. It has been suggested that cultural and educa
tional differences between European and American children may, in par
account for the differences.[16] Whatever the final outcome of research o
the development of understanding in the child, Piaget's studies are un
excelled for the richness and spontaneity of children's verbalizations of thei
own experiences and attempts to understand the world around them.

Finally, we might note that Piaget believes that the study of the devel
opment of understanding in the child leads directly to the problem of th
evolution of human knowledge in general. In his own words,

> it may very well be that the psychological laws arrived at by means of our re
> stricted method can be extended into epistemological laws arrived at by th
> analysis of the history of the sciences: the elimination of realism, of substantial
> ism, of dynamism, the growth of relativism, etc., all are evolutionary laws whic
> appear to be common both to the development of the child and to that of scien
> tific thought (*32*, p. 240).

While the argument presented in the preceding quotation is, at this stag

[16] See *2*, *25*, and *36*.

of psychological knowledge, no more than an interesting parallel, *any* promising approach to the all-important goal of the better understanding of human thought processes is to be encouraged.

CURRENT TRENDS IN THE PSYCHOLOGY OF THINKING

At the present writing it is impossible to discern any overall trends in contemporary systematic developments in the area of thinking. There is no dearth of research in the field, as well as in related fields, such as linguistic behavior and learning. There are, however, no distinct miniature systems in the area of thinking, such as we found to be true of perception and learning. Rather, the overall approach in recent years has been an empirical one in which various matters of interest relative to the thought processes have been investigated without regard to elaborate theoretical considerations or systematic biases. We shall conclude our discussion of thinking by outlining what seem to us to be the three major research areas of greatest concern to American psychologists, from which miniature systems are most likely to develop. These are: (1) studies of abstracting ability and representative factors in thinking, (2) studies of concept formation, and (3) studies of creative thinking.

Studies of abstraction and representative factors. Studies of abstraction and representative factors are best exemplified by the work of Goldstein and his associates on human patients with brain injuries and by the research of various physiologists and physiological psychologists on animals. We shall briefly outline the general findings in these areas.

Goldstein's work spans the period from the end of World War I to the present.[17] He became interested in the conceptual abilities of soldiers suffering from brain injuries (especially injuries in the frontal lobes) during the first World War. Such patients, he found, were unable to think in abstract terms. For example, when asked to classify skeins of wool of assorted hues into appropriate *classes* of colors, they were unable to do so. Obvious greens or reds could be grouped correctly by such patients, but they were unable to deal with hues that deviated markedly from the standard.

By way of interpretation, Goldstein postulated two levels of conceptual ability, *concrete* and *abstract*. The concrete functions are not seriously impaired in brain-injured patients, but abstracting ability is either deficient or absent. The greatest impairment to abstracting ability occurs in cases of injury to the frontal lobes.

[17] See *9* and *10*.

In 1941, Goldstein and Scheerer (*10*) reported a further series of studies of hospital patients with brain injuries in the frontal regions. The studies in question involved the administration of various tests of abstracting ability to the patients. Some of the tests were standardized by Goldstein and his associates for clinical use. Descriptions of these may be found in the Goldstein-Scheerer monograph referred to above. Others were simple qualitative tests improvised by the investigators. Because of space limitations, we cannot undertake an analysis of Goldstein and Scheerer's results with standard tests; however, a brief summary of the more informal tests and results with them will convey the flavor of this interesting approach to the study of human thought processes.

Goldstein and Scheerer discuss eight general behavioral modes which test the individual's ability to abstract. First, the normal individual is able to detach his ego from the outer or inner worlds of experience; the brain-injured cannot. One patient, for example, when asked to repeat the sentence, "The snow is black," refused to do so on the grounds that it was contrary to his knowledge. Another patient, when requested to take a comb from the table and bring it to the examiner, could not do so without combing her hair. Thus, one price the patient pays for brain injury is the inability to detach himself from concrete experience or situations.

Second, brain-injured patients cannot assume a certain mental set. For example, the patient is unable to set the hands of a clock to a certain hour. Similar actions cannot be initiated by the patient even though he is able to carry them out if prompted by the experimenter.

Third, the patient may be unable to account for spatial relationships. Even though the patient is able to indicate where a noise originates, by pointing to the source, he cannot *verbally* state the direction of origin. The verbalization of abstract space is beyond his ability even though the more concrete ability involved in pointing out spatial directions has not suffered as a result of the injury.

Fourth, the brain-injured may be unable to shift a mental set from one aspect of a task to another. When asked to recite the alphabet, he is unable to follow the recitation by giving the days of the week. Similarly, if shown an ambiguous figure containing two faces, the brain-injured will see only one of the faces. Stated in terms of the normal individual, the average person can readily shift his set from one activity to another. The brain-injured patient's concrete orientation makes him rigid in his behavior.

Fifth, the patient whose abstracting ability is impaired is unable to keep two tasks in mind simultaneously. For example, he can respond correctly to one light in a reaction-time test, but when instructed to respond to one of several lights presented in irregular order the patient begins to react to all lights indiscriminately.

Sixth, the patient cannot synthesize parts into an integrated whole.

He may be unable to work jigsaw puzzles or put together performance tests. The formation of wholes from parts requires a perception of the whole into which the parts must be fitted. Since, at the beginning of the test, the whole is an abstraction, the patient cannot visualize it.

Seventh, the brain-injured cannot abstract out the common properties embedded in a variety of test situations. When requested to find the common denominator of a set of fractions, the patient is unable to do so. For the same reason, such individuals have difficulty with reasoning problems in general.

Finally, the patient is unable to plan ahead. He cannot draw a map of his way home from the hospital, and on the ball-and-field test in the Binet Scale, cannot make an intelligent plan of search.

While the descriptions given above are stated in more or less absolute terms, it must be recognized that brain-injured patients show various degrees of inability depending upon their original capacities, the site and extent of their lesions, and so on. However, Goldstein and Scheerer emphasize that abstraction is *not* merely a higher degree of concrete ability; nor is it a synthesis or compounding of a number of lower order functions. Rather, they believe that abstract thinking is a recent evolutionary type of ideational activity which is qualitatively different from the phylogenetically older concrete ability. According to these writers, the paramount factor in abstract thinking is *conscious will*. In other words, the individual must consciously reflect, judge, and look ahead before his thinking can qualify as abstract.

Goldstein's work on human subjects has been paralleled by animal research directed toward discovering the symbolic processes or representative factors which mediate thought. The investigations which are most closely related to Goldstein's studies are experiments on the memory trace in monkeys. These experiments originated out of the finding that animals have the ability to make delayed reactions. For example, a normal monkey can be shown where a reward is hidden under one of two cups which are placed some distance apart and in front of the animal. Even though the monkey is forced to delay up to thirty seconds, he can still go to the correct cup. But Jacobsen (*17, 18*) found that monkeys with bilateral lesions in the frontal lobes were unable to delay more than a few seconds, if at all.

Jacobsen believed his animals had suffered an amnesia of the "representative factor" by means of which they remembered the cues utilized in finding the reward. However, a number of investigators have challenged Jacobsen's interpretation on the basis of their own investigations of brain-injured animals. Finan (*7*), for example, gave prefrontal monkeys "predelay reinforcement" which took the form of allowing the animals a bit of food on the correct side just before the delay period. Despite their lesions, the reinforced animals could delay successfully. Finan's results suggest that the basic loss in prefrontal animals is not one of memory but of attention. The prefrontal monkey is excitable, readily distracted, and it is possible that Jacobsen's animals were not sufficiently attentive to the experimenter's activities and as a consequence had no cues to remember. Additional evidence that the deficiency is in the area of attention comes from a number of studies in which prefrontal monkeys were given sedatives, kept in the dark during the delay, or otherwise rendered less distractable during the test situation (17, 26, 35, and 38). The general findings suggest that the disturbance is, indeed, in the process of attention.

If we stretch a point and look for the common factor running through studies of human and animal subjects whose frontal lobes have been injured, the general picture is a deficiency in the *planning, management,* and *control of behavior.* The human patient's lack of abstracting ability is, in part, the result of his inability to concentrate, keep a set, and maintain a consecutive series of activities without constant guidance from the physician. Thus, the frontal lobes exercise a restraining, guiding influence on other brain centers —especially emotional centers—as revealed by the personality changes accompanying prefrontal lobotomy in psychotics.

While both animal and human studies have led to an increased knowledge of the functions of the frontal lobes, no real theory of thinking has emerged from such investigations. Goldstein and Scheerer admit that their eight criteria of abstracting ability are descriptive rather than explanatory. Similarly, the animal studies tell us nothing about the nature of the representative factors that animals utilize in making delayed reactions. The nearest contribution to a theory of thinking that has emerged from research on brain functions in ideational activity is Goldstein's analysis of concrete and abstract levels of thought; and, here again, the categories are more descriptive than explanatory.

Concept formation.   Much the same can be said of contemporary studies of concept formation. Two representative studies will be cited to illustrate the experimental approach to the study of concept formation. The classic study of concept formation carried out by Hull in 1920 (15) laid the ground work for subsequent research; hence we shall outline his experiment first Hull presented his subjects with a series of twelve packs of cards. Each card carried a Chinese character, and one of the characters in each pack included a "concept" (see Figure 10-10). For example, the concept "oo" was represented by a checklike character as illustrated for each series in Figure 10–10 The subjects were practiced on a given series until they could give the correct concept. In a later part of the experiment (Series VI to XII), the subjects were tested for their ability to generalize the learned concepts, or in other words, recognize them in new situations.

Hull analyzed his results in terms of ordinary discrimination learning The subject, he argued, learns to discriminate the *common element* in th

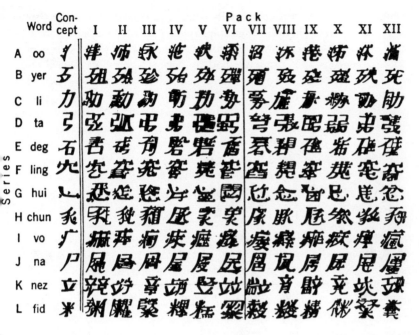

Fig. 10-10. Chinese characters used in studies of concept formation. For explanation see text. (From Hull, *15*.)

characters, and, on the basis of his experiences, can recognize and utilize similar elements when they appear in new settings. Thus, the child comes to appreciate the meaning of "round" from his experiences with apples, oranges, balls, beads, and similar objects, and is able to recognize roundness in unfamiliar situations. Obviously Hull's interpretation reduces concept formation to the principles of conditioned learning—reinforcement, generalization and selective discrimination.

In a recent and extensive series of studies, Heidbreder (*12* to *14*) investigated the formation of various *types* of concepts. Utilizing a series of drawings presented on a memory drum, Heidbreder instructed her subjects to anticipate nonsense names for the concepts embedded in the drawings. For example, when series I was presented, the subject watched as the experimenter pronounced the name of each figure (see Figure 10-11). On the next trial the subject tried to give the name associated with the picture and was prompted by the experimenter whenever necessary. In each series of sixteen figures, nine concepts were embedded. In series I, faces were always named "RELK," and buildings "LETH." After the subject had learned series I, he began with series II and so on, until all were learned. At some point during the experiment, the subject recognized concepts learned in previous series and began to anticipate all "faces" by responding with "RELK," all buildings by responding with "LETH," and the like.

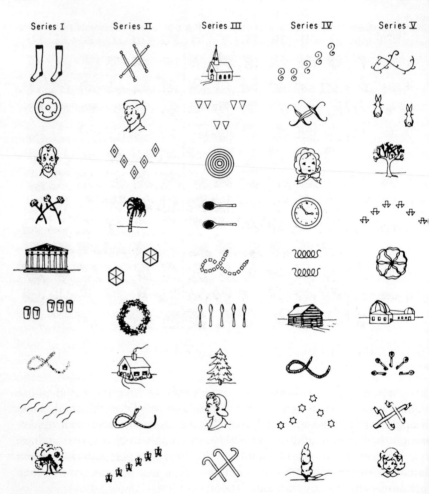

Fig. 10-11. Materials used by Heidbreder to study concept formation. For explanation see text. (From Heidbreder, *11.*)

Three general types of concepts occurred in Heidbreder's series: *concrete objects, spatial forms,* and *abstract numbers.* She found that concrete concepts are readily attained. Spatial forms are intermediate in difficulty and abstract numbers most difficult to learn. By way of interpretation, Heidbreder suggests that concrete forms are the concepts which are not only first experienced in childhood, but also those which occur most frequently in the everyday life of the adult. At first a ball is a concrete object to be manipulated by the child, and only secondarily to be thought of as round or something to be counted. Thus, there is an order of "dominance" in human thinking ranging from the concrete to the abstract, with the latter type requiring more than mere perception. The parallels between Heidbreder's hypothesis and Goldstein's analyses of thinking into concrete and abstract levels are obvious.

Finally, it must be emphasized that Hull and Heidbreder employed the *inductive* method of concept formation, in which many examples are presented from which the concept must be differentiated by the subject. In the *deductive* approach, a principle is given, and the subject must then develop examples from it. Clearly, in the history of human thought both types of concept formation have been utilized—often in mixed form—by original thinkers. This is especially true of the scientific mode of thought, which is always a mixture of inductive empiricism and deductive rationalism.

Creative thinking. Interest in creativity and creative thinking had its scientific origins in studies of individual differences in abilities and their genetic transmission. Sir Francis Galton (1822 to 1911), the great British scientist and cousin of Charles Darwin, published a series of studies on genius and creativity which have become classics. In *Hereditary Genius* (1869), he demonstrated by means of careful biographical and ancestral studies that genius tends to run in families. This work was followed by *English Men of Science* (1874) and by *Inquiries into Human Faculty and Its Development* (1883).

Galton's studies are not inquiries into the nature of creative thinking as such. Much the same can be said for James McKeen Cattell's famous study of eminent American scientists, which was stimulated by Galton's work. But these and similar biographical investigations reveal a deeply rooted interest in the kind of outstanding intellectual ability and other personal characteristics which are associated with creative thinking.

More direct attempts to get at the processes involved in creative thinking originated in anecdotal accounts of original thinking provided by such outstanding men as Helmholtz and the brilliant French mathematician Poincaré. Both stressed the sudden, seemingly "inspired" nature of many of their solutions to difficult problems—inspirations which came only after arduous preparation followed by several unsuccessful attempts to solve the problem by more or less habitual means. These impressionistic reports were supplemented during the 1930's by questionnaires sent to eminent scientists asking for descriptions of their methods of work. Earlier (1926) Graham Wallas (*39*) had formalized the results of some of the early studies into a four-stage theory of creative thinking which held that periods of preparation, incubation, illumination, and verification were characteristic of creative thinking.

In preparation, the thinker "loads up" on all relevant information that is pertinent to his problem and may attempt tentative solutions. If an immediate solution is not forthcoming, a period of incubation follows during which the thinker makes no deliberate efforts to solve the problem, having temporarily "given up." But, according to Wallas, "unconscious cerebration" is nevertheless going on, leading to a sudden illumination which often occurs at unexpected times and places. This "Eureka experience" must of course, be followed by an attempt to verify its validity by observation or experimentation.

In an attempt to subject Wallas' four stages to an experimental test Patrick (27, 28) had poets and painters come to the laboratory where they were assigned a creative task which was carried out during a living-in period in the laboratory. They were asked to write impressionistic reports of their mental processes during the creative activities, and these, upon analysis, supported Wallas' theory, particularly the interesting hypothesis that incubation or unconscious cerebration occurs during creative thinking About three-fourths of the subjects testified to experiencing incubation periods followed by sudden and unexpected illuminations. However, Patrick found that many admitted that the incubation period was by no means free of thinking. The problem recurred from time to time with tentative stabs at a solution. It has also been pointed out that many people experience a change of perspective on a problem after a period of no active work This change may lead to a sudden solution. The combined effect of these factors of rehearsal and change of perspective leading to the solution appears less mysterious than "unconscious cerebration." However, no one has disproved the possibility that the latter process may go on as well.

More recently the study of creativity has once more returned to the approach pioneered by Galton and Cattell—that is, through a study of individual differences. However, the work to which we have reference involves large-scale analysis of the intellectual and personal characteristics of creative persons who were studied directly. Our summary is based on a report of a team project by Barron (1) which was carried out at the University of California at Berkeley and which was still underway at the time of publication and may be expected to continue for some years.

In this multifaceted approach under the leadership of Donald W MacKinnon and Frank Barron, measurements of the personal and intellectual traits of outstanding architects, research scientists, writers, engineers and mathematicians were carried out using a variety of tests and rating scales.

In one set of studies the method of "living-in assessment" was employed. An assessment typically involved a Friday to Sunday weekend in which the research staff and the subjects being evaluated actually lived together in a former fraternity house near the Berkeley campus. Meals were taken together, and every effort was made to create a friendly atmosphere in order to make the situation as natural as possible. At the end of an assessment session each member of the staff wrote down his impressions of each subject, utilizing several check lists to aid in completeness and objectivity. In other sessions scientists and creative writers took a variety of standardized tests designed to measure personality traits and intellectual abilities. For a complete description of the method, tests, and results the reader is referred to Barron's article (*1*). Here we shall attempt to give only a sample of the extensive results obtained thus far.

We may begin with a summary of Q-sort items[18] which were found to be correlated with creativity. As Table 10-1 shows, creativity is positively correlated with such traits as unconventionality of thought and behavior, a positive evaluation of intellectual values, high intellectual capacity and is negatively correlated with dependability, sympathy, and conventional morality. Table 10-2 also shows some of the composite Q-sort descriptions

Table 10-1.
Clinical Q-sort Items Correlated with Creativity

r WITH CREATIVITY RATING	Q-SORT ITEM
Positive correlations:	
0.64	Thinks and associates to ideas in unusual ways; has unconventional thought processes.
0.55	Is an interesting, arresting person.
0.51	Tends to be rebellious and nonconforming.
0.49	Genuinely values intellectual and cognitive matters.
0.46	Appears to have a high degree of intellectual capacity.
0.42	Is self-dramatizing; histrionic.
0.40	Has fluctuating moods.
Negative correlations:	
−0.62	Judges self and others in conventional terms like "popularity," the "correct thing to do," "social pressures," and so forth.
−0.45	Is a genuinely dependable and responsible person.
−0.43	Behaves in a sympathetic or considerate manner.
−0.40	Favors conservative values in a variety of areas.
−0.40	Is moralistic.

[18] As used in this study the Q-sort technique refers to a personality assessment in which raters sort a number of statements into piles representing the degree to which the statements apply to the subjects. Each statement can then be given a score representing the degree of strength to which a given subject possesses traits. The Q-sort is also widely used as a technique for having subjects judge their own traits.

Table 10-2.
Composite Staff Q-sort Description of Creative Writers

9's

Appears to have a high degree of intellectual capacity.
Genuinely values intellectual and cognitive matters.
Values own independence and autonomy.
Is verbally fluent; can express ideas well.
Enjoys esthetic impressions; is esthetically reactive.

8's

Is productive; gets things done.
Is concerned with philosophical problems; for example, religion, values, the meaning of life, and so forth.
Has high aspiration level for self.
Has a wide range of interests.
Thinks and associates to ideas in unusual ways; has unconventional thought processes.
Is an interesting, arresting person.
Appears straightforward, forthright, candid in dealings with others.
Behaves in an ethically consistent manner; is consistent with own personal standards.

for the two highest categories (8 and 9 on a nine-point scale) which are associated with creative writers, again revealing such traits as high intellectual capacity, independence, and fluency in thinking and expression, and high esthetic reactivity. A similar profile was obtained with creative architects, although the latter are more socially conventional and practical-minded, as is no doubt necessitated by the demands put upon them in the world of business.

Data obtained from personality inventories such as the Minnesota Multiphasic Personality Inventory, the California Psychological Inventory, and the Type Indicator based on Carl Jung's types show consistently more psychopathological deviation among creative persons than control samples. However, Barron and his associates strongly emphasize that the creative individual also possesses greater ego-strength and self-control, thus being able to contain his tendency toward deviation. No evidence was found to support the popular contention that creative individuals show psychotic traits or the "madness of genius."

Finally, we may briefly note a composite characterization of the productive young research scientist so important in our scientific and technocratic culture, as revealed by a number of studies whose authorship is given by Barron (1, p. 85). Table 10-3 shows these characteristics and, as the reader may judge for himself, bears a close relationship to many of the traits revealed in the Berkeley studies.

These interesting and provocative investigations of creative persons' traits are, it must be remembered, largely descriptive. Much more research will be needed before we have a complete picture of the dynamics of creative thinking and how it is related to these intellectual and personality traits. We do not know, for example, to what extent being a successful creative thinker generates some of the modes of behavior measured and described in these studies. Correlations, we must always bear in mind, are not necessarily revealing of causation. We do not mean to imply anything as extreme as the generalization that one can *become* intelligent by engaging in creative thinking over a long period of time, but it is possible that under the same circumstances one might become unconventional, more interested in abstract impersonal activities, and less interested in warm, personal contacts. Certainly, there is much biographical data to show that many famous writers and artists became increasingly unconventional as they became more successful and withdrawn from ordinary society.

We do not, however, mean to call into question the general validity of studies such as these. Rather, we commend the entire report to the interested reader for many additional facets of methodology and results. Moreover, we shall be considering the problem of outstanding individuals again in connection with Maslow's theory of motivation.[19]

Table 10-3.
A Unified Picture of Traits Found in Productive Scientists

---

1. High ego strength and emotional stability
2. A strong need for independence and autonomy; self-sufficiency; self-direction
3. A high degree of control of impulse
4. Superior general intelligence
5. A liking for abstract thinking and a drive towards comprehensiveness and elegance in explanation
6. High personal dominance and forcefulness of opinion, but a dislike of personally toned controversy
7. Rejection of conformity pressures in thinking (although not necessarily in social behavior)
8. A somewhat distant or detached attitude in interpersonal relations, though not without sensitivity or insight; a *preference* for dealing with things or abstractions rather than with people
9. A special interest in the kind of "wagering" which involves pitting oneself against the unknown, so long as one's own effort can be the deciding factor
10. A liking for order, method, exactness, together with an excited interest in the challenge presented by contradictions, exceptions, and apparent disorder

---

SUMMARY AND EVALUATION

In reviewing the topic of thinking, one cannot help but be impressed by the complexity and variety of mental processes that psychologists have

---

[19] The reader who wishes to anticipate will find Maslow's theory discussed in Chapter 11.

subsumed under this heading. Undoubtedly this diversity accounts, in part, for the lack of satisfactory theoretical offerings in the area as compared with other areas in psychology. Moreover, psychologists have found it difficult to apply those quantitative techniques to the thought processes that are readily utilized in the study of learning, intelligence, sensation, and, to some degree, perception. As a result, much of the research on thinking has been exploratory in nature; and, as a consequence, the resulting interpretations are descriptive rather than explanatory. However, we do not wish to minimize the work of those whose names appear in the literature of thinking. Certainly the provocative implicit speech theory of Watson, the challenging investigations of the Gestalt psychologists on productive thinking, and the brilliant clinical studies of Goldstein and his associates, as well as the work of more recent investigators, have deepened and broadened our understanding of the thought processes. Nevertheless, it is fair to say that progress toward the formation of more comprehensive theories of thinking has been necessarily slow. In looking to the future, it seems likely that the empirical approaches pioneered by Hull, Heidbreder, and the comparative psychologists will generate comprehensive theories of thinking in terms of learned mediating processes.

REFERENCES

1. Barron, F. The psychology of creativity. In *New directions in psychology*, II. New York: Holt, Rinehart and Winston, 1965.
2. Berlyne, D. E. Recent developments in Piaget's work. In R. C. Anderson and D. Ausubel (eds.), *Readings in the psychology of cognition*. New York: Holt, Rinehart and Winston, 1965.
3. Boring, E. G. *A history of experimental psychology*, ed. 1. New York: Appleton, 1929.
4. Carr, H. A. *Psychology: A study of mental activity*. New York: Longmans, Green, 1925.
5. Dement, W., and E. Wolpert. The relation of eye movements, body motility, and external stimuli to dream content. *Journal of Experimental Psychology*, **55**, 1958, pp. 543–553.
6. Duncker, K. On problem solving. *Psychological Monographs*, **58**, 1945, No. 270.
7. Finan, J. L. Delayed responses with pre-delay reinforcement in monkeys after removal of the frontal lobes. *American Journal of Psychology*, **55**, 1942, pp. 202–214.
8. Gelb, A., and K. Goldstein. Über Farbennamenamnesie. *Psychologische Forschung*, **6**, 1924, pp. 127–186.
9. Goldstein, K. *The organism*. New York: American Book, 1939.
10. Goldstein, K., and M. Scheerer. Abstract and concrete behavior. An experimental study with special tests. *Psychological Monographs*, **53**, 1941, No. 239.
11. Heidbreder, E. The attainment of concepts: I, Terminology and methodology. *Journal of General Psychology*, **35**, 1946, pp. 173–189.
12. Heidbreder, E. The attainment of concepts: II, The problem. *Journal of General Psychology*, **35**, 1946, pp. 191–223.
13. Heidbreder, E. The attainment of concepts: III, The process. *Journal of Psychology*, **24**, 1947, pp. 93–138.

14. Heidbreder, E. The attainment of concepts: VI, Exploratory experiments on conceptualization at perceptual levels. *Journal of Psychology,* **26,** 1948, pp. 193–216.
15. Hull, C. L. Quantitative aspects of the evolution of concepts. *Psychological Monographs,* **28,** 1920, No. 123.
16. Humphrey, G. *Directed thinking.* New York: Dodd, Mead, 1948.
17. Jacobsen, C. F. Influence of motor and pre-motor lesions upon the retention of skilled movements in monkeys and chimpanzees. *Research publications, Journal of Nervous and Mental Diseases,* **13,** 1934, pp. 225–247.
18. Jacobsen, C. F. Functions of the frontal association areas in primates. *Archives of Neurology and Psychiatry,* **33,** 1935, pp. 558–569.
19. Jacobsen, C. F. Studies of cerebral functions in primates: I, The functions of the frontal association areas in monkeys. *Comparative Psychology Monographs,* **13,** 1936.
20. Jacobsen, C. F. The effects of extirpations on higher brain processes. *Physiological Review,* **19,** 1939, pp. 303–322.
21. Jacobsen, C. F., and G. M. Haslerud. Studies of cerebral functions in primates: III, A note on the effect of motor and premotor area lesions on delay responses in monkeys. *Comparative Psychology Monographs,* **13,** 1936, No. 3.
22. Jacobson, E. *Progressive relaxation.* Chicago: University of Chicago Press, 1929.
23. Jacobson, E. Electrophysiology of mental activities. *American Journal of Psychology,* **44,** 1932, pp. 677–694.
24. James, W. *Principles of psychology:* Vol. I. New York: Holt, 1890.
25. Jersild, A. *Child psychology.* Englewood Cliffs, N. J.: Prentice-Hall, 1954.
26. Malmo, R. B. Interference factors in delayed response in monkeys after removal of frontal lobes. *Journal of Neurophysiology,* **5,** 1942, pp. 295–308.
27. Patrick, C. Creative thought in poets. *Archives of Psychology,* **26,** 1935, No. 178.
28. Patrick, C. Creative thought in artists. *Journal of Psychology,* **4,** 1937, pp. 35–73.
29. Piaget, J. *The language and thought of the child.* New York: Harcourt, Brace, 1926.
30. Piaget, J. *The child's conception of the world.* New York: Harcourt, Brace, 1929.
31. Piaget, J. *Judgment and reasoning in the child.* New York: Harcourt, Brace, 1928.
32. Piaget, J. *The child's conceptions of physical causality.* New York: Harcourt, Brace, 1930.
33. Piaget, J. *The construction of reality in the child.* New York: Basic Books, 1954.
34. Piaget, J. *Play, dreams, and imitation in childhood.* New York: Norton, 1962.
35. Spaet, T., and H. F. Harlow. Problem solution by monkeys following bilateral removal of the prefrontal areas: II, Delayed-reaction problems involving the use of the matching-from-sample method. *Journal of Experimental Psychology,* **32,** 1943, pp. 424–434.
36. Thompson, G. G. *Child psychology.* Boston: Houghton Mifflin, 1952.
37. Titchener, E. B. *A textbook of psychology.* New York: Macmillan, 1910.
38. Wade, M. The effect of sedatives upon delayed responses in monkeys following removal of the prefrontal lobes. *Journal of Neurophysiology,* **10,** 1947, pp. 57–61.
39. Wallas, G. *The art of thought.* New York: Harcourt, Brace, 1926.
40. Watson, J. B. *Behavior: An introduction to comparative psychology.* New York: Holt, 1914.
41. Watson, J. B. *Psychology from the standpoint of a behaviorist.* Philadelphia: Lippincott, 1919.
42. Wertheimer, M. *Productive thinking.* New York: Harper, 1945.
43. Wertheimer, M. *Productive thinking.* (Expanded edition edited by Michael Wertheimer). New York: Harper, 1959.
44. Woodworth, R. S. *Experimental psychology.* New York: Holt, 1938.

11

Motivation

In this and the following chapter, we are entering upon the study of systems and theories in *dynamic psychology*. As it is used in the language of everyday life, the term "dynamic" carries with it the implication of "power," "energy," "force," or "action." In the technical literature of psychology the concept has the same connotation as it does in everyday speech, but its denotation is much more specific. Technically, dynamic psychology is the psychology of motivation and emotion. The two processes are grouped under the broad heading of *dynamic psychology* because psychologists look upon motives and emotions as *conditions which arouse, regulate, and sustain behavior*. It is also interesting to note that both terms come from the same Latin root, *movere,* meaning to move or incite to action. Thus, psychological usage is sanctioned by etymological tradition. However, in psychological research and in the systematic literature, motivational and emotional processes are conventionally treated separately, partly for practical reasons and partly on theoretical grounds. We shall follow the more or less conventional pattern of considering the two processes independently, devoting the present chapter to motivational theory and the following to systematic theories of emotion.

Before we begin our examination of historical conceptions of motivation, it will be helpful by way of orientation to consider what has traditionally been included within this area. As we examine the scope of motivational psychology, it will become apparent that the field is both broad and complex, in the sense that motivation is intimately related to a number of other psychological processes.

First, the psychology of motivation is concerned with those *changing physiological states* that are associated with hunger, thirst,

390

sex, and so forth. Because of this, many of the early experimental studies of motivation were directed toward the investigation of the strength of drives which are known to be related to bodily needs and physiological processes. More recently, there has been a great deal of research and theorizing in this same area whose aim has been the understanding of the fundamental neurological, metabolic, and psychological factors underlying the primary drives.

Second, *emotional states,* as already indicated, are sometimes treated as motivating conditions. Psychologists have demonstrated experimentally that emotional states, through learning, can act as drives. Moreover, as common experience tells us, emotions often reinforce motives in progress. When we strongly desire something, the accompanying emotional tone increases the strength of our desire to attain a goal.

Third, *habits* enter the realm of motivational psychology because of the fact that well-established habits can incite the individual to action. The monkey who has been experimentally habituated to morphine is highly motivated to get his daily injections and may die if he fails to receive them. Similarly, the professional man or office worker who has spent thirty or forty years on the job often finds retirement an exceedingly difficult adjustment. He reminds us of the proverbial fire horse who, though officially "retired," charged off at the sound of the alarm. Habits are also considered to be at the heart of social motives. It is generally agreed that such motives as prestige, affection, the desire for possessions, security, and the like are learned patterns of behavior, or, as some authorities prefer to put it, culturally determined.

Fourth, *sets, attitudes, and values* are complex cognitive processes compounded, in part, of motivational factors and, because of this dynamic component, are properly considered to be within the scope of motivational psychology. Sets, indeed, may be defined as temporary states of motivation which make for greater selectivity of perception and increased specificity of response. Attitudes are more enduring mental states and are motivational in the sense that where they are strongly held they predispose the individual to react in a certain way, as is so clearly illustrated by racial and religious prejudices. Values, too, may be thought of as enduring cognitive processes which function as guides to conduct and as goals to which the individual directs his behavior. As is true of deeply ingrained religious beliefs, values, too, can act as powerful and lifelong influences on the individual's conduct.

Fifth, *incentives* and other *environmental influences* which play upon motivational processes are properly included within the scope of both theoretical and experimental studies of motivation. Lewin, for example, made incentives and environmental conditions in general an important aspect of his system of dynamic psychology. (See Chapter 11.)

Our brief outline of the major areas of motivational psychology should serve to indicate the complexity of the task facing those psychologists who undertake the formulation of a comprehensive theory of motivation. However, the broad scope of the field is by no means the only problem confronting the systematist. Motivational processes are hidden states, often outside the conscious awareness of the individual and, as a consequence, must be inferred from behavior. While the same is true of learning, perception, intelligence, and other mental processes, the problem is accentuated in motivational studies because of the difficulty of establishing "anchoring points" on the stimulus and response side.

Finally, we should like to point to another factor which retarded the evolution of motivational psychology. We refer to the dominance of the structuralistic psychology of consciousness for which motivation was not a recognized area of investigation. Moreover, the atomistic approach of the early behaviorists, directed as it was toward externally observable behavior failed to develop the orientation which is required to get at inferred processes. It was not until the impact of Freud's psychoanalytic theory was felt in academic circles that psychologists began to turn their attention to the development of techniques for the investigation of motivation.

Because the representatives of the early academic schools of psychology had little to say about motivational processes in their systematic literature we shall, following a brief historical introduction, begin with Freud's theory of human motivation. Following our discussion of this system, we shall examine several modern academically nurtured systems in which motivational theories have played a significant role. Finally, we shall discuss contemporary trends in motivational theory, which, we shall discover, are developing rapidly along many diverse lines.

MOTIVATIONAL PSYCHOLOGY
IN THE PRESCIENTIFIC ERA

Ever since men first began to speculate about human nature, the question of man's motives has inevitably arisen. In ancient philosophical and theological works, human nature is treated as a "problem," in the sense that ethical philosophy and moral theology have traditionally sought to guide and control the individual for the betterment of society. Consequently, the reasons why people do the things they do and want the things they want become of paramount importance. Closely related to the problem of the underlying basis of human wants and desires is the question of freedom of will—a question that is still something of an issue in philosophy, theology, and humanistic psychology. Is man free to act as he wills? Is he the pawn of fate? Or is he the "puppet" of hereditary and environmental forces over which he has no control?

In seeking the answers to the basic driving forces in human nature, the ancient Greek philosophers favored a humoral or bodily basis for motivation. Perhaps it was the enlightened, scientific approach to knowledge characteristic of the Golden Age of Greece that was responsible for the Greek biological analysis of man's motives, or it may have been their rapidly developing interest in medicine. Whatever the reason, Greek philosophical speculation on human motivation took the form of relating patterns of action and thought to differences in physique and underlying physiological states. We have already touched upon Plato's physiological theory of human nature (Chapter 1), but the most influential of all classical theories of human motivation was Hippocrates' fourfold-type theory of personality. The "father of medicine" believed that people could be understood in terms of their temperaments, and held that there are four basic personality types, to each of which is related a different underlying bodily "humor." The "sanguine" individual's optimistic and hopeful attitude is associated with a predominance of the "blood humor." The "melancholic" temperament he believed to be due to a predominance of "black bile," while an abundance of "yellow bile" gives rise to the "choleric," or irascible, disposition. Finally, the "phlegmatic" temperament is associated with an excess of "phlegm."

Typological theories of individual differences have persisted down through the ages with incredible pertinacity and, as will be brought out in the chapter on personality, remain a part of modern psychology. But because they attempt to encompass the whole of personality, typologies are only tangential to the psychology of motivation. The point at which the two overlap is in the search for the underlying energetics of behavior. The typologist is rarely satisfied with formulating broad descriptive categories of personality or temperament, but, in addition, endeavors to explain individual differences in terms of the biological substratum of motivation—usually on the basis of bodily build or the endocrine system.

Another motivational doctrine that has played a considerable role in both ancient and modern accounts of human motivation is that of psychological hedonism. The doctrine of hedonism stems from ethical philosophy, where it took the form of affirming that the attainment of happiness is the highest good in life. For this reason, ethical hedonism is a nonscientific, philosophical value system and, as such, has little relevance for psychology. Psychological hedonism, on the other hand, does not impute value judgments to the pursuit of good or evil, but simply postulates that man seeks pleasure and avoids pain.

The philosopher Bentham was the first writer to formulate clearly psychological hedonism as the basis for human motivation. Largely as a result of the applications of his doctrine to criminal law, our present penal code is based on the assumption that punishment acts as a deterrent to crime by balancing the pleasure to be gained from the commission of a crime with an equal degree of pain. Thus, in traditional British common

law, the problem for jurists was "to make the punishment fit the crime.'
However, it eventually became apparent that the doctrine of hedonism was
an oversimplification of human motivation. More and more severe penalties
had to be written into law in an effort to deter criminals, until some 250
offenses carried the supreme penalty. Pickpocketing was one of the infrac-
tions calling for the death penalty. But at the public hangings of convicted
pickpockets, those still out of custody gathered in large numbers to ply their
trade among the spectators. Obviously, hedonism as an explanation of
human behavior proved defective and in its original form no longer occupies an important place in most systems of motivation. Hedonism is now
considered not so much a *determiner* of conduct but an emotional accom-
paniment of motivated behavior. Pleasantness of hedonic tone indicates an
overall attitude of approach and acceptance, while unpleasantness implies
a tendency to reject and withdraw.

The next historical development of importance in motivational psychology was the rise of the "instinct" school of motivation. Largely as a
result of the growing interest in animal behavior around the middle of the
nineteenth century, biologists and early comparative psychologists were
impressed with the repertoire of complex unlearned behavior patterns exhibited by lower forms. The concept of "instinct" achieved widespread
popularity among those attempting to account for behavior patterns which
are unlearned and for which the organism has no foresight of the consequences of its own behavior. Thus, the wasp, without education or insight
into the nature of her activities, builds a complicated cellular nest. Similarly, yearling birds migrate thousands of miles without guidance or fore-
knowledge of their ultimate goal.

The doctrine of instinct as an explanatory concept was given support
by the theory of evolution and the science of genetics. Once the mechanisms
of heredity had been identified, the somatic, or bodily, basis of instinct could
with considerable logical justification, be attributed to propensities for certain patterns of behavior mediated by inherited "chains" of reflexes or
"prepotent" nervous pathways. At a certain stage in the organism's development, certain stimulus patterns "trigger off" a sequence of behavior
which, taken as a whole, is described by the outside observer as an
"instinct." Because of its apparent "explanatory" power, the concept of
instinct became highly popular in late nineteenth-century biology and
psychology. Undoubtedly a great deal of its attractiveness lay in the fact
that it offered a mechanistic explanation for behavior, apparently reducing
complex behavior to simpler elements in the hereditary nervous and
glandular processes.

However, as is so often true in the history of science, "first" explanations lose their attractiveness as mature reflection displaces initial enthusiasm. It became increasingly clear that in accounting for behavior in terms

of instincts, nothing had been accomplished after all. To attribute the wasp's nest-building ability to an "instinct for nest building" is little more than a circular explanation. Basically, the difficulty arises from the fact that instinctive behavior is defined as behavior which is unlearned and that unlearned behavior is, in turn, "explained" as "instinctive." In terms of an example, we say that the wasp's ability to build a nest must be instinctive since she has no opportunity to learn the behavior in question. But if we then raise the question as to what enables wasps to build nests, and take as the answer, "instinct," the circularity of the reasoning involved is apparent. Moreover, to "explain" instincts as "hereditary propensities" is substituting one mystery for another. As a result, the concept of instinct fell from its position of preeminence to become, for a time, a "bad word" in psychology, especially from the point of view of the behaviorists with their distrust of the "unseen." But as has already been pointed out, there are cycles of ascendance and descendance in psychological theory. In the past several decades, the investigation of instinctive behavior has enjoyed a resurgence of interest, largely as a result of the work of European ethologists who are seeking to discover the environmental-physiological relationships in the behavior of lower forms. We shall return to the problem of instincts later in the chapter when we discuss this new and challenging approach to comparative psychology, but we must first consider several important motivational systems which reached their development during the early decades of the present century.

FREUD AND THE LIBIDO THEORY[1]

In many ways, Freudian psychoanalysis is an outgrowth of instinct psychology. As his biographers emphasize, Freud was strongly attracted to both Darwin and Goethe, whose evolutionary systems appealed to his biological interests. As a young man, Freud studied medicine at the University of Vienna, where a brilliant academic staff numbered among its members some of Europe's outstanding biologists, physiologists, and neurologists. Moreover, Darwinism was in the air in Viennese academic circles, and Freud, finding himself drawn more and more toward psychology, believed he saw a way to keep the science of mind firmly on a biological basis by founding the motivational aspect of his psychoanalytic system on a modification of the reproductive instinct, which he called the *libido*.

The term *libido* is best understood as a psychophysical concept meaning both *the bodily and mental aspects of the sex instinct* (*24*, Vol. II, pp. 282–283). In other words, the libido is at once raw sexuality and the mental desire or

[1] See *10, 11, 12, 23, 24,* and *46* for both primary and secondary sources.

longing for sexual relations. Freud, however, emphasized the mentalistic aspect of the libido in his writings, and for all practical purposes, libidinal energy may be equated with mental or psychic energy. Moreover, he employed the term to cover a range of behavior and motivational phenomena ordinarily not considered sexual in the narrower sense. Self-love, a mother's love for her child, religious love—in fact, any pleasurable activities in which the individual engages—are but broader aspects of the basic desire to achieve sexual satisfaction.

In his later writings Freud further generalized his libido theory into an all-inclusive "life instinct," *eros*. Eros includes the instinct for self-preservation, the desire to propagate the species, self-love, love for others, and the tendency to grow and realize one's potentialities. In short, eros is the creative force that underlies life itself. However, Freud also saw in his patients the urge to destroy—sometimes to destroy the self, sometimes others. Man, he believed, is inevitably drawn toward death. If the death instinct is turned inward, it results in suicidal destruction; if outward, in hate or aggression, and, in its worst form, murder. This all-embracing instinct of death and destruction he called *thanatos*.

Since eros and thanatos exist side by side, we are all driven by conflicting unconscious forces. Love, then, is a fusion of eros and thanatos. In fact, every human motive is an alloy of both constructive and destructive impulses. Freud agreed in principle with the poet, Oscar Wilde, who said that in wish or in deed each man kills the things he loves.

On the basis of these fundamental instincts, Freud built his entire system of motivation. The elaboration of eros and thanatos as the child develops determines his relationships with members of the family constellation and his reactions to the social order into which he is born, and to those with whom he will have interpersonal relations during his adult life. From the point of view of Freudian psychoanalytic theory, the most important phase of development occurs during the early years, especially the infantile period, which, as Freud defined it, lasted up to five or six years of age. During the very early infantile period, the child, according to him, is "autoerotic." That is, he derives erotic or sexual satisfaction from stimulation of his own body or from having the "erogenous" zones such as the lips, cheeks, nipples, or genital organs stimulated by the mother incidental to feeding and bathing. More specifically, the early infantile period can be subdivided into three stages: (1) the *oral stage,* in which stimulation of the mouth gives rise to pleasurable sensations; (2) the *anal stage,* in which libidinal pleasure is obtained in connection with the activities of the lower bowel; and (3) the early *genital stage,* in which manipulation of the sexual organs is the chief source of erotic pleasure.

Throughout these early stages, the child's libido is said to be undergoing localization in increasingly more pleasurable regions of the body

But at the same time, the libido seeks "object attachment" in the form of another human being. Obviously, during the autoerotic stages, the object choice is the child's own body. Because the infantile libido is centered on the child himself during the autoerotic stage, Freud referred to the infant as narcissistic, after the legend of Narcissus of Greek mythology, who was in love with himself. During the genital stage, however, the child becomes attached to the parent of the opposite sex. This early parental attachment Freud described as the *Oedipus complex* after the Greek tragedy *Oedipus Rex,* which tells of Oedipus' murder of his father and marriage to his own mother to fulfill the decree of the Fates. Eventually the child overcomes the Oedipus complex because of his increasing fear of retaliation on the part of the parent of the same sex for whom the child is a "rival." In overcoming his incestuous impulses, the child makes use of three mechanisms: *repression, sublimation,* and *identification.* Repression is the forceful ejection from consciousness of forbidden impulses or of shameful, traumatic experiences. Sublimation involves the conversion of sexual impulses into socially acceptable forms of behavior. It is a kind of transformation of energy from one form to another in which the progression is from a baser to a more "sublime" type of motivation. Identification involves the child's putting himself in the place of the parent of the same sex and thereby obtaining vicarious sexual satisfaction from that parent's sexual relations with the spouse.

When the child has successfully resolved the Oedipus complex, he enters upon the second major stage of motivational development, namely, the *latent period.* During this stage, which lasts from the end of the infantile period to the onset of puberty, the child is primarily engaged in the development of social feelings. Narcissism is diminished, there is a further decline of autoeroticism, and, as the term *latent* implies, sexuality as such is not evident.

After the onset of puberty the genital organs become capable of sexual functioning, and a revival of zone sensitivity occurs. A resurgence of narcissism and autoeroticism accompanies the development of the sexual organs. Typically autoeroticism takes the form of masturbation at this stage of development. There may also be a revival of the Oedipus-object choice at puberty, but in the normal course of events a heterosexual choice is made outside the family, and marriage follows.

During the course of psychosexual development, *fixations* may occur at any stage, with the result that the child's motivational system fails to develop properly, and, further, personality growth is seriously hampered. For example, if fixation occurs during the early oral stage as a result of overindulgence on the part of the mother, the child or adult will be excessively carefree, generous, overoptimistic, and will, in general, behave as if the world owed him a living. Presumably, he expects a continuous flow of pleasure from life just as he experienced an overabundant flow of milk from the mother's breast. However, if the child is frustrated during the early oral stage, he will become pessimistic, demanding and socially dependent upon others. If fixation occurs at the anal stage, the child may develop into an overorderly adult who, in his concern for detail, cleanliness, and possessiveness, reflects parental overemphasis on bowel training accompanied by evidence of emotional revulsion or disgust at the sight of feces.

Freud believed that the normal frustrations which accompany weaning, bowel training, and the suppression of the Oedipus complex strengthen the child's character. This assumes that the training is not carried out in a harsh manner and that the child has an adequate supply of libidinal energy to maintain repressions as well as to meet the demands of reality. In an atmosphere of warmth and affection, the expanding personality of the child derives more and more pleasure from the stimulation afforded by dealing with reality and less from indulgence in primitive bodily satisfactions. Thus, in the normal adult, crude sexual curiosity has been sublimated into mature intellectual interests. The characteristic broadening of interests that goes with the process of maturation means, in effect, that the libidinal energy is becoming attached to more and more objects. Moreover, with changing situations and varying age levels, the type of object attachment changes. The young adolescent in the first throes of true love is at a stage of development when all his libidinal energy is attached to one object. The mature man with diverse intellectual interests shows a constellation of libido attachments that spread far beyond primary sexual satisfaction.

The preceding discussion of libidinal development illustrates the highly deterministic nature of Freud's system of motivation. Eros represents all of the tendencies within the individual toward living, expanding, and realizing the self. But all of the energy available to eros stems from the libido. Thus, from birth onward there is a limited, determined supply of energy which can neither be augmented nor decreased in any fundamental sense. Thanatos Freud regarded as far more difficult to study, and he did not specify the source of energy behind destructive impulses. However, it will be recalled that thanatos, as well as eros, is an instinct with which the individual is born and, as such, is presumably part of the same stuff of life which supplies the libidinal energies.

Since Freud's theories range over such diverse phenomena as infantile sexuality, neurotic behavior patterns, the structure of primitive societies, and the Judaeo-Christian religious tradition, a *complete* discussion of his motivational system would require several volumes rather than a section in a single chapter. However, even a summary of Freud's theory of human motivation would be incomplete without some mention of the interesting and highly characteristic methods he employed to assess the motivational structure of his patients. Indeed, as the historical accounts of the development of psychoanalysis reveal, methodology and theory marched hand in hand throughout the evolution of the Freudian system. As Freud himself has pointed out (12), psychoanalysis began with Breuer's[2] discovery that patients under hypnosis revealed memories for experiences which they were unable to recall in the waking state. In treating his own patients Freud eventually dispensed with the hypnotically induced states in favor of free association. Theoretically, the free-associating patient's "guard" is down and unconscious material is therefore able to escape the "censorship" normally exerted during directed, conscious thinking. This does not mean that the patient's associations are entirely lacking in direction or are unrelated to an overall goal. The very fact that he is a suffering human being who is voluntarily seeking help lends a general purpose to the analytic session; the patient is there to explore the inner self, not simply to reminisce idly. Consequently, his associations tend to be concentrated within emotional and motivational areas. Indeed, if the patient wanders too far afield, the analyst interprets this as a sign of "resistance" and strives to bring him back to more significant productions.

An important submethod within the larger technique of free association is dream analysis. So critical is the process of analyzing dreams that it is sometimes considered as a separate method of uncovering unconscious motivational processes. However, in practice, dreams are analyzed by having the patient free-associate around the content of the dream so that its dynamics may be revealed. Since Freud considered dreams a "royal road" to the unconscious, it will be necessary to go into the process of dream analysis in some detail.

To begin with, it is important to recognize that, upon analysis, dreams reveal two distinct types of content, the *manifest content* and the *latent content*. The dream as remembered by the dreamer upon awakening is the manifest content. Psychoanalytically, the manifest content is not the significant portion of the dream, since in the process of becoming conscious, it has undergone considerable distortion in order to make it acceptable to the dreamer's conscious self. The hidden or latent content of the dream, therefore, must be discovered by searching deep below the surface of the manifest content. This depth analysis is accomplished in two ways. First, the patient is required to associate around elements within the dream. If, for example, the dream involves swimming, the patient is asked to associate around the word "water." Presumably, water in the manifest content has some hidden significance for the dreamer, and the memories and impulses which it calls to the patient's mind during free association help to reveal just what that significance is.

The second method for discovering the latent meaning of dreams is symbol analysis. Since symbolism in dreams is largely a private affair, the

[2] Breuer was a Viennese physician who pioneered in the therapeutic use of hypnotism in the cure of hysteria.

meaning of symbols must be determined in relation to the psyche of the individual dreamer. This involves the discovery of partial or incomplete identities between the manifest symbols and hidden wishes or impulses buried in the patient's unconscious. In general, the majority of symbols in dreams are sexual (*9*, p. 161). Because sexual impulses are "forbidden," the *dream work* utilizes several processes to convert them into acceptable and apparently harmless symbols. A number of these are common from individual to individual and may therefore be considered as "universal" symbols.

For example, the male sex organ will appear in the form of sticks, poles, steeples, snakes, or some form of pointed object. The female genitals are symbolized as pocketbooks, trunks, caves, or enclosed places. The process of birth is symbolized as running water or swimming. The dreamer's body takes the form of a house, and if the dreamer is male, the walls of the house will be smooth; if female, the house will have ledges and balconies (breasts).

In the foregoing examples the partial identities are easily recognized. But in many dreams the manifest content is extremely distorted and sometimes bizarre. In such cases the symbolism in the dream and the events depicted have undergone considerable modification by the dream work. The first, and one of the most important processes of the dream work, is *condensation*, in which the manifest content is translated into a highly abbreviated form. Some elements of the dream are omitted altogether, and others appear only in fragmentary form. In other cases several elements may be blended into one. Frequently, in the latter instance, one person in the manifest content may stand for several individuals in the latent content.

A second process employed by the dream work is *displacement*. The latter takes two forms: first, a latent element may be replaced by something more remote—something that is virtually an allusion instead of a direct representation of a significant event in the dreamer's life. Second, the accent in the manifest content may be displaced. For example, latent accent on the male genital organ may appear in the dream as accent on the nose. Not infrequently displacement takes the form of accenting opposites: thus, clothing often represents nakedness; love may be a disguise for hate, and vice versa. Finally, the process of *secondary elaboration* helps to disguise the real significance of dreams. In secondary elaboration, the dreamer, upon awakening, makes a "good story" or good Gestalt out of the dream. He therefore tends to add elements that were not in the original dream and omits others. In some cases elaboration may go so far that the dream is modified to such an extent as to give rise to total misunderstanding of its significance (*9*, p. 190).

In general, the process of dream interpretation is designed to reverse the dream work. In other words, the purpose of the analysis is to reveal precisely what the dream work is trying to repress. Basically, what is repressed is a wish—a wish that is strongly desired by the dreamer's unconscious but which is incompatible with the dreamer's evaluation of himself. Because such unconscious repressed impulses are at the root of the patient's symptoms, their importance for successful therapy is obvious.

Freud was also convinced that slips of the tongue, errors in writing or behaving, and accidental or symptomatic acts reveal hidden motivation. Of special importance in indicating a strong desire to repress or hide unconscious motives is the process of *resistance* which is encountered in neurotic patients during therapy. The operation of resistance is revealed when the patient's free associations become unproductive, when he refuses to go on, "forgets" appointments, or otherwise behaves as if he were on the defensive. According to Freud, the appearance of resistance indicates that a sensitive, painful area of the unconscious is being approached; and, in order to protect himself from the anxiety attendant upon the exposure of deeply repressed impulses or experiences, the patient strengthens his defenses. In such cases the analyst moves slowly, reassures the patient as the analysis proceeds, and helps him to understand the meaning of his defensive behavior.

Finally, neurotic symptoms themselves reveal the operation of unconscious motives. The unsatisfied libido, frustrated by reality, is forced to seek its satisfaction in other ways. The symptoms are substitutes for the suppressed urges of the libido. Symptoms are less shocking to the individual's conscious than the direct wishes lurking in the unconscious. Thus, compulsive symptoms such as hand washing, counting steps, or touching certain objects are symbolic, disguised wish fulfillments of repressed desires. By carrying out the compulsive act, the individual achieves tension reduction. Consequently, symptoms act as safety valves for relieving pent-up libidinal energies which might otherwise explode catastrophically.

We shall have more to say about Freud's concepts of human motivation when we consider his theory of personality structure in Chapter 15. Meanwhile, we shall briefly consider the motivational aspects of several of the more important variants of Freudian theory.

ADLER AND INDIVIDUAL PSYCHOLOGY[3]

Alfred Adler (1870 to 1937) was an associate of Freud's during the years 1902 to 1911 while psychoanalysis was still in its formative stages. After making a number of contributions to psychoanalytic theory, he disagreed with Freud on certain fundamental issues, with the result that he

For sources, see *1*, *2*, and *3*.

resigned from the international association for the promotion of psych
analysis which Freud had established some years earlier. After his departu
from the Freudian circle, Adler founded a rival society of "Individu
Psychology," wrote extensively on his theoretical views, and, in collabor
tion with his colleagues, founded a number of clinics for the treatment
both children and adults.

Adler's theory of human motivation takes as its point of departure th
initial weakness and helplessness of the child. Although the child is awa
of his comparative inferiority, he possesses an inherent urge to grow,
dominate, to be superior. His goal is the goal of security and superiorit
and he is driven toward his objective by insecurity and feelings of inferiorit
Children with organic defects, female children, and those born in
minority groups bear an added burden of inferiority and are likely
develop "inferiority complexes." [4] In striving to overcome inferiority fee
ings, the child adopts compensatory patterns of behavior, which in extrem
cases take the form of overcompensation. Thus, the child with an inferi
body may, by a supreme effort, become a great athlete. A girl with po
eyesight might strive to become an artist or dress designer. Adler pointe
to many outstanding men of past ages—Julius Caesar, Demosthenes, Ale
ander the Great, Theodore Roosevelt—who overcame serious organ
defects to be numbered among the great leaders of history.

Not all compensation, however, is direct and socially useful. Th
neurotic, the psychotic, and the delinquent are striving to overcome infer
ority feelings indirectly and according to a "style of life" which is social
unacceptable or even destructive. Such individuals, Adler believed, are lac
ing in "social sense" and are overly preoccupied with individual goals. H
was firmly convinced that no human being can achieve happiness in th
pursuit of egocentric, fictional goals. Therefore, the focal point of therap
is the patient's style of life. Adler helped his patients explore the vario
ramifications of the neurotic style of living to which the patient had becom
enthralled. The unrealistic, fictional goals toward which the patien
energies were directed must be revealed, understood, and redirected towa
socially useful goals. In this connection, Adler laid special emphasis on th
exploration of the marital, vocational, and social aspects of the patien
life style, since each of these areas is so crucial in the individual's adjustmen

It is also important to note that Adler, in contrast to Freud, nev
practiced psychoanalysis. Adler's was a face-to-face technique in which th
psychologist and patient were on an equal footing. During the course
the therapeutic conversations, Adler explored with his patient the latter

---

[4] In his later writings Adler put less emphasis on feelings of inferiority as negative states whi
must be overcome by compensatory mechanisms. Rather, he came to interpret feelings of infer
ority as states of imperfection or incompletion. He saw man's restlessness and incessant strivi
not so much as a desire to rid himself of deficiencies but as a more positive process in which m
seek to grow and to move forward to higher things.

arly recollections and present dreams, since he felt both were highly signifi-
ant in revealing the patient's life style. He also stressed the patient's posi-
on in the family constellation and his relationships to the parents. In
eneral, his therapeutic technique was more "permissive" than Freud's
nd more directed toward contemporaneous as opposed to genetic prob-
ms. In modern psychiatric practice, Adler's therapy would be charac-
rized as "ego therapy" as opposed to the deeper Freudian procedures.

Like Freud, Adler stressed the family situation and the early years as
ae critical factors in the development of the child's character structure.
Inlike Freud, however, Adler did not assign a fundamental role in person-
lity development to sexuality. He believed that Freud had greatly exag-
erated the importance of the sex motive while neglecting the importance
f the child's social relationships with its parents and siblings. Both the
verpampered child and the rejected child are in danger of becoming
aaladjusted. The pampered child cannot develop confidence in himself,
xpects too much from others, and attempts to dominate them just as he
ominated his mother. The rejected child becomes insecure, anxious, or in
ome instances hostile and rebellious. In any event, both overprotected and
ejected children never acquire the spirit of cooperation that makes for
ound, productive human relationships.

In summary, Adler's theory of human motivation emphasizes social
s opposed to biological factors. The individual's style of life as it impinges
pon his interpersonal relations in marriage, work, and community living
, the reflection of his basic motivational structure. Adler, therefore, in con-
ast to Freud, advocated a molar rather than a molecular approach to
uman behavior. The individual's entire program of living is the focus of
aerapy—not the sexual side of life alone. In his system the self is a central
oncept. In many ways, Adler anticipated the neo-Freudian psychoanalysts
hose theories will be summarized later in this chapter.

JUNG AND ANALYTIC PSYCHOLOGY[5]

Carl Jung (1875 to 1961) was another close associate of Freud's during
ae early period of psychoanalysis, but ultimately disagreed with the master
n theoretical issues and, like Adler, founded his own school. Jung's system
s known as "analytical psychology," and, as the name implies, is closer
oth in spirit and practice to Freud's system than is Adler's individual
sychology.

Jung's major point of disagreement with Freud was over the nature of
ae libido. Years before Freud had integrated the concept of the libido with
ros, Jung had defined it as a general life urge. He held that Freud's con-

For sources see 25, 26, and 27.

ception of infantile sexuality was incorrect and that the child's libido e:
pressed itself in terms of growth and the urge to excel rather than in dire
sexuality. Moreover, Jung disagreed with Freud on the nature of the u
conscious, arguing that it exists on two levels, the *individual unconscious* an
the *collective unconscious*. The former arises from repressions; the latter co
sists of inherited neural patterns which predispose the individual towar
primitive modes of thought such as autistic thinking and belief in magic
superstitions. Since it is a racial instinct, the libido is contained in the co
lective unconscious.

Jung is most famous for his concepts of *introversion* and *extroversio*
terms which have become part of our everyday speech. The motivation
and interest patterns of the introvert dispose him toward self-centerednes
In dealing with the physical and social worlds the introvert is governed b
the relation of things and individuals to himself. He is inclined to be rigi
in his behavior, and if he develops a neurosis, it will most likely be of tl
obsessive-compulsive variety. The extrovert, on the other hand, is external
oriented. He is adaptable, sociable, and is governed by objective realit
rather than by subjective considerations. If the extrovert becomes psych
neurotic, he typically develops hysteria.

Jung, like Freud, tended to think in terms of opposites or polaritie
The individual whose dominant personality pattern is that of introversio
is unconsciously extroverted, and vice versa. The male has in his makeu
elements of femininity, and the woman correspondingly has masculir
tendencies in her unconscious. To complicate the picture even furthe
mental activity takes four dominant forms: sensation, thinking, intuitio
and feeling. See Figure 11-1. Thinking and feeling are polar opposite
and both tendencies are always present in the individual at the same tim
If his dominant mental activity is thinking, the individual's unconsciou
tends toward feeling. Similarly, sensing and intuition are opposites, anc
as is true of the other polarities, both are operative in the individual at th
same time.

Clearly, where so many diverse and conflicting tendencies are presen
there is a great danger of one-sided development. One aspect of the ind
vidual's personality tends to become overdominant, totally overshadowin
the unconscious, latent portion of self. If the extroverted masculine-thinkin
aspects of the self gain a unilateral ascendance, the individual cannot utiliz
the introverted, more feminine, and intuitive potentialities which remai
untapped in his unconscious. The problem for the therapist in such case
is to help the individual realize these hidden potentialities and to integrat
them with the more active side of the self. Moreover, the Jungian therapi
must help the patient explore his collective unconscious in order to achiev
a sense of oneness with the entire human race. One of the most powerfu
factors in the collective unconscious is man's religious instinct. Jung, there
fore, encourages his patients to strengthen their religious sense and searc

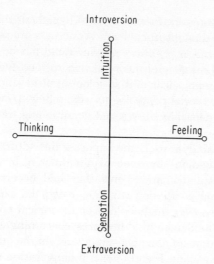

Fig. 11-1. Jung's fundamental polarities of introversion-extraversion, and of modes of response.

for their souls. A cure is not achieved until the patient is able to integrate and harmonize the personal and collective unconscious and to arrive at a working synthesis of the complementary polarities which divide him from his true self.

MOTIVATIONAL THEORY IN NEO-FREUDIAN PSYCHOLOGY

By the third decade of the present century, psychoanalysis had made its impact felt in every department of human thought. Its influence, however, was most marked within the arts, social sciences, and medicine. The violent reaction born of conservatism and prudery during the first two decades of the twentieth century had given way to enthusiastic acceptance in some quarters, and in others to at least a limited recognition of the value of the Freudian insights. However, Freud's influence on the arts and sciences was no longer a one-way process. Developments within the rapidly expanding sciences of anthropology, sociology, social psychology, and medicine began to exert a reciprocal influence on psychoanalysis. Cultural anthropologists were discovering that many of the taboos and other social practices which Freud had interpreted in terms of libido theory and the Oedipus complex either did not occur in all primitive social orders or took an entirely different form from those making up the warp and woof of civilized societies. Malinowski, for example, found that incest taboos among the Trobriand Islanders were directed against relations with the sister rather than the mother. Moreover, Freud's general hypothesis that neurotic symptoms and modes of thought in civilized Westerners are similar to attitudes and behavior patterns in primitive peoples could not be confirmed. However, the validity of his general theory of unconscious dynamics did receive support from anthropological and sociological field studies. At the same time, sociologists and social psychologists were piling up evidence that much of our behavior is determined by social conditioning, rather than by biological factors.

Within psychoanalysis itself, the impact of the cultural sciences resulted in a strong "neo-Freudian" movement quite different in spirit and purpose from the various splinter movements that had occurred earlier within Freud's international association. In most cases, the earlier schisms grew out of disagreements over methodology or theoretical emphasis, and were not the result of fundamental differences concerning libido theory and psychosexual development. The neo-Freudians, on the other hand, rejected both the libido theory and Freud's general emphasis on sexuality. Instead, neuroses were envisioned as being partly a product of cultural conflicts and partly the result of unsound social development. The child was no longer considered to be at the mercy of his biological instincts. Instead, his normal development was believed to be contingent upon secure and affectionate family relationships on the one hand, and the cultural and social influences that play upon him on the other hand. Moreover, the very definition of what is normal and what is abnormal was held to be culturally determined.

The outstanding exponent of the neo-Freudian point of view is Karen Horney (1885 to 1952), who for many years was associated with the New York Psychoanalytic Institute. In her book *The Neurotic Personality of Our Time* (20), which appeared in 1937, Horney emphasizes her dissatisfaction with orthodox Freudian theory. In the first chapter, entitled significantly "Cultural and Psychological Implications of Neuroses," Horney strongly emphasizes the cultural definition of neurosis as a deviation from a pattern of behavior commonly accepted in a given society. She believes that the driving force behind the neurosis is "basic anxiety" generated originally by a genuine lack of love and affection in childhood. In striving to overcome anxiety, the child develops "neurotic trends" which are essentially compensatory behavior patterns whose purpose is to promote security. In a later book, *Our Inner Conflicts* (22), she argues that there are three fundamental and mutually incompatible neurotic trends: (1) moving toward people, (2) moving against people, and (3) moving away from people.

If the child's dominant compensatory trend is moving toward people he is attempting to overcome anxiety and insecurity through his excessive demands on others for love and affection. If the child's predominant mode is moving against people, he seeks to overcome insecurity by the excessive development of power, prestige, and dominance. Finally, moving away from people implies a search for security through withdrawal. The child who is hurt and rejected retreats from the source of pain and eventually refuses to try at all lest he fail.

According to her own clinical experience, Horney found that neurotic trends do not exist in isolation in the individual but occur together, thus giving rise to inner conflicts. For example, if a neurotic's predominant trend is moving against people, he nevertheless unconsciously wishes to move *toward* people. Because his hostile behavior antagonizes others, it becomes more and more difficult for him to make friends despite the fact that he needs them desperately, albeit unconsciously. The result is increased anxiety leading to greater hostility, which, in turn, is accompanied by rapidly deteriorating interpersonal relations. The neurotic, to employ Horney's phrase, is caught in a "vicious circle." The problem for the therapist is to help the neurotic realize his inner conflicts and the various secondary defense mechanisms to which they give rise. This is accomplished through psychoanalysis.

A detailed examination of neo-Freudian theory is beyond the scope of this volume.[6] However, the brief sketch that it has been possible to present here is representative of the strong socially oriented nature of the new movement. While retaining Freud's methods, his emphasis on determinism, unconscious motivation, repression and conflict, the neo-Freudians show considerably more theoretical and methodological flexibility than is characteristic of conservative Freudians. In the last analysis, this new spirit of freedom and experimentation which the neo-Freudians have brought to psychoanalysis may prove to be more significant than the specific theoretical and methodological issues which now divide them. Certainly the willingness of the neo-Freudians to recognize the relevance of contributions from the social sciences has commanded respect from the academic psychologists who work in the areas of motivation and personality. They have found the study of recent psychoanalytic theory both stimulating and enlightening, and many of the neo-Freudian concepts of personality development have close parallels in contemporary theories of motivation and personality.

McDOUGALL'S HORMIC PSYCHOLOGY

At approximately the same time that Freud and his associates were launching the psychoanalytic movement, a British psychologist,[7] William McDougall (1871 to 1938), was formulating his hormic, or purposive, system of psychology—a system which was granted an enthusiastic hearing

For a detailed comparative study of both Freudian and neo-Freudian schools of psychoanalysis, e Munroe (46).

McDougall came to Harvard after World War I and subsequently accepted an appointment Duke.

by psychologists, anthropologists, sociologists, and political scientists durir the first two decades of the twentieth century. Despite the fact th McDougall's early views were crystallized before he had become acquaint∈ with Freudian psychology, his systematic orientation resembles Freud in several aspects. First, both founded their theories of human nature c instincts. Second, both sought to create dynamic systems whose centr theme is the psychology of motivation or purpose. Finally, both attempt∈ to revolutionize the scope of psychology by extending it into the soci. area. McDougall sought to accomplish this by creating a system deliberate oriented toward the field of social psychology, whereas Freud "socialized his system by generalizing his account of the neurotic character structur to the behavior of both primitive peoples and the societies of Wester civilization. However, there were profound differences in methodology an outlook between the two men, differences which will become clear as v examine McDougall's system.[8]

McDougall's introductory text in social psychology, first published i 1908, was an immediate and continued success. It went through fourtee editions by 1921, and for a time was one of the most influential texts i the entire field. In his introduction to the fourteenth edition, McDouga deplored the fact that for decades academic psychologists had emphasize the study of consciousness to the virtual exclusion of other aspects of huma behavior. The result is that dynamic psychology is in a "backward state in which the greatest obscurity, vagueness and confusion still reign (40, p. 3

After pointing out that the psychology of motivation, impulse, an emotion is the foundation of social psychology, ethics, philosophy, an sociology, McDougall announces that his purpose is to build a psycholog of ". . . those most fundamental elements of our constitution, the inna∙ tendencies to thought and action that constitute the native basis of mind (40, p. 16). In the course of the next four chapters he identifies the natur of instincts and discusses both the principal human instincts and broad∈ innate tendencies or propensities that are not as specific as instincts b∙ are nevertheless part of man's native equipment.

McDougall considers instincts as:

> innate or inherited tendencies which are the essential springs or motive powe of all thought and action, whether individual or collective, and are the bas∈ from which the character and will of individuals and nations are graduall developed under the guidance of the intellectual faculties (40, p. 20).

Basically, there are two broad types of innate propensities: (1) the specif tendencies or instincts, and (2) the general or nonspecific tendencies. Sp∈ cific instincts may be exemplified by flight, curiosity, pugnacity, and th

---

[8] Our exposition is based chiefly on McDougall's *An Introduction to Social Psychology,* 14th ed. (40

Table 11-1.
The Principal Instincts[a]

INSTINCT	ACCOMPANYING EMOTION
Flight	Fear
Curiosity	Wonder
Repulsion	Disgust
Pugnacity	Anger
Self-abasement	Subjection
Self-assertion	Elation
Parental	"Tender emotion"
Reproduction ⎫	No well-defined
Gregariousness ⎬	emotional
Acquisition ⎪	accompaniment
Construction ⎭	

[a]According to McDougall, *40*.

like (see Table 11-1), while the more general innate propensities are exemplified by sympathy, suggestibility, and imitation. Further differences between basic types of propensities will be brought out as we take up each type in more detail.

The specific instincts such as fear, anger and sexual desire are describable in terms of the same three fundamental characteristics that apply to all mental processes—*cognitive, affective,* and *conative.* In the language of contemporary psychology, McDougall is saying that instinctive behavior shows the following attributes: (1) a sensory (cognitive) aspect, in which environmental situations provide the stimuli necessary to arouse instinctive behavior; (2) a motivational (conative) aspect, which is characteristic of all purposive or goal-directed behavior; and (3) an emotional (affective) aspect.

Because instincts have a sensory side, inherent behavior can be modified through learning and experience. The human child learns to respond to stimuli that are not originally capable of arousing instinctive behavior. Thus the infant, inherently afraid of loud noises, becomes conditioned to fear the lightning which accompanies thunder. On the motor or response side, too, modifications in instinctive behavior develop as the child grows older. The very young child literally flees from a fear-inducing stimulus, whereas older children may merely verbalize their anxiety in the presence of danger.[9]

Finally, instinct may also undergo a more complex type of modification by combining into "sentiments." Love, for example, obviously includes the sexual instinct, but at the same time, depending upon the situation, may

*The similarity of McDougall's theory of sensory-motor modification of instincts bears obvious parallels to contemporary conditioning theory.

include any of the following: the propensity to care for the young, anger when love is threatened, fear if it is in danger of being lost, joy when the object of love is joyful. In addition to being complexes or combinations of instinctive propensities, the sentiments are further characterized by their enduring quality. By contrast, pure animal instincts are quickly aroused and quickly disappear. Sentiments such as love, jealousy, and patriotism are persistent motivating conditions which, like attitudes, may endure for years.

McDougall's second category of innate propensities includes the "general" or "nonspecific" tendencies. The chief distinction between the basic instincts and the general innate tendencies lies in the broad, nonspecialized range of reactions to which the latter give rise. Specific instincts, regardless of how modified they may be, retain an essentially unchanged nucleus, are aroused by definite stimulus conditions, and give rise to relatively predictable reactions. The general tendencies, on the other hand, have no specific character. Sympathy, for example, may be aroused by a wide variety of stimulating conditions and expresses itself in many forms. One may sympathize with another's grief, joy, fear, achievement—indeed with virtually any human (or animal) reaction. The reaction may vary all the way from experiencing a mild subjective feeling to strong emotional and behavioral responses resembling those displayed by the object of sympathy. Whatever the case, it is extremely difficult to predict the precise cause of sympathetic reactions, in the first place, and equally difficult to predict their behavioral outcome once they have been initiated.

By way of summary and conclusion, McDougall's hormic system is basically an instinct theory of human behavior. The object of psychological study is to discover the specific and general innate propensities and to reveal how these become combined into sentiments. The behavior of the adult is not motivated directly by instincts but by the learned modifications and combinations of instincts which McDougall calls sentiments. The emotional, impelling force of sentiments is derived from their instinctive substratum.

As we indicated in the introduction to this section, McDougall's system enjoyed a considerable initial success among social scientists. Undoubtedly a great deal of the popularity of his theories can be attributed to two factors. First, there was strong interest in Darwinism and animal behavior among social and biological scientists around the end of the nineteenth century and the beginning of the twentieth. Since McDougall's system bridged the gap, so to speak, between animal and human behavior, it fitted into the intellectual *Zeitgeist*. A second, and even more important, factor in accounting for the popularity of the system was McDougall's insistence on a *purposive* psychology. The sociologist, anthropologist, political scientist, and applied psychologist could find little of relevance for their sciences in either a structuralistic psychology of consciousness or a behaviorism devoid of motivation purpose, and will. In this respect McDougall's system filled a need. However, about the same time that the last edition of his *Social Psychology* appeared, McDougall's system went into an eclipse. As we pointed out earlier (p. 394), the concept of instinct is, in the last analysis, descriptive rather than explanatory, and psychologists were coming to recognize its descriptive nature. Moreover, the growing evidence of the importance of purely social factors in the behavior of both individual and social groups pointed to the culture as the most important source of those aspects of human behavior which are truly human as distinct from animalistic. As a consequence of this change in emphasis and interest, McDougall's doctrines rapidly lost ground until they are now mainly of historical importance. Nevertheless, he must be credited with pioneering a purposive system which has its counterpart in Tolman's psychology, and with developing the first true behavioristically oriented social psychology.

GOLDSTEIN'S ORGANISMIC PSYCHOLOGY[10]

We are already familiar with Kurt Goldstein's conceptions of the thought processes (Chapter 10). He is also well known in psychological circles for his "organismic" theory of human nature. Goldstein's system stands somewhere between instinct-based theories such as Freud's and McDougall's, on the one hand, and Gestalt or field theories on the other. He is unwilling to completely divorce his system from a neurophysiological foundation, but at the same time finds a holistic or Gestalt-like point of view the only acceptable general framework for the exposition of his conceptions of human personality. Goldstein does not, however, consider himself a Gestalt psychologist, since he believes Gestalt theory to be too preoccupied with mental processes in isolation. For Goldstein the slightest degree of reductionism is unacceptable. Because we are concerned with motivation in the present chapter, we shall not attempt to outline his theory in its entirety but instead summarize the motivational aspects of the system.

True to his holistic viewpoint, Goldstein asserts that there is but one fundamental human motive, *self-actualization,* from which all other motives arise. Hunger, thirst, the reproductive drive, the desire for knowledge, power, prestige, and other primary and "social" motives are but special manifestations of the basic tendency to realize the self. The fulfillment of needs is not the mere release of tension and elimination of deficiencies, but the more positive goal of joy in achievement and the pleasures of exercising one's capacities and abilities (*14*, p. 203).

[10] The exposition is based primarily on Goldstein's *The Organism* (*14*). See also reference numbers *5* and *35*.

Goldstein believes the common impression among behavioristic psychologists that the organism is "driven" by isolated drives has arisen as a
result of the fact that there is a kind of hierarchy of drives in the individual,
with one becoming more important than others under certain conditions
and apparently dominating the behavior of the individual as a whole. If,
for example, the individual is forced to go without food for an extended
period of time, his behavior is dominated by the hunger motive, and the
self-actualization of the personality as a whole is temporarily disrupted in
the face of a crisis. But under ordinary conditions, the hunger drive can be
suppressed if the organism is involved in something of greater importance
for the realization of the self. In essence, isolated drives arise only as a result
of deficiencies and emergencies and for this reason are special motivating
conditions (*14*, p. 202). Ordinarily the organism seeks to *fulfill* its capacities
or potentialities, and the satisfaction of specific drives or needs is a means
to this global end, not an end in itself.

Goldstein goes on to deal with the question of habits in relation to
drives. He takes cognizance of the fact that a number of psychologists emphasize the transformation of habits into automatic mechanisms as the
child matures, without the necessity for postulating any overall self-actualization tendency. While he admits that habits do contribute to self-actualization once they are established, he argues that all fundamental habit
mechanisms arise out of an innate impulse to grow and realize potential
hereditary capacities. Goldstein identifies this fundamental impulse to grow
and develop as the "tendency to perfection." Without this original tendency
arising from the organism as a whole, habits and fundamental skills such
as walking and talking could never develop in the first place. When habits
become autonomous and mechanistic, psychologists fall into the error of
studying them as isolated phenomena torn out of their contextual background, when, in reality, they are "embedded in the activities of the *organism
as a whole*" (*14*, p. 204).

Finally, an important aspect of Goldstein's motivational theory centers
around his concept of the "constancy of the organism." He likens the activities of the organism to the Gestalt concept of figure-ground in perception.
In any given activity, "part" of the organism "stands out," while the rest
remains in the background. The foreground of behavior is determined by
the nature of the task confronting the organism at any given point in time.
Expressions of self-actualization are the behavior patterns which the organism displays in interacting with his environment. But while thus engaging
in active give-and-take relations with his environment, the organism tends
to maintain constancy and identity. To put it negatively, the organism is
not at the mercy of its surroundings, but whenever "stimulated" by the
environment, tends to regain an "average state which corresponds to its
nature . . ." (*14*, p. 112).

Common experience tells us that the organism is not always successful in "coming to terms with the environment." Failure to do so is most common when the organism's neurological or psychological capacities are defective. In such cases the organism will be overwhelmed by anxiety and feelings of inability to carry out a given task. In severe cases the individual goes into a "catastrophic" reaction or complete breakdown. But such instances are the exception rather than the rule. The normal individual is not dominated by anxiety or driven by "isolated" needs commonly observed in accentuated form in those who are physically ill or neurotic. The normal person responds in terms of the single, comprehensive need to realize the self.

In summary, Goldstein's system of motivation centers around three basic concepts: (1) the fundamental motive of self-actualization, (2) "coming to terms" with the environment, and (3) the maintenance of constancy in the face of continuous environmental change. Coming to terms with the environment and the maintenance of constancy are subservient to self-actualization. Consistency and orderliness of behavior in the face of environmental change affords the best means of realizing the self. The organism, however, is not pulled hither and yon by the flux of events, but is moved from within. The organism does not seek relief from annoying tensions and drives but strives toward the goal of perfection.

As we leave Goldstein's theory to turn our attention to Kurt Lewin's field theory, we are moving from a holistic theory based on neurological research and formulated within the biological orientation of environmental interactionism to a "pure" psychological theory. In a sense Freud and McDougall represent an extreme biological point of view, whereas Goldstein stands for a psychobiological viewpoint. Lewin falls in the opposite extreme, since he favors psychological rather than physiological or biological determiners in his account of human behavior.

LEWIN'S FIELD THEORY[11]

As was pointed out in Chapter 5, Lewin may be considered as a member of the Gestalt school or as the developer of a separate system. Neither characterization is correct if taken literally, since Lewin's system is Gestalt-like in its orientation, yet at the same time differs strikingly from orthodox Gestalt psychology in its emphasis on needs, will, personality, and social factors. The founders of the Gestalt school stressed the study of perception, and to a lesser degree learning, emphasizing in their theoretical writings physiological constructs in accounting for behavior. Lewin's orientation,

[1] Our account is drawn primarily from Lewin's *Principles of Topological Psychology* (28). See also , 29, 30, and 31.

on the other hand, is toward psychology as a social science. In their experimental work he and his associates have emphasized the study of behavior as a function of the total social and physical situation. Much of this research was carried out on children, often utilizing elaborate experimental setups in which an attempt was made to control (or at least get detailed information about) the child's total environment during the course of the investigation. We shall meet with examples of Lewin's experimental techniques as we examine his theoretical position.

Lewin lays the foundation for his theoretical system by analyzing the basic structure of science in general. He believes that science has evolved over three developmental epochs, which he designates as "speculative," "descriptive," and "constructive." Early Greek science exemplifies the speculative stage of scientific evolution. Its goal is to discover the essence behind natural phenomena. A science in this phase of development is friendly to speculative theorizing. In general, scientific systems at this stage of development are characteristically "all-inclusive" and are derived from a few basic concepts. Plato's mind-body dichotomy, Heraclitus' reduction of all things to fire, and Aristotle's laws of association are all illustrative of science during the speculative epoch of scientific evolution.

In its descriptive phase, science seeks to accumulate as many facts as possible and to describe them with precision. Classifications take the form of broad abstractions, and theorizing is looked upon with disfavor. Perhaps the best illustration of this mode of scientific development is to be found in pre-Darwinian biology, in which classification in terms of phylogenetic categories and descriptions of life cycles of animals and plants was the essence of the science. Similarly, structuralism as a system of psychology was largely a descriptive science held together purely by a logical ordering of its phenomena with little or no underlying theory.

The constructive, or as Lewin also calls it, "Galilean" mode of science has as its goal the discovery of laws by means of which the scientist can predict individual cases. He is no longer satisfied with descriptive categorization, but envisions his system in terms of a group of interrelated concepts held together by laws. Constructive or Galilean science is friendly to empirical theories and laws, but does not demand that either be treated as "universals." Events are lawful even if they occur only once in an individual. The proof of a law depends upon the "purity of the case" and not necessarily upon the frequency with which it occurs.

Reduced to its simplest terms, Lewin's argument holds that psychological laws need not be formulated solely on the basis of statistical averages. Rather, the individual case is equally important. Even if all general psychological laws were known, we would still need to understand the concrete individual and the total situation in which that individual exists before we could make any predictions about his behavior. Thus, Lewin avors a psychology in which the focus is on the *individual,* or *genotype,* as opposed to a system where the emphasis is on the statistical average, or *phenotype.* Lewin reduces his thesis to the following formula: $B = f(PE)$ where: B represents behavior; f is a function (or in the more general case, a law); P, the person; and E, the total environmental situation.

In light of his emphasis on the study of the individual as a factor in the total situation, Lewin devoted a great deal of effort to devising a theoretical schema for representing environmental variables as they impinge upon the psychological individual. As a result, his system leans heavily on concepts derived from: *topology,* a branch of higher mathematics which deals with transformations in space; *vector analysis,* the mathematics of directed lines; the sciences of chemistry and physics, from which Lewin borrowed such concepts as "valence," "equilibrium," "field force," and others. Because most of the concepts of field theory can be represented in diagrammatic form by making use of planes, surfaces, vectors, valence signs, fields of equilibria, and disequilibria, Lewin's books and research papers are filled with diagrammatic analyses of various psychological phenomena. Because he felt that he could not adequately represent psychological phenomena with the conventional concepts of mathematics, physics, and chemistry, Lewin invented a new system of geometry called *hodological space,* which consisted of a qualitative geometry that emphasizes locomotion along psychological paths, the dynamic interaction of individuals in their environments and behavior at borders and barriers. Indeed, it has been said that Lewin's system grew out of his blackboard drawings. In the preface to his *Principles of Topological Psychology,* Lewin admits that "it occurred to me that the figures on the blackboard which were to illustrate some problems for a group in psychology might after all be not merely illustrations but representations of real concepts" (*28,* p. vii).

Let us begin, appropriately enough, with a diagram illustrating Lewin's fundamental concept of "the life space." Figure 11-2 (a) represents the life space of a child, while Figure 11-2 (b) shows the more "differentiated" life space of an adult. The life space is the *totality of all possible events that influence the individual.* Thus the individual's life space contains a past, present, and future, for, *psychologically,* each of these three aspects of life determines behavior in a given situation. The goal-directed individual looks to the future and is influenced in his present behavior by the future life space toward which he is striving. The past, of course, influences the individual in terms of his experiences of success and failure, attitudes, and the like, which are important in determining present goals, methods of approach to goals and reactions to failure. Sometimes the individual's life space may be entirely in the past, as for example, when he is thinking about his childhood. Sometimes, on the other hand, a person's life space is wholly in the future. If he is imagining the anticipated pleasures of a picnic on the mor-

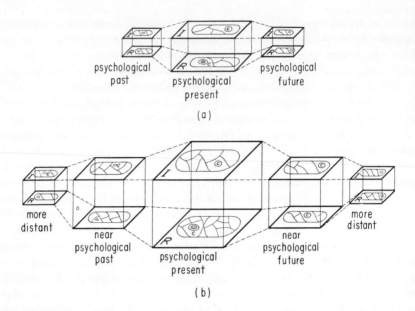

Fig. 11-2. Diagrams representing the life space of the individual at two different levels of maturity. (From Lewin, *31.*)

row, his life space is where he expects to be—on the beach or in the woods—not where he happens to be in the present.

"Differentiation" of the life space depends upon the richness of experiences which the individual has enjoyed throughout the course of his development. The life space of the newborn infant can be represented by a blank circle, since he is too immature to have differentiated regions in his life space. The highly educated and imaginative adult, on the other hand, shows a well-differentiated life space. It is differentiated in the three aspects of past, present, and future and also on the dimension of reality-irreality. The latter dimension of the life space may exist, in turn, on several levels. The reality level represents behavior which has been, is, or will be carried out. Realistic planning for the future represents an intermediate level of irreality, while pure daydreaming or fantasy lies on the extreme irreality end of the dimension.

The concept of the person in the total life space represents the *descriptive* or *structuralistic* aspects of field theory to which we may now relate Lewin's *dynamic* concepts. In doing so we shall be dealing with the motivational aspects of the system. The fundamental concepts in the motivational system are as follows: *need, tension, valence, vector, barrier,* and *equilibrium.* Each of these will be defined and illustrated in the following sections.

Need is Lewin's concept for any motivated state which can be brought about by a physiological condition, the desire for an environmental object, or intention to achieve a goal (see Figure 11-3).

Tensions are emotional states which accompany needs. When the infant needs food he is thrown into a state of tension which is reduced by food. Tensions may also be induced by environmental objects which have potential need significance for the individual. Thus, the child who is apparently playing contendedly may experience need arousal and the accompanying state of tension by the sight of a delicious apple which is brought into the room (see Figure 11-3).

Objects may have either positive or negative *valence*. Objects which satisfy needs or are attractive have positive valence, while objects which threaten the individual or are repellent have negative valence. It is important to recognize that objects do not *literally* possess "valence" in the sense that the concept is used in chemistry. Valence, as Lewin uses the term, is a *conceptual* property of objects. Thus, to a hungry child, an apple has positive valence. To a child who is experiencing the ill effects of having eaten a half-dozen green apples, the apple has a negative valence (see Figure 11-3).

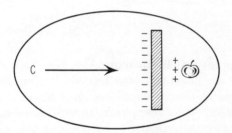

Fig. 11-3. The large ellipse represents the child's life space at the moment. C represents the child. The vector indicates that he is motivated to get the apple which is shown with positive valence. The crosshatched barrier is shown with negative valence. The barrier in this case might be the mother who has forbidden the child to eat the apple.

Mathematically, a *vector* is a directed line. Lewin utilized the concept to represent the direction and strength of attraction of objects. If only one vector impinges upon the individual, he will move in the direction indicated by the vector (see Figure 11-3). If two or more vectors are impelling him in different directions, the effective movement will be the resultant of all the forces. If two equally balanced vectors are operating, the result is a conflict (see Figure 11-4).

Lewin's analysis of conflict situations is one of his best-known conceptual schemes. Consequently, we will discuss each of these basic types in turn. The *approach-approach conflict* is that which exists between two positive

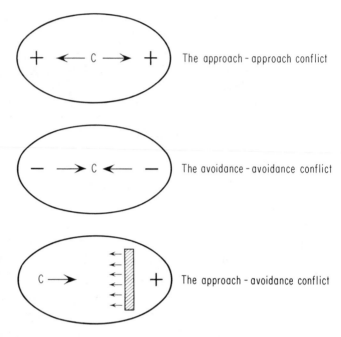

Fig. 11-4. The three basic types of conflict according to Lewin.

goal objects of approximately equal attractiveness. Such a situation might be illustrated by an individual who receives two equally attractive job offers simultaneously. The choice of one goal object clearly implies the rejection of the other. As a consequence, the individual remains in a state of equilibrium poised between the two goals in a state of indecision. The equilibrium is, however, an unstable one. As the individual moves toward one of the goals, a goal gradient effect occurs in which the attractiveness of the nearer goal increases while the unattractiveness of the goal which has been moved away from decreases. Because the individual is now in a state of imbalance he will be drawn rapidly toward the goal toward which he moved.

More serious is the *avoidance-avoidance conflict* in which the individual finds himself between two negative things which he wishes to avoid. Yet he is compelled to choose one of the alternatives. Such a situation might be illustrated by the case of a soldier who is suffering from combat fatigue and who wishes to escape from the battlefield but who is compelled to remain by social and military pressure. In this case the equilibrium tends to be a stable one, and the individual remains torn by indecision. If he moves toward one alternative the negative repelling force grows stronger and he is thrown back toward the other. But as he approaches the other alternative, its negative force increases and so he tends to vacillate close to the middle. The solutions of such conflicts may require a choice as the lesser of two evils; or the individual may "leave the field" as the soldier does when he experiences an incapacitating psychological breakdown.

The *approach-avoidance conflict* is likely to be extremely disruptive since the individual is both drawn and repelled by the same situation at the same time. Thus, the drug addict may be strongly drawn toward a cure but dreads the process of withdrawal symptoms and the return to a lonely, meaningless life. The approach-avoidance conflict is a stable equilibrium, since at a certain distance from the goal the positive and negative forces are balanced. If the individual attempts to move toward the positive goal, negative factors in the situation repel him; consequently movement tends to be minimal.

Lewin's analysis of conflict also admits the possibility of more complex types of situations with two or more goals and more possible alternative courses of action. Moreover, individuals do not remain forever balanced between two poles; life is a great resolver of conflicts. The value of Lewin's analysis does not lie in the inclusiveness with which all possible situations are treated but in providing a model of basic patterns of conflict which have led to experimental analyses of approach and avoidance gradients. Figure 11-5 shows in graphic form an analysis of an approach-avoidance gradient

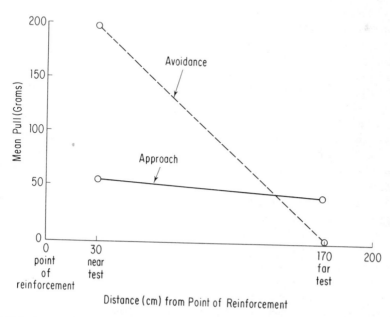

Fig. 11-5. Approach-avoidance gradients. For explanation see text. (From Miller, *41*.)

developed by Miller (41), who trained rats to run along an alley to a food box and then gave them an electric shock as they were eating. On the next trial the animals still ran to the goal, but more slowly, stopping short of the goal itself. This was defined as the point of balance where approach tendencies were equal to avoidance tendencies and an equilibrium was reached. The degree of hunger and the strength of shock could, of course, modify the steepness of the gradient and point of equilibrium.

Barriers may be objects, people, social codes—anything which thwarts the motivated individual as he is moving toward a goal. As the barrier is reached, it tends to take on negative valence. Barriers typically give rise to exploratory behavior in which the individual tests the strength of the barrier. Exploration may also lead to getting around the barrier. Or, if he finds it to be impassable, the individual may launch an "attack" on the barrier.

In Lewin's system, the arousal of needs leads to a state of *disequilibrium*. Generally speaking, disequilibrium may be defined as a state of unequal tension throughout the individual. The ultimate goal of all motivated behavior is to return to a state of equilibrium in which the individual obtains relief from tension. For example, needs such as hunger, sexual desire, or the wish to be recognized by others create states of disequilibrium accompanied by strong tensions. When the needs are satisfied, the tension disappears, and equilibrium is once again restored.

Because there is a serious danger of leaving the reader with the impression that Lewin's system is based on nothing more substantial than strange terms and rather complex diagrammatic representations of psychological phenomena, several characteristic experiments carried out by Lewin and his associates will be summarized in the following paragraphs. It will also be possible by this means to reinforce some of the more important concepts which we have introduced in preceding pages.

The first of our illustrative experiments was conducted at the University of Berlin by one of Lewin's pupils, Bluma Zeigarnik (53). The purpose of the experiment was to compare the ability to recall finished *versus* unfinished tasks. According to field theory, interrupting a subject in the middle of a task should have the effect of leaving him in a state of tension and disequilibrium. Moreover, the interruption should serve as a "barrier" to the goal of completing the task, and this should increase the subject's desire to finish the task. If the foregoing hypothetical analysis is correct, then the subjects should recall more unfinished than finished tasks under the conditions of Zeigarnik's experiment.

Zeigarnik assigned to her subjects eighteen to twenty-two simple problems such as completing jigsaw puzzles, working out arithmetic problems, making clay models, and the like. Each subject was allowed to finish half the tasks, the remainder being arbitrarily interrupted by the experimenter and the subject requested to go on to another task. The interrupted tasks were randomly scattered throughout the entire series.

When all tasks had been either completed or experimentally interrupted, Zeigarnik requested the subjects to recall *all* tasks. Approximately 80 percent of the subjects recalled more *uncompleted* tasks than completed tasks. Moreover, tasks in which the subjects were strongly engrossed were more often recalled than those in which the subject showed only a moderate degree of interest. The experiment demonstrates the influence of experimentally aroused tensions on the persistence of needs. Tensions aroused by the task remain undischarged until the task is completed. If uncompleted, the persistent tension is revealed by selective recall. However, subsequent experiments have demonstrated that the "Zeigarnik effect" depends to a large degree on the subject's ego involvement (*32*). Tasks in which the subject is ego-involved are more likely to be recalled *whether completed or not*. In this case personal failure or success is the important factor, and subjects tend to recall selectively those tasks for which they experienced success.[12]

Our second illustrative experiment is particularly interesting since it is an application of the techniques and theoretical interpretations of field theory to one of Freud's concepts. More specifically, Barker *et al.* (*5*) studied the effects of experimentally induced frustration on the constructiveness of children's play. If, as Freud held, one reaction to frustration is regression or returning to more primitive levels of behavior, then children's play should show some degree of deterioration as a result of frustration. The subjects were thirty children between two and five years of age. They were first allowed to play with a set of toys, some of which had parts missing. For example, an ironing board was available without an iron; there were "floating toys" but no water. However, most of the children made up in imagination what they lacked in reality and played happily. Observers rated the children in terms of the constructiveness of their play. Since there was a close correlation between the mental age of the child and the constructiveness of play, it was possible to rate constructiveness of play in mental-age units.

Following the pretest session, the children were permitted to play with highly attractive and complete toys in a part of the experimental room that was normally inaccessible. They were then returned to the less desirable toys but could still see the more fascinating toys through a wire screen. Again the constructiveness of play was rated by the observers. On the average, the children's play regressed 17.3 months of mental age. In terms of the number of children, twenty-five out of thirty showed some degree of destructiveness in their play. It was also possible to study "behavior at

---

[12] The literature on conditions affecting the Zeigarnik effect is complex and contradictory. See Osgood (*48*) for a discussion of the empirical findings and various theoretical interpretations.

barriers," since the wire screen interposed between the children and the highly desirable toys functioned as a barrier. Some children approached the screen and attempted to reach through it to the toys beyond; some even tried to "escape" from the room altogether ("leave the field"). Typically children who demonstrated greater evidence of disturbance at the barrier also showed a higher degree of "regression" in their play.

The experiment reported in the preceding paragraphs represents a later phase of Lewin's work. In the early years his chief concern was with theoretical problems and issues, but as time went on he became more and more interested in social psychology. Nevertheless, the experiment is an excellent illustration of the holistic approach characteristic of field theory. The analysis of the results in terms of barrier behavior, and reduction of the degree of differentiation in the constructiveness of play are also typical of field-theory analyses.

Finally, we shall briefly summarize the studies of authoritarian and democratic atmospheres carried out by Lewin, Lippitt, and White (30, 33, and 34). The objective of this series of experiments was to determine the effects of inducing "democratic" and "authoritarian" atmospheres on the productiveness and general behavior of small groups of boys.

During the course of meetings held over an extended period, groups of boys engaged in small crafts work under the direction of a group leader. All groups were exposed to all leaders and both types of atmospheres were induced for each group.[13] While the experiment was in progress, the "life space" of each child was under intensive investigation. Parents, teachers, and group leaders were questioned at length about the children's behavior during various phases of the experimental program. Personality tests were also administered during the course of the experiment in order to determine whether or not the child's personality was undergoing modification as a result of his group experiences.

The following techniques were utilized by the adult leaders to create an authoritarian atmosphere. To begin with, the autocratic leader made all decisions. The final objectives of the work projects were not revealed to the children in advance. Rewards and punishments were directed at individual children. Finally, the authoritarian leader remained "aloof" from the children unless actively engaged in directing a project.

The democratic leader made all decisions a matter for group discussion. Alternative solutions were suggested whenever problems arose. Goals were announced in advance, and whenever it was necessary to administer praise or reproof, this was done objectively.

In general, the democratic groups were more productive, less demanding of the leader's time, more friendly in their approach to the leader and

[13] A "laissez faire" atmosphere was also studied partly for reasons of control. We are summarizing only the results of the main experimental variables.

less riven by internal dissention within the group. The democratic group's productiveness remained relatively high even though the leader came in late or left during the course of a session. The authoritarian groups tended to be either more aggressive or more apathetic than the democratic groups. However, the apathetic groups frequently broke out in aggressive behavior on those occasions when the leader was "called out" of the clubhouse. This suggests that the "apathy" was more the result of suppressive measures on the part of the leader than a true absence of aggression in the boys themselves. During the course of an experimentally arranged "attack" on the groups, the authoritarian groups showed poor morale and a tendency to break up, while the democratic group became more closely knit than before the attack. Finally, one of the most interesting (and disturbing) findings concerned the discovery that the children were able to move from a democratic to an authoritarian atmosphere more readily than they were able to shift from an authoritarian to a democratic atmosphere.

This experiment in social psychology has obvious implications for those concerned with morale, leadership, and political theory. For our purposes (along with the other experiments summarized earlier) it illustrates the novel and ingenious experimental programs developed under Lewin's inspiration.

By way of conclusion, it should be pointed out that Lewin's experimental programs have proved more acceptable to psychologists in general than have his particular theoretical views. This must not be taken to mean that his theoretical influence has not been considerable. His writings and concepts have influenced the fields of social, child, and experimental psychology. But Lewin failed to convince psychologists that his special topological and vectorial representations of psychological phenomena were superior to those derived from more conventional mathematical and verbal approaches. In the last analysis, it is premature to attempt any serious evaluation of Lewin's motivational or topological theories, since his students and associates continue to push forward the program of research in the broad area of social psychology that came into fruition under his leadership.

CONTEMPORARY TRENDS IN MOTIVATIONAL THEORY

As is true in the fields of perception and learning, contemporary motivational theorists align themselves according to the traditional systematic orientations. The neobehaviorists continue to emphasize the study of the animal drives; the organismic orientation is represented in the work of several contemporary theorists; and there are still others who seek to establish "miniature" theories around the intensive study of a certain motive or class of motives. We cannot, of course, undertake a summary of the entire field of contemporary motivation. Those who wish to explore the diverse theoretical and research literature in this fascinating area are referred to sources *6, 35, 52,* and *54.* In the concluding pages of this chapter we shall once again invoke the sampling technique and present a summary of what appear to be the most significant and active developments within the broad area of contemporary motivational theory. For this purpose we have chosen four contemporary systematic approaches: (1) the current behavioristic approach to motivation through drive theory, as represented by the physiological theory of C. T. Morgan; (2) the contemporary organismic point of view, as represented by the hierarchical theory of A. H. Maslow; (3) a specialized or "miniature" theory approach to social motivation, as represented by the studies of the achievement motive by D. C. McClelland and his associates; and (4) H. F. Harlow's studies of intrinsic drives.

Morgan's central motive state. In a series of books and papers (*42* to *45*), C. T. Morgan has developed what he calls his "physiological theory of drive," to which he relates a great deal of empirical research carried out by comparative and physiological psychologists. Morgan, incidentally, does not refer to himself as an adherent of any particular school, but his academic training, research interests and theoretical inclination qualify him as a neobehaviorist.

After introducing certain background and historical considerations, Morgan delimits his physiological drive theory as follows: He seeks to provide an explanation of motivated behavior in terms of underlying physiological mechanisms within the organism. Consequently, he does not attempt to account for the so-called social motives for which there is no known physiological basis. He goes on to state that the aims of a physiological theory of motivation are as follows: First, to define the internal conditions that arouse motives; second, to discover how these conditions are related to each other; and third, to reveal how they control motivated behavior. Moreover, Morgan makes it clear that he favors a *central* as opposed to a peripheral theory of drive. He proposes the concept of a "central motive state" to emphasize the central locus of the drive-control mechanisms.

Central motive states have the following properties:

1. They are persistent. Once aroused, central motive states do not require support from stimuli outside the organism or from within. Rather they are maintained by reverberatory circuits or tonicity in the centers themselves.
2. A central motive state results in selectivity of reaction to stimuli. The hungry animal is selectively set to accept food; the adrenalectomized animal to ingest salt.
3. The central motive state may be responsible for emitting certain behavior patterns directly. It is always responsible for the general activity observed in motivated animals, and in some instances may be responsible for the specific form of activity which satisfies the need. Thus, the sexually aroused animal

is generally restless and, at the same time, displays certain characteristic patterns of mating behavior.

Morgan admits that "releasers" or external stimuli in general may also elicit behavior that is dependent on central motive states. However, external stimuli are but triggering factors in such instances; the fundamental inciting mechanism is the central motive state.

Finally, the theory seeks to account for the mechanism of drive reduction. How, in other words, are central motive states satisfied or eliminated? For systems of psychology that emphasize the law of effect, this is the problem of "satisfaction." For theories of learning it is the problem of reinforcement. There are several possibilities. First, the removal of stimuli which aroused the drive in the first place may account for its diminution. Second, hormonal factors may, in some cases, explain drive reduction. For example, there is a possibility that hunger is reduced by hormones discharged by the small intestine into the bloodstream following the ingestion of food. Third, continued stimulation of receptors during the course of drive-initiated behavior may reduce the drive itself. In eating sweets, for example, there is a relatively rapid satiation effect which can be accounted for on the basis of the strong receptor stimulation from sugar. Finally, central motive states may be reduced as a result of the "running out" of the behavior initiated by such states, analogous to the manner in which a clock eventually runs down.

Morgan then marshals the evidence in favor of central motive states by first presenting negative evidence against peripheral theories of motivation, and second, by citing positive evidence in favor of central states. Under the category of negative evidence, he reviews the literature on hunger and thirst, showing how Cannon's local (peripheral) theory is inadequate to account for the facts. In the case of hunger, Cannon held that the discomfort of stomach contractions impels the organism to restless food-seeking behavior. In thirst, dryness of the mouth and throat accounts for water-seeking behavior. Citing various lines of evidence from a number of investigators, Morgan shows that such a view of hunger and thirst is inadequate. A few examples will have to suffice here. Dogs deprived of water and then allowed to drink ad libitum tend to make up the loss in body weight resulting from deprivation. More strikingly, dogs with esophageal fistulas drink vast quantities of water every day despite the fact that their mouths and throats are quite wet from continuous drinking. Similarly, in the case of hunger, animals in food cafeterias are able to select and balance their diets and do not eat indiscriminately, even though the latter course would stop general hunger contractions. Female animals deprived of innervation to their sexual organs nevertheless mate with normal frequency.

Morgan surveys the results from studies of food preference, self-selec-

tion feeding, and sexual behavior, which, he asserts, provide *indirect* support
for central motive states. Briefly the evidence is as follows:

1. Studies which show that an adequate supply of sex hormones is necessary
   for sexual behavior presumably mean that such hormones sensitize or excite
   the central motive state, which, in turn, leads to sexual behavior.
2. Studies of food selection reveal that animals generally demonstrate a "wisdom
   of the body" by taking what they need in terms of nutritional requirements.
   The weight of the evidence at present seems to indicate that some kind of
   hormonal control is exerted on the central motivating mechanisms to make
   the animals more sensitive to needed substances.

Evidence *for* central motive states is discussed by Morgan under several
major headings: (1) direct neurophysiological studies of peripheral mechanisms in motivated behavior, (2) humoral factors, and (3) studies involving
electrical stimulation of neural centers. The neurophysiological studies
cited take the general form of tests of whether or not peripheral mechanisms
involved in motivated behavior are altered by states of need. For example,
do adrenalectomized rats take more salt because the taste buds on the
tongue have been sensitized to salt as a result of sodium insufficiency
brought about by the operation? The evidence is by and large negative.
He cites the experiments of Pfaffmann and Bare (49) who demonstrated
that adrenalectomized rats' thresholds for weak salt solutions were not
altered by the operation even though they needed and took greater quantities of salt than normal animals. Earlier Richter (50) had proposed that
the taste buds of adrenalectomized animals might be altered by their
increased need for salt. Consequently, Morgan believes that such results
may be interpreted as *positive* evidence in favor of central mechanisms as
the responsible factors for the alteration in feeding behavior.

Under humoral factors, Morgan points out that a variety of experiments have shown that humoral or blood factors influence drive. For example, rats with stomach fistulas are not reinforced by inflated balloons
or nonnutritive foods. Nutritive foods, on the other hand, are reinforcing,
although not as reinforcing as food eaten in the normal manner. However,
the fact that food by fistula is reinforcing at all is interpreted to mean that
a hormonal factor must be produced by the digestive tract which, when it
reaches the central mechanisms by way of the circulatory system, "reduces"
need and indirectly reinforces learning. Similarly, "preloading" the stomach
or injecting substances directly into the blood stream influences the rate
at which the animal ingests those substances. In either case, the effect is
presumably humoral in nature and mediated by the circulatory
system.

Finally, under neural centers, Morgan finds support for a central
theory in the wave of recent experiments involving direct electrode stimu-

lation of brain centers. Perhaps the most dramatic of these experiments, partly because the findings were unexepected, is the discovery by Olds and Milner (47) that subcortical stimulation of regions around the septal area of a rat's brain have a reinforcing effect on the animal's behavior. Indeed, the effect is stronger than that demonstrable in any normal drive state. The technique involves the chronic implantation of very fine electrodes directly into the brain. The exposed terminal outside the rat's skull can be connected to a source of low voltage which is activated whenever the animal presses a bar. Rats will press such bars thousands of times per hour to receive shocks to their "pleasure centers." Since the pioneer work of Olds and Milner, negative reinforcing centers have also been discovered. That is, centers which when stimulated result in a decreased rate of bar pressing. Moreover, "centers" for alertness, somnolence, the control of hunger and thirst, sexual activity, and emotional behavior have been delineated by stimulation and extirpation techniques.[14] Animals can be made to eat, drink, awaken, and even run mazes correctly as a result of stimulation of appropriate brain centers. Obviously, the discovery of such "central" reinforcing and control centers is convincing evidence for some kind of central motive states. However, the existence of such centers does not necessarily preclude the possibility of the contributory regulation of drives through sensory and other peripheral mechanisms.

In the final sections of his most recent statement of the central theory of motivation, Morgan presents some of the broader implications of his theory for various problems in motivational psychology. To the present writers, the most significant of these implications is Morgan's attempt to relate his central theory to certain empirical findings that have been difficult to explain. We refer, first, to the well-established fact that animals exhibit curiosity and manipulative and exploratory "drives" which appear to be equally as basic and just as inherent as the common visceral drives of hunger, thirst, sex, and the like. Second, the discovery of hierarchies of food preferences has been difficult to relate to any kind of specific physiological mechanisms. Finally, there is the work of the ethologists on instinctive behavior, in which they have convincingly demonstrated that certain behavior patterns are "released" at an appropriate developmental period by environmental stimuli. For example, "imprinting" (the instinct of ducklings to follow the mother) is "released" by the stimulus of the moving mother duck about twelve hours after hatching, and can be released experimentally by a moving decoy. At first reading, these findings appear to emphasize the role of stimulus factors rather than central states.

With regard to the curiosity, manipulative and similar motives, Morgan suggests the concept of "somatic" drives to characterize such states.

[14] For a concise review of the literature especially as it relates to reinforcement theory, see 6. See also Chapter 13 of this volume for additional discussion of the subcortical motivational centers.

The behavior of animals in food-preference situations, he suggests, demonstrates "sensory" drives. By grouping somatic and sensory drives under the general concept of "sensory hunger," that is, a drive to explore, manipulate, taste, see, or to otherwise receive stimulation from the environment, the two concepts are, in effect, related to each other.

Morgan has no "explanation" for sensory hungers at the present time. He suggests they may be internally controlled by nervous circuits in the reticular formation, or that "stimuli may be drive-reducing in and of themselves" (45, p. 662). Thus, the hungry rat in a food cafeteria may quickly shift preferences from one food to another, so rapidly, in fact, that its behavior cannot be accounted for on the basis of humoral mechanisms. If sensory stimulation reduces the drive for each food in turn, causing the animal to shift to another, it would further have to be assumed that stimulation of the sense organs is capable of "inhibiting" central motive states. Presumably such inhibition would be mediated by subcortical "inhibitory" centers such as have been found for sleep and hunger.

Finally, Morgan finds no difficulty in relating the "releasers" of contemporary instinct theory to his concept of central motive states. The releaser mechanism, as Morgan interprets its role in initiating the animal's behavior, is simply an afferent burst of impulses which sets into motion behavior patterns under the control of central mechanisms. The central motive state "primes" or sensitizes the organism to respond to the releaser.

With the foregoing discussion of sensory drives and releasers, we have concluded our summary of Morgan's theory of physiological drives. As he himself points out, it is a "modest" theory which, at the present time, makes no pretense of being anything more than a descriptive theory under which a great deal of empirical data from the comparative laboratory may be brought together and related to a general unifying concept, the central motive state. Morgan's theory is clearly in step with the *Zeitgeist*, for the recent wave of interest in direct electrical simulation of brain centers *is*, indeed, revealing hitherto unsuspected cerebral control of the physiological drives. Undoubtedly, many more centers will be discovered in the years to come. With an increased fund of empirical data upon which to draw, psychologists will be in a better position to evaluate the relative role of central versus peripheral mechanisms in primary motivation.

Maslow's hierarchical theory of motivation.[15]   A. H. Maslow's hierarchical theory of human motivation is a contemporary organismic theory. Since we have already outlined the general viewpoint of the organismic theorist in our discussion of Goldstein's system, we shall confine our summary of Maslow's views to two characteristic aspects of his theory in which he

[15] The exposition follows Maslow's *Motivation and Personality* (35). See especially Chapters 5 and 12.

attempts to extend the organismic point of view into relatively unexplored aspects of motivational psychology. These are: (a) his hierarchical conception of motivation, and (b) his efforts to develop a more valid and comprehensive psychology of motivation through the study of "self-actualizers."

Maslow assumes that human motives are arranged along a hierarchy of potency. Those needs which have the greatest potency at any given time dominate behavior and demand satisfaction. The individual feels "driven," so to speak, by a high-priority need. When the need is satisfied, a higher-order motive (or class of motives) makes its appearance and demands satisfaction, and so on to the top of the hierarchy. Figure 11-6 is a schematic representation of the hierarchy of human motives. Its point of departure, it will be observed, is the physiological needs. If one of these needs is unsatisfied, the individual is dominated by that need. Thus, the hungry man is dominated by hunger. His emotions, perceptions, thought processes, and behavior in general are preoccupied solely with getting food and satisfying hunger. Similarly, the sexually deprived individual is overdriven by sexual desire, and other considerations become unimportant in the light of his overwhelming need.

Let us, however, assume that the basic physiological needs are satisfied. The next high order of needs emerges and dominates the individual. He seeks safety or security. Maslow believes that the safety needs are most readily observable in the child because of his relative helplessness and dependence on adults. The child prefers some kind of predictable, orderly routine, and he reacts with feelings of fear and insecurity if confronted with novel, threatening, or terrifying stimuli. Parental quarrels and threats of

Fig. 11-6. A schematic representation of Maslow's hierarchical theory of motivation.

separation are particularly harmful to the child's sense of well-being. On the adult level, the individual seeks safety by establishing bank accounts, building a home, and finding a job with an assured future.

Maslow considers the physiological and safety needs truly lower-order needs. The good society provides for the basic needs of its members, and few healthy, normal people are dominated by hunger, thirst, sex, or other animal needs. The neurotic adult is more likely to be driven by such lower order motives. Perhaps he engages in excessive eating or sexual promiscuity as a means of winning love and affection. Or, his lack of security and consequent preoccupation with safety measures may, in reality, be in the service of frustrated higher needs such as love or prestige. As these examples illustrate, Maslow allows for the possibility of one need substituting for another in cases of severe deprivation and lack of opportunity for satisfaction.

Maslow refers to the next higher order of motives as the "belongingness and love needs." These emerge if the two lower orders are reasonably well satisfied. The individual seeks friends, longs for affectionate relationships, and strives to find a place in some group, however small. Again, in our society such needs are generally well satisfied, and it is only in the neurotic or more severely pathological cases that serious deprivation occurs.

The fourth order of needs is the esteem needs.[16] These include the desire for a firmly based high evaluation of the self. There is, in all of us, a desire for strength, for mastery and competence leading to a feeling of independence and freedom. In addition, individuals in our society seek prestige, dominance and recognition from others. Satisfaction of the esteem need generates feelings of worth, self-confidence, and adequacy. Lack of satisfaction of these needs results in discouragement, feelings of inferiority, and inadequacy.

Finally, if all the foregoing needs are satisfied, the need for self-actualization impels the individual to activity. In Maslow's own words: "A musician must make music, an artist must paint, a poet must write if he is ultimately to be at peace with himself. What a man *can* be he *must be*. This need we may call self-actualization" (*35*, p. 91).

Self-actualization need not, however, take the form of creative activity characteristic of genius. A fine mother, an athlete, a good workman may be actualizing their potential abilities in doing well what they can do best. It is nevertheless true that self-actualizers are comparatively rare and disproportionately represented among the gifted. Most of us, apparently, are seeking the satisfaction of lower-order needs.

In his theoretical papers Maslow has argued for a number of years that psychologists have been overly preoccupied with neurotics, delinquents, and other varieties of psychologically underdeveloped individuals. The result

---

[16] Maslow makes the interesting point that these are the needs stressed by Adler and the neo Adlerians and relatively neglected by Freud and his followers.

he believes, is a one-sided psychology lacking in comprehensiveness and based on the abnormal. In a unique study, he has attempted to correct this deficiency by investigating the personalities of self-actualizers. Among the individuals studied were both outstanding historical figures such as Whitman, Thoreau, Beethoven, Lincoln, Einstein, and Spinoza, and people who were living at the time the study was carried out, such as Eleanor Roosevelt, Albert Schweitzer, and Fritz Kreisler. A holistic analysis of the personalities and achievements of such individuals revealed that self-actualizers show the following characteristics: (1) They demonstrate an efficient perception of reality and acceptance of it. (2) They accept themselves and others. (3) They show a high degree of spontaneity. (4) They have a problem-centered orientation to life rather than a self-centered orientation. (5) Such individuals have a need for privacy and detachment. (6) They are autonomous or relatively independent of their environments. (7) They appreciate the "basic goods of life" with continued freshness and pleasure. (8) They show, at times, profound mysticism. (9) They are able to identify with mankind. (10) They develop deep interpersonal relations with others. (11) They are democratic. (12) They keep means and ends distinguishable. (13) They possess a well-developed and unhostile sense of humor. (14) They are creative. (15) They tend to be nonconformists.

In recent years Maslow has made a special study of the discovery that outstanding or creative individuals have mystical experiences ". . . moments of great awe, moments of most intense happiness, or even rapture, ecstasy, or bliss." (*36*, p. 45.) During these "peak experiences," as Maslow describes them, the individual tends to lose his self-consciousness and becomes one with the world. He sees the veil of mystery which ordinarily keeps him from the meaning of life ripped aside, and he experiences the essence of truth and seems to grasp the secret of life, if only for a short time.

Maslow hastens to point out that peak experiences are not supernatural; nor are they limited to highly creative people or to those who practice Zen Buddhism or Taoism. They occur in ordinary people, although they may not be recognized for what they are. A musician may have a peak experience during an especially good performance when all goes well. It is as if he goes far beyond the mere rendition of music to become a kind of creator in his own right. A mother may experience a peak when she sees her children playing happily with their father. The sexual experience, the experience of great love, or of joy may all be peak experiences.

Maslow believes that peak experiences may be therapeutic, that they may have ". . . ennobling and beautifying effects on the character, on the life outlook, on the way the world looks, on the way that the husband looks, or the baby." The problem or puzzle of so many individuals is why they refuse to allow peak experiences to counteract the fear, hostility, and misery of life. Indeed, many people who are aware of having such experiences actually suppress or reject them because of the rationalistic or mechanistic attitudes characteristic of our century.

Maslow recognizes that many unresolved issues remain before psychologists in general are willing to accept the validity of a concept traditionally associated with religious and mystical writings. We shall make no attempt to evaluate a theory which is still in its infancy except to point out that it is entirely congruent with the positions advocated by Rogers (51), Fromm (13), and Adler (3), which emphasize that healthy development depends upon openness to new experience—a willingness to be spontaneous, creative, and free from deterministic attitudes about one's own future.

In summary, Maslow has attempted to broaden organismic theory by extending it to the study of fine, outstanding and healthy individuals. He believes that Goldstein, as well as psychologists in general, have been too concerned with the diseased, the neurotic, and the stunted personality. Moreover, he has consistently urged that motivational psychology has overstressed the physiological and lower-order needs, which, in his opinion, are not the chief motivating forces in the normal human adult. He believes that motivational psychology has much to contribute to ethics, philosophy, and the good life by turning its attention to the study of abundancy needs and self-actualization. In this lies his unique contribution to motivational theory.

McClelland and the achievement motive.[17]   In their initial long-range research program, D. C. McClelland and his associates have investigated primarily human motivation through the intensive study of a single motive, the achievement motive. Moreover, their dissatisfaction with current motivational theory has led them to elaborate their own systematic views in the form of an "affective arousal model" of motivation. We shall first summarize the McClelland investigators' motivational theory,[18] and following this, we shall outline the results of their investigations of the achievement motive.

We have referred to the motivational theory of McClelland and his associates as a "miniature theory." This is not strictly true. These investigators hope ultimately to provide a comprehensive system of motivation rather than a restricted theory. We are employing the characterization "miniature" in the same sense that the concept has been applied to contemporary learning theories. That is, such theories are based on an intensive study of a restricted range of phenomena and in a particular area of psychology. In any case, McClelland and his associates base their theory of motivation on the assumption that motives arise from changes in emotional states. Specifically, they define a motive in the following terms: "*A motive is*

---

[17] The primary source for this summary is *The Achievement Motive* by McClelland and his associates (37). For further applications of the techniques see Atkinson (4).

[18] The theory as elaborated in *The Achievement Motive* is far too extensive to permit more than a bare outline treatment in the present volume.

the redintegration by a cue of a change in an affective situation" [19] (*37*, p. 28). Redintegration, as the term has been traditionally employed in psychology, means the reinstatement in consciousness of a psychological process as a result of stimulation by an environmental cue. Thus, a scene from one's past may be redintegrated by the sight of a long-forgotten childhood friend, a toy discovered in the attic, or perhaps an old photograph.

The term "affect" is a traditional concept for denoting *conative* processes such as feeling, will, emotional, and motivational states (*37*, Chapter 5). The term is little used in contemporary psychology, but our theorists are employing it in the more restricted sense of states of feeling and emotion. Thus, returning to the definition, motives arise when learned cues reinstate emotional states or feelings. It should also be noted that McClelland and his colleagues, by making emotional arousal contingent upon a cue, are arguing that *all motives are learned whether they are primary physiological drives or the "social" motives.* Moreover, by postulating that motives result from affective arousal, they are "reversing" the dominant trend of contemporary psychology, which has accounted for emotional states as concomitants of motivation. Finally, it should be noted that the redintegrated affect, according to the present theory, involves a change in the present affective state of the individual at the time of arousal. If there is no change, there is no motive.

McClelland and his associates justify their choice of affective states as basic to motives on the grounds that: (1) Affective states "control" behavior in everyday life (psychological hedonism); (2) "selective sensitivity" is of great importance in food preferences, "releaser" behavior in submammalian forms, sexual behavior, and the like. Presumably, such sensitivity is based on sensitization of the central nervous system by affective states. Thus, the rat takes one food in preference to another because of the higher palatability value of the former. Palatability, in turn, is dependent upon how the food stimulus is related to the organism's adaptation level. Either stimuli or complex perceptual situations which are not widely disparate from the organism's preadaptation level give rise to positive affective states, while those which are widely disparate give rise to negative affective states. Thus, strong solutions, harsh sounds, pungent odors, and the like tend to be unpleasant, while milder forms of stimulation give rise to pleasant states.

In essence, then, McClelland and his coworkers postulate that the immature organism at first reacts to simple sensory stimuli with either a positive or a negative affective state. Whether the reaction is negative or positive depends upon both the nature of the stimulus and how great a discrepancy exists between the stimulus and the organism's present adaptation level. Some stimuli, such as sugar, quite naturally give rise to pleasantness;

Italics in original.

others, such as quinine, to unpleasantness. However, it should be repeate
that the critical factor is the individual's adaptation level. An extreme
sweet taste may be so far from the individual's normal adaptation level th
it will be judged unpleasant. Similarly, very mild bitter solutions or dilu
whiffs of normally unpleasant odors, such as musk, may be pleasant.

As the individual develops, he acquires, through learning, comple
perceptual and cognitive processes. Nevertheless, the theory holds that tl
latter are essentially more complex variations in stimulus events, and th
the basic principle of affective arousal as a result of discrepancies still holc

Motives are formed by the pairing of cues with affective states. In di
grammatic terms McClelland and his associates portray the process
follows (after McClelland 37, p. 67):

Large discrepancy from adaptation level ⟶ Negative affective state —
    Autonomic response ⟶ Distinctive cues --→ Avoidance response

Because it is learned, the final sequence is shown as a dotted line. The ir
tial sequences, on the other hand, are inherent. Naturally, in the case
small discrepancies, the end result is an approach reaction.

The final highlight from the theory of motivation developed I
McClelland and his group that we shall present here involves the proble
of defining a particular motive. How do we know an individual is exhibi
ing a given motive? After reviewing various alternatives, our authors co
clude that motives should be "distinguished primarily in terms of the *typ
of expectations involved,* and secondarily in terms of types of action, insofar
they exist, which confirm those expectations in varying degrees and th
yield positive or negative affect" (*37*, pp. 76–77). The achievement motiv
therefore, develops out of the expectations based on various experiences tl
individual has had with the common problems of life, from learning to wa
to learning a life's trade or profession.

The achievement motive, then, can be identified on the basis of tl
individual's expectation of success, provided he is personally involved.
mere intellectual attitude of achievement does not necessarily indicate tl
operation of a true motive, since intellectual attitudes need not imply tl
presence of affective states which, according to the theory being outline
here, are a necessary aspect of motivated behavior. Consequently, in ord
to ensure valid measures in their elaborate studies of the achievement m
tive, McClelland and his associates required that their subjects be eg
involved in the testing situations.

The general technique employed in measuring the achievement m
tive was as follows: College students were shown pictures on a screen ar
asked to write brief stories about the pictures. The pictures employed we
taken either from Murray's Thematic Apperception Test or were simil:

in design. Sometimes a combination of original TAT and specially developed pictures was employed. In one series of experiments, the investigators attempted to manipulate the achievement motive by inducing varying degrees of need for achievement in their subjects through appropriate instructions at the beginning of the experiment. Three general levels of achievement motivation were studied: (1) a relaxed condition, (2) a neutral condition, and (3) an achievement-oriented condition. In addition, various success-failure conditions were superimposed on the three basic conditions in order to test the effects of success and failure on the achievement motive.[20] The relaxed condition was induced largely by the examiner's lighthearted attitude as he told the student-subjects that he was trying out "some new ideas." The subjects were given to understand that various tests—anagrams, paper and pencil tests, and the like—they were asked to do, were "in the developmental stage." Following completion of the tests, whose purpose was to provide cues for the arousal of the achievement motive, the subjects were given the group TAT as "a test of the creative imagination."

For the neutral condition the examiner attempted neither to increase nor decrease the level of motivation. Instructions for the tests were presented seriously, but no attempt was made to ego-involve the subjects in the tasks. In the case of the achievement-oriented condition, a serious effort was made to get the subjects personally involved by presenting the cue tests as "intelligence tests" and indices of potential leadership. The TAT in this case was referred to as a test of "creative intelligence."

McClelland and his associates carried out both qualitative and quantitative studies of the TAT stories written by their subjects. In general, the results were positive in the sense that the higher the level of the achievement motive, the greater number of achievement responses in the TAT situation. There were, of course, instances of failure and of mixed types of imagery revealed in the stories. These do not necessarily indicate that the method is a bad one or that the hypothesis is invalid. As the investigators themselves point out, the project was in the nature of exploratory research, and subsequent work along the same lines has resulted in many refinements.

We cannot undertake to present the extensive quantitative data from the original study. However, we shall include several examples of the TAT stories written by the subjects. The picture upon which the following stories are based shows a workshop with a workbench about which are suspended various tools. A machine stands on the floor, activated from below by a large flywheel which is half sunk in a pit. Two men are in the picture. One is shown in profile; he is working at the machine. The other man is shown in rear view, watching the first.

See 37, Chapter III, for details.

The first story shows a high level of achievement motivation. Not particularly the words and phrases italicized by the original investigators

> Something is being heated in a type of furnace which appears to be c metal. The men are blacksmiths. The men have been doing *research* on an allo of some type, and *this is the crucial test* that spells success or failure of the experi ment. They want a specific type of metal. They are working for government in terests. They may be successful this time. They have *invented* a metal that is ver light, strong, durable, heat resistant, etc. A *real step in scientific progress (37*, p. 117

A much lower degree of motivation is revealed in the following ex ample. Note the absence of affective terms. Some achievement, however, i indicated by the goal of making a bolt and the indication of a probabl successful outcome:

> There are two men working in some sort of machine shop. They are makin some sort of a bolt or something. One of the men's car broke down, and he ha discovered that a bolt is broken. So, being a fairly good forger, he is making new bolt. He is discussing with the other man just how he is making the bolt an telling him about all of the details in making this bolt. When he is finished, h will take the bolt and replace the broken bolt in the car with it. He will then b able to get his car going (*37*, p. 119).

The following protocol illustrates unsuccessful achievement. Again, th italicized terms should be noted.

> The scene is a workshop. Two men are doing a very important job. The are grinding an important cog for a new jet engine which will attempt a fliglit t the moon. The inventor who doesn't want to let his secret out has hired thes two men to work secretly for him. They are not very well known, but if the jo is a success, they will be famous. They are both very tense, each knowing that on little mistake will mean *months of hard work* lost and wasted. When they are fir ished, they find that the piece is too small for the engine, and they have *faile* and must start again (*37*, p. 127).

With these illustrative stories from the study of the achievement motive we have indicated something about this promising attempt to measure mo tivation through fantasy. The work of McClelland and his associates is a extension of the pioneer work of Rorschach, who designed the famous "in blot" test which bears his name, and of the personality investigations carrie out by Murray and his associates, who developed the thematic apperceptio method and the original TAT as one of the techniques for the assessmen of personality. By way of a conclusion, we might note that the fantasy tech nique for the measurement of human motivation has the great advantage c being a "free" technique. The subject need not know he is being "tested," and, in his responses, he is at liberty to express himself as he sees fit. Since most of the traditional techniques for measuring animal motivation are obviously inappropriate for human beings, the techniques developed by McClelland and his associates are promising developments in a difficult field.

McClelland has recently extended the theory of achievement motivation into the area of society as a whole (38). The achieving society, he suggests, is not one especially favored by population growth, favorable economic conditions or natural resources but one that is high in achievement motivation. The entrepreneurial spirit, the presence of executives with high levels of drive, and a social orientation that emphasizes achievement in the training of children are factors which are necessary for high levels of social achievement.

McClelland has utilized such indices of economic development as the consumption of electric power, the importation of coal, and general trade as objective measures of the extent to which a society is achieving. Because it is not practical or, in the case of past societies, is impossible to obtain the achievement indices of executives and other leaders by means of fantasy, McClelland has utilized the nation's popular literature—poems, songs, plays, funeral orations, and books for the education of children—as indices of achievement motivation. By means of a coding system the level of achievement can be rated with reasonable objectivity and correlated with the indices of economic achievement.

Figures 11-7 and 11-8 show two such relationships graphically. Figure 11-7 shows how achievement motivation in Ancient Greece dropped sharply from about 850 B.C. to 200 B.C. and was accompanied by a sharp decrease in trade beginning about 550 B.C. The trade area in square miles was established by means of maps of trade drawn from the discovery of dated amphorae or jars which were used for carrying wine and olive oil and which can be recovered from the bottom of the sea in the area of wrecks. The lag in the decline of trade shows that the destruction of the Golden Age of Greece was not the result of Peloponnesian wars but was caused by a loss in achievement motivation. A nation of low achievers is not strongly motivated to protect what they have.

Similarly, Figure 11-8 shows how achievement motivation is correlated with rate of industrial growth in a modern nation. Change in industrial growth lags about a generation behind changes in achievement motivation, again suggesting a causal relationship. As nonachieving children grow up, economic growth declines. If subsequent adult generations begin to emphasize achievement, then, as their children reach maturity, the economic index rises.

McClelland has made a number of interesting comparisons between

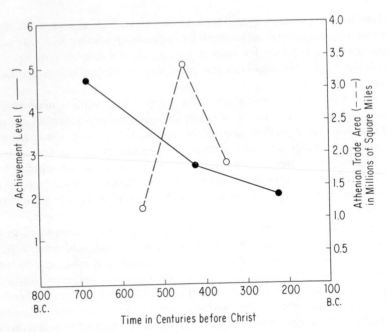

Fig. 11-7. Level of *n* Achievement as related to dispersion of trade in ancient Athens. (From McClelland, *38.*)

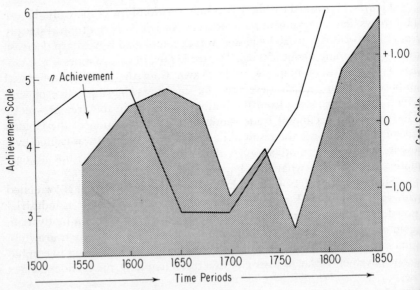

Fig. 11-8. A comparison of the level of *n* Achievement and utilization of coal from 1550 to 1850. (From McClelland, *39.*)

dern European nations and the United States and between capitalist
d communist nations (*38* and *39*). In each case he presents evidence to
ow that it is not the economic system, political considerations, or geo-
aphical factors which are responsible for economic success but the pres-
ce or absence of achievement motivation.

By way of general summary, we may point out that in regard to the
eoretical analysis of motivation presented by the authors, the concepts
d principles are in no sense revolutionary. Instead, the theory is built
ound a modification of the old concept of psychological hedonism. Per-
ps the only novel aspect of the theory is the hypothesis that motives
velop out of the affective states. As we pointed out previously, this view
ns counter to the current body of psychological opinion. At the present
ne we can only invoke the Scotch verdict "not proven." The studies of
e achievement and other motives certainly demonstrate that experi-
entally cued redintegration of affective states can be measured by fantasy
havior. Whether these results will be accepted as sufficient evidence for
e support of a general theory of human motivation in which motives arise
t of affective states is, at the present writing, impossible to predict.

Harlow's studies of intrinsic drives.   Traditionally, behavioristic psycholo-
sts have explained motivated activities in terms of certain inherent and
rived drives. Hunger, thirst, sex, maternal behavior, and other basic
ysiological drives are considered to be inherent and referable to tissue
eds. The more complex motives, such as those for affection, gregarious-
ss, safety, prestige, and the like are assumed to be derived from physiolog-
al drives through a process of learning. Thus, the infant is born with a
inger drive which is satisfied by the mother. But, because her presence is
sociated with the pleasantness of drive reduction, she comes to be de-
anded for her own sake. We may now speak of the presence of a motive
r affection or gregariousness.

The merits of the derived drive theory have been debated, particularly
organismic psychologists. They point out that drive reduction implies
at the animal or individual is seeking to reduce some kind of stimulation.
he irritations associated with sex, hunger, thirst, pain, and extremes of
vironmental stimulation act as goads impelling the organism to take
ch action as will reduce or eliminate the stimuli. However, as we have
ready pointed out (Chapter 5), studies of sensory deprivation show that
ople seek stimulation—indeed, find its absence intolerable. We also
ow from everyday experience that man is a curious, restless animal who
joys activity for its own sake without any extrinsic rewards.

Psychologist Harry Harlow (*16* to *19*) has brought the study of intrin-
cally motivated behavior into the animal laboratory and has shown that
onkeys will solve complicated puzzles without the necessity of introducing

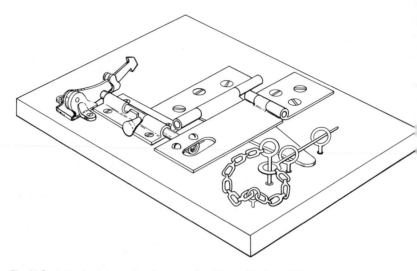

Fig. 11-9. A six-device mechanical puzzle. (From Harlow, *16*.)

extrinsic rewards—indeed, introducing an extrinsic reward made learnir less efficient.

Figure 11-9 shows the type of mechanical puzzle confronting tl monkeys in Harlow's experiment. For twelve days they were presented wit an assembled puzzle without any association between the puzzle and foc or water. A control group was presented with an already disassemble puzzle during the same period. On test days the experimental anima proved to be more efficient in disassembling the puzzles than the contr animals. The monkeys had learned to work the puzzle for the intrins reward of manipulation. When food rewards were subsequently introduce for solving the problem, the nature of the animals' behavior was marked altered. They now worked at the puzzle only to get at the food and showe little further interest in manipulation for the sake of manipulation.

Harlow has also shown that monkeys can be trained to make discrin inations by utilizing the curiosity drive as a motive (*19*). In this type experiment the animals are confined in a closed box which has two opaqi doors with different stimulus cards attached to the inside. One door wa selected by the experimenter as positive; and when the monkey pushed th door it opened, and he was allowed to look out. The other door was locke The animals showed high rates of response to the positive door and lo rates to the negative door. Moreover, studies have shown that the mo interesting the scene upon which the animal looks out (such as a toy tra moving) the more rapid the learning.

There have been a number of studies utilizing both animal and human subjects which involve other types of exploratory, manipulatory, and curiosity motives. These have been reviewed by Cofer and Appley (7, Chapter 6). As these authors point out, research with exploratory, manipulatory and curiosity drives is still in its infancy and much more work is needed before we can be sure that these are true drives which are under the primary control of a stimulus as opposed to external conditions. They do not deny that external stimulating conditions have the capacity to arouse behavior. However, it is possible that emotional arousal brought about by placing the animal in a dark room or a novel situation may be partially responsible for the observed activity. It is also suggested that deviations from a state of complete internal homeostasis or adaptation may be rewarding and therefore sought after by the animals.

Whatever the ultimate resolution of these points of controversy, studies of exploratory and manipulatory behavior have introduced a challenging problem for those interested in the psychology of motivation. Until it can be conclusively demonstrated that such drives are dependent upon some hidden extrinsic factor we must accept the possibility of intrinsically motivated behavior.

SUMMARY AND EVALUATION

Motivational psychology, the most central of all fields, is one of the least well-developed areas in psychology. The great variety of points of view and diverse experimental approaches summarized in this chapter leaves one wondering if any progress is being made toward an integrated theory of animal and human motivation. The fundamental dichotomies of atomism-holism, hard determinism, and the somatic versus the psychic basis for motivation sharply divide the behavioristic-comparative theorists from those whose concern is primarily with the human species.

However desirable it might be to conclude on a hopeful note, the gulf between these conflicting points of view seems too wide for any early or easy resolution.[21] Perhaps the most hopeful sign on the horizon is the increasing concern on the part of psychologists over the present unsatisfactory state of motivation theory. The increasing interest in the area, the greater quantity of research, and the attention given by learning theorists to motivational problems by way of a particular concern with reinforcement theory may, in the not too distant future, bring a new order to this important segment of the science of psychology.

[21] Such, certainly, is the impression gleaned from the yearly symposia at Nebraska (54).

REFERENCES

1. Adler, A. *Understanding human nature.* New York: Greenberg, 1927.
2. Adler, A. *The practice and theory of individual psychology.* New York: Harcourt, 1929.
3. Ansbacher, H. L., and R. Ansbacher. *The individual psychology of Alfred Adler.* New York: Basic Books, 1956.
4. Atkinson, J. (ed.). *Motives in fantasy, action, and society.* Princeton, N. J.: Van Nostrand, 1958.
5. Barker, R. G., T. Dembo, and K. Lewin. Frustration and regression: an experiment with young children. *University of Iowa Studies in Child Welfare,* **18,** No. 386, 1941.
6. Bindra, D. *Motivation: A systematic reinterpretation.* New York: Ronald, 1959.
7. Cofer, C. N., and M. Appley. *Motivation: Theory and research.* New York: Wiley, 1964.
8. Ellis, W. *A source book of Gestalt psychology.* London: Routledge, 1938.
9. Freud, S. *A general introduction to psychoanalysis.* New York: Boni & Liveright, 1920.
10. Freud, S. *Collected papers* (5 vols.). London: Hogarth Press, 1924–1950.
11. Freud, S. *New introductory lectures on psychoanalysis.* New York: Norton, 1933.
12. Freud, S. *The basic writings of Sigmund Freud.* New York: Modern Library, 1938.
13. Fromm, E. *Escape from freedom.* New York: Holt, Rinehart and Winston, 1941.
14. Goldstein, K. *The organism.* New York: American Book, 1939.
15. Goldstein, K. Organismic approach to the problem of motivation. *Transactions of the New York Academy of Sciences,* **9,** 1947, pp. 218–230.
16. Harlow, H. F. Learning and satiation of response in intrinsically motivated complex puzzle performance by monkeys. *Journal of Comparative and Physiological Psychology,* **43,** 1950, pp. 289–294.
17. Harlow, H. F., N. Blazek, and G. McClearn. Manipulatory motivation in the infant rhesus monkey. *Journal of Comparative and Physiological Psychology,* **49,** 1956, pp. 444–448.
18. Harlow, H. F., M. Harlow, and D. Meyer. Learning motivated by a manipulation drive. *Journal of Experimental Psychology,* **40,** 1950, pp. 228–234.
19. Harlow, H. F., and G. McClearn. Object discrimination learned by monkeys on the basis of manipulation motives. *Journal of Comparative and Physiological Psychology,* **47,** 1954, pp. 73–76.
20. Horney, K. *The neurotic personality of our time.* New York: Norton, 1937.
21. Horney, K. *New ways in psychoanalysis.* New York: Norton, 1939.
22. Horney, K. *Our inner conflicts.* New York: Norton, 1945.
23. Jones, E. *The life and work of Sigmund Freud,* (3 vols.). New York: Basic Books, 1953.
24. Jones, M. (ed.). *Nebraska symposium on motivation.* Lincoln: University of Nebraska Press, 1954.
25. Jung, C. *Psychology of the unconscious.* New York: Dodd, Mead, 1931.
26. Jung, C. *Psychological types.* New York: Harcourt, 1923.
27. Jung, C. *Modern man in search of a soul.* New York: Harcourt, 1933.
28. Lewin, K. *Principles of topological psychology.* New York: McGraw-Hill, 1936.
29. Lewin, K. *Contributions to psychological theory.* Durham, N. C.: Duke University Press, 1938.
30. Lewin, K., R. Lippitt, and R. White. Patterns of aggressive behavior in experimentally created "social climates." *Journal of Social Psychology,* **10,** 1939, pp. 271–299.

31. Lewin, K. Behavior and development as a function of the total situation. In Carmichael, L. (ed.), *Manual of child psychology*. New York: Wiley, 1946.
32. Lewis, H. B., and M. Franklin. An experimental study of the role of the ego in work, II. The significance of task-orientation in work. *Journal of Experimental Psychology*, **34**, 1944, pp. 195–215.
33. Lippitt, R. Field theory and experiment in social psychology: autocratic and democratic group atmospheres. *American Journal of Sociology*, **45**, 1939, pp. 26–49.
34. Lippitt, R., and R. White. The "social climate" of children's groups. In Barker, R. G., J. S. Kounin, and H. F. Wright (eds.), *Child behavior and development*. New York: McGraw-Hill, 1943.
35. Maslow, A. *Motivation and personality*. New York: Harper, 1954.
36. Maslow, A. Lessons from the peak experiences. In Farson, R. E. (ed.), *Science and human affairs*. Palo Alto, Calif.: Science and Behavior Books, 1965.
37. McClelland, D. C., J. Atkinson, R. Clark, and E. Lowell. *The achievement motive*. New York: Appleton, 1953.
38. McClelland, D. C. *The achieving society*. Princeton, N. J.: Van Nostrand, 1961.
39. McClelland, D. C. *The roots of consciousness*. Princeton, N. J.: Van Nostrand, 1964.
40. McDougall, W. *An introduction to social psychology*, ed. 14. Boston: J. W. Luce, 1921.
41. Miller, N. E. Experimental studies of conflict. In Hunt, J. McV. (ed.), *Personality and the behavior disorders*. New York: Ronald, 1944.
42. Morgan, C. *Physiological psychology*. New York: McGraw-Hill, 1943.
43. Morgan, C., and E. Stellar. *Physiological psychology*. New York: McGraw-Hill, 1950.
44. Morgan, C. Physiological mechanisms in motivation. In Jones, M. R. (ed.), *Nebraska symposium on motivation*. Lincoln: University of Nebraska Press, 1957.
45. Morgan, C. Physiological theory of drive. In Koch, S. (ed.), *Psychology: A study of science*, Vol. 1, New York: McGraw-Hill, 1959.
46. Munroe, R. *Schools of psychoanalytic thought*. New York: Dryden, 1955.
47. Olds, J., and P. Milner. Positive reinforcement produced by electrical stimulation of septal area and other regions of rat brain. *Journal of Comparative and Physiological Psychology*, **47**, 1954, pp. 419–427.
48. Osgood, C. E. *Method and theory in experimental psychology*. New York: Oxford, 1953.
49. Pfaffmann, C., and J. K. Bare. Gustatory nerve discharges in normal and adrenalectomized rats. *Journal of Comparative and Physiological Psychology*, **43**, 1950, pp. 320–324.
50. Richter, C. P. Total self-regulatory functions in animals and human beings. *The Harvey Lecture Series*, **38**, 1942, pp. 63–103.
51. Rogers, C. R. *Client-centered therapy; its current practice, implications, and theory*. Boston: Houghton Mifflin, 1951.
52. Young, P. T. *Motivation and emotion*. New York: Wiley, 1961.
53. Zeigarnik, B. On finished and unfinished tasks. In Ellis, W. (ed.), *A source book of Gestalt psychology*. London: Routledge, 1938.
54. In addition to the above, the student will find The Nebraska Symposia (issued yearly since 1953) a valuable source of papers on contemporary issues in motivational theory by leaders in the field. The volumes are issued by The University of Nebraska Press, Lincoln, Nebraska.

12

Feeling
and Emotion

In some respects the systematic psychology of the emotions is in an even more unsatisfactory state than that of motivation. One of the difficulties that has stood in the way of an acceptable theory of the emotions has been disagreements over the definition of the emotional processes. Some psychologists have held that the emotions are disruptive states of the organism which result from a loss of cortical dominance. Others assert that the opposite is nearer the truth, namely, that the emotions are organizing states which ready the individual for action in emergency situations. Still others take a middle-of-the-road position, treating emotional states as "activating" or "energizing" processes. We shall meet with representatives of some of these divergent viewpoints later in this chapter.

Another factor that has stood in the way of developing a valid psychology of the emotions is the lack of reliable experimental data upon which to erect a system. The emotions are not easy to isolate for experimental investigation in the artificial atmosphere of the psychology laboratory. Ethical or human considerations preclude studies of the more violent emotions of hate, sexual excitement, grief, or rage. There are equally cogent reasons why the more tender and complex emotions such as love are unsuitable for laboratory study. Moreover, even where it is possible to create reasonable facsimiles of genuine emotions in the laboratory, the techniques of investigation are likely to interfere with the emotions under study. For example, if the subject is asked to give a verbal report on how he feels, the calm "intellectual" attitude which he must assume tends to destroy the emotion.

However, despite the difficulties of definition and experimentation just enumerated, the emotional processes have by no means been neglected by the systematists and theo-

444

rists. Indeed, in the centuries comprising the prescientific era of psychology, we find a rich literature bearing on the emotions. Some of this we have touched upon from time to time in preceding chapters. We found that classical Grecian speculation on the dynamics of human behavior took the form of postulating humoral or blood factors which serve to arouse motivational and emotional states. The classical ethical philosophers and the Christian theologians, such as Thomas Aquinas and Saint Augustine, were also concerned with the dynamics of human behavior, and both advocated the control of the undesirable "passions" while encouraging the gentler emotions of love for God and man.

As we move down the centuries to the modern period in philosophy, we are again confronted with interest in the emotions from the orientation of ethical and practical problems. Indeed it has been said the underlying philosophical attitude toward the emotions that is characteristic of Western civilization has been one of suppression. In the older philosophical and moral literature the emotions are frequently characterized as "base," or as constituting man's "animal" nature. Such expressions are, of course, tinged with prejudice growing out of a particular point of view. It is interesting to note that one result of the recent scientific study of the emotions and the ascendance of the scientific point of view has been a more tolerant attitude toward man's irrational and emotional side. However, there would be little to be gained by dwelling on these traditional ethical issues and controversies. What we wish to emphasize is essentially this: The study of psychological processes from moral or ethical points of view, although legitimate within these special orientations, has little interest from the scientific frame of reference. The experimental psychologist seeks primarily to *predict* behavior and secondarily to *understand* it. The consequences of behavior from a moral or ethical standpoint are outside his purview.

In accordance with the preceding argument, we shall begin our study of the emotions with the systematic views of Titchener.[1] Following a summary of the structuralistic point of view, we shall examine the doctrines of representatives of the other schools of psychology and conclude with a note on contemporary studies of emotion.

AFFECTION AND EMOTION IN THE STRUCTURALISTIC PSYCHOLOGY OF TITCHENER[2]

Titchener introduces his systematic view of affection and emotion by considering certain problems of definition. Affection is defined as the ele-

Those interested in the prescientific psychology of the emotions will find an exhaustive treatment in *Feeling and Emotion* by Gardiner, Metcalf and Beebe-Center (9).
The exposition follows Titchener (25).

mentary mental process characteristic of feeling and of the emotions such as love, hate, joy, and sorrow. The term *feeling*[3] is used to denote a simple connection of sensation and affection in which the affective process dominates consciousness. For example, hunger is a sensation—a sensation which is coupled with an affective state of feeling. It may be a "gnawing" hunger or a pleasant, anticipatory hunger. In either case the affective element is added to the bare sensation. Similarly, pain, a sensation, arouses feelings of unpleasantness.

Feeling may also be used in a narrow sense to denote sensations of touch, roughness, solidity, and the like. Such experiences, Titchener believes, are more properly termed perceptions or touch blends and, as such, do not enter into the psychology of feeling and emotion.

Titchener next raises the question of how affection differs from the element sensation. He reiterates his definition of sensation as an elementary process constituted of four attributes: quality, intensity, clearness, and duration. Affection, however, has but three attributes: quality, intensity, and duration. Consequently, sensations and affections are processes of the same general type inasmuch as they have three attributes in common. They differ in that affection lacks clearness.

Affection has two qualities, *pleasantness* and *unpleasantness*. In other words, *any* affective state is introspectively either pleasant or unpleasant. Intensity is the dimension along which affection is described as "mildly pleasant," "disagreeable," "unbearable," or in similar terms. Finally, an affective state may be of short or long duration. A mild pinprick gives rise to a momentarily unpleasant state, whereas a bad mood may persist for days.

The affective processes resemble sensations in that both show adaptation. Placing the hand in lukewarm water arouses a mild sensation of warmth which quickly fades away as the skin temperature adapts to the surrounding water. Similarly, a musical composition or popular tune may initially excite strong feelings of pleasantness which gradually fade out with repetition of the selection.

Finally, affection also resembles organic sensation in the sense that pleasantness is closely associated in experience with bodily comfort, health, and drowsiness. Unpleasantness, on the other hand, is typically associated with pain, discomfort, fatigue, and illness.

However, despite the many resemblances which exist between sensations and the affective states, Titchener emphasizes that the two are nevertheless different. As has been pointed out, affection lacks clearness. On the other hand, if we attend to a sensation, it becomes clearer and clearer. If we attend to an affective state, the state disappears. There is, however, a further

---

[3] In practice, Titchener falls into the habit of using feeling and affection synonymously.

difference between the two processes. Pleasantness and unpleasantness are opposites. There is no such antagonism among the sensory processes. Two or more sensory qualities may, in fact, be combined. We cannot, however, experience pleasantness and unpleasantness at the same time. Titchener admits that popular speech favors the point of view that we can experience "mixed feelings." Despair is lightened by hope; there is no pleasure without pain; crying may be mixed with laughter. Titchener suggests that these are, in reality, alternating states of feeling or affection. He states that in his laboratory experience he has never found an unmistakable case of mixed feeling.

Titchener next deals with the question of laboratory techniques for investigating the affective processes. Basically, there are two: (1) the method of impression, and (2) the method of expression. The method of impression is illustrated by the psychophysical method of paired comparisons. If, for example, the problem is to arrange fifty mixed color samples along a scale ranging from most pleasant to least pleasant, the observer begins by comparing the first color with every other, meanwhile recording his impressions as he goes along. Color number two is then compared with every other one, and so forth. At the end of the experiment the preferences can be summarized or averaged for each color. The introspective task, Titchener adds, is simple; the lengthy comparisons, "laborious."

The method of expression involves the measurement of bodily changes which accompany the affective processes. The measures Titchener describes are the still familiar techniques for recording the respiratory, circulatory, and muscular changes which occur during emotional states. Interestingly enough, he points out that the psychogalvanic response has within "a year or two been brought into the psychological laboratory." Since the method had not yet been extensively used, Titchener prefers not to "judge of its merit."

The bulk of the remainder of Titchener's chapter on affection is devoted to a refutation of Wundt's "Tridimensional Theory of Feeling." Wundt published his famous theory in 1896. In essence, he argued that feelings cannot be described in terms of their pleasantness-unpleasantness, but require three dimensions for a valid description: (1) pleasantness-unpleasantness, (2) tension-relaxation, and (3) excitement-depression (see Figure 12-1). Each feeling moves, first, between the poles of P-U, then between E-D, and finally between T-R. For example, the feeling associated with mirth would move rapidly out along the dimension of pleasantness, while at the same time excitement and tension would be added. The feeling, in this case, would then drop back to relaxation tinged, perhaps, with depression and slight unpleasantness. Other feelings, depending on their nature, would take different courses.

Wundt's theory gained many adherents, but Titchener believes that

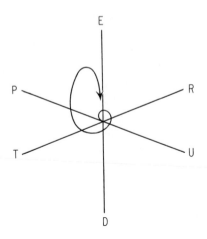

Fig. 12-1. Diagram to represent Wundt's tridimensional theory of feeling. For explanation see text.

it is incorrect and maintains that feelings can vary only along the dimensions already discussed in the preceding paragraphs. More specifically, he denies that the dimensions of tension-relaxation and excitement-depression are simple, elementary mental processes, as Wundt believed, but instead that they are "muscular attitudes." Moreover tension and relaxation are not true opposites. Relaxation, he insists, is the zero point of tension—not its opposite. Similarly, excitement and depression are not true opposites. Is not calm, he asks, a more logical opposite for excitement than depression?

With these and similar objections, Titchener attempts to show that the theory is not logically constructed and cannot, moreover, meet certain experimental tests which we need not go into here. This old controversy is no longer an issue in the psychology of emotions, but this much can be said for Titchener's side of the argument: The weight of the introspective evidence suggests that pleasantness-unpleasantness is the best-established of the possible affective dimensions.

Turning to Titchener's treatment of the emotions, we have already pointed out that he considers the affective states or feelings to be the characteristic element in the emotional process. Because the organic or visceral reactions and the expressive or bodily aspect of the affective states are equally characteristic of the emotions, Titchener addresses himself to the problem of how the several aspects of emotional behavior are integrated. He examines and rejects the James-Lange theory,[4] then outlines his own views.

[4] See the following section.

The organic or visceral responses, Titchener holds, are intensified and extended forms of the affective reaction. That is, increased heart rate, respiratory changes, glandular disturbances, and other organic reactions are, in mild form, characteristic of the affective states. More intense forms of these visceral changes occur in emotional states because the affective element is intensified as a result of the more primitive nature of the adjustment involved. Titchener believes that the organic reactions in ordinary emotions are essentially carry-overs or vestigial processes from a period of evolutionary development when strong overt emotional reactions were invariably associated with adjustments to critical situations. In civilized society, man tends to suppress his emotional reactions so that organic responses are primarily covert or visceral except in emergency situations. However, it should be emphasized that Titchener considers the core of emotional states to be the affective reaction. The organic processes are merely associated or parallel processes, which are exaggerated forms of the more subtle organic reactions typical of the affective states.

Finally, with regard to the expression of the emotions in behavioral and facial reactions, Titchener holds that we must look to biology for the explanation of these processes. He invokes Darwin's three principles to account for such expressions. The principles in question are: (1) the principle of "serviceable associated habits," (2) the principle of "antithesis," and (3) the principle of "direct action of the excited nervous system on the body." The first principle assumes that many expressive behavioral and facial reactions are vestigial reflections of once practical or serviceable movements. The bared fangs of primitive jungle combat become the grimace of rage in civilized society. The expression of grief is a toned-down version of the wild sobbing of primitive people or of the infant. Presumably as evolution proceeds, there is less need for the strongly overt reactions and, as a consequence of their decreasing usefulness, they become more and more reduced in intensity.

Darwin's second principle, that of "antithesis," is the hypothesis that opposite emotional processes tend to give rise to opposite reactions. For example, laughter, the opposite of sobbing, is explained as spasmodically interrupted *expiration*—the opposite being interrupted *inspiration* or sobbing.

Finally, the principle of "the direct action of the excited nervous system of the body" explains violent trembling, the paralysis characteristic of panic, and other extreme emotional reactions in which there is an overflow or spill-over of the nervous processes because of the extremity of the reaction.

The remainder of Titchener's treatment of the emotions concerns such problems as the classification of emotions; the definition of such complex processes as moods, temperament, and sentiments; and the description of the characteristics of the emotive memory. We need not, however, be con-

cerned with his treatment of these problems, since they are not fundamenta
to his systematic psychology of emotion. Indeed, he was far more interested
in the psychology of feeling and the affective states than in the emotiona
processes. Because feeling and affection are elementary processes from
Titchener's point of view, they lend themselves to the structuralists' char
acteristic method of introspection. The distinctive attributes of the emo
tional processes, on the other hand, are behavioral. Since these are obviously
physiological rather than conscious, Titchener's interest in them is only
tangential. In conclusion, Titchener's system offers no unique contribution
to the psychology of the affective or emotional processes. Rather, affection
or feeling is treated as an element co-ordinate with sensations and images

FUNCTIONALISM AND EMOTION

Carr[5] treats the emotions as part of the "background of mental life."
Emotions are defined as *organic readjustments* which occur automatically in
the face of appropriate behavioral situations. Thus, the emotion of ange
arises when the organism is confronted with a serious obstacle to freedom
of movement. In this instance the organic readjustment involves a mobiliza
tion of energy to aid the individual in his efforts to overcome the obstacle
The quickened pulse, the withdrawal of blood from the viscera, more rapid
respiration, and other bodily changes enable the organism to react more
energetically and vigorously. Clearly, in the case of anger and fear, Carr'
definition is in keeping with his overall viewpoint. However, it would be
a mistake to assume that he holds *all emotions to be biologically useful*. On
the contrary, as Carr himself points out, such emotions as grief and joy
may have no biological utility whatever in some situations.

Driving to the heart of the problem, Carr states that "the various emo
tions can be readily identified and defined only in terms of the behaviora
situation in which they occur . . ." (2, p. 278). Moreover, he points out tha
the reaction in emotional states is highly similar to that found in any kind
of vigorous exercise or activity. The distinguishing feature of emotiona
states arises from the fact that they occur in cases where there is a *lack o
adequate motor outlets*. Once the individual begins to react to the situation
the emotional response dies down. In the following paragraph Carr sum
marizes his point of view on the basic nature of the emotional processes

> The emotional reactions thus occur in the absence of any correlative act
> or they develop and run their course with some degree of independence of the

[5] The exposition follows Carr's *Psychology* (2).

act and hence largely determine the character of that act. We thus suggest that it is these surging, seething, tumultuous, impulsive, and explosive features that constitute the distinctive characteristic of an emotional type of organic readjustment. Thus an emotion may well be called an organic commotion. In support of this conception, we may call attention to the well-known fact that the emotions tend to disappear with action. Our anger soon cools and wanes when we begin to fight, and terror no longer holds us in its grip when we indulge in strenuous flight. The difference between these two conditions does not consist of the presence and absence of an organic disturbance, for both fighting and flight obviously involve a very pronounced readjustment on the part of the vital activities. Evidently the disappearance of the emotions with overt action is due to a change in the character of the organic reaction. Given an adequate motor outlet, these organic activities gradually become adapted to the exigencies of the act, and hence they lose their initial tumultuous and impulsive character and the experience is no longer labelled an emotion (2, pp. 282–283).

He then summarizes the James-Lange[6] theory of emotions and shows how his own conceptions differ from those postulated by James and Lange. The James-Lange theory identifies the emotion with the perception of the organic changes. In James's own words:

Common-sense says, we lose our fortune, are sorry and weep; we meet a bear, are frightened and run; we are insulted by a rival, are angry and strike. The hypothesis here to be defended says that this order of sequence is incorrect, that the one mental state is not immediately induced by the other, that the bodily manifestations must first be interposed between, and that the more rational statement is that we feel sorry because we cry, angry because we strike, afraid because we tremble, and not that we cry, strike, or tremble because we are sorry, angry, or fearful, as the case may be. Without the bodily states following on the perception, the latter would be purely cognitive in form, pale, colorless, destitute of emotional warmth. We might then see the bear and judge it best to run, receive the insult and deem it right to strike, but we should not actually *feel* afraid or angry (17, pp. 375–376).

Further on in his famous chapter on the emotions, James attempts to support his theory by an appeal to the reader's sense of logic:

If we fancy some strong emotion, and then try to abstract from our consciousness of it all the feelings of its bodily symptoms, we find we have nothing left behind, no "mind-stuff" out of which the emotion can be constituted, and that a cold and neutral state of intellectual perception is all that remains (17, p. 379).

Finally, we might note that in support of his position James asked Broadway actors and actresses if they experienced emotions while going through the

---

[6] Lange was a Danish physiologist who postulated a theory of the emotions similar to James's. Consequently the two names are linked.

motions of acting out emotional scenes. Theoretically, a stage fight or "love scene" ought to create the organic changes, and these, in turn, should arouse the appropriate emotion. James was told that such, indeed, was frequently the case. However, the evidence he was able to marshal in support of this theory is not very convincing, and as will be brought out later in this chapter, the Cannon-Bard theory accounts for the facts of emotional experience more satisfactorily than does the James-Lange theory.

Carr differs from James and Lange in two respects. First, Carr insists on the psychophysical nature of the emotions and, as a consequence, is unable to accept the view that emotions are explicable solely as the perception of the organic processes. Carr, in other words, believes there is a conscious aspect to the emotions *which is independent of the organic* processes. Second, he argues that the emotion is partly responsible for the behavioral act. To relate his argument to James's example of fleeing from a bear, Carr believes the emotion of fear is partly the cause of running. James, on the other hand, made fear contingent upon the behavioral act of running.

In summary, Carr treats emotions as psychophysical events which are organic readjustments occurring in certain behavioral situations. The name given to the emotions depends upon the situation in which it occurs. Whereas emotions are organic readjustments, not all emotions are biologically useful. Again, the utility value of an emotion must be defined in terms of the behavioral situation in which that emotion occurs. In general, we might note that his treatment of the emotions offers nothing unique or even highly characteristic of the functional point of view. As we have noted earlier, Carr is particularly interested in perception and learning. Emotions are treated somewhat incidentally as part of the "background" of mental life.

EMOTION IN GESTALT PSYCHOLOGY

As has been emphasized throughout this survey of systematic psychology, the Gestalt school's primary interest was in the field of perception. Consequently, none of the original leaders of the movement developed a particular point of view on the emotions. Even Lewin with his strong interest in dynamic psychology did not formulate a characteristic theory of emotion. Moreover, in contemporary Gestalt-oriented treatments of the subject, the emotions are typically treated as inevitable concomitants of motivated behavior which have little significance if abstracted out of the motivational context. Because the Gestalt school failed to elaborate a special systematic point of view on the emotions, we shall go on to the more fertile ground of behaviorism.

FEELING AND EMOTION
FROM THE BEHAVIORISTIC POINT OF VIEW[7]

In his *Behavior: An Introduction to Comparative Psychology,* Watson admits that affection is one of two serious "stumbling blocks" in the way of a strictly objective psychology. The other is thinking. If the thought processes and affective states cannot be reduced to behavioristically observable phenomena, the whole behavioristic program is in grave danger of collapse.

We have already found that Watson solved the problem for the thought processes by reducing thinking to laryngeal habits or "implicit" speech (see Chapter 10). In dealing with the affective states he followed essentially the same line of reasoning, arguing that pleasantness-unpleasantness are reducible to implicit muscular and glandular reactions. More specifically, he assumed that the reproductive organs and associated erogenous zones function in affection in much the same manner that laryngeal habits function in the thought processes. The erogenous areas he believed to be capable of initiating two fundamental kinds of impulses: (1) a group of impulses associated with tumescence and rhythmical contractions of muscular tissues and increased glandular secretions; (2) a group connected with the detumescence of the sex organs, relaxation of associated muscular tissues, and inhibition of secretions.

The complete, overt functioning of the structures described under Group 1 occurs during sexual excitement and the unfolding of the reproductive act. Similarly, as gross sexual excitement dies down, the processes described under Group 2 are in the ascendance. Watson goes on to argue that *the afferent impulses associated with the phenomena in Group 1 are the bodily substrata of pleasantness, and the afferent impulses associated with Group 2 processes are the substrata of unpleasantness.* Originally, then, pleasantness and unpleasantness are aroused by sexual stimulation. If the organism is sexually receptive, the result is an approach reaction accompanied by tumescence, muscular tension, and increased glandular secretions. These reactions are pleasant. If, on the other hand, the organism is sexually unreceptive, the result is an avoidance reaction accompanied by inhibition of the sexual processes and the arousal of the affective state of unpleasantness.

Watson next deals with the problem of how objects or stimuli not originally connected with the sexual processes come to arouse feelings of pleasantness or unpleasantness. The answer to this difficulty is to be found in the ordinary mechanisms of habit or conditioning. Stimuli not originally associated with sexual behavior (therefore not capable of arousing the pattern of reactions associated with either pleasantness or unpleasantness) can,

[7] Our exposition of Watson's views on feeling follows his *Behavior: An Introduction to Comparative Psychology* (26). The discussion of emotion follows *Psychology from the Standpoint of a Behaviorist* (27).

through substitution or conditioning, arouse such reactions to a faint degree (implicit behavior). He presents no direct evidence for his assertions other than to note that phallic symbols, fetishes, and other phenomena from the area of sexual pathology support his contentions.

Finally, Watson suggests several avenues of approach for assessing the validity of his theory and, at the same time, carrying out behavioristic studies of the affective processes. First, the behaviorist will attempt to determine whether the muscular and glandular processes presumed to be associated with affective reactions do indeed set up afferent impulses. He will also be able to carry out plethysmographic and galvanometric studies of the sex organs themselves. Finally, by eliminating the sensory tracts leading from the glands, the behaviorist can determine the effects of the absence of afferent impulses. Watson is convinced that the sexual impulses play "an enormous role" in artistic, esthetic, and religious behavior. He believes that the more liberal views toward the study of sex are rapidly making people lose their prejudice toward acknowledging the possibility of the sexual reference of all behavior.

In summary, Watson treated the affective consciousness as an epiphenomenon unworthy of serious study. By identifying the affective states of pleasantness and unpleasantness with their bodily substrata in the erogenous zones, he believed that he had opened an avenue of approach to the behavioristic investigation of these processes. While admitting that no such studies had been carried out successfully, Watson was nevertheless satisfied that he had succeeded in bringing the difficult problem of affective psychology into his behavioristic program.

As is evident in his definition, Watson's view of the emotions is highly similar to his earlier position on feeling or affection. He defined an emotion as a "*hereditary 'pattern-reaction' involving profound changes of the bodily mechanism as a whole, but particularly of the visceral and glandular systems*" (*27*, p. 195). By pattern-reaction Watson refers to the various components of the response which appear with some degree of regularity each time the appropriate stimulus situation arises. He believes that there are three such fundamental patterns in the human infant. These are: *fear, rage,* and *love.* The appropriate stimulus situation for the evocation of fear is either a sudden loss of support or a loud sound. For rage, the stimulus is hampering the infant's movements; and for love, stroking or manipulating one of the erogenous zones.

The hereditary reaction-pattern characteristic of fear consists of a sudden catching of the breath, closing the eyes, puckering the lips, and random clutching movements of the hands and arms. For rage, the responses are stiffening of the body, screaming, and slashing or striking movements of the arms and legs. For love, the responses consist of smiling, cooing, and extension of the arms as if to embrace the experimenter.

Again, Watson faced the problem of demonstrating how the vast anorama of human emotions arises from the basic three. Once more the nswer is through conditioning and habit. Environmental conditioning, rst of all, brings about a partial inhibition of the more obvious external motional responses. Thus, the violent responses of the infant become the mplicit glandular and smooth muscular reactions of the adult. The second ffect of environmental conditioning is the attachment of the basic herediary responses to a variety of stimuli which are originally not capable of liciting them. Watson, himself, proceeded to show how this was possible >y conditioning an eleven-month-old boy to fear a rat. Watson's description •f this famous experiment follows:

(1) White rat suddenly taken from the basket and presented to Albert. He began to reach for rat with left hand. Just as his hand touched the animal the bar was struck immediately behind his head. The infant jumped violently and fell forward, burying his face in the mattress. He did not cry, however.

(2) Just as his right hand touched the rat the bar was again struck. Again the infant jumped violently, fell forward, and began to whimper.

In order not to disturb the child too seriously no further tests were given for one week.

Eleven months, ten days old. (1) Rat presented suddenly without sound. There was steady fixation but no tendency at first to reach for it. The rat was then placed nearer, whereupon tentative reaching movements began with the right hand. When the rat nosed the infant's left hand the hand was immediately withdrawn. He started to reach for the head of the animal with the forefinger of his left hand but withdrew it suddenly before contact. It is thus seen that the two joint stimulations given last week were not without effect. He was tested with his blocks immediately afterwards to see if they shared in the process of conditioning. He began immediately to pick them up, dropping them and pounding them, etc. In the remainder of the tests the blocks were given frequently to quiet him and to test his general emotional state. They were always removed from sight when the process of conditioning was underway.

(2) Combined stimulation with rat and sound. Started, then fell over immediately to right side. No crying.

(3) Combined stimulation. Fell to right side and rested on hands with head turned from rat. No crying.

(4) Combined stimulation. Same reaction.

(5) Rat suddenly presented alone. Puckered face, whimpered, and withdrew body sharply to left.

(6) Combined stimulation. Fell over immediately to right side and began to whimper.

(7) Combined stimulation. Started violently and cried, but did not fall over.

(8) Rat alone. The instant the rat was shown the baby began to cry. Almost instantly he turned sharply to the left, fell over, raised himself on all fours and began to crawl away so rapidly that he was caught with difficulty before he reached the edge of the table.[8]

---

[8] From *Psychology from the Standpoint of a Behaviorist*, ed. 2, pp. 232–233.

Watson went on to show that Albert, though originally conditionec to fear a rat, generalized his fear to a variety of furry animals. He als showed fear of a fur coat and Santa Claus whiskers. Watson suggests tha many adult aversions, phobias, fears, and anxieties for which the individua has no rational explanation may well have arisen years before by a proces of conditioning.

Finally, the native or fundamental emotions and their substitute deriv atives become combined and consolidated into more and more comple emotions. Love, by such an evolutionary process, gives rise to tenderness sympathy, love-sickness, and related emotions; fear, to embarrassment anguish, anxiety, and similar derivatives; and rage to hate, jealousy, anger and similar emotions.

Watson's insistence on a behavioristic approach to the emotions, alon with his interest in the physiological changes which accompany emotiona behavior, was highly influential in stimulating a great deal of research or emotional development in children and on the specific reaction pattern in specific emotions. However, subsequent experiments failed to substan tiate the specific responses postulated by Watson. When the experimente is unaware of the stimulating situation, infantile reactions do not necessaril conform to those announced by Watson. If observers are aware of th stimuli applied to the infant, agreement as to the emotional nature of th infant's reaction is much better (23, 24). Apparently, adults tend to read their own feelings into the child's behavior. Consequently, if he *observes* th infant being dropped, the adult assumes the observed reaction is fear. I addition to the likelihood that Watson fell victim to this error, his observa tions were limited to a relatively small number of infants. Bridges (1), wh has observed a large number of infants and young children over a wide ag range, believes that infants show only general excitement which, with in creasing age, differentiates into the basic emotions of distress and delight The latter, in turn, undergo differentiation into more and more comple emotions.

Similarly, a number of studies of the physiological changes accompany ing emotional behavior have failed to verify the hypothesis that a specifi pattern of changes is correlated with specific emotions. The one clear-cu exception is the startle pattern studied extensively by Landis and Hunt (19) Unexpected stimuli result in a rapid "hunching" of the body. The head i thrown forward; the eyes blink; and the mouth widens. However, in th case of the other emotions, the degree of activation of the various orgar systems appears to be the only reliable index of differentiation.

One significant outcome of the broad research program directec toward the investigation of the physiological substrata of the emotions wa the development of the famous Cannon-Bard theory of the emotions. Th theory belongs to no particular "school" of psychology, but because it i essentially behavioristic in orientation, we have chosen to include it in this section. The theory emphasizes the fact that strong emotions ready the individual for emergency reactions. For this reason, it is frequently called the "emergency" theory of the emotions. In essence, the theory postulates that the sympathetic division of the autonomic nervous system is dominant during emotional states. The effects of massive sympathetic stimulation are well known. The heart is speeded; digestion is inhibited; respiration is deeper and more rapid; blood is shunted to the periphery from the viscera. However, of all the visceral changes that occur the most significant is the release of large quantities of adrenalin into the blood stream. In general, adrenalin mimics a massive sympathetic discharge. Consequently, all of the sympathetic effects already described are reinforced by the action of adrenalin on the various internal organs. In addition, adrenalin causes the blood to clot faster in the event that the individual is injured during the emergency, and it also acts on the muscles in such a way as to lessen fatigue.

Cannon and Bard identified the hypothalamus as the main integrating center in the brain for the control of behavioral reactions in emotions.[9] They found that when the hypothalamus is removed from animals, emotional responses become fragmentary and disintegrated. Approaching the problem from another direction, they demonstrated that electrical stimulation of the hypothalamus results in a full-fledged rage and attack pattern. Removal of the cerebral cortex lowers the threshold for rage responses in animals, indicating that it normally exerts an inhibiting influence over the hypothalamus. It has also been demonstrated that rage responses in decorticate animals are short-lived and disappear almost as soon as the stimulus is withdrawn. Moreover, the rage responses of such animals are lacking in direction. It is as if the animal fails to appreciate the source of the irritating stimulus. Such a view seems entirely justified, since decorticate animals lack the neurological mechanisms for perceiving, judging, and directing their behavior toward a goal.

As a result of their classic researches on the hypothalamus, Cannon and Bard postulated a "thalamic theory" of the emotions in opposition to the James-Lange theory. The thalamic theory states that nervous impulses coming into the hypothalamus from the receptors stimulate that center to send impulses to the cortex and viscera simultaneously. (See Figure 12-2.) The arrival of the impulses in the cortex gives rise to the conscious experience of an emotion. The motor impulses sent to the viscera by way of the sympathetic nervous system result in the emergency state described earlier. Thus, while James and Lange made the emotional experience dependent upon afferent impulses from the viscera and consequently a *result* of emotional behavior, Cannon and Bard held that the emotional experience and

---

[9] See *20*, *28*, and *29* for more extensive discussions of the theory and summaries of the relevant experimental literature.

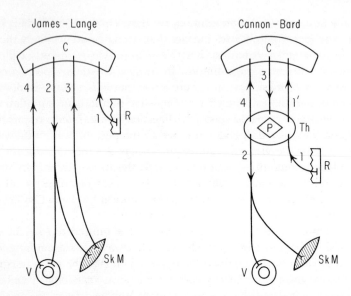

Fig. 12-2. Diagrams of the nerve connections in the James–Lange and Cannon–Bard theories. *C*, cortex; *R*, a receptor; *Th*, thalamus; *V*, viscera; *SkM*, skeletal muscle; *P*, pattern of simultaneous thalamic impulses. Lines 1–4 represent nervous pathways. (From Walter B. Cannon, Again the James–Lange and the Thalamic Theories of Emotion. *Psychological Review, 38,* 1931, p. 282.)

the expressive responses both occur *at the same time* as a result of hypothalamic activity. In diagrammatic terms the two theories can be contrasted as follows:

James-Lange: Perception → motor reaction → visceral arousal → emotion

Cannon-Bard: Perception → hypothalamic arousal ↗ emotion
                                                    ↘ visceral arousal

Whereas the Cannon-Bard theory "explains" more of the phenomena associated with emotional behavior than the James-Lange theory and, at the same time, is more thoroughly grounded in experimental evidence, it must not be concluded that the latter theory has been "disproved." Although the majority of psychologists have come to accept the Cannon-Bard theory as the better of the two, there remains a grain of truth in the contention that visceral and behavioral responses do, in part, determine how we feel. Anyone who has been frightened knows that sensations arising from the shaking limbs, the dry mouth, the quivering stomach, and reac-ions in the other organs reinforce the feeling of fear; and, when it is possible to pull oneself together," fear is to some degree alleviated. To this extent he James-Lange theory remains good phenomenological psychology, and, s such, cannot be summarily dismissed.

In bringing to a conclusion our survey of the contributions from within he behavioristic orientation to the psychology of feeling and emotion, the ollowing generalizations appear to be justified. First, of all the contribu- ions to the area of feeling and emotion within the *academic* schools, the ehaviorists have done more to further our understanding *of the emotions* han any other group. It should be noted that we are careful to specify that his contribution lies within the restricted area of the *emotions*—not feeling r affective psychology. Watson's assumptions that affective psychology ould be reduced to its objective manifestations in the sex organs and glands as never been substantiated. In the case of the emotions, however, the ehaviorists may be credited with two significant contributions. First, Wat- on's own research on the emotional reactions of children, although erro- eous in its conclusions, led to widespread studies in this area which have ast considerable illumination on the development of the emotions during hildhood.[10] Second, studies of the physiological concomitants of emotional ehavior, though not exclusively of behavioristic origin, have either temmed largely from that orientation or have been stimulated by it. In his same connection, we might point to the close parallel in the direction f research now taking place on the identification of the central brain nechanisms in both the emotional and motivational processes. (See Chap- er 13.) It is too early to predict a merger between these two areas, but the ast several decades have witnessed a growing rapprochement between hese rapidly developing fields.

THE PSYCHOANALYTIC VIEW OF THE EMOTIONS[11]

Freud, it will be recalled, postulated that the sexual instinct, or libido, as the fundamental motive or driving force in the infant. Because of the rgency of the instinct, the child seeks pleasure by reduction of tension in he sexual organs and erogenous zones. For this reason Freud spoke of the hild's behavior as governed by the pleasure principle. In his own words: It seems that our entire physical activity is bent upon *procuring pleasure and voiding pain,* that it is automatically regulated by the pleasure-principle" 5, p. 365).

Opposed to the sexual, or libido, instincts are the "ego instincts." The go is Freud's equivalent for the "I" or self. One of the functions of the ego

) See *18* for an account of the work in this area.
 The pertinent references are *5* to *8* and *21*.

is to serve as a mediator between the libido and the environment. The ego in other words, strives to give the libido satisfaction within the limits set b the demands of the environment. For this reason, Freud spoke of th "reality principle" as the guiding force behind the ego. Consequently, th child is operating according to the demands of two sets of instincts—th sexual, or libido, instincts which are governed by the pleasure principl and the ego instincts operating according to the reality principle.

Freud believed that the pleasure principle is dominant in the earl years, whereas in the adult, the reality principle gains ascendance. Obv ously, in the normal course of development such a transition would b necessary if the individual is to successfully meet the demands of society.

It was within this theoretical framework that Freud developed his doc trines of the emotions. However, he did not attempt to formulate a system atic view of all the emotions, but instead concentrated on the problem c anxiety, the emotion which has the greatest relevance for psychoanalyti theory.

Freud distinguishes three main types of anxiety: *objective anxiety, neuroti anxiety,* and *moral anxiety.* All three types represent reactions of weakness o the part of the ego in the face of demands made on the individual b reality, the id, and the superego. Objective anxiety is the consequence c weakness toward the id, and moral anxiety stems from weakness towar the superego—Freud's equivalent for conscience.

The individual confronted by heavy demands arising from the environ ment becomes anxious. Such a condition first occurs at birth when the in fant is suddenly overwhelmed by massive stimulation from the environmen The "birth trauma," as Freud referred to primary objective anxiety, is th prototype for the recurrence of secondary anxiety reactions later in the indi vidual's life. Thus, whenever the individual is confronted by the likelihoo of a traumatic experience, there is a reinstatement of the feelings associate with the original trauma of birth. It should be noted that anxiety is a reac tion to an *anticipated* danger. Hence it is only correct to speak of anxiet when the individual expects trouble. If the danger or trauma actuall occurs, the consequent reaction is *fear*, not anxiety.

By relating primary and secondary anxiety, Freud sought to explai the symptoms characteristic of adult anxiety. The tense, restricted breath ing, the trembling which results from massive motor nerve discharge, th rapid heart beat, and so on, which are found in a typical anxiety attack mimic the emotional conditions exhibited by the infant shortly after birt

Neurotic anxiety is, in the last analysis, reducible to the objectiv anxiety from which it is derived. In neurotic anxiety, the individual fear the possible consequences of giving in to the demands of his own libido. Th real basis of his fear, however, is apprehension about the objective conse quences of his own behavior. Specifically, he is afraid of the social conse

iences of engaging in forbidden sexual behavior. Thus, it is proper to con-
der neurotic anxiety a special form of objective anxiety.

Neurotic anxiety may take one of two forms. The first is "free-floating"
ixiety, in which the individual continually anticipates the worst possible
itcomes, is inclined to misinterpret chance happenings as evil omens, and
especially fearful of ambiguous situations, from which he foresees the
orst consequences. The second is a more circumscribed form in which the
notion is aroused by specific objects and situations. The second type is
ost clearly exemplified in the various phobias wherein the individual may
e afraid of such objects or situations as snakes, open spaces, thunder,
seases—indeed, almost any stimulus object or situation can become the
ndition for a phobic reaction.

However, the particular form that neurotic anxiety takes is not the
ndamental problem for psychotherapy. Whether the individual is suffer-
g from free-floating anxiety or specific phobias, the basic cause is an un-
nscious fear of the libidinal impulses which must be resolved.

The third form of anxiety, moral anxiety, is also based on objective
ixiety. Because the superego is developed as a result of introjected moral
rohibitions and restrictions from the parents, the original source of all
ioral anxiety or guilt is environmental and consequently objective. More
articularly, moral anxiety may be understood as a derivative of the original
iildhood fear of losing the love and good will of the parents, and possibly
being punished. Obviously, in the adult, the whole mechanism is no longer
iediated through a conscious fear of parental loss or retaliation for immoral
ehavior, but instead is a secondary or derived consequence of such early
ars, just as secondary objective anxiety is genetically related to the primary
irth trauma.

Finally, we should like to point out that Freud attributed a motiva-
onal function to both neurotic and moral anxiety, in the sense that either
iay lead to repression. As the ego becomes aware of danger, it takes steps
reduce the attendant anxiety by repressing the impulse which gave rise
the emotion in the first place. Looked at from this point of view, repres-
on becomes a mechanism for dealing with anxiety.

In concluding our discussion of Freud's theory of anxiety, it should be
nphasized that his conception of this emotion is congruent with the
ehavioristic-physiological view of the emotions. More particularly, Freud
oked upon primary anxiety as an instinctive reflex (birth trauma) which
ecomes attached to all sorts of stimuli through a process of conditioning.
his formulation closely follows both Watson's and the neobehavioristic
iew in which hereditary emotional responses become attached through
inditioning to a variety of originally neutral or nontraumatic stimuli. In
ie following section we shall find that Freud's organic-dynamic view of
ie emotions has been broadened into an entirely new branch of medicine,

"psychosomatic medicine," which recognizes the close relationship betwee
emotional (psychic) disorders and bodily (somatic) disorders.

EMOTION IN NEO-FREUDIAN AND CONTEMPORARY PSYCHIATRIC PRACTICE

Among adherents of the neo-Freudian psychoanalytic group, th
problem of anxiety continues to be of central importance in accounting fo
the structure of the neuroses. Karen Horney, our representative of tha
school, considers anxiety to be ". . . the dynamic center of the neuroses . .
(15, p. 41). According to her interpretation, unconscious hostile impulse
are the main source of neurotic anxiety. Hostile impulses, in turn, aris
from conflict. According to Horney, the individual in a conflict situation
caught between two incompatible motives, as we brought out more full
in the previous chapter (see Chapter 11). For example, the individual wh
is at one and the same time attempting to move toward and against peop
becomes anxious because of the repressed hostility underlying his attituc
toward others. Because the neurotic is aware that others meet his excessiv
demands with rebuffs, more anxiety is generated. Therefore, the very mear
employed to reduce anxiety lead to its increase. The end result is the deve
opment of what Horney calls "vicious circles." She believes that such ci
cular reactions account, in part, for the tendency of the neurotic to gro
worse unless the root of the problem is unearthed through appropria
therapeutic procedures.

While placing considerably more emphasis on the contemporaneou
nature of neurotic conflicts than is characteristic of the traditional Freudia
school, Horney nevertheless agrees that every neurosis is a disturbance
the individual's character structure in childhood. In a particularly chara
teristic passage Horney puts the problem as follows:

> The basic evil is invariably a lack of genuine warmth and affection. A chi
> can stand a great deal of what is often regarded as traumatic—such as sudde
> weaning, occasional beating, sex experiences—as long as inwardly he fee
> wanted and loved. Needless to say, a child feels keenly whether love is genuin
> and cannot be fooled by any faked demonstrations. The main reason why a chi
> does not receive enough warmth and affection lies in the parents' incapacity
> give it on account of their own neuroses. More frequently than not, in my exper
> ence, the essential lack of warmth is camouflaged, and the parents claim to hav
> in mind the child's best interest. Educational theories, oversolicitude or the se
> sacrificing attitude of an "ideal" mother are the basic factors contributing to a
> atmosphere that more than anything else lays the cornerstone for future feeling
> of immense insecurity (15, p. 80).

While the theoretical significance attributed to anxiety differs in var ous neo-Freudian systems, there is general agreement that the emotion is generated by a lack of security or personal adequacy in stress situations. Because of the neo-Freudian emphasis on the importance of security in childhood, the concept has loomed large in recent years in pediatric and educational literature. Similarly, as a result of the close causal relationship between anxiety and security, our time, with its succession of hot and cold wars, has been characterized as "the age of anxiety."

Although not all academic psychologists are in agreement with recent psychoanalytic theory, there has been increasing recognition of the role of anxiety as a driving force in human behavior. In their *Psychology of Adjustment* (22), Shaffer and Shoben agree with the neo-Freudian point of view that anxiety arises as a result of conflict—a conflict of the individual's inner impulses—and, because it is inwardly determined, creates a particularly pervasive and personal sense of helplessness. Shaffer and Shoben go on to point out that anxiety once aroused acts as a drive. Consequently, individuals in the grip of powerful conflicts will do virtually anything to alleviate the attendant anxiety.

In turning from the special field of psychoanalysis to the more general area of modern medicine, we encounter one of the most challenging and significant developments in contemporary medical practice. We refer to the relatively recent growth of that specialized branch of medical practice known as *psychosomatic medicine*.[12] As the term *psychosomatic* implies, this recent development recognizes the fact that emotional disturbances are at the root of a number of illnesses formerly believed to be purely organic in origin. Actually, the pioneers in clinical psychology such as Janet, Freud, Prince, and others recognized that conversion hysteria is the result of psychological disturbances. In this type of hysteria, the individual develops functional paralyses, anesthesias, or sensory defects which are indistinguishable from true organic illnesses. However, in psychosomatic disorders the underlying conflicts and chronic emotional disorders actually produce tissue changes in the bodily organs, whereas in hysteria the limbs or sense organs, even though disabled, do not undergo pathological modification. The hysteric's paralyzed arm can be temporarily restored to its normal function by placing the individual in a hypnotic trance and suggesting that the limb's function has been restored. It is not possible to abolish a peptic ulcer in such a manner, since the mucosal lining of the stomach or duodenum has undergone corrosion by the hydrochloric acid in the digestive secretions. In the latter case *both* the psychological and organic involvement must be treated concomitantly.

Psychosomatic reactions may involve any of the major organs or physiological systems that are energized during strong emotional states. Conse-

---

12 See *4* for a nontechnical account of this field. For an excellent brief account see *22*.

quently, such disorders are typically associated with the circulatory system, digestive tract, and respiratory system. Some of the more common specific reactions are ulcers, colitis, tachycardia, various allergies, chronic constipation, diarrhea, and essential hypertension or high blood pressure. It must be emphasized, however, that each of these disease entities has an organic as well as a psychological basis. Allergies, for example, are probably originally reactions to pollen irritation in those persons who are "sensitive" to certain plants, notably goldenrod or pigweed. However, once such reactions become well developed, they are subsequently affected by psychological factors. Allergic individuals suffer more severe attacks during periods of emotional stress. Similarly, many individuals develop mild digestive derangements which may be accompanied by actual inflammation of the mucous membranes. But if such a person becomes involved in a strong conflict situation in which a chronic "emergency reaction" is set into motion by the sympathetic nervous system, the gastrointestinal tissues may break down with the consequent formation of an ulcer.

In some cases, there appears to be no predisposing organic factor involved. Many individuals consult physicians, complaining of "heart trouble," "shortness of breath," or "fatigue." Physical examinations reveal that nothing is organically wrong. Theoretically, such reactions can be explained on the basis of conditioning. Perhaps at some time in his past, the individual has experienced a strong reaction of fear in the presence of a real threat. If the individual subsequently develops a neurosis, the anxiety attendant upon the arousal of conflicts or threats to the self may serve as cues to reinstate the same reaction which was previously experienced in a "real" emergency.

A major theoretical question which arises in explaining psychosomatic reactions is why certain individuals develop this particular syndrome as opposed to some other type of neurosis. Although peptic ulcers are typically associated with the active, hard-driving business or professional man who may be either openly hostile toward people or has repressed his hostility, not *all* such personality types develop peptic ulcers. There are two hypotheses that have been proposed to account for such individual differences in susceptibility to psychosomatic disorders.

The first hypothesis proposes that some individuals are "constitutionally" predisposed toward such complaints. Presumably, such people have inherited inadequate organ systems which, under the ordinary stress of daily living, manage to function adequately. However, under the increased tensions of severe emotional crises, the system breaks down, and the individual develops a more or less chronic psychosomatic disorder. It is also possible that previous organic illness might so weaken an organ system as to render it susceptible to psychosomatic disorders.

The second hypothesis accounts for the development of particular patterns of disorders on the basis of the type of conflict the individual is experiencing. For example, the typical psychological symptom among patients suffering from gastric ulcers is hostility. However, instead of directing their hostility outward against the source of the frustration, it is directed inward against the self. The chronic digestive disturbances associated with anger or hostility eventually result in a breakdown of the mucosa. Similarly, migraine headaches are commonly found in middle-aged women of higher than average intelligence who tend to be ambitious, hard-driving individuals. Presumably, in the face of an added emotional strain their chronically over-energized nervous systems produce a high degree of intercranial pressure which, in turn, results in a headache.

Neither theory can account for the facts adequately. Moreover, the two theories need not be considered mutually independent. It is likely that both constitutional factors and the nature of the psychological conflict are important in the etiology of the psychosomatic disorders, as is now believed to be true of the major mental disorders such as schizophrenia. Any definitive explanation of psychosomatic illnesses will have to await the outcome of research now in progress on the role of the glandular and other organic factors in mental disorders. Moreover, recent discoveries relating to the dramatic effects of the tranquilizing drugs on neurotic and psychotic disturbances must be integrated into any comprehensive theory of the emotional disorders.

CURRENT DEVELOPMENTS IN EMOTIONAL THEORY

A note on subcortical centers and emotional behavior. The most important breakthrough in the study of emotional behavior during the past half-century has been the discovery of electrically stimulable areas in the subcortical regions of the cerebrum. Because an understanding of research in this area presupposes a fairly detailed knowledge of the anatomical structures concerned, we have chosen to defer discussion of theories of emotional processes as related to brain centers to the chapter to follow on the physiological basis of behavior. Meanwhile, we shall go on to a program of research which has excited considerable interest in recent years among psychologists who are concerned with the dynamics of affectional responses in infant organisms and the influence of such early experience on adult behavior.[13]

Affectional responses in monkeys. Harry Harlow, with whose studies of manipulatory motivation we are already familiar, has carried out extensive

[3] See also Chapter 5.

investigations with infant monkeys in an attempt to clarify the nature (
affectional responses between young animals and the mother.

It will be recalled that drive reduction theory assumes that the attacl
ment of the young for the mother is a derived or secondary motive based o
satisfactions associated with the primary drive of hunger. (See Chapter 7
Harlow has expressed strong reservations about this position in a series
theoretical and experimental papers published during the past ten yea
(*10* to *14*). Harlow's fundamental position is that young animals (and, l
extension, human infants) demonstrate affectional responses which are ind
pendent of the drives and satisfactions associated with hunger and feedin

To test this hypothesis experimentally, Harlow and his associates ha
been utilizing surrogate or substitute mothers. Some of these mothers a
made of wire; others are fabricated from wooden frames covered by spon
rubber and soft terry cloth (Figure 12-3). The "mothers" can be heated l
means of electric light bulbs and baby bottles can be installed in either
the substitutes.

In a fundamental experiment newly born monkeys were placed

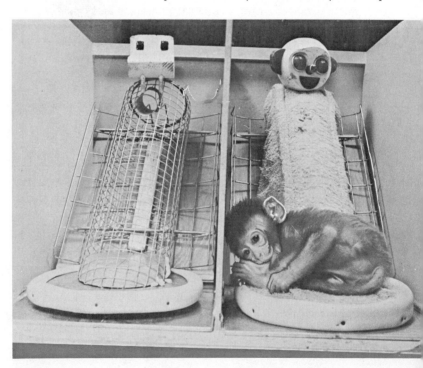

Fig. 12-3. Wire and terry cloth mothers. Infant monkeys spend most of the time c
cloth mothers regardless of which mother provides milk. (Photograph courtesy
Dr. Harry Harlow.)

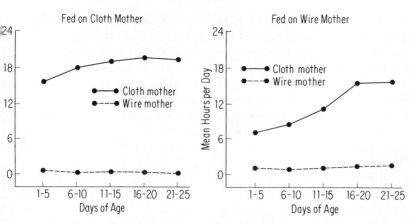

12-4. The mean hours per day spent on cloth and wire mothers by monkeys fed both types of mother. Note that regardless of whether the animals were fed on wire cloth mothers nearly all free time was spent on the cloth mother. (From Harlow, *10.*)

ges containing one wire and one cloth mother. Half of the group was fed ly through the wire mother and the other half through the cloth mother. he animals were free to spend as much time as they pleased on either other. Regardless of which mother provided the milk, the animals spent arly all their time clinging to the cloth mother, leaving her only long ough to feed (Figure 12-4). Those animals who were fed through the cloth other formed attachments to it faster than those fed on the wire mother, t after a few weeks the strength of the attachment for the cloth mother as identical for both groups.

In order to test whether or not the baby monkeys obtained a sense of curity from their substitute mothers as human infants do, various tests ere run in which the animals were subjected to stress. For example, in en field tests they were placed in a strange, empty room in the company a large mechanical bug. When released the monkeys would run in a nic to the cloth mother—often surmounting obstacles to do so—and cling her while gradually relaxing. In a few minutes they would begin tentative ploratory behavior, quickly returning if frightened. The wire mother ovided no such creature comfort or security.

Subsequent tests have shown that the early experiences of the experi- ental animals had far-reaching and durable influences on their subse- ient development. Monkeys reared on either cloth or wire mothers show normal social responses, including uncooperativeness, aggression, and ck of sexual reactions. Other forms of aberrant behavior include stereo- ped or ritualistic acts, self-inflicted wounds, and aggressive responses to xual advances from normally reared animals. While the monkeys reared on cloth mothers did not show as extreme forms of aberrant behavior, tl results nevertheless demonstrated that the cloth mother is not a substitu for the real mother. Moreover, animals who showed such abnormalities behavior do not develop into normal animals if subsequently given oppo tunities to interact with other animals. As is so often true in behavior development, there is a "critical" period during which behavioral patter must be allowed to develop or be permanently retarded or perhaps even fa to appear altogether.

Research by Harlow and his associates (12) has shown that to son degree social contact with other young monkeys may make up for lack of real mother. Animals reared on cloth surrogates that were also allowed dai periods of interaction with other young animals appear to develop normal in terms of social and sexual behavioral patterns.

Thus, Harlow's work, while demonstrating that warm contact is partially rewarding experience independent of physical drive reinforcemer also shows contact is not a sufficient substitute for live social interaction far as normal social development is concerned. The question of precise what is established in the young monkeys by real mothers or peer contac cannot be decided on the basis of present evidence. It may be that soci motives and satisfactions are created by social interaction, or it may be th skills and habits of adjustment can be developed only through creatu contacts. We do not know. We do know that Harlow's results show strikir parallels to studies of deprived children whose inadequate or absent conta with the mother leads to severe behavioral disorders (See 3, pp. 685–69(

In a recent symposium on the behavior of nonhuman primates, Ha low and Harlow (13) have provided a theoretical organization for tl empirical studies on affection emanating from the Wisconsin laborator The Harlows point out that there are five affectional systems which occi in a hierarchical order of development: (1) the infant-mother affection system which develops the strong ties of the infant to the mother; (2) tl mother-infant relationship which is the reciprocal of the infant-moth system; (3) the infant-infant or peer affectional system which develops b tween age mates; (4) the sexual affectional systems leading to adult repr ductive patterns; and (5) the paternal affectional system where the adu males exhibit positive responses toward infants, juveniles and other anima in their particular social group.

From the point of view of a better understanding of Harlow's wo with monkeys the infant-mother affectional system is the most importan Moreover, Harlow and Harlow characterize it as ". . . enormously powe ful and probably less variable than any of the other systems" (13, p. 288 This, they point out, is undoubtedly a natural adaptation for survival, sin strong infant ties to the mother are essential in the animal's natural enviror ment.

Harlow and Harlow subdivide the infant-mother affectional system
to four stages: (1) a reflex stage, (2) a comfort and attachment stage, (3) a
curity stage, and (4) a separation stage.

The reflex stage persists from birth to the second or third week of the
fant's life and consists of two groups of reflexes, those associated with nurs-
g and those associated with grasping. The nursing reflex consists of
ienting and "rooting" movements of the head to bring the mouth into
ontact with the nipple, whereupon sucking begins. The grasping reflex
onsists of strong clinging responses which insure that the infant can main-
in contact with the mother as she travels from place to place during the
ay.

Harlow and Harlow identify the second stage, the period of comfort
nd attachment, as one in which ". . . the infant receives little from the
other, other than the satisfaction of its basic bodily needs, nursing, con-
ct, warmth, and probably proprioceptive stimulation and protection from
anger" (*13*, p. 291). Even though the mother displays strong protective
havior during this period, which ends between sixty to eighty days, the
fants appear to derive only a moderate sense of security from contact with
e mother.

By contrast, during the stage of security when the infant is tested with
ar-producing stimuli, he runs quickly to the mother and clings to her fear-
lly, only gradually relaxing as we pointed out above in connection with
sts of infant's reactions to surrogate mothers. Here we need only add that
the absence of the mother, infants show "freezing" behavior—crouching
d clutching with their arms as if to protect or comfort themselves.

Finally, in the normal course of development, the separation stage
adually begins to terminate the infant-mother affectional relationship. In
e normal environment the lure of objects, the increasing tendency to ex-
lore farther and farther away from the mother, and the development of
xtrafamilial social contacts weaken the bonds between mother and child.

Those familiar with the literature of developmental and child psychol-
zy will recognize many interesting parallels between the behavior of the
fant monkey and that of the human infant. Harlow's empirical research
nd theoretical organization of affectional systems constitute important
omparative and developmental contributions on the frontiers of psychology
f motivation and emotion.

SUMMARY AND EVALUATION

In little more than half a century, the psychology of feeling and emo-
on has undergone a gradual evolution in the direction of becoming more
nd more "somatically" oriented. In the older, prescientific literature, and

in the structuralistic psychologies of Wundt and Titchener, the empha:
was primarily on the affective states as conscious phenomena and on
secondarily on the emotions. Moreover, in their treatment of the emotior
nineteenth- and early twentieth-century psychologists stressed the conscio
or introspective aspect of the emotional states. Beginning with the fun
tionalistic-behavioristic studies of the behavioral expressions of the emotior
the latter came to be emphasized more and more in both experiment
research and the theoretical literature.

The trend in research on the emotions has, in a sense, been from tl
periphery inward. The early behavioral studies emphasized either the faci
expressions characteristic of the various emotions or the associated viscer
changes. More recently, beginning with the researches and theoretical i:
terpretations of Cannon and Bard, the emphasis has shifted toward tl
central or cerebral mechanisms in emotional behavior. Moreover, in ve·
recent years, the discovery of the subcortical centers associated with anim
drives, which we touched upon toward the end of the preceding chapte
has reinforced interest in formulating an empirically grounded centr
theory of the dynamic states. While a comprehensive systematic account
feeling and emotion lags behind the wealth of recent experimental di
coveries, the twentieth-century trend toward a behavioral science of tl
emotions appears to be a distinct improvement.

REFERENCES

1. Bridges, K. M. B. Emotional development in early infancy. *Child Development,*
   1932, pp. 324–341.
2. Carr, H. A. *Psychology: A study of mental activity.* New York: Longmans, Green, 192
3. Cofer, C. N., and M. Appley. *Motivation: Theory and research.* New York: Wile
   1964.
4. Dunbar, F. *Mind and body: Psychosomatic medicine.* New York: Random House, 194
5. Freud, S. *A general introduction to psychoanalysis.* New York: Boni & Liveright, 192
6. Freud, S. *Collected papers* (5 vols.). London: Hogarth Press, 1924–1950.
7. Freud, S. *New introductory lectures on psychoanalysis.* New York: Norton, 1933.
8. Freud, S. *The basic writings of Sigmund Freud.* New York: Modern Library, 1938.
9. Gardiner, H. M., R. C. Metcalf, and J. G. Beebe-Center. *Feeling and emotion:
   history of theories.* New York: American Book, 1937.
10. Harlow, H. F. The nature of love. *American Psychologist,* **13,** 1958, pp. 673–685.
11. Harlow, H. F. The heterosexual affectional system in monkeys. *American Psycho·
    gist,* **17,** 1962, pp. 1–9.
12. Harlow, H. F., and M. K. Harlow. Social deprivation in monkeys. *Scientific Ame:
    can,* **207,** 1962, pp. 136–146.
13. Harlow, H. F., and M. K. Harlow. The affectional systems. In Schrier, A. M
    H. F. Harlow, and F. Stollnitz (eds.). *Behavior of nonhuman primates,* Vol. II. Ne
    York: Academic Press, 1965.
14. Harlow, H. F., and R. R. Zimmermann. Affectional responses in the infant mo·
    key. *Science,* **130,** 1959, pp. 421–432.

15. Horney, K. *The neurotic personality of our time.* New York: Norton, 1937.
16. Horney, K. *Our inner conflicts.* New York: Norton, 1945.
17. James, W. *Psychology, briefer course.* New York: Holt, 1892.
18. Jersild, A. *Child psychology.* Englewood Cliffs, N.J.: Prentice-Hall, 1954.
19. Landis, C., and W. Hunt. *The startle pattern.* New York: Rinehart, 1939.
20. Morgan, C., and E. Stellar. *Physiological psychology.* New York: McGraw-Hill, 1950.
21. Munroe, R. *Schools of psychoanalytic thought.* New York: Dryden, 1955.
22. Shaffer, L. F., and E. J. Shoben. *The psychology of adjustment,* ed. 2. Boston: Houghton Mifflin, 1956.
23. Sherman, M. The differentiation of emotional responses in infants: I. Judgments of emotional responses from motion picture views and from actual observation. *Journal of Comparative Psychology,* **7,** 1927, pp. 265–284.
24. Sherman, M. The differentiation of emotional responses in infants: II. The ability of observers to judge the emotional characteristics of the crying of infants, and of the voice of an adult. *Journal of Comparative Psychology,* **7,** 1927, pp. 335–351.
25. Titchener, E. B. *A textbook of psychology.* New York: Macmillan, 1910.
26. Watson, J. B. *Behavior: An introduction to comparative psychology.* New York: Holt, 1914.
27. Watson, J. B. *Psychology from the standpoint of a behaviorist.* Philadelphia: Lippincott, 1919; also second edition, 1924.
28. Woodworth, R. S., and H. Schlosberg. *Experimental psychology,* rev. ed. New York: Holt, 1954.
29. Young, P. T. *Emotion in man and animal.* New York: Wiley, 1943.

13

Physiological
Theories
of Behavior

In discussing the emergence of psychology as a natural science (Chapter 1) we emphasized the close relationship which existed between the new discipline and experimental physiology. Weber, Fechner, and Wundt—the men who were responsible for applying the methods of the natural sciences to psychological problems—brought those methods to psychology from physiology. The early psychology of the latter half of the nineteenth century not only emerged from physiology but also was often indistinguishable from it. And it is a testimony to cyclical trends in history that a large segment of psychology in the mid-twentieth century is scarcely to be distinguished from neurophysiology. Indeed, as we hope to demonstrate in this chapter, the explosive developments in the physiology of the nervous system in recent years have resulted in an increasing rapprochement between the two sciences. The psychologist's long quest for a better understanding of mental and behavioral activities inevitably leads to the brain as the seat of all behavior. However, the early hopes of the physiological psychologists who looked to the nervous system for the biological basis of the cognitive, conative, and affective processes are only now being realized with the development of the precise electronic and biochemical tools that have made possible the recent revolutionary discoveries in this oldest of psychological fields.

In attempting to trace the development of physiological theories of behavior, we shall have to abandon our customary approach of examining the position of the leaders of the older schools and then tracing the subsequent fate of their systematic positions as these evolved into contemporary psychology. Despite the fact that psychology was founded by men who were physiologists by training, these leaders did not have well

472

ırmulated theories of brain function and behavior, with the possible excep-
on of the Gestalt school whose strongly physiological orientation in treating
ertain aspects of perception we examined in Chapter 5. In general, the
ystematists of the early schools were not strong physiological theorists; and,
aditionally, the physiological psychologists have not been strong system-
tists in the sense of developing schools or broad positions encompassing the
hole of psychology. With some exceptions their theorizing has been con-
ned to hypothetical explanations of specific functions rather than to
ttempts to integrate the entire field within the strucure of a physiological
reory. We may begin with just such an attempt, as we consider the develop-
ient of theories of cortical localization in learning, which remains one of
le broadest and most central problems of physiological psychology, as it
ras throughout the nineteenth century.

EARLY THEORIES OF CORTICAL LOCALIZATION
F FUNCTION

Phrenology.   By one of those strange accidents that occur from time to
ime in the history of science, the study of cortical localization of function

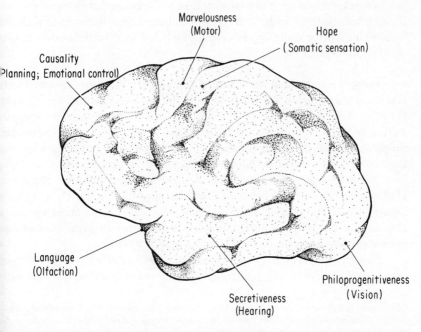

ig. 13-1. A lateral view of the cerebrum showing areas of localization according to the
hrenologists. The actual functions of the areas are shown in parentheses.

developed out of the pseudoscience of phrenology then under the vigorou leadership of Franz Joseph Gall (1758 to 1828) and his pupil, J. G. Spur. heim (1776 to 1832). Gall and Spurzheim took the position that mind made up of a number of faculties some of which are *affective*, consisting (instincts and propensities such as the will to live, aggressiveness, acquisitive ness, self-esteem, benevolence, and the like; and others which are *intellectiv* in nature, such as the linguistic, spatial, temporal, numerical, and music; faculties. Figure 13-1 shows a phrenological chart with the location of som of the more important faculties as localized by the phrenologists.

Gall and Spurzheim further believed that the possession of a high) developed faculty indicates a correspondingly well-developed area in th cerebral cortex and, most importantly, that the configuration of the ove: lying skull reflects this cerebral development. Thus, in order to assess th individual's mental faculties one need only make measurements of th degree of development of the localized "bumps" on the skull.

Although phrenology enjoyed enormous popular appeal, it never wc widespread scientific support. Indeed, Gall and Spurzheim were ridicule by most anatomists and neurologists, who found their assumptions about th correlation between the brain and skull untenable. However, their opp(nents had no specific alternative evidence to show precisely how cortic; function is localized or, if not localized, how the brain functions as a whol Indeed, historians (5 and 20) credit opposition to the doctrines of Gall an Spurzheim with stimulating research which led to a better understandir of cerebral localization.

Hall and Flourens and the method of extirpation. We have already brief described the work of Marshall Hall (1790 to 1857) and Pierre Floures (1794 to 1867) who were responsible for carrying out the first scientif studies of the functions of the brain. Hall, it will be recalled, performe simple experiments which involved decapitation of animals showing th; they could make motor responses if appropriately stimulated.

Flourens, the more important of the two men, although confirmir Hall's concept of broad levels of functioning (see Chapter 1), denied th precise localization of faculties or functions[1] in the cerebral cortex : claimed by the phrenologists, espousing instead the doctrine of a unitai principle of function in which the cortex acts as a whole.

Flourens was a model experimenter. He relied entirely on direct obse vation in formulating his conclusions about brain functions. In his exti

---

[1] The distinction between "faculty" and "function," although not made by the early anatomis and physiologists, is an important one. Faculties were assumed to be inherent "powers" of th mind such as will, memory and calculational ability. These powers were held to be responsible f mental activities. The now favored term "function" refers to a process or activity characterist of a given organ without the implication that "powers" lie behind such activities.

Table 13-1.
Functional Levels of the Brain According to Flourens

ANATOMICAL CENTER	RESULTS OF DESTRUCTION	FUNCTION
Cerebrum	Loss of judgment, inability to initiate voluntary movement, inability to remember	Perceiving, willing, memory, intelligence
Cerebellum	Loss of coordination	Coordination of voluntary movement
Corpora quadrigemina	Disturbances in visual and auditory processes	Mediation of visual and auditory reflexes
Medulla	Death of animal	Vital functions—respiration and heartbeat

pative work he carefully isolated a part of the brain for study, removed it, and then observed the subsequent reaction in the animal. He investigated the functions of the cerebrum, cerebellum, corpora quadrigemina (the superior and inferior colliculi), medulla, and spinal cord by removing these parts in different animals, primarily in birds. Table 13-1 summarizes his findings.

On the basis of his results, Flourens concluded that: (1) the brain is a multiple organ whose functions are diverse and which exist at several levels; (2) the cerebrum proper functions as a whole for the higher mental processes of cognition, volition, association, and intellectual processes. More specifically, he showed that while the brain behaves as if it were several distinct organs, it nevertheless functions in a unitary manner. Thus, he could point to the cerebellum as the organ of coordination, the corpora quadrigemina as centers for vision and the medulla as a vital center; but he could not *localize* volition, intelligence, and perceptual processes in the cerebrum. All were coextensive functions existing inseparably from each other.

Paul Broca and the clinical method. Flourens' conclusions set back the cause of cortical localization for nearly a quarter of a century. His generalization that the cerebrum functions as a unity at first failed to generate serious opposition on the part of those who championed some form of localization. It was not until Paul Broca (1824 to 1880), a professor of surgery at the Bicêtre, announced the discovery of the speech center which bears his name (See Figure 13-2) that the issue of cortical localization once more

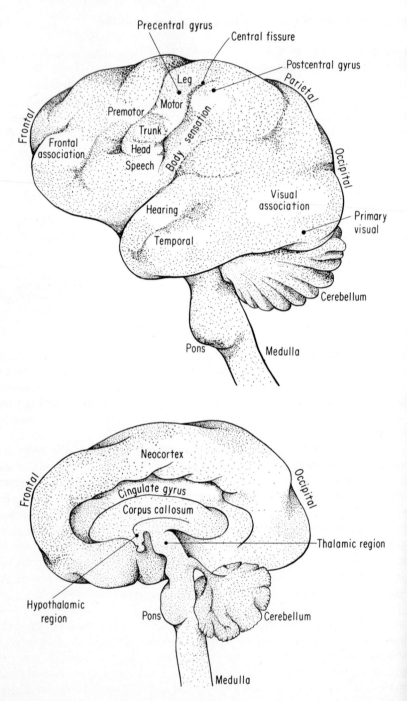

Fig. 13-2. Lateral views of the exterior and interior structures of the cerebrum showing the principal parts and areas of functional localization.

came to the fore. The historian, Boring, tells of the discovery in the following account.

Broca's observation was in itself very simple. There had in 1831 been admitted at the Bicêtre, an insane hospital near Paris, a man whose sole defect seemed to be that he could not talk. He communicated intelligently by signs and was otherwise mentally normal. He remained at the Bicêtre for thirty years with this defect and on April 12, 1861, was put under the care of Broca, the surgeon, because of a gangrenous infection. Broca for five days subjected him to a careful examination, in which he satisfied himself that the musculature of the larynx and articulatory organs was not hindered in normal movements, that there was no other paralysis that could interfere with speech, and that the man was intelligent enough to speak. On April 17 the patient—fortunately, it would seem, for science —died; and within a day Broca had performed an autopsy, discovered a lesion in the third frontal convolution of the left cerebral hemisphere, and had presented the brain in alcohol to the Société d'Anthropologie (5, p. 69).

Broca had not only made an important anatomical discovery, he had also introduced a new technique, the clinical method. Other physicians had, of course, been using the clinical method as a diagnostic tool in the treatment of disease since it was described by the Greek physician, Hippocrates. But Broca was the first to utilize it successfully for demonstrating localization of function in the cerebral cortex.

Broca had also chanced upon another discovery: one side of the brain is dominant over the other. His patient, Leborgne, showed no defect on the right side of the brain. This finding, that speech functions are localized on the dominant side of the brain—usually the left—was quickly confirmed on other patients with similar behavioral difficulties. Incidentally, the phenomenon of laterality of function in the brain has been a puzzle whose solution has occupied a large share of research among neurophysiologists and physiological psychologists.

Electrical stimulation. The first experimental discovery of a localized area in the brain using the method of electrical stimulation was made by G. Fritsch (1838 to 1927) and E. Hitzig (1838 to 1907), who, in 1870, applied a weak electric current to the surface of a dog's brain and showed that the animal made movements on the opposite side of the body. They had, in effect, both discovered the motor area of the cortex which lies along the precentral gyrus and had inaugurated the use of what was to become a fundamental method in experimental neurophysiology.

Subsequent experiments on dogs, monkeys, and isolated reports on the stimulation of the cortex in man confirmed Fritsch and Hitzig's observations and established not only that the cortex contains a highly localized motor center for the control of the limbs and body, but also that several other centers concerned with eye movements, ears, mouth and with sensory processes could be localized in the brain.

By the end of the nineteenth century there was general agreement that localization of both motor and sensory functions had been established as a fact of cortical functioning.

To summarize the contributions of the nineteenth century to the problem of cortical localization, we may say that there were two principal discoveries: First was the development of three important methods of investigation—extirpative, clinical, and electrical. Second, the principle of cortical localization of function was well established by the turn of the century. However, localization was neither as precise nor as widespread as had been asserted by Gall and Spurzheim. What had been shown was that motor and sensory functions could be localized with considerable precision, but no one had yet demonstrated that the so-called higher mental processes were localized in specific areas of the cortex in the same manner as electrically excitable points on the motor cortex. Moreover, in the case of sensory localization, only very guarded generalizations could be made. There was no way for investigators to communicate with an animal whose sensory cortex was being stimulated in order to determine what the animal was experiencing. By contrast, upon stimulation of the motor cortex, it was easy to observe motor movements on the periphery. The method of ablation did, of course, reveal gross sensory deficiencies, such as blindness, but experimenters had to await the development of reliable psychological tests of sensory processes before more precise generalizations could be formulated about the role of the cortex in sensory discrimination.

THE ROLE OF THE CEREBRAL CORTEX
IN MAZE LEARNING

It was Karl Lashley (1890 to 1959) who utilized the psychological methods of studying learning in animals in order to investigate the role of the cerebral cortex in learning and retention.

We may begin with his now classical studies of maze learning in rats, which were conducted for the purpose of testing (1) the relationship between the complexity of the problem and cerebral lesions, and (2) the effects of destruction of various sizes and locations on the maze habit. Diagrams of Lashley's three mazes, known as Mazes I, II, and III are reproduced from his *Brain Mechanisms and Intelligence* (23) in Figure 13-3. Maze I, it will be noted, is a simple discrimination problem involving only a single choice. Maze II is much more difficult since it is a three-blind maze, and Maze III, the most difficult, has eight blinds.

The results left no doubt that there is a close relationship between the difficulty of the problem and the effect of cerebral lesions. Figure 13-4 shows this relationship in a three-dimensional surface. A careful study of the

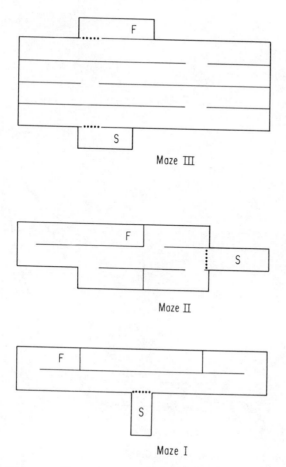

Fig. 13-3. Floor diagrams of Lashley's three mazes. (From Lashley, *23.*)

diagram reveals that small destructions—10 percent or less—have little effect on learning in any of the mazes. However, for Maze III the number of errors increases very rapidly with increasing magnitude of cortical destructions. For Mazes I and II destructions of over half of the cortex do not have a serious effect on the acquisition of the habit.[2]

The purely quantitative effects of cerebral lesions in learning might well have been predicted in advance on purely logical grounds. We would expect that a close relationship should exist between the magnitude of a

[2] Another way of showing the relationship between the difficulty of the problem and the magnitude of the lesion is to compare the correlations between the extent of cerebral destruction and errors for the three mazes. As reported by Lashley (*23*, p. 67) these are: Maze I 0.20; Maze II 0.58; and Maze III 0.75.

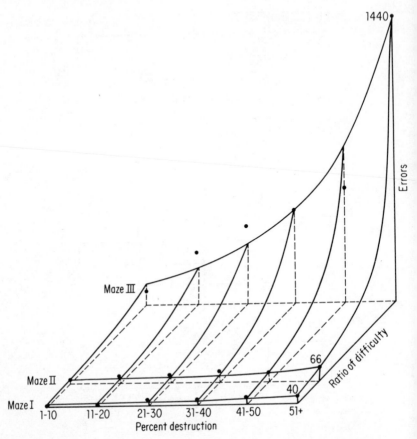

Fig. 13-4. Lashley's three-dimensional surface showing the relationships between percent destruction, ratio of difficulty, and errors in the three mazes. (From Lashley, 23.)

cerebral injury and the ability to learn in situations of varying difficulty. However, not so readily predictable was Lashley's discovery that the locus or site of the lesion was not an important factor in retardation. Rather, the *mass* of the lesion was the crucial factor. This finding led Lashley to formulate his well-known principles of mass action and equipotentiality.

> *Mass action.* I have already given evidence which is augmented in the present study, that the equipotentiality is not absolute but is subject to a law of mass action whereby the efficiency of performance of an entire complex function may be reduced in proportion to the extent of brain injury within an area whose parts are not more specialized for one component of the function than for another (*23*, p. 25).

> *Equipotentiality.* The term "equipotentiality" I have used to designate the apparent capacity of any intact part of a functional area to carry out, with o

without reduction in efficiency, the functions which are lost by destruction of the whole. This capacity varies from one area to another and with the character of the functions involved. It probably holds only for the association areas and for functions more complex than simple sensitivity or motor co-ordination (*23*, p. 25).

In effect, the principle of equipotentiality states that a 50 percent destruction in the anterior half of the brain would cause the same retardation as a 50 percent destruction of the posterior half *in maze learning*. We emphasize that the generalization applies to maze learning, since there are many cases of cerebral functioning where locus is important—for example, in speech.

We may pause and raise the question as to the meaning of mass action and equipotentiality. Are we to assume that in the maze problem the brain acts as a whole, thus exhibiting the operation of a general learning factor which is dispersed over the entire cortex? Such a possibility would be entirely consistent with both the principle of mass action and that of equipotentiality. However, there is another possibility, namely that maze learning depends upon the total sensory input coming to the cortex from the various receptors—the eyes, ears, nose, the pads of the feet, the vibrissae, and so forth. If so, then Lashley's increasingly massive destructions would involve more and more of the localized centers for these senses until eventually all input would be affected and the animal would be unable to show a significant degree of learning.

In the latter case we would be dealing with localized factors which in combination destructions would give the appearance of a mass action effect. That this may, in fact, be true is strongly suggested by an experiment of Honzik's in which the sense organs of animals were systematically destroyed both singly and in combination. As Figure 13-5 shows, the destruction of even one important sense organ, such as vision or smell, has a severe retarding effect on maze learning. But combinations of destructions are much more serious in their effects, indicating that in the absence of one sense the animal is falling back on another, just as blind people will utilize the sense of audition in place of vision. Clearly, then, as more sense organs are destroyed, the animal has fewer and fewer alternatives; consequently, retardation becomes more and more severe—a mass action effect.

Honzik, of course, carried out peripheral ablations of sense organs while Lashley employed central lesions. However, each receptor on the periphery is represented by a cortical projection center with its surrounding association area, and to destroy the visual cortex is, in effect, to blind the animal just as if his eyes were removed.

It is still possible that each of the projection-association areas for the various senses may have two functions: (1) a specific or localized function and (2) a generalized function. To test this hypothesis it would be necessary

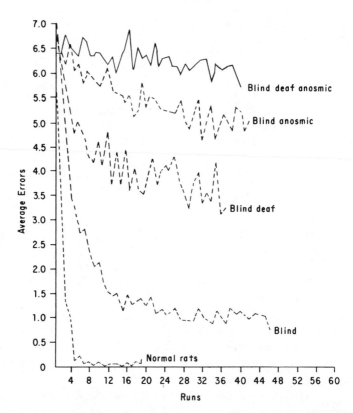

Fig. 13-5. Errors in the maze as a function of single and multiple destructions. (After Honzik, *14a.*)

to destroy the sense peripherally, measure the amount of retardation, and then destroy the appropriate cortical center, in order to determine whether a further retardation occurs because of loss of a general factor in the cortex associated with that sensory function. Unfortunately, the results of experiments bearing on the question are conflicting and inconclusive. The interested reader will find a summary of the results in Morgan (*33*) with citations of original studies.

CORTICAL LOCALIZATION IN DISCRIMINATION LEARNING

Broadly speaking, there are two kinds of discrimination, one involving the subject's ability to differentiate between two intensities or brightnesses and the other requiring a discrimination between two qualities, such as two orms or two tonal patterns. Intensity discriminations are much easier for he animal subject than are form discriminations; and, not surprisingly, t turns out that the role of the cortex differs in the two situations. We shall discuss each problem separately, indicating the general experimental results and using data from visual intensity and form discrimination problems as ypical of those involving other sensory modalities.

Brightness discrimination. Again, it was Lashley who carried out the pioneer studies of the role of the cerebral cortex in brightness discrimination. Figure 13-6 shows the type of apparatus used for training the animals in his brightness discrimination problems. The unexpected result of his studies was that animals whose occipital cortices were destroyed showed no decrement in the ability to learn a brightness discrimination habit (23, p. 47). However, if the animal was trained in the problem before cerebral lesions were imposed, the habit was abolished by destruction of the occipital cortex (23, p. 86). If the animal was then given retraining, the habit could be relearned; and, unless the conditions of learning were modified, the course

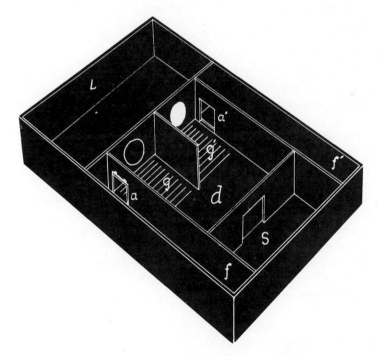

ig. 13-6. A brightness discrimination box. The starting compartment is at a. Food may be obtained at f or f' depending on the discrimination required. The areas labeled and g' are grids which may be used to apply shock; a and a' are openings leading to the food compartments. (From Lashley, 23.)

of relearning in operated animals did not appear different from that in normals. Thus, we may conclude that while the occipital cortex is normally involved in the acquisition of a brightness discrimination habit, it is not essential to its formation.

If, however, the problem is made more difficult, say by requiring the animal to distinguish between two lights of different intensities rather than between a light and a dark area, the postoperative animals have more difficulty in relearning the habit. This result is not inconsistent with the first if we assume that subcortical centers are capable of mediating relatively simple brightness discriminations but that increasingly more difficult discriminations involve the striate cortex. As we shall see, when discriminations become very difficult (form discrimination), the integrity of the cortex is essential to the learning of the problem.

We may at this point raise the question as to why animals trained in brightness discrimination fail to retain the habit after extirpation of the striate cortex even though they can learn it without the cortex. A recent experiment by Thompson (45) indicates that there is a lack of transfer between the pre and postoperative situations. Thompson trained animals in the discrimination problem and then operated in two stages in which one side of the striate cortex was first removed, the animals allowed to recover for a period of several days during which training went on, followed by removal of the other half. There was no loss of the habit. Apparently the cortex remaining after the first operation serves as a "bridge" allowing the subcortical nuclei to "acquire" the habit.

Form discrimination. As noted in the preceding discussion, the integrity of the striate area is necessary for visual form discrimination. Figure 13-7 shows the apparatus used by Lashley in his extensive experiments on visual form discrimination problems. He found that animals lacking the striate cortex could not learn a form discrimination. Moreover, those who had learned the problem before the lesion was imposed suffered complete and permanent postoperative amnesia. Furthermore, no amount of retraining could reinstate the habit (24). If, however, the animals suffered only partial lesions the habit was not abolished even though only remnants of the cortex remained. Apparently animals with partial lesions are able to overcome the resultant gaps or scotomata in their visual fields.

If we compare Lashley's results on form discrimination with those obtained in the maze situation, we find that while equipotentiality applies to the latter, it does not apply to the former. In other words, when learning involves a specific sensory input, such as the eye, and no alternative path is present, another part of the brain cannot take over and function vicariously. Equipotentiality, then, is a concept which is limited in scope and which indicates that the brain, like other organ systems in the body, possesses flexibility—but not unlimited flexibility. There is localization of

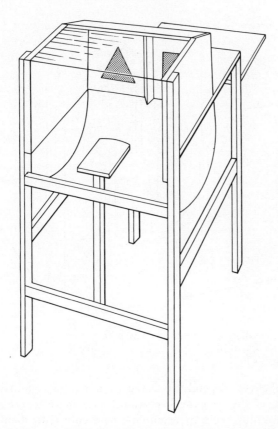

Fig. 13-7. Lashley's form discrimination apparatus. One of the doors (triangle or square) is left unfastened. If the animal jumps to this door he obtains food on the rear platform. If he jumps to the incorrect side he falls into the net below. (After Lashley, '23a.)

function as well as mass action and equipotentiality. As is true when dealing with other concepts in psychology, we must be careful to be operationstic and to specify precisely what experimental tests we have in mind before we attempt to generalize or to assess the validity of mass action and equipotentiality.

PROBLEM SOLVING AND THE CEREBRAL CORTEX[3]

The most complex form of learning involves solutions where both the stimulus factors and the response pattern are highly complex and, as many

---

[3] The student should review for himself the studies of Jacobsen and Goldstein on the role of the cerebral cortex in delayed reaction problems and concept formation (Chapter 10).

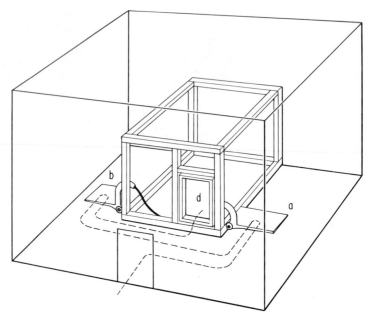

Fig. 13-8. A double alternation problem. The animal must shuttle between levers *a* and *b*, pressing them in turn before being allowed in door *d* where a reward is obtained. (From Lashley, *23*.)

psychologists believe, depends upon representative or cognitive factors for the mediation of the response. Returning once more to Lashley's classic studies (*23*), we may begin by examining his results with the double alternation box, a relatively simple form of problem in which the animal is required to press down successively two platforms mounted on opposite sides of an enclosure containing food (Figure 13-8). Animals suffering lesions involving 14 to 50 percent of the cortex, with an average destruction of 28.4 percent, required no more trials on the average to master the problem than normals. Similarly, animals who had learned the problem and then suffered injuries were found to be somewhat retarded in their performance but could easily relearn. There was evidence to show that the frontal lobes were more important in the successful solution of the problem than other portions of the brain. This finding is not surprising in view of the fact that the problem involves the use of the forelimbs, whose motor innervation is, of course, localized in the frontal regions.

The double alternation problem is a relatively simple one. In more difficult latch boxes involving a hard-to-reach lever which must be manipulated by one hand (the preferred hand), a high degree of localization involving only 1 to 2 percent of the cortex in the frontal region has been found to abolish the performance, although the habit can be relearned

(*38, 39*). Again, we are dealing with a specialized motor function which is dependent upon a restricted area of the cortex. However, Maier (*31*) showed that small lesions involving 10 to 15 percent of the cortex could seriously disturb a reasoning problem in which the animal was required to put two previous experiences together in order to solve a present problem (Figure 13-9).

Finally, we may briefly outline an interesting pair of experiments by Krechevsky (*21, 22*), in which he found that animals which are given alternate paths involving visual and spatial cues in a discrimination maze utilize both alternatives, some favoring spatial cues, some visual, and others using both. In the case of the "spatial" rats, lesions in the frontal region disrupted the habit, whereas the "visual" animals suffered a loss of ability if the lesions were in the striate area. Once again we see that the issue of cortical localization is contingent upon the type of problem employed. If the problem requires the use of specialized cues or demands skilled manipulation, then we find cortical localization. If the problem can be solved by utilizing

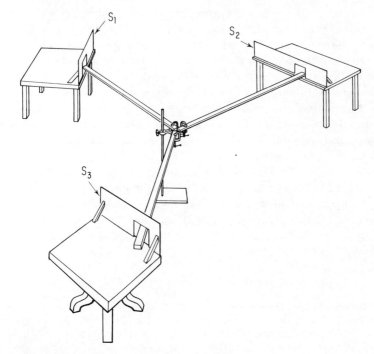

Fig. 13-9. Maier's reasoning problem. The animal is first allowed to explore thoroughly all runways and tables (Experience I). Food is then placed on one of the tables and the animal permitted to eat (Experience II). The reasoning test consists of placing the animal on one of the other two tables and seeing if it will go directly to the table with food, thus showing it has put together two previous experiences. (From Maier, *31*.)

various cues or does not require skilled manipulation, then we are unlikely to find a high degree of cortical localization.

CORTICAL LOCALIZATION IN MAN

We have been emphasizing studies of cortical localization carried out on animals under conditions of precise experimental control. From the point of view of the experimental psychologist this is the best type of evidence. Lesions can be localized in animals. The experimenter has complete control over the genetic and environmental history of his subjects; and, most important of all, he is able to devise precise pre and postoperative tests of the psychological function under investigation. However, the physiological psychologist is ultimately interested in cortical localization in man, and man is the one subject unavailable for experimental research. He must therefore, go to the clinician in order to obtain knowledge of cortical localization.

In recent years it has been possible to carry out brain operations on patients suffering from surgically correctable neurological disorders, such as focal epilepsy, while the patient is under local anesthesia and can therefore remain conscious. Local anesthetics are injected into the scalp which is then reflected along with the bone of the skull and the brain is exposed. Paradoxically, although the brain is the seat of all pain, it does not respond with sensations of pain when stimulated directly. Thus, the neurosurgeon can stimulate the cortex with a weak electric current and "map" the motor, sensory, and association areas according to the subject's reports or his movements.

An impressive collection of such clinical investigations has been provided by the famous Canadian neurosurgeon, Wilder Penfield (36, 37).

A typical case from *The Excitable Cortex of Conscious Man* is presented in summary form because of its special interest in showing the localization of complex memories as well as in demonstrating the excitability of the traditional motor and sensory areas. (See Figures 13-10, 13-11, and 13-12.)

CASE M. M. The patient was a woman of 26 years who was afflicted by recurring cerebral seizures. The first manifestation of each attack was a sudden "feeling—as though I had lived through this all before." At times there was also a feeling of fear. On other occasions she experienced what she called a flashback.

The initial feeling of familiarity she described as applying to the whole of any experience she might be having at the moment. On the other hand, the flashbacks were experiences from her earlier life. They came suddenly while she retained awareness of her actual surroundings. She gave the following example: Without warning she seemed to be sitting in the railroad station of a small town, which might be Vanceburg, Kentucky, or perhaps Garrison. "It is winter and the wind is blowing outside and I am waiting for a train." This was apparently an experience from her earlier life but it was one she had "forgotten."

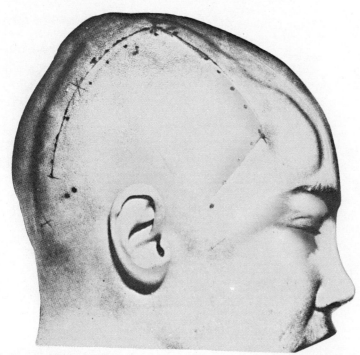

Fig. 13-10. The subject injected with a local anesthetic and marked for surgery. (From Penfield, *36.*)

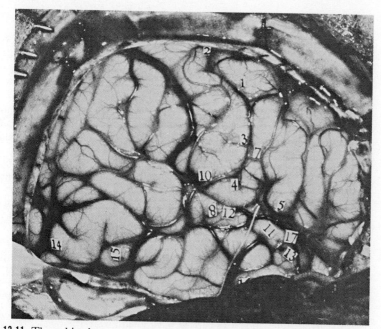

Fig. 13-11. The subject's cortex exposed and functional areas labeled. (From Penfield, *36.*)

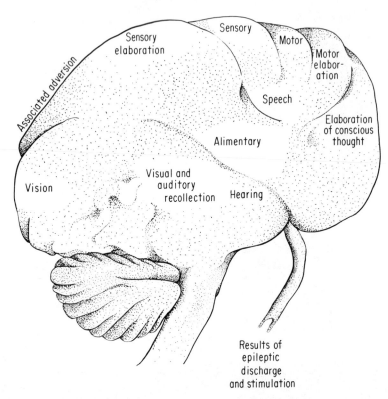

Fig. 13-12. The functional areas of the cerebral cortex as revealed by Penfield's clinical studies of the living cortex in conscious man. (After Penfield and Rasmussen, *37*.)

These minor seizures (psychical seizures) were often followed by automatisms, periods of irresponsible behavior of which she would have no memory. During these periods she might fall or walk about in a confused state, speaking unrelated and disjointed words and sentences.

Thus, in summary, the localized epileptic discharges in the right temporal lobe of this young woman were causing her to experience, from time to time: (1) a sense of false familiarity (déjà vu), (2) a feeling of fear, (3) reproductions of previous experience. The first was an illusion, the second an emotion, the third an hallucination. These are all to be considered psychical phenomena, any one of which the operator might hope to reproduce by stimulation.

Osteoplastic craniotomy carried out under local anaesthesia disclosed atrophy and sclerosis of the first temporal convolution, and the uncus and hippocampus as well. Electrographic recordings taken directly from the cortex by my associate, Dr. Herbert Jasper, showed spontaneous "spike" discharges from this area. The area of abnormality is shown by shading. The EEG abnormality is marked A, C, D, and E.

Electrical stimulation was carried out (Square wave generator, 60 cycles 2 millisecond pulses). She was ordinarily warned by the operator each time the electrode was applied. But, as usual, at intervals the warning was given with no stimulus and at other times, stimulation without warning. This serves to eliminate with certainty false or imaginary responses.

Sensory and Motor Responses

A current of two volts (about 0.2 milliamperes) proved to be the minimum threshold strength that would produce responses from the sensory and motor areas.

Stimulation at point 2—sensation in thumb and index finger. She called it "quivering," "tingling."

3—"Same feeling on the left side of my tongue."

7—Movement of the tongue.

4—"Yes, a feeling at the back of my throat like nausea."

8—She said, "No." Then she said, "Yes, I suddenly cannot hear." This is, obviously, the border of auditory sensory cortex.

The foregoing responses were motor and sensory in character much like those obtained routinely. They serve only to identify the Rolandic sensory and motor cortex and Heschl's auditory gyrus, most of which is buried within the fissure of Sylvius.

Psychical Responses

The following were the "psychical" results of stimulating the interpretive cortex. The strength of current was increased from 2 to 3 volts.

11—"I heard something familiar, I do not know what it was."

11—(repeated without warning)—"Yes, Sir, I think I heard a mother calling her little boy somewhere. It seemed to be something that happened years ago." When asked to explain, she said, "It was somebody in the neighbourhood where I live." She added that it seemed that she herself "was somewhere close enough to hear."

Warning without stimulation—"Nothing."

11 repeated—"Yes, I hear the same familiar sounds, it seems to be a woman calling, the same lady. That was not in the neighbourhood. It seemed to be the lumber yard." Then she added reflectively, "I've never been around the lumber yard much."

This was an incident of childhood which she could never have recalled without the aid of the stimulating electrode. Actually she could not "remember" it but she knew at once, with no suggestion from us, that she must have experienced it sometime.

12—"Yes. I heard voices down along the river somewhere—a man's voice and a woman's voice calling."

When she was asked how she could tell that the calling had been "along the river," she said, "I think I saw the river." When asked what river it was, she said, "I don't know. It seems to be one I was visiting when I was a child."

Warning without stimulation—"Nothing."

Three minutes later without any warning, stimulation was carried out again probably near 13. While the electrode was held in place, she exclaimed: "Yes, I hear voices. It is late at night, around the carnival somewhere—some sort of travelling circus." Then, after removal of the electrode: "I just saw lots of big wagons that they use to haul animals in."

These simple re-enactments of experience had auditory and visual elements in them.

Eleven minutes later, stimulation was carried out without warning at a point just posterior to 11—"I seemed to hear little voices then," she said, "the voices of people calling from building to building somewhere—I do not know where it is but it is very familiar to me. I cannot see the buildings now but they seemed to be run-down buildings."

14 (just posterior to 15)—This stimulation caused her to say: "The whole operation now seems familiar."

Warning without stimulation—"Nothing."

15—"Just a tiny flash of familiarity and a feeling that I knew everything that was going to happen in the near future." Then she added, "as though I had been through all this before and thought I knew exactly what you were going to do next."

At point 17, an electrode, covered with an insulating coat except at its tip, was inserted to different depths and the current switched on and off at will so as to stimulate in various buried portions of the superior temporal convolution and uncus.

17c (1 cm deep)—"Oh, I had the same very, very familiar memory, in an office somewhere. I could see the desks. I was there and someone was calling to me, a man leaning on a desk with a pencil in his hand."

Warning without stimulation—"Nothing."

11 (forty minutes after first stimulation of this point)—"I had a flash of familiar memory. I do not know what it was."

13 (repeated three times)—"Nothing."

11 (after four minutes)—"Nothing."

Conditions seemed to have changed and stimulation now would summon no experiences.

The plan of surgical excision had now been formulated. Accordingly the second and third temporal convolutions were removed, exposing the first temporal convolution and the uncus and hippocampal gyrus deep within the temporal fossa.

Stimulation near uncus or just lateral to it, at 18a—"I had a little memory—a scene in a play—they were talking and I could see it. It was just seeing it in my memory."

Stimulation at a point nearby—"I feel very close to an attack—I think I am going to have one—a familiar memory."

20 (Stimulation of the lateral aspect of the hippocampal gyrus)—"Oh, it hurts and that feeling of familiarity—a familiar memory—the place where I hang my coat up, where I go to work."

The patient M. M., described in this case, was a good witness, self-critical, understanding, and tolerant. I have reported the features which are of psychological interest throughout the whole procedure of exploration and cortical excision, a three-hour period (37, pp. 25–30).

Figure 13-12 shows Penfield's conception of cortical localization of function in man based on his studies of the living brain.[4] It will be noted that the old anatomical division of the brain into primary projection areas and association areas (called "interpretative areas" by Penfield) is con-

---

[4] Figure 13-13 is a composite of Penfield's and Rasmussen's Figures 110 and 120 from *The Cerebral Cortex of Man* (36).

irmed. The Fissure of Rolando separates the pre- and postcentral gyri, which govern the motor and somasthetic processes respectively. There are also visual and auditory centers associated with the projection fibers arising from the appropriate sense organs. An interesting area is that revealed along the border between the occipital and parietal lobes labeled "visual and auditory recollection." As was demonstrated in the case of M. M., Penfield has been able to elicit elaborate memory sequences in patients in which this area was stimulated.

Thus man's brain, like that of his animal ancestors, functions partly in terms of highly localized areas which serve specific functions and also in terms of more loosely localized regions which subserve the complex skills and verbal processes. In this connection, it might be noted that the proportion of tissue devoted to projection centers *decreases* as we ascend the phylogenetic scale and the proportion of association tissue *increases*. At the risk of being teleological we may argue that man's brain is better adapted for learning complex skills and planning for the future, whereas the animal's brain is more at the mercy of immediate stimuli to which it makes immediate and ad hoc reactions.

Summary and recapitulation.   We have come a long way in our understanding of the role of localization of the cerebral cortex. The history of the problem shows that theorists have oscillated between the extreme localization position first promulgated by the phrenologists to the position which assumes extreme unity of function or complete nonlocalization championed by Flourens. The truth, using our present knowledge, lies somewhere between these extremes. We have seen that there is localization, and that the precision of that localization depends upon the specificity of the function under consideration. Simple sensory and motor problems may show a fairly high degree of localization. Problems involving more general functions show less localization. We have also noted the astonishing degree to which the cortex is capable of recovery of function (equipotentiality); and, for maze learning and certain other problems, how mass of cortex destroyed is more important than specific location.[5]

THE MEMORY TRACE

Common sense tells us that the fact that we can remember the past means that experience leaves some kind of modification in the nervous

---

We have made no attempt to cover all phases of cortical localization of function. For a more extensive treatment the reader is referred to Morgan (*33*). For a report on the utilization of the method of electrical stimulation to map the somatic sensory and motor areas in detail see Woolsey (*48*). For more detail on cortical localization in man, Penfield and Rasmussen (*36*) provide excellent and readable accounts based on case histories.

system. This popular assumption is also good psychology. From the point of view of the experimental psychologist, memories do not exist in a vacuum but are presumed to be a reflection of the functions of neural traces or engrams. This concept of the neural trace is a very old one in psychology, first finding implicit expression in Locke's doctrine of the *tabula rasa* (Chapter 1). If experience "writes" on the blank tablet of mind, the traces of that experience must be somewhere in the mind, or more properly, in the functions of its parallel physiological organ, the brain.

Locke did not give explicit physiological status to memory traces. His successor in the British empirical school of philosophy and the founder of associationism, David Hartley (Chapter 1), supplied this deficiency. He accepted Newton's concept of the vibratory action of infinitely small "medullary particles" whose vibrations result in either sensation (if over afferent nerves) or movements of the limbs (if over efferent nerves). These minute disturbances of the inner substratum of the nerves—called "vibratiuncles" by Hartley—were held to be responsible for ideas as well as sensations and motor movement. The vibrations for ideas are simply fainter and more diminutive than those for sensation. Hartley accounted for associations or the bonds between ideas on the basis of a law of contiguity, arguing that if two sets of vibratiuncles occur in close temporal proximity, one develops the power to excite the other.[6]

Although Hartley's doctrine is stated in a very general way and in terms of physiological processes which are no longer acceptable, the doctrine *in essence* states both the problem and the solution that every subsequent theory of the memory trace has invoked in some manner. The heart of the problem is that of accounting for the linkage of two or more neuronal systems previously unrelated before having been modified by a new learning experience. Moreover, any theory of memory has to explain the nature of the persistence of the connection during intervals of no practice or rehearsal.

No responsible modern theory of memory holds that neural activity persists as long as memories last. Such a theory would demand that the nervous impulses for all memories from the beginning of earliest childhood persist in many instances throughout life—a physiological impossibility. However, assuming that a new linkage or network of neurons is formed as a result of a new experience, contemporary theory does assume that the network, once formed, persists. All that is required to reinstate a memory is the reactivation of the network. For example, let us assume that a piano player learned Yankee Doodle years ago and shows that he remembers it by sitting down and playing. We may assume that the sight of the piano and the pattern of keys in particular, serves to reactivate the motor circuits

[6] Summarized from Boring (5).

ıediating the responses by way of neural impulses arriving over afferent
eurons.

Hebb's theory of perceptual learning, which we discussed in detail
ı Chapter 5 makes a similar assumption. The cell assembly is his term
ɔr the linkage of neurons that activate any fundamental part of a concept;
ıe phase sequence is the total functional linkage that mediates the entire
ɔncept or memory.

In attempting to provide a theoretical account of the exact mecha-
ism by means of which one neuron can be functionally linked to another
y practice or experience, physiological psychologists have invoked a num-
er of models and hypotheses. We shall examine several of the more in-
uential of these in turn.

Chronaxie. An early theory of neural linkage assumed that a change
ı the *chronaxie* of the neurons in question had taken place as a result of
timulation by practice. Chronaxie is a term originated by Louis Lapicque
1866 to 1952), a professor of physiology at the Sorbonne, to refer to the
ensitivity of nervous tissue as determined by the speed with which a neuron
eacts to a stimulus which is twice the strength of the threshold stimulus.
ʌapicque found that some neurons react faster than others and at the same
ime discovered a precise quantitative measure of excitability. The propo-
ents of the chronaxie theory applied the concept to the synapse, arguing
hat contiguous excitation of anatomically adjacent neurons could link
hem functionally or physiologically by bringing their chronaxies into phase.
'recisely why practice should have this effect on neural tissue was not
xplained.

Neurobiotaxis. A somewhat more sophisticated theory of neural linkage
vas developed around the concept of *neurobiotaxis,* a theoretical formulation
ʙy C. U. A. Kappers (*18*). Neurobiotaxis refers to the discovery that areas
ɔf high metabolic activity result in electrical gradients which favor the
rowth of tissue toward such areas. As applied to the memory trace, the
heory assumes that additional synaptic knobs can be developed by activity
n the region of the synapse. Thus, two anatomically connected neurons
night be functionally separate and unable to transmit an impulse from
ɔne to the other because of insufficient terminal buttons until these had
leveloped as a consequence of excitation reaching the end-brush of one of
he neurons. As indicated in Chapter 5, Hebb has adopted this hypothesis
n accounting for the development of cell assemblies and phase sequences.

Sensitization. Because it has long been known that chemical substances
ιre secreted at synaptic junctions (adrenergic and cholinergic substances

in the autonomic nervous system; acetylcholine in the central nervous system), a number of neurologists (13, p. 125–126) have speculated that during learning, activity on the part of the neurons might facilitate the secretion of the transmitter substance thus establishing a functional connection between the neurons. Presumably, once sensitization occurred during practice the resultant modification in the neurons would persist, making the connection relatively permanent. A recent version of the sensitization theory has been advanced by Milner (32).

Milner assumes that in forming associations some synaptic knobs do not fire, regardless of how many impulses arrive along their axons, except when the cell upon which they terminate happens to be fired from another source at the same instant that impulses are arriving at the nonfiring knob. Under these conditions the impulse is able to

> . . . invade that synaptic knob, and in the process the membrane of the knob is changed so that it can subsequently be fired, at least for a time, by any further impulses coming down its axon. This sensitization of the synaptic knob to its input may only last for a few seconds on the first occasion it takes place, but if the same thing keeps happening (i.e., if the two cells concerned often fire together), the sensitization may eventually become permanent (32, p. 122).

Milner makes it clear that his theory does not imply a neurobiotaxic process in which new knobs develop. Rather, he assumes that nonfunctional knobs already present become functional by a process of sensitization. In this way complex networks of neurons can develop through learning or experience. The reader will note that the theory is very similar to Hebb's in all essential respects except in the manner in which synaptic linkage is achieved.

DNA and RNA. The discovery of deoxyribonucleic acid and ribonucleic acid has made possible a highly sophisticated theory of learning which has excited considerable attention among neurophysiologists in recent years. Essentially, the theory, as proposed by Hydén (15), assumes that learning causes changes in RNA, and these altered RNA substances govern the metabolic activities of the cell and obtain "instructions" from DNA, the macro-molecular substances which form the genetic information complement in the cell nucleus. Since, as has been pointed out, learning involves a relatively permanent change in behavior, it is presumably related to a relatively permanent change in cellular structure, in this case in the neuron. Possibly such changes are reflected as changes in the cell's ribonucleic acid components. Most other cellular substances are too transitory to account for the durability of modifications due to learning. More specifically, the proponents of the RNA theory argue that practice excites metabolic changes in the cell causing changes in RNA, which then manufactures new proteins, and these presumably become the permanent end products of learning and are capable of facilitating neural transmission.

A number of experiments too extensive to review here have been carried out in support of the RNA hypothesis. These are summarized in Deutsch and Deutsch (*11*, pp. 89–93) with references to appropriate primary sources. Here we may briefly outline two typical experiments bearing on the question in order to illustrate the technique and design of research in this area.

Hydén (*15*) trained rats to climb a rope. An analysis was then made of the composition of RNA in the nuclei of cells in the first vestibular relay nucleus and in the nuclei of the surrounding glial cells. Changes in the composition of RNA were found. Control animals were subject to rotation to induce vestibular stimulation but these animals did not show significant changes in RNA. Critics have pointed out that the vestibular relay nucleus is a peripheral nucleus and that, despite Hydén's controls, we cannot be sure the changes in the nuclei of the cells comprising the relay nucleus might be due to vestibular disturbances rather than to learned modifications. However, if confirmed for higher centers, the results would be highly significant, showing as they do that fundamental cellular changes can occur as a result of experience.

In a widely quoted experiment by Thompson and McConnell (*46*) planaria (flatworms which have the ability to regenerate parts that have been cut off) were conditioned to contract to a light by repeatedly pairing a light with a shock. They were then cut in two and both halves allowed to regenerate. Again the worms were tested in the conditioning situation, and they showed significant retention of the response. Presumably, this experiment indicates that the memory trace was transferred to the new halves by means of RNA transfer.

As yet, we cannot be sure that RNA transfer is the biological basis of memory. A vast amount of research[7] is in progress on the psychochemistry of learning—research on animals in which experimenters are testing the effects of RNA injections in the bloodstream and brain and experiments in which various pharmocological substances are administered either orally or by injections to test out whether RNA transfer is inhibited or facilitated. Careful assays of the brain are being made before and after experiences to determine whether changes in the level of various substances, believed to be associated with neural transmission and memory such as acetylcholine,

See Morgan (*33*, Chapter 20) for a review of the literature on psychochemistry. Deutsch and Deutsch (*11*, Chapter 3) discuss the physiological basis of memory and learning with extensive references to the recent research on drug facilitation, RNA transfer, and electrochemical studies. Both of these standard texts provide numerous references to original papers.

are increased (43). As yet, we can draw no firm conclusions from this work, but it is possible to say that neurologists and physiological psychologists are not far from identifying the physiological basis for memory.

DYNAMIC PROCESSES AND THE SUBCORTEX

By dynamic processes we refer to motivational and emotional activities or those behavioral and physiological functions which come under the old classification of conative (motivational) and affective (emotional) processes as opposed to cognitive (sensory and perceptual) processes. Traditionally, the cognitive processes have been identified with the functions of the cerebral cortex. Sensing, perceiving, intellectual activities, associational or learned processes—all have been ascribed to the "higher" centers in the cortex. It has also long been assumed that the "lower" or subcortical centers mediate the dynamic aspects of behavior. As we shall see, this distinction has considerable merit. We have already found that the cortex is highly specialized for sensory and associational functions. However, there are also centers in the cortex which are concerned with visceral processes; and, as will be brought out, the subcortex and cortex are by no means isolated in their respective activities, but instead work as a team.

We cannot undertake a detailed anatomical and physiological account of the many nuclei that make up the subcortical centers, many of which are primarily concerned with motor processes. Rather, we have selected for study those centers which recent research has linked with motivational and emotional behavior. Even in this limited area research activities and the flood of new knowledge have been phenomenal. Neurologists have taken a new look at the older portions of the brain which man inherited from his animal forebears and found hitherto unsuspected functional correlations between these centers and dynamic processes. Much of this work has been made possible through the discovery of the feasibility of electrode implantation into areas that were virtually inaccessible using older techniques.

For convenience of discussion we shall divide these centers into three major categories—the reticular, the hypothalamic, and the limbic. We hasten to admit that divisions such as the above are inevitably arbitrary to some degree, following as they do old, anatomical considerations which prevailed before physiological techniques revealed a surprising degree of integration among the so-called lower centers. However, the *primary* functions of these several centers are identifiable, and we shall point out their interrelations from time to time, thus minimizing the risk of separating the inseparable.

The Reticular Formation and Activation[8]

Psychologists and physiologists have always associated consciousness ith the activities of the cerebral cortex. And in a sense this position has ver been challenged. An infant whose cortex is nonfunctional is "con- ious" only for brief periods. Those born with the congenital defect of encephaly (absence of the cortex) never achieve any real appreciation of eir surroundings. They remain vegetative idiots. However, a complex stem of fibers in the medulla and brain stem has been shown to make an portant contribution to consciousness, alertness, and sleep. When this nter is seriously damaged, the individual becomes comatose and cannot e aroused (Figure 13-13).

The reticular formation or, as it is commonly known, the reticular acti- ating system (RAS), is a loosely organized network (reticulum = network) fibers which runs up through the medulla to the brain stem and beyond. s Figure 13-14 shows, sensory impulses coming in from the periphery over e afferent neurons must go through the RAS, where they are either in- bited or facilitated. Inhibited impulses never reach the cortex and there- re are not paralleled by a conscious awareness of stimulation. Impulses hose passage is facilitated spread out upon the appropriate projection nters in the cortex, arousing functional activity and awareness of stimula- on. Facilitation takes the form of collateral impulses generated by the RAS hich "alert" the cortex for the reception of peripheral impulses.

This phase of RAS activity is known as the ascending reticular system. would be a mistake, however, to assume that all RAS functions are peri- herally controlled. A descending reticular system is intimately concerned ith regulation of peripheral reflexes and muscle tone. Moreover, impulses om parts of the cortex itself play upon the RAS and can stimulate it into ction. For example, stimulation of certain areas in a monkey's cortex will waken the sleeping animal. If the stimulation is delivered to a monkey that already awake, the animal stops its ongoing activity, looks around in- ntly, and appears puzzled as if taken unawares by a stimulus (12).

Relating the ascending and intracranial channels of RAS activity to veryday life, we may take the example of a sleeping person who is bom-

Our account has been taken from a variety of sources. For good general treatments with refer- ces to primary sources see Morgan (33, Chapter 12), and Deutsch and Deutsch (11, Chapter 5). D. French (12) has prepared an article for the Scientific American which is an excellent summary the general functions of the formation. Horace Magoun's The Waking Brain (30) is the "classic" the field written by the man who did most of the research establishing the importance of the rmation. A short technical article by the same author appears in The Biological and Biochemical ses of Behavior (29). In the same volume Jasper deals with the more theoretical aspects of the AS.

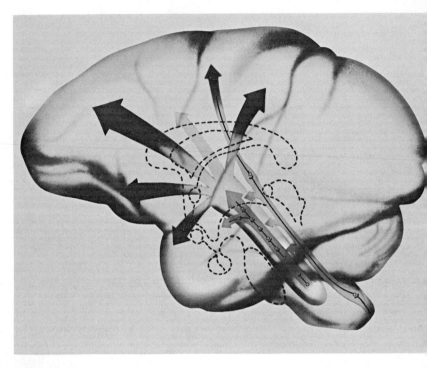

Fig. 13-13. A diagrammatic representation of the principal pathways of the reticul. system. (From Magoun, *29.*)

barded during the night by all sorts of exteroceptive and propriocepti stimuli.[9] Only "important" stimuli get through—the smell of smoke, th distress cries of the baby, and growling of the family dog. Clearly, if a stimuli got through, sleep would be impossible. Yet, as our examples shov parts of the cortex are sufficiently alert to "direct traffic," instantly con manding a flood of alerting stimuli to pass the reticular formation if nece sity demands. The close interplay between cortex and RAS is even mo dramatically revealed by the ability of most people to awaken at or near certain hour if necessity demands. They "tell" themselves that they wish awaken; and, at the appropriate time, signals go out from the cortex to th RAS and back again alerting the cortical centers.

We do not mean to imply that all the phenomena of sleep and wak fulness can be accounted for by the activities of the RAS. There are oth centers both in the hypothalamus and thalamus which are closely connecte to the RAS and which contribute to cycles of sleep and wakefulness (*33*, p

[9] It has been estimated that over four million impulses *per second* reach the RAS. Obviously, only small fraction of these ever get through to the cortex.

16-348). However, it is generally conceded by neurologists that the RAS the primary mechanism that controls alertness and somnolence.

While we have been emphasizing the role of the RAS in sleep and ertness, we would also like to suggest that in this diffuse network of cells sychologists may have the key to the old problems of set, attention, and lectivity of perception. It has always been assumed that these processes ave their neurological counterparts, but until the RAS was identified no seful working model had been suggested. We now know that the RAS lapts to repeated sensory stimulation by a tonal pattern (loss of attention), it if the sound pattern is changed the animal is once again alert (*17*). In is connection French (*12*) has concluded that the RAS is, indeed, an ntegrating machine" which functions in the manner that we have sug- ested:

> The RAS seems to be such a machine. It awakens the brain to consciousness and keeps it alert; it directs the traffic of messages in the nervous system; it moni- tors the myriads of stimuli that beat upon our senses, accepting what we need to perceive and rejecting what is irrelevant; it tempers and refines our muscular activity and bodily movements. We can go even further and say that it contrib- utes in an important way to the highest mental processes—the focusing of atten- tion, introspection, and doubtless all forms of reasoning.

Much more research remains to be done before our knowledge of these omplex mechanisms is complete. But in the course of a generation we have ained the equivalent of centuries of knowledge on the fundamental prob- ms of the neurological basis of cognition.

The Hypothalamus, the Regulation of Bodily Needs, and Emotion

Although the hypothalamic area was described by the medieval natomists, our knowledge of its functions is relatively recent. It was not ntil the early part of this century that neurophysiologists first attempted xperimental investigations of the region. In 1909 two German investigators, . P. Karplus and A. Kreidl,[10] showed that stimulation of the hypothalamus auses changes in autonomic functions—specifically in heart rate, blood ressure, sweating, and vasoconstriction. In the 1920's Bard began his now lassic studies of hypothalamic functions showing that the caudal or osterior portion is involved in the expression of rage. It was on the basis f this work and his own investigations that Cannon postulated the hypo- halamic theory of the emotions which we discussed earlier (Chapter 12).

Between the early electrical and extirpative investigations of the 1920's nd the present time, a vast amount of research on the hypothalamic region

Cited by Fulton (*14*).

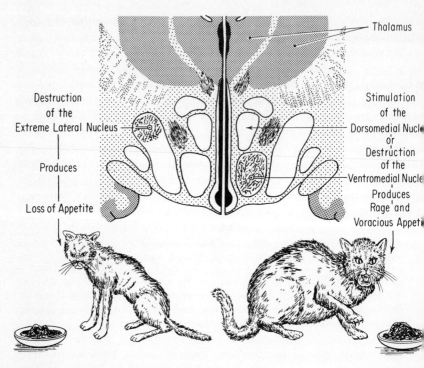

Fig. 13-14. A diagrammatic representation of the principal nuclei of the hypothalamu (From Krech and Crutchfield, *20a*.)

has identified it not only as an area concerned in the expression of emc tional behavior but also as a center for the control of hunger and thirs sexual behavior, heat control, and the regulation of visceral processe through the autonomic nervous system. Moreover, a number of investigator have pointed to the close anatomical and functional relationships betwee the RAS and hypothalamus and between the limbic system (see followin section) and the hypothalamic nuclei. Here we shall be primarily concerne with the role of the hypothalamus in the regulation of hunger, thirst, an general emotional expression.

1. The hypothalamus and hunger. There are two centers for the regula tion of hunger which work in opposite ways. The ventromedial nuclei exer a restraint or control over eating and the lateral nuclei stimulate eatin (Figure 13-14). A number of investigators have produced lesions in th ventromedial nucleus with the consistent result that the animal becomes hypothalamic hyperphagic or excessive eater. Immediately after the opera tion such animals eat several times as much as normal; and, as a conse

NAMIC PROCESSES AND THE SUBCORTEX

ience of their excessive appetites, become extremely obese. After several eeks their intake tends to level off; nevertheless, they remain obese. A milar condition has been observed in human beings who suffer from mors which invade the ventromedial area, pressing on the cells and estroying them. Lesions in the lateral thalamic nuclei, on the contrary, roduce aphagic (without appetite) animals who refuse to eat to the oint of starvation and special methods must be employed to keep them ive.

Because numerous investigators have confirmed the role played by the entromedial and lateral nuclei, these have come to be known as *satiety* and *ding* centers respectively. In other words, if the ventromedial nuclei are tact, they serve as "STOP" centers in the regulation of eating whereas the teral nuclei are "GO" centers. We should also note that *stimulation* of the teral nucleus (*10*) produces increased intake—an interesting fact which rroborates the GO function of the lateral nuclei. In the normal animal, en, the balance between the two centers serves to regulate the animals' take of food.

Investigators have also found that emotional and appetitive behavior e correlated. Ingram (*16*) showed that cats with lesions in the ventro-edial nuclei become savage as well as hyperphagic. Animals with lesions the lateral system of nuclei tend to become placid, possibly as a result of creasing weight loss and general debility.

It would be misleading to assume that eating and appetite are solely nder the control of the hypothalamic nuclei. These centers appear to gulate the *amount* of food eaten. We do not know what central nervous ctors play upon them to initiate eating—possible impulses from the cortex enerated by the sight and smell of food. Nor do we know what governs ecial appetites for certain foods and aversions for others. We know from e extensive researches of Richter (*41*) and others that biochemical and idocrine factors are important in protein, fat, carbohydrate, mineral, and tamin appetites. And we also know from numerous studies carried out by oung and his associates (*49, 50*) that psychological factors of habit and alatability are also of great importance in governing the choice of specific ods.

However, if we invoke the Richter-Young theory of specific appetites governed by biochemical and psychological factors and add to it the re-ent knowledge of intake regulation by hypothalamic nuclei, we have a elatively complete theory of hunger motivation. That is, we may confi-ently postulate that overall intake is governed through the hypothalamic uclei. However, the initiation of eating and the quality of foods eaten epend upon environmental factors, such as availability, the attractiveness f foods, their palatability, and the habits and preferences that the individ-al has built up through experience.

2. The hypothalamus and thirst. The early accounts of the regulation of water intake tended to emphasize local stimulus factors in the mouth and throat. Thus Cannon's (8) local theory explained the thirst motive as dependent upon dryness and stickiness in the oral cavity which, in turn, results from decreased salivary functioning due to a general depletion of water in the blood. There is no question that such local factors play some part in the initiation of drinking, but a variety of experiments (42) have shown that total water intake—the primary factor in maintaining proper water metabolism—is not dependent upon these local factors. In addition to oral factors, the condition of the blood, the hydration of body cells, secretions from the posterior pituitary gland and hypothalamic factors are also involved in the regulation of water intake. Here we are concerned with the role of the hypothalamus, and the evidence seems conclusive that, as in the case of eating, there are special centers which regulate water intake.

There have been several general approaches utilized in establishing the precise location of nuclei concerned with water intake: extirpative, electrical, and chemical. We shall consider each, briefly, in turn.

Extirpation of the region near the supraoptic nucleus causes excessive drinking or polydipsia (40). The high intake of water is accompanied by a high output of urine; however, the latter does not develop until the animal has already become "waterlogged." Moreover, excessive drinking may be demonstrated in animals with esophageal fistulas (4). Taken together, these factors show that the polydypsia is a primary consequence of the lesion and is not a secondary result of polyuria.

Lesions in the medial and anterior hypothalamus can cause cessation of drinking in animals to the point of severe dehydration and death (3). This finding suggests that for thirst, as for hunger, there may be STOP and GO centers in the hypothalamus which regulate water intake.

That such regulatory mechanisms exist in the normal animal is supported by studies involving electrical stimulation (2). Weak currents applied to the midregion of the hypothalamus evoke almost immediate drinking which continues to the point of water intoxication.

Finally, the results of chemical injections directly into the hypothalamic nuclei further strengthen the position that precise regulatory mechanisms exist in this part of the brain. In a widely cited investigation, Andersson (1) injected both hypotonic and hypertonic solutions directly into the hypothalamus of goats. Hypertonic injections initiated drinking—even in animals that had all the water they needed. Hypotonic solutions, on the other hand, caused a cessation of drinking even in animals suffering from water deprivation who were in the act of drinking at the time of the injection.

It has been suggested by Verney (47) and others that the cells of the hypothalamus concerned with water intake may be osmoreceptors which are sensitive to the level of saline and other minerals in solution in the blood nd body fluids. As the saline level becomes higher (greater than normal osmotic pressure) due to water loss resulting from perspiration, respiration, urination, and the like, the cells stimulate drinking behavior. Then as the surrounding fluids become hypotonic (less than normal osmotic pressure), the cells inhibit drinking.

The osmotic theory is attractive because of its logical simplicity. However, we know that the thirst drive and the regulation of water intake is an extremely complex process dependent in part on hypothalamic factors but also on the posterior pituitary, oral cavity, gastric receptors, blood factors, and probably cortical centers as well. Moreover, in man, thirst, like hunger, is involved with habits and preferences which are learned but which may be as important in the selection and regulation of fluids as are primary bodily factors.

By way of summary, we are now in a position to attempt to integrate hypothalamic with other regulatory factors. Stellar (*44*) has offered a model of a central process theory of motivation centering around hypothalamic regulation. As Figure 13-15 shows, the model provides for the influence of sensory stimuli and a variety of internal factors both physical and chemical which play upon the hypothalamus. The theory is essentially a homeostatic model since it emphasizes feedback and regulatory mechanisms. While Stellar's organization of the role of neural, sensory and humoral factors is useful as a conceptual device, we shall see (in the final section of this chapter) that an old part of the brain anterior to the hypothalamus, the limbic system, is also an important center of behavior dynamics.

3. The hypothalamus and emotion.

We have already pointed out how the Cannon-Bard theory of the emotions developed out of Bard's discovery that destruction of the posterior hypothalamus leaves the animal unable to initiate a complete rage reaction. We also indicated how in the absence of the cerebral cortex the animal can still manifest a complete rage response but that the threshold for rage is lower and the response lacks directionality.

The fact that complete rage responses are possible only with an intact hypothalamus led Cannon and Bard to identify that division of the brain as the center of the emotions. Today we know that this is an oversimplified view. It is true that rage responses appear to be mediated by the lateral hypothalamus. Most recently Delgado (*9*) has shown that a full-fledged integrated and meaningful attack pattern in cats can be initiated by stimulation of the lateral hypothalamus (Figure 13-16). However, this same investigator has also shown that centers for fear may be located more anteriorly in the posteroventral nucleus of the thalamus. However, other investigators have obtained a variety of emotional responses by stimulation of the hypothalamus—not always with consistent results (*7*). Apparently the topography of the region is complex, with a variety of closely associated nuclei that mediate emotional or emotional-like reactions. Even a few millimeter difference in the placement of an electrode can result in an entirely different response.

The safest generalizations that can be made about the role of the hypo-thalamus in the emotions are: (1) that the posterior nuclei are involved in the expression of rage and attack patterns, since if these nuclei are destroyed the animal becomes placid and unemotional; (2) the ventromedial nuclei are centers for the suppression or control of rage, since if these are destroyed the animal becomes ferocious (Figure 13-15); and (3) the hypothalamus in conjunction with the limbic system is involved in other aspects of emotional behavior in as yet a poorly understood manner.

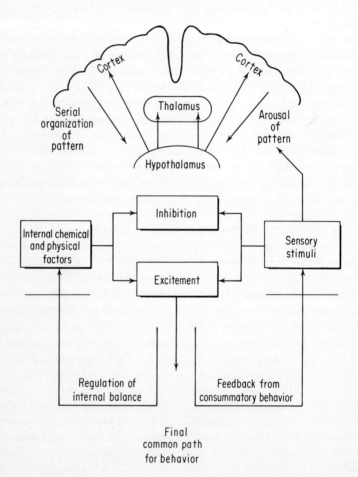

Fig. 13-15. The various physiological processes which contribute to motivated behavior (After Stellar, *44*.)

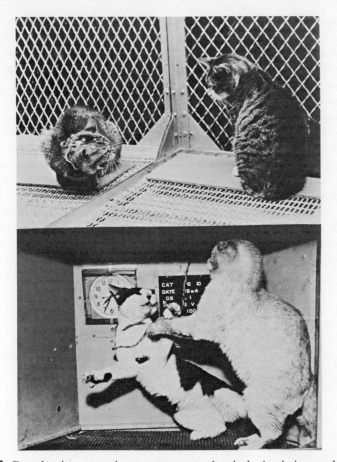

ig. 13-16. Cats showing aggressive patterns upon electrical stimulation to the hypo-nalamic region. (Photographs courtesy of Dr. Jose Delgado.)

The limbic system.[11] Theoretical accounts of the role played by the mbic system in the emotions date from what is now regarded as a classic aper by James W. Papez which appeared in 1937 (*35*). Entitled a "Pro-osed Mechanism of Emotion," the report described the limbic system natomically, tracing its known connections with higher centers and sum-narizing the then meager clinical evidence in support of the hypothesis hat the system is an emotional center rather than part of the olfactory

---

[1] The volume of research on the limbic system has become so large as to virtually defy summariz-ng. Moreover, much of it is highly technical and only poorly related to theoretical interpreta-ions of behavior. We have followed our usual practice of sampling and have based our discussion rimarily on the work of Paul D. MacLean whose research has centered around a theoretical osition and to whose theory the work of other investigators can readily be related. References MacLean's research will be made at appropriate places.

brain, a commonly held opinion of its function that had prevailed for over a century. In his revolutionary account, Papez concluded that ". . . the hypothalamus, the anterior thalamic nuclei, the gyrus cinguli, the hippocampus and their interconnections constitute a harmonious mechanism which may elaborate the functions of central emotion, as well as participate in emotional expression" (*35*, p. 743).

Because of the dominance of the Cannon-Bard theory, with its emphasis on hypothalamic mechanisms, Papez' theory received little attention from neurophysiologists or psychologists at the time of its publication. It was not until the introduction of microelectrode stimulating techniques following World War II that his remarkable chain of reasoning began to obtain sound experimental support.

Considerable credit is due Paul D. MacLean (*25, 28*), who called the attention of neurophysiologists to Papez' original statement and at the same time extended its theoretical implications. He also cited considerable experimental evidence in its support. In the intervening years the limbic system has attracted a legion of experimenters seeking to delimit its functional connections and to relate them to emotional behavior.

Figure 13-17 shows the various parts of the limbic system. It will be noted that the system consists basically of two divisions, cortical and subcortical. The largest of the cortical areas is the *cingulate gyrus* which lies deep within the longitudinal fissure above the corpus callosum. The *hippocampal gyrus* also lies deep within the longitudinal fissure but posteriorly to the

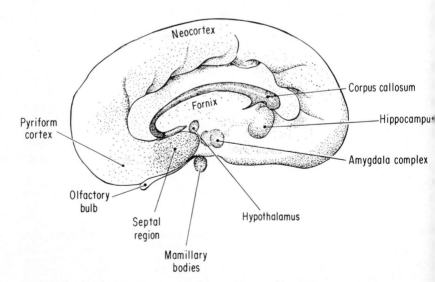

Fig. 13-17. A diagrammatic view of the principal structures of the limbic system.

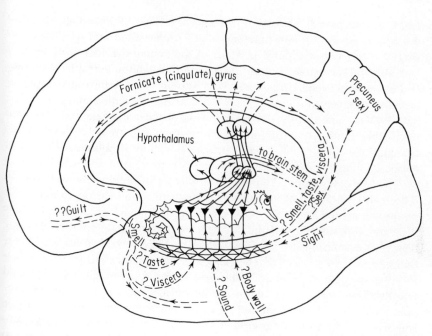

Fig. 13-18. The circuits of the limbic system as conceived by MacLean on the basis of his own work and Papez' theory of the function of the system. (From MacLean, *25.*)

corpus callosum. Finally, the *pyriform lobe* near the olfactory bulbs is the third cortical center commonly associated with the limbic system.

The subcortical portions of the limbic system are the *fornix,* lying under the corpus callosum; the *hippocampus,* a sea-horse shaped structure, lying below the fornix; the *septum* in the anterior or frontal region; the *amygdala,* a nuclear mass in the lower portion of the brain; and the *mamillary bodies* in the front and central region of the subcortex. There is general agreement about the inclusion of the foregoing cortical and subcortical centers in the limbic system. However, some authorities would also include the hypothalamic nuclei, the nonspecific nuclei of the thalamus, the olfactory bulbs, and other and less familiar subcortical structures. Because of its close connections with the amygdala complex, the temporal lobe is often included in a discussion of the limbic system.

Figure 13-18 shows the Papez-MacLean circuit, as it is now called, in simplified form. The various sensory systems stream into the region from the special sense organs in the head and up through the reticular formation from the lower parts of the body. Upon reaching the limbic system they are channeled into the hippocampus and from there radiate out to the amygdala complex, the cingulate gyrus, hippocampal gyrus, pyriform cortex,

and other structures.[12] Broadly speaking, MacLean (28) has suggested tha
the system serves the joint functions of self-preservation and species preser
vation. The fronto-temporal portions of the system are identified by hin
with survival mechanisms of self-protection (fear and anger) and obtainin;
and assimilating food. In general, wild animals with lesions in this regio
become extremely docile and show peculiarities of feeding and sexual be
havior. More specifically, bilateral lesions of the amygdala complex giv
reasonably consistent results in rendering animals extremely docile—eve
changing the social dominance hierarchy in groups of monkeys (33). For
merly dominant and aggressive monkeys become fearful and submissive.

If the fronto-temporal cortex is included in the lesions, the well-know
Klüver–Bucy (19) syndrome appears immediately after the operations. Th
syndrome, named for its discoverers, consists of dramatic changes in feedin;
behavior and sexuality. Animals become indiscriminate in their feedin;
behavior, attempting to eat nuts and bolts, bits of wood, feces, and food
that are ordinarily rejected. They also show extreme sexuality and attemp
to copulate with cage mates regardless of sex or even species. Frequen
masturbation and oral eroticism are also evident in the behavior of suc
animals. Thus, we may assume that in the normal animal, sexual restrain
is exerted by the fronto-temporal cortex and its associated subcortical cen
ters; and, as MacLean suggests, oral behavior—licking, chewing, eatin¢
and the like—also appear to be under the control of that region.

MacLean also points out that fear, dread and feelings of thirst an
nausea have been reported in conscious human subjects who are stimulate
in the temporal region during brain operations or in those people wh
suffer from epilepsy whose discharges are focused on the fronto-tempora
cortex. This clinical evidence, he believes, further strengthens the sel
preservative and alimentary nature of fronto-temporal functioning.

MacLean attributes species-preservative behavior to the hippocampal
septal-cingulate centers. This behavior includes sexual pleasure, sexua
reflexes, and grooming in animals. Support for this aspect of his theor
comes, in part, from the well-known studies of Olds and Milner (34), wh
discovered that animals with electrodes implanted in the septal region wil
press bars rapidly to the point of exhaustion in order to continue to obtai
shocks—presumably because they are pleasurable. In addition, MacLea
(26, 27, and 28) has shown that stimulation of the hippocampus which re
sults in after-discharge to the cingulate gyrus and septal nuclei leads cat
to begin grooming and licking themselves. In males, penile erections appear
and the animals show evident signs of pleasure—purring, fanning the fore
paws, rolling over, and so forth. It is behavior patterns such as these whicl
are associated with sexuality that have led MacLean to postulate that th

[12] For a more detailed and highly technical account of the connections of the limbic system see 6

hippocampal-cingulate-septal circuits are concerned with species preservation or, in short, reproductive responses and associated sexual behavior.

In the nearly two decades which have followed MacLean's rediscovery of the Papez theory of emotions, a vast number of studies investigating the effects of electrode stimulation and ablation of limbic centers have been carried out.[13] Unfortunately, there are numerous disagreements both in empirical findings and interpretation among investigators, particularly concerning the results of electrical stimulation in various limbic centers. Part of the problem appears to be one of interpreting the nature of emotional behavior in animals. It may be difficult to decide whether a hissing cat with an arched back is afraid or is angry and about to attack. Also, if animals are frequently tested for emotional reactions after brain operations, they may become more and more irritable (or fearful) as a result of being disturbed, particularly if the tests involve noxious or punitive stimuli. In recent years there have been increasing attempts to develop learning methods which will yield more objective indices of animal emotionality. This means that the emotional state may be employed as a drive to stimulate a learned avoidance or escape reaction. Presumably, if the animal avoids or escapes he is experiencing fear or anxiety, and his behavior in escaping is a more objective index of emotion than an experimenter's estimate of what the animal is experiencing. In the future we may expect to see more and more investigations carried out utilizing these behavioral indices.

Nevertheless, despite the disagreements, a sound body of knowledge is slowly evolving from the experimental laboratories which is revealing the long-hidden nature of the neurophysiology of the emotions.

SUMMARY AND CONCLUSIONS

Most of our knowledge of the neurological foundations of behavior is less than a century old. The vast bulk of what we know has been learned in the twentieth century. Progress in neurophysiology has been slower than in other fields both because of the forbidding complexity of the structures involved and because discovery in this area had to await the development of techniques in other fields, particularly in electronics. Nevertheless, great progress has been made. We have seen how cortical localization for sensory, motor, and associative functions has been established with the help of experimental and clinical techniques. In the functions of the reticular system we now have a sound theoretical explanation of sleep, arousal, and attention. The recent breakthrough in the study of the limbic system has provided a major stride forward in understanding the neurological basis of the

---

[13] See *11* for a summary of these studies with references to recent primary sources.

emotions. And, within a few years after the identification of DNA and RNA as the biological memory code, neurophysiologists and psychologists had adapted their remarkable bioarchitectural abilities to provide a model of the memory trace.

REFERENCES

1. Andersson, B. The effect of injection of hypertonic NaCl solutions into different parts of the hypothalamus of goats. *Acta Physiologica Scandinavica,* **28,** 1953, pp. 188–201.
2. Andersson, B., and S. M. McCann. A further study of polydipsia evoked by hypothalamic stimulation in the goat. *Acta Physiologica Scandinavica,* **33,** 1955, pp. 333–346.
3. Andersson, B., and S. M. McCann. The effect of hypothalamic lesions on water intake of the dog. *Acta Physiologica Scandinavica,* **35,** 1956, pp. 312–320.
4. Bellows, R. T., and W. P. Van Wagenen. The relationship of polydipsia and polyuria in diabetes insipidus. *Journal of Nervous and Mental Diseases,* **88,** 1938, pp. 417–473.
5. Boring, E. G. *A history of experimental psychology,* ed. 1. New York: Appleton, 1929.
6. Brady, J. V. The paleocortex and behavioral motivation. In Harlow, H. F., and C. N. Woolsey (eds.), *Biological and biochemical bases of behavior.* Madison, Wisconsin: University of Wisconsin Press, 1958.
7. Brady, J. V. Emotional behavior. In Field, J., H. W. Magoun, and V. E. Hall (eds.), *Handbook of physiology,* Vol. 3. Washington, D. C.: American Physiological Society, 1960.
8. Cannon, W. B. *Bodily changes in pain, hunger, fear, and rage.* New York: Appleton, 1929.
9. Delgado, J. M. R. Emotions. In Vernon, J. A., (ed.), *Introduction to general psychology: A self-selection textbook.* Dubuque, Iowa: Wm. C. Brown, 1966.
10. Delgado, J. M. R., and B. K. Anand. Increased food intake induced by electrical stimulation of the lateral hypothalamus. *American Journal of Physiology,* **172,** 1953, pp. 162–168.
11. Deutsch, J. A., and D. Deutsch. *Physiological psychology.* Homewood, Illinois: The Dorsey Press, 1966.
12. French, J. D. The reticular formation. *Scientific American,* **196,** 1957, pp. 54–60.
13. Fulton, J. F. (ed.). *Howell's textbook of physiology.* Philadelphia: W. B. Saunders 1946.
14. Fulton, F. F. *The physiology of the nervous system,* ed. 3. New York: Oxford University Press, 1949.
14a. Honzik, C. H. The sensory basis of maze learning in rats. *Comparative Psychological Monographs,* **13,** 1936, No. 4.
15. Hydén, H. Satellite cells in the nervous system. *Scientific American,* **205,** 1961, pp. 62–70.
16. Ingram, W. R. The hypothalamus. *Clinical Symposia,* **8,** No. 4, 1956, Ciba Pharmaceutical Products, Inc.
17. Jasper, H. Reticular-cortical systems and theories of the integrative action of the brain. In Harlow, H. F., and C. N. Woolsey (eds.), *Biological and biochemical bases of behavior.* Madison, Wisconsin: University of Wisconsin Press, 1958.

8. Kappers, C. U. A. On the structural laws in the nervous system. The principles of neuro-biotaxis. *Brain,* **44,** 1921, p. 125.

9. Klüver, H., and P. C. Bucy. Preliminary analysis of functions of the temporal lobes in monkeys. *Archives of Neurology and Psychiatry,* **42,** 1939, pp. 979–1000.

0. Krech, D. Cortical localization of function. In Postman, L. (ed.), *Psychology in the making.* New York: Knopf, 1962.

0a. Krech, D., and R. S. Crutchfield. *Elements of psychology.* New York: Knopf, 1958.

1. Krechevsky, I. Hereditary nature of "hypotheses." *Journal of Comparative Psychology,* **16,** 1933, pp. 99–116.

2. Krechevsky, I. Brain mechanisms and "hypotheses." *Journal of Comparative Psychology,* **19,** 1935, pp. 425–468.

3. Lashley, K. S. *Brain mechanisms and intelligence.* Chicago: University of Chicago Press, 1929.

23a. Lashley, K. S. The mechanism of vision: XV. Preliminary studies of the rat's capacity for detailed vision. *Journal of General Psychology,* **18,** 1938, 123–193.

4. Lashley, K. S. The mechanism of vision: XVII. The functioning of small remnants of the visual cortex. *Journal of Comparative Neurology,* **70,** 1939, pp. 45–67.

5. MacLean, P. D. Psychosomatic disease and the "visceral brain": recent developments bearing on the Papez theory of emotion. *Psychosomatic Medicine,* **11,** 1949, 338–353.

6. MacLean, P. D. Some psychiatric implications of physiological studies on fronto-temporal portions of the limbic system (visceral brain). *Neurosurgery,* **11,** 1954, pp. 29–44.

7. MacLean, P. D. Chemical and electrical stimulation of hippocampus in unrestrained animals, Part II: Behavioral findings. *Archives of Neurology and Psychiatry,* **78,** 1957, pp. 128–142.

8. MacLean, P. D. The limbic system with respect to self-preservation and the preservation of the species. *Journal of Nervous and Mental Diseases,* **127,** 1958, pp. 1–11.

9. Magoun, H. W. Nonspecific brain mechanisms. In Harlow, H. F., and C. N. Woolsey (eds.), *Biological and biochemical bases of behavior.* Madison, Wisconsin: University of Wisconsin Press, 1958.

0. Magoun, H. W. *The waking brain,* ed. 2. Springfield, Illinois: Charles Thomas, 1963.

1. Maier, N. R. F. Cortical destruction in the posterior part of the brain and its effects on reasoning in rats. *Journal of Comparative Neurology,* **56,** 1932, pp. 179–214.

2. Milner, P. M. The application of physiology to learning theory. In Patton, R. (ed.), *Current trends in psychological theory.* Pittsburgh: University of Pittsburgh Press, 1961.

3. Morgan, C. T. *Physiological psychology,* ed. 3. New York: McGraw-Hill, 1965.

4. Olds, J., and P. Milner. Positive reinforcement produced by electrical stimulation of septal area and other regions of rat brain. *Journal of Comparative and Physiological Psychology,* **47,** 1954, pp. 419–427.

5. Papez, J. W. A proposed mechanism of emotion. *Archives of Neurology and Psychiatry,* **38,** 1937, pp. 725–743.

6. Penfield, W., and T. Rasmussen. *The cerebral cortex of man.* New York: Macmillan, 1950.

7. Penfield, W. *The excitable cortex of conscious man.* Liverpool: Liverpool University Press, 1958.

8. Peterson, G. M. Mechanisms of handedness in the rat. *Journal of Comparative Psychology,* **9,** 1934, pp. 1–67.

39. Peterson, G. M., and L. Fracarol. The relative influence of the locus and mass of destruction upon the control of handedness by the cerebral cortex. *Journal of Comparative Neurology*, **68**, 1938, pp. 173–190.

40. Ralph, C. L. Polydipsia in the hen following lesions in the supraoptic hypothalamus. *American Journal of Physiology*, **198**, 1960, pp. 528–530.

41. Richter, C. P. Total self-regulatory function in animals and human beings. *Harvey Lectures*, **38**, 1942, pp. 63–103.

42. Rosenzweig, M. R. The mechanisms of hunger and thirst. In Postman, L. (ed.), *Psychology in the making*. New York: Knopf, 1962.

43. Rosenzweig, M. R., D. Krech and E. Bennett. Heredity, environment, brain biochemistry, and learning. In Patton, R. (ed.), *Current trends in psychological theory*. Pittsburgh: University of Pittsburgh Press, 1961.

44. Stellar, E. The physiology of motivation. *Psychological Review*, **61**, 1954, pp. 5–22.

45. Thompson, R. Retention of a brightness discrimination following neocortical damage in the rat. *Journal of Comparative and Physiological Psychology*, **53**, 1960, pp. 212–215.

46. Thompson, R., and J. V. McConnell. Classical conditioning in the planarian Dugesia dorotocephala. *Journal of Comparative and Physiological Psychology*, **48**, 1955, pp. 65–68.

47. Verney, E. B. The antidiuretic hormone and the factors which determine its release. *Proceedings of the Royal Society*, **135**, 1947, pp. 25–106.

48. Woolsey, C. N. Organization of somatic sensory and motor areas of the cerebral cortex. In Harlow, H. F., and C. N. Woolsey (eds.), *Biological and biochemical bases of behavior*. Madison, Wisconsin: University of Wisconsin Press, 1958.

49. Young, P. T. Psychologic factors regulating the feeding process. In *Symposium on nutrition and behavior*. New York: The National Vitamin Foundation, 1957, pp. 52–59.

50. Young, P. T., and Chaplin, J. P. Studies of food preference, appetite, and dietary habit, III: Palatability and appetite in relation to body need. *Comparative Psychology Monographs*, **18**, 1945, No. 3.

14

Quantitative Psychology

In this and the following chapter we shall be concerned primarily with theories within the broad division of the field known as *differential psychology*. The differential psychologist approaches human behavior through the investigation of individual differences—largely in the areas of intelligence and personality. On the other hand, psychologists in the field of *general psychology* are primarily concerned with establishing broad general laws of behavior within such traditional areas as motivation, learning, thinking, and perception.

Looked at from a somewhat different point of view, general psychology studies people in terms of how they are alike, while differential psychology looks at people in terms of how they differ. In reality, the two fields are complementary, since if we could know all the ways in which people are alike, it follows that we would know the ways in which they differ, and conversely. The distinction between the two fields is, in part, historical and, in part, a matter of convenience. Traditionally, those psychologists whose primary interest was the development of aptitude and personality tests came to be associated with differential psychology, while those whose interests remained within the areas of greatest concern to the schools were considered general experimental psychologists.

Because the investigation of individual differences has relied heavily on quantitative techniques, psychologists working in the area of differential psychology are sometimes known as "quantitative" psychologists. But again the distinction is merely a question of emphasis, since all contemporary psychologists rely on quantitative methods in designing experiments and interpreting the results. Furthermore, a number of psychologists in the area of learning (traditionally a "general" area) are developing mathematical models of the learning process and are more "quantitative" in their orientation and methodology than many differential psychologists. For this reason we have decided to include mathematical models of learning in this chapter. Another recent development within the field is the utilization of information theory in model making. Again, because information theory relies heavily on data processing techniques, we have chosen to include it here.

ORIGINS AND DEVELOPMENT OF QUANTITATIVE METHODS

The first application of statistical methods and the theory of the normal probability curve to the interpretation of biological and social data was made by Quetelet (1796 to 1874), a Belgian astronomer. The normal curve had been discovered earlier by mathematicians who applied it to the distribution of measurements and errors in scientific observations. However, until Quetelet demonstrated that anthropometric measurements carried out on unselected samples of people typically yield a normal curve, the law had never been applied to human variability. Quetelet employed the phrase, *l'homme moyen,* to express the fact that most individuals tend toward the average or center of the normal curve, with fewer and fewer cases represented near the extremes.

Sir Francis Galton (1822 to 1911), famous for his studies of hereditary genius, became interested in Quetelet's applications of the normal curve and greatly extended the latter's work. Galton also established a laboratory for the purpose of large-scale testing of individual differences. For these investigations, he designed a number of pieces of equipment, among which was a whistle for determining the upper limit for pitch, a bar for measuring the individual's ability to judge visual extents, and a pendulum-type reaction time device for measuring simple reactions. For decades, during the "brass instrument" phase of psychology, the Galton Whistle and Galton Bar were standard equipment in laboratories throughout the world.

However, of even greater importance was Galton's invention of various statistical tools—the median, the standard score, and the method of correlation. The last-named constitutes his single greatest contribution to quantitative psychology. The modern techniques for establishing the validity and reliability of tests, as well as the various factor analytic methods, are direct outgrowths of Galton's discovery. It is interesting to note that the method of correlation resulted from his observation that inherited characteristics tend to "regress" toward the mean of a distribution of those characteristics. Specifically, the sons of tall men are, on the average, not as tall as their fathers. Conversely, the sons of very short men are, on the average, taller than their fathers. More generally, the unusual combinations of genes that make for extreme deviations in any human characteristic occur only rarely, while the most probable combinations result in average characteristics. The symbol for the coefficient of correlation, r, is taken from the first letter of "regression" in recognition of its origin in Galton's discovery of the tendency toward mediocrity in the inheritance of human traits.

Finally, among the originators of the basic tools of descriptive statistics was Karl Pearson (1857 to 1936), who developed a large number of formulas for the treatment of psychological data. Pearson was also responsible for the present form of the product-moment coefficient of correlation which frequently bears his name. It is also worthy of note that in collaboration with Galton and Weldon he founded a journal, *Biometrika*, for the publication of the results of quantitative researches in biology and psychology.

While the basic measures of descriptive statistics were undergoing development in the hands of Quetelet, Galton, Pearson, and others, the psychophysical tradition was already well underway in the work of Weber and Fechner. As we pointed out in Chapter 2, the evolution of the psychophysical methods went hand in hand with the growth of experimental psychology. For this reason, some historians (*4, 13*) distinguish between the "mental test tradition," embracing the work of the "statisticians" and test developers, and the "psychophysical tradition," which evolved out of the researches of Weber and Fechner. Despite the fact that both traditions utilize the same fundamental statistical approaches, each has developed relatively independently of the other. The mental-test tradition has attracted those psychologists whose main interest lies in the area of individual differences, while the psychophysical tradition has remained closely allied to the general-experimental area.

However, as is so often the case with broad generalizations and dichotomies, there have been psychologists who, though trained in the experimental-psychophysical tradition, have made some of their most significant contributions in the area of individual differences. Such was true in the case of James McKeen Cattell (1860 to 1944), one of America's greatest psychologists and one who in many ways best epitomizes the spirit of American psychology. Cattell's postgraduate education in psychology was primarily German—but German with Cattell's highly individualistic stamp impressed upon it. Indeed, one of the most famous anecdotes in the history of psychology concerns Cattell's introduction to Wundt. As reported by Boring (*4*), Cattell became Wundt's first assistant—self-appointed, it might be noted. He appeared at Wundt's laboratory and said, "Herr Professor, you need an assistant, and I will be your assistant!" Cattell, moreover, made it clear that he would choose his own research problem—the psychology of individual differences. Wundt, according to Boring, is said to have characterized Cattell and his project as "*ganz amerikanisch.*"

Cattell's investigations of individual differences were centered largely around the reaction time experiment which at that time was enjoying tremendous popularity. In fact, the whole field of differential psychology may be said to have originated out of the discovery that individuals differ in respect to the speed with which they react to a stimulus. The discovery came about in 1796, when Maskelyne, the royal astronomer at Greenwich Observatory, dismissed his assistant, Kinnebrook, because the latter observed stellar transits approximately a second later than he did. This "error," as it was originally supposed to be, eventually became known as the "personal equation" in astronomy. Years later, in Wundt's laboratory, the investigation of reaction time under various conditions appeared to provide an avenue for the precise measurement of the mental processes. In general, the early investigators set for themselves the problem of attempting to measure "conduction time" over the sensory and motor nerves. Once this had been accomplished, it was hoped that conduction time could be "subtracted out," thus yielding accurate measures of such mental processes as sensory and motor sets, discriminations of various types, will, and association.[1]

Many of the classic experiments in the area of reaction time were carried out by Cattell. He investigated the speed of reaction as a function of the sense modality stimulated, simple as opposed to discrimination and association reaction time. In addition to his investigations of reaction time, he also contributed to psychophysics by inventing the order-of-merit method, in which stimuli ranked by a number of judges can be placed in a final rank order by calculating the average rating given to each item. For example, as Cattell applied the method to eminent American scientists, he asked ten scientists to rank a number of their outstanding colleagues, and averaged the results by assigning an order of merit to the scientists on the basis of the pooled results. Finally, Cattell and an associate devised a number of simple mental tests, which they administered to Columbia freshmen, marking the first large-scale testing of human subjects for the purpose of determining the range of individual differences.

In general, Cattell is credited with having influenced the overall development of American psychology in the direction of an eminently practical, test-oriented approach to the study of the mental processes. His was a psychology of human abilities as opposed to a psychology of conscious content. In this sense he comes close to being a functionalist, though he was never formally associated with that school. Thus, he represents a transition between the Germanic psychophysical tradition and the American functionalistic spirit, which has always emphasized the study of mental processes in terms of their utility to the organism.

[1] For a detailed history of reaction time experiments see Woodworth (*32*).

THE MENTAL TESTING MOVEMENT
AND THEORIES OF INTELLIGENCE

The mental testing movement began with the development of the first intelligence test by Binet and Simon in 1905. The test, as is well known, sprang from the purely practical goal of discovering an objective method of assessing the intellectual level of French school children. The Minister of Public Education had become concerned with the problem of how to identify and eliminate subnormal children who were unable to profit from public school education. He commissioned Binet and Simon to devise a scale that would select such children and, at the same time, indicate the nature of special instruction from which they could profit. A secondary objective was the improved diagnosis of hospitalized feebleminded children.

The Binet-Simon scale was developed around a theoretical framework involving three main conceptions of the nature of intelligence: (1) a goal or direction to the mental processes involved, (2) the ability to show adaptable solutions, (3) the capacity to show selectivity of judgment and self-criticism of choices. In attempting to measure these processes, Binet and Simon constructed their test from items of common information, word definitions, reasoning items, ingenuity tests, and the like. By giving the test to a large sample of children, they were able to arrange the items according to an age scale by placing them at a point where 50 to 75 percent of the children passed. For example, if a given item was passed by 50 percent of four-year-olds, it was considered appropriate for that level. Generalizing this reasoning to the test as a whole, Binet and Simon were obviously assuming that intelligence grows or develops in parallel with the child's chronological age. By comparing the child's rate of intellectual growth to the average rate of growth of the standardization group, it was then possible to measure any given child's intellectual level. Thus, as the Binet and other mental-age scales are now used, the child who passes all the items at the seven-year level *is mentally seven years of age irrespective of his chronological age.* In other words, he is able to do test items which 50 to 75 percent of seven-year-old children can pass. This concept of *mental age* as measured by a graded scale was Binet and Simon's great contribution.[2]

Such, briefly, was the reasoning behind the Binet-Simon Test. The critics, however, quickly began to voice their objections to the theoretical assumptions underlying the scale. First, is intelligence goal direction, adaptability, and critical judgment? If so, did the hodgepodge of test items employed by Binet and Simon measure the abilities they were designed to

The almost universally employed I.Q. which is calculated by dividing MA by CA was suggested by a German psychologist, Stern.

measure? Moreover, is intelligence a unitary or general ability as implied by the practice of lumping scores on a variety of items into a single mental-age score? The answers to these seemingly straightforward questions are still being sought half a century after the publication of the Binet scales. Broadly speaking, psychologists have taken two avenues of approach in attempting to formulate a definition of intelligence and to solve the problems involved in its measurement. The first is the "armchair" or deductive method, wherein the psychologist seeks to define intelligence on the basis of his expert opinion and then proceeds to construct a test which he believes will measure the processes identified in the definition. Clearly, this technique was the one employed by Binet and Simon. The second approach involves the analysis of already existing tests in an attempt to discover just what the tests are measuring. Obviously, the second technique involves the a priori assumption that existing tests are *generally valid*. That is to say, already existing tests do measure intelligence, not perfectly perhaps, but with sufficient precision to make the proposed analyses meaningful.

Because the deductive technique is nonquantitative, we shall not attempt to review the many definitions that have been offered by those in the field. Rather, the present discussion will be limited to theories of intelligence which depend upon mathematical analyses for the identification of intellectual functions. Following our usual "sampling technique," we shall explore the three leading quantitative theories of intelligence: Charles Spearman's two-factor theory, G. H. Thomson's sampling theory, and L. L. Thurstone's weighted group-factor theory.

Spearman's two-factor theory.[3]   Charles Spearman (1863 to 1945) announced his two-factor theory of intellectual ability in 1904, thus antedating the Binet Test by one year. However, his theory did not come into prominence until the mental-testing movement had been given impetus by the development of intelligence tests. Once it had come into its own, the theory became the center of international discussion and controversy as well as the starting point for rival theories of intelligence formulated on the basis of mathematical analyses of tests.

Spearman's basic assumption is that all mental tasks require two kinds of ability, a general ability, G, and a specific ability, s. G, or general ability, as the term implies, is common to all intellectual tasks, whereas s is always specific to a given task. Consequently, there is one G but as many s's as there are different intellectual tasks. For the sake of simplicity, let us assume that we are dealing with two tests, a vocabulary test and an arithmetic test. Both tests draw upon the common general ability, G; yet, in addition, each requires specialized abilities which are independent of each other. In this

---

[3] For primary sources see *22* and *23*.

case we may assume that the vocabulary test draws upon a specific verbal ability, s_1, and the arithmetic test a specialized numerical ability, s_2. Moreover, it follows that because the two tests require a common ability, they will be positively correlated. The correlation will not be perfect, however, because of the fact that s_1 and s_2 are independent or specialized abilities which have nothing in common. The situation which we have been describing can be represented graphically as follows (see Figure 14-1):

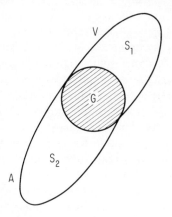

Fig. 14-1. A diagram to represent Spearman's G and s theory of intellectual abilities. For an explanation see text.

Let ellipses V and A represent the vocabulary and arithmetic tests, respectively. Because the tests are correlated, the ellipses overlap. The area of overlap represents G. The areas of independence represent s_1 and s_2 as indicated. Applying the same reasoning more generally, *all* intellectual tests, according to Spearman, "center" around G, since all are positively correlated. Indeed, the basic evidence for the two-factor theory was derived from Spearman's finding that various intellectual tests are positively correlated and to a moderately high degree. By a complex process involving the use of tetrad equations,[4] Spearman was able to show mathematically that his two-factor theory could account for the empirical interrelationships existing among tests.

Spearman's theory is able to explain the observed fact that children who show ability in one intellectual area also show ability along other lines. In short, the theory supports the Binet-Simon concept of an all-around general intellectual ability. However, because specific abilities are held to be independent of G and of each other, the theory also allows for the ob-

---

[4] The tetrad difference method of establishing factors is now considered obsolete. For the mathematical processes involved, the reader may consult *23*.

served fact that individuals do show differences in their more specialized aptitudes. For example, an individual of average ability as measured by a general intelligence test may, if given appropriate special tests, demonstrate more verbal than numerical ability. On the general test, the two more specialized abilities "balance out," and the overall average rating is the result. Such fluctuations in abilities are most marked in the case of highly specific aptitudes, such as musical ability or mechanical ability. Being relatively independent of G, highly specific aptitudes may be well developed in persons of generally low overall ability or may be poorly developed in individuals of relatively high general intelligence.

Spearman's theory as originally formulated subsequently underwent revision in the light of further findings. He discovered that tests of mental abilities which are highly similar correlate to a greater extent than can be accounted for on the basis of their common overlap with G. As a result, he acknowledged the possibility of group factors such as verbal ability and spatial ability. He did not, however, abandon his original position with regard to G and s. The new group factors are conceived to be intermediate in scope, while G remains the overall factor of greatest importance. Finally, he proposed the existence of additional *general* factors, p, o, and w, which stand for perseveration, oscillation, and will, respectively. Perseveration and oscillation are additional intellective factors which Spearman accounts for as follows. Perseveration represents the inertia of the individual's supply of mental energy, and oscillation the extent to which it fluctuates from time to time. Finally, w represents will, a motivational-personality factor which enters into the taking of intelligence tests.

Before leaving Spearman's two-factor theory, some mention ought to be made of his assumptions as to the nature of G. He believes that it is basically the ability to grasp relationships quickly and use them effectively. Because his definition of G is so broad, he is able to account for the ability required to solve virtually any kind of intellectual problem. Thus, the child who knows word definitions understands relationships between concepts and their definitions. Similarly, the ability to solve arithmetic reasoning problems, such as occur in the Binet Test, requires a knowledge of relationships between the elements of the problem. Even the duck hunter must have the ability to take into account such factors as distance, speed of flight, wind direction, and force, as well as the power of his shotgun if he is to solve the "problem" of shooting down the duck. While Spearman's views as to the nature of G are relatively little known as compared to his operationally formulated G and s theory, he devoted an entire volume (22) to the elaboration of his conceptions of the nature of the cognitive processes with special reference to intellective factors. We shall return to Spearman's two-factor theory near the end of this section. Meanwhile, we shall go on to examine two rival factor theories.

Thomson's sampling theory. G. H. Thomson[5] (1881 to 1955) has proposed a *sampling theory*[6] of intellectual organization in opposition to both Spearman's two-factor theory and Thurstone's group-factor theory to be considered next. Thomson argues that intellectual behavior depends upon a large number of independent abilities which, though restricted in scope, nevertheless enter into a wide variety of tasks. Consequently, the taking of any one intelligence test would involve a particular *sample* of intellectual elements, while a different test would draw upon a somewhat different sample. The positive correlations found among various cognitive tests result from overlapping of the different samples or patterns of abilities. Thomson's argument can be represented graphically as follows (see Figure 14-2):

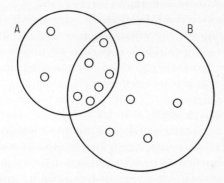

Fig. 14-2. A diagrammatic representation of Thomson's sampling theory of intellectual abilities. For an explanation see text.

The small circles represent specific factors; the large circles, tests. Test A draws upon or samples eight specific factors, while Test B samples eleven. Since the two tests have six specific factors in common, they are positively correlated. If a number of tests draw extensively upon a relatively large number of common factors, then we have the appearance of a "general factor" *for that set of tests.* Clearly, Thomson does not agree with Spearman that there is a universal G factor entering into all intellectual tasks; but he does allow for a kind of group factor which is not so narrow in scope as Spearman's *s* or as broad as G.

Thomson's theory can account for the relationships among mental abilities as well as Spearman's and in some cases better. For example, it is a well-known fact that more complex tests correlate more highly with each

[5] The exposition is based on Thomson's *Factorial Analysis of Human Ability* (25).
[6] E. L. Thorndike, whose associationistic theory of learning we considered in Chapter 6, has a highly similar theory in which neuronal "bonds" or "connections" form the basis of the specific abilities.

other than do simple tests. It is difficult to account for this finding on the basis of Spearman's theory, but in terms of Thomson's theory more overlapping specific factors are included in the two measurements. Similarly, the theory provides a sound basis for pooling a variety of tests, such as is the practice in the Binet, and deriving from the result a single, comprehensive score. By employing this technique a wide range of the individual's abilities can be measured. Finally, Thomson's theory lends support to programs of vocational and aptitude testing, since it assumes a wider variety of abilities than does Spearman's theory. The Spearman s factors, in his original formulation at least, are so specialized that any practical program of testing would be impossible unless each specific task entering into the job or profession under consideration was measured separately.

In passing, we might note that Thomson's theory is, in reality, highly similar to Spearman's revised theory in the sense that both allow for group factors in accounting for the organization of mental abilities. The chief point of difference is Spearman's insistence on G. Moreover, as will be brought out in the paragraphs to follow, the sampling theory is also closely related to Thurstone's group-factor theory.

Thurstone's weighted group-factor theory. L. L. Thurstone[7] (1887 to 1955), our third representative of the quantitative theorists, has been identified since the early 1930's with a weighted group-factor theory of primary mental abilities. Thurstone is equally well known for his development of the method of *factor analysis,* which he used in isolating group factors. Both Thurstone's theory of primary mental abilities and his factor analytic methods have gained international recognition not only in the area of intelligence testing but also in those fields where factor analysis can be used as a tool for identifying the variables responsible for observed relationships.

Thurstone denies the existence of G and s. Rather, he conceives of mental organization in terms of group factors of intermediate scope. However, his group factors are not believed to be the result of the overlapping of highly specific abilities of narrow range. Rather, such factors are revealed by correlation clusters which occur among similar tests which, in turn, are drawing upon certain primary mental abilities. For example, let us assume that a group of individuals is given a large variety of tests, among which are included tests of verbal, spatial, arithmetic, and perceptual ability. Let each of these tests be represented by small ellipses with appropriate subscripts v_1, v_2, v_3, s_1, s_2, s_3, and so on. If all tests are intercorrelated, the result will be the appearance of clusters of tests which are highly correlated among themselves but which show only a low correlation *between* clusters. See Figure 14-3.

---

[7] For sources, see *26–29.*

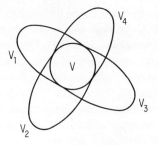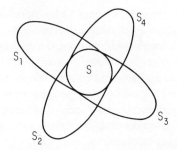

Fig. 14-3. A diagrammatic representation of Thurstone's group-factor theory. The ellipses v_1, v_2, v_3, and v_4 represent four tests of verbal ability; the ellipses s_1, s_2, s_3, and s_4, spatial tests. The verbal tests correlate highly with each other as indicated by the area of common overlap. Similarly, the spatial tests show relatively high correlations. V and S represent Verbal and Spatial ability respectively and are defined by the correlation clusters found among tests of verbal and spatial ability. Note that the group factors are independent and do not correlate with each other.

As indicated in Figure 14-3, the area of common overlap in each cluster defines a primary mental ability. In one large-scale investigation (28) Thurstone found evidence for seven primary mental abilities. Briefly, these are:

1. *Verbal ability:* the ability to understand and utilize verbal ideas effectively.
2. *Number:* the ability to carry out the fundamental arithmetic operations of addition, subtraction, multiplication, and division.
3. *Spatial:* the ability to deal with objects in space and spatial relationships such as is demanded in geometric problems.
4. *Perceptual:* the ability to identify objects quickly and accurately such as is required in reading, map work, and the like.
5. *Memory:* the ability to learn and retain information.
6. *Reasoning:* the ability to perceive and utilize abstract relationships; to be able to put together past experiences in the solution of new problems.
7. *Word fluency:* the ability to think of words rapidly. Word fluency may be related to personality variables as well as to intellective factors.

On the basis of his findings, Thurstone undertook a program of test construction for the purpose of developing more refined measures of the primary mental abilities. He believed that the traditional method of rating the individual's intellectual ability by means of a single, overall score was wrong. Instead, the testee's standing on each of the primary mental abilities is reported in terms of percentiles. In this way a psychogram of the individual's particular pattern of abilities can be reported. Thurstone believes that this method gives a more valid and useful appraisal of the abilities than the traditional I.Q. score which, he feels, obscures the underlying pattern of mental aptitudes.

Finally, it should be noted that Thurstone's analytic techniques reveal
that various tests show different "factor loadings" or varying degrees of
relationship to the several correlation clusters. For example, Test A might
correlate 0.76 with a verbal factor; 0.10 with a numerical factor; and -0.06
with a perceptual factor. In this case we are obviously dealing with a test
of verbal ability. In the same factor analysis, Test B correlates 0.16 with the
verbal factor, 0.80 with number and 0.28 with the perceptual factor. In this
instance the test is drawing primarily upon number ability and to a lesser
extent upon perceptual ability. More generally, the degree of refinement
of a battery of tests determines, in part, how closely each test will correlate
with each of the underlying factors. Theoretically, if we had perfectly reli
able tests that measured one and only one mental ability with complete
accuracy, the relations of each test to its underlying factor would be
perfect.

The last statement also presumes that there is no general ability, or, to
put it another way, that there is no intercorrelation among the various
abilities. Such is not the case. Thurstone discovered low positive correlations
among the various primary abilities, indicating the existence of a low order
of general ability. Moreover, he found that for adults the correlations among
primary abilities are low, while for children the correlations are higher.
Independent confirmation of this finding has been provided by H. E. Garrett and his associates (11), who, in a series of investigations reaching down
to the third and fourth grades, found that the intercorrelations among
various tests *increase* with samples of younger children and decrease markedly with high school and college students. On the basis of these findings
Garrett has postulated a developmental theory of intelligence in which he
argues that with increasing age abilities differentiate out of general abstract
intelligence into relatively independent factors. He believes that the differentiation occurs as a result of both maturation and increasing specialization
of interests on the young adult level.

Thurstone's and Garrett's findings with respect to intellective factors
suggest that the general-factor and group-factor theories may not be as far
apart as they first appeared to be when they were originally postulated. The
present evidence indicates that both points of view are partially correct and
practically useful when appropriately applied. The concept of a unitary
intelligence measured by a general intelligence test appears to be valid for
young children, while the concept of more specialized aptitudes or group
factors measured by appropriate tests would seem to be more valid for older
children and adults.

In concluding our survey of factor theories of intelligence, several generalizations appear to be warranted regarding the significance of the
developments within this area of psychological investigation. First, it must
be emphasized that factor analytic methods are purely descriptive tech-

niques. The mathematical manipulation of tables of intercorrelations by factorial methods reveals the smallest number of factors which can account for the correlations. The psychologist must then make assumptions about the nature of the psychological processes involved. He names the factors which he discovers on the basis of these assumptions. If a number of verbal tests correlate highly among themselves, he assumes that the relationship is logically and validly explained by hypothesizing that all of the tests draw upon the same underlying ability. When the smallest number of factors which can account for the correlations has been discovered and when the factors have been identified with their corresponding psychological processes, the psychologist is in possession of a *theoretical description of the system he is seeking to establish.* The validity of the system, however, is contingent upon both the validity of the operations from which it was derived and the psychologist's judgment upon which the assumptions are based.

Second, as has been previously noted, factor analytic methods must begin with already existing tests which are assumed to have overall validity. Since most of the widely used tests of intelligence are heavily loaded with verbal and numerical items, it is natural that these factors—especially the verbal—should show heavy weightings on the factor loadings. In the last analysis, one gets out of a factorial study only what has been put into the correlation matrix in the first place. This does not mean that the method itself is invalid, but only that we must not jump to the conclusion that because certain factors show up strongly in the final correlation clusters, these *are* the essence of intelligence. Given a different set of initial assumptions, a different set of factors would emerge from the analysis. At least one psychologist (*24*) believes that we have neglected a number of aspects of intelligent behavior in the design of our tests. However, in fairness to those engaged in research on the nature of intelligence through the factorial approach, it should be pointed out that their programs are not static but dynamic. The factor analysts are not only active in analyzing already existing tests, but are striving to develop better measures of the intellectual functions which their techniques have revealed.

Finally, we should like to note that factor analytic techniques have proved useful in a variety of applications outside of the area of intelligence. They have been successfully applied to the isolation of personality traits (see Chapter 15), to problems in human engineering, to the measurements of interests, and to a limited extent in the field of experimental psychology.[8] We have been able to do no more than summarize the usefulness of this interesting and powerful statistical tool in the limited area of intelligence. There can be little doubt that as time goes on the technique will continue to find increasingly wider ranges of application in other areas of psychology.

[8] For a more extensive treatment of factor analysis and its potential applications see *13*.

QUANTITATIVE THEORIES AND MODELS IN LEARNING

Early models. In Chapter 6 we noted that Ebbinghaus utilized quantitative techniques in his pioneer studies of rote memory. We also pointed out that his famous retention curve, $R = K/(\log t)c$, is an empirical formulation of the retention process based on experimentally obtained data. Empirical equations such as Ebbinghaus' are descriptive, shorthand expressions of the relationships among the variables studied. As such, they are practically useful in that predictions can be made on the basis of the equations. However, the psychologist is not justified in making predictions beyond the limits of his own observations. To put it another way, the data are plotted and the curve and its equation are selected on the basis of how well they fit the data. Finally, we noted that rational equations are attempts to discover the nature of the phenomena involved and to support the type of equation selected with logically justifiable arguments. Obviously, the development of rational equations puts much heavier demands on the psychologist, and for this reason, such formulations are of relatively recent origin. Because both types of models have played a significant role in the evolution of quantitative psychology, we shall discuss examples of each.

Following Ebbinghaus' attempt to formulate an empirical curve for the process of retention, a number of psychologists sought to discover a generalized curve for the acquisition process. Most of these attempts took the form of a negatively accelerated curve. The basic assumption underlying the curve was that rate of learning is proportional to the material still to be learned. Another way of stating the assumption is this: The rate of learning is proportional to the difference between present attainment and the psychological limit of attainment. The general mathematical formulation for such curves as given by Gulliksen (*14*) is as follows:

$$y = a + be - cx$$

where y = a measure of learning; x = a measure of practice; a = the asymptote or limit of attainment; b = a correction factor for curves that do not start at zero; e = the base for natural logarithms; c = the slope of the curve.

Exponential curves of this general type show relatively rapid gains during the initial stages of learning followed by progressively decreasing gains during the latter trials. For example, Hull's learning curve of habit strength plotted against successive reinforcements is a typical negatively accelerated curve (Figure 7-2). The formula for the curve may be expressed as follows:

$$_SH_R = M(1 - e^{-kt})$$

where $_sH_R$ = habit strength; M = the physiological maximum of habit strength; t = time or trials; k = a constant expressing maximum habit strength as limited by the quality and quantity of reinforcement; e = the base of the natural logarithms.

In Hull's own words, the fundamental assumption underlying the curve is that "*the amount of growth resulting from each unit of growth opportunity will increase the amount of whatever is growing by a constant fraction of the growth potentiality as yet unrealized*"[9] (*17*, p. 114). It might be noted that the two curves just discussed are basically of the same type. Both are negatively accelerated. The chief difference lies in Hull's assumptions about habit strength and reinforcement.

Another popular type of empirical learning curve took as its point of departure monomolecular autocatalytic chemical reactions, or more simply, chemical reactions in which the rate of reaction is proportional to the concentration of the remaining reaction substance.[10] Learning curves of this type follow the general equation as formulated by Gulliksen (*14*):

$$y = \frac{be^{Ax}}{c + e^{Ax}}$$

where y = a measure of learning; x = a measure of practice; A = a constant depending upon the individual learner and the task to be learned; b = a limit of achievement; c = a mathematical constant of integration; e = the base of the natural logarithms.

Graphically, such curves are similar in form to the normal ogive or S-shaped learning curve (Figure 14-4).

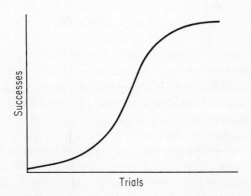

Fig. 14-4. The general shape of the autocatalytic learning curve.

9 Italics in original.
10 Compare Hecht's reasoning for photochemical processes in the retina (Chapter 3).

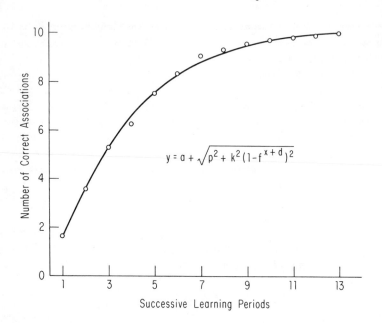

Fig. 14-5. Data from paired associates learning fitted to Woodrow's curve. (From Woodrow, *31*.)

Finally, Woodrow (*31*) has proposed a highly generalized type of curve which was found to fit not only a variety of data from human and anima learning experiments, but also sensory discrimination problems, reaction time, and mental growth curves as well. Woodrow's formula is given a follows:

$$y = a + \sqrt{p^2 + k^2(1 - f^{x+d})^2}$$

where y = the function measured; a = the origin of the y scale; p = potenti ality of response; k = the upper limit of response; and the expressio $1 - f^{x+d}$ expresses how rapidly the upper limit of the response is reached

Figures 14-5 and 14-6 reproduce two of Woodrow's curves fitted t data from experiments in paired associate learning and maze learning i rats. The satisfactory fit is obvious by visual inspection. However, the diff culty with Woodrow's equation turns out to be its very generality. An equa tion that fits too wide a variety of data is of limited theoretical interest, sinc it offers little by way of hints as to the nature of the psychological processe involved. More generally, as has already been implied, empirical curv fitting is not enough. Given a sufficiently large number of parameters, an set of data can be fitted with reasonable accuracy. However, when this ha been accomplished, all that we have is a purely descriptive system which fails to choose the function on the basis of the underlying mental processes involved.

L. L. Thurstone undertook to remedy this inherent defect of empirical curves by formulating a rational equation on the basis of two fundamental hypotheses as to the nature of the learning process. His first assumption is "that learning consists in a series of separate acts, that some of these are counted as successful and that others are counted as errors. Each act whether right or wrong will be counted as a unit of practice" (27, p. 469).

Thurstone's second assumption has to do with the second main variable in learning, attainment. For the purpose of measurement, the latter can be expressed as the "probability that an act will be counted as successful" (27, p. 469). Clearly, at first, the probability of success will be low but with increasing practice rises until it approaches unity. In terms of mathematical formulas Thurstone's assumptions can be expressed as follows:

$$p = \frac{s}{s + e}$$

$$q = \frac{e}{s + e}$$

where s = the total number of acts which can be credited as successes; e = the total number of acts which would lead to failure; p = the probability

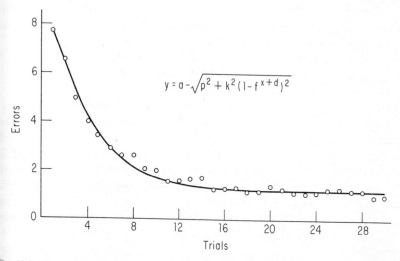

$$y = a - \sqrt{p^2 + k^2(1 - f^{x+d})^2}$$

Fig. 14-6. Maze learning data fitted to Woodrow's theoretical curve. (From Woodrow, 1.)

that the act initiated at any moment of time will lead to successful compl╴
tion; q = the probability that the act initiated at any moment of time wi╴
lead to failure or error.

By introducing an additional constant, k, to represent rate of learnin╴
Thurstone was able to cast his equations into differential form:

$$\frac{de}{dt} = -kq \text{ to express probability of success}$$

$$\frac{de}{dt} = \frac{-ke}{s+e} \text{ to express probability of failure}$$

Finally, by introducing the constant, m, to represent the complexity ╴
the learning task, Thurstone could integrate[11] his equations, yielding th╴
following final formulation:

$$\frac{2p-1}{\sqrt{p-p^2}} = \frac{kt}{\sqrt{m}} + z$$

The symbol t represents practice time, and z represents a constant of int╴
gration.

Basically, Thurstone's formula assumes that for simple homogeneo╴
learning tasks, an S-shaped curve with an inflection point at $p = 0.50$ wi╴
be generated. If the task is heterogeneous, or composed of elements of ur╴
equal difficulty, a nonsymmetrical curve will be obtained with the inflectio╴
point somewhere in the lower half of the curve. In cases where a variety ╴
different elements are present in the learning task, the inflection point ma╴
be missing altogether, and a negatively accelerated curve will result. Fc╴
insight learning, Thurstone assumes that the task must contain a very sma╴
number of psychological elements to be mastered. Thus Thurstone's ration╴
equation accounts for most varieties of learning curves.

Thurstone carried out a number of studies in which he tested the agre╴
ment between his rational equation and empirical data obtained by ╴
number of other investigators who employed relatively heterogeneous an╴
meaningless verbal material in their experiments. Three of Thurstone╴
curves are presented in Figure 14-7. Obviously, from the close fit existin╴
between the theoretical curves and the empirical curves, Thurstone's a╴
sumptions concerning the interrelated variables of practice and attainmer╴
are well borne out. Whether or not the results can be generalized to variou╴
other types of learning situations, such as prose or poetry, has not bee╴
established.

[11] For the mathematical steps involved see 27, pp. 473–477.

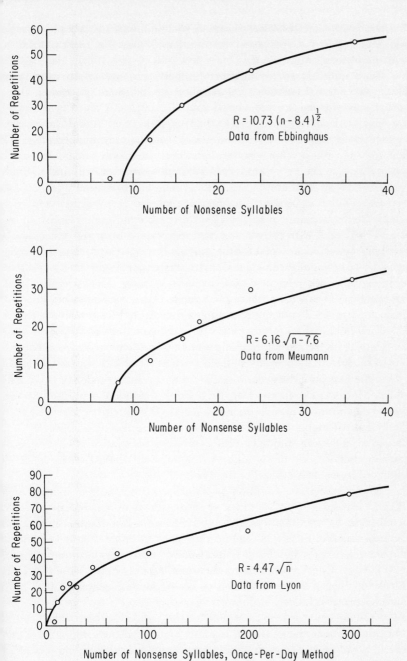

$$R = 10.73 \, (n - 8.4)^{\frac{1}{2}}$$
Data from Ebbinghaus

$$R = 6.16 \sqrt{n - 7.6}$$
Data from Meumann

$$R = 4.47 \sqrt{n}$$
Data from Lyon

Fig. 14-7. Thurstone's theoretical curve fitted to nonsense syllable learning data from several sources. (From Thurstone, *26*.)

Contemporary mathematical models of learning.   Immediately after the sec ond World War psychologists began to show increasing interest in mathe matical models of learning. This development was partly the result c stimulation from the new sciences of cybernetics and information theor along with related technological advances in computer processing. But i part it was also due to disenchantment with currently existing theories c learning, particularly in respect to their lack of precision and the disagree ments among theorists over the nature of learning and reinforcement. Th new quantitative psychologists are less concerned with understanding th nature of the learning process (or why reinforcers reinforce) and are mor concerned with formulating models which will accurately predict per formance. They argue that if a phenomenon can be predicted with preci sion, it does not matter if it is not completely understood. The astronome is able to make extremely accurate predictions about the placement c heavenly bodies at any given time, but he has only an incomplete under standing of celestial mechanics. Gravity, his major "intervening variable, remains undefined and, in reality, explains nothing. Similarly, the mathe matical model maker has sidestepped the explanatory issues that divide h: theoretical minded colleagues and has concentrated on prediction.

Two publications that appeared a year apart marked the beginning c the postwar interest in mathematical models in learning. William K. Estes (6) initial formulation of his statistical sampling model was announced i 1950. The first published report of the linear operator model by R. R. Bus and F. Mosteller (5) appeared in 1951. Estes' theory has been modified an revised in a number of subsequent publications and has become the leadin mathematical model in the literature of learning. For this reason we hav chosen to include a summary of it here as representative of contemporar mathematical models of learning. A summary of the Bush-Mosteller mode appeared in the first edition of this book.[12]

Estes' model, in common with other contemporary mathematica models, utilizes the probabilities of responses as its dependent variable From these the model attempts to derive various interrelationships amon the experimental measures, such as response rate, time, frequency, latency and the effects of schedules of reinforcement, by the applications of proba bility theory. Estes' model is not a theory of learning in the sense that Hull theory is, since it makes no claim to be a complete representation of th learning process. Indeed, it does not matter whether it is "true" or not in conventional sense as long as it enables the psychologist to make accura predictions about the course of learning under various conditions. There fore, it is not necessary to make assumptions about the learning process pe se, only about its outcome. Put somewhat differently, the statistical mode

[12] A book-length treatment of the Bush-Mosteller model by its originators appeared in 195: See 5.

of learning treats learned performance as processes or sequences of events which can be treated in terms of the probability of their occurrence or nonoccurrence. Assumptions are made about how the course of performance may change from trial to trial depending upon changes in both subject and environmental conditions.

Estes begins by assuming that all possible responses can be grouped into two categories: those which result in a given outcome and those which do not (7). The rat either presses the bar or he does not; the human learner reports a nonsense syllable correctly or he does not. Similarly, any learned response—a conditioned response, a turn in a discrimination box, a chess move—can be treated in terms of its probability of occurrence.

On the stimulus side, Estes assumes that any situation is made up of many stimulus elements which are further assumed to be independently variable. Moreover, on any given experimental trial only a sample of elements is operative. If the experimental situation is rigidly defined, we may assume that the stimulus elements will vary less from trial to trial than in situations which are highly complex.

Since for any given trial only a sample of elements is operative, a particular sample has only a certain probability of occurring. The situation is analogous to the classic probability problem of drawing balls from a jar which are then replaced immediately and intermixed before the next sample is taken. Under these conditions any given sample of balls will have only a certain probability, p, of being sampled on subsequent trials independently of how many other balls are sampled. Estes assumes the same set of conditions holds for stimulus elements and represents this as probability θ.

It was pointed out above that Estes assumes that all responses may be divided into two classes, those that produce a given outcome and those that do not. Following Estes, we may designate these classes as A_1 and A_2 respectively. Now it is further assumed that each stimulus element is conditioned (connected or attached) to one of the responses, A_1 or A_2. In a bar-pressing experiment, for example, some elements would be conditioned to pressing (A_1) and others to not pressing (A_2). Naturally, at the beginning of the experiment all elements are conditioned to not pressing. Learning, then, means that more and more elements become conditioned to A_1 as time goes on.

It is not necessary to know which of the stimulus elements are conditioned to which response in order to be able to predict response probability. All that needs to be known is what proportion of the stimulus elements are conditioned to each response. We may, in fact, assume that all elements have the same probability of being sampled on any given trial. This is the probability that is represented by θ. Under these conditions the probability of obtaining A_1 is equivalent or equal to the proportion of stimulus elements connected to A_1. Clearly, under conditions of reinforcement, this probability keeps changing. On any given trial n, the probability that an element conditioned to A_1 on the next trial or $n + 1$ is given by the formula: (p. 398)

$$p_{n+1} = p_n + \theta(1 - p_n)$$

The equation states that the probability of a response on the next tria p_{n+1}, is equal to the probability on the given trial, or p_n, plus a fraction of th probability required to reach $p = 1.00$—or in other words $(1 - p_n)$.

This equation is called a difference equation since it expresses th change in probability which occurs from one trial to the next. If the equa tion is written over and over beginning with the first trial and ending o any given trial, n, it may be given the form: (7, p. 401)

$$p_n = 1 - (1 - p_1)(1 - \theta)^{n-1}$$

We now have a generalized equation for a learning curve expressing th increments (or decrements) of reinforcing events on a trial by trial basis.

Figure 14-8 shows the Estes equations transformed to apply to fou learning situations in order to test their goodness of fit. It will be noted tha curves A and B are plotted from data from bar-pressing experiments; an curves C and D, from T-maze data. All are excellent fits.

Estes' model must, of course, do more than provide a generalize curve for predicting acquisition of response. It must also be able to handl situations involving stimulus generalization, discrimination, extinction drive, and reinforcement.

Stimulus generalization can be accounted for by assuming that gen eralization will occur when and only when similar situations actually con tain a number of identical elements. Aside from the fact that Estes dea with acts rather than movements, the assumption is the same as Guthrie or Thorndike's.

In simple discrimination learning situations it must be assumed tha the subject learns a response (A_1) to one set of stimulus elements and anothe response (A_2) to another set. If the stimulus elements occur in nonover lapping sets, then the extension of the model to cover the situation involve only the additional assumption that A_1 is reinforced in the presence of on set of stimuli and A_2 in the presence of the other with consequent independ ent curves developing over time. If, however, the two stimulus situation have some elements in common, the situation is much more complicated nevertheless, the model has proved successful in predicting the outcome i some situations. However, Estes reports (7, p. 432) instances of failure an difficulties in developing tests of the model with highly complex discrimina tion problems, such as the Lashley jumping stand. These are some of th current problems being worked out by Estes and his associates.

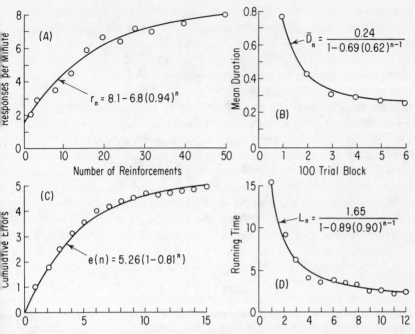

Fig. 14-8. Estes' model applied to four learning situations. Curves A and B are from a bar-pressing experiment. C and D are from a T-maze experiment. Clearly, the curves are an excellent fit.

Extinction, retroactive inhibition, forgetting, and spontaneous recovery provide no formidable difficulties for the theory. Extinction involves only the assumption that stimulus elements originally conditioned to A_1 are, during extinction, reconditioned to A_2.

Figure 14-9 shows a schematic representation of how Estes accounts for retroactive inhibition by assuming that new stimulus elements become associated with original material during interpolated learning and persist into the retention tests.

Forgetting is accounted for by assuming that during learning a certain set of stimulus elements is sampled but that after an interval of time some of these elements are no longer available for sampling. For example, we may assume that the characteristics of the learner and the conditions in the environment during learning vary from time to time, thus producing varying stimulus complexes. If such variations occur between the learning and retention situations, then stimulus elements conditioned to A_1 will no longer be available to A_1 and will now be connected with A_2.

Spontaneous recovery can be accounted for by postulating the forgetting of extinction. More specifically, stimulus elements reconditioned to A_2

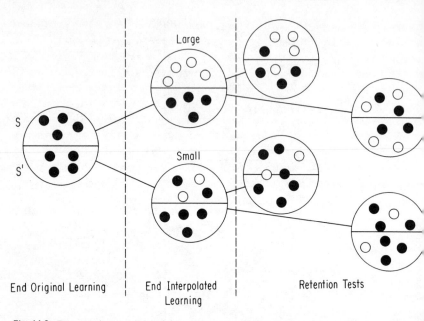

Fig. 14-9. Retroactive inhibition according to Estes' theory. New stimulus elements (open circles) become associated with original learning (black dots) during interpolated learning. "Large" and "small" denote relative amounts of interpolated learning. (From Estes, 7.)

during extinction may, after an interval, become reconnected to A_1 because of changes in the learning situation or the learner.

Reinforcement is handled by Estes in much the same manner as it is by Skinner. That is, a reinforcer is a set of conditions which determines to which response category a given set of stimulus elements will be conditioned. It is not necessary to specify "explanatory" principles of reinforcement such as Hull attempted to do in relating it to drive reduction or drive stimulus reduction. In Estes' own words:

> Upon reviewing the many attempts to formulate simple, closed explanatory principles of reinforcement and the still more numerous attempts to test the formulations, I have been led strongly to suspect that no hypothesis as simple or unitary as those envisaged by contemporary contiguity or drive-reduction theorists is going to prove adequate. It appears, rather, that associative learning depends upon a complex of causal factors or conditions. The experimental operation we refer to as a reinforcement for a given response in a given situation is one which supplies the factor or factors missing from the complex needed for acquisition in that situation (7, p. 460).

Drive is a set of stimulus elements. It need not be regarded as "ener gizing," as Hull so regarded it. Instead, the level of energy may be accounted for in terms of the number of stimulus elements that are operative under various degrees of drive. If, under conditions of low drive, we assume only a small number of stimulus elements is present, then clearly the probability of sampling these is small. If, on the other hand, we assume that under conditions of high drive a large number of stimulus elements is present, the probability of sampling them becomes greater. Thus, the apparently higher energizing effect of drive could be accounted for in terms of the number of drive stimulus elements which are conditioned to different responses.

We have summarized the simplest formulation of Estes' statistical model in order to illustrate a contemporary mathematical model of learning. Estes' model has been tested in a wide variety of learning situations, including verbal learning (2, 7, 8, 18) and is currently undergoing further testing and development. In its simplicity of assumptions, dealing as it does with contiguously connected S–R elements, it strongly resembles Guthrie's theory —indeed, is, in a sense, a precise mathematical formulation of the theory but one with a potentially wider range of applicability.

More recently Estes and his associates have shown increasing interest in extending mathematical models to deal with stimulus configurations or patterns and to make predictions in situations which involve small numbers of stimulus elements on the order of one to three. Particular interest has developed in making predictions on the basis of one-element models which are special cases of the more general stimulus sampling theory. These recent developments in Estes' theory are far too extensive and technical to include here, and the reader is referred to the references cited at the end of this chapter for original reports by Estes and others which provide numerous examples of mathematical models of learning with their mathematical derivations.

By way of summary and evaluation, we may point out that mathematical models of learning provide information in a form which is suitable both for making predictions and testing their validity. Because mathematics is a rigorous discipline, the psychologist must define his position carefully and with greater precision than is possible in ordinary language. Moreover, he is able to manipulate and test the soundness of the mathematical system before it is applied to experimental data. This, of course, does not guarantee that the assumptions themselves are correct. One can set up irrational mathematical systems that are internally logical but which have no relationship to the world of reality. The moral is this: the psychologist must choose his mathematics wisely, but if he chooses a mathematical system in the first place, the logical thinking required tends to insure rigor and precision in the definitions, predictions, and applications of the system.

However, as Hilgard (15) points out, there are certain additional dangers and cautions which must be observed by those working with mathematical theories and models. First, he emphasizes the fact that most great scientific discoveries in the physical sciences which involved mathematic came about through the use of simple mathematical relationships such a Mendel's 3:1 ratio in genetics or Mendelyeev's periodic arrangement of th elements. Hilgard further suggests that the complex mathematical pro cedures employed by learning theorists may be more appropriate for a late stage of theory development, while the more fundamental (and simpler mathematical interpretations are perhaps being overlooked.

Hilgard also points out that the proponents and critics of models often overlook the fact that all models thus far developed in the area of learning are limited in their scope and consequently should neither be overgeneral ized in terms of their applicability nor criticized for failing to fit situations for which they were never intended in the first place.

Finally, he suggests that despite their usefulness, models will not make other types of theorizing obsolete. "Verbal" theories may suggest new type of mathematical models which, in turn, may supplement or complement already existing models and theories.

In a similar vein Hilgard and Bower (16) suggest that although mathe matical models of learning have demonstrated their usefulness and shows that it is possible to make very accurate predictions, model making appear to lack an overall integrating frame of reference. One result of this has been a proliferation of small-scale models of limited usefulness. However, the further suggest that this state of affairs is most likely attributable to th essential newness of the field. Model making, they conclude, will remain a strong current in the literature of learning.

Information theory.   Information theory is an aspect of mathematica models which is attracting increasing attention among psychologists in re cent years and which therefore requires special comment. Information theorists assume that psychological processes can best be understood i analyzed as though they were physical communications systems. The organ ism is treated as if it were a "black box" which receives, processes, and act upon messages in the same way that electronic devices are able to detec and encode information in the form of signals, to store it or modify it in some way, and to reproduce it upon demand in decoded form.

The home television receiver provides a handy example of an informa tion processor which has certain broad parallels to human behavior (Figure 14-10). Sensors in the form of the elements of the antenna system detec and pick up "messages" or electrical signals from the transmitter, encode and amplify them within the internal circuits of the receiver, and then de code them to produce electrical impulses which excite the phospher screen of the picture tube. In this communication system we have a kind of S-O-R mechanism capable of sensing, modifying, and responding just as living

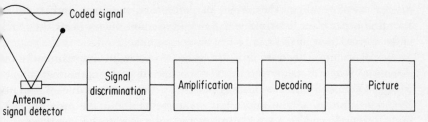

Coded signal

Antenna–
signal detector

Signal discrimination — Amplification — Decoding — Picture

ig. 14-10. A schema of the functional parts of a television receiver.

rganisms respond to cues in the environment on the basis of their sense rgans, contribution of O-factors, and central processes and then respond ehaviorally.

With the development of digital computers we have an even more triking analogy to organismic systems. The computer is "instructed" by neans of a special language, such as FORTAN, which can be punched into apes or cards. Special sensors detect the information and convey it to the "memory" banks, where it is stored until required for the solution of a roblem. When the machine is presented with a problem, it solves it by lrawing on its memory in order to apply the appropriate variables and ransformations. Answers are given in printed form, either in mathematical ymbols or in ordinary language. By proper programming, computers can lay games with their human operators, "sing" Christmas carols, do in a ew seconds the work of several hand calculators working over a period of nonths, decide on the compatability of two matrimonial candidates, or letect and accurately plot the course and target area of an enemy missile econds after it leaves the launching pad.

These fantastic technological developments of the postwar years were f immediate interest to psychologists who saw in them the possibility of leveloping information processing models of human behavior. If a machine an be built that is capable of reading or translating a foreign language, he engineer who built it has given a convincing demonstration that he has considerable understanding of the processes involved. Psychologists, how-ver, who specialize in information theory are careful to point out that analogies and simulators are not explanations, nor do they provide psycho-ogical or physiological interpretations of behavior. Information theory (or ligital computers) can be used by anyone without regard to his knowledge f behavioral processes or his systematic or theoretical biases. Moreover, the nachine can make decisions and carry them out, but not policy. Computers vhich tell us that an enemy missile is on the way do not say what ought to e done about it. Nevertheless, psychologists who are interested in informa-ion theory believe that the design and analysis of such models can lead to fruitful thinking about the nature of perception, memory, and thinking. We shall provide an illustration of how information theory deals with each of these areas after introducing a few basic concepts.

The information theorist uses the term *information* in approximately the same way that it is employed in everyday life. It is the opposite of uncertainty. Thus, as Attneave has suggested (*3*), the parlor game of Twenty Questions illustrates how informative statements about the animal, vegetable, mineral, and so forth nature of the substance to be identified, can reduce uncertainty until the precise answer is obtained. In order to be able to quantify information, the *"bit"* (from binary digit) has been chosen as the unit of information. More precisely, the bit is defined as the unit of information gained when the number of alternatives is reduced by one-half. Of course, it is necessary to formulate questions in advance in such a manner that the uncertainty is reduced by half, or some other measure will have to be employed.

In dealing with bits of information, the theorist usually must apply stochastic or probability processes to the problem. The difficulty here is similar to that found in learning situations. The theorist can only make assumptions about what the learner will do on the next trial. He cannot be certain. In information theory, the concept of *redundancy* defines the property of messages which reduce the error of prediction to less than chance probability by virtue of the fact that the message contains information which describes what will probably happen next. For example, the message that an infantry position is soon to be under attack by either Able or Charley artillery companies is not redundant insofar as providing information at better than chance accuracy about which unit will attack. If the message is "You may expect an attack by Able company," the message is redundant.

Information systems may be subject to *noise*. In the television receiver this often takes the form of "snow" or "tearing" of the picture. Noise, therefore, reduces the amount of useful information which can get through. Technically, noise is said to raise the level of *entropy* or uncertainty. The term *entropy* has been borrowed by information theorists from physical systems where it is the amount of heat generated, or wasted energy which is unavailable for work.

Finally, two additional basic concepts may be mentioned, *input* and *output*. These terms refer to the signals entering a communications system and the decoded message coming out of the system respectively. They are often used as broadly analogous to sensory data and responses in organisms.

By way of illustrating the complexity and range of problems studied by means of information theory we may begin with the most fundamental of all perceptual problems: How do we recognize or discriminate a pattern? Can a machine be built that will model the human organism's ability to recognize and classify printed material?

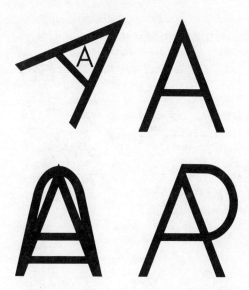

Fig. 14-11. Template matching. If the unknown letter (large *A* on left) is different in size or orientation than the template, the match may be impossible. If the template is too close in size and shape to an incorrect letter (*R*), a match may be made which is better than one made to a correct letter. (After Selfridge and Neisser, *21*.)

If the problem is the relatively simple one of recognizing standard and invariable patterns, such machines are not difficult to build. Indeed, banks all over the world have been employing them for years to "recognize" checks for the purpose of charging and crediting accounts. The numbers printed in special characters on the face of the check are scanned by a photosensitive machine which matches each digit of the number to a programmed pattern or template which is stored in the memory bank. However, if the input signals are variable (as they are for example in reading books set in different type or in handwriting) the problem is vastly more complicated. As Figure 14-11 shows, the machine might make a better match between an incorrect template and an unknown letter than a correct one. One solution to the problem is shown in Figure 14-12, where sequential processing analysis reveals how a machine might discriminate among several letters on the basis of their characteristics (*21*).

Machines have been built which can solve the problem of recognizing cursive writing or Morse code signals. However, thus far these machines do not show perceptual learning in the sense that they can build their own storehouse of future information on the basis of past experience. Rather, they are only able to apply information already put into the memory banks.

Machines have also been shown to be capable of solving reasoning

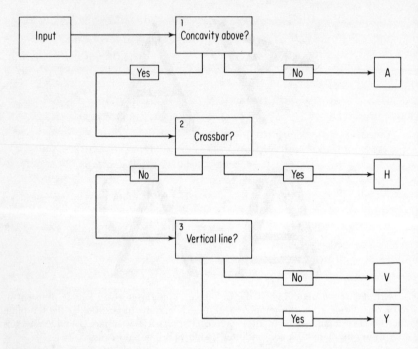

Fig. 14-12. A sequential-processing solution to the problem of distinguishing four letters. (From Selfridge and Niesser, *21*.)

problems, such as proving geometric theorems (*12*). That machines are able to solve such problems is more than a mere *tour de force* of technological wizardry. It is a rigorous demonstration of the fundamental processes involved. Moreover, once the machine solves such a problem, it can often specify additional problems or solutions that were not recognized by the programmers.

Perhaps the problem with the greatest fascination for those who are utilizing model making in order to understand the mental processes involved is chess. As Feigenbaum and Feldman put it:

> Game playing has many fascinating aspects to the researcher. Affectively, it provides a direct contest between man's wit and machine's wit. On a more serious level, game situations provide problem environments which are relatively highly regular and well defined, but which afford sufficient complexity in solution generation so that intelligence and symbolic reasoning skill play a crucial role. In short, game environments are very useful task environments for studying the nature and structure of complex problem solving processes (*10*, p. 39).

The authors go on to point out that a number of programs have been written

for computers, some of which have been developed with sufficient sophistication to be able to beat a weak human player. These are reviewed by Newell
et al. (20). One of these authors, Newell (*19,* p. 85), has provided a schematic
diagram which shows the essential operations involved in programming a
computer for chess, Figure 14-13. The complexity of programming for such
a game is a formidable task. For each move there are, in a normal game,
about 30 legal alternatives, and for the machine to look ahead even two
moves involves 30^4 or 810,000 decisions. Clearly, it will be some time before
machines can enter master chess tournaments. However, it is a testimony
to the versatility and ingenuity of the computer-processing model that so
much has been accomplished thus far.[13]

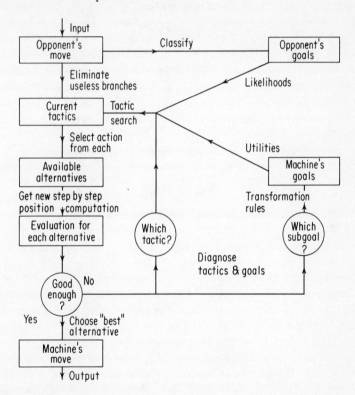

Fig. 14-13. A diagrammatic representation of a programmed sequence for chess. (From
Newell, *et al.,19.*)

Finally, by way of illustrating how information theorists are attempting
to design models of verbal learning behavior, we shall briefly note a model

[3] For an actual game with notations see *10,* pp. 66–67. For a notated checkers game see p. 99 of
the same volume.

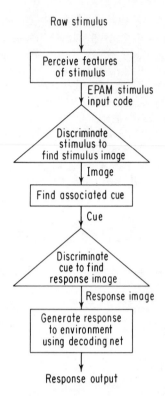

Fig. 14-14. The EPAM process for producing the response which has been associated with a stimulus. (From Feigenbaum, *9*.)

developed by E. A. Feigenbaum (*9*). The model is designed around a computer program called EPAM or Elementary Perceiver and Memorizer. Figure 14-14 shows in diagrammatic form the EPAM performance process for input to output for producing a response that is to be associated with a stimulus. The stimulus or bits of information must be detected, discriminated, and linked with the proper response just as is true in paired associate verbal learning. The process of learning consists in developing a discrimination net such as that shown in Figure 14-15. As will be noted by an examination of Figure 14-15, the stimuli which are detected by the machine are sorted to a terminal node where they are compared with an image, if an image is present. If there is no image, then part of the stimulus is copied at that node for future reference; if an image is present, the incoming stimulus is compared with it; and if there are any fundamental differences, a new branch of the network is formed to increase its discriminative capacity. Thus, the machine modifies itself on the basis of past experience. An EPAM then builds internal associations by storing, along with stimulus images, sufficient information to retrieve the response image from the network.

EPAM has been able to carry out paired associate learning and to show mediation and transfer, retroactive inhibition and serial position effects. Because it is still undergoing revision, it is not possible to predict how comprehensive the final model will be in stimulating human verbal learning phenomena.

At this writing no psychologist is in a position to evaluate the probable outcome of information theory and computer processing models of behavior. The pioneers in this new movement are still carrying forward their programs, most of which are either incomplete or have yet to undergo thorough testing. It is to their credit that they have already been able to synthesize or reconstruct complex mental processes with considerable precision—an accomplishment which was considered impossible not many years ago because of the complexity of the processes involved. To what extent these models will lead to improved theories with greater "truth" value than those we have at the present time is for the research of the future to decide.

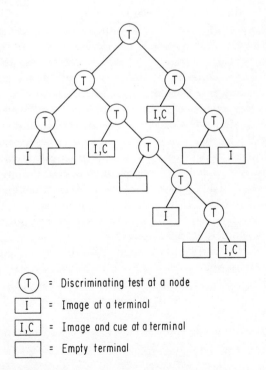

T = Discriminating test at a node

I = Image at a terminal

I,C = Image and cue at a terminal

= Empty terminal

Fig. 14-15. A typical EPAM discrimination net. (From Feigenbaum, 9.)

MODELS IN OTHER AREAS OF PSYCHOLOGY

Since the end of World War II model making, along with the related development of drawing analogies between physical machines and the human nervous system, has achieved the proportions of a fad. A great deal of the impetus for the movement stems from the work of the cyberneticists, a group of scientists working in a kind of "no man's land" whose area lies primarily between physiology and mathematics but is also bounded by the fields of engineering, psychology, biology, and economics. Cybernetics originated[14] at Harvard University in 1938 under the sponsorship of Norbert Wiener, a mathematician, and Arturo Rosenbleuth, a physiologist and associate of Walter Cannon's. The name *cybernetics*—a term coined by Wiener—means "steersman" and reflects the cyberneticists' interest in devices and circuits which control the behavior of machines and animals.

The original group of cyberneticists at Harvard held seminars at regular intervals during the prewar years in order to explore the possibilities of creating a hybrid science concerned primarily with communications— communications not only within the nervous system and physical machines, but in the field of the social sciences as well. With the onset of World War II, the two principals in the movement became involved in defense work. Professor Wiener was associated with Vannevar Bush, who, in turn, was given responsibility for the development of electronic computers capable of solving complex partial differential equations. Rosenbleuth was appointed head of the National Institute of Cardiology in Mexico, where he continued his research on the mechanisms of the transmission of the nervous impulse.

Immediately after the war, Wiener, Rosenbleuth, and others, with the support of the Rockefeller Foundation, founded an association whose purpose was to engage in both theoretical and practical research in the new field of cybernetics. Among the original members of the group were such eminent persons as Kurt Lewin, Margaret Mead, and O. Morgenstern. Wiener's book, *Cybernetics*, published in 1948, is a report on the theoretical and practical developments within the new science up to that time.

During the same period, British scientists were thinking along much the same lines as their American colleagues. One of the leaders in the more restricted British movement is Ross Ashby, whose *Design for a Brain* (1), published in 1952, described a complex electronic device, the "homeostat," which is capable of solving simple problems in "adjustment."

During the decade of the 1950's, the proliferation of mathematical and physical models resulted in the development of whole new fields, such as mathematical biophysics, information theory, the theory of games and the

---

[14] The historical summary is based on Wiener's book (*30*).

like, which reflect both the great interest in applying mathematics to the social sciences and the tremendous strides made in a short time in a new area of science.

For the student of psychology, perhaps the most interesting and immediately relevant "models" formulated by the cyberneticists are those within the area of nervous physiology. The reasoning, in brief, is this: If analogies can be drawn between the nervous system and electronic circuits, many of the puzzling aspects of nervous behavior may be better understood. In a sense, then, the model or analogy serves as a hypothesis—a hypothesis, however, with no "truth" value. For example, the operation of neurons is held to be analogous to the operation of digital computing machines. These so-called "brain machines" are composed of thousands of relays which operate in an "all or nothing" (on-off) manner, as is also true of the single neuron which either fires or does not fire. The electronic computer can "remember" sets of numbers which are fed into it just as the brain "remembers" events. Presumably, brain memory is under the control of reverberatory circuits (see Chapter 5), in the same way that computer memory depends on the electronic loops which store information.

However, the most interesting comparisons between the nervous system and the machine center around the operation of "feedback" mechanisms. We are all familiar with a feedback mechanism in our home heating plant. When the house temperature falls to a certain critical level, a relay closes, turning on the furnace. When the temperature rises to a certain point, "information" to this effect is fed back to the furnace, turning it off. This is a simple example of a stepwise negative feedback system. A more complex type of continuous negative feedback occurs in radios equipped with automatic volume control. If the signal from the station begins to weaken because of atmospheric disturbances, the output circuit which drives the loudspeaker "informs" the input circuit that more signal amplification is required. If, on the other hand, the signal begins to "blast" for any reason, the output circuit dampens the input circuit by activating negative feedback loops in the set.

Positive feedback occurs in machines only when they get out of order. If, for example, the governor on a steam engine calls for more and more steam the faster the machine runs, the machine will tear itself to pieces.

There are many analogies that can readily be drawn between the physiological mechanisms of behavior and both negative and positive feedback circuits. For example, the more we eat, the less voracious our appetite and the more slowly we consume additional food. Negative feedback circuits from the stomach inform the brain that the digestive organ is approaching a state of fullness. Similarly, the focusing mechanisms in the eye operate according to a negative feedback principle. The lens accommodates for far and near vision because it is controlled by the contraction and relaxation of the ciliary muscle, which, in turn, is governed by brain centers that "inform" the muscle whether to contract or relax, depending upon the clarity of the image arriving in the brain. Similarly, most of our reflex and voluntary movements depend upon kinesthetic feedback circuits which prevent us from over- or undershooting the mark. The hand, in reaching for an object, is guided by the eye, which, through its connections with appropriate brain centers, "slows down" the reaching arm as the hand approaches the object in question. Incidentally, one of the practical objectives of cybernetic research is to improve the quality of artificial limbs by designing into them feedback circuits which will enable the wearer to make smoother and less machine-like movements.

Finally we might note that positive feedback also has its analogies to behavioral phenomena. The psychotic individual in a manic state seems to be operating on a positive feedback principle. Like the runaway engine, his activity level spirals to greater and greater heights until he collapses into a depression as a result of sheer physical exhaustion. Perhaps part of the explanation for the dramatic effects of the tranquilizer drugs lies in their ability to slow down positive feedback circuits in the brain which are responsible for such out-of-control behavior.

There are many more possible analogies which can be drawn between the operation of electronic machines and the nervous system. Two others are worthy of note here. The reticular formation which seems to serve as an alerting system for the cerebral cortex might be likened to the carrier wave broadcast by radio or television stations. The program signals (musical, vocal, or video) are then impressed upon the carrier frequency. It may be that incoming sensory impulses are similarly impressed upon the background impulses supplied by the reticular formation before they arrive at the cortex. A similar argument has been offered for the function of the alpha rhythm associated with the activities of the occipital cortex. It has been suggested that the alpha wave is a fundamental scanning wave such as a television set employs. The scanning wave is then modified by light waves reflected off objects in the television studio, and the alpha wave by incoming sensory impulses from the visual system. Whatever the validity of the analogy, it has been demonstrated that the alpha wave is, indeed, influenced by incoming nervous impulses. (See Chapter 5.)

However interesting they may be, such analogies as we have been describing do not and cannot prove anything about the nervous system. More generally, no model has "truth" value. Models can only serve as devices to aid understanding and to suggest new lines of inquiry. As such, no one can deny that they have played an important role in the development of the sciences. We must, however, continually remind ourselves that they do not necessarily correspond to reality in any fundamental way.

CONCLUDING REMARKS

Our survey of quantitative systems in psychology has emphasized two main subdivisions within the general area: the evolution of quantitative systems of intelligence and the development of mathematical systems in learning. We have deliberately omitted any attempt to trace the evolution of descriptive and inferential statistical methods in psychology. Statistics, per se, does not belong to psychology; nor does this branch of mathematics constitute a psychological system. Instead, statistical methods are tools belonging to all sciences and employed by all psychologists in summarizing data and drawing inferences from their research. However, as we have shown, the emergence of sophisticated mathematical approaches to psychological processes has, in recent decades, led to the formulation of theories and models in many areas, especially in intelligence, learning, and physiological psychology.

Most specialists in these fields are quite cautious in assessing the significance of this strong trend in contemporary psychology. All new developments which promise interesting leads tend to be exploited rapidly. In the long history of science some apparently significant approaches have led nowhere, while others have resulted in gigantic strides forward. We have no intention of dismissing recent developments in quantitative psychology as a temporary fad. Indeed, the whole history of science shows that each science as it matures tends to become more and more quantitative in its approach.

However, the ultimate test of the values of mathematical laws and constructs is their power to predict the phenomena with which they are concerned. As our brief survey of recent work in this area of psychology suggests, we are at the stage of developing and testing *limited* quantitative systems which have validity only over a highly restricted range of phenomena. At the present time, it appears that in psychology, at least, the development of general quantitative laws with the universality and predictive value of those in the physical sciences lies far in the future.

REFERENCES

1. Ashby, W. R. *Design for a brain.* New York: Wiley, 1952.
2. Atkinson, R. C., and W. K. Estes. Stimulus sampling theory. In Luce, R. D., R. R. Bush, and E. Galanter (eds.). *Handbook of mathematical psychology.* New York: Wiley, 1963.
3. Attneave, F. *Application of information theory to psychology.* New York: Holt, Rinehart and Winston, 1959.
4. Boring, E. G. *A history of experimental psychology,* ed. 1. New York: Appleton, 1929.

5. Bush, R., and F. Mosteller. *Stochastic models for learning*. New York: Wiley, 1955.
6. Estes, W. Toward a statistical theory of learning. *Psychological Review,* **57,** 1950, pp. 94–107.
7. Estes, W. The statistical approach to learning theory. In Koch, S. (ed.). *Psychology: A study of a science,* Volume 2. New York: McGraw-Hill, 1959.
8. Estes, W., K. S. Koch, K. MacCorquodale, P. E. Meehl, C. G. Mueller Jr., W. N. Schoenfeld, and W. S. Verplank. *Modern learning theory.* New York: Appleton, 1954.
9. Feigenbaum, E. A. The stimulation of verbal learning behavior. In Feigenbaum, E. A., and J. Feldman (eds.). *Computers and thought.* New York: McGraw-Hill, 1963.
10. Feigenbaum, E. A., and J. Feldman (eds.). *Computers and thought.* New York: McGraw-Hill, 1963.
11. Garrett, H. A developmental theory of intelligence. *American Psychologist,* **1,** 1946, pp. 372–377.
12. Gelernter, H. Realization of a geometry-theorem proving machine. *Proceedings of the international conference on information processing.* New York: UNESCO, pp. 273–282.
13. Guilford, J. *Psychometric methods,* ed. 2. New York: McGraw-Hill, 1954.
14. Gulliksen, H. A rational equation of the learning curve based on Thorndike's law of effect. *Journal of General Psychology,* **11,** 1934, pp. 395–434.
15. Hilgard, E. *Theories of learning,* ed. 2. New York: Appleton, 1956.
16. Hilgard, E. R., and G. H. Bower *Theories of learning,* ed. 3. New York: Appleton, 1966.
17. Hull, C. *Principles of behavior.* New York: Appleton, 1943.
18. Keller, L., M. Cole and W. K. Estes. Reward information values of trial outcomes in paired-associate learning. *Psychological Monographs,* **79,** No. 12, 1965.
19. Newell, A. The chess machine. In Sayre, K. M., and F. J. Crosson. *The modeling of mind.* South Bend, Indiana: University of Notre Dame Press, 1963.
20. Newell, A., J. C. Shaw, and H. A. Simon. Chess-playing programs and the problem of complexity. In Feigenbaum, E. A., and J. Feldman (eds.). *Computers and thought.* New York: McGraw-Hill, 1963.
21. Selfridge, O., and U. Neisser. Pattern recognition by machine. *Scientific American,* **203,** 1960, pp. 60–80.
22. Spearman, C. *The principles of cognition and the nature of intelligence.* New York: Macmillan, 1924.
23. Spearman, C. *The abilities of man.* New York: Macmillan, 1927.
24. Stoddard, G. *The meaning of intelligence.* New York: Macmillan, 1943.
25. Thomson, G. *The factorial analysis of human ability,* ed. 3. Boston: Houghton Mifflin, 1948.
26. Thurstone, L. L. The relation between learning time and length of task. *Psychological Review,* **37,** 1930, pp. 44–53.
27. Thurstone, L. L. The learning function. *Journal of General Psychology,* **3,** 1930, pp 469–491.
28. Thurstone, L. L. *Vectors of mind.* Chicago: University of Chicago Press, 1935.
29. Thurstone, L. L. *Multiple factor analysis.* Chicago: University of Chicago Press, 1947.
30. Wiener, N. *Cybernetics.* Cambridge, Mass.: Technology Press, 1948.
31. Woodrow, H. The problem of general quantitative laws in psychology. *Psychological Bulletin,* **39,** 1942, pp. 1–27.
32. Woodworth, R. S. *Experimental psychology.* New York: Holt, 1938.

15

Personality

Theories of personality, like systematic theories of intelligence, evolved largely outside of the traditional academic schools. As we pointed out in the introduction to the preceding chapter, the differential psychologist approaches human behavior through the study of individual differences rather than by seeking general laws that apply to all mankind. In the case of personality, as is also true of intelligence, the differential psychologist's program is most readily accomplished through the psychometric analysis of personality and individual clinical studies.

There is, however, another reason why personality theory has never been closely identified with the traditional schools. The concept of personality itself implies the study of the individual as a whole; and, as we have emphasized throughout this volume, the schools were atomistic in their approach to behavior. The chief exception was, of course, the Gestalt school, and it is significant that of the traditional schools only Lewin in his Gestalt-like field theory attempted to encompass personality. Finally, as Hall and Lindzey (*10*) have pointed out, personality theorists have typically been "rebels"; consequently, they have been loath to remain within the framework of a conventional school.

The study of personality, however, has never wanted adherents. The challenge and interest inherent to the field is reflected by the fact that the Hall-Lindzey volume on *Theories of Personality* deals with twelve major contemporary theories. Even this relatively large number represents a severe selection from among the many existing theories. In fact, the great diversity of viewpoints in the area creates considerable difficulty for anyone who attempts to survey the field. However, as is true of all psychological theories, it is possible to group the various systems of personality according to such dimensions as the relative weight given to biological as opposed to social factors, the emphasis on learning as opposed to perception, the relative importance of the self-structure in the system, and so forth. Because of space limitations our usual sampling approach will be invoked; consequently, we shall limit our discussion to theories representative of the following general orientations: (1) the psychoanalytic, as represented by Freud; (2) the constitutional, as represented by Sheldon; (3) the factorial, as represented by R. B. Cattell; (4) the individual approach, as represented by Allport; (5) the personalistic, as represented by H. A. Murray; and (6) the self or ego-integrative, as represented by Carl Rogers. The student should also note that Goldstein's organismic theory and Lewin's field theory (see Chapter 11) are often considered theories of personality as well as general systems of psychology. We believe that the six theories discussed in the present chapter along with the two discussed in Chapter 11 represent a fair sample of the chief orientations to personality in contemporary psychology.

FREUD'S PSYCHOANALYTIC THEORY[1]

In our discussion of Freud's system of motivation and emotion (Chapters 11 and 12), we found it necessary to introduce a number of concepts that bear on personality. In view of this, there will obviously be a certain amount of overlap with the present chapter. Such a situation is virtually unavoidable in dealing with a highly integrated deterministic theory such as Freud's. However, in the last analysis, this partial duplication can be looked upon as an advantage from the student's point of view, since it will serve to bring together these interrelated aspects of Freudian theory.

Freud's anatomy of personality is built around the concepts of the id, ego, and superego. Each of these aspects of personality is related to the other two both genetically and functionally. The id is the primary aspect of personality, of which little is known. It is, in Freud's own words, "a chaos, a cauldron of seething excitement" (9, p. 104). Freud believed that the id is "somewhere" in direct contact with the somatic or bodily processes from which it accepts the instinctual needs for conversion into wishes. Because the id is a mass of blind instincts, it has no logical organization. Indeed, in it contradictory impulses may exist side by side. There is, moreover, no sense of time; thus either impulses originally in the id or those forced into it by repression can remain unaltered for an indefinite period. In this way Freud is able to account for the persistence of repressed traumatic experiences from childhood into adulthood. Finally, the id is amoral. It possesses

[1] The primary source from which our exposition is taken is *New Introductory Lectures on Psychoanalysis* (9, Chapter 3).

no sense of values and therefore cannot distinguish between good and evil but instead is dominated entirely by the pleasure principle.

Freud's evidence for the structure of the id is entirely indirect for the very good reason that id processes are unconscious. He deduced its characteristics behavioristically from the study of dreams and neurotic symptom formation. Because dreams represent wishes, and since symptoms are essentially compromises between the direct impulses of the id and the demands of the ego and superego (see Chapter 11), the id is best characterized as the conative, unconscious aspect of personality. Thus, Freud conceives of a confluence of instincts as the driving force which constitutes the substratum of personality. These instincts originate out of tissue needs and are expressed in the form of wishes or desires to get rid of the accompanying bodily excitation. Of these instincts, the most important from the Freudian point of view is, of course, the sexual or libidinal instinct (see Chapter 11).

The ego is "that part of the id which has been modified by its proximity to the external world and the influences the latter has on it, and which serves the purpose of receiving stimuli and protecting the organism from them, like the cortical layer with which a particle of living substance surrounds itself" (9, p. 106). Freud further characterizes the ego-id relationship as one in which the ego represents external reality to the id, at the same time effecting a compromise between the blind, chaotic striving of the id and the superior forces and demands of the environment. If the id were not so protected, it would be destroyed. The essential mechanism by means of which the ego accomplishes its protective function is through the "reality test." Specifically, the ego, after observing the external world, searches its own perceptions in order to determine whether traces of internal impulses have crept in and thus distorted the memory picture. In this way the ego "dethrones" the pleasure principle in favor of the reality principle which, in the long run "promises greater security and greater success" (9, p. 106).

The ego, as has been previously pointed out, is a logical, ordered aspect of personality, as it needs must be if it is to function effectively in dealing with reality. It is this latter aspect of the ego which Freud believes chiefly distinguishes it from the id. The organizational, critical, and synthesizing ability of the ego makes possible a life of reason despite the fundamentally animalistic nature of man. However, it must be emphasized that the ego's power is derived entirely from the id and that its ultimate goal is to try insofar as is possible to meet the demands of the id by compromising with reality. Consequently the ego is in the position of an executive whose powers have been delegated to him from below. He must try to run the organization in such a way as to maximize both owner and customer satisfaction.

The superego is that aspect of the ego which makes possible the processes of self-observation and what is commonly called conscience. While Freud believes that the superego is an aspect or function of the ego, it is, at

the same time, more or less autonomous in function; he therefore deals witl
it as if it were a separate entity. The self-observation function of the ego is a
necessary prerequisite to the critical and judicial aspects of the superego
In other words, the individual must first be able to stand apart from him
self before he can serve as his own critic. The moral and judicial aspects c
the superego come largely from internalization of parental restrictions, pro
hibitions, customs, and the like, through the process of *identification* (9, p. 90)
The child wishes to be like his parents; he therefore unconsciously acquire
the parents' moralistic point of view. Freud further points out that the
child's superego is not modeled directly on the parents' behavior, but in
stead on the parents' superego. Thus, the superego becomes the vehicle o
tradition, for, in a sense, it is handed down from generation to generation
Freud believes that this helps to explain why racial traditions tend to re
main relatively fixed and yield but slowly to new developments. Finally, the
superego is the source of man's idealism. All striving for perfection arise
out of the superego.

Because of their antithetical nature, the id, ego and superego canno
exist side by side as a harmonious triumvirate. Instead, the id and superego
are in constant conflict with the ego. The id, of course, demands satisfaction
which the superego cannot tolerate. Consequently, the ego is at the mercy
of both of the two remaining aspects of personality. Moreover, as indicated
previously, the ego must meet the demands of reality if the individual is to
function in society. As Freud puts it, "the poor ego . . . has to serve three
harsh masters, and has to do its best to reconcile the demands of all three"
(9, p. 108). Because of the imminent danger inherent in allowing the id the
satisfaction of its demands, the ego, when hard pressed, experiences anxiety
But if it then rids itself of intolerable anxiety by giving in to the demands o
the id, the superego punishes it with a sense of guilt and inferiority.

In its attempts to mediate between the pressures of the environment or
the one hand, and the demands of the superego and id on the other hand
the ego develops defense mechanisms which are essentially modes of be
havior that serve to relieve ego-tensions. Generally speaking, the defense
mechanisms function unconsciously in the sense that the ego is unaware o
what is taking place. Because of this, the mechanisms are able to fulfill thei
primary function of distorting reality in such a way as to take the pressure
off the ego. We shall discuss each of the principal defense mechanisms ir
turn.

First, and of greatest significance for both the individual and Freudiar
theory, is the mechanism of *repression*. In modern psychoanalytic theory
repression has two related meanings. First, it refers to the forceful ejection
from consciousness of painful or shameful experiences. Second, repression
refers to the process of preventing unacceptable impulses or desires from
reaching consciousness. A soldier's inability to remember fleeing the battle-

field exemplifies the first type of repression, while the child's unconscious sexual attraction for the parent of the opposite sex exemplifies the second. In either case, the purpose is essentially the same, namely, to protect the ego from processes which are incompatible with the individual's high evaluation of himself.

When repressions occur, they are maintained by an expenditure of libidinal energy. Consequently, the individual's limited store of energy is partly used up and is therefore unavailable to the ego. Moreover, because of the dynamic nature of repressions, they are exceedingly difficult to resolve. Consequently, the individual who suffers from too many repressions becomes weakened and eventually experiences a neurosis or psychosis. The tenacity with which such individuals maintain repressions is revealed in a general way by the length of a typical Freudian psychoanalysis and more specifically by resistance during analysis. In a sense, therefore, the chief goal of psychoanalysis is the resolution of repressions.

Reaction formation is a mechanism that functions to replace repressed wishes by their opposites. Thus, the husband whose wife is a hopeless invalid may unconsciously wish to be rid of her, but because any direct wish that she die would be abhorrent, the negative wish, through reaction formation, is expressed as unusual concern for her welfare and attentiveness to her needs. If the process were conscious, we would say that the husband "leans over backwards" to show love and concern in a trying situation.

Regression occurs when the individual reverts to satisfactions more appropriate to an earlier level of development. The older child who begins to wet the bed when a new baby arrives may be seeking the mother's attention yet cannot bring himself to demand it consciously because his need arises out of jealousy and is therefore unacceptable to him. Similarly, but far more serious in its nature, is the adult psychotic's playing with dolls. Here regression has progressed to a truly remarkable degree.[2]

Rationalization is a defense mechanism commonly observed in daily life. We all rationalize whenever we give "good" or socially acceptable reasons for our conduct in place of real reasons.

Less common, and more undesirable from an adjustmental point of view, is the related mechanism of *projection* which means attributing to others one's own undesirable impulses or behavior patterns. The classic example of projection occurs in paranoia, where the psychotic's delusions of persecution take the form of projecting destructive impulses to other people or social groups.

Fantasy is another commonly observed variety of behavior which, as an ego-defense mechanism, takes the form of seeking imaginary satisfactions in place of real ones (see also Chapter 11).

[2] See Chapter 11 for an experimental demonstration of regression.

In addition to these, we have already encountered *identification* (see Chapter 11), wherein the individual's directly unattainable desires are satisfied by putting himself in another's place. Similarly, *sublimation*, or the transformation of libidinal urges into socially acceptable interests and activities, we found to be one of the normal mechanisms of psychosexual development (Chapter 11). Finally, *conversion*, or the changing of mental conflicts into physical symptoms has been discussed in connection with psychosomatic medicine (Chapter 12).

In concluding our discussion of id, superego, and ego functions, it must be emphasized that Freud did not conceive of these aspects of personality as real entities or little spirit-like creatures which inhabit the mind and control the individual as if he were a puppet which they work by a system of strings. Rather, he utilized the concepts as symbolic of *processes* or systems of thought. As Hall and Lindzey have pointed out (*10*, p. 36), the id may be considered the *biological* component of personality, the ego the *psychological*, and the superego the *social*. Thinking of the three interacting processes in this way makes them seem less mysterious and, at the same time, avoids the danger of personification.

The dynamics underlying the development of personality have already been discussed in Chapter 11. It will be recalled that the child moves through three basic stages of psychosexual development, the *oral, anal,* and *genital,* and that differences in the adult personality are related to the manner in which the individual resolves the various conflicts associated with his early development. The student should also review Freud's theory of anxiety in the chapter on emotion, since the various types of anxiety are closely related to the functions of the ego and superego.

Freud's system has been the most widely influential of all theories of personality. His views have had a profound influence not only in the fields of psychology and psychiatry, but in art, literature, ethics, philosophy, and related disciplines as well. While all psychologists acknowledge psychology's debt to Freud, not all are in agreement as to the validity of his basic assumptions and the relative emphasis which he placed on the various aspects of psychological development. Perhaps the chief target of criticism of academic psychologists is Freud's methodological procedures (*10* to *12*). His biased samples, uncritical acceptance of his patient's statements, and his instinct-oriented approach to personality have come under heavy fire in the past half-century. On the other hand, his concept of the unconscious determination of much of our behavior, his causal determinism, and his emphasis on childhood as the critical period for personality development have been well-received by academic psychologists, especially the behaviorists. In recent years Freudian theory has undergone considerable evolution in the hands of his followers, and academic psychologists have made a serious attempt to subject many of his basic concepts to experimental verification

(*12, 27,* and *28*). While the psychoanalysts and academicians have not yet discovered a sufficient number of broad areas of agreement to effect a rapprochement between the two disciplines, the once bitter antagonisms have largely disappeared. It appears likely that this desirable trend will continue in the future.

SHELDON'S CONSTITUTIONAL THEORY OF PERSONALITY[3]

In our study of motivational theory we found that type theories of human behavior go back at least to the ancient Greeks. Moreover, we found that nearly all typologies assume that behavior characteristics are related in some fundamental way to underlying biological factors (see Chapter 11). In contemporary psychology, however, the concept of "types" has acquired a bad name largely because it violates the common empirical finding that the psychological characteristics of unselected samples of individuals are not distributed according to the manner in which typologies would predict, that is, in bimodal or completely separate distributions. Indeed, the very concept of the *normal* distribution implies that psychological traits follow the familiar bell-shaped distribution.

William Sheldon has always recognized the validity of antitype criticism and insists on the measurement of traits as continuous variables. On the other hand, he has staunchly defended a psychology of personality which recognizes the importance of biological or constitutional factors. Here again Sheldon has insisted on a continuous-variable approach to the measurement of constitutional factors as opposed to the earlier methods of classification on the basis of broad discontinuities. However, his system does resemble the older typologies in the sense that he postulates that both the human physique and personality can be adequately described in terms of three basic bodily components to which are related three fundamental temperamental patterns. We shall first discuss Sheldon's dimensions of the human physique, and following this, the related temperamental components.

There are three primary components of the human physique of which any given individual is a mixture. These are: (1) *Endomorphy,* or the degree to which the individual shows rotundness, and an underdevelopment of muscle and bone in favor of an overdevelopment of fat and viscera, especially the latter. Shakespeare's Sir John Falstaff exemplifies an extreme endomorphic physique. (2) *Mesomorphy* is the degree to which the individual shows a predominance of development of bone and muscle as opposed to the other bodily components. The person who is predominantly mesomorphic

[3] For primary sources see *30* to *33*.

possesses an athletic body which is hard, well proportioned, and muscular. The Greek Olympic athlete exemplifies mesomorphy to an extreme degree. (3) *Ectomorphy* is the component which determines the relative development of skin and central nervous tissue over the other components. The extreme ectomorph shows a high ratio of skin surface to total bodily mass, and, for this reason, is tall, thin, and underdeveloped muscularly. Among historical figures, Abraham Lincoln possessed an ectomorphic physique to an extreme degree.

Sheldon has suggested (*30*) that the individual's physique is related to the relative preponderance of development of the three fundamental embryonic tissues, the *endoderm, mesoderm,* and *ectoderm.* In fact, the names for his basic components of physique are derivatives of the latter. The endoderm is the innermost layer of embryonic cells and is the primary tissue from which the inner organs or viscera are differentiated during fetal life. Thus, the endomorph with his predominantly visceral development is made up primarily of endodermal tissue. The mesoderm is the embryonic layer from which the muscles, bones, and blood are derived. Consequently, the mesomorph is one in whom this type of tissue predominates. Finally, the ectoderm is the primary cellular layer from which the skin, hair, and central nervous system are derived. Thus the ectomorph with his large central nervous system and high surface area is constituted largely of ectodermal tissue. (See Figure 15-1.)

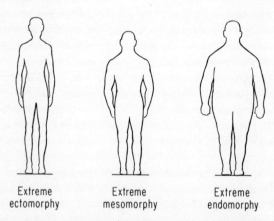

Extreme ectomorphy	Extreme mesomorphy	Extreme endomorphy

Fig. 15-1. A diagrammatic representation of Sheldon's three fundamental somatotypes.

The degree to which the individual possesses each of the three primary physical components of endomorphy, mesomorphy, and ectomorphy is determined by comparing him to a standard set of photographs of representative somatotypes (patterning of the three primary components) which,

turn, has been derived by Sheldon from careful anthropomorphic meas-
rements of thousands of individuals. Once the individual's approximate
omatotype has been selected, actual physical measurements are then
arried out on the nude subject. The measurements, besides taking the
ibject's height, girth, and weight, involve the calculation of a complex set
f ratios of limb length to diameter, trunk length to girth, and so on.[4]

When the measurements are completed, the individual is then assigned
n individual somatotype in which he is rated on each of the components
long a seven-point scale.[5] The extreme endomorph would be assigned a
ating of 7-1-1 indicating an excessive development of fat and viscera with
ery low development of the other bodily components. Similarly, 1-7-1 and
-1-7 indicate extreme mesomorphy and ectomorphy, respectively. In
heldon's colorful language, the 1-1-7 is the human "walking stick," the
-7-1 is the "golden eagle" while the 7-1-1 is compared to manatees and
ugongs. An individual who is average in all three components would be
ssigned the median value for each component, resulting in a somatotype
f 4-4-4.

In addition to these basic or primary components, the individual may
lso be rated on the degree to which he demonstrates *dysplasia, gynandro-
orphy,* and *texture.* Dysplasia is the extent to which a person shows a lack
f harmony or displays a markedly uneven mixture of the basic components
n any part of his body. For example, an otherwise ectomorphic individual
vith the legs of an endomorph would show the bodily discrepancy Sheldon
alls dysplasia. Dysplasia, according to preliminary findings, may be asso-
iated with a tendency toward delinquency and mental disease. Gynandro-
norphy is the extent to which the individual has the bodily characteristics
ommonly identified with members of the opposite sex. Gynandromorphy
nay range from true hermaphroditism to the more everyday varieties of
nasculinity or femininity of appearance.

Physical texture, or *t,* is the degree to which the individual possesses a
ine, esthetically pleasing body as revealed by the texture of his skin, hair,
nd perhaps underlying body cells.

Sheldon suggests that texture is an indication of how successful the
biological experiment" was that gave rise to the particular individual (*30,*
. 21). However, precisely what significance texture, gynandromorphy, and
lysplasia have for temperament Sheldon is not yet certain, since under-
tanding them ultimately depends upon a more thorough knowledge of the
ignificance of the primary components.

With this somewhat oversimplified account of Sheldon's technique of
omatotyping to serve as a background, we may now turn to his system of

For even greater accuracy a series of half steps may be employed which allows a thirteen-point
ange of measurements.
For a complete description of the technique see *32,* Appendix 3.

identifying the primary dimensions of temperament. The term *temperamen* refers to the individual's fundamental emotional and motivational nature Behaviorally it is perhaps best described as his reactive disposition. Sheldon began by attempting to discover the source traits which, in turn, make up temperament. By means of correlation analyses of a variety of personalit' tests, he found that three primary clusters of traits could account for th 1,225 correlations among the traits studied (*31*). Table 15-1 shows th characteristics associated with the three clusters.

Table 15-1.
The Three Original Clusters of Traits[a]

GROUP I	GROUP II	GROUP III
V–1 Relaxation	S–1 Assertive posture	C–1 Restraint in posture
V–2 Love of comfort	S–3 Energetic character-	
V–6 Pleasure in digestion	istic	C–3 Overly fast reactions
V–10 Greed for affection and approval	S–4 Need of exercise	C–8 Sociophobia
	S–7 Directness of manner	C–9 Inhibited social address
V–15 Deep sleep	S–13 Unrestrained voice	C–10 Resistance to habi
V–19 Need of people when troubled	S–16 Overmaturity of appearance	C–13 Vocal restraint
	S–19 Need of action when troubled	C–15 Poor sleep habits
		C–16 Youthful intentness
		C–19 Need of solitude when troubled

[a] From Sheldon, *31*.

Sheldon was next faced with the task of naming the primary tempera mental components revealed by the three trait clusters. Because the trait which are positively correlated with the first cluster are also closely asso ciated both anatomically and functionally with the digestive and viscera processes, the concept of *viscerotonia* was chosen as the name for the firs component. *Somatotonia* was selected as the name of the second componen since the traits with which it is correlated are associated with the voluntar muscular system (somatic structures). Finally, *cerebrotonia,* the third com ponent, was so designated because the traits associated with it are "activi ties which have to do chiefly with attentional consciousness" (*31*, p. 21 Essentially, the cerebrotonic tends to substitute thought (cerebration) fo direct action.

By organizing the twenty most important traits associated with th primary components into a scale, Sheldon constructed his *Scale for Tempera ent,* which is reproduced in Table 15-2. In using the scale, Sheldon recommends an intensive study of the individual for at least a year, in the course f which he is observed in as many situations as possible and during which t least twenty analytic interviews are conducted. The interviews are for ae purpose of covering such important aspects of the individual's life as his enetic, educational, economic, social, sexual, and medical history. After ach such interview the subject is rated on as many traits as possible, revisons being made whenever indicated.

For Sheldon the most significant problem in the constitutional approach to personality is the question of what, if any, relationship exists etween physique and temperament. In a study of two hundred adult males e found that viscerotonia is most closely related to endomorphy, somatonia to mesomorphy, and cerebrotonia to ectomorphy. The complete matrix f intercorrelations is given in Table 15-3. Sheldon's results quite clearly aggest that there is a close correspondence between physique and temperanent—so close, in fact, *that temperament can be predicted from physique with nsiderable accuracy, and concomitantly, physique from temperament.*

The possibility of predicting temperament from a study of physique is of onsiderable theoretical and practical significance. It is of theoretical interst, since it would point to a biological foundation for personality. Precisely rhich biological factors are responsible is, of course, not revealed by the xistence of correlations but depends instead upon the results of further esearch. However, the age-old belief that *some* set of biological factors nderlies at least the temperamental core of personality has received conrmation in Sheldon's findings.

Sheldon's findings are of considerable practical importance in that he elieves the individual's basic somatotype remains relatively constant in ae absence of gross pathological or nutritional changes. If this is true, then ong-range prediction of temperament on the basis of present physique is ossible. Of special interest is the possibility that young children could be omatotyped and personality descriptions formulated on the basis of such hysical analyses. Sheldon and his collaborators (*32*) attempted such an vestigation on delinquent boys. While there was considerable variation a somatotypes, the *characteristic* delinquent physique is endomorphic mesoaorphy. Similarly, Sheldon suggests that various mental disorders are rpically associated with certain somatotypes.[6] While preliminary and argely empirical studies such as these are by no means conclusive evidence f biological-temperamental relationships of high predictive value, they evertheless suggest interesting and potentially useful relationships.

See especially the interesting verbal descriptions accompanying the photographic plates in the *tlas of Men* (*33*) where many such relationships are suggested.

Table 15-2.
The Scale for Temperament[a]

I VISCEROTONIA	II SOMATOTONIA	III CEREBROTONIA
( ) 1. Relaxation in posture and movement	( ) 1. Assertiveness of posture and movement	( ) 1. Restraint in posture and movement, tightness
( ) 2. Love of physical comfort	( ) 2. Love of physical adventure	___ 2. Physiological overresponse
( ) 3. Slow reaction	( ) 3. The energetic characteristic	( ) 3. Overly fast reactions
___ 4. Love of eating	( ) 4. Need and enjoyment of exercise	( ) 4. Love of privac
___ 5. Socialization of eating	___ 5. Love of dominating, lust for power	( ) 5. Mental overin tensity, hyper-attentionality, apprehensive-ness
___ 6. Pleasure in digestion	( ) 6. Love of risk and chance	( ) 6. Secretiveness c feeling, emo-tional restraint
( ) 7. Love of polite ceremony	( ) 7. Bold directness of manner	( ) 7. Self-conscious motility of the eyes and face
( ) 8. Sociophilia	( ) 8. Physical courage for combat	( ) 8. Sociophobia
___ 9. Indiscriminate amiability	( ) 9. Competitive aggressiveness	( ) 9. Inhibited socia address
___ 10. Greed for affection and approval	___ 10. Psychological callousness	___ 10. Resistance to habit, and po routinizing
___ 11. Orientation to people	___ 11. Claustrophobia	___ 11. Agoraphobia

[a] From Sheldon, *31*. The thirty traits with parentheses constitute collectively the short form of the scale.

By way of concluding this summary of Sheldon's constitutional theory it must be emphasized that his work has engendered considerable criticism and controversy. The correlations he reports between physique and temperament are unusually high as correlations between physical and mental traits go. It has been suggested by his critics that because Sheldon does both the somatotyping and temperamental ratings of his subjects the high correlations obtained reflect his bias or preconceptions rather than true relationships between the variables studied. Sheldon, himself, recognizes the danger of such cross-contamination and, in part, offers the following defense of his position.

I VISCEROTONIA	II SOMATOTONIA	III CEREBROTONIA
) 12. Evenness of emotional flow	___ 12. Ruthlessness, freedom from squeamishness	___ 12. Unpredictability of attitude
) 13. Tolerance	( ) 13. The unrestrained voice	( ) 13. Vocal restraint, and general restraint of noise
) 14. Complacency	___ 14. Spartan indifference to pain	___ 14. Hypersensitivity to pain
___ 15. Deep sleep	___ 15. General noisiness	___ 15. Poor sleep habits, chronic fatigue
) 16. The untempered characteristic	( ) 16. Overmaturity of appearance	( ) 16. Youthful intentness of manner and appearance
) 17. Smooth, easy communication of feeling, extraversion of viscerotonia	___ 17. Horizontal mental cleavage, extraversion of somatotonia	___ 17. Vertical mental cleavage introversion
___ 18. Relaxation and sociophilia under alcohol	___ 18. Assertiveness and aggression under alcohol	___ 18. Resistance to alcohol, and to other depressant drugs
___ 19. Need of people when troubled	___ 19. Need of action when troubled	___ 19. Need of solitude when troubled
___ 20. Orientation toward childhood and family relationships	___ 20. Orientation toward goals and activities of youth	___ 20. Orientation toward the later periods of life

Table 15-3.
Intercorrelations and Intracorrelations among the Primary Components[a]

	VISCEROTONIA	MESOMORPHY	$N = 200$ SOMATOTONIA	ECTOMORPHY	CEREBROTONIA
Endomorphy	+0.79	−0.29	−0.29	−0.41	−0.32
Viscerotonia		−0.23	−0.34	−0.40	−0.32
Mesomorphy			+0.82	−0.63	−0.58
Somatotonia				−0.53	−0.62
Ectomorphy					+0.83

[a] From Sheldon, *31*.

In attempting to define an individual in terms of so general a concept as a patterning of his static and dynamic components, we of course expose ourselves more or less recklessly to the danger of the halo error. Having once set up criteria for the measurement of ectomorphy, for example, and having established (or even suspected) the existence of a relationship between cerebrotonia and ectomorphy, it is admittedly difficult not to see cerebrotonic characteristics wherever ectomorphy is observed. Moreover, there is no way of removing the influence of the morphological patterning totally from the picture, for any investigator who has learned to think in constitutional terms observes the general morphological patterns of individuals as inevitably (and as subconsciously) as a trained ornithologist notes the identity of birds he meets. It cannot be denied that whenever the writer talks with an individual, he becomes as aware of the fellow's somatotype as of the general state of his physical and mental health. Also a preliminary estimate of the relative strength of the various temperamental components is inevitably formed. The early estimate is not always correct, but it is always present.

Perhaps the strongest defense we can offer against the halo is simply the fact that we are well aware of its nature. We look for it suspiciously behind every bush in the psychological garden. Darwin, too, was aware of this danger. Concerned as he was with tracing out the broad outlines of a basic taxonomy according to an hypothesis which ran against the conventional academic stereotypes of his day, he sensed a particular danger from that "inward emotional glee" which he found to accompany observations diametrically refuting his ("smugly complacent") critics. He noticed too that observations supporting his hypotheses stood out in consciousness and were well remembered, while apparent exceptions tended to slip lightly by. He therefore took to writing down the latter, for emphasis and preservation (31, pp. 423–424).

Others have criticized Sheldon's assertion that the somatotype is relatively invariant (17). Again, Sheldon recognized the possibility that the somatotype taken at a given cross-section in time of the individual's life may not adequately reflect his true biological structure. Aside from repeated longitudinal studies of the individual *and* his ancestors, the somatotype plus a medical history is the only practical way of assessing the individual's physique.

Finally, a third important criticism of Sheldon's research is directed at the fact that most of it has been done on male subjects. However, Sheldon is engaged on a study of female somatotypes and their temperamental relationships, and is preparing an *Atlas of Women* as a companion volume to his *Atlas of Men*. At this writing, however, the volume has not yet been published. From his preliminary studies of women, it is likely that significant differences between the two sexes will be found among both the physical and temperamental variables.

In the last analysis, criticism in any scientific field can be answered only by further research and repetition of the work toward which the criticism is directed—preferably by those not involved in the original studies. Until such time as Sheldon offers a "finished" system and those who chalnge it have shown that the results cannot be duplicated, *both* Sheldon's sults *and* the criticism must stand.[7]

R. B. CATTELL'S FACTORIAL SYSTEM[8]

Since we are already familiar with the factor analytic method in the nvestigation of psychological problems we may begin our study of Cattell's actorial theory with a definition. Personality is defined as *"that which permits prediction of what a person will do in a given situation"* (*6*, p. 2). More recently 7) Cattell has formulated his definition as follows: $R = f(S \cdot P)$ which eads, *R*, the nature and magnitude of a response, is a function of both nvironmental situations in which the individual finds himself and his personality. However, he makes it clear that this is a working definition nore denotative than connotative. Because personality connotes all of the behavior of the individual, precise description and measurement which are he first stages of the scientific study of personality must begin with a rela- ively restricted definition. When adequate descriptions and measurements ave been carried out, the more restricted units of behavior must be inte- rated into the larger whole which, in the last analysis, is the true picture f the functioning personality as it exists in its natural environment.

After discussing both types and traits as possible units of description nd measurement, Cattell makes it clear that he favors the trait approach is the more fruitful. Traits are defined as a "characterological or relatively permanent feature of personality" (*8*, p. 500). Traits are inferred from the ndividual's behavior and are of two fundamental kinds, *surface traits* and *ource traits*. Surface traits are revealed by correlating "trait-elements" or 'trait-indicators" which, in turn, are essentially behavior samples that "go ogether." For example, tests or ratings of independence, boldness, alertness, enthusiasm, and energy level tend, when correlated, to form a cluster re- vealing the existence of a surface trait of "Energy, Boldness, Spiritedness" (*5*, p. 147). By means of such correlation techniques Cattell found that the hundreds of traits used to describe and measure personality could be re- duced to between fifty and sixty "nuclear clusters." Obviously, if two trait tests correlate positively to a relatively high degree they are describing or measuring essentially the same behavior. One might expect, for example, that tests of "dominance" and "ascendance" would show high positive correlations. In this case both are evidently measures of the same trait, and, even more important, are both related to the same underlying functional unity.

In order to exemplify Cattell's general approach, we have reproduced

---

[7] For a more extensive critique see *10*.

[8] The exposition is primarily based on Cattell's *Personality* (*6*) except as otherwise indicated.

Table 15-4.
List of Ten Rating Traits[a]

1. *Adaptable:* flexible; accepts changes of plan easily; satisfied with compromises; is not upset, surprised, baffled, or irritated if things are different from what he expected.	*vs.*	*Rigid:* insists that things be done th way he has always done them; doe not adapt his habits and ways of think ing to those of the group; nonplusse if his routine is upset.
2. *Emotional:* excitable; cries a lot (children), laughs a lot, shows affection, anger, all emotions, to excess.	*vs.*	*Calm:* stable, shows few signs of emo tional excitement of any kind; remain calm, even underreacts, in dispute danger, social hilarity, and the like
3. *Conscientious:* honest; knows what is right and generally does it, even if no one is watching him; does not tell lies or attempt to deceive others; respects others' property.	*vs.*	*Unconscientious:* somewhat unscrupu lous; not too careful about standard of right and wrong where persona desires are concerned; tells lies and given to little deceits; does not respec others' property.
4. *Conventional:* conforms to accepted standards, ways of acting, thinking, dressing, and the like; does the "proper" thing; seems distressed if he finds he is being different.	*vs.*	*Unconventional, eccentric:* acts different! from others: not concerned abou wearing the same clothes or doing th same things as others; has somewha eccentric interests, attitudes, and way of behaving; goes his own rather pecu liar way.
5. *Prone to jealousy:* begrudges the achievement of others; upset when others get attention, and demands more for himself; resentful when attention is given to others.	*vs.*	*Not jealous:* likes people even if they d better than he does; is not upset whe others get attention, but joins in prais

[a] From Cattell (7), pp. 63–64.

a sample list of ten rating traits in Table 15-4. As Cattell suggests (7, p. 62), such traits might be used by raters in assessing the personality traits of young men or women with whom they are well acquainted. When fifty to sixty such traits are rated and correlated they form the clusters of related traits referred to above.

It will be observed that traits are described as bipolar opposites. This convention is typical of personality systems which depend upon statistical methods of description and measurement. The underlying assumption is that traits are normally distributed in a continuous manner with few individuals showing extreme degrees of the trait under consideration and with most people falling in the middle or median range. (See Figure 15-2.)

Source traits are revealed by factor analysis, and represent deeper, less variable, more significant aspects of personality. While surface traits are

Table 15.4 (*Continued*)

6. *Considerate, polite:* deferential to needs of others; considers others' feelings; allows them before him in line, gives them the biggest share, and the like.

vs.

Inconsiderate, rude: insolent, defiant, and "saucy" to elders (in children); ignores feelings of others; gives impression that he goes out of his way to be rude.

7. *Quitting:* gives up before he has thoroughly finished a job; slipshod; works in fits and starts; easily distracted, led away from main purposes by stray impulses or external difficulties.

vs.

Determined, persevering: sees a job through in spite of difficulties or temptations; strong-willed; painstaking and thorough; sticks at anything until he achieves his goal.

8. *Tender:* governed by sentiment; intuitive, empathetic, sympathetic; sensitive to the feelings of others; cannot do things if they offend his feelings.

vs.

Tough, hard: governed by fact and necessity rather than sentiment; unsympathetic; does not mind upsetting others if that is what has to be done.

9. *Self-effacing:* blames himself (or nobody) if things go wrong; reluctant to take credit for achievements; does not seem to think of himself as very important or worthwhile.

vs.

Egotistical: blames others whenever there is conflict or things go wrong; often brags; quick to take credit when things go right; has a very good opinion of himself.

10. *Languid, fatigued, slow:* lacks vigour; vague and slow in speech; dawdles, is slow in getting things done.

vs.

Energetic, alert, active: quick, forceful, active, decisive, full of pep, vigorous, spirited.

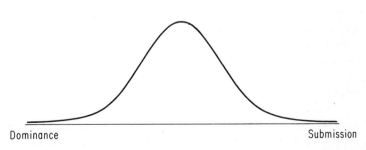

Dominance   Submission

Fig. 15-2. The theoretical distribution of the personality trait dominance-submission in the population at large. Few individuals are extremely dominant or submissive; most individuals fall in the median range.

merely *descriptive* units, the source traits upon which they depend are, in part, *explanatory* and therefore represent underlying causes of the observed correlations among surface traits. Cattell believes that with further research source traits will be found to correspond to the most fundamental influences —physiological, temperamental, and social—which give rise to personality.

In repeated factorial studies of surface trait correlation clusters, Cattell has found evidence for the existence of as many as twenty source traits. Table 15-5 shows a list of Cattell's personality factors with both their technical and popular names.

It will be noted that Factor A is the familiar trait of being reserved, withdrawn, and lacking in affective or emotional reactivity toward others as opposed to outgoingness, sociability, and warmth in emotional reactions toward others. Cattell formerly referred to this trait as cyclothymia-schizothymia but modified the name because of the connotations of mental disorder associated with the earlier terms derived as they were from schizophrenia and manic-depressive psychoses. Other neologisms such as "harria," "alaxia," "threctia," and "praxernia" have been coined by Cattell to avoid the connotations which have accrued to the more popular descriptions of the corresponding personality traits or to such shopworn technical terms as "extroversion" or "introversion."

Not all of this relatively extensive list of traits has been repeatedly confirmed by studies. The list of Cattell's traits is constantly undergoing revision on the basis of empirical research and clinical data, as is to be expected in the case of a viable theory.

Source traits, such as those shown in Table 15-5, may be further categorized according to whether they arise out of the operation of environmental or hereditary influences. Those which result from environmental forces are *environmental-mold traits,* and those which are hereditarily determined are called *constitutional traits.* Source Trait A (Sizothymia vs. Affectothymia) exemplifies a constitutional trait, while Q (Conservatism vs. Radicalism) is probably an environmental-mold trait. Surface traits, on the other hand, may reflect the operation of more than one source trait and therefore cannot be divided into environmentally versus constitutionally determined classes.

Finally, in regard to the descriptive phase of Cattell's system, traits may be categorized as *dynamic, ability,* or *temperamental.* This threefold category refers to the manner in which the trait is expressed. Dynamic traits are concerned with goal-directed behavior; ability traits, with how well or effectively the individual works toward a goal; and temperamental traits with the emotional reactivity, speed, or energy with which he responds. Cattell believes that there is a practical advantage in identifying traits according to their manner or modality of expression. If, for example, one

Table 15-5.
**Technical and Popular Labels for Personality Factors A to Q_4
(The Technical Labels Appear in Parenthesis)** [a]

LOW-SCORE DESCRIPTION	FACTOR		FACTOR	HIGH-SCORE DESCRIPTION
Reserved (sizothymia)	A−	vs.	A+	Outgoing (affectothymia)
Less intelligent (low "g")	B−	vs.	B+	More intelligent (high "g")
Emotional (low ego strength)	C−	vs.	C+	Stable (high ego strength)
Humble (submissiveness)	E−	vs.	E+	Assertive (dominance)
Sober (desurgency)	F−	vs.	F+	Happy-go-lucky (surgency)
Expedient (low superego)	G−	vs.	G+	Conscientious (high superego)
Shy (threctia)	H−	vs.	H+	Venturesome (parmia)
Tough-minded (harria)	I−	vs.	I+	Tender-minded (premsia)
Trusting (alaxia)	L−	vs.	L+	Suspicious (protension)
Practical (praxernia)	M−	vs.	M+	Imaginative (autia)
Forthright (artlessness)	N−	vs.	N+	Shrewd (shrewdness)
Placid (assurance)	O−	vs.	O+	Apprehensive (guilt-proneness)
Conservative (conservatism)	Q_1−	vs.	Q_1+	Experimenting (radicalism)
Group-tied (group adherence)	Q_2−	vs.	Q_2+	Self-sufficient (self-sufficiency)
Casual (low integration)	Q_3−	vs.	Q_3+	Controlled (high self-concept)
Relaxed (low ergic tension)	Q_4−	vs.	Q_4+	Tense (ergic tension)

After Cattell (7).

is concerned with the measurement of intelligence, the testee's dynami*
and temperamental traits should be at an optimum level. If not, the result
of the test will reflect combinations of traits rather than single traits. Simi*
larly, in clinical investigations, abilities may be ignored in favor of dynami
and temperamental traits.

Thus far we might summarize Cattell's personality theory as follows
From the psychological point of view human personality may be considere(
as an integration of traits. The individual's behavior as he interacts with
his environment reflects a relatively large number of *surface traits.* In an
given culture such traits are common to most individuals and can therefor*
be measured by objective tests and ratings. Surface traits are dependen*
upon underlying *source traits* which, in turn, may be identified by facto*
analytic studies of surface trait correlation clusters. Such studies have thu*
far revealed a limited number of such traits, some of which are related t*
basic constitutional factors and others to environmental influences. Trait
may also be described in terms of how they are expressed—as abilities, a*
dynamic or goal-directed traits, or as reactive-temperamental traits.

In the further development of his system, Cattell is primarily concerne(
with (a) the dynamics of the functioning personality, and (b) its develop*
ment. Central to the problem of dynamics are his concepts of *ergs* an*
metaergs. Equally crucial to the problem of development are a number o
principles of personality formation. We shall consider each of these aspect*
of the theory in turn.

In essence, an *erg* is a dynamic, constitutional source trait. In terms c
a formal definition an erg is:

> *an innate psychophysical disposition which permits its possessor to acquire reactivity (atten*
> *tion, recognition) to certain classes of objects more readily than others, to experience a specifi*
> *emotion in regard to them, and to start on a course of action which ceases more complete*
> *at a certain specific goal activity than at any other. The pattern includes also preferre*
> *behavior subsidiation paths to the preferred goal* (6, p. 199).

Cattell points out that the definition emphasizes four main points
First, the goal-directed individual is selectively tuned toward certain en*
vironmental objects. Second, an ergic pattern carries with it a certain char*
acteristic emotion. Third, the pattern results in a specific type of goa*
satisfaction. Fourth, there is an innate preference for certain paths leadin*
to the goal.[9]

Cattell is not yet ready to present a list of human ergs, but on the basi
of preliminary research indicates that sex, self-assertion, fear, gregarious*

---

[9] The reader should compare Cattell's definition of an erg to McDougall's concept of instinc*
If, as Cattell suggests, the third and fourth aspects of his definition are combined, the three char*
acteristics of ergic behavior are *cognitive, affective,* and *conative,* as is true in McDougall's theor*

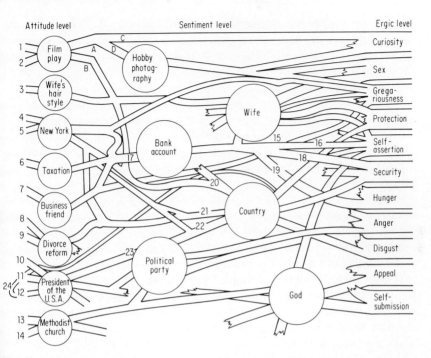

Fig. 15-3. A dynamic lattice showing subsidiation of attitudes, sentiment, and ergic levels. (From Cattell, 6.)

ness, parental protectiveness, appeal or self-abasement, play, curiosity, and narcissism are fundamental (6, p. 198).[10] Recently (7, pp. 185–186), Cattell has emphasized the essentially instinctive nature of fundamental motives or ergs. Referring to his *dynamic lattice* (Figure 15-3), Cattell notes that various attitudes, sentiments, and motives eventually reduce to basic, instinctive goals.

A *metaerg* is in all respects like an erg except that it is an environmental-mold source trait rather than a constitutional source trait. In short, meta-ergs are learned, whereas ergs are innate. Following McDougall (see p. 409), Cattell considers sentiments as the most important of the various metaergs. By definition, sentiments are ". . . major acquired dynamic trait structures which cause their possessors to pay attention to certain objects or classes of objects, and to feel and react in a certain way with regard to them" (6, p. 161).

Following Cattell's own example, the concept of sentiment can be conveniently illustrated by an individual's feelings toward his home. Home means first of all the partial satisfaction of the basic ergs such as sex, gre-

---

[10] See also 6, pp. 180–181, for a more extensive "preliminary" list of possible ergs.

gariousness, and parental protection. Furthermore, one's sentiment toward home is compounded of attitudes and opinions about insurance, marriage gardening, children, education, and so forth. Such an interrelated complex of processes Cattell describes as a "dynamic lattice." Attitudes are evolved out of sentiments, and these, in turn, arise out of the fundamental ergs For example, the sentiment toward one's country is developed on the basis of security, protection, and disgust (presumably one is not always satisfied with one's country!). The sentiment, in turn, governs attitudes toward the movies, New York, divorce, the President of the United States, and so forth. Cattell's general term for the interdependence of attitudes, sentiments, and ergs is *subsidiation.*

Finally, one of the most important of the sentiments is the *self-sentiment* or ability to contemplate one's own self. The self-sentiment is, of course, founded on the concept of the self which Cattell considers to be an integration of the ego and superego. Cattell admittedly favors the Freudian conception of self, but believes that he has discovered independent evidence in factor analytic studies to support Freud's clinically derived concepts of the ego and superego as aspects of the self. In any case, Cattell argues that the ". . . ultimate integration (of sentiment structures) is to be accounted for only by a conscious sentiment centered in the self and including ego and superego" (*6*, p. 267).

The development of the human personality is viewed as the unfolding of maturational processes and their modification through learning and experience. Generally speaking, maturation contributes the basic perceptual and motor abilities, while learning is responsible for the modification of innate ergs, the elaboration of metaergs, and the organization of the self. The course of personality development and the "principles of personality formation" are contained in Chapters 19 to 21 of Cattell's *Personality* and are far too extensive in scope to summarize here. Instead, we shall attempt only to present a broad outline of his views.

During the period from conception to puberty, the child's personality undergoes its most significant developmental phases. The years from one to five are critical for the development of both normal and abnormal traits. Either type of trait remains remarkably constant from five until puberty. About the ages of seven to eight the child begins to be weaned from parental influence. He acquires the social code of his culture, the dominant trends in interests, characteristic emotional patterns, and, finally, leader-follower characteristics also begin to appear. Around the age of ten or eleven secondary groups, such as the gang and school, begin to exert as much influence on the developing personality as does the home. Depending upon the rate of development, some children at this age begin to experience the cleavage between home and peer-group approved forms of behavior. At the end of the period, the adolescent interests start to emerge.

Adolescence is a period which makes great demands on the child. At one and the same time he is confronted with the many biological and intellectual changes typical of the period. He must adjust to the demands of sex accompanied as it is by increasing self-assertion, but at the same time is under pressure to postpone the satisfaction of sexual needs. He must also strive to maintain parental approval in the face of his growing independence. In short, he must attempt to satisfy four different sets of demands which arise from the following sources: (1) the parents, (2) his adolescent peers, (3) the adult culture pattern, and (4) the internal "residues" of childhood (superego).

The period of maturity is one of a gradual but steady decline of most of the biologically based mental processes. During this period the average individual tends to substitute familial for social interests, grows more philosophical and is increasingly more stable emotionally. With the onset of old age, new adjustments are demanded as a result of both loss of occupation and the decreased social evaluation put upon the aged in our culture.

Finally, Cattell summarizes his theory of personality development under seventeen "principles of personality formation." The laws or principles are concerned with learning, the effects of deprivation, frustration and blockage, the formation of sentiments, the development of the self, and the individual in the social context.

In his laws of learning, Cattell accepts both contiguity (classical conditioning) and a modified law of effect. His treatment of goal-directed behavior, frustration, and responses to frustration closely follows the functionalistic point of view (see Chapter 5); however there are also strong overtones of Gestalt and field theory noticeable throughout his elaboration of the principles. The principles underlying the formation of sentiments consist, for the most part, in the application of the laws of learning, whereas the principles underlying the formation of the self lean heavily on Freudian concepts. The most characteristic of Cattell's contributions to the formation of personality is his concept of the development of dynamic lattices involving subsidiation chains of ergs, metaergs, sentiments, attitudes, and opinions. (Figure 15-3.) Finally, because the individual personality is embedded in the larger social context, prediction of individual behavior is contingent upon the psychologist's knowledge of the individual's relationship to the social context.

In recent years Cattell's highly active research program has led him to apply his theoretical findings to practical situations. In his *Meaning and Measurement of Neuroticism and Anxiety* (8), written with I. H. Scheirer, he has returned to his early clinical interests to offer techniques for the assessment of neuroticism and anxiety. In a more recent semipopular book, *The Scientific Analysis of Personality* (7), he shows how his factor-analytic approach may be applied to problems in the areas of vocational, educational, and clinical psychology. Special attention is given to personality testing of school children and to the relationship of personality theory to the broad social problems involved in psychotherapy and mental health.

In attempting to evaluate Cattell's factorial theory of personality, we are confronted with many of the same problems that arise in trying to assess factor theories of intelligence (see Chapter 14). That the method itself is precise and highly quantitative, if correctly applied, cannot be doubted. Moreover, as Hall and Lindzey (10) point out, the entrance of factor theories into the area of personality has provided a refreshingly empirical emphasis in a field otherwise overweighted with subjective theories. However, as is true in the study of intelligence, the factor analyst must at some stage in his research name the factors revealed by his empirical manipulations of the correlational matrices. It is at this point that subjectivity is likely to creep into the picture. However, as Cattell and others who employ factorial techniques have pointed out, refinement of the tests upon which the studies depend will, to a great extent, meet this particular criticism.

The whole question of whether the highly objective, trait-dominated approach to personality is to be preferred to the clinically oriented, ideographic approach is, of course, a long-standing controversy in the field. The objective method has the advantage of providing general principles of personality development and operation, whereas the clinical, individual approach has the advantage of dealing with real individuals instead of statistical abstractions. However, in the long run, the two orientations are not truly antagonistic but complementary. The clinician needs tests—tests which must be standardized by means of large-scale testing programs. The quantitative psychologist, on the other hand, cannot afford to lose sight of the individual personality. Consequently, he needs the clinician's insights and observations to provide points of departure for the construction of tests and design of research programs. There is every reason to believe that the future will see an ever increasing rapprochement between the two schools of thought.

GORDON W. ALLPORT'S PSYCHOLOGY OF INDIVIDUALITY[11]

G. W. Allport's systematic views on personality span a period of over thirty years. During this time he has been guided by two basic principles: (1) to do justice to the *complexity* of personality, compounded as it is of

[11] Except as noted the exposition follows *1, 2, 3,* and *4.*

hereditary, temperamental, social, and "psychological" factors; and (2) to recognize the uniqueness of each individual personality despite the many communalities that exist among different people. To put it another way, he has attempted to develop a psychology of personality which recognizes the value of the nomothetic approach, especially in regard to the problem of the foundations of personality and its quantitative measurement, but at the same time takes cognizance of the value of the ideographic method.

In his first book-length treatment of personality, published in 1937, Allport emphasized the concept of the *functional autonomy* of motives and the organization of personality in terms of traits. The principle of functional autonomy as stated in 1937 holds that adult motives are varied "self-sustaining, *contemporary* systems, growing out of antecedent systems, but functionally independent of them" (*1*, p. 194). We shall have more to say about this principle later, but for the present it is sufficient to emphasize that by casting his basic principle of personality dynamics in this form, Allport allowed for *both* the general, nomothetic approach in terms of a universal law, while emphasizing the unique and ahistorical nature of individual motivation. Similarly, in dealing with traits, Allport recognized both the generalized nature of traits, in the sense that many traits are exhibited in common by all adult members of a given culture, but at the same time provided for an *individual* functional autonomy in the actual operation of traits in a given personality.

We do not mean to give the impression that the first formulation of Allport's system is nothing more than an attempt to straddle both sides of the nomothetic-ideographic dichotomy. Rather, we wish to emphasize that the system originated as an attempt to synthesize and integrate the relevant contemporary body of psychological knowledge on the subject of personality in such a way as to do justice to both points of view.

It seems fair to say that in recent years Allport has become less concerned with traits and the more elemental aspects of personality dynamics and increasingly interested in the foundations of personalistic psychology as a science. Certainly his choices for his volume of selected papers on the nature of personality, as well as his *Becoming*, lean heavily in the direction of exploring the foundations of personality theory and at the same time show an increasing emphasis on the uniqueness of personality and what might be called "ego psychology."

We have dwelled at length on these introductory considerations in order to point up the difficulty in summarizing a system which has been evolving vigorously over more than three decades. We shall attempt to do justice to Allport's theory by first considering his basic definitions, and following this, outline the more "open-ended" psychology characteristic of his more recent publications.

Let us begin with his well-known definition of personality.[12] "Personality is the dynamic organization within the individual of those psychophysical systems that determine his characteristic behavior and thought" (*4*, p. 28). Allport characterizes his definition as a "synthesis" of contemporary definitions and goes on to point out the denotation of the more important elements within the definition.

By "dynamic organization" he means that personality is a developing, changing organization which reflects motivational conditions. By stressing an active organization, Allport avoids what he terms the "sterile enumerations of the omnibus definitions."

"Psychophysical," as Allport uses the phrase, refers to habits, attitudes, and traits. Obviously, the choice of the term "psychophysical" is a recognition of the fact that both bodily *and* mental factors must be taken into consideration in the description and study of personality.

"Systems" refers to complexes of more elemental processes. Habits, traits, and concepts exemplify such systems.

"Characteristic" refers to the uniqueness of each individual's behavior.

"Behavior and thought . . . are a blanket to designate anything whatsoever an individual may do." In general, they make for survival and growth in the environment.

The inclusion of the term "determine" is a natural consequence of Allport's psychophysical point of view. Personality is *not* synonymous with mere activity or behavior, but instead is that which *underlies* behavior. The psychophysical systems that constitute personality are "determining tendencies" which, when set into motion by appropriate stimuli, give rise to those behavioral acts through which we come to know personality.

Basic to Allport's definition is the underlying idea of personality as a *dynamic* (motivated), *growing* system. The concept of the functional autonomy of motives to which we have already alluded provides the necessary foundation for the system. We must now examine the concept at some length, for in many ways it constitutes the core of Allport's system.

Functional autonomy ". . . *refers to any acquired system of motivation in which the tensions involved are not of the same kind as the antecedent tensions from which the acquired system developed*" (*4*, p. 229).[13] Thus, a child originally may be motivated to practice the piano because of tensions associated with fear of parental retaliation if he fails to put in his daily stint. Indeed, he might prefer to be out playing baseball. However, after five or six years of training, the child may practice for the sole reason that he enjoys playing for its own

---

[12] In the 1937 edition of his *Personality* (*1*, p. 48) the definition read: "Personality is the dynamic organization within the individual of those psychophysical systems that determine his unique adjustments to his environment." Thus, the present definition is only slightly modified from the original.

[13] Italics in original.

sake. The activity of piano playing once serving to reduce the fear of punishment has now become self-motivating. Moreover, we may assume in this case that the original motive has long since subsided. Allport cites as examples of functionally autonomous behavior such everyday instances as the good workman continuing to do an excellent job even though his income no longer depends on it, the "unwilling" mother's eventual acquisition of love for her child, the urban citizen's longing for the hills of home, and the businessman's amassing of wealth beyond the possibility of ever spending it.

Allport distinguishes between two types of functionally autonomous systems—the *perseverative* and the *propriate*. Perseverative functional autonomy refers to physiologically based motivational systems which, once activated, can continue to function for a time without further environmental stimulation. Thus, the animal or man who becomes habituated to cycles of feeding or to drugs becomes restless and active at regular intervals corresponding to the usual time of ingestion of the food or drug. Allport also cites task perseveration, such as occurs in the Zeigarnik effect (Chapter 9), as an example of perseverative striving.

Propriate functional autonomy involves higher order processes such as interests, attitudes and the life style. Allport suggests that interests tend to follow abilities, with people tending to do what they can do best. Such interests are functionally autonomous when the present reason for exercising the ability is no longer related to the original reason except in a historical sense. Thus, the college student who is required to take a course of study and does so only reluctantly may, nevertheless, develop an interest in it, perhaps even majoring in the subject area. Similarly, one may acquire values and an entire life style through training programs in childhood which are accepted reluctantly but later become functionally autonomous of the original fear or coercion which compelled their acceptance. It is these latter processes which are central to the major trends of life and become the organizing core of personality. In discussing propriate motivation Allport also stresses the close relationship between motives and cognitive processes. All motives are a blend of both. Because of these blends the individual develops a "cognitive style" in part dependent upon how he perceives the culture but also as dependent upon his self-perception.

The principle of functional autonomy of motivation, as the examples indicate, stresses both the *contemporaneity* and *variety* of adult human motives. Clearly, Allport is in direct opposition to the psychoanalytic view of personality dynamics in which all present behavior must be traced to its genetic origins. Present motives, Allport admits, are *continuous* with original motives, just as a modern city is historically related to its origins. But neither the adult human being nor the modern city *depends* on its origins for its present "drive." Similarly, Allport divorces his system from the earlier instinct psychologies, such as McDougall's. Instincts may appear in the course of development, but once having appeared, are transformed under the influence of learning. The principle of functional autonomy is also in opposition to the behaviorists' theory of acquired drives. It will be recalled (see Chapter 11) that the behaviorist accounts for acquired drives by invoking the principle of generalization of conditioned stimuli. That is, if a fear is originally acquired by conditioning it to an arbitrary stimulus, theoretically it can become attached to a multitude of additional stimuli by further conditioning. But in such cases the determining factor in arousing and maintaining behavior is the continuing reinforcement provided by the various conditioned stimuli, not the activity itself.

Finally, Allport's concept of functional autonomy is in opposition to the principle of homeostasis, since once a motive becomes functionally autonomous it is self-sustaining, whereas homeostasis implies the cyclic appearance of motivation dependent upon changes in physiological rhythms.

On the positive side, the principle of functional autonomy explains the transformation of the selfish child into the socialized adult. It accounts for the force of phobias, delusions, and other forms of compulsive behavior. Further, the driving force behind such complex activities as craftsmanship, artistic endeavor, and genius is explained as love of the activity for its own sake. In all these cases, Allport feels, it requires a strained and illogical interpretation of human nature to account for adult motivation in terms of its genetic origins. Functional autonomy is, in Allport's words, "a declaration of independence" for personality theory (*1*, p. 207). While the concept of functional autonomy is a central principle in Allport's system, it cannot account for all complexities of personality. Rather, the principle is concerned with how the dynamics underlying those "psychophysical systems" that constitute personality develop and serve the adult. Allport is perfectly willing to admit the importance of the role of learning in personality development. However, he makes it clear that learning as he defines it is not the quasi-mechanical learning of the behaviorists (*4*, p. 108).

Allport makes it clear that he favors the trait as the most valid concept for the description of personality. By definition a trait is "*a neuropsychic structure having the capacity to render many stimuli functionally equivalent, and to initiate and guide equivalent (meaningfully consistent) forms of adaptive and expressive behavior*" [14] (*4*, p. 347).

The definition further implies that traits are *consistent* modes of behavior which are similar to habits but are more generalized. In principle, traits are more like attitudes than habits, since they are determining tendencies rather than specific modes of behavior. Consistency is revealed by the Uriah Heep who is always sycophantic in all situations and who always puts himself in an obsequious position. Similarly, the honest man is presumably consistent

[14] Italics and parentheses in the original.

in his behavior. We must, however, be careful to recognize that traits are not necessarily generalized from situation to situation. A boy may be *consistently* honest in a given situation, say, in handling money in a grocery store, but occasionally dishonest in school. Thus, the consistency of traits is, in part, dependent upon the consistency of the situation in which they are aroused. Obviously, such considerations are important for the practical measurement and prediction of traits.

Allport then distinguishes between *individual* traits and *common* traits. In a sense every trait is an individual trait, since each personality is different from every other. However, such a view of traits, if taken quite literally, would make cross-comparisons between individuals impossible. Indeed, if such conditions prevailed there could be no science of personality. However, because members of a given culture are subject to common evolutionary and social influences, there are many aspects of behavior on which members of a given culture can be compared. These are common traits. In terms of a more formal definition:

> *A common trait is a category for classifying functionally equivalent forms of behavior in a general population of people. Though influenced by nominal and artifactual considerations, a common trait to some extent reflects veridical and comparable dispositions in many personalities who, because of a common human nature and common culture, develop similar modes of adjusting to their environments, though to varying degrees (4, p. 349).*

In his research programs employing tests, rating scales, and the like, the psychologist is making use of the common trait (nomothetic approach). Allport, himself, has provided such a technique in the *Allport-Vernon-Lindzey Scale.* The scale allows for a cross-comparison of the individual with a standardization group on the relative strength of common values—theoretical, economic, esthetic, social, political, and religious.

Allport further distinguishes between *cardinal traits, central traits,* and *secondary traits.* A trait which is outstanding, all-pervasive, and dominant in the individual's life is a cardinal trait. It is, so to speak, a "ruling passion." For this reason cardinal traits are relatively rare. Central traits, on the other hand, are the foci of personality. They are the traits ordinarily measured by rating scales, mentioned in conversation, and described in letters of recommendation. Secondary traits are the less important or minor traits which usually escape notice except by the careful observer or close acquaintance.

To summarize thus far, Allport's theory of personality revolves around the central concepts of *traits* and *the functional autonomy of motives.* Relating the two, *traits are functionally autonomous reaction tendencies which are aroused by certain classes of stimulus situations.* Such reaction tendencies are, in a sense, unique for each individual personality; but, because of common biological and environmental influences, many traits may be considered as *common traits*, thus allowing for the measurement and prediction of behavior. In some individuals a trait may be of such central importance as to be the dominant factor in life. Such rare traits are *cardinal traits*. For the most part the psychology of personality is concerned with *central traits*, which are the building blocks of personality, and to a minor extent with *secondary traits*.

No psychologist, least of all Allport, believes that a human personality is a mere congeries of unrelated traits. Personality demonstrates a unity and integration of traits. Such terms as the "ego" or the "self" reflect the traditional psychological view that there is an overall unifying principle to which traits, motives, experiences and so forth are related. In his recent publications Allport has shown an increasing concern with the problem of identifying and describing the inner essence of personality. We shall now consider his position on this aspect of the psychology of personality.

The pivotal problem for the psychology of growth, as well as the question around which the integration and uniqueness of personality revolve, is the concept of the self. As Allport points out, the self lost out in the dominant psychological systems of the late nineteenth and early twentieth centuries. But more recently the concept has regained favor, at least in those systems which have been characteristically subjective in their approach. However, while Allport is wholeheartedly in favor of a self-psychology or ego psychology, he warns of the danger of personifying the ego or self, thus making of these concepts a kind of *deus ex machina* to account for all behavior (*2*, p. 139; *3*, p. 39; *4*, p. 138).

Allport suggests the concept of the *proprium* to represent what psychology has traditionally included under the terms "self," "ego," "style of life," and so forth. As he employs it, the proprium includes the bodily sense (coenesthesis); self-identity, or the awareness of the continuity of self; ego enhancement; ego extension, or the identification of external objects with the self; rational and cognitive functions; the self image; and propriate striving. The last-named concept, that of propriate striving, is of first importance in Allport's system.

Propriate striving refers to that motivated behavior which is of central importance to the self as opposed to behavior which is peripheral to the self. Examples of propriate striving include all forms of behavior that serve self-realization. The scientist, the explorer, the craftsman, the parent, the artist—all strive for goals that are in a sense forever unattainable but which confer unity to motivation and which make life meaningful. In Allport's words:

> Here seems to be the central characteristic of propriate striving: its goals are, strictly speaking, unattainable. Propriate striving confers unity upon personality, but it is never the unity of fulfillment, of repose, or of reduced tension. The devoted parent never loses concern for his child; the devotee of democracy

adopts a lifelong assignment in his human relationships. The scientist, by the very nature of his commitment, creates more and more questions, never fewer. Indeed the measure of our intellectual maturity, one philosopher suggests, is our capacity to feel less and less satisfied with our answers to better and better problems (3, p. 67).

Propriate striving represents *growth* or abundancy motivation as opposed to deficiency motivation. In Allport's opinion, too much emphasis has been placed on such concepts as tension reduction, homeostasis, and drive reduction by contemporary psychologists. These are fragmentary, peripheral aspects of personality which, while important for survival, represent but one side of human motivation. Man seeks variety, new horizons, and the freedom to explore, as well as relief from the irritations attendant upon deficiencies. The essence of personality is the individual's *way of living*. The ego or self, then, becomes the integration of the propriate functions that constitute the unified style of life.[15] In the last analysis, the style of life for the normal, healthy individual is, to use the title of Allport's recent volume, one of "becoming."

In a special chapter in his *Pattern and Growth in Personality* (Chapter 7), Allport discusses Freud's theory of personality, characterizing it as a strata theory because of its emphasis on the three levels of consciousness and the division of the personality into id, ego, and superego. He believes that Freud developed too passive an ego theory, allowing too little room for self-determination. He also characterizes psychoanalytic theory as most descriptive of neurotic as opposed to healthy personalities. However, he does believe that the Freudian ego-defense mechanisms (repression, rationalization, projection, and the like) are of value in understanding both normal and abnormal people.

By way of concluding our summary of Allport's personalistic theory we should like to make several evaluative comments.

First of all, the theory has been widely influential among those psychologists whose major concern is the area of personality. Perhaps one reason for its success in this respect is Allport's insistence from the very beginning on the individuality of personality, while, at the same time, allowing for the possibility of the quantitative, nomothetic approach through his principle of functional autonomy and his trait-theory orientation.

Second, his insistence on a psychology which recognizes the self as a central concept, although launched in a period when subjective concepts were still unpopular, has been vindicated. As he himself points out, the self has crept back into psychology in recent years. However, it is to Allport's credit that he has never accepted a personified self, and in his recent publi-

---

[15] It should be noted that Allport's psychology of the proprium is closely related to Adlerian theory (Chapter 11) and to Maslow's system of motivation (Chapter 11).

cations has emphasized his concern with this danger by developing the concept of the proprium to represent ways of behaving traditionally subsumed under self-functions. Because of his emphasis on the self and ego functions Allport's is an "academic" theory that has been acceptable to clinically oriented psychologists.

Third, Allport's system as a whole may be characterized as on the subjective, tender-minded side of psychological theorizing. In terms of the systems reviewed in this volume, its closest affiliations are with the systems advocated by Adler, Maslow, the functionalists, and the Gestalt psychologists. This must not be taken to mean that Allport has simply "borrowed" from other systems. Rather, the influence of these systems "show through" Allport's original contributions.

Finally, in the concluding chapter of his *Pattern and Growth in Personality,* Allport shows his individualism and humanism in maintaining that psychology cannot sever all links with philosophy. He believes that a purely psychological conception of the individual neglects the broader problem of human nature and man's place in the cosmos. By thus accepting the validity of a broader philosophical point of view, Allport aligns himself with those humanistic psychologists who oppose the dominant *S-R* approach of contemporary American psychology. In his own words, he pleads that "Ancient wisdom, both philosophical and theological, should be consulted and incorporated lest we find ourselves dealing with elaborate trivialities."

H. A. MURRAY'S PERSONOLOGY[16]

Murray's system, like Allport's, has been developed over a period of several decades. Moreover, Murray's theory also resembles Allport's in its humanistic, holistic, and eclectic orientation to the problems involved in developing a science of personality. Unlike Allport's, Murray's theory has been strongly influenced by psychoanalytic conceptions of personality and has also placed greater stress on the importance of environmental influences on the individual. Finally, by way of introduction, it should be noted that Murray has consistently stressed the fundamental significance of the physiological processes which underlie behavior. The latter perhaps is a reflection of its author's medical training (*16*, pp. 9–12).

As a point of departure for examining Murray's theory let us begin with a definition: "Personality is the continuity of functional forms and

[16] The exposition is based on the following primary sources: *13*, *14*, *15*, and *16*. For the best brief summary of Murray's theory see *14*. However, the need-press theory is not elaborated in this article, which is intended only to outline certain basic considerations for personality theory.

forces manifested through sequences of organized regnant processes and overt behaviors from birth to death" (*15*, p. 49). There are several principal components contained within this definition. First, personality exhibits *continuity*. In other words, it evolves as a continuous process over the entire lifetime of the individual. Second, "regnant processes" refers to dynamically organized brain activities. Murray has always emphasized the functional dependence of personality and mental events in general on brain processes. In Murray's own words:

> Since in the higher forms of life the impressions from the external world and from the body that are responsible for conditioning and memory are received, integrated, and conserved in the brain, and since all complex adaptive behavior is evidently coordinated by excitations in the brain, the unity of the organism's development and behavior can be explained only by referring to organizations occurring in this region (*13*, p. 45).

Elsewhere Murray has said that "Personality may be biologically defined as the governing organ, or superordinate institution of the body. As such, it is located in the brain. No brain, no personality" (*14*, p. 267). Thus, personality as the reflection of regnant processes is the organizing and integrating agency in the individual's life which governs all the organismic processes.

Third, the definition emphasizes the "functional forms," or more simply the activities of personality as it contributes to the individual's adaptation to his environment. It is with this latter aspect of Murray's definition that we shall begin our detailed study of his system, since the most characteristic aspect of the theory is the dynamic or functional nature of personality as it mediates between the individual and his needs and demands of the environment.

It will be convenient to begin with Murray's definition of need, followed by a list of the more important needs as revealed in the elaborate studies of human personality carried out by Murray and his associates. Needs are defined as follows:

> A need is a construct (a convenient fiction or hypothetical concept) which stands for force (the physicochemical nature of which is unknown) in the brain region, a force which organizes perception, apperception, intellection, conation, and action in such a way as to transform in a certain direction an existing, unsatisfying situation (*13*, pp. 123–124).

The fundamental needs are:[17]

---

[17] For more extended definition of these and other needs listed see *13*, pp. 146–227.

1. Positive cathexis
   Supra:
   (a) Mother
   (b) Female
   (c) Father
   (d) Male
   (e) Brother
   (f) Sister
   Infra:
   (g) Brother
   (h) Sister
   (i) Contemporary
   (j) Animal
   (k) Possessions

2. n Affiliation
   (a) Friendliness
   (b) n Suc: Dependence
   (c) n Def: Respect
   (d) n Nur: Kindness

3. n Deference
   (a) n Blam: Compliance
   (b) n Aff: Respect
   (c) n Nur: Devotion
   (d) Ego ideal emulation
   (e) Suggestibility

4. n Nurturance
   (a) Sympathy
   (b) n Aff: Kindness
   (c) n Def: Devotion

5. n Succorance
   (a) Crying
   (b) n Aff: Dependence
   (c) n Harm: Appealance

6. n Harmavoidance
   (a) Timidity
   (b) n Suc: Appealance
   (c) Nightmares
   (d) Fears
      i. Insup., heights and
         falling
      ii. Water
      iii. Darkness
      iv. Fire
      v. Isolation
      vi. Assault, lightning
      vii. Assault, animals

   viii. Assault, Human
         General hostility
         Father
         Mother
         Contemporaries
   ix. Illness and death
   x. Miscellaneous

7. n Infavoidance
   (a) Narcisensitivity
   (b) Shyness, embarrassment
   (c) Avoidance of competition
   (d) Inferiority feelings
      i. General
      ii. Physical
      iii. Social
      iv. Intellectual

8. n Blamavoidance and superego
   (a) Sensitivity to blame
   (b) n Def: Compliance
   (c) n Aba: Shame and self-
       depreciation
   (d) Directive superego
   (e) Religious inclination

9. n Abasement
   (a) n Blam: Blame-acceptance
   (b) n Def: Subservience
   (c) n Harm or n Inf: Surrender

10. n Passivity
    (a) Inactivity
    (b) n Aba: Acceptance

11. n Seclusion
    (a) Isolation
    (b) Reticence
    (c) n Inf: Shyness

12. n Inviolacy
    (a) n Dfd: Vindication
    (b) n Ach: Restriving
    (c) n Agg: Retaliation
    (d) n Auto: Resistance

13. Negative cathexis
    Supra:
    (a) Mother
    (b) Female
    (c) Father
    (d) Male

Negative cathexis (*continued*)
   (e) Brother
   (f) Sister
   (g) Contemporaries
Infra:
   (h) Brother
   (i) Sister

14. n Aggression
   (a) Temper
   (b) Combativeness
   (c) Sadism
   (d) n Dom: Coercion
   (e) n Auto: Rebellion
   (f) n Suc: Plaintance
   (g) Destruction

15. n Autonomy
   (a) Freedom
   (b) Defiance
   (c) Inv: Resistance
   (d) n Ach: Independence

16. n Dominance
   (a) Leadership
   (b) Inducement
   (c) n Agg: Coercion

17. n Rejection
   (a) Hypercriticalness
   (b) n Inf: Narcisensitivity
   (c) n Sec: Inaccessibility

18. n Noxavoidance
   (a) Hypersensitivity, gen.
   (b) Food

19. n Achievement
   (a) General
   (b) Physical
   (c) Intellectual
   (d) Caste
   (e) Rivalry
   (f) Ego ideal
   (g) n Inv: Restriving
   (h) n Auto: Independence

20. n Recognition
   (a) Recitals of superiority
   (b) Cathection of praise
   (c) n Exh: Public performance

21. n Exhibition
   (a) n Rec: Public performance
   (b) n Sex: Exhibitionism

22. n Sex
   (a) Masturbation
   (b) Precocious heterosexuality
   (c) Homosexuality
   (d) Bisexuality

23. n Acquisition
   (a) Greediness
   (b) Stealing
   (c) Gambling

24. n Cognizance
   (a) Curiosity, general
   (b) Experimentation
   (c) Intellectual
   (d) Sexual, birth
   (e) Genitals

25. n Construction
   (a) Mechanical
   (b) Aesthetic

26. n Order
   (a) Cleanliness
   (b) Orderliness
   (c) Finickiness about details

27. n Retention
   (a) Collectance
   (b) Conservance

28. n Activity
   (a) Physical
   (b) Verbal

An explanation of the more technical and unfamiliar terms follows. Positive cathexis means the investment of an object, such as the mother, with special significance. The child becomes attached to the mother, father, animals, toys, and the like, and needs their presence. Supra and

Infra are abbreviations for supravertive and infravertive, respectively. Supravertive needs are those directed toward a superior person, while infravertive needs are directed toward inferiors. Other commonly used abbreviations with their full equivalents are: Suc—Succorance; Def—Deference; Nur—Nurturance; Blam—Blame avoidance; Aff—Affiliation; Dfd—Defendance; Ach—Achievement; Agg—Aggression; Auto—Autonomy or Independence; Dom—Dominance; Inv—Inviolacy; Exh—Exhibition.

In general it should be noted that Murray's needs lean heavily on Freudian and other psychoanalytic conceptions of childhood and developmental patterns. Moreover, with other psychologists, Murray recognizes the interrelatedness of needs. As has already been pointed out, needs may fuse so that behaviorally two needs may have the same outcome. Needs may also be in conflict. The child may experience both feelings of love and hate for the same person. In addition, needs may be interrelated by *subsidiation.* This concept refers to instances in which one need is in the service of another. Thus, an individual who is anxious and who feels inferior in social situations may nevertheless desire close personal attachments (n Affiliation). But, because of his anxiety and inferiority, he can only approach others with extreme deference. He conforms strictly to custom. He showers excessive praise on those he admires. He yields eagerly to their wishes. This pattern (n Deference) is, therefore, in subsidiation in respect to the need for affiliation.

Needs may be either latent or overt. Those needs which are latent are repressed or restrained. Those which are overt are expressed freely and are consciously recognized by the individual. In thus distinguishing between latent and overt needs, Murray again reveals the influence of the psychoanalytic systems of Freud and Jung.

Needs are also defined in terms of whether they are *proactive* or *reactive.* Proactive needs are those which arise from within the individual without the necessity of environmental stimulation. The strong need of the creative individual to produce artistic or intellectual works exemplifies proactive needs in operation. Reactive needs are those aroused by stimulation from the environment. Thus, the sight of an attractive member of the opposite sex may arouse strong reactive needs in a young man. However, in the final analysis, all needs are processes within the individual whether aroused centrally or environmentally.

Finally, we may distinguish between Murray's concept of *process activities, modal,* and *effect needs.* Process activities are actions performed for their own sake without regard to some definite goal or the reduction of tensions associated with physiological needs. Thus, the musician will make music on many occasions when he is alone, only because he enjoys playing for its own sake. The concept of process activities is obviously closely related to Allport's functional autonomy.

Modal needs refer to the individual's desire for excellence. The musician not only plays; he strives to play well, to achieve a high degree of facility or excellence in rendition.

An effect need is one that leads to a goal. Playing a piano concerto in order to compete in a contest is an effect need. Many additional examples of effect needs could be found in the direct reduction of viscerogenic drives, such as hunger, thirst, sex, and the like.

Finally, in commenting on needs, we may note that Murray accepts the widely used concept of tension reduction or the search for homeostasis or equilibrium as a fundamental class of needs. However man also has needs to generate tension, to seek excitement, novelty, and experiences which temporarily disturb his equilibrium. Thus, in Murray's system, man is not a creature entirely at the mercy of tensions or viscerogenic irritations, but one who, in part, governs his own need states.

At this point we should like to pause for the purpose of interpolating a brief outline of the method employed by Murray and his collaborators in identifying the needs discussed above and the perceptual press to be considered subsequently. Briefly the need-press findings grew out of an elaborate series of investigations of fifty normal adults by Murray and a team of experts associated with the Harvard Psychological Clinic. All told, twenty-eight specialists worked together for a period of two and one-half years in planning, carrying out and evaluating the results of the project. In order to give some idea of the scope and penetrating quality of the study, twenty-five different procedures were employed for assessing the subject's personality. Among these were conferences, questionnaires, the Rorschach Test, various experimental tests, hypnotic and analytic sessions, and the Thematic Apperception Test. The last-named, familiarly known as the TAT, was especially designed by Murray and C. D. Morgan for the investigation of fantasy and is now one of the "classic" projective techniques. As should be evident from even this brief outline of the procedures employed in need-press studies, Murray's conceptions are well grounded in empirical evidence. With this in mind we may go on to examine his theory of perceptual press.

A perceptual press of an object or person is "what it can *do to the subject* or *for the subject*—the power that it has to affect the well-being of the subject in one way or another" (*13*, p. 121). The common press of childhood, as revealed in the study by Murray and his coworkers referred to above, are shown in the following list (*13*, pp. 291–292):

1. p Family insupport
   (a) Cultural discord
   (b) Family discord
   (c) Capricious discipline
   (d) Parental separation
   (e) Absence of parent:
       Father
       Mother
   (f) Parental illness:
       Father
       Mother

p Family insupport (*continued*)
  (g) Death of parent:
      Father
      Mother
  (h) Inferior parent:
      Father
      Mother
  (i) Dissimilar parent:
      Father
      Mother
  (j) Poverty
  (k) Unsettled home

2. p Danger or misfortune
  (a) Physical insupport, height
  (b) Water
  (c) Aloneness, darkness
  (d) Inclement weather, lightning
  (e) Fire
  (f) Accident
  (g) Animal

3. p Lack or loss
  (a) of nourishment
  (b) of possessions
  (c) of companionship
  (d) of variety

4. p Retention, withholding objects

5. p Rejection, unconcern and scorn

6. p Rival, competing contemporary

7. p Birth of sibling

8. p Aggression
  (a) Maltreatment by elder
      Male
      Elder female
  (b) Maltreatment by
      contemporaries
  (c) Quarrelsome contemporaries

9. Fp Aggression-dominance,
      punishment
  (a) Striking, physical pain
  (b) Restraint, confinement

10. p Dominance, coercion and
       prohibition
  (a) Discipline
  (b) Religious training

11. Fp Dominance-nurturance
  (a) Parental ego idealism
      Mother
      Father
      Physical
      Econ, vocation
      Caste
      Intellectual
  (b) Possessive parent
      Mother
      Father
  (c) Oversolicitous parent, fears:
      Accident
      Illness
      Bad influences

12. p Nurturance, indulgence

13. p Succorance, demands for
       tenderness

14. p Deference, praise, recognition

15. p Affiliation, friendships

16. p Sex
  (a) Exposure
  (b) Seduction
      Homosexual
      Heterosexual
  (c) Parental intercourse

17. Deception or betrayal,
       intraorganic press

18. p. Illness
  (a) Prolonged, frequent illness
  (b) Nervous
  (c) Respiratory
  (d) Cardiac
  (e) Gastrointestinal
  (f) Infantile paralysis
  (g) Convulsions

19. p Operation

20. p Inferiority
  (a) Physical
  (b) Social
  (c) Intellectual

There are no technical terms in the list that have not already been defined in connection with Murray's manifest and latent needs. However, the symbol Fp (see Numbers 9 and 11 in the list) needs clarification. Fp stands for a fusion of two press. In the case of Number 9, both aggression and dominance fuse, with the result that the child perceives the threat of punishment. Similarly, a fusion of Dominance and Nurturance results in a variety of perceptual press characterized by solicitude, possessiveness, and parental idealism.

It must be emphasized that press are perceptual processes and do not represent objects or persons in the environment in any literal sense. The distinction between press and environment in Murray's theory parallels the distinction between the situation and the field in Gestalt theory (see Chapter 5). Moreover, it should be noted that needs and press are interrelated in the sense that needs are fundamental to press. Invoking once more the example of a boy and an apple, if the boy is satiated the apple has little or no interest for him. If he is hungry, or at least not satiated, the apple is perceived as a desirable object. Murray, in relating needs and press, refers to the interaction of the individual and his needs and the environment and perceptual press in a behavior episode as a *thema*. Thus in using the Thematic Apperception Test, or one of the other projective techniques, the psychologist *infers* the individual's needs from the themas revealed as he "interacts" with the test stimuli.

The discussion of the interrelation of needs and press leads us to what Murray considers the basic data of psychological observation—*proceedings*. Proceedings are the concrete activities of an individual during a specific period of time. *Internal proceedings* are the individual's consciousness of memories, fantasies, plans for the future, bodily events, and so forth. *External proceedings,* on the other hand, refer to the individual's active coping with the environment during a given temporal period. The external proceeding is ". . . the psychologist's *real entity,* the thing he should observe, analyze, try to reconstruct, and represent if possible with a model, and thus explain it . . ." (*15*, p. 9).[18]

It has already been emphasized that the individual personality possesses continuity. The concept of proceedings, it should be noted, does not contradict the principle of continuity. Proceedings leave traces behind them. In some little way each experience makes the individual different from what he was before that event occurred. Moreover, Murray employs the concept of *serials* to represent the functional interrelatedness of proceedings which, though occurring discretely in time, are nevertheless dynamically related. Perhaps one of the best examples of serials is the long-term striving necessary to reach an important goal. Many proceedings stretching into programs of serials are involved in reaching an important objective such as a degree in medicine.

[18] See also *14*, pp. 268–269.

So much for the building blocks of Murray's conception of personality. In terms of the *development* of personality, Murray leans heavily on Freudian concepts. The concepts of the id, ego, and superego are accepted by Murray with modifications. Specifically, the id, from Murray's point of view, is not entirely constituted of unacceptable impulses, especially during the infancy period. There is, at this stage of the individual's development, nothing unacceptable about the various spontaneous and natural emotions and impulses which make possible the child's continued existence.

The ego's functions are complex, but in the main involve perception, intellection, and conation (or will).[19] In general, Murray's view of the ego is consistent with Freud's. However, in Murray's system, the ego is less like an authoritarian principle or the personification of a police force whose primary function is id-suppression. He believes that the ego can achieve important and socially acceptable satisfactions and that the individual is not necessarily torn by unresolved conflicts.

Similarly, the superego is viewed as a product of cultural internalization, as is the case in Freudian theory. Murray also distinguishes a fourth aspect of mind, the ego-ideal, which, while intimately related to the superego, is distinguishable from it. The ego-ideal is the individual's guiding image of himself; it is his view of himself at some future date. The ego-ideal may correspond approximately to the superego, as it does in the normal, average individual, or, in other cases, such as the criminal or psychotic, may be far removed from the superego's essentially social conceptions of morality.

Murray also accepts the psychoanalytic concept of infantile complexes and fixations which lead to certain recognizable modes of adult behavior. Specifically, he recognizes the anal, oral, and castration complexes of classical Freudian theory and, in addition, has emphasized several varieties of "claustral" complexes which are related to the individual's prenatal existence. Some people wish to reinstate the comforts of the prenatal life. In others, the complex may revolve around the anxiety attendant upon separation from the mother (birth trauma), and in still others it may take the form of anxiety over the possibility of confinement (claustrophobia). Finally, Murray recognizes the existence of a *urethral complex*. In childhood this complex involves enuresis and urethral eroticism. In the adult, it takes the form of an interest in fires (presumably spraying fires with water is symbolic of urination), a tendency toward narcissism, and ambition which dissolves (becomes fluid) in the face of frustration.

There is a danger in emphasizing Murray's use of the psychoanalytic complexes that sight will be lost of the fact that he also strongly emphasizes the role of environmental determinants in the ontogenesis of behavior. It

---

[19] The best source for Murray's views of personality organization is *15*.

ill be recalled that in his concepts of thema, proceedings, and press he lows his strong interest in constantly relating the individual and his environment. Moreover, in a statement of the background of his theory, he becifically acknowledges the influences of culture, anthropology, and sociology in the formulation of his principles (16).

It has been possible to present only the barest summary of what appears b us to be the main outlines of Murray's complex theory. Despite this limitation, however, the more salient features and emphases should be pparent. First, the theory is eclectic in that Murray recognizes contribu-ons from many other points of view. Moreover, his interest in anthropology, medicine, literature, and their allied disciplines has contributed both chness and diversity to his system. Second, the theory ranks high in its mphasis on dynamic and perceptual factors but does not, on the other and, put a premium on self and individuality. It is difficult, therefore, b "classify" the theory with any degree of ease or precision.[20] However, s emphasis on genetic factors in personality development, unconscious eterminants in behavior, free use of Freudian concepts, and its essentially nalytic methodology place it in the psychoanalytic camp, broadly speak-ig. Third, Murray's theory is perhaps the most detailed and complex of ll current theories of personality. In part, this is a reflection of his broad nterests and, in part, a reflection of his eclecticism. But more basically reflects Murray the man—a theorist who is highly imaginative, complex ı personality, and very much the rebel in his orientation to psychology.

Finally, it is fair to say that Murray's theoretical system has made ess of an impression on "academic" psychologists than on those whose rofessional work is in the clinical field. In part, this can be attributed to he psychoanalytic orientation of the system, in part to its sometimes highly peculative nature, and finally to clinical interest in the purely methodo-bgical technique of the Thematic Apperception Test. It is impossible to redict which aspects of the theory *as a theory* will persist to become part f the body of psychology. Whatever the future holds, Murray's careful nalysis of motivational and perceptual processes in the dynamics of the nnctioning personality is in and of itself a significant contribution.

ROGERS' SELF THEORY[21]

Carl Rogers' self theory is unique among the academic theories of ersonality that we have examined in that it grew directly out of clinical ractice—a world-famous practice which began over forty years ago and

---

This difficulty is related to the richness of the background influences which have gone into furray's system (16).
For primary sources drawn upon see reference numbers 18 to 26.

which has continued in the service of maladjusted people to the present
writing. Client-centered therapy, or as some prefer to call it, nondirective
counseling, has attracted a group of loyal followers from both the United
States and Europe. But regardless of whether or not a contemporary ther
apist practices nondirective therapy, he must take cognizance of Rogers
challenging and novel conception of the therapeutic process. Because the
present chapter does not attempt to give an account of the psychothera
peutic foundations of personality theory in detail, we cannot undertake
to present more than a bare outline of Rogers' technique of nondirective
counseling. However, because the self theory developed directly out of
clinical practice *some* understanding of the method is necessary in order to
appreciate the personality theory.

Table 15-6.
Basic Conditions of the Therapeutic Process According to Rogers

---

For therapy to occur, it is necessary that these conditions exist:

1. That two persons are in *contact.*

2. That the first person, whom we shall term the client, is in a state of *incongruence*
   being *vulnerable,* or *anxious.*

3. That the second person, whom we shall term the therapist, is *congruent* in the
   relationship.

4. That the therapist is *experiencing unconditional positive regard* toward the client.

5. That the therapist is *experiencing* an *empathic* understanding of the client's *internal
   frame of reference.*

6. That the client *perceives,* at least to a minimal degree, Conditions 4 and 5, the
   unconditional positive regard of the therapist for him, and the *empathic* understanding
   of the therapist.

The therapeutic background.   Table 15-6 presents in a highly summarized
form Rogers' formulation of the basic conditions necessary for effective
therapy. We shall comment on each of the conditions briefly, in turn.
Contact refers to a relationship between two persons, such as a client and
the therapist, in which "each make a perceived or subceived difference in
the experiential field of the other" (*20*, p. 207). Rogers has consistently
taken the position that the best atmosphere for achieving psychological
contact is a warm, permissive atmosphere in which the therapist uncon-
ditionally accepts the client or shows positive regard for his feelings and
for him as a person (Condition 4).

Moreover, the therapist must experience an empathic understanding
of the client from the viewpoint of the latter's internal frame of reference

Condition 5). This means that the therapist must feel with and understand the client "as if" he were the client. In other words, feeling and understanding in the therapeutic situation must be from the client's point of view, not the therapist's. In order to make this clear let us take a simple example. A client expresses the attitude "I dislike my father." The counselor's response might be, "You resent your father's criticism?" expressed in a warm tone of voice which indicates that the therapist understands the client's statement and empathizes with his attitude. The tone and manner in which the therapist expresses his reactions to the client's verbalizations are critical. The same statement as illustrated in the hypothetical example just given but delivered in a nonsympathetic tone and harsh manner would convey disapproval or criticism on the part of the therapist. Or, in still another setting a nonempathetic, indifferent tone might indicate mere objective curiosity on the part of the therapist. As Condition 6 indicates, the client must perceive that the therapist understands and empathizes with him or therapy will be impossible or unsuccessful. Therefore, this condition is central to the practice of nondirective counseling.

Condition 2 indicates that the client is in a state of incongruence, is vulnerable and anxious. Incongruence refers to a condition in which the individual has not properly symbolized and admitted to awareness his significant experiences. It is for this reason that he is vulnerable—particularly vulnerable to anxiety, which is a strong emotional reaction that arises when the individual's protective mechanisms are challenged and incongruent experiences therefore threaten to come suddenly to awareness. To exemplify: an individual may have experienced homosexual desires at some time in his development but because of the strong parental and social disapproval attendant upon such practices, he has not made his impulses congruent with his conception of himself as one who would like to stand high in the regard of others. Thus he must distort and deny to awareness all homosexual impulses; and when there is a danger that they are approaching consciousness, he experiences anxiety and becomes vulnerable. Happily, in the therapeutic situation vulnerability can mean the possibility of bringing distorted and denied experiences to full awareness where they can be made congruent with the self and so reduce anxiety. Vulnerability and anxiety, although subjectively unpleasant, are the price the person has to pay for change.

Finally, Condition 3 specifies that the therapist must be congruent in the therapeutic relationship which signifies that:

> the therapist's symbolization of his own experience in the relationship must be accurate, if therapy is to be most effective. Thus, if he is experiencing threat and discomfort in the relationship, and is aware only of an acceptance and understanding, then he is not congruent in the relationship, and therapy will suffer.

It seems important that he could accurately "be himself" in the relationship whatever the self of that moment may be (*20*, p. 214).

As Rogers is quick to point out, these primary conditions do not partake of an all-or-nothing status. Therapists, like clients, are imperfect and are not always congruent in the therapeutic situation. Hopefully, further research will enable therapists to better understand themselves and more skillfully conduct therapeutic processes. Moreover, this bare outline of fundamental conditions is by no means all there is to nondirective therapy. Like other forms of therapy it requires careful training and a broad understanding of the human personality if it is to be effective. We are careful to point this out because of all forms of psychotherapy, nondirective counseling is most likely to be misunderstood, since, superficially, it appears to put so few demands on the therapist.[22]

The personality theory. Table 15-7 presents the essence of Rogers' view of the normal, fully functioning person. Using the propositions in the Table as points of departure, we may summarize Rogers' theory of personality.

Actualization of the self is his single dynamic construct. All other motives whether viscerogenic or socially conditioned are aspects of this fundamental motive. From Rogers' point of view growth and development involve a constant tendency toward autonomy away from control by external forces. The concept of actualizing as he employs it is very similar to the concepts of self-actualization and self-realization postulated by Maslow and Goldstein (Chapter 11). By adopting this point of view, Rogers therefore aligns himself with the organismic and holistic theorists.

We have already commented on the importance of symbolization of experiences in connection with the therapeutic process. Here we might add that for the normal individual such experiences may be ignored, they may be symbolized and made a part of the self, or they may be distorted and denied symbolization. This proposition is central to Rogers' theory of the neuroses and is broadly analogous to Freud's theory of repression and the unconscious. Therapy, as we have already pointed out, consists in bringing distorted experiences to full awareness so that they may be made congruent with the self. Clearly, the fully functioning and healthy person cannot have large segments of noncongruent or distorted experiences.

Positive regard and positive self-regard refer to (1) attitudes of warmth, respect, liking, and acceptance on the part of others towards the self, and (2) similar attitudes with regard to one's own experiences as independent

[22] For a more detailed account of the process of nondirective counseling, see *18*, *19*, and *26*. The earlier books contain a number of illustrative cases. The article in *Psychology: A Study of a Science* (*20*) represents a more definitive statement of the theory and its supporting research programs.

able 15-7.

ssence of Rogers' View of the Normal, Fully Functioning Person

A. The individual has an inherent tendency toward *actualizing* his organism.

B. The individual has the capacity and tendency to *symbolize experiences* accurately in *awareness.*
   1. A corollary statement is that he has the capacity and tendency to keep his *self-concept* congruent with his *experience.*

C. The individual has a *need for positive regard.*

D. The individual has a *need for positive self-regard.*

E. Tendencies A and B are most fully realized when needs C and D are met. More specifically, tendencies A and B tend to be most fully realized when
   1. The individual *experiences unconditional positive regard* from significant others.
   2. The pervasiveness of this *unconditional positive regard* is made evident through relationships marked by a complete and communicated *empathic* understanding of the individual's *frame of reference.*

F. If the conditions under E are met to a maximum degree, the individual who experiences these conditions will be a fully functioning person. The fully functioning person will have at least these characteristics:
   1. He will be *open to his experience.*
      a. The corollary statement is that he will exhibit no *defensiveness.*
   2. Hence all *experiences* will be *available to awareness.*
   3. All *symbolizations* will be as accurate as the experiential data will permit.
   4. His *self-structure* will be congruent with his *experience.*
   5. His *self-structure* will be a fluid Gestalt, changing flexibly in the process of assimilation of new *experience.*
   6. He will *experience* himself as the *locus of evaluation.*
      a. The *valuing process* will be a continuing *organismic* one.
   7. He will have no *conditions of worth.*
      a. The corollary statement is that he will *experience unconditional self-regard.*
   8. He will meet each situation with behavior which is a unique and creative adaptation to the newness of that moment.
   9. He will find his *organismic valuing* a trustworthy guide to the most satisfying behaviors, because
      a. All available experiential data will be available to *awareness* and used.
      b. No datum of *experience* will be *distorted in,* or *denied to, awareness.*
      c. The outcomes of behavior in *experience* will be *available to awareness.*
      d. Hence any failure to achieve the maximum possible satisfaction, because of lack of data, will be corrected by this effective reality testing.
   10. He will live with others in the maximum possible harmony, because of the rewarding character of reciprocal *positive regard.*

of social transactions with others. What Rogers is saying is that every healthy individual needs both types of regard, social and personal, and that one cannot be normal and function adequately if he does not experience regard for others as well as possessing a realistically based sense of his own worth. And, as indicated in E in Table 15-7, self-actualizing tendencies and the congruent symbolization of experience are most full realized under conditions of social and self-regard. It might also be note that in therapeutic situations regard must be unconditional and be com municated emphatically by the therapist (1 and 2 under E).

Rogers' characteristics of the full-functioning person are given unde the ten subpropositions listed under F in Table 15-7.

Openness to experience (1 and 2) means that all stimuli whether ex ternal or internal in origin are freely transmitted through the individual nervous system without undergoing distortion by defense mechanisms Obviously, such experiences are fully available to awareness and are als available to symbolization and self-congruency. Situations of threat, as ha been suggested earlier, preclude the possibility of openness to experienc It is for this reason that children in threatening situations, or individual in therapy who feel threatened, cannot adequately symbolize experience and bring them to full awareness.

Here we must give the concept of symbolization more explicit mean ing. It is essentially synonymous with awareness or consciousness. Conse quently, accuracy of symbolization (Characteristic 3) means that in hi transactions with the environment the individual will form hypothese about reality that can be tested or validated by acting upon them. Thu the individual who has a reasonable estimate of his ability as dependen upon his experience of success or failure will neither seriously underestimat nor overestimate his future potential, whereas the psychotic's estimates ar likely to bear little relationship to reality.

In Rogers' own words, the self-structure (Characteristics 4, 5 and 6 refers "to the organized, consistent conceptual Gestalt composed of per ceptions of the characteristics of the I or me and the perception of the rela tionships of the I or me to others and to various aspects of life, togethe with the value attached to these perceptions" (20, p. 200).

The self is the central concept in Rogers' theory. He confesses that th concept evolved very slowly out of his clinical experience and in oppositior to his own early scepticism that such a concept could be defined in an meaningful and accurate manner. He found, however, that individual undergoing therapy experienced violent fluctuations in their evaluatior of themselves, how they perceive the world about them, and how they ar perceived by others. Even minor incidents can, in some cases, change th entire configuration (Gestalt) of the individual's self-perception. However regardless of how real the self may appear to the client or to the therapist the problem nevertheless remains of discovering an operational definition This was realized, Rogers believes, in the development of the Q-technique As he and his associates use it, the technique consists of having the indi vidual sort a pack of cards containing statements applicable to himsel along a continuum or distribution. For example, seven or nine categorie or reference points might be placed before the subject expressing varying degrees of self-evaluative statements ranging from most like, to least like, himself. These could be taken directly from clinical protocols. When the subject has sorted the pack of statements according to the way he believes they describe his present condition, a median or average rating for the various categories can be calculated, thus giving a specific rating to each card. In this manner a quantitative estimate of the individual's self-picture can be obtained before and after therapy. Subjects who make initial sorts but who do not undergo therapy for a significant interval of time can be used as members of a control group in order to assess the effect of therapy. Clearly, if therapy changes the subject in a positive direction, we have an operational definition not only of the self but of the therapy.[23]

The self not only undergoes changes as a result of the flux of environmental events, it also experiences changing self-evaluation as the result of these events. The healthy individual refers to his own self-structure for evaluation; the neurotic or the submissive child perceives the locus of evaluation in others. Thus, Rogers offers the tragic-comic example of the little girl who when asked her name replied, "Mary Ann Don't." Such a child would have only the weakest sense of self-evaluation and a strong sense of value judgments localized in others.

The seventh characteristic of the fully functioning person is that "he will have no conditions of worth." Conditions of worth refer to self experiences which are sought or avoided because they are perceived as being either more or less worthy of self-regard. Thus, a mother may stress the importance of eating a certain food, and the child may accept this value judgment even though it is incongruent with the self because he cannot risk incurring her displeasure. A fully functioning creative artist, on the other hand, will reject either praise or criticism which he knows to be invalid. Beethoven's last quartets, for example, were dismissed by his contemporaries as the meanderings of a failing mind. Beethoven judged them quite differently and, as it turns out, more accurately. Today they are regarded as examples of the most profound music ever composed. To put this in the corollary phrase of Characteristic 7, Beethoven, the master composer, experienced unconditional self-regard.

Characteristic 8 needs little interpretative comment. It refers to the essentially creative and adaptive adjustment of the healthy, mature personality. The neurotic, on the contrary, reacts obsessively and with rigidity to new experiences.

Characteristic 9 and the corollaries summarize concepts which we have already considered in outlining Rogers' theory of therapy. These characteristics refer to the opposite of those in the neurotic who fails to bring signifi-

[23] For research reports utilizing the Q-technique see *20* and *26*.

cant experiences to awareness, denies, or distorts them. The healthy, fully functioning person accepts and utilizes all experiences. He grows with each novel experience, utilizing it fully and relating it to the self-construct.

Finally, Rogers describes the tendency of the fully functioning individual to live in harmony because of "the rewarding character of reciprocal positive regard." The fully functioning person is, in other words, one who has achieved an optimal adjustment in his interpersonal relations. More specifically, positive regard, as it is used here, is the same as it is employed in characteristic C and D—that is, attitudes of warmth, liking, and respect.

Even this most casual reading of Rogers' theory reveals his deep optimism about the possibility of human growth, in contrast to Freud's essential pessimism. Moreover, he shows himself in an antithetical position with respect to Freud in his willingness to accept what the individual says about himself at face value. It is in this latter respect that client-centered therapy has been severely criticized as "superficial." The psychoanalysts, whether of the Freudian persuasion or not, believe that there is overwhelming evidence for the unconscious determination of behavior. Moreover, Rogers has been challenged on the grounds that self-deception and the unreliability of subjective reports cast doubt on the validity of the subject's statements. However, Rogers does subscribe to the notion that the subject distorts experiences and, as we pointed out above, may deceive himself. Nevertheless, his profound optimism leads him to conclude that given the proper environment, the individual will arrive at a nondistorted, nondefensive view of the self.

Rogers' theory is still evolving as a conception of human personality with an enthusiastic group of followers. For this reason it would be premature to attempt to evaluate it at this time. We can only agree with Hall and Lindzey (*10*, p. 499) that it has been highly influential in bringing the self back into psychology and making it a valid object of empirical investigation. In this respect Rogers must share credit with Allport, the neo-Freudians, and a small group of humanistic motivational theorists who have returned the person to his rightful place in personality theory.

SUMMARY AND EVALUATION

In reflecting on the theories of personality that we have examined, one cannot help but be impressed by the diversity of theoretical and methodological orientations. In part, this may be attributed to the fact that the subject matter of personality is so broad, that the field has attracted psychologists with widely divergent points of view. Indeed, it is difficult to conceive of *any* orientation which cannot encompass the study of the human personality. As we have seen, it may be approached from such divergent points of view as the factor-analytic, constitutional, and psychoanalytic. But aside from this diversity in orientation and despite disputes over specific issues, there is more agreement among the theorists than is apparent on the surface. Indeed, it is our contention that differences in *methodological* orientation are responsible for creating a not insignificant portion of surface disagreement which tends to obscure many fundamental areas of agreement.

With the exception of the learning theorists, whose position we have not examined, there is general agreement that personality, whatever its other attributes might be, is characterized by *purpose*. Purpose, in turn, reflects the dynamic, motivated nature of personality. Again, noting the same previous exception and adding Sheldon to the dissenters, there is a common, ever increasing emphasis upon the self, or ego functions, as the core of personality. The self that is thus gaining ground is not the mechanistic Freudian ego, but a more "psychological" self perhaps best represented by Allport's concept of the proprium or Rogers' self.

There is also good agreement among the various theories on the continuity and consistency of behavior both as a theoretical aspect of personality and as an important practical issue. After all, there would be little value in measuring personality if it were discontinuous, thereby making prediction, the final goal of measurement, impossible. The enduring quality of personality, along with the necessity for measurement, has resulted in the postulating of "units of behavior" in the form of traits (Cattell, Allport), syndromes (Sheldon), mechanisms (Freud), proceedings and serials (Murray), characteristics (Rogers), which, in the last analysis, are different ways of looking at aspects of *behavior*. While no one would pretend that these similar modal units of analysis spell present agreement, it cannot be denied that they provide a fundamental basis for future agreement.

The more important areas where *disagreement* is the rule are: (a) the relative emphasis on unconscious determination of behavior, (b) the role of learning, and (c) contemporaneity of motivation. Freud and Murray strongly emphasize unconscious determinants, while the other theorists either give a moderate role to such determinants, or deemphasize them in favor of conscious ego-determinants. Obviously, the critical factor here is the degree of influence of psychoanalytic concepts on the theory in question. The psychoanalysts and those who favor psychoanalytic formulations have traditionally emphasized unconscious motives and mechanisms, while those from other background orientations tend more toward conscious, modifiable determinants.

Similarly, the less psychoanalytically inclined tend to emphasize contemporaneity in motivation and at the same time maximize the role of learning and cultural determinants in the development of personality. Naturally, those who favor a constitutional approach, such as Sheldon, deemphasize learning, contemporary motivation and cultural factors.

Once more, in this, our final look at systems of psychology, it is apparent how heavily contemporary theories are influenced by the background systems from which they evolved. At the same time the mutual interaction between method and theory is once again apparent. All systems and theories are compounded of the man, the background, and the method. Yet each, like human personality from which it springs, maintains its uniqueness and individuality.

REFERENCES

1. Allport, G. *Personality: A psychological interpretation.* New York: Holt, 1937.
2. Allport, G. *The nature of personality: Selected papers.* Reading, Mass.: Addison-Wesley, 1950.
3. Allport, G. *Becoming: Basic considerations for a psychology of personality.* New Haven: Yale University Press, 1955.
4. Allport, G. W. *Pattern and growth in personality.* New York: Holt, Rinehart and Winston, 1961.
5. Cattell, R. The principal trait clusters for describing personality. *Psychological Bulletin,* **42,** 1945, pp. 129–161.
6. Cattell, R. *Personality.* New York: McGraw-Hill, 1950.
7. Cattell, R. B. *The scientific analysis of personality.* Chicago: Aldine, 1965.
8. Cattell, R. B., and I. H. Scheirer. *The meaning and measurement of neuroticism and anxiety.* New York: Ronald, 1961.
9. Freud, S. *New introductory lectures on psychoanalysis.* New York: Norton, 1933.
10. Hall, C., and G. Lindzey. *Theories of personality.* New York: Wiley, 1957.
11. Heidbreder, E. *Seven psychologies.* New York: Appleton, 1933.
12. Hilgard, E. *Theories of learning,* ed. 2. New York: Appleton, 1956.
13. Murray, H., (and collaborators). *Explorations in personality.* New York: Oxford, 1938.
14. Murray, H. Some basic psychological assumptions and conceptions. *Dialectica,* **5,** 1951, pp. 266–292.
15. Murray, H., and C. Kluckhohn. Outline of a conception of personality. In Kluckhohn, C., H. Murray, and D. Schneider (eds.), *Personality in nature, society and culture,* ed. 2. New York: Knopf, 1953.
16. Murray, H. Preparations for scaffold of a comprehensive system. In Koch, S. (ed.), *Psychology: A study of a science,* Vol. 3. New York: McGraw-Hill, 1959.
17. Newman, R. Age changes in body build. *American Journal of Physical Anthropology,* **10,** 1952, pp. 75–90.
18. Rogers, C. R. *Counseling and psychotherapy.* Boston: Houghton Mifflin, 1942.
19. Rogers, C. R. *Client-centered therapy: Its current practice, implications, and theory.* Boston: Houghton Mifflin, 1951.
20. Rogers, C. R. A theory of therapy, personality, and interpersonal relationships as developed in the client-centered framework. In Koch, S. (ed.), *Psychology: A study of a science,* Vol. 3. New York: McGraw-Hill, 1959.
21. Rogers, C. R. *On becoming a person: A therapist's view of psychotherapy.* Boston: Houghton Mifflin, 1961.
22. Rogers, C. R. Two divergent trends. In May, R. (ed.), *Existential psychology.* New York: Random House, 1961.

23. Rogers, C. R. Toward a science of the person. *Journal of Humanistic Psychology*, **3,** 1963, pp. 72–93.

24. Rogers, C. R. Some questions and challenges facing a humanistic psychology. *Journal of Humanistic Psychology*, **5,** 1965, pp. 1–5.

25. Rogers, C. R. Some thoughts regarding the current philosophy of the behavioral sciences. *Journal of Humanistic Psychology*, **5,** 1965, pp. 182–195.

26. Rogers, C. R., and R. F. Dymond. *Psychotherapy and personality change.* Chicago: Univ. of Chicago Press, 1954.

27. Sears, R. Survey of objective studies of psychoanalytic concepts. *Social Science Research Council Bulletin,* 1943, No. 51.

28. Sears, R. Experimental analyses of psychoanalytic phenomena. In Hunt, J. McV. (ed.), *Personality and the behavior disorders.* New York: Ronald, 1944.

29. Shaffer, L. F., and E. J. Shoben. *The psychology of adjustment,* ed. 2. Boston: Houghton Mifflin, 1956.

30. Sheldon, W. (with the collaboration of S. S. Stevens and W. B. Tucker). *The varieties of human physique.* New York: Harper, 1940.

31. Sheldon, W. (with the collaboration of S. S. Stevens). *The varieties of temperament.* New York: Harper, 1942.

32. Sheldon, W. (with the collaboration of E. M. Hart and E. McDermott). *Varieties of delinquent youth.* New York: Harper, 1949.

33. Sheldon, W. (with the collaboration of C. W. Dupertuis and E. McDermott). *Atlas of men.* New York: Harper, 1954.

16

Epilogue

Our survey of systems of psychology has covered twenty centuries and perhaps as many different theoretical points of view. But, psychology is truly a child of the nineteenth and twentieth centuries, for only within the past hundred years has it emerged from philosophy as an independent discipline. It is also true that psychology is a product of the Age of Analysis—an age which has witnessed an ever increasing proliferation of scientific disciplines as the analytic method of the natural sciences rolls back the frontiers of knowledge. Thus, within the brief period of a single century, psychologists have sought to define their subject and to establish its broad foundations as a science.

As we have seen, the problem of definition proved to be a knotty one. Each emergent leader sought to establish psychology in the image of his own preconceptions, with the result that psychology's infancy was characterized by a diversity of opinions as to the nature of the new science. An inevitable consequence of the multiplicity of definitions was disagreement over methodology. Because controversies attract supporters to either side, divergent viewpoints come to be organized into "schools" of psychology. While schools as such no longer exist in academic psychology, the old viewpoints are still evident, as we have tried to show in tracing the emergence of contemporary trends and theoretical orientations.

Despite the fact that so many divergent points of view have had their day in court, it must be admitted that no generally acceptable definition of psychology has emerged. Rather, the disharmony engendered by the schools gave rise to an attitude of distrust of all systematic orientations which pretended to be sufficiently comprehensive to encompass the whole of psychology. As a result "miniature systems" began to emerge around

he end of the 1930's and to become the dominant trends in psychology
prior to World War II. Since the war, miniature systems have, in turn,
given way to more limited theories and models. Looked at in retrospect,
he collapse of the schools appears to have been a salutary development.
Theory and systematizing had far outrun its empirical foundation—a state
of affairs which is never healthy in science. However, the miniature systems
still show the dominant characteristics of their ancestry in the parent schools.
A study of Table 16-1, which summarizes the major systems and their
derivatives, will help to bring out these genetic relationships.

In emphasizing differences among schools, miniature systems and
theories, there is a danger that we shall leave the reader with the impression
that contemporary psychology is hopelessly divided by theoretical controversies. In point of fact such is not the case. The original sharpness of
the old conflicts has been dulled with the passage of time; and, for the
most part, psychologists from one orientation not only recognize the value
of other points of view, but borrow freely from each other. An examination
of the journals in the field which, in the last analysis, best represent psychology as it is today, gives one the impression that, broadly speaking,
American psychology is a functionalistic behaviorism.

If our analysis is correct, then American psychologists have come
to recognize that whereas science deals with objective events, those events
are of little interest in and of themselves but only become significant when
they are viewed as manifestations of functional processes within the individual. Thus, while the *definition* of psychology has become more behavioristic, its *spirit* has remained functionalistic. There are several consequences
of the dominance of the behavioristic-functionalism characteristic of contemporary psychology. First, most psychologists now look upon their discipline as an inferential science. Experimental observations of behavior are
designed in such a way as to reveal the nature of intervening variables
and the principles which govern their interrelationships.

Second, psychologists have become increasingly concerned with dynamic or motivational processes. In part, this has resulted from the already
noted increased emphasis on intervening variables but, in part, is also
related to the functionalistic spirit of contemporary psychology. The current
interest in dynamics is revealed in the traditionally experimental areas of
perception and learning by the increasingly large number of studies concerned with the influence of motivational variables on those processes. In
the area of personality it is responsible for the return of the dynamic ego
or self as opposed to the traditionally mechanistic self. In the area of physiological psychology the great interest in the dynamics of central processes
is revealed in studies of the limbic system and related structures in the subcortex. In short, psychology has never lost its interest in "human nature"
while maintaining its hard-won natural science orientation.

Table 16-1.
The Major Systems of Psychology and Their Derivatives

MAJOR SYSTEMS	FOUNDER(S) OR CHIEF EXPONENTS	CHIEF METHOD OF ORIGINAL SCHOOL
Associationism	Hartley and the British Empiricists	Philosophical analysis
Psychophysics and quantitative psychology	Weber, Fechner, Galton, Binet	Quantitative measurement
Structuralism	Wundt, Titchener	Introspectionism
Functionalism	James, Dewey, Angell, Carr	Objective experimental studies, introspection
Behaviorism	Watson	Objective experimentation, especially conditioning
Gestalt	Wertheimer, Köhler, Koffka	Phenomenological experimentation
Psychoanalysis	Freud	Free association and dream analysis

[a] It should be noted that not *all* behaviorists are physiologically oriented. There is, however, a tendency for the two to go together.

Subject matter or object of study	Chief areas of concern of original school	Representative derivatives or related systems and exponents
Cognitive processes	Laws of memory, nature of learning	Experimental associationism —Ebbinghaus, Thorndike, Robinson
Sensory processes and individual differences	Sensory processes and individual differences	Factor analysis—Thurstone, model making; Cybernetics
Consciousness	Sensation, attention, images, affective processes	None
Mind viewed in terms of its adaptive significance for the organism	Perception, learning, mental testing	Dynamic psychology— Robert S. Woodworth. Functionalistic perceptual theorists—Egon Brunswik, the "Ames Group." Functionalistic learning theorists—McGeoch, Melton
Behavior	Sensation, animal learning	Purposive behaviorism— Tolman. Conditioning theorists—Guthrie, Hull, Skinner "Physiological" theorists[a] Lashley, Hebb, Morgan
Mental and behavioral processes as wholes	Perception; thinking	Field theory—Lewin. Organismic and holistic psychology—Goldstein, Maslow. Most contemporary perceptual theories show the Gestalt influence
Analysis of unconscious dynamic processes	Psychotherapeutic treatment of the neurotic	Individual psychology— Adler. Analytic psychology —Jung. Neo-Freudian psychoanalysis— Horney, Fromm, Kardiner, Sullivan

Third, the behavioral-functionalistic spirit of the times is revealed by the close connection which exists between theory and practice. That is, contemporary theories are far less *programmatic* than their forerunners, the systems of the late nineteenth and early twentieth centuries. Instead of dealing in broad generalities, today's theorists strive to maintain a close functional bond between theorizing and experimentation.

Finally, the behavioral-functionalistic spirit of American psychology has resulted in the large-scale development of the practical applications of the science. It will be recalled that one of Watson's aims was to carry psychology into the applied fields (see Chapter 2). This has been abundantly accomplished in such areas as clinical, industrial, legal, military, advertising, and educational psychology. American psychologists have shown a willingness to make the practical fields a kind of adjunct to the experimental laboratory. While systematic and theoretical issues play a less important role in the applied fields, the vigor of applied psychology testifies to its highly functionalistic orientation.

There remains but one important question. What of the future? Will psychology continue along the traditional lines that have guided its development throughout its past? There is every reason to believe that it will in the larger sense, for the simple reason that it is committed to the experimental method of the natural sciences and like its sister sciences must continue to follow the methodology common to all. However, the areas of high activity in psychology today do not necessarily represent trends that will extend far into the future. As we have pointed out from time to time, interest in certain phases of knowledge tends to follow cycles, and with cyclic interests go corresponding ups and downs in progress. Each area of psychology is related to every other, and new insights in one field often result in considerable advances in others. We have seen how the field of perception has been influenced in recent years by the contemporary interest in motivation. Moreover, as has been true in vision, hearing, and central motivational theory, purely technical considerations influence the pattern of development of a given area. We have seen how there is an especially close correlation between the improvement of electronic equipment and advances in the "physiological" areas of psychology. Similarly, it may be that the development and application of new mathematical techniques will give the learning theorists their long-sought general laws of learning.

But whatever the future may hold with respect to progress in the various fields of psychology, one final task remains for the psychologists of tomorrow. That is to relate all points of view to a central theme just as the chemist and physicist have related their sciences to atomic theory and the biologist has organized his discipline around evolution. Whether this unification will be accomplished gradually as more and more empirical findings point the way toward a unifying theory, or whether some future genius will bring to psychology a comprehensive theoretical structure with the integrating force of atomic theory in the physical sciences, it is impossible to say. Whatever the way, no more challenging or important task lies ahead in any science.

Name Index

Aborn, M., 343, 346
Ades, H., 117, 121
Adler, A., 60, 71, 148, 149, 290, 430, 432, 442, 584, 607
  biography, 74
  on motivation, 401–403
Aiken, E. G., 305, 318
Alexander the Great, 402
Allport, F. H., 72, 159, 170, 180, 191
Allport, G., 153, 191, 601, 602
Alper, T. G., 347
Ames, A., Jr., 170, 187, 191
Anand, B. K., 512
Anderson, B., 504, 512
Angell, J. R., 47, 48, 172, 286, 352, 606
  biography, 74–75
Ansbacher, H. L., 71, 72, 442
Ansbacher, R. R., 71, 72, 442
Appley, M., 441, 442, 470
Aquinas, Thomas, 445
Aristotle, 15, 17, 18, 84, 362, 414
  biography, 28–29
Aronfreed, J. M., 179, 191
Ashby, W. R., 548, 551
Atkinson, J. W., 432, 442, 443, 551
Attneave, F., 72, 542, 551
Auerbach, E., 191
Augustine, Saint, 445
Bacon, F., 18
Bard, P., 452, 456, 457, 458, 459, 470, 501, 505
Bare, J. K., 426, 443
Barker, R. G., 421, 442, 443
Barrett, W., 19, 28
Barron, F., 384–388
Bartlett, F. C., 153, 154, 191
Bartley, S. H., 121, 190, 191
Beebe-Center, J. G., 445, 470
Beethoven, L., 431, 599
Bellows, R. T., 512
Bennett, E., 514
Bentham, J., 393
Bergmann, G., 318
Berkeley, G., 21, 23, 123, 125, 126, 196
  biography, 29
  views on perception, 126–127
Berlyne, D., 373, 388
Bernard, C., 25, 26
Bindra, D., 442

Binet, A., 355, 606
  views on intelligence, 519–520
Birch, H. G., 223, 225, 255
Blake, R. R., 191
Blazek, N., 442
Boring, E. G., 15, 19, 23, 38, 41, 72, 87, 105, 113, 121, 127, 133, 150, 255, 388, 477, 494, 512, 517, 551
Bower, G. H., 540, 552
Brady, J. V., 512
Bray, C. W., 114, 122
Brentano, F., 356
Brett, G. S., 15, 28, 150, 225
Breuer, J., 59, 399
Bricker, P. D., 179, 191
Bridges, K. M. B., 456, 470
Bridgman, P. W., 7, 28
Broca, P., 27, 475–477
Brown, C. T., 192
Brown, C. W., 28
Brown, P. K., 110, 121
Brown, W., 191
Brownfield, C. A., 191
Bruner, J. S., 66, 73, 180, 181, 182, 191, 193
Brunswik, E., 172, 191, 607
Bucy, P. C., 510, 513
Bugelski, B. R., 287
Burtt, H. E., 225
Bush, R. R., 534, 551, 552
Caesar, J., 402
Cannon, W. B., 26, 28, 425, 452, 470, 501, 512, 548
  biography, 30
  theory of emotions, 456–459
  theory of thirst, 504–505
Cantril, H., 191
Carmichael, L., 155, 192, 243, 287
Carr, H., 48, 49, 50, 73, 95, 121, 150, 172, 225, 246, 272, 286, 352, 388, 470, 606
  biography, 75
  definition of psychology by, 48–49
  on emotion, 450–452
  on learning, 212–217
  on perception, 137–140
  on sensation, 90–92
  on thinking, 357–359
Cattell, J. McK., 383, 384, 517

Subject Index